Time Series
Volume II

The International Library of Critical Writings in Econometrics

Series Editors: Mark Blaug
Professor Emeritus, University of London
Consultant Professor, University of Buckingham
Visiting Professor, University of Exeter
Adrian C. Darnell
Senior Lecturer in Economics, University of Durham

1. The Econometrics of Panel Data (Volumes I and II)
   G.S. Maddala

2. Macroeconometric Modelling (Volumes I and II)
   Kenneth F. Wallis

3. Simultaneous Equation Estimation
   Carl F. Christ

4. The History of Econometrics (Volumes I and II)
   Adrian C. Darnell

5. Time Series (Volumes I and II)
   Andrew Harvey

6. The Methodology of Econometrics (Volumes I and II)
   Dale J. Poirier

Future titles will include:

Bayesian Inference
George C. Tiao and Nicholas Polson

General to Specific Modelling
Neil R. Ericsson

Selection Bias
James J. Heckman

Specification Problems

Nonlinear Models

Time Series
Volume II

Edited by

Andrew Harvey

Professor of Econometrics, Department of Statistics
London School of Economics and Political Science

THE INTERNATIONAL LIBRARY OF CRITICAL WRITINGS IN ECONOMETRICS

An Elgar Reference Collection

Published by
Edward Elgar Publishing Limited
Gower House
Croft Road
Aldershot
Hants GU11 3HR
England

Edward Elgar Publishing Company
Old Post Road
Brookfield
Vermont 05036
USA

British Library Cataloguing in Publication Data
Time Series. – (International Library of
Critical Writings in Economics; Vol. 5)
I. Harvey, A.C. II. Series
330.0151955

Library of Congress Cataloguing in Publication Data
Time series / edited by Andrew Harvey.
p. cm. — (International library of critical writings in econometrics : 5)
"An Elgar reference collection."
1. Time-series analysis. 2. Econometrics. I. Harvey, Andrew, 1947– . II. Series.
HB139.T53 1995
330'01'51955—dc20 94–27602
CIP

ISBN 1 85278 662 0 (2 volume set)

Printed in Great Britain at the University Press, Cambridge

Contents

Acknowledgements

The editor and publishers wish to thank the following who have kindly given permission for the use of copyright material.

American Economic Association for article: Christopher A. Sims (1972), 'Money, Income, and Causality', *American Economic Review*, **LXII** (4), September, 540–52.

American Society of Mechanical Engineers for article: R.E. Kalman (1960), 'A New Approach to Linear Filtering and Prediction Problems', *Journal of Basic Engineering, Transactions of the ASME*, Series D, **82**, March, 35–45.

American Statistical Association for articles: D.B. Duncan and S.D. Horn (1972), 'Linear Dynamic Recursive Estimation from the Viewpoint of Regression Analysis', *Journal of the American Statistical Association*, **67** (340), December, 815–21; Richard H. Jones (1980), 'Maximum Likelihood Fitting of ARMA Models to Time Series with Missing Observations', *Technometrics*, **22** (3), August, 389–95; Richard J. Meinhold and Nozer D. Singpurwalla (1983), 'Understanding the Kalman Filter', *American Statistician*, **37** (2), May, 123–27; Genshiro Kitigawa (1987), 'Non–Gaussian State–Space Modeling of Nonstationary Time Series', *Journal of the American Statistical Association*, **82** (400), December, 1032–41.

Basil Blackwell Ltd for articles: R.L. Brown, J. Durbin and J.M. Evans (1975), 'Techniques for Testing the Constancy of Regression Relationships over Time', *Journal of the Royal Statistical Society*, Series B, **37** (2), 149–63; A.I. McLeod and W.K. Li (1983), 'Diagnostic Checking ARMA Time Series Models Using Squared–Residual Autocorrelations', *Journal of Time Series Analysis*, **4** (4), 269–73; R.L. Smith and J.E. Miller (1986), 'A Non–Gaussian State Space Model and Application to Prediction of Records', *Journal of the Royal Statistical Society*, Series B, **48** (1), 79–88.

Biometrika Trustees for article: Ruey S. Tsay (1986), 'Nonlinearity Tests for Time Series', *Biometrika*, **73** (2), August, 461–66.

Econometric Society for articles: C.W.J. Granger (1969), 'Investigating Causal Relations by Econometric Models and Cross–Spectral Methods', *Econometrica*, **37** (3), July, 424–38; Kenneth F. Wallis (1980), 'Econometric Implications of the Rational Expectations Hypothesis', *Econometrica*, **48** (1), January, 49–73; Robert F. Engle (1982), 'Autoregressive Conditional Heteroscedasticity with Estimates of the Variance of United Kingdom Inflation', *Econometrica*, **50** (4), July, 987–1007; Robert F. Engle, David F. Hendry and Jean–François Richard (1983), 'Exogeneity', *Econometrica*, **51** (2), March, 277–304; James D. Hamilton (1989), 'A New Approach to the Economic Analysis of Nonstationary Time Series and the Business Cycle', *Econometrica*, **57** (2), March, 357–84.

Elsevier Science Publishers B.V. for excerpt: Arnold Zellner (1979), 'Causality and Econometrics', *Three Aspects of Policy and Policymaking: Knowledge, Data and Institutions*, Karl Brunner and Allan H. Meltzer (eds), Carnegie-Rochester Conference Series on Public Policy, Volume 10, 9–54.

Elsevier Sequoia S.A. for article: Tim Bollerslev (1986), 'Generalized Autoregressive Conditional Heteroskedasticity', *Journal of Econometrics*, **31** (3), April, 307–27.

Institute of Electrical and Electronics Engineers, Inc. for article: Fred C. Schweppe (1965), 'Evaluation of Likelihood Functions for Gaussian Signals', *IEEE Transactions on Information Theory*, **11**, January, 61–70.

Institute of Mathematical Statistics for article: Piet de Jong (1991), 'The Diffuse Kalman Filter', *Annals of Statistics*, **19** (2), 1073–83.

National Bureau of Economic Research, Inc. for article: Barr Rosenberg (1973), 'Random Coefficient Models: the Analysis of a Cross Section of Time Series by Stochastically Convergent Parameter Regression', *Annals of Economic and Social Measurement*, **2** (4), October, 399–428.

Every effort has been made to trace all the copyright holders but if any have been inadvertently overlooked the publishers will be pleased to make the necessary arrangement at the first opportunity.

In addition the publishers wish to thank the Library of the London School of Economics and Political Science, the Marshall Library of Economics, Cambridge University and the Photographic Unit of the University of London Library for their assistance in obtaining these articles.

Part I
Causality, Exogeneity and Expectations

[1]

Econometrica, Vol. 37, No. 3 (July, 1969)

INVESTIGATING CAUSAL RELATIONS BY ECONOMETRIC MODELS AND CROSS-SPECTRAL METHODS

BY C. W. J. GRANGER

There occurs on some occasions a difficulty in deciding the direction of causality between two related variables and also whether or not feedback is occurring. Testable definitions of causality and feedback are proposed and illustrated by use of simple two-variable models. The important problem of apparent instantaneous causality is discussed and it is suggested that the problem often arises due to slowness in recording information or because a sufficiently wide class of possible causal variables has not been used. It can be shown that the cross spectrum between two variables can be decomposed into two parts, each relating to a single causal arm of a feedback situation. Measures of causal lag and causal strength can then be constructed. A generalisation of this result with the partial cross spectrum is suggested.

1. INTRODUCTION

THE OBJECT of this paper is to throw light on the relationships between certain classes of econometric models involving feedback and the functions arising in spectral analysis, particularly the cross spectrum and the partial cross spectrum. Causality and feedback are here defined in an explicit and testable fashion. It is shown that in the two-variable case the feedback mechanism can be broken down into two causal relations and that the cross spectrum can be considered as the sum of two cross spectra, each closely connected with one of the causations. The next three sections of the paper briefly introduce those aspects of spectral methods, model building, and causality which are required later. Section 5 presents the results for the two-variable case and Section 6 generalises these results for three variables.

2. SPECTRAL METHODS

If X_t is a stationary time series with mean zero, there are two basic spectral representations associated with the series:

(i) the Cramer representation,

$$X_t = \int_{-\pi}^{\pi} e^{it\omega}\, dz_x(\omega), \tag{2.1}$$

where $z_x(\omega)$ is a complex random process with uncorrelated increments so that

$$\begin{aligned} E[dz_x(\omega)\,\overline{dz_x(\lambda)}] &= 0, \qquad \omega \neq \lambda, \\ &= dF_x(\omega), \quad \omega = \lambda; \end{aligned} \tag{2.2}$$

(ii) the spectral representation of the covariance sequence

$$\mu_\tau^{xx} = E[X_t \overline{X}_{t-\tau}] = \int_{-\pi}^{\pi} e^{i\tau\omega}\, dF_x(\omega). \tag{2.3}$$

If X_t has no strictly periodic components, $dF_x(\omega) = f_x(\omega)\,d\omega$ where $f_x(\omega)$ is the power spectrum of X_t. The estimation and interpretation of power spectra have been discussed in [4] and [5]. The basic idea underlying the two spectral representations is that the series can be decomposed as a sum (i.e. integral) of uncorrelated components, each associated with a particular frequency. It follows that the variance of the series is equal to the sum of the variances of the components. The power spectrum records the variances of the components as a function of their frequencies and indicates the relative importance of the components in terms of their contribution to the overall variance.

If X_t and Y_t are a pair of stationary time series, so that Y_t has the spectrum $f_y(\omega)$ and Cramer representation

$$Y_t = \int_{-\pi}^{\pi} e^{it\omega}\,dz_y(\omega),$$

then the cross spectrum (strictly power cross spectrum) $Cr(\omega)$ between X_t and Y_t is a complex function of ω and arises both from

$$\begin{aligned} E[dz_x(\omega)\,\overline{dz_y(\omega)}] &= 0, \qquad \omega \neq \lambda, \\ &= Cr(\omega)\,d\omega, \quad \omega = \lambda, \end{aligned}$$

and

$$\mu_\tau^{xy} = E[X_t\overline{Y}_{t-\tau}] = \int_{-\pi}^{\pi} e^{i\tau\omega} Cr(\omega)\,d\omega.$$

It follows that the relationship between two series can be expressed only in terms of the relationships between corresponding frequency components.

Two further functions are defined from the cross spectrum as being more useful for interpreting relationships between variables:

(i) the coherence,

$$C(\omega) = \frac{|Cr(\omega)|^2}{f_x(\omega)f_y(\omega)},$$

which is essentially the square of the correlation coefficient between corresponding frequency components of X_t and Y_t, and

(ii) the phase,

$$\phi(\omega) = \tan^{-1}\frac{\text{imaginary part of } Cr(\omega)}{\text{real part of } Cr(\omega)},$$

which measures the phase difference between corresponding frequency components. When one variable is leading the other, $\phi(\omega)/\omega$ measure the extent of the time lag.

Thus, the coherence is used to measure the degree to which two series are related and the phase may be interpreted in terms of time lags.

Estimation and interpretation of the coherence and phase function are discussed in [**4**, Chapters 5 and 6]. It is worth noting that $\phi(\omega)$ has been found to be robust under changes in the stationarity assumption [**4**, Chapter 9].

If X_t, Y_t, and Z_t are three time series, the problem of possibly misleading correlation and coherence values between two of them due to the influence on both of the third variable can be overcome by the use of partial cross-spectral methods.

The spectral, cross-spectral matrix $\{f_{ij}(\omega)\} = S(\omega)$ between the three variables is given by

$$E\begin{bmatrix} dz_x(\omega) \\ dz_y(\omega) \\ dz_z(\omega) \end{bmatrix} [\overline{dz_x(\omega)}\ \overline{dz_y(\omega)}\ \overline{dz_z(\omega)}] = \{f_{ij}(\omega)\}\, d\omega$$

where

$$\begin{aligned} f_{ij}(\omega) &= f_x(\omega) \quad \text{when} \quad i = j = x, \\ &= Cr^{xy}(\omega) \quad \text{when} \quad i = x, j = y, \end{aligned}$$

etc.

The partial spectral, cross-spectral matrix between X_t and Y_t given Z_t is found by partitioning $S(\omega)$ into components:

$$S = \left[\begin{array}{c|c} S_{11} & S_{12} \\ \hline S_{21} & S_{22} \end{array}\right]$$

The partitioning lines are between the second and third rows, and second and third columns. The partial spectral matrix is then

$$S_{xy.z} = S_{11} - S_{12}S_{22}^{-1}S_{21}.$$

Interpretation of the components of this matrix is similar to that involving partial correlation coefficients. Thus, the partial cross spectrum can be used to find the relationship between two series once the effect of a third series has been taken into account. The partial coherence and phase are defined directly from the partial cross spectrum as before. Interpretation of all of these functions and generalisations to the n-variable case can be found in [4, Chapter 5].

3. FEEDBACK MODELS

Consider initially a stationary random vector $X_t = \{X_{1t}, X_{2t}, \ldots, X_{kt}\}$, each component of which has zero mean. A linear model for such a vector consists of a set of linear equations by which all or a subset of the components of X_t are "explained" in terms of present and past values of components of X_t. The part not explained by the model may be taken to consist of a white-noise random vector ε_t, such that

$$(3.1)\qquad \begin{aligned} E[\varepsilon_t'\varepsilon_s] &= 0, \quad t \neq s, \\ &= I, \quad t = s, \end{aligned}$$

where I is a unit matrix and 0 is a zero matrix.

Thus the model may be written as

$$(3.2) \qquad A_0 X_t = \sum_{j=1}^{m} A_j X_{t-j} + \varepsilon_t$$

where m may be infinite and the A's are matrices.

The completely general model as defined does not have unique matrices A_j as an orthogonal transformation. $Y_t = \Lambda X_t$ can be performed which leaves the form of the model the same, where Λ is the orthogonal matrix, i.e., a square matrix having the property $\Lambda\Lambda' = I$. This is seen to be the case as $\eta_t = \Lambda\varepsilon_t$ is still a white-noise vector. For the model to be determined, sufficient a priori knowledge is required about the values of the coefficients of at least one of the A's, in order for constraints to be set up so that such transformations are not possible. This is the so-called "identification problem" of classical econometrics. In the absence of such a priori constraints, Λ can always be chosen so that the A_0 is a triangular matrix, although not uniquely, thus giving a spurious causal-chain appearance to the model.

Models for which A_0 has nonvanishing terms off the main diagonal will be called "models with instantaneous causality." Models for which A_0 has no nonzero term off the main diagonal will be called "simple causal models." These names will be explained later. Simple causal models are uniquely determined if orthogonal transforms such as Λ are not possible without changing the basic form of the model. It is possible for a model apparently having instantaneous causality to be transformed using an orthogonal Λ to a simple causal model.

These definitions can be illustrated simply in the two variable case. Suppose the variables are X_t, Y_t. Then the model considered is of the form

$$(3.3) \qquad \begin{aligned} X_t + b_0 Y_t &= \sum_{j=1}^{m} a_j X_{t-j} + \sum_{j=1}^{m} b_j Y_{t-j} + \varepsilon_t', \\ Y_t + c_0 X_t &= \sum_{j=1}^{m} c_j X_{t-j} + \sum_{j=1}^{m} d_j Y_{t-j} + \varepsilon_t''. \end{aligned}$$

If $b_0 = c_0 = 0$, then this will be a simple causal model. Otherwise it will be a model with instantaneous causality.

Whether or not a model involving some group of economic variables can be a simple causal model depends on what one considers to be the speed with which information flows through the economy and also on the sampling period of the data used. It might be true that when quarterly data are used, for example, a simple causal model is not sufficient to explain the relationships between the variables, while for monthly data a simple causal model would be all that is required. Thus, some nonsimple causal models may be constructed not because of the basic properties of the economy being studied but because of the data being used. It has been shown elsewhere [**4**, Chapter 7; **3**] that a simple causal mechanism can appear to be a feedback mechanism if the sampling period for the data is so long that details of causality cannot be picked out.

4. CAUSALITY

Cross-spectral methods provide a useful way of describing the relationship between two (or more) variables when one is causing the other(s). In many realistic economic situations, however, one suspects that feedback is occurring. In these situations the coherence and phase diagrams become difficult or impossible to interpret, particularly the phase diagram. The problem is how to devise definitions of causality and feedback which permit tests for their existence. Such a definition was proposed in earlier papers [**4**, Chapter 7; **3**]. In this section, some of these definitions will be discussed and extended. Although later sections of this paper will use this definition of causality they will not completely depend upon it. Previous papers concerned with causality in economic systems [**1, 6, 7, 8**] have been particularly concerned with the problem of determining a causal interpretation of simultaneous equation systems, usually with instantaneous causality. Feedback is not explicitly discussed. This earlier work has concentrated on the form that the parameters of the equations should take in order to discern definite causal relationships. The stochastic elements and the natural time ordering of the variables play relatively minor roles in the theory. In the alternative theory to be discussed here, the stochastic nature of the variables and the direction of the flow of time will be central features. The theory is, in fact, not relevant for nonstochastic variables and will rely entirely on the assumption that the future cannot cause the past. This theory will not, of course, be contradictory to previous work but there appears to be little common ground. Its origins may be found in a suggestion by Wiener [**9**]. The relationship between the definition discussed here and the work of Good [**2**] has yet to be determined.

If A_t is a stationary stochastic process, let $\bar{A}_t$ represent the set of *past* values $\{A_{t-j}, j = 1, 2, \ldots, \infty\}$ and $\bar{\bar{A}}_t$ represent the set of *past and present values* $\{A_{t-j}, j = 0, 1, \ldots, \infty\}$. Further let $\bar{A}(k)$ represent the set $\{A_{t-j}, j = k, k + 1, \ldots, \infty\}$.

Denote the optimum, unbiased, least-squares predictor of A_t using the set of values B_t by $P_t(A|B)$. Thus, for instance, $P_t(X|\bar{X})$ will be the optimum predictor of X_t using only past X_t. The predictive error series will be denoted by $\varepsilon_t(A|B) = A_t - P_t(A|B)$. Let $\sigma^2(A|B)$ be the variance of $\varepsilon_t(A|B)$.

The initial definitions of causality, feedback, and so forth, will be very general in nature. Testable forms will be introduced later. Let U_t be all the information in the universe accumulated since time $t - 1$ and let $U_t - Y_t$ denote all this information *apart* from the specified series Y_t. We then have the following definitions.

DEFINITION 1: *Causality*. If $\sigma^2(X|U) < \sigma^2(X|\overline{U - Y})$, we say that Y is causing X, denoted by $Y_t \Rightarrow X_t$. We say that Y_t is causing X_t if we are better able to predict X_t using all available information than if the information apart from Y_t had been used.

DEFINITION 2: *Feedback*. If

$$\sigma^2(X|\bar{U}) < \sigma^2(X|\overline{U - Y}),$$

$$\sigma^2(Y|\bar{U}) < \sigma^2(Y|\overline{U - X}),$$

we say that feedback is occurring, which is denoted $Y_t \Leftrightarrow X_t$, i.e., feedback is said to occur when X_t is causing Y_t and also Y_t is causing X_t.

DEFINITION 3: *Instantaneous Causality*. If $\sigma^2(X|\overline{U}, \overline{\overline{Y}}) < \sigma^2(X|\overline{U})$, we say that instantaneous causality $Y_t \Rightarrow X_t$ is occurring. In other words, the current value of X_t is better "predicted" if the present value of Y_t is included in the "prediction" than if it is not.

DEFINITION 4: *Causality Lag*. If $Y_t \Rightarrow X_t$, we define the (integer) causality lag m to be the least value of k such that $\sigma^2(X|U - Y(k)) < \sigma^2(X|U - Y(k + 1))$. Thus, knowing the values $Y_{t-j}, j = 0, 1, \ldots, m - 1$, will be of no help in improving the prediction of X_t.

The definitions have assumed that only stationary series are involved. In the nonstationary case, $\sigma(X|\overline{U})$ etc. will depend on time t and, in general, the existence of causality may alter over time. The definitions can clearly be generalised to be operative for a specified time t. One could then talk of causality existing at this moment of time. Considering nonstationary series, however, takes us further away from testable definitions and this tack will not be discussed further.

The one completely unreal aspect of the above definitions is the use of the series U_t, representing *all* available information. The large majority of the information in the universe will be quite irrelevant, i.e., will have no causal consequence. Suppose that all relevant information is numerical in nature and belongs to the vector set of time series $Y_t^D = \{Y_t^i, i \in D\}$ for some integer set D. Denote the set $\{i \in D, i \neq j\}$ by $D(j)$ and $\{Y_t^i, i \in D(j)\}$ by $Y_t^{D(j)}$, i.e., the full set of relevant information except one particular series. Similarly, we could leave out more than one series with the obvious notation. The previous definitions can now be used but with U_t replaced by Y_t and $U_t - Y_t$ by $Y^{D(j)}$. Thus, for example, suppose that the vector set consists only of two series, X_t and Y_t and that all other information is irrelevant. Then $\sigma^2(X|\overline{X})$ represents the minimum predictive error variance of X_t using only past X_t and $\sigma^2(X|\overline{X}, \overline{Y})$ represents this minimum variance if both past X_t and past Y_t are used to predict X_t. Then Y_t is said to cause X_t if $\sigma^2(X|\overline{X}) > \sigma^2(X|\overline{X}, \overline{Y})$. The definition of causality is now relative to the set D. If relevant data has not been included in this set, then spurious causality could arise. For instance, if the set D was taken to consist only of the two series X_t and Y_t, but in fact there was a third series Z_t which was causing both within the enlarged set $D' = (X_t, Y_t, Z_t)$, then for the original set D, spurious causality between X_t and Y_t may be found. This is similar to spurious correlation and partial correlation between sets of data that arise when some other statistical variable of importance has not been included.

In practice it will not usually be possible to use completely optimum predictors, unless all sets of series are assumed to be normally distributed, since such optimum predictors may be nonlinear in complicated ways. It seems natural to use only linear predictors and the above definitions may again be used under this assumption of linearity. Thus, for instance, the best linear predictor of X_t using only past X_t and past Y_t will be of the form

$$P_t(X|\overline{X}, \overline{Y}) = \sum_{j=1}^{\infty} a_j X_{t-j} + \sum_{j=1}^{\infty} b_j Y_{t-j}$$

where the a_j's and b_j's are chosen to minimise $\sigma^2(X|\overline{X}, \overline{Y})$.

It can be argued that the variance is not the proper criterion to use to measure the closeness of a predictor P_t to the true value X_t. Certainly if some other criteria were used it may be possible to reach different conclusions about whether one series is causing another. The variance does seem to be a natural criterion to use in connection with linear predictors as it is mathematically easy to handle and simple to interpret. If one uses this criterion, a better name might be "causality in mean."

The original definition of causality has now been restricted in order to reach a form which can be tested. Whenever the word causality is used in later sections it will be taken to mean "linear causality in mean with respect to a specified set D."

It is possible to extend the definitions to the case where a subset of series D^* of D is considered to cause X_t. This would be the case if $\sigma^2(X|Y^D) < \sigma^2(X|Y^{D-D^*})$ and then $Y^{D^*} \Rightarrow X_t$. Thus, for instance, one could ask if past X_t is causing present X_t. Because new concepts are necessary in the consideration of such problems, they will not be discussed here in any detail.

It has been pointed out already [**3**] that instantaneous causality, in which knowledge of the current value of a series helps in predicting the current value of a second series, can occasionally arise spuriously in certain cases. Suppose $Y_t \Rightarrow X_t$ with lag one unit but that the series are sampled every two time units. Then although there is no real instantaneous causality, the definitions will appear to suggest that such causality is occurring. This is because certain relevant information, the missing readings in the data, have not been used. Due to this effect, one might suggest that in many economic situations an apparent instantaneous causality would disappear if the economic variables were recorded at more frequent time intervals.

The definition of causality used above is based entirely on the predictability of some series, say X_t. If some other series Y_t contains information in past terms that helps in the prediction of X_t and if this information is contained in no other series used in the predictor, then Y_t is said to cause X_t. The flow of time clearly plays a central role in these definitions. In the author's opinion there is little use in the practice of attempting to discuss causality without introducing time, although philosophers have tried to do so. It also follows from the definitions that a purely deterministic series, that is, a series which can be predicted exactly from its past terms such as a nonstochastic series, cannot be said to have any causal influences other than its own past. This may seem to be contrary to common sense in certain special cases but it is difficult to find a *testable* alternative definition which could include the deterministic situation. Thus, for instance, if $X_t = bt$ and $Y_t = c(t + 1)$, then X_t can be predicted exactly by $b + X_{t-1}$ or by $(b/c)Y_{t-1}$. There seems to be no way of deciding if Y_t is a causal factor of X_t or not. In some cases the notation of the "simplest rule" might be applied. For example, if X_t is some complicated polynomial in t and $Y_t = X_{t+1}$, then it will be easier to predict X_t from Y_{t-1} than from past X_t. In some cases this rule cannot be used, as the previous example showed. In any case, experience does not indicate that one should expect economic laws to be simple in nature.

Even for stochastic series, the definitions introduced above may give apparently silly answers. Suppose $X_t = A_{t-1} + \varepsilon_t$, $Y_t = A_t + \eta_t$, and $Z_t = A_t + \gamma_t$, where ε_t,

η_t, and γ_t are all uncorrelated white-noise series with equal variances and A_t is some stationary series. Within the set $D = (X_t, Y_t)$ the definition gives $Y_t \Rightarrow X_t$. Within the set $D' = (X_t, Z_t)$, it gives $Z_t \Rightarrow X_t$. But within the set $D'' = (X_t, Y_t, Z_t)$, neither Y_t nor Z_t causes X_t, although the sum of Y_t and Z_t would do so. How is one to decide if either Y_t or Z_t is a causal series for X_t? The answer, of course, is that neither is. The causal series is A_t and both Y_t and Z_t contain equal amounts of information about A_t. If the set of series within which causality was discussed was expanded to include A_t, then the above apparent paradox vanishes. It will often be found that constructed examples which seem to produce results contrary to common sense can be resolved by widening the set of data within which causality is defined.

5. TWO-VARIABLE MODELS

In this section, the definitions introduced above will be illustrated using two-variable models and results will be proved concerning the form of the cross spectrum for such models.

Let X_t, Y_t be two stationary time series with zero means. The simple causal model is

$$X_t = \sum_{j=1}^{m} a_j X_{t-j} + \sum_{j=1}^{m} b_j Y_{t-j} + \varepsilon_t,$$

(5.1)

$$Y_t = \sum_{j=1}^{m} c_j X_{t-j} + \sum_{j=1}^{m} d_j Y_{t-j} + \eta_t,$$

where ε_t, η_t are taken to be two uncorrelated white-noise series, i.e., $E[\varepsilon_t \varepsilon_s] = 0 = E[\eta_t \eta_s]$, $s \neq t$, and $E[\varepsilon m_s] = 0$ all t, s. In (5.1) m can equal infinity but in practice, of course, due to the finite length of the available data, m will be assumed finite and shorter than the given time series.

The definition of causality given above implies that Y_t is causing X_t provided some b_j is not zero. Similarly X_t is causing Y_t if some c_j is not zero. If both of these events occur, there is said to be a feedback relationship between X_t and Y_t. It will be shown later that this new definition of causality is in fact identical to that introduced previously.

The more general model with instantaneous causality is

$$X_t + b_0 Y_t = \sum_{j=1}^{m} a_j X_{t-j} + \sum_{j=1}^{m} b_j Y_{t-j} + \varepsilon_t,$$

(5.2)

$$Y_t + c_0 X_t = \sum_{j=1}^{m} c_j X_{t-j} + \sum_{j=1}^{m} d_j Y_{t-j} + \eta_t.$$

If the variables are such that this kind of representation is needed, then instantaneous causality is occurring and a knowledge of Y_t will improve the "prediction" or goodness of fit of the first equation for X_t.

Consider initially the simple causal model (5.1). In terms of the time shift operator U—$UX_t = X_{t-1}$—these equations may be written

$$(5.3)\qquad \begin{aligned} X_t &= a(U)X_t + b(U)Y_t + \varepsilon_t, \\ Y_t &= c(U)X_t + d(U)Y_t + \eta_t, \end{aligned}$$

where $a(U)$, $b(U)$, $c(U)$, and $d(U)$ are power series in U with the coefficient of U^0 zero, i.e., $a(U) = \sum_{j=1}^{m} a_j U^j$, etc.

Using the Cramer representations of the series, i.e.,

$$X_t = \int_{-\pi}^{\pi} e^{it\omega}\, dZ_x(\omega), \qquad Y_t = \int_{-\pi}^{\pi} e^{it\omega}\, dZ_y(\omega),$$

and similarly for ε_t and η_t, expressions such as $a(U)X_t$ can be written as

$$a(U)X_t = \int_{-\pi}^{\pi} e^{it\omega} a(e^{-i\omega})\, dZ_x(\omega).$$

Thus, equations (5.3) may be written

$$\int_{-\pi}^{\pi} e^{it\omega}[(1 - a(e^{-i\omega}))\, dZ_x(\omega) - b(e^{-i\omega})\, dZ_y(\omega) - dZ_\varepsilon(\omega)] = 0,$$

$$\int_{-\pi}^{\pi} e^{it\omega}[-c(e^{-i\omega})\, dZ_x(\omega) + (1 - d(e^{-i\omega}))\, dZ_y(\omega) - dZ_\eta(\omega)] = 0,$$

from which it follows that

$$(5.4)\qquad A\begin{bmatrix} dZ_x \\ dZ_y \end{bmatrix} = \begin{bmatrix} dZ_\varepsilon \\ dZ_\eta \end{bmatrix}$$

where

$$A = \begin{bmatrix} 1 - a & -b \\ -c & 1 - d \end{bmatrix}$$

and where a is written for $a(e^{-i\omega})$, etc., and dZ_x for $dZ_x(\omega)$, etc.

Thus, provided the inverse of A exists,

$$(5.5)\qquad \begin{bmatrix} dZ_x \\ dZ_y \end{bmatrix} = A^{-1}\begin{bmatrix} dZ_\varepsilon \\ dZ_\eta \end{bmatrix}.$$

As the spectral, cross-spectral matrix for X_t, Y_t is directly obtainable from

$$E\begin{bmatrix} dZ_x \\ dZ_y \end{bmatrix}[\overline{dZ_x}\, \overline{dZ_y}],$$

these functions can quickly be found from (5.5) using the known properties of dZ_ε and dZ_η. One finds that the power spectra are given by

$$(5.6)\qquad \begin{aligned} f_x(\omega) &= \frac{1}{2\pi\Delta}(|1 - d|^2\sigma_\varepsilon^2 + |b|^2\sigma_\eta^2), \\ f_y(\omega) &= \frac{1}{2\pi\Delta}(|c|^2\sigma_\varepsilon^2 + |1 - a|^2\sigma_\eta^2), \end{aligned}$$

where $\Delta = |(1-a)(1-d) - bc|^2$. Of more interest is the cross spectrum which has the form

$$Cr(\omega) = \frac{1}{2\pi\Delta}[(1-d)\bar{c}\sigma_\varepsilon^2 + (1-\bar{a})b\sigma_\eta^2].$$

Thus, the cross spectrum may be written as the sum of two components

$$Cr(\omega) = C_1(\omega) + C_2(\omega), \tag{5.7}$$

where

$$C_1(\omega) = \frac{\sigma_\varepsilon^2}{2\pi\Delta}(1-d)\bar{c}$$

and

$$C_2(\omega) = \frac{\sigma_\eta^2}{2\pi\Delta}(1-\bar{a})b.$$

If Y_t is not causing X_t, then $b \equiv 0$ and so $C_2(\omega)$ vanishes. Similarly if X_t is not causing Y_t then $c \equiv 0$ and so $C_1(\omega)$ vanishes. It is thus clear that the cross spectrum can be decomposed into the sum of two components—one which depends upon the causality of X by Y and the other on the causality of Y by X.

If, for example, Y is not causing X so that $C_2(\omega)$ vanishes, then $Cr(\omega) = C_1(\omega)$ and the resulting coherence and phase diagrams will be interpreted in the usual manner. This suggests that in general $C_1(\omega)$ and $C_2(\omega)$ can each be treated separately as cross spectra connected with the two arms of the feedback mechanism. Thus, coherence and phase diagrams can be defined for $X \Rightarrow Y$ and $Y \Rightarrow X$. For example,

$$C_{\overrightarrow{xy}}(\omega) = \frac{|C_1(\omega)|^2}{f_x(\omega) f_y(\omega)}$$

may be considered to be a measure of the strength of the causality $X \Rightarrow Y$ plotted against frequency and is a direct generalisation of coherence. We call $C_{\overrightarrow{xy}}(\omega)$ the causality coherence.

Further,

$$\phi_{\overrightarrow{xy}}(\omega) = \tan^{-1} \frac{\text{imaginary part of } C_1(\omega)}{\text{real part of } C_1(\omega)}$$

will measure the phase lag against frequency of $X \Rightarrow Y$ and will be called the causality phase diagram.

Similarly such functions can be defined for $Y \Rightarrow X$ using $C_2(\omega)$.

These functions are usually complicated expressions in a, b, c, and d; for example,

$$C_{\overrightarrow{xy}}(\omega) = \frac{\sigma_\varepsilon^4 |(1-d)c|^2}{(\sigma_\varepsilon^2|1-d|^2 + \sigma_\eta^2|b|^2)(\sigma_\varepsilon^2|c|^2 + |1-a|^2\sigma_\eta^2)}.$$

Such formulae merely illustrate how difficult it is to interpret econometric models in terms of frequency decompositions. It should be noted that $0 < |C_{\overrightarrow{xy}}(\omega)| < 1$ and similarly for $C_{\overrightarrow{yx}}(\omega)$.

As an illustration of these definitions, we consider the simple feedback system

$$X_t = bY_{t-1} + \varepsilon_t, \tag{5.8}$$
$$Y_t = cX_{t-2} + \eta_t,$$

where $\sigma_\varepsilon^2 = \sigma_\eta^2 = 1$.

In this case

$$a(\omega) = 0,$$
$$b(\omega) = b\,e^{-i\omega},$$
$$c(\omega) = c\,e^{-2i\omega},$$
$$d(\omega) = 0.$$

The spectra of the series $\{X_t\}$, $\{Y_t\}$ are

$$f_x(\omega) = \frac{1 + b^2}{2\pi|1 - bc\,e^{-3i\omega}|^2}$$

and

$$f_y(\omega) = \frac{1 + c^2}{2\pi|1 - bc\,e^{-3i\omega}|^2},$$

and thus are of similar shape.

The usual coherence and phase diagrams derived from the cross spectrum between these two series are

$$C(\omega) = \frac{c^2 + b^2 + 2bc\cos\omega}{(1 + b^2)(1 + c^2)}$$

and

$$\phi(\omega) = \tan^{-1}\frac{c\sin 2\omega - b\sin\omega}{c\cos 2\omega + b\cos\omega}.$$

These diagrams are clearly of little use in characterising the feedback relationship between the two series.

When the causality-coherence and phase diagrams are considered, however, we get

$$C_{\vec{xy}}(\omega) = \frac{c^2}{(1 + b^2)(1 + c^2)}, \qquad C_{\vec{yx}}(\omega) = \frac{b^2}{(1 + b^2)(1 + c^2)}.$$

Both are constant for all ω, and, if $b \neq 0, c \neq 0$, $\phi_{\vec{xy}}(\omega) = 2\omega$ (time lag of two units),[1] $\phi_{\vec{yx}}(\omega) = \omega$ (time-lag of one unit).

The causality lags are thus seen to be correct and the causality coherences to be reasonable. In particular, if $b = 0$ then $C_{\vec{yx}}(\omega) = 0$, i.e., no causality is found when none is present. (Further, in this new case, $\phi_{\vec{xy}}(\omega) = 0$.)

[1] A discussion of the interpretation of phase diagrams in terms of time lags may be found in Granger and Hatanaka [4, Chapter 5].

Other particular cases are also found to give correct results. If, for example, we again consider the same simple model (4.8) but with $\sigma_\varepsilon^2 = 1, \sigma_\eta^2 = 0$, i.e., $\eta_t \equiv 0$ for all t, then one finds

$$C_{\overrightarrow{xy}}(\omega) = 1,$$

$$C_{\overrightarrow{yx}}(\omega) = 0,$$

i.e., X is "perfectly" causing Y and Y is not causing X, as is in fact the case.

If one now considers the model (5.2) in which instantaneous causality is allowed, it is found that the cross spectrum is given by

$$Cr(\omega) = \frac{1}{2\pi\Delta'}[(1 - d)(\bar{c} - c_0)\sigma_\varepsilon^2 + (1 - \bar{a})(b - b_0)\sigma_\eta^2] \tag{5.9}$$

where

$$\Delta' = |(1 - a)(1 - d) - (b - b_0)(c - c_0)|^2.$$

Thus, once more, the cross spectrum can be considered as the sum of two components, each of which can be associated with a "causality," provided that this includes instantaneous causality. It is, however, probably more sensible to decompose $Cr(\omega)$ into three parts, $Cr(\omega) = C_1(\omega) + C_2(\omega) + C_3(\omega)$, where $C_1(\omega)$ and $C_2(\omega)$ are as in (5.7) but with Δ replaced by Δ' and

$$C_3(\omega) = \frac{-1}{2\pi\Delta}[c_0(1 - d)\sigma_\varepsilon^2 + b_0(1 - a)\sigma_\eta^2] \tag{5.10}$$

representing the influence of the instantaneous causality.

Such a decomposition may be useful but it is clear that when instantaneous causality occurs, the measures of causal strength and phase lag will lose their meaning.

It was noted in Section 3 that instantaneous causality models such as (5.2) in general lack uniqueness of their parameters as an orthogonal transformation Λ applied to the variables leaves the general form of the model unaltered. It is interesting to note that such transformations do not have any effect on the cross spectrum given by (5.9) or the decomposition. This can be seen by noting that equations (5.2) lead to

$$A\begin{bmatrix} dz_x \\ dz_y \end{bmatrix} = \begin{bmatrix} dz_\varepsilon \\ dz_\eta \end{bmatrix}$$

with appropriate A. Applying the transformation Λ gives

$$\Lambda A\begin{bmatrix} dz_x \\ dz_y \end{bmatrix} = \Lambda\begin{bmatrix} dz_\varepsilon \\ dz_\eta \end{bmatrix}$$

so that

$$\begin{bmatrix} dz_x \\ dz_y \end{bmatrix} = (\Lambda A)^{-1}\Lambda\begin{bmatrix} dz_\varepsilon \\ dz_\eta \end{bmatrix}$$

$$= A^{-1}\begin{bmatrix} dz_\varepsilon \\ dz_\eta \end{bmatrix}$$

which is the same as if no such transformation had been applied. From its definition, Λ will possess an inverse. This result suggests that spectral methods are more robust in their interpretation than are simultaneous equation models.

Returning to the simple causal model (5.3),

$$X_t = a(U)X_t + b(U)Y_t + \varepsilon_t,$$
$$Y_t = c(U)X_t + d(U)Y_t + \eta_t,$$

throughout this section it has been stated that $Y_t \not\Rightarrow X_t$ if $b \equiv 0$. On intuitive grounds this seems to fit the definition of no causality introduced in Section 4, within the set D of series consisting only of X_t and Y_t. If $b \equiv 0$ then X_t is determined from the first equation and the minimum variance of the predictive error of X_t using past X_t will be σ_ε^2. This variance cannot be reduced using past Y_t. It is perhaps worthwhile proving this result formally. In the general case, it is clear that $\sigma^2(X|\overline{X}, \overline{Y}) = \sigma_\varepsilon^2$, i.e., the variance of the predictive error of X_t, if both past X_t and past Y_t are used, will be σ_ε^2 from the top equation. If only past X_t is used to predict X_t, it is a well known result that the minimum variance of the predictive error is given by

$$\text{(5.11)} \qquad \sigma^2(X|\overline{X}) = \exp \tfrac{1}{2}\pi \int_{-\pi}^{\pi} \log \tfrac{1}{2}\pi\, f_x(\omega)\, d\omega.$$

It was shown above in equation (5.6) that

$$f_x(\omega) = \frac{1}{2\pi\Delta}(|1 - d|^2\sigma_\varepsilon^2 + |b|^2\sigma_\eta^2)$$

where $\Delta = |(1-a)(1-d) - bc|^2$. To simplify this equation, we note that

$$\int_{-\pi}^{\pi} \log|1 - \alpha\, e^{i\omega}|^2\, d\omega = 0$$

by symmetry. Thus if,

$$f_x(\omega) = \alpha_0 \frac{\pi|1 - \alpha_j\, e^{i\omega}|^2}{\pi|1 - \beta_j\, e^{i\omega}|^2},$$

then $\sigma^2(X|\overline{X}) = \alpha_0$. For there to be no causality, we must have $\alpha_0 = \sigma_\varepsilon^2$. It is clear from the form of $f_x(\omega)$ that in general this could only occur if $|b| \equiv 0$, in which case $2\pi f_x(\omega) = \sigma_\varepsilon^2/|1 - a|^2$ and the required result follows.

6. THREE-VARIABLE MODELS

The above results can be generalised to the many variables situation, but the only case which will be considered is that involving three variables.

Consider a simple causal model generalising (5.1):

$$X_t = a_1(U)X_t + b_1(U)Y_t + c_1(U)Z_t + \varepsilon_{1,t},$$
$$Y_t = a_2(U)X_t + b_2(U)Y_t + c_2(U)Z_t + \varepsilon_{2,t},$$
$$Z_t = a_3(U)X_t + b_3(U)Y_t + c_3(U)Z_t + \varepsilon_{3,t},$$

where $a_1(U)$, etc., are polynomials in U, the shift operator, with the coefficient of U^0 zero. As before, $\varepsilon_{i,t}$, $i = 1, 2, 3$, are uncorrelated, white-noise series and denote the variance $\varepsilon_{i,t} = \sigma_i^2$.

Let $\alpha = a_1 - 1, \beta = b_2 - 1, \gamma = c_3 - 1$, and

$$A = \begin{bmatrix} \alpha & b_1 & c_1 \\ a_2 & \beta & c_2 \\ a_3 & b_3 & \gamma \end{bmatrix},$$

where $b_1 = b_1(e^{-i\omega})$, etc., as before. Using the same method as before, the spectral, cross-spectral matrix $S(\omega)$ is found to be given by $S(\omega) = A^{-1}k(A')^{-1}$ where

$$k = \begin{bmatrix} \sigma_1^2 & 0 & 0 \\ 0 & \sigma_2^2 & 0 \\ 0 & 0 & \sigma_3^2 \end{bmatrix}.$$

One finds, for instance, that the power spectrum of X_t is

$$f_x(\omega) = |\Delta|^{-2}[\sigma_1^2|\beta\gamma - c_2 b_3|^2 + \sigma_2^2|c_1 b_3 - \gamma b_1|^2 + \sigma_3^2|b_1 c_2^2 - c_1\beta|^2]$$

where Δ is the determinant of A.

The cross spectrum between X_t and Y_t is

$$C_r^{xy}(\omega) = |\Delta|^{-2}[\sigma_1^2(\beta\gamma - c_2 b_3)\overline{(c_2 a_3 - \gamma a_2)} + \sigma_2^2(c_1 b_3 - b_1\gamma)\overline{(\alpha\gamma - c_1 a_3)}$$
$$+ \sigma_3^2(b_1 c_2 - c_1\beta)\overline{(c_1 a_2 - c_2\alpha)}].$$

Thus, this cross spectrum is the sum of three components, but it is not clear that these can be directly linked with causalities. More useful results arise, however, when partial cross spectra are considered. After some algebraic manipulation it is found that, for instance, the partial cross spectrum between X_t and Y_t given Z_t is

$$C_r^{xy,z}(\omega) = -\frac{[\sigma_1^2\sigma_2^2 b_3 a_3 + \sigma_1^2\sigma_3^2\beta a_2 + \sigma_2^2\sigma_3^2 b_1\alpha]}{f_z'(\omega)}$$

where

$$f_z'(\omega) = \sigma_1^2|\beta\gamma - c_2 b_3|^2 + \sigma_2^2|c_1 b_3 - b_1\gamma|^2 + \sigma_3^2|b_1 c_2 - c_1\beta|^2.$$

Thus, the partial cross spectrum is the sum of three components

$$C_r^{xy,z}(\omega) = C_1^{xy,z} + C_2^{xy,z} + C_3^{xy,z}$$

where

$$C_1^{xy,z} = -\frac{\sigma_1^2\sigma_2^2 b_3 a_3}{f_z'(\omega)}, \text{ etc.}$$

These can be linked with causalities. The component $C_1^{xy,z}(\omega)$ represents the interrelationships of X_t and Y_t *through* Z_t, and the other two components are direct generalisations of the two causal cross spectra which arose in the two variable case and can be interpreted accordingly.

In a similar manner one finds that the power spectrum of X_t, given Z_t is

$$f_{x,z}(\omega) = \frac{\sigma_1^2\sigma_2^2|b_3|^2 + \sigma_1^2\sigma_3^2|\beta|^2 + \sigma_2^2\sigma_3^2|b_1|^2}{f'_z(\omega)}.$$

The causal and feedback relationships between X_t and Y_t can be investigated in terms of the coherence and phase diagrams derived from the second and third components of the partial cross spectrum, i.e.,

$$\text{coherence}\,(\overrightarrow{xy}, z) = \frac{|C_2^{xy,z}|^2}{f_{x,y}f_{y,z}}, \quad \text{etc.}$$

7. CONCLUSION

The fact that a feedback mechanism may be considered as the sum of two causal mechanisms and that these causalities can be studied by decomposing cross or partial cross spectra suggests methods whereby such mechanisms can be investigated. Hopefully, the problem of estimating the causal cross spectra will be discussed in a later publication. There are a number of possible approaches and accumulated experience is needed to indicate which is best. Most of these approaches are via the model-building method by which the above results were obtained. It is worth investigating, however, whether a direct method of estimating the components of the cross spectrum can be found.

The University of Nottingham

REFERENCES

[1] Basman, R. L.: "The Causal Interpretation of Non-Triangular Systems of Economic Relations," *Econometrica*, Volume 31, 1963, pp. 439–448.

[2] Good, I. J.: "A Causal Calculus, I, II," *Brit. J. Philos. Soc.*, Volume 11, 1961, pp. 305–318 and Volume 12, 1962, pp. 43–51.

[3] Granger, C. W. J.: "Economic Processes Involving Feedback," *Information and Control*, Volume 6, 1963, pp. 28–48.

[4] Granger, C. W. J., and M. Hatanaka: *Spectral Analysis of Economic Time Series*, Princeton University Press, 1964.

[5] Nerlove, M.: "Spectral Analysis of Seasonal Adjustment Procedures," *Econometrica*, Volume 32, 1964, pp. 241–286.

[6] Orcutt, G. H.: "Actions, Consequences and Causal Relations," *Review of Economics and Statistics*, Volume 34, 1952, pp. 305–13.

[7] Simon, H. A.: "Causal Ordering and Identifiability," *Studies in Econometric Method* (edited by W. C. Hood and T. C. Koopmans), Cowles Commission Monograph 14, New York, 1953.

[8] Strotz, R. H., and H. Wold: "Recursive versus Non-Recursive Systems: An Attempt at Synthesis," *Econometrica*, Volume 28, 1960, pp. 417–427.

[9] Wiener, N.: "The Theory of Prediction," *Modern Mathematics for Engineers*, Series 1 (edited by E. F. Beckenback), Chapter 8, 1956.

[2]

Money, Income, and Causality

By Christopher A. Sims*

This study has two purposes. One is to examine the substantive question: Is there statistical evidence that money is "exogenous" in some sense in the money-income relationship? The other is to display in a simple example some time-series methodology not now in wide use. The main methodological novelty is the use of a direct test for the existence of unidirectional causality. This test is of wide importance, since most efficient estimation techniques for distributed lags are invalid unless causality is unidirectional in the sense of this paper. Also, the paper illustrates the estimation of long lag distributions without the imposition of the usual restrictions requiring the shape of the distribution to be rational or polynomial.

The main empirical finding is that the hypothesis that causality is unidirectional from money to income agrees with the postwar *U.S.* data, whereas the hypothesis that causality is unidirectional from income to money is rejected. It follows that the practice of making causal interpretations of distributed lag regressions of income on money is not invalidated (on the basis of this evidence) by the existence of "feedback" from income to money.

* Associate professor of economics, University of Minnesota. Work for this paper was carried out during my tenure as a research fellow at the National Bureau of Economic Research, and a more extended paper on this topic may appear as a *NBER* publication. Numerous members of the *NBER* staff provided support at various stages of the research. Special thanks are due to Philip Cagan, John Hause, Milton Friedman, the Columbia Monetary Economics Workshop, and a seminar at the Cowles Foundation, whose objections and advice have sharpened the paper's argument. Josephine Su carried out the computational work. H. I. Forman drew the charts.

I. The Causal Ordering Question for Money and Income

It has long been known that money stock and current dollar measures of economic activity are positively correlated. There is, further, evidence that money or its rate of change tends to "lead" income in some sense.[1] A body of macro-economic theory, the "Quantity Theory," explains these empirical observations as reflecting a causal relation running from money to income. However, it is widely recognized that no degree of positive association between money and income can by itself prove that variation in money causes variation in income. Money might equally well react passively and very reliably to fluctuations in income. Historically observed timing relations between turning points have also for some time been recognized not to be conclusive evidence for causal ordering. James Tobin and William Brainard and Tobin provide explicit examples of the possibilities for noncorrespondence between causal ordering and temporal ordering of turning points. People in close connection with the details of monetary policy know that some components of the money supply react passively to cyclical developments in the economy. Frank DeLeeuw and John Kalchbrenner, for example, argue that the monetary base (currency plus total reserves) is not properly treated as an exogenous variable in a regression equation because of the known dependence be-

[1] See Milton Friedman and Anna Schwartz (1963b), Friedman (1961), (1964) reprinted in chs. 10–12 of Friedman (1969).

tween certain of its components and cyclical factors.

Phillip Cagan uses an analysis of the details of money-supply determination to argue convincingly that the long-run relation between money supply and the price level cannot be due primarily to feedback from prices to money. His application of the same analytical technique to cyclical relations of money with income measures fails to yield a firm conclusion, however.

Friedman and Schwartz have argued on the basis of historical analysis that major depressions have been caused by autonomous movements in money stock.[2]

The issues between the monetarists and the skeptics are not easily defined on the basis of the literature cited in the preceding paragraphs. Probably few of the skeptics would deny *any* causal influence of money on income. But, on the other hand, leading exponents of the monetarist approach seem ready to admit that there is "clear evidence of the influence of business change on the quantity of money,"[3] at least for the mild cycles which have characterized the postwar United States.

Now if the consensus view that there is some influence of business conditions on money is correct, if this influence is of significant magnitude, and if current dollar *GNP* is a good index of business conditions,[4] then distributed lag regressions treating money as strictly exogenous are not causal relations. Since such regressions are now treated as causal relations by some economists, it is important to test the assumption of causal priority on which they rest.

As will be shown below, there is a natural analogue in a dynamic system to Wold's "causal chain" form for a static econometric model.[5] This analogue turns out to be exactly a model in which causation is unidirectional according to the criterion developed by C. W. J. Granger. But Wold's form is in general not testable in a static context; any multivariate set of data with a specified list of endogenous variables can be fit by a recursive model. The dynamic analogue is, however, easily testable: If and only if causality runs one way from current and past values of some list of exogenous variables to a given endogenous variable, then in a regression of the endogenous variable on past, current, and future values of the exogenous variables, the future values of the exogenous variables should have zero coefficients.

Application of this test to a two-variable system in a monetary aggregate and current dollar *GNP* with quarterly data shows clearly that causality does not run one way from *GNP* to money. The evidence agrees quite well with a null hypothesis that causality runs entirely from money to *GNP*, without feedback.

II. The Meaning of the Results

Before giving a rigorous explanation of the notion of causal direction and the detailed description of statistical results, it is worthwhile to consider in a nontechnical way what the results do and do not prove. That the test applied in this paper shows no feedback from y to x is a necessary condition for it to be reasonable to interpret a distributed lag regression of y on current and past x as a causal relation or to apply any of the common estimation methods involving use of lagged dependent variables or corrections for serial cor-

[2] See Friedman and Schwartz (1963b), p. 217–18 as reprinted in Friedman (1969).

[3] The quoted phrase is from Milton Friedman's introduction to Cagan, p. xxvi, and summarizes one of Cagan's main results.

[4] As I will argue below, it may be that the one-dimensional current dollar *GNP* index is so inadequate a measure of those aspects of business conditions which influence money supply that there is no feedback from current dollar *GNP* to money despite the existence of feedback from business conditions to money.

[5] See Edmond Malinvaud, p. 511 ff., for a description of causal chain models.

relation. Hence the most conservative way to state the results for money and income is that they show it to be unreasonable to interpret a least squares lag distribution for money on *GNP* as a causal relation, and that they provide no grounds for asserting that distributed lag regressions of *GNP* on money do not yield estimates of a causal relation. It is natural, and I believe appropriate, to phrase the result more positively: the data verify the null hypothesis that distributed lag regressions of *GNP* on money have a causal interpretation. However, it is possible to concoct models in which a money on *GNP* regression does not yield a causal relation and yet this paper's test would not detect feedback.

The test will fail to detect within-quarter feedback of a certain type. The "innovation" in the stochastic process x_t is that part of x_t which cannot be predicted from x_t's own past (i.e., the residual in a regression of x_t on its own past). If x_t and y_t are connected by two causal relations—one from x to y involving a distributed lag, and the other from y to x but with only the current innovation in y_t on the right-hand side—then the test used in this paper will not detect the y to x feedback.[6]

Where the data show negligible serial correlation, this failing of the test becomes important. For then y and x are their own innovations and one expects that causal relations may be purely contemporaneous. In the general case, with serially correlated data, the failing is not likely to be important. It can result in false conclusions only where there is a certain sort of exact relation between the lag distributions defining the causal structure and the autocorrelation functions of the error terms. With one important class of exceptions, there is seldom reason to suppose any relation at all between the causal structure and the properties of the error terms.

The exception arises for models in which some elements of optimal control enter. If one of the two relations in a bivariate system is chosen optimally, then the innovations in the variables become structural elements of the system. This fact is important for money and income, since it is easy to imagine that money may have been controlled to influence or to conform to income. It can be shown that in a bivariate system with optimal control of one variable, there will be in general two-way causality by the Granger criterion. The only exception is that if the information lag in the control process is just one period and if the criterion for control is minimal variance in, say, y, then causality will spuriously appear to run from y to x.[7] But then the only way optimal control would be likely to hide income-to-money feedback would be if income were controlled to hold down variance in money. This seems farfetched.

The fact that this paper finds no evidence of feedback from *GNP* to money is not direct evidence on the structure of money-supply determination. All that is necessary to allow interpretation of the money on *GNP* distributed lags as causal relations is the hypothesis that in this particular historical sample (1947–69), the determinants of money supply showed no *consistent* pattern of influence by *GNP*. Thus it would be enough if, for example, money supply were influenced quite differently by real and price components of *GNP* movements, so long as actual *GNP* movements were not dominated by one

[6] One elementary consequence is that it is possible for the test to show no feedback in either direction, despite the existence of well-defined lag distributions in both x on y and y on x regressions. This is the case where all the relation between y and x consists of contemporaneous correlation of their innovations.

[7] Proving this in any generality would require stretching the length and increasing the technical level of the paper. I expect to take up this point at greater length in a subsequent paper.

component or the other. Alternatively, a consistent pattern of feedback from *GNP* to money could have been swamped in this sample period by extraneous influences on money. The situation is analogous to that in a supply and demand estimation problem, where we have evidence that in a particular sample elements other than price dominated supply. Such evidence proves that in the sample the price-quantity relation traces the demand curve, but it does not in itself prove anything about the supply curve. Thus one can imagine that if heightened awareness of the importance of monetary policy makes money respond more consistently to the business cycle, single-equation estimates of the money-to-*GNP* relation will become unreliable.

Finally, we ought to consider whether the bivariate model underlying this paper could be mimicking a more complicated model with a different causal structure. The method of identifying causal direction employed here does rest on a sophisticated version of the *post hoc ergo propter hoc* principle. However, the method is not easily fooled. Simple linear structures with reversed causality like the one put forth by Tobin cannot be constructed to give apparent money-to-*GNP* causality. Complicated structures like that put forward by Brainard and Tobin in which both *GNP* and money are endogenous will except under very special assumptions yield a bivariate reduced form showing bidirectional causality. The special assumptions required to make endogenous money appear exogenous in a bivariate system must make money essentially identical to a truly exogenous variable. Thus, if money has in the sample been passively and quickly adjusted to match the animal spirits of bankers and businessmen, and if animal spirits is a truly exogenous variable affecting *GNP* with a distributed lag, then money might falsely appear to cause *GNP*. However, if there is substantial random error in the correspondence between animal spirits and money and that error has a pattern of serial correlation different from that of animal spirits itself, then the bivariate relation between money and *GNP* will appear to show bidirectional causality.[8]

An assumption that future values of money or income cause current values of the other, via economic actors' having forecasts of the future better than could be obtained from current and past money and *GNP*, will affect the apparent direction of causality. However, the effect is much more likely to make a truly unidirectional structure appear bidirectional than vice versa. For example, it is easy to see that if current money supply is determined in part by extraneous knowledge of *GNP* for several future quarters, past money could spuriously appear to affect current *GNP*. However, it is difficult to imagine in such a situation why past *GNP* and all the variation in future *GNP* which can be predicted from past *GNP* should *not* affect money. Without such an artificial assumption, one cannot explain a one-sided lag distribution of *GNP* on money by a "reversed-causation-with-accurate-anticipations" model.

III. Testing for the Direction of Causality[9]

In a single, static sample, the "direction of causation" connecting two related groups of variables is ordinarily not identified. That is, one can construct many different models of causal influence all of which are consistent with a given pattern

[8] This point is not obvious, but to prove it would, as in the case of the previous point about optimal control, overextend the paper. The technically sophisticated reader may easily verify the proposition for himself.

[9] It is my impression that many of the results in this section, even where they have not previously been given formal expression, are widely understood. For example, H. Akaike clearly understands that a two-sided transfer function implies the existence of feedback.

of covariances amongst the variables. If one is willing to identify causal ordering with Wold's causal chain form for a multivariate model, and if enough identifying restrictions are available in addition to those specifying the causal chain form, one can test a particular causal ordering as a set of overidentifying restrictions. The conditions allowing such a test are seldom met in practice, however.

Granger has given a definition of a testable kind of causal ordering based on the notion that absence of correlation between *past* values of one variable X and that part of another variable Y which cannot be predicted from Y's own past implies absence of causal influence from X to Y. More precisely, the time-series Y is said to "cause" X relative to the universe U (U is a vector time-series including X and Y as components) if, and only if, predictions of $X(t)$ based on $U(s)$ for all $s<t$ are better than predictions based on all components of $U(s)$ except $Y(s)$ for all $s<t$.

We will give content to Granger's definitions by assuming all time-series to be jointly covariance-stationary, by considering only linear predictors, and by taking expected squared forecast error as our criterion for predictive accuracy.

Consider the jointly covariance-stationary pair of stochastic processes X and Y. If X and Y are jointly purely linearly indeterministic (linearly regular in the terminology of Yu. S. Rozanov), then we can write

$$(1)\qquad \begin{aligned} X(t) &= a^*u(t) + b^*v(t) \\ Y(t) &= c^*u(t) + d^*v(t) \end{aligned}$$

where u and v are mutually uncorrelated white noise[10] processes with unit variance, a, b, c, and d all vanish for $t<0$, and the notation

$$g^*f(t) = \sum_{s=-\infty}^{\infty} g(s)f(t-s)$$

The expression (1) is the moving average representation of the vector process $\left[\begin{smallmatrix} X \\ Y \end{smallmatrix}\right]$ and is unique up to multiplication by a unitary matrix.[11]

A useful result, not proved by Granger, is

THEOREM 1: *Y does not cause X in Granger's definition if, and only if, a or b can be chosen identically 0.*[12]

This result gives us another intuitive handle on Granger causality. If causality is from X to Y only, then of the two orthogonal white noises which make up X and Y, one is X itself "whitened" and the other is the error in predicting Y from current and past X, whitened. (A whitened variable is one which has been passed through a linear filter to make it a white noise.)

Granger has shown that if there is an autoregressive representation, given by

$$(2)\qquad B^*\begin{bmatrix} X \\ Y \end{bmatrix}(t) = \begin{bmatrix} u \\ v \end{bmatrix}(t),$$

$B(t)=0$ for $t<0$, u, v defined by (1), then the absence of causality running from Y to X is equivalent to the upper right-hand element of B being zero. That is, causality runs only from X to Y if past Y does not influence current X. From this point it is not hard to show:

THEOREM 2: *When $\left[\begin{smallmatrix} X \\ Y \end{smallmatrix}\right]$ has an autore-*

[10] A "white noise" is a serially uncorrelated process.

[11] Actually, the statement that (1) is the moving average representation of $\left[\begin{smallmatrix} X \\ Y \end{smallmatrix}\right]$ is a condition for uniqueness. There will be forms of (1) for which a, b, c, and d are all 0 for $t<0$ and u and v are white noises but do not yield moving average representations. These forms of (1) will not be unitary transformations of the moving average representation and can be distinguished from the true moving average representation by the fact that in a true moving average representation $a(0)u(t)+b(0)v(t)$ is the limiting forecast error in forecasting $X(t)$ from all past X and Y.

[12] Proofs of both theorems appear in the Appendix.

gressive representation, Y can be expressed as a distributed lag function of current and past X with a residual which is not correlated with any values of X, past or future, if, and only if, Y does not cause X in Granger's sense.

We can always estimate a regression of Y on current and past X. But only in the special case where causality runs from X to Y can we expect that no future values of X would enter the regression if we allowed them. Hence, we have a practical statistical test for unidirectional causality: Regress Y on past and future values of X, taking account by generalized least squares or prefiltering of the serial correlation in $w(t)$. Then if causality runs from X to Y only, future values of X in the regression should have coefficients insignificantly different from zero, as a group.

An implication of Theorem 2 is that many commonly applied distributed lag estimation techniques are valid only if causality runs one way from independent to dependent variable. The condition that the independent variable X be "strictly exogenous," central to most statistical theory on time-series regression, is exactly the Theorem 2 condition that $X(t)$ be uncorrelated with the residual $U(s)$ for any t, s. For example, quasi differencing to eliminate serial correlation in residuals will produce inconsistent estimates without the one-way causality condition; and the "Koyck transformation" which is invoked to allow interpretation of regressions with autoregressive terms as estimates of infinite lag distributions depends on one-way causality. Hence in principle a large proportion of econometric studies involving distributed lags should include a preliminary test for direction of causality.

Remarks on Distributed Lag Methodology

Especially in a study of this kind, where we wish to make fairly precise use of F-tests on groups of coefficients, it is important that the assumption of serially uncorrelated residuals be approximately accurate. Therefore all variables used in regressions were measured as natural *logs* and prefiltered using the filter $1-1.5L+.5625L^2$; i.e., each logged variable $x(t)$ was replaced by $x(t)-1.5x(t-1)+.5625x(t-2)$. This filter approximately flattens the spectral density of most economic time-series, and the hope was that regression residuals would be very nearly white noise with this prefiltering.

Two problems are raised by this prefiltering. First, if the filter has failed to produce white noise residuals, it is quite unlikely to fail by leaving substantial positive first-order serial correlation. Durbin-Watson statistics are therefore of little use in testing for lack of serial correlation, and tests based on the spectral density of the residuals were used instead. Second, as I pointed out in an earlier paper (1970), prefiltering may produce a perverse effect on approximation error when lag distributions are subject to prior "smoothness" restrictions. Therefore, no Koyck, Almon, or rational lag restrictions were imposed a priori, and the length of the estimated lag distributions was kept generous.

In applying the F-tests for causal direction suggested in the previous section, one should bear in mind that the absolute size of the coefficients is important regardless of the F value. It is a truism too often ignored that coefficients which are "large" from the economic point of view should not be casually set to zero no matter how statistically "insignificant" they are. Thus, the fact that future values of the independent variable have coefficients insignificantly different from zero only shows that unidirectional causality is possible. If the estimated coefficients on future values are as large or larger than those on past values, bidirectional causality may be very important in practice, despite insignificant F's. Moreover, small coefficients on future values of the independent variable may sometimes be safely ignored even when they are statistically significant. This is especially true in the light of my observation (1971) that nonzero coefficients on future values may be generated in discrete-time data from a "one-sided" continuous-time distributed lag.[13]

All the data used in the regressions presented in this paper were seasonally adjusted at the source. This creates potential problems of a sort which has not been widely recognized heretofore. Most seasonal adjustment procedures in common use allow for a seasonal pattern which shifts slowly over time, and the rate at which the seasonal pattern is taken to shift varies from one series to another. It can be shown[14] that in distributed lag regressions relating two variables which have been deseasonalized by procedures with different assumed rates of shift in the seasonal pattern, spurious "seasonal" variation is likely to appear in the estimated lag distribution. The lag distributions estimated in this paper are long enough and free enough in form that bias from this source should be obvious wherever it is important (and it is important in one regression). However, it would be better to start from undeseasonalized data, being sure that both variables in the relation are deseasonalized in the same way. A check along these lines, using frequency-domain procedures, was carried out for this paper and is mentioned in the discussion of results below.

[13] The definition of causality given in the previous section generalized easily to continuous time. One simply reinterprets (1) as a continuous-time relation, and "Y does not cause X" still corresponds to "b identically zero."

[14] I showed this in an earlier mimeographed version of this paper. A separate short paper on this topic is in preparation.

IV. Time Domain Regression Results

The data used cover the period 1947–69, quarterly. Money was measured both as monetary base (MB)—currency plus reserves adjusted for changes in reserve requirements—and as $M1$—currency plus demand deposits. Figures for MB were taken from the series prepared by the Federal Reserve Bank of St. Louis and supplied to the National Bureau of Economic Research data bank. Results were similar for $M1$ and MB, so we sometimes use M or money to refer to both $M1$ and MB in what follows.

Regressions of the *log* of GNP (in current dollars) on future and lagged *log* M were significant, as were the reversed regressions of *log* M on future and lagged *log* GNP. (See Table 1.) Table 2 reports tests for homogeneity between the pre-1958 and post-1958 sections of the sample. No significant differences between the subsamples appeared in the regressions. Future values of GNP were highly significant in explaining the M dependent variable, but future values of M were not significant in explaining the GNP dependent variable. (See Table 3.) The largest individual coefficients in each GNP on M regression occur on past lags,

TABLE 1—SUMMARY OF *OLS* REGRESSIONS[a]

	F for Independent Variables	$\bar{R}^2$	Standard Error of Estimate	Degrees of Freedom
$GNP=f(M1$, 8 past lags)	1.89*	0.7927	0.01018	64
$GNP=f(M1$, 4 future, 8 past lags)	1.37	0.7840	0.01040	60
$GNP=f(MB$, 8 past lags)	2.24**	0.8004	0.00999	64
$GNP=f(MB$, 4 future, 8 past lags)	1.61	0.7924	0.01019	60
$M1=f(GNP$, 4 future, 8 past lags)	11.25**	0.8385	0.00403	60
$MB=f(GNP$, 4 future, 8 past lags)	5.89**	0.8735	0.00410	60

* Significant at 0.10 level.
** Significant at 0.05 level.
[a] All regressions were fit to the period 1949III-1968IV. $M1$ is currency plus demand deposits. MB is monetary base as prepared by the Federal Reserve Bank of St. Louis. The F-tests shown are for the null hypothesis that all right-hand side variables except trend and seasonal dummies had zero coefficients. See also notes to Table 4.

TABLE 2—*F*'S FOR COMPARISONS OF SUBPERIODS 1948III–1957III VS. 1957IV–1968IV[a]

Regression Equation	*F*	Degrees of Freedom
$GNP=f(M1$, 8 past lags)	1.44	(14, 50)
$GNP=f(MB$, 8 past lags)	0.64	(14, 50)
$M1=g(GNP$, 4 future, 8 past lags)	0.88	(18, 46)
$MB=f(GNP$, 4 future, 8 past lags)	1.01	(18, 46)

[a] Tests are for the null hypothesis that all coefficients (including trend and seasonals) remained the same in both subsamples.

TABLE 3—*F*-TESTS ON FOUR FUTURE QUARTERS' COEFFICIENTS[a]

Regression Equation	*F*
GNP on *M*1	0.36
GNP on *MB*	0.39
*M*1 on *GNP*	4.29**
MB on *GNP*	5.89**

** Significant at 0.05 level

[a] All tests apply to regressions run over the full sample and are assumed distributed as $F(4, 60)$.

and the estimated shapes for those regressions appear broadly reasonable on the assumption that coefficients on future lags are small and coefficients on past lags are nonzero and fairly smooth. (See Table 4 and Figures 1 and 2.)

These results allow firm rejection of the hypothesis that money is purely passive, responding to *GNP* without influencing it. They are consistent with the hypothesis that *GNP* is purely passive, responding to *M* according to a stable distributed lag but not influencing *M*.

But let us note a few statistical *caveats.* Though the estimated distribution looks like what we expect from a one-sided true distribution, the standard errors on the future coefficients are relatively high. These results are just what a unidirectional causality believer would expect, but they are not such as to necessarily force a believer in bidirectional causality to change his mind. Also, seasonality problems are

TABLE 4—LAG DISTRIBUTIONS FROM TIME-DOMAIN REGRESSIONS[a]

Coefficient on lag of:	*GNP* on *MB* past only	*GNP* on *MB* with future	*MB* on *GNP*	*GNP* on *M*1 past only	*GNP* on *M*1 with future	*M*1 on *GNP*
−4		−0.65	.162		−.300	.050
−3		.290	−.013		.120	.117
−2		−.088	.105		.126	.069
−1		−.110	.179		.105	.125
0	.603	.532	.171	.570	.484	.181
1	.593	.507	.015	.370	.412	.089
2	.509	.515	.052	−.034	−.017	.116
3	−.029	.080	.264	.543	.582	.107
4	−.011	.023	.107	−.242	−.363	.027
5	−.865	−.822	−.009	−.178	−.147	.027
6	−.037	−.053	.016	−.180	−.136	.025
7	−.296	−.282	.147	−.157	−.139	.123
8	.072	.039	.130	−.326	−.405	.112
Standard errors of coefficients:						
Largest s.e.	.313	.338	.052	.293	.318	.051
Smallest s.e.	.272	.276	.045	.274	.294	.044
Sum of coefficients	.540	—	—	.365	—	—
Standard error of sum	.442	—	—	.523	—	—

[a] Regressions were on *logs* of variables, prefiltered as explained in the text. Each regression included, in addition to the leading and lagging values of the independent variable for which coefficients are shown, a constant term, a linear trend term, and three seasonal dummies. Trends were in all cases significant. Seasonal dummies were insignificant. (The data were seasonally adjusted.)

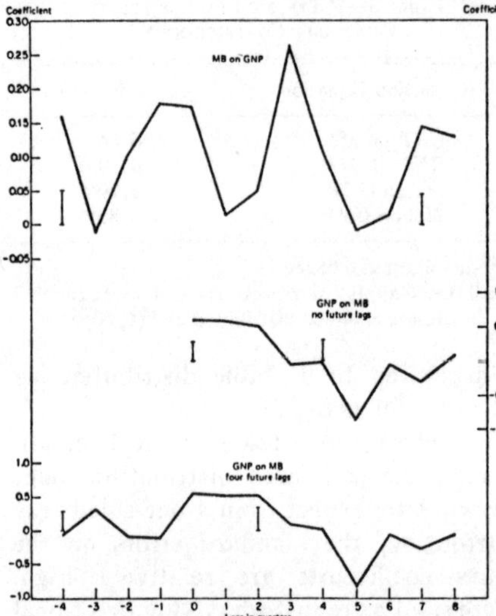

FIGURE 1. LAG DISTRIBUTIONS FOR *MB* AND *GNP*
Note: Smallest and largest standard errors are displayed as vertical lines above or below corresponding coefficients.

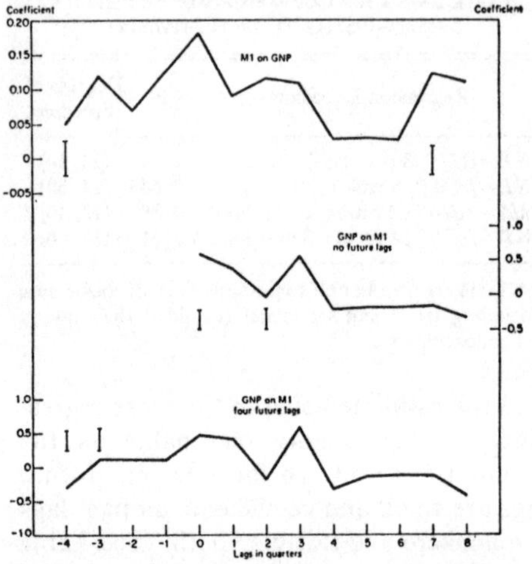

FIGURE 2. LAG DISTRIBUTIONS FOR *M*1 AND *GNP*
Note: Smallest and largest standard errors are displayed as vertical lines above or below corresponding coefficients.

clearly present in the *MB* on *GNP* regression. Seasonality effects appear to be less of a problem with *M*1 than with *MB*.

DeLeeuw and Kalchbrenner have argued, in attacking the "reduced form" money vs. *GNP* regressions put out by the St. Louis Fed, that the monetary base is not truly exogenous. We have discussed above the substance of that argument. Suffice it to say here that they claim that one could make the monetary base more "exogenous" by extracting from it borrowed reserves and (possibly) cash in hands of the public. Attempts to use these adjusted *MB* series (one of them is actually unborrowed reserves) failed, in the sense that relations were less significant statistically and *GNP* on adjusted *MB* regressions did not show one-sided lag distributions.

The same regression equations used for *GNP* and *M* were estimated also with *GNP* replaced by the *GNP* deflator (*PGNP*) and then by real *GNP* (*RGNP*) with *MB* the money variable. Quantity theory even in its modern guise does not claim to have firm implications about the way income changes divide into real and price components, but it seemed useful to examine the possibility that monetary variables would predict the components separately as well as their product. Standard errors of the (logarithmic) equations regressing *RGNP* on *MB* were slightly larger than corresponding standard errors for current dollar *GNP*. Values of coefficients and *F*-statistics were much the same with *RGNP* as dependent variable as with *GNP* the dependent variable. Future lags were again highly significant for *MB* on *GNP* regressions and highly insignificant for the reversed relation. However, with *RGNP*, current plus eight past lagged values of *MB* were not as a group significantly different from zero at the .10 level. With *PGNP*, standard errors of estimate were small, but almost every *F*-test failed to attain significance, including the test on future lags in the *MB* on *PGNP* relation.

V. Tests for Serial Correlation in Residuals

Durbin-Watson statistics for all reported regressions are close to two. This is to be expected because of the prefiltering. The test on the cumulated periodogram of the residuals, described by James Durbin, yields results in the indeterminate range for each regression.[15] The test on the cumulated periodogram is in principle capable of detecting departures from serial independence even when there is no first-order serial correlation, and in this sense is a stronger test than the Durbin-Watson for the case at hand.

The central difficulty here, though, is that a total of 17 of the available 78 degrees of freedom have been used up in the regression, so that the easily-computed bounds tests leave a wide range of indeterminancy. An alternative to the bounds tests is to use the likelihood ratio test for the null hypothesis that the periodogram of the residuals has constant expectation across a number of intervals. This test is described in E. J. Hannan (1960), p. 98.[16] In application to regression residuals this test is justified only when the number of observations is much larger than the number of independent variables, which is clearly not the case here. The statistics reported in Table 5 would be distributed as chi-square with 7 degrees of freedom if asymptotic results applied, but the true significance levels of the test will be higher than the nominal ones. Even at nominal significance levels, though, only the residuals from the regression of *GNP* on *M*1 are significantly "nonwhite" at a 5 percent level.

Table 5—Likelihood-Ratio Tests for White Noise Residuals[a]

GNP on *MB*	*GNP* on *M*1	*MB* on *GNP*	*M*1 on *GNP*
13.02	19.01	11.04	12.64

Note: .05 significance level for chi-squared with 7 degrees of freedom. 14.1

[a] The statistics shown are each distributed asymptotically as chi-square with 7 degrees of freedom on the null hypothesis of white noise residuals. As noted in the text, the asymptotic distribution is probably not a good approximation to the true distribution here. For the *GNP* on *M* equations, residuals were taken from the form with no future lags. For the *M* on *GNP* equations, residuals were taken from the form including future lags.

The conclusion from this list of approximate or inconclusive tests can only be that there is room for doubt about the accuracy of the *F*-tests on regression coefficients.

As a check on the least squares results, these same regressions were estimated also using a frequency-domain procedure, Hannan's (1963) "inefficient" procedure.[17] This procedure has some disadvantages relative to least squares, but it has the two advantages that 1) it makes it computationally simple to estimate the variance-covariance structure of the residuals and use the estimate in constructing tests on the estimated regression coefficients and 2) it makes it easy to deseasonalize raw data directly. Not all the tests for significance of groups of coefficients came out

[15] The test carried out was actually based on cumulation of the periodogram over 128 equally spaced points, instead of over the 39 harmonic frequencies as would be appropriate to get Durbin's test. This difference is, however, demonstrably asymptotically negligible (as sample size increases Durbin's test converges in distribution to any test based on more points than half the sample size) and seems unlikely to have been very important even at this particular sample size.

[16] Hannan's description includes Bartlett's small-sample correction to the likelihood ratio test. The results reported in Table 5 do not include the Bartlett correction, since it was small.

[17] The theory of these estimates has been extended in Hannan (1967) and Wahba. It is worthwhile noting that Wahba's proof that the Hannan inefficient estimates are "approximately" least squares estimates is not a proof that the Hannan inefficient estimates have the same asymptotic distribution as least squares, and their asymptotic distributions are in fact different.

the same way at the same significance levels in the frequency-domain estimates, but the general agreement with the least squares results was so close that there is no point in reproducing the frequency-domain results here.[18] Raw data for the monetary base was not readily available, but frequency-domain estimates using raw data on $M1$ and GNP, symmetrically deseasonalized, gave results very similar to those obtained with least squares on published deseasonalized data.

VI. The Form of the Lag Distribution

The lag distribution estimated here to relate GNP to M has only a loosely determined form because of the lack of prior restrictions on its shape. Still, it is worthwhile noting that it agrees in general shape with many previous estimates, and that it can be given an economic explanation. The distribution is positive at first, then becomes mostly negative beyond the fourth lag. The initial positive coefficients sum to a number greater than one, though the sum of all the coefficients is less than one. (Note, though, that the standard error on the sum of coefficients is very large. See Table 4.) The pattern of a short-run elasticity exceeding unity and a long-run elasticity below unity agrees with the theoretical speculations of Friedman (1969), pp. 138–39, concerning the effects of a demand for money dependent on permanent rather than on current income. However, note that the contemporaneous quarter response is less than unitary, and that negative response does not set in for several quarters. To explain this, one must either introduce an averaging procedure into the other side of the equation, making "permanent money" depend on permanent income, or one must introduce the possibility of transactional frictions which keep the economy off its demand curve for money in the short run. At least the latter of these elements is not novel. Alan Walters pointed out that over short enough time intervals people are likely to be off their demand curves. It seems only natural that, since individuals' money balances always fluctuate over short periods due to random timing of transactions, it should take time for changes in money balances to affect individuals' spending behavior.

[18] The frequency-domain results were presented and discussed in an earlier mimeographed version of this paper.

VII. Conclusion

The main conclusions of the paper were summarized in the introduction. I repeat them more briefly here: In time-series regression it is possible to test the assumption that the right-hand side variable is exogenous; thus the choice of "direction of regression" need not be made entirely on a priori grounds. Application of this test to aggregate quarterly data on $U.S.$ GNP and money stock variables shows that one clearly should not estimate a demand for money relation from these data, treating GNP as exogenous with money on the left-hand side; no evidence appears to contradict the common assumption that money can be treated as exogenous in a regression of GNP on current and past money.

Appendix

THEOREM 1: *Y does not cause X in Granger's definition if, and only if, in the moving average representation*

$$\text{(A)} \qquad \begin{bmatrix} X(t) \\ Y(t) \end{bmatrix} = \begin{bmatrix} a & b \\ c & d \end{bmatrix} * \begin{bmatrix} u \\ v \end{bmatrix} (t),$$

a or b can be chosen to be identically zero.

PROOF:

Following Rozanov we introduce the notation $H_z(t)$ to stand for the completion under the quadratic mean norm of the linear space of random variables spanned by $z(s)$ for $s \leq t$. Suppose b is zero. Clearly $X(t)$ then lies in $H_u(t)$. By the definition of a moving average (*m.a.*) representation, $H_{X,Y}(t)$ is identical to $H_{u,v}(t)$. But it follows from Rozanov's "Remarks" on pages 62–63 that if $H_u(t)$ and $H_X(t)$ are not identical, then with b zero the identity of $H_{X,Y}(t)$ and $H_{u,v}(t)$ fails. Therefore, $H_u(t)$ and $H_X(t)$ are identical. But then the projection of $X(t)$ on $H_{X,Y}(t-1)$ is in $H_X(t-1)$, which is to say that given past X, past Y does not help in predicting current X. One side of the double implication is proved.

In Granger's definition, Y not causing X is the same thing as the projection of $X(t+1)$ on $H_{X,Y}(t)$ lying in $H_X(t)$. Assuming this condition holds, define $u(t)$ as the difference between $X(t)$ and the projection of $X(t)$ on $H_X(t-1)$. Define $w(t)$ as the difference between $Y(t)$ and the projection of $Y(t)$ on $H_{X,Y}(t-1)$. Finally, define $v(t)$ as that part of $w(t)$ orthogonal to $u(t)$ (i.e., the residual in a regression of $w(t)$ on $u(t)$). By definition, $u(t)$ and $w(t)$ and therefore, $v(t)$ are uncorrelated with past values of each other. Also, $u(t)$ and $v(t)$ are contemporaneously uncorrelated and $H_{u,v}(t)$ is identical to $H_{X,Y}(t)$. Expressing $X(t)$ and $Y(t)$ in terms of the coordinates $u(s)$, $s \leq t$, will give us a moving average representation of the form (A).

THEOREM 2: *When* $\begin{bmatrix} X \\ Y \end{bmatrix}$ *has an autoregressive representation, Y can be expressed as a distributed lag function of current and past X with a residual which is not correlated with any X(s), past or future if, and only if, Y does not cause X in Granger's sense.*

PROOF:

Suppose Y can be expressed as a distributed lag on X with a residual $w(t)$ independent of $X(s)$ for all s. Let $u(t)$ be the fundamental white noise process in the moving average representation of $X(t)$ alone and $v(t)$ be the fundamental white noise process in the *m.a.* representation of $w(t)$ alone. Write the assumed distributed lag relation

$$\text{(B)} \qquad Y(t) = \mu^* X(t) + w(t)$$

Then clearly

$$\text{(C)} \qquad Y(t) = \mu^* a^* u(t) + d^* v(t),$$

where a^*u and d^*v are the *m.a.* representations of X and w, respectively. The equation (C) together with the *m.a.* representation of X are clearly in the form (A) with $b \equiv 0$. Now we need only verify that u and v are jointly fundamental for X and Y, and for this we need only show that $H_{X,Y}(t)$ includes $H_{u,v}(t)$. $H_u(t)$ is in $H_X(t)$ by definition. $H_v(t)$ is in $H_w(t)$ which is in turn (by inspection of (B)) in $H_{X,Y}(t)$. One side of the double implication is proved. Suppose that we have the autoregressive representation

$$\text{(D)} \qquad \begin{bmatrix} \alpha & \beta \\ \gamma & \delta \end{bmatrix} * \begin{bmatrix} X \\ Y \end{bmatrix}(t) = \begin{bmatrix} u \\ v \end{bmatrix}(t)$$

and that the *m.a.* representation has the form (A) with $b \equiv 0$. Let G be the matrix on the right-hand side of (A) and H be the matrix on the left-hand side of (D). Then almost everywhere $\tilde{G}^{-1} = \tilde{H}$. (The tilde denotes a Fourier transformation.) Since $\tilde{G}$ can be written in triangular form, $\tilde{H}$ (and thus H) can be written triangular also. But then we can substitute the first equation of (D) into the second euqation of (A) to obtain

$$\text{(E)} \qquad Y(t) = c^* \alpha^* X(t) + d^* v(t) x$$

Equation (E) has the desired properties, since X can be expressed entirely in terms of u and v is uncorrelated with u.

REFERENCES

H. Akaike, "Some Problems in the Application of the Cross-Spectral Method," in B. Harris, ed., *Advanced Seminar on Spectral Analysis of Time Series,* New York 1967.

W. Brainard, and J. Tobin, "Pitfalls of Financial Model Building," *Amer. Econ. Rev. Proc.,* May 1968, *58,* 99–122.

P. Cagan, *Determinants and Effects of Changes in the Stock of Money,* Nat. Bur. Econ. Res. *Stud. Business Cycles,* No. 13, New York 1965.

F. DeLeeuw, and J. Kalchbrenner, "Monetary and Fiscal Actions: A Test of Their Relative Stability—Comment," *Fed. Reserve Bank St. Louis Rev.,* Apr. 1969, *51,* 6–11.

J. Durbin, "Tests for Serial Correlation in Regression Analysis Based on the Periodogram of Least Squares Residuals," *Biometrika*, Mar. 1969, *56*, 1–16.

M. Friedman, "The Monetary Studies of the National Bureau," Nat. Bur. Econ. Res. *Annual Report* 1964; reprinted in Friedman (1969).

———, "The Lag in the Effect of Monetary Policy," *J. Polit. Econ.*, Oct. 1961, *69*, 447–66; reprinted in Friedman (1969).

———, *The Optimum Quantity of Money and Other Essays*, Chicago 1969.

——— and A. Schwartz, (1963a) *Monetary History of the United States 1867–1960*, Nat. Bur. Econ. Res. *Stud. Business Cycles*, No. 12, Princeton 1963.

——— and ———, (1963b) "Money and Business Cycles," *Rev. Econ. Statist.*, Feb. 1963, supp., *45*, 32–64; reprinted in Friedman (1969).

C. W. J. Granger, "Investigating Causal Relations by Econometric Models and Cross-Spectral Methods," *Econometrica*, July 1969, *37*, 424–38.

E. J. Hannan, *Time Series Analysis*, London 1969.

———, 'Regression for Time Series," in M. Rosenblatt, ed., *Time Series Analysis*, New York 1963.

———, "Estimating a Lagged Regression Relation," *Biometrika*, 1967, *54*, 409–18.

E. Malinvaud, *Statistical Methods of Econometrics*, Chicago 1965.

Y. S. Razanov, *Stationary Random Processes*, San Francisco 1967.

C. A. Sims, "The Role of Approximate Prior Restrictions in Distributed Lag Estimation," *J. Amer. Statist. Ass.*, Mar. 1972, *67*, 169–75.

———, "The Role of Approximate Prior Restrictions in Distributed Lag Estimation," mimeo 1970.

———, "Discrete Approximation to Continuous-Time Distributed Lags in Econometrics," *Econometrica*, May 1971, *39*, 545–63.

J. Tobin, "Money and Income: Post Hoc Ergo Propter Hoc?" *Quart. J. Econ.*, May 1970, *84*, 301–17.

G. Wahba, "Estimation of the Coefficients in a Multi-Dimensional Distributed Lag Model," *Econometrica*, July 1969, *37*, 398–407.

A. Walters, "Professor Friedman on the Demand for Money," *J. Polit. Econ.*, Oct. 1965, *73*, 545–55.

[3]

Excerpt from Karl Brunner and Allan H. Meltzer (eds), *Three Aspects of Policy and Policymaking: Knowledge, Data and Institutions*, 9–54.

CAUSALITY AND ECONOMETRICS

Arnold ZELLNER*

University of Chicago

1. Introduction

Although the concept of causality has been treated extensively in the philosophical literature and used extensively in interpreting data in many sciences including econometrics, almost all, if not all, textbooks treating the methodology of econometrics, that is, econometric theory and/or principles, exclude terms like *causality* and *cause* from their subject indexes. Indeed these econometrics textbooks also say little, if anything, even about the age-old issue of the relationship between the concepts of correlation and causality.

The glaring failure of econometrics texts to treat the fundamental concept of causality could be excused if this concept were irrelevant to or unimportant for economics and econometrics. That such is not the case is easily established by taking note of the following observations:

1. On the opening page of Stigler's (1949, p. 3) influential textbook on price theory, he writes, "The important purpose of a scientific law is to permit prediction, and prediction is in turn sought because it permits control over phenomena. That control requires prediction is self-evident, for unless one knows what 'causes' a particular phenomenon, one cannot effect or prevent its occurrence." Although the word *causes* in this quotation is central, it is not defined, perhaps because its meaning is thought to be self-evident or, more likely, because its meaning is rather controversial, hence the use of quotation marks. Be that as it may, causation is clearly a central concept in Stigler's discussion of the purpose of scientific laws that appear in price theory and econometrics.
2. Cowles Commission Monograph 14, *Studies in Econometric Method*, edited by T.C. Koopmans and W.C. Hood, a key contribution to the development of econometrics, includes a paper by H. Simon (1953) on the nature of causal orderings.
3. In the 1950s and 1960s, controversies regarding the causal interpretation of econometric models involving H.A.O. Wold, R.L. Basmann, R.H. Strotz, and others raged in the literature, giving evidence of much concern and no little confusion regarding the causal interpretation of fully recursive and interdependent or simultaneous econometric models. Given confusion about the

* Research financed in part by National Science Foundation Grant 77-15662 and by income from the H.G.B. Alexander Endowment Fund, Graduate School of Business, University of Chicago.

causal interpretation of econometric models, there was also confusion regarding the relation of these models to the scientific laws that they were supposed to represent.

4. The more recent economic and econometric literature abounds with papers in which the Wiener-Granger concept of causality appears. In addition, various tests of causality have been formulated and applied, sometimes with startling results.

The few observations listed above, and many more that could be added, testify to the importance of the concept of causality in economics and econometrics. The fact that many textbooks have little or nothing to say about causality is thus considered to be an important omission, one that may be in large part responsible for the difficulties that some have in understanding the results of recent analyses that purport to be tests of causality.

Further difficulties in understanding recent analyses of causality are produced by statements like that of T. Sargent (1977, p. 216):

> It is true that Granger's definition of a causal relation does *not*, in general, coincide with the economist's usual definition of one: namely, a relation that is invariant with respect to interventions in the form of imposed changes in the processes governing the causing variables.

The statement is accompanied by the following footnote:

> Sims suggests to me that it is not really so clear that economists' use of the word cause typically coincides with "invariance under an intervention" rather than "a one-sided relation with a strictly exogenous variable on the right-hand side." Certainly in the mathematics and engineering literature the concept of a causal relation coincides with the latter one.

From these statements, it seems apparent that the man in the street may not be the only one who is at a loss to understand the nature of causality and causal relations.

Further, in his Report on the NBER-NSF Seminar on Time Series (1977), C.F. Ansley states:

> Granger said that he wanted to clarify the notion of causality. Causality is defined as a reduction in forecasting variance with respect to a given information set; this idea dated back to Wiener. The various tests that had been proposed were equivalent only in the population, not in the sample. Given a stationary series, one should use postsample forecasting as a test. Cross-correlation methods are tests of identification [in the time series analysts' sense] only. (p.20)

While Ansley's statement may provide clarification for some, it is pertinent to note that Granger and Newbold (1977) write:

> It is doubtful that philosophers would completely accept this definition [their definition of causality], and possibly *cause* is too strong a term, or one too emotionally laden, to be used. A better term might be *temporally related*, but since cause is such a simple term we shall continue to use it. (p.225)

While the five letter word *cause* is indeed a simple word, Granger and Newbold's remarks attest to the fact, long appreciated by philosophers, that cause is a rather subtle and difficult concept, which is not completely synonymous with *temporally related* or with *a reduction in forecasting variance with respect to a given information set*.

The discussion presented above reveals that concepts of causation, causality, cause, causal relations, etc. have been important in economics and econometrics. Indeed Simon (1953) writes, "The most orthodox of empiricists and antideterminists can use the term 'cause,' as we shall define it, with a clear conscience" (p.51). As this statement implies, a satisfactory definition of cause is relevant for many. However, as is clear from the above discussion, many different definitions of cause, causation, causal relation, etc. have appeared in the literature, some of them inconsistent with each other and inconsistent with definitions provided by philosophers. There is thus a need to reconsider these definitions and try to arrive at a better understanding of the issues involved and how they relate to current econometric practice.

In what follows, I will attempt to arrive at a better understanding of causation and associated concepts. I will begin by reviewing a philosophical definition of causation and its implications in Section II. In Section III, the discussion in Section II will be brought to bear on some major definitions of causation that have appeared in the econometric literature. In Section IV, the implications of the preceding sections for tests of causality will be explored. Finally, in Section V, a summary of findings and some concluding remarks will be presented.

II. Review of a Philosophical Definition of Causality and Its Implications

At the end of the last section, we recognized a need for a clear-cut definition of causation. Fortunately, a sophisticatedly simple and deep definition of causation is available in a paper by H. Feigl (1953), which "was written with the purpose of summarizing succinctly some results of the logical and methodological analyses of the concept of causation" (n., p. 408). According to Feigl:

> The clarified (purified) concept of causation is defined in terms of *predictability according to a law* (or more adequately, according to a set of laws). (p. 408)

This deceptively simple definition is noteworthy both for what it includes and what it excludes. Most importantly it links causation *not just to predictability* but to *predictability according to a law or set of laws.* According to this philosophical definition, predictability without a law or set of laws, or as econometricians might put it, without theory, is *not* causation. As will be seen, linking predictability to a law or set of laws is critical in appraising various tests of causality that have appeared in the econometric literature. This view also coincides with that of Jeffreys (1967), who remarks that the most important part of our knowledge "consists of making inferences from past experience to predict future experience. This part may be called generalization or induction" (p. 1). Jeffreys emphasizes the important role of laws, such as Newton's or Einstein's laws, in efforts to predict future experience or as yet unobserved outcomes. With respect to causality, Jeffreys (1957) writes, "If we can say with high probability that a set of circumstances would be followed by another set, that is enough for our purposes" (p. 190). Since, for Jeffreys, the process of prediction is identified with generalization, his concept of causality is very close to that presented above. Note, however, that Jeffreys mentions "a high probability," while Feigl does not similarly qualify his use of the term *predictability*. Consideration will be given to this point below.

In his definition of causation, Feigl speaks of the "clarified (purified) concept of causation." By *clarified* or *purified*, he means a concept of causation that is purged of "metaphysical, i.e. in principle unconfirmable, connotations that had traditionally obscured, if not eclipsed, the only meaning of causation that is logically tenable and methodologically adequate and fruitful" (p. 408).

What are some of these so-called unconfirmable connotations? First, there is the teleological conception (final cause or causes, considered by Aristotle and others). According to Feigl, final cause is eliminated from the modern concept of causation. In this connection, it is interesting to consider J.M. Keynes's (1921) analysis of the issue of final causes. Keynes writes:

> The discussion of *final* causes and of the argument from design has suffered confusion from its supposed connection with theology. But the logical problem is plain and can be determined upon formal and abstract considerations. The argument is in all cases simply this--an event has occurred and has been observed which would be very improbable *a priori* if we did not know that it had actually happened; on the other hand, the event is of such a character that it might have been not unreasonably predicted if we had assumed the existence of a conscious agent whose motives are of a certain kind and whose powers are sufficient. (p. 297)

Keynes then provides the following analysis of the problem:

> Let h be our original *data*, a the occurrence of the event, b the existence of the supposed conscious agent. Then a/h [the probability of a given h] is assumed very small in comparison with a/bh [the probability of a given b and h]; and we require b/ah [the probability of b given a and h], the probability, that is to say, of b after a is known. The inverse principle of probability [Bayes's theorem]. . .shows that $b/ah = a/bh \cdot \frac{b/h}{a/h}$, and b/ah is therefore not determinate in terms of a/bh and a/h alone. Thus we cannot measure the probability of the conscious agent's existence *after* the event, unless we can measure its probability *before* the event. . . .The argument tells us that the existence of the hypothetical agent is more likely after the event than before it; but, . . .unless there is an appreciable probability first, there cannot be an appreciable probability afterwards. No conclusion, therefore which is worth having, can be based on the argument from design *alone*; like induction, this type of argument can only strengthen the probability of conclusions, for which there is something to be said on *other* grounds. (p. 298)

Keynes has thus shown that the hypothesis of final causes can be subjected to scientific logical analysis and that the critical result that emerges is one of degree of confirmation; that is, if the initial or prior probability (*b/h* in Keynes's notation) is very small, the posterior probability (*b/ah*) will also be very small under Keynes's conditions. This does not lead to a "conclusion worth having." This analysis has relevance for those who argue that an unusual event, for example, World War I or the Great Depression of the 1930s, is the result of some final cause or grand design. Unless there are other grounds or evidence leading to enhancing the value of our prior probability, the result of Keynes's analysis will be an inconclusive result regarding the hypothesis that the supposed conscious agent or grand design exists.

In closing this discussion of final causes or grand design, it is important to point out that Keynes's analysis indicates that these concepts are not to be ruled out a priori. The concepts, according to Keynes, are amenable to scientific deductive and inductive analysis. This important finding is in accord with one of Jeffreys's rules governing any theory of scientific learning or induction, namely, Jeffreys's (1967) Rule 5, which states, "The theory must not deny any empirical proposition *a priori*; any precisely stated empirical proposition must be formally capable of being accepted. . .given a moderate amount of relevant evidence" (p. 9).

A second conception of causation that Feigl has purged from his modern definition is the animistic conception. He explains that the animistic conception of causation implies that:

> there is an internal (but unconfirmable) compulsion (conceived anthropomorphically in analogy to coercion as experienced on the human level when forced against our own impulses), which supposedly accounts for the invariable connection of causes with their effects. One fallacious inference from this conception is the doctrine of *fatalism*. (p. 408)

Taking a cue from Keynes's treatment of final causes, I think it may be possible to sharpen and explicate the animistic concept to render it in the form of a clear-cut empirical proposition. If this were done, it seems that an analysis similar to Keynes's analysis of final causes would apply. In this case, however, the hypothesis of the existence of an internal compulsion would replace the hypothesis of the existence of a final cause. The proposition would then become susceptible to empirical investigation in accord with Jeffreys's theory of scientific induction, and the application of Keynes's analysis would lead to a conclusion similar to that reached in the case of his analysis of final causes. Since the animistic concept of causation is sometimes encountered in the economic and historical literature in the guise of "*A* is the inevitable consequence of *B* by the very nature of the circumstances," having an explicit analysis of the nature of such statements is valuable.

The third concept of causation eliminated by Feigl is "the *rationalistic* conception which identifies (I should say, confuses) the causal relation with the logical relation of implication (or entailment)" (p. 408). Feigl says that this conception of causation was repudiated by Hume and that attempts by Kant and others to revive a conception of causation based on conceptions of logical identity, entailment, or necessity "may be said to have failed (for diverse reasons such as mistaken conceptions of logical identity or necessity, . . .)" (p. 408).

The rationalistic conception of causality is rejected, because it conflicts with basic principles of scientific methodology that distinguish the rules of induction and deduction in scientific work. As Jeffreys (1967) puts it:

> Traditional or deductive logic admits only three attitudes to any proposition: definite proof, disproof, or blank ignorance. But no number of previous instances of a rule [or law] will provide a deductive proof that the rule [or law] will hold in a new instance. There is always the formal possibility of an exception. (pp. 1-2)

This statement embodies the negative findings of Hume's analysis of the nature of causality, namely that there is no logically necessary relationship connecting cause and effect. Jeffreys (1967) comments further that in much writing on scientific method there is a "tendency to claim that scientific method can be reduced in some way to deductive logic, which is the most fundamental fallacy of all: it can be done only by rejecting its chief feature, induction" (p. 2). Jeffreys (1957) also states, ". . .inference from past observations to future ones is not deductive. The observations not yet made may concern events either in the future or simply at places not yet inspected. It is technically called induction. . . .There is an element of uncertainty in all inferences of the kind considered" (p. 13).

The unavoidable uncertainty involved in making inferences from past data to as yet unobserved data is a basic reason for rejecting the rationalistic conception of causality, which involves the concept of deductive logical necessity, or entailment. Thus, using deduction to prove that, according to economic theory, event *A* must produce or cause event *B* obviously does not imply that there is a logical necessity that event *B* will actually be observed given the occurrence of *A*. What is needed in such a case is an application of inductive logic that would produce a statement like "Given the occurrence of *A*, *B* will *probably* occur." Most important, there is no element of deductive logical necessity in this last statement. The appropriate concept of probability to be utilized in such a statement yielded by inductive logic and the quantification of the phrase *will probably occur* are issues treated at length by Jeffreys (1957, 1967) in his development of a theory of scientific induction. He states, ". . .*the essence of the present theory* is that no probability. . .is simply a frequency. The fundamental idea is that of a reasonable degree of belief, which satisfies certain rules of consistency and can in consequence of these rules be formally expressed by numbers. . ." (1967, p. 401).

Thus, Jeffreys, along with Hume, provides compelling arguments against the rationalistic conception of causality. Further, while perhaps more controversial, Jeffreys's theory of scientific induction requires a particular concept of probability, and in his work he provides many applied analyses illustrating how his concept of probability can be employed to obtain numerical probabilities associated with alternative laws, models, or hypotheses, many of which are frequently encountered in econometrics. In summary, the deductive, rationalistic conception of causality is considered inappropriate and can be replaced by one grounded in inductive rather than deductive logic.

Returning to Feigl's definition of causality, we see that it involves the concept of "laws." It is relevant to consider the types and forms of laws and the domains and levels of their application. Feigl (1953) presents the following list of characteristics:

A. *Types of Laws*

1. Deterministic
2. Statistical

B. *Forms of Laws*

1. Qualitative
2. Semi-quantitative (topological)
3. Fully quantitative (metrical)

C. *Domains of Laws*

1. Temporal (sequential)
2. Coexistential (simultaneous)

D. Levels of Laws

1. Macro
2. Micro

In addition, he recognizes that certain laws may have combinations of these characteristics.

Although the above list may not be all inclusive, it does contain many of the characteristics of laws. A brief discussion of these characteristics is worth undertaking. With respect to deterministic laws and determinism, Feigl writes:

> The principle of determinism [i.e., ideally complete and precise predictability, given the momentary conditions, the pertinent laws, and the required mathematical techniques] may therefore be interpreted as a--to be sure, very bold and hence extremely problematic--hypothesis concerning the order of nature. (p. 412)

He goes on to say that most of the younger-generation physicists have definitely abandoned determinism. Jeffreys (1967) also writes, "We must also reject what is variously called the principle of causality, determinism, or the uniformity of nature, in any such form as 'Precisely similar antecedents lead to precisely similar consequences'" (p. 11). He explains that no two sets of antecedents are ever identical. He even rejects a looser form of determinism such as "In precisely the same circumstances very similar things can be observed, or very similar things can usually be observed," with the observations that "If 'precisely the same' is intended to be a matter of absolute truth, we cannot achieve it" (pp. 11-12). He also states:

> The most that can be done is to make those conditions the same that we believe to be relevant--"the same" can never in practice mean more than "the same as far as we know", and usually means a great deal less. The question then arises, How do we know that the neglected variables are irrelevant? Only by actually allowing them to vary and verifying that there is no associated variation in the result; but this requires the use of significance tests, a theory of which must therefore be given before there is any application of the principle, and when it is given it is found that the principle is no longer needed. . .(p. 12)

While the existence of quantum theory, a probabilistic theory, is often cited as evidence against determinism, Jeffreys's critique of determinism goes much deeper and relates to the operational uses of systems, not just their deductive logical structure. Thus, Burks's (1977) observations that "John von Neumann argues that quantum mechanical systems are inherently probabilistic and cannot be embedded in deterministic systems" (p. 589), and that "Einstein believed that when a complete theory of quantum phenomena is developed, it will be deterministic" (p. 590), while interesting, do not have much bearing on the issues raised by Jeffreys's critique of determinism. It is thus concluded that laws to which Feigl's definition of causality relates are in the main, if not exclusively, nondeterministic, statistical or probabilistic laws.

Next, we take up the forms of laws. There does not appear to be any compelling reason to limit the concept of causality to laws that are "fully quantitative (metrical)." Qualitative laws that yield predictions about the presence or absence of qualities or characteristics and semi-quantitative laws involving, as Feigl puts it, "only the relations of 'equal' or 'greater than'" (p. 409) are just as relevant as fully quantitative laws in defining causality.

As regards the forms of mathematical functions appearing in laws, it is sometimes convenient to assume them, and perhaps their first and second derivatives, to be continuous. However, other representations are not precluded. In fact at various stages of the development of a subject, two alternative formulations may coexist. For example, Jeffreys (1967) remarks that:

> The quantum theory and the continuous emission theory both accounted for one set of facts, but each, in its existing form, was inconsistent with the facts explained by the other. The proper conclusion was that both explanations were wrong and that. . .some new explanation must be sought. . . . But meanwhile, physicists based their predictions on the laws; in types of phenomena that had been found predictable by quantum methods, they made their predictions by quantum methods; in phenomena of interference they made predictions by assuming continuous wave trains. (pp. 411-12)

Another point about forms of laws is that they be capable of yielding verifiable predictions about as yet unobserved data. This requirement does not place overly severe restrictions on the forms of laws or of mathematical functions appearing in them. However, many including G.E.P. Box, R.A. Fisher,

M. Friedman, H. Jeffreys, the present writer, and a number of others do emphasize the virtues of simplicity in formulating laws. Some exhibit a preference for simplicity by appealing to Ockham's Razor, the Principle of Parsimony, or the Jeffreys-Wrinch Simplicity Postulate. With respect to the Simplicity Postulate, Jeffreys (1967) states that contrary to the widespread belief that the choice of the simplest law is merely a convention, "...the simplest law is chosen because it is the most likely to give correct predictions; that the choice is based on a reasonable degree of belief. . ." (pp. 4-5). Further Jeffreys (1967) writes:

> Precise statement of the prior probabilities of the laws in accordance with the condition of convergence requires that they should actually be put in an order of decreasing prior probability. . .All we have to say is that the simpler laws have the greater prior probabilities. This is what Wrinch and I called the *Simplicity Postulate*. (p. 47)

He goes on to suggest a tentative numerical rule for assessing the complexity of laws expressible by differential equations. Jeffreys (1957) also presents an analysis of developments in the history of science that provides support for the Simplicity Postulate. Thus, if the Simplicity Postulate is accepted as probably valid, it involves a most important ordering of causal laws.

We now consider several aspects of the domains of laws involved in Feigl's definition of causation. The domains of many laws are temporal or temporal-spatial. In regard to the temporal-spatial aspects of laws, Feigl (1953) writes:

> This principle [the homogeneity and isotropy of space, and homogeneity of time], clearly formulated by Maxwell, states the irrelevance of absolute space or time co-ordinates, and in this sense the purely relational character of space and time as seen already by Leibniz and re-emphasized in Einstein's theory of relativity. The place and the time at which events occur do not by themselves have any modifying effect on these events. (p. 412)

He goes on to say, "Differences in effects must always be accounted for in terms of differences in the *conditions*, not in terms of purely spatio-temporal location" (p. 412). These considerations and considerations of the reversibility (symmetry) of the cause-effect relation in molecular processes that is assumed in the work of Gibbs and Boltzmann and empirically observed in the case of Brownian motion lead Feigl to state:

> Since the basic laws of classical mechanics and electrodynamics as well as those of modern quantum mechanics are temporally symmetrical, it would seem that the direction of causality may indeed be reducible to Boltzmann's explanation [the probabilities for a transition from a more highly ordered state to one of lower order (greater disorder) are always higher than those for the process in the opposite direction]. Once this is assumed, such statements as "earlier actions can influence later events but not vice versa" are recognized as sheer tautologies. . . (p. 414)

These considerations of time and space as they relate to physical laws indicate an important probabilistic reversibility of laws in time. As regards laws in the social sciences, it has been customary to think in terms of chronological time and to require that laws be such that causes precede their effects in chronological time. From what has been presented above, it is clear that such a requirement is at odds with important physical laws. In addition, if Allais's (1966) concept of psychological time is considered, then there is no assurance that laws stated in a psychological time frame will necessarily meet the requirement that cause precede effect in chronological time.

Another issue regarding the temporal domain of laws is whether laws relate to continuous or discrete time. There does not seem to be any compelling reason to favor either continuous or discrete time formulations of laws, and, in fact, mixed difference-differential equation formulations of laws are not only possible but have been employed.

Finally with respect to temporal matters, there is the problem of laws that involve "simultaneity" or "instantaneous causality." As Feigl notes, ". . .an equally well established usage [of the crude concepts of cause and effect] seems to prevail even if the two events (factors, processes) are contemporaneous" (p. 417). In terms of the discussion of temporal ordering presented above, it seems clear that simultaneous or instantaneous formulations of laws cannot be ruled out, provided that these laws are capable of yielding predictions about as yet unobserved data. If they can, then such laws are causal laws according to Feigl's definition.

As regards the levels, macro or micro, to which laws relate, it is of course possible to have laws relating specifically to macro phenomena, specifically to micro phenomena, or to combined micro and macro phenomena. While there is a natural desire to have a consistent law applicable to both micro and macro phenomena, the fact that in some areas such a law does not exist does not preclude the use of laws relating to one level until an improved, more general law is formulated.

In the above discussion of some characteristics of a philosopher's definition of causation, namely, "predictability according to a law" (or, more adequately, "according to a set of laws"), not much has been said about the deductive, logical nature of causal laws; rather, more emphasis has been placed on the inductive logical nature of causation, since this aspect seems very relevant to the tasks of working scientists. Also, it must be mentioned that the calculus of inductive logic plays a central role in comparing and testing alternative laws' predictions. Jeffreys (1967, ch. 5-6) and Burks (1977, pp. 65-91) describe the theory and some applications of this use of inductive logic that involves Bayes's theorem to compute probabilities associated with alternative laws or hypotheses. This inductive logical analysis is needed to provide information about the quality of the predictability of various laws.

In the next section attention is directed to reviewing and discussing several works dealing with causation that have appeared in the econometric literature.

III. Review of Selected Discussions of Causation in the Econometric Literature

The objectives of this review are to establish the extent to which concepts of causation in the econometric literature coincide with or differ from those considered in Section II and to provide a basis for approaching the tests of causality to be considered in the next section. Because not all discussions of causality that have appeared in the econometric literature can be covered, I have selected several leading works that appear important and relevant for assessing the meaningfulness of tests of causality.

A. Simon's "Causal Ordering and Identifiability"

H. Simon's essay "Causal Ordering and Identifiability" (1953) was published as chapter III in one of the most influential monographs on econometric methodology. For this reason and because some recent work by Sims (1977) builds on Simon's contribution, it is worthwhile to review Simon's analysis.

Simon agrees with Feigl that the concept of causation is in need of purification and clarification. In fact, Simon mentions ". . .objectionable ontological and epistemological overtones that have attached themselves to the causal concept. . ." (p. 49). He also notes:

> In view of the generally unsavory epistemological status of the notion of causality, it is somewhat surprising to find the term in rather common use in scientific writing (when the scientist is writing about his science, not about its methodology). Moreover, it is not easy to explain this usage as metaphorical, or even as a carry-over of outmoded language. (p. 50)

Thus Simon is in agreement with the view, expressed above, that the notion of causality is in widespread use in science.

In view of the impure connotations associated with the term *causation* and of "Hume's critique that necessary connections among events cannot be perceived (and hence can have no empirical basis)," (p. 49), Simon opts for a narrower concept of causality. Simon's narrower notion of causality is "that causal orderings are simply properties of the scientist's model, properties that are subject to change as the model is altered to fit new observations. . ." (p. 50). He rightly points out that such a notion of causality can be applied to probabilistic as well as deterministic models. Applicability to probabilistic models is important, since Simon believes that ". . .the viewpoint is becoming more and more prevalent that the appropriate model of the world is not a deterministic model but a probabilistic one" (p. 50).

Whether this last statement is true or not, it is evident that Simon's notion of causality is a deductive logical concept relating to models' characteristics, not to empirical features of the world that require statements of inductive logic. Indeed, Simon (p. 51) states, "It is the aim of this chapter. . .to provide a clear and rigorous basis for determining when a causal ordering can be said to hold between two variables or groups of variables in a model [and not the 'real' world]," and ". . .the concepts to be defined all refer to a model--a system of equations--and not to the "real" world the model purports to describe." Thus, Simon's narrower notion of causality or causation is radically different from Feigl's concept of causation, i.e., predictability according to a law or set of laws. For Feigl predictability means predictability of empirically observable outcomes, certainly not just a deductive logical property of a model or of a law. While Simon's notion of causality can be used to describe logically the laws that Feigl mentions, it involves no necessary relation to the prediction of "real" world outcomes. Obviously a law that is causal in Simon's sense need not be causal in Feigl's; that is, the law may be incapable of predicting "real-world" outcomes. Such a law would not be termed causal in an inductive, empirical sense.

In addition to this important distinction between Simon's and Feigl's concepts of causation, it is relevant to note that even within his narrower concept of causality Simon explains that:

> . . .we might say that if *A* and *B* are functionally related and if *A* precedes *B* in time, then *A* causes *B*. There is no logical obstacle to this procedure. Nevertheless, we shall not adopt it. We shall argue that time sequence does, indeed, sometimes provide a basis for asymmetry between *A* and *B*, but that asymmetry is the important thing, not the sequence. By putting asymmetry, without necessarily implying a time sequence, at the basis of our definition we shall admit causal orderings where no time sequence appears (and sometimes exclude them even where there is a time sequence). By so doing we shall find ourselves in closer accord with actual usage, and with a better understanding of the meaning of the concept than if we had adopted the other, and easier, course. We shall discover that causation (as we shall define it) does not imply time sequence, nor does time sequence imply causation. (p. 51)

Thus, Simon is in agreement with the discussion in the previous section regarding the non-necessity of a chronological time ordering between cause and effect. While Simon agrees with this position in the early part of his essay, in his concluding section he remarks,

> There is no necessary connection between the asymmetry of this relation [among certain variables] and asymmetry in time, although an analysis of the causal structure of dynamical systems in econometrics and physics will show that lagged relations can generally be interpreted as causal relations. (pp. 73-74)

Since it is not clear to what specific lagged relations Simon is referring, it is difficult to evaluate this last remark. Suffice it to say that there are many examples of empirically fitted dynamical systems in econometrics in which a lagged relation cannot be regarded as causal in Feigl's sense.

To illustrate the nature of Simon's analysis of causal orderings, we will review the simplest example presented in his paper. In this example, he considers the following three-equation, linear, deterministic system (p. 58):

$$a_{11}x_1 = a_{10}, \tag{1}$$

$$a_{21}x_1 + a_{22}x_2 = a_{20}, \tag{2}$$

$$a_{32}x_2 + a_{33}x_3 = a_{30}, \tag{3}$$

where x_1 is an index measuring the favorableness of weather for growing wheat; x_2 is the size of the wheat crop; x_3 is the price of wheat; and the a's are parameters. Simon writes, "We suppose the weather to depend only on a parameter; the wheat crop, upon the weather (we ignore a possible dependence of supply on price); and the price of wheat, on the wheat crop. . ." (p. 58).

Since the value of x_1 can be determined from (1) alone, it is possible to substitute this value in equations (2) and (3) to get a reduced system involving x_2 and x_3. The substitution from (1) into (2) yields a relation determining the value of x_2, which when substituted in (3) along with the value of x_1 from (1), determines the value of x_3. This ordering of the algebraic solution of the system in (1)-(3) results in Simon's writing:

$$(1) \longrightarrow (2) \longrightarrow (3),$$

which Simon interprets as "(1) has direct precedence over (2), and (2) over (3)," (p. 58) and

$$x_1 \longrightarrow x_2 \longrightarrow x_3,$$

which he interprets as "x_1 is the direct cause of x_2, and x_2 of x_3" (p. 58).

While Simon analyzes systems more complicated than that shown above, this simple system reveals well the nature of his notions of causality and causal orderings, which are, as he emphasizes, just logical properties of the model considered. He leaves the inductive relevance of the model aside, probably on purpose; yet, it is the inductive aspect of this and other models that is critical for appraising the degree to which the model is causal.[1] In discussing a concept of causality close to Simon's, Jeffreys (1967) expresses a similar point of view:

> Causality, as used in applied mathematics, has a more general form, such as: "Physical laws are expressible by mathematical equations, possibly connecting continuous variables, such that in any case, given a finite number of parameters, some variable or set of variables that appears in the equations is uniquely determined in terms of the others." . . .The equations, which we call laws, are inferred from previous instances and then applied to instances where the relevant quantities are different. This form permits astronomical prediction. But it still leaves the questions "How do we know that no other parameters than those stated are needed?" "How do we know that we need consider no variables as relevant other than those mentioned explicitly in the laws?" and "Why do we believe the laws themselves?" It is only after these questions have been answered that we can make any actual application of the principle, and the principle is useless until we have attended to the epistemological problems. (p. 12)

B. *The Basmann-Strotz-Wold Discussion of Causality*

In three papers, published together as "a triptych on causal chain systems," R.H. Strotz and H.O.A. Wold (1960), R.H. Strotz (1960) and H.O.A. Wold (1960), bring together and extend earlier work of Wold (See references in Strotz and Wold, 1960) attempting to clarify the causal nature and properties of econometric models, including entire models and particular equations and parameters appearing in models. In a paper dealing with the Strotz-Wold papers, Basmann (1963) writes:

[1] In a letter, dated May 2, 1978, to the author, Simon emphasizes that while in earlier work he ". . .neglected to emphasize the correspondence principle that connects the syntactic with the semantic dimensions of any theory," in more recent work he does recognize this important link.

> . . .Wold and Strotz have not stated from what specific definition of causality they argue to the conclusion that only *triangular* recursive systems are causal. Their own view lacks several essential features of the classical notion of causality; the classical notion. . .is not mentioned by them as a possible alternative to their own. It is the purpose of this note to show constructively, by an example, that, contrary to the Wold-Strotz assertion, the hypothethical structural equations which underlie "interdependent," i.e., non-triangular, systems can be validly given a straightforward causal interpretation, at least in the classical sense. . . (pp. 441-42)[2]

As the quotation reveals, two of the basic issues in this discussion are (*a*) the definitions of causality employed by the participants in this discussion and (*b*) the relationship between concepts of causality and the forms of econometric models. These two aspects of the Strotz-Wold and Basmann discussion are considered below.

With respect to the definition, or definitions, of causality, Strotz and Wold (1960) are rather eclectic. They write, "No one has monopoly rights in defining 'causality.' The term is in common parlance and the only meaningful challenge is that of providing an explication of it. No explication need be unique, and some may prefer never to use the word at all" (p. 418). Also, Wold (1960) states that ". . .in the treatment of the models at issue, problems come up for which the natural sciences give no guidance, an unusual situation in the social sciences. This is in particular so with regard to the causal interpretation of econometric models" (p. 461). These comments raise the issue of whether a single definition of causality, such as Feigl's, is adequate for work in both the natural and social sciences. While it is recognized that improvements in a definition of causality are possible, it would have to be shown that entertaining different concepts of causality in the natural and social sciences is necessary and empirically fruitful. Since this has not been done, as far as the present writer is aware, the proposition that different concepts of causality are required is purely speculative. It is also noteworthy that Strotz and Wold adopt a definition of causality that they believe is in agreement with "common scientific and statistical-inference usage." Strotz and Wold write,

---

[2]References cited in original have been omitted.

> For us, however, the word [*causality*] in common scientific and statistical-inference usage has the following general meaning. *z* is a cause of *y* if, by hypothesis, it is or "would be" possible by *controlling z* indirectly to control *y*, at least stochastically. But it may or may not be possible by controlling *y* indirectly to control *z*. A causal relation is therefore in essence asymmetric, in that in any instance of its realization it is asymmetric. Only in special cases may it be reversible and symmetric in a causal sense. These are the cases in which sometimes a controlled change in *z* may cause a change in *y* and at other times a controlled change in *y* may cause a change in *z*, but *y* and *z* cannot both be subjected to simultaneous controlled changes independently of one another without the causal relationship between them being violated. (p. 418)

The Strotz-Wold definition, presented above, differs from Feigl's most markedly by bringing in the concept of controlled changes in variables. Feigl's definition of causality or causation can be fruitfully applied to areas of science in which no variables are under control. In addition, the Feigl definition can also apply in cases in which laws or models contain one or more variables that can actually be controlled. Note too that Strotz and Wold say, ". . .it is or 'would be' possible by *controlling z* . . ." What do they mean by *would be*? If they mean that *z* cannot actually be controlled but that they are considering a hypothetical controlled variation of *z*, then they appear to be admitting impossible experiments into their definition of causality. Whether impossible experiments are admissible in an operational theory of scientific induction incorporating a consistent definition of causality is a controversial issue. Jeffreys (1967), for example, takes the position that "the existence of a thing [e.g., causality] or the estimate of a quantity must not involve an impossible experiment" (p. 8). While the issue of the admissibility of impossible experiments may be relevant to the Strotz-Wold definition, it is still the case that their definition is subsumed under Feigl's more general definition of causation and causal laws.

In his comment on the Strotz-Wold papers, Basmann (1963) presents the following definition of causality:

> The classical scientific notion of causality to which we shall appeal, can be expressed satisfactorily as follows: *Assume that* [the] *mechanism under investigation can be isolated*

> *from all systematic*, i.e., *non-random external influences; assume that the mechanism can be started over repeatedly from any definite initial condition. If, every time the mechanism is started up from approximately the same initial condition, it tends to run through approximately the same sequence of events, then the mechanism is said to be causal.* (p.442, references omitted).

Also, directly following his definition, Basmann writes,

> Any model that (1) represents a mechanism in *isolation* from non-random external influences and (2) asserts that, when started up from approximately the same initial conditions the mechanism always tends to run through approximately the same sequence of states, is a causal model expressing a causal hypothesis about the mechanism under investigation. (p. 442)

In a footnote to this last sentence, he remarks, "It is not necessary that such experiments be feasible; it is sufficient that they are not ruled out in principle" (p. 442).

If we equate Feigl's concept of "law or set of laws" with Basmann's concept of a "model that represents a mechanism," and Feigl's concept of "predictability" with Basmann's requirement that a model assert that "when started up from approximately the same initial conditions the mechanism always tends to run through approximately the same sequence of states. . . ," we see that Feigl's and Basmann's concepts of causality or causation and causal laws or models are similar from a logical point of view. There may, however, be some question as to whether Feigl's concept of predictability is precisely the same as Basmann's, a point considered below.

Feigl does not rule out the concept of causation; i.e., predictability according to a law or set of laws, in cases in which, as is common in mainly nonexperimental sciences, a single realization of a process is the rule rather than the exception. Indeed, Feigl (1953) writes,

> In the case of unrepeatable (unique) events, as described in the historical disciplines (as in the history of the inorganic, organic, mental, social, cultural or individual-biographical occurrences), the assertion of causal relations (as in statements

> regarding who or what influenced events to what degree and in which direction) is often methodologically precarious, i.e., only very weakly confirmable. But it is not meaningless. (p. 410)

Similarly Jeffreys (1967), who has applied his causal concept to much nonexperimental data from astronomy and geophysics, remarks,

> There must be a uniform standard of validity for all hypotheses, irrespective of the subject. Different laws may hold in different subjects, but they must be tested by the same criteria; otherwise we have no guarantee that our decisions will be those warranted by the data and not merely the result of inadequate analysis or of believing what we want to believe. (p. 7)

Thus, predictability and confirmation of predictability are relevant in situations in which repetition of outcomes is impossible. Thus, Basmann's requirement that the experiment mentioned in his definition "not be ruled out in principle" appears to be superfluous. Of course, however, repetition of experiments, when possible, is usually highly desirable, since it provides a greater degree of confirmation, or lack thereof, for a particular model.

On the issue of the forms of econometric models or laws and causality, it is apparent that Feigl's, Jeffreys's, and Basmann's definitions of causality apply to complete econometric models, whether the models are formulated in fully recursive, triangular, or interdependent forms. Models in any of these forms can embody economic laws and are capable of providing predictions about as yet unobserved phenomena. Thus, they are all causal in a logical, deductive sense. Whether particular parts or single equations of such models are capable of yielding predictions and thus can, in isolation, be interpreted causally is a separate issue that can be decided by a careful examination of the structures of particular models as, for example, carried through by Simon (1953) and Basmann (1963). That models be built so as to have *each* equation capable of a causal interpretation in the above sense is an a priori restriction on the forms of models that cannot be justified methodologically. This requirement could be justified if it were found empirically that models so constructed performed better in prediction than models not so constructed. Since this empirical issue has not been settled, or perhaps cannot be settled in view of Basmann's (1965) demonstration of the observational equivalence of fully recursive and interdependent models, it is inappropriate to require that econometric models necessarily be of one form or another simply on a priori grounds.

A similar conclusion applies to the Strotz-Wold view, expressed in Strotz (1960):

> If a causal interpretation of an interdependent system is possible it is to be provided in terms of a recursive system. The interdependent system is then either an approximation to the recursive system or a description of its equilibrium state. This was the conclusion of the preceding paper, written jointly with Professor Wold.[3] (p. 428)

This statement is an a priori view about the forms of causal laws and, as indicated above, it is methodologically unsound to rule out, on a priori grounds alone, logically consistent laws that assume particular forms. Aside from the observational equivalence of fully recursive and interdependent systems, discrimination among different laws is an inductive issue involving empirical confirmation procedures. Thus, the Strotz-Wold position that interdependent systems are in some sense approximations to "true" underlying recursive systems and that the former systems involve, as Strotz puts it, ". . .some form of specification error. . ." (p. 428) is unacceptable as a general proposition.

C. *The Wiener-Granger Concept of Causality*

Granger (1969) considers a theory of causality that he views as an alternative to those of Simon, Strotz, Wold, and Basmann reviewed above. Granger writes,

> In the alternative theory to be discussed here, the stochastic nature of the variables and the direction of the flow of time will be central features. The theory is, in fact, not relevant for nonstochastic variables and will rely entirely on the assumption that the future cannot cause the past. This theory will not, of course, be contradictory to previous work but there appears to be little common ground. Its origins may be found in a suggestion by Wiener. . . (p. 428)

Contrary to what Granger says, it is apparent that his theory is contradictory to previous work on causality in at least two important respects.

---

[3]Footnote included in original has been omitted.

First, in the previous work of Feigl, Jeffreys, Simon, Strotz, Wold, Basmann, and others, *both* stochastic and nonstochastic variables are considered. The analysis is not limited to stochastic variables, and such limitation is certainly not warranted on either methodological or subject matter considerations. Second, Granger, in contrast to Feigl, Simon and Basmann, embeds the notion of temporal asymmetry in his theory of causality. Feigl and Simon, as explicitly pointed out above, do not identify causal asymmetry with succession of "cause" and "effect" in chronological time. These requirements of the Granger concept of causality that appear contrary to previous concepts of causality are stated explicitly in Granger and Newbold (1977) as follows: "(i) The future cannot cause the past. Strict causality can occur only with the past causing the present or future." "(ii) It is sensible to discuss causality only for a group of stochastic processes. It is not possible to detect causality between two deterministic processes" (pp. 224-25). As stated above, these restrictions, which do not appear in other concepts of causality, definitely restrict the range of applicability of the Granger concept. If an inductive case could be made that such restrictions are required, then they would be acceptable. Because, as far as the present writer is aware, no such convincing case has been made, it is questionable that the restrictions are required for a fruitful definition of causality. In fact, Granger's restrictions appear to rule out economic laws which state that *nonstochastic* variation in one variable causes variation in a second variable or that a nonstochastic trend in one variable causes a nonstochastic trend in a second variable. As discussed above, such a priori restrictions on the forms of economic laws have to be justified on inductive grounds.

Despite the restrictiveness of his theory of causality, Granger (1969) regards his definition of causality as ". . .very general in nature" (p. 428). In developing this definition, Granger considers a stationary stochastic process, A_t. He lets $\bar{A}_t$ represent the set of *past* values of A_t, and $\bar{\bar{A}}_t$ the set of *past and present* values of A_t. Further, he lets $\bar{A}(k)$ represent the set $\{A_{t-j}, j = k, k + 1, \ldots, \infty\}$. He also denotes the optimum, unbiased least squares predictor of A_t using the set of values B_t by $P_t(A|B)$, the predictive error series by $\epsilon_t(A|B) = A_t - P_t(A|B)$, and the variance of $\epsilon_t(A|B)$ by $\sigma^2(A|B)$. Then Granger (1969) writes,

> Let U_t be all the information in the universe accumulated since time t-1 and let $U_t - Y_t$ denote all this information *apart* from the specified series Y_t. We then have the following definitions.

Definition 1: *Causality*. If $\sigma^2(X|U) < \sigma^2(X|\overline{U-Y})$, we say that Y is causing X, denoted by $Y_t \Rightarrow X_t$. We say that Y_t is causing X_t if we are better able to predict X_t using all available information than if the information apart from Y_t had been used.

Definition 2: *Feedback*. If

$$\sigma^2(X|\bar{U}) < \sigma^2(X|\overline{U-Y}),$$

$$\sigma^2(Y|\bar{U}) < \sigma^2(Y|\overline{U-X}),$$

We say that feedback is occurring, which is denoted $Y_t \Leftrightarrow X_t$, i.e., feedback is said to occur when X_t is causing Y_t and also Y_t is causing X_t.

Definition 3: *Instantaneous Causality*. If $\sigma^2(X|\bar{U},\bar{\bar{Y}}) < \sigma^2(X|\bar{U})$, we say that instantaneous causality $Y_t \Leftrightarrow X_t$ is occurring. In other words, the current value of X_t is better "predicted" if the present value of Y_t is included in the "prediction" than if it is not.

Definition 4: *Causality Lag*. If $Y_t \Rightarrow X_t$, we define the (integer) causality lag m to be the least value of k such that $\sigma^2(X|U-Y(k)) < \sigma^2(X|U-Y(k+1))$. Thus, knowing the values of Y_{t-j}, $j = 0,1, \ldots, m-1$, will be of no help in improving the prediction of X_t. (pp. 428-29)

Granger's definition of causality, his definition 1 above, states that if the variance of the forecast error of an unbiased least squares predictor of a stationary stochastic variable X_t, based on all the information in the universe accumulated since time t-1, is smaller than the variance of the forecast error of an unbiased least squares predictor of X_t, based on all the information in the universe since time t-1 except for the past values of Y_t, then "Y is causing X." Several important characteristics of this definition follow. First, as recognized by Granger (1969), "The one completely unreal aspect of the above definitions is the use of the series U_t, representing *all* available information" (p. 429). In fact, this requirement makes the Granger definition nonoperational and in violation of one of Jeffreys's (1967) rules for theories of scientific induction, namely, "Any rule given must be applicable in practice. A definition is useless unless the thing defined can be recognized in terms of the definition when it occurs. The existence of a thing or the estimate of a quantity must not involve an impossible experiment" (p. 8). In dealing with this problem, Granger suggests replacing "all the information in the universe" with the concept of "all relevant information" (p. 429). While this modification is a step in the direction of making his definition operational, Granger does not explicitly mention the important role of economic laws in defining the set of "all relevant information." By not mentioning the role of economic laws or theory, Granger gives the impression that purely statistical criteria can be employed in defining causality.

Second, Granger's definition of causality is unusual in that embedded in it is a particular confirmatory criterion, the variance of the forecast error of an unbiased least squares predictor. This confirmatory criterion is not applicable to processes that do not possess finite moments. Also, for most processes, even just stationary processes, which involve parameters whose values must be estimated from finite sets of data, an unbiased least squares "optimum" predictor is often not available. Recognizing some of these difficulties, Granger (1969) writes,

> In practice it will not usually be possible to use completely optimum predictors, unless all sets of series are assumed to be normally distributed, since such optimum predictors may be nonlinear in complicated ways. It seems natural to use only linear predictors and the above definitions may again be used under this assumption of linearity. (p. 429)

Even in the case of linear systems with parameters that must be estimated from finite sets of data, an "optimum" (in finite samples) linear unbiased predictor will not always be available. In fact, the restriction that a predictor be linear and unbiased can result in an inadmissible predictor relative to a quadratic loss function even in linear normal models, given the results of Stein. Thus, it is not clear that the confirmatory procedures embedded in the Granger definition of causality are entirely satisfactory.

Third, as regards the implied quadratic criterion involved in the use of unbiased predictors and variance of forecast or prediction errors, Granger (1969) writes:

> It can be argued that the variance is not the proper criterion to use to measure the closeness of a predictor P_t to the true

> value X_t. Certainly if some other criteria were used it may be possible to reach different conclusions about whether one series is causing another. The variance does seem to be a natural criterion to use in connection with linear predictors as it is mathematically easy to handle and simple to interpret. If one uses this criterion, a better name might be "causality in mean." (p. 430)

Thus linking the confirmatory procedure to comparisons of variances is viewed as a matter of convenience. However, as Granger notes, it is not applicable in general. Further, Granger's confirmation procedures depart from those based on posterior probabilities associated with laws that are adopted by Jeffreys (1967), Burks (1977), and others. The posterior probability concept of confirmation is much more general than Granger's; however, it must be recognized that not all technical problems of applying it to a number of cases encountered in practice have been solved.

Fourth, in commenting on the general concept of causality, Granger and Newbold (1977) write,

> The definition as it stands is far too general to be testable. It is possible to reach a testable definition only by imposing considerable simplification and particularization to this definition. It must be recognized that, in so doing, the definition will become less intuitively acceptable and more error-prone. (p. 225)

Some of the simplifications and particularizations have been mentioned above. Most important, though, is the failure of Granger and Newbold to recognize explicitly the role of economic laws or theories in defining causality. They, perhaps inadvertently, give the impression that the concept of causality can be defined entirely in terms of statistical considerations, a point of view that is contrary to those of Feigl, Jeffreys, Basmann, and others. The simplifications and particularizations that Granger and Newbold discuss appear to be statistical in nature and not of the kind involved in the Jeffreys-Wrinch Simplicity Postulate that deals with the forms of laws.

Fifth, Granger's definitions 2-4 are also subject to the criticisms brought up in connection with his definition 1. In addition, since the two processes X and Y are not considered within the context of particular economic laws, it is hard to determine whether the modified, operational Granger concepts are indeed applicable and lead to unambiguous results. On this latter point, Granger (1969) himself points out, "Even for stochastic series, the definitions introduced above may give apparently silly answers" (p. 430). After analyzing a case illustrating this point, he goes on to say, "It will often be found that constructed examples which seem to produce results contrary to common sense can be resolved by widening the set of data within which causality is defined" (p. 431). Perhaps a more satisfactory position would be to define causality, as Feigl and others have, in terms of predictability according to well-thought-out economic laws.

Last, while Granger (1969) does not completely rule out the concept of instantaneous causality, he does remark that in some cases,

> . . .although there is no real instantaneous causality, the definitions will appear to suggest that such causality is occurring. This is because certain relevant information, the missing readings in the data, have not been used. Due to this effect, one might suggest that in many economic situations an apparent instantaneous causality would disappear if the economic variables were recorded at more frequent time intervals. (p. 430)

This statement and what has been presented above reveal that Granger generally adopts a temporal asymmetrical view of cause and effect. As mentioned earlier, such a view is not compatible with certain physical science considerations and is not a necessary component of a definition of causality.

In summary, Granger's definition of causality, his definition 1 above, is a nonoperational definition involving consideration of predictability in a very special confirmatory setting. The definition does not involve mention of laws, economic or otherwise. In fact, the conditions surrounding the definition and the suggestions for making the definition operational have important implications for the forms of laws. For example, nonstochastic variables are excluded, and forms of laws for which least squares unbiased predictors are not at least approximately optimal are not covered. Perhaps in principle such variables could be covered if definition 1 were broadened. However, if definition 1 is so broadened, it appears to the present writer that it may as well be broadened to coincide with Feigl's definition of causality, namely predictability according to a law or set of laws. Given careful attention to the formulation of such laws, confirmatory procedures that are appropriate for them can be applied. Indeed, this last approach seems very similar to that employed traditionally in econometrics.

IV. Empirical Tests of Causality

In this section several empirical studies involving issues discussed in the preceding sections will be analyzed. First, consideration will be given to studies that employ what has been referred to above as the "traditional econometric approach." Then recent studies employing the Granger-Wiener concept of causality will be reviewed. In the discussion, it will be assumed that readers are familiar with standard econometric terminology.

Haavelmo's (1947) early paper, reprinted in Cowles Commission Monograph 14, involves an econometric formulation and estimation of a simple Keynesian macroeconomic model that appeared and appears in many introductory economics textbooks. The simple model that Haavelmo considered is given by:

$$c_t = \beta + \alpha y_t + u_t \tag{4}$$

$$t = 1, 2, \ldots, T$$

$$y_t = c_t + z_t \,. \tag{5}$$

Equation (4) is a consumption function relating two endogenous variables, (*a*) consumption in period *t*, c_t and (*b*) income in period *t*, y_t. β and α are parameters with unknown values, and u_t is an unobservable random disturbance. In Haavelmo's empirical work, he employs U.S. Department of Commerce data on consumers' expenditures in constant dollars per capita to measure c_t, and disposable income in constant dollars per capita, to measure y_t. No attention will be given here to the adequacy of these empirical measures. If they are adopted, then equation (5) is an identity satisfied by the data with z_t equal to "investment expenditures, in constant dollars," the difference between disposable income and consumers' expenditure, which Haavelmo points out is equal to private net investment minus corporate savings plus government deficits. While much more could be said about the interpretation of (5) in terms of an equilibrium condition involving aggregate demand and supply with special assumptions regarding aggregate supply, this matter will not be pursued. Haavelmo then completes his model by assuming (*a*) that the u_t's have zero means, constant common variance, and are serially uncorrelated and (*b*) that the time series z_t is autonomous in relation to u_t and y_t, a condition that is fulfilled if the sequence z_t is a sequence of given numbers, or if each z_t is a random variable which is stochastically independent of u_t. Further, he assumes that sample variance of the z_t's converges, either mathematically in the case of nonstochastic z_t's or in a weak probability sense in the case of stochastic z_t's, to a positive, finite constant. In a deductive logical sense, Haavelmo's model is a causal model, since it allows us to obtain predictions of future values of c_t and y_t given parameter estimates and future values of z_t. In an inductive sense, the model may not yield good predictions if it is difficult to obtain (in the case of nonstochastic z_t's) future values of the z_t's or to predict (in the case of stochastic z_t's) the future z_t's very well. Also, the model may not predict very well if there are errors in specifying the consumption function's form or the disturbance term's properties, or if it is assumed that z_t is autonomous. Thus, the autonomous or exogenous assumption regarding z_t is just one of several possible reasons for the model's possible poor performance in actual prediction.

In his paper, Haavelmo gives special attention to the assumption that z_t is autonomous or exogenous. His approach involves elaborating his simple model to provide two alternative models in which z_t is no longer autonomous. His third model involves the following equations:

$$c_t = \beta + \alpha y_t + u_t \quad , \tag{6}$$

$$r_t = \upsilon + \mu(c_t + x_t) + w_t \quad , \tag{7}$$

$$y_t = c_t + x_t - r_t \quad , \tag{8}$$

$$x_t = \text{an autonomous variable} \tag{9}$$

in which c_t, y_t, and r_t are endogenous variables, (7) is a business saving equation, and u_t and w_t are disturbance terms, not necessarily uncorrelated but with zero means, constant covariance matrix, and serially uncorrelated. Note from (5) and (8) that $z_t = x_t - r_t$ so that if r_t is endogenous, z_t will be also. Given future values of x_t and parameter estimates, it is clear that the expanded model in (6)-(9) can be employed to generate predictions of corresponding future values of c_t, y_t, and r_t.

In his analysis of Haavelmo's expanded model, (6)-(9), Chetty (1966, 1968) points out that if the parameter μ in (7) has a zero value and if the covariance between the disturbance terms u_t and w_t is zero, then the expanded model collapses to become the original model shown in (4)-(5) with z_t autonomous or exogenous. Thus a test of the joint hypothesis $\mu = 0$ and $\text{cov}(u_t, w_t) = 0$ is a test of the hypothesis that z_t is autonomous or exogenous and that the original model (4)-(5) may be adequate if it is not defective in other respects.

The review of Haavelmo's models provides some elements of what might be called the traditional econometric approach to building causal econometric models. In this approach, one uses economic theory and other outside information to formulate a tentative model. If the Simplicity Postulate is taken seriously, the initial formulation will be sophisticatedly simple. Such simplicity does not necessarily stand in a one-to-one relationship with the size (number of equations) of a model. Clearly, it is possible to have complicated single-equation models. Given the initially entertained model, it is subjected to a number of diagnostic and prediction checks. In this connection, economic considerations, as in Haavelmo's case, may suggest certain broader formulations. After diagnostic and prediction checks have been performed, the model may have to be reformulated. Then the reformulated version is subjected to diagnostic and prediction checks, and so on. Various aspects of this approach to model-building have been discussed both in the econometric and in the statistical literature. For present purposes, it is most important to emphasize the central role of economic considerations, including economic theory, in developing causal economic models. To state this point more generally, subject matter considerations, including theory, play an important role in developing causal models in science. While some may regard this point as obvious, as several empirical tests of causality considered below will show, adequate account is not taken of this "obvious" point.

Since it is impossible to consider all reported tests of causality that employ the Granger concept of causality, attention will be given to just three leading examples, namely Sims (1972), Feige and Pearce (1976), and Pierce (1977). Sims (1972) writes, "The main empirical finding is that the hypothesis that causality is unidirectional from money to income agrees with the postwar U.S. data, whereas the hypothesis that causality is unidirectional from income to money is rejected" (p. 540). On the other hand, Pierce (1977), who analyzed similar data for the U.S., concludes, "Results of this type [independence or lack of causal relations between important economic variables] have also been obtained in several other studies. Using a similar methodology, Feige and

Pearce. . .have found little or no association between the money supply (or the monetary base) and gross national product, using quarterly data" (p. 19). Thus, it appears that the findings of Sims (1972), on the one hand, and of Feige and Pearce (1976) and Pierce (1977), on the other hand, are diametrically opposite. This and other features of these tests of causality are considered in what follows.

First, on the issue of whether the three empirical tests of causality cited above embody anything resembling what Feigl would call a law or set of laws, Pierce (1977) is most explicit when he writes, "The present study centers around an empirical specification of relations between economic time series. The data themselves are permitted, insofar as feasible, to suggest, at least in general terms, the patterns of interrelationships that do or do not exist" (p. 11). Thus, Pierce's approach is described quite frankly as one that involves "measurement without [economic] theory." The phrase *measurement without theory* is not used to condemn Pierce's approach as useless; his approach may be capable of generating important empirical results that can then, perhaps, be explained by old or new economic theories. Until this latter task is accomplished, however, by not incorporating economic law or laws, his analysis is not causal according to Feigl's definition, presented in Section II. Similarly, Sims (1972) and Feige and Pearce (1976), while not as explicit about the omission of theory as Pierce (1977), do not develop the relationships that they examine in the context of a detailed specification of economic laws or theories. As is well-known, if relevant economic theory is not considered, incorrect forms of variables, e.g., nominal variables rather than real variables, may be included, or relevant economic variables may be excluded. Failure to include more than two variables in these analyses has been recognized as a serious problem by Pierce (1977, p. 18) and by Sims (1977, p. 40). In a conversation with the author, Newbold[4] described the problem as simply analogous to the problem of left-out variables in regression models. Because they do not pay attention to subject matter theory, the studies considered offer little assurance that, in each case, the two variables examined are appropriate and/or the only two relevant for the analyses performed. Thus, the attempt to establish causality without use of economic theory or economic laws is a departure from investigation of causal laws in the sense of Feigl. Sims (1972) appears to realize this fact when he writes, "The method of identifying causal direction employed here does rest on a sophisticated version of the *post hoc ergo propter hoc* principle" (p. 543). Whether the version is "sophisticated" or just "obscure" will not be argued here.

Second, in order to make Granger's definition of causality operational, all three studies introduce specific statistical operations and assumptions that

[4]Newbold (1978), Personal communication.

have implications for the forms of economic laws and, probably, for the particular results of these and similar studies. Sims (1972) states some of these assumptions quite cryptically, "We will give content to Granger's definitions by assuming all time-series to be jointly covariance-stationary, by considering only linear predictors, and by taking expected squared forecast error as our criterion for predictive accuracy" (p. 544). Some implications of these assumptions have already been discussed in Section III. Here it is relevant to emphasize that most economic time series are nonstationary, not, as Sims assumes, covariance-stationary. Sims may mean that he will consider filtered series that are stationary. In fact, he mentions that

> all variables used in [his] regressions were measured as natural *logs* and prefiltered using the filter $1 - 1.5L + 0.5625L^2$ [where L is the lag operator]. . . .This filter approximately flattens the spectral density of most economic time-series, and the hope was that regression residuals would be very nearly white noise with this prefiltering. (p. 545)

It is very questionable that this specific filter does what Sims claims (or should do what he claims in terms of producing flat spectra). Further, if his regression error terms were generated by a particular AR(2) process, $u_t - 1.5u_{t-1} + 0.5625\, u_{t-2} = \epsilon_t$, where ϵ_t is white noise, his procedure would produce white noise errors. The results of his empirical tests for disturbance autocorrelation throw considerable doubt on the adequacy of his filtering procedure. However, there may be some filter or filters that, when applied to highly nonstationary variables, render them stationary. Feige and Pearce (1976) and Pierce (1977), following Box and Jenkins, employ differencing to render series approximately stationary; that is, their filters are $(1-L)^a$, where a assumes an integer value, usually 1 or 2, and need not be the same for different variables. Then relationships to be studied are formulated in terms of the transformed or filtered variables, certainly an important restriction on the forms of economic laws. It might be asked, "Why filter?" and "What are the possible effects of filtering?"

On the question "Why filter?" it appears that forms of laws are being thereby restricted so that stationary, *statistical* theory can be applied. In terms of stationary variables, one can employ autocorrelation functions, cross-correlation functions, etc. However, if it makes economic sense to formulate a law or model in terms of nonstationary variables, e.g., nonstochastic variables or trending stochastic variables, it is not necessary to filter variables in order to estimate parameters' values and to predict from such estimated models.

Thus, it can be seen that the filtering of variables to produce variables that are covariance-stationary is not necessary in general and is inapplicable to nonstochastic variables. This is not to say, however, that use of prefiltered, stationary variables is never appropriate. Rather, it is to say that subject matter considerations are very relevant in this regard. An excellent example illustrating some of these considerations is provided by Hendry (1977, p. 196). In addition, in terms of analyses using a money variable, it is obvious that controlled non-stochastic changes in the rate of growth of money can produce a series that is difficult, if not impossible, to be made covariance stationary by filtering.

On the question "What are the possible effects of filtering?" it must be remarked that the effects of filtering, whether by differencing or by use of more general filters, can be drastic enough in some circumstances to justify Friedman's phrase[5] "*throwing the baby out with the bath.*" Also, Friedman's remarks in his letter regarding an earlier draft of the Pierce (1977) paper led me to formulate the following example to dramatize the effects of filtering on tests of causality of the type carried through in the papers under consideration. Consider the nonstationary processes $\ln C_t$ and $\ln Y_t$, where C_t and Y_t are measured real consumption and income, respectively. Assume that

$$\ln C_t = \ln C_t^p + u_t ,$$

$$\ln Y_t = \ln Y_t^p + v_t ,$$

where C_t^p and Y_t^p are real permanent consumption and real permanent income, respectively. Further, assume that $\ln C_t$ and $\ln Y_t$ are each filtered (if $C_t^p = kY_t^p$, with k assumed constant, the same filter can be employed) to produce the stationary innovations, u_t and v_t. If u_t and v_t are cross-correlated or subjected to the Sims regression techniques and found to be totally uncorrelated, what is being obtained is a confirmation of one form of Friedman's theory of the consumption function; the conclusion that filtered $\ln C_t$ and filtered $\ln Y_t$ are uncorrelated or independent says nothing about the causal relation between C_t^p and Y_t^p and/or the causal relation between C_t and Y_t. The nature of the underlying economic theory is critical in interpreting results based on pre-filtering. In addition, measurement considerations are relevant, since u_t and v_t

[5]Friedman (1975), Personal communication.

contain errors in measuring consumption and income. It is also the case that filtering is not required in a "nonstationary" version of the Granger (1969, p. 429) definition of causality. This consumption-income example illustrates how important economic laws are in defining causality. While Pierce (1977) recognizes in a special case that "...the deterministic detrending/deseasonalization procedure possibly took too much out of the series" (p. 19), he does not link up this possibility with any economic theory. Thus, it is difficult to interpret what is "too much" or "too little."

In general then, it has to be recognized that filtering economic time series is not usually a mechanical, neutral procedure that necessarily produces satisfactory results. The issues of whether to filter and what kinds of filters to employ, e.g., seasonal filtering (Sims, 1972, uses seasonally adjusted data), are most fruitfully resolved in relation to specific economic laws or theories and other serious subject matter considerations.

In terms of analyses involving money and either GNP or the rate of inflation, there is the issue of monetary policy and its possible impact on the results of tests of causality. Sims (1972) and Pierce (1977) mention this complication, but Feige and Pearce (1976) do not seem to appreciate it adequately. Pierce (1977) writes, "Thus if the money supply grows by exactly 5 percent over the sample period, it will show up as unrelated to anything else, despite what its actual relationship to interest rates, reserves, income, etc., might be" (p. 18). He also explains:

> The data may be even worse than happenstance [in terms of experimental design considerations] insofar as closed-loop control has probably been operative over the sample period for many macroeconomic series, including such instruments as money, interest rates and government spending and such targets as inflation, unemployment and income. If in the context of the dynamic regression model. . . ,suppose x [the input variable] has been adjusted to keep y [the output or dependent variable] on a desired path according to a control strategy $x_t = C(B)y_t$ [where $C(B)$ is a polynomial in the backshift or lag operator B]. Then it can be shown that not only is the lag distribution [$V(B)$ in $y_t = V(B)x_t + u_t$] unidentifiable, but that identical residuals and model forecasts can result from

i. a model with $V(B)$ chosen so that the disturbances [the u_t's] will be white noise;
ii. a "model" with $V(B) = 0$ so that y is formally related only to its own past;
iii. an infinite number of intermediate models.

Perhaps this is not surprising; if x is determined from present and past y then, knowing y, knowing x in addition tells us nothing new. Certainly control strategies over the past 30 years have been imprecise in the short run and shifting in the long run; but certainly they have existed. (p. 20)[6]

Pierce's thoughtful and insightful remarks regarding the possible effects of monetary control policies on the results of causality tests highlight the importance of serious study of what monetary policies have been pursued in the particular sample period being analyzed. Without such study, as Pierce's remarks indicate, the results of mechanical tests of causality cannot be unambiguously interpreted. Irritating as it may be to those who seek purely statistical panaceas, the nature of policy control requires detailed consideration in formulating causal economic laws and testing their performance in prediction, a problem appreciated, if not completely solved, in the traditional econometric approach.

To return to some other aspects of how "operationalizing" Granger's nonoperational definition of causality leads to restrictions, some of them severe, on the nature of economic laws and some specific test results, consider Sims's (1972) analysis of money, X_t, and income, Y_t, variables. Since these variables are nonstationary, as mentioned above, Sims prefilters the natural logarithms of these variables to obtain x_t and y_t, assumed stationary. He then considers the following linear autoregressive representation of the assumed stationary variables x_t and y_t:

$$\begin{bmatrix} b_{11}(L) & b_{12}(L) \\ b_{21}(L) & b_{22}(L) \end{bmatrix} \begin{pmatrix} x_t \\ y_t \end{pmatrix} = \begin{pmatrix} u_t \\ v_t \end{pmatrix}, \qquad (10)$$

where $b_{ij}(L)$ is a polynomial in the lag operator L, $i, j = 1, 2$, and u_t and v_t are mutually uncorrelated white noise errors.

[6] References cited in original have been omitted.

As Sims (1972, p. 544) mentions, Granger has shown that if there is an autoregressive representation as given in (10), then the *absence* of causality, in the Granger sense, running from y_t to x_t is equivalent to the condition that $b_{12}(L) \equiv 0$. Given this condition, (10) reduces to

$$b_{11}(L)x_t = u_t , \qquad (11a)$$

$$b_{22}(L)y_t + b_{21}(L)x_t = v_t . \qquad (11b)$$

Since u_t and v_t are mutually uncorrelated and non-serially correlated disturbance terms, (11) is an extreme form of a fully recursive model, extreme since no lagged values of y_t appear in (11a), *an added restriction* to the usual definition of a fully recursive model. From (11b), it is possible to write the dynamic regression for y_t as

$$y_t = -\frac{b_{21}(L)}{b_{22}(L)} x_t + \frac{1}{b_{22}(L)} v_t , \qquad (12)$$

$$= V(L)x_t + \frac{1}{b_{22}(L)} v_t ,$$

with $V(L) \equiv - b_{21}(L)/b_{22}(L)$. As can be seen from (12), the disturbance term is in the form of an infinite moving average, $b_{22}^{-1}(L)v_t$, and hence will in general be autocorrelated. Under the special assumption that $b_{22}(L)$ is of degree zero in L, the disturbance term will not be autocorrelated. On the other hand, if nonstationary variables Y_t and X_t are related by $Y_t = V(L)X_t + w_t$, and a common filter, $C(L)$, is applied to both sides, $C(L)Y_t = V(L)C(L)X_t + C(L)w_t$, or $y_t = V(L)x_t + C(L)w_t$. Then *if* $w_t = v_t/C(L)$, $y_t = V(L)x_t + v_t$. The disturbance term, v_t, in this last equation differs from that in (12), namely, $b_{22}^{-1}(L)v_t$. Thus, in terms of the system (11) with $x_t = C(L)Y_t$ and $y_t = C(L)Y_t$, the result in (12) indicates that disturbance terms will generally be autocorrelated. If the relationship $Y_t = V(L)X_t + w_t$ is viewed as a starting point, it is clearly not derived from (11), and on filtering both sides using $C(L)$, it will generally have autocorrelated disturbances, except in very special cases. Indeed, Sims

(1972) reports results of tests for serial correlation of disturbance terms in (11) and concludes, "The conclusion from this list of approximate or inconclusive tests can only be that there is room for doubt about the accuracy of the F-tests on regression coefficients" (p. 549). Also, Quenouille (1957, pp. 43-44) has pointed out explicitly that serial correlation in the error terms in (10) can be produced by the omission of relevant variables.

For the empirical implementation of (12), it is necessary to make assumptions regarding the form of $V(L)x_t$, an *infinite* distributed lag. Sims (1972) chooses to approximate this infinite distributed lag term by a finite distributed lag term and explains ". . .the length of the estimated lag distributions was kept generous" (p. 545). Keeping the length "generous" is understandable in terms of avoiding a misspecification of the lag pattern. However, this approach does involve a finite truncation of the lag and introduction of many lag parameters, an important consideration when only 78 degrees of freedom are available in his data. A basic result of this approach is evident from the reported standard errors associated with the estimates of the distributed lag coefficients in Sims's Table 4 (p. 547). In his regression of quarterly filtered GNP on eight past, current and four future quarterly values of filtered monetary base, his largest standard error is 0.338, while his smallest is 0.276. The absolute values of his coefficient estimates for the four future values of the monetary base range from 0.088 to 0.65. In the case of GNP on M1, his coefficient standard errors range from 0.294 to 0.318, while the future coefficient estimates range from 0.105 to 0.300 in absolute value. These results indicate that the precision of estimation is quite low even when possible autocorrelation of disturbance terms is overlooked. The same can be said of his other two-sided regressions. This lack of precision in estimation is noted as a statistical caveat by Sims (1972) in about the middle of his paper:

> Though the estimated distribution looks like what we expect from a one-sided true distribution, the standard errors on the future coefficients are relatively high. These results are just what a unidirectional causality believer would expect, but they are not such as to necessarily force a believer in bidirectional causality to change his mind. (p. 547)

In other words, Sims is saying that his analyses, viewed from an estimation point of view, *have yielded inconclusive results*. The results would be even more inconclusive if one were to do a detailed analysis of the validity and power of the *F*-tests employed in the paper. In view of these considerations, it must be stated that Sims's strong conclusions about the exogeneity of money, stated at the opening and end of his paper, are not convincingly supported by his empirical analyses. As pointed out above, his estimates are imprecise and his tests are not very powerful, even when no consideration is given to autocorrelated errors, seasonal complications, effects of filtering, left-out variables, and forms of monetary policies. When these latter points are considered, Sims's conclusion becomes even more uncertain.

Unlike Sims, Feige and Pearce (1976) and Pierce (1977) do not directly estimate a dynamic regression. Instead, they (*a*) use differencing to make their variables stationary, (*b*) construct autoregressive-moving average (ARMA) models for their differenced variables, and (*c*) then compute contemporaneous and lagged cross-correlations from the estimated innovations of their ARMA schemes for the pairs of variables under consideration and test their significance. Enough has been said above about the possible important effects of differencing or other filtering techniques on results of analyses as well as complications associated with policy control, errors of measurement, etc. As regards step (*b*) of the process, there is often some difficulty in determining the forms of ARMA schemes from data. Any errors in this operation would be carried over to affect the operation in (*c*). Finally, in step (*c*), a large sample χ^2 test is employed to test the hypothesis that population cross-correlations are all zero. As lucidly explained by Pierce (1977, p. 15), step (*c*) is closely related to, but not exactly the same as, analyzing a dynamic regression directly, as Sims (1972) does.

In the one explicitly reported example in Pierce's (1977, p. 15) paper, he investigates the relationship between weekly retail sales and currency in circulation. After completing steps (*a*)-(*c*) above, he obtains a sample test statistics' value, $n\sum_{k=-10}^{k=10}\hat{r}_k^2 = 39.1 > \chi^2_{0.01}(21) = 38.1$. Thus, at the 1 percent level of significance, his large sample χ^2 test, using the estimated cross-correlations of the innovations, the $\hat{r}_k$'s, yields a "significant" result. Pierce comments,

> One could tentatively conclude that there is unidirectional causality from retail sales to currency (although the situation concerning feedback is somewhat unclear): evidently a rise in retail sales results in a somewhat greater demand for currency. . .The explanatory power of this relationship is quite small, however, as the cross correlations are not large. (p. 16)

These remarks are quite confusing to the uninitiated reader. Pierce's statistical test yields "significant" results at the 1 percent level of significance; yet, he has doubts about the results of the test. A similar methodological statement is made by Sims (1972):

> In applying the F-tests for causal direction suggested in the preceding section, one should bear in mind that the absolute size of the coefficients is important regardless of the F value. It is a truism too often ignored that coefficients which are "large" from the economic point of view should not be casually set to zero no matter how statistically "insignificant" they are. (p. 545)

Apparently, Pierce and Sims are pointing to a defect of mechanical significance tests. The information in the testing procedures does not reflect all the relevant information. Nowhere is what Sims suggests is reasonable done by Pierce or by Feige and Pearce; that is, Pierce and Feige and Pearce do not look at the absolute sizes of the individual dynamic regression coefficients and/or their sum. In a simple regression of y on x, the regression coefficient is $\beta = \sigma_{xy}/\sigma_x^2$, while the correlation coefficient is $\rho = \sigma_{xy}/\sigma_x\sigma_y = (\sigma_x/\sigma_y)\beta$. Clearly, a small ρ need not necessarily imply a small β. Similar considerations carry over to apply to cross-correlations and dynamic regression coefficients. Thus, there is an element of uncertainty regarding an analysis of causality that relies only on the estimated cross-correlations and standard significance tests, as employed by Pierce and Feige and Pearce, without adequate concern for the power of these tests relative to precisely specified alternative hypotheses. This point was raised by the author in connection with the Feige-Pearce analysis several years ago in a meeting of the University of Chicago Money Workshop.

From this review of three papers in which tests of causality have been applied, it is concluded that for a variety of reasons the tests' results are inconclusive with respect to the basic issues considered. The inconclusive nature of the results may, in part, be due to technical problems discussed quite extensively by the authors, particularly Pierce and Sims. However, the problem goes deeper than just "technical issues." The fundamental lack of subject matter considerations and theory exhibited in these studies is probably at the heart of the inconclusive nature of the results. Instead of formulating sophisticated models, which take account of subject matter considerations and relevant economic theory, the authors attempted to operationalize a nonoperational definition of causality. This operation led to consideration of an extreme form of a fully recursive model as the null hypothesis with little or no attention paid to economically motivated, *specific* alternatives. The very special null hypothesis appears to have been tested against a very wide range of loosely specified, from an economic point of view, alternatives. Given such a broad range of alternatives, it is no wonder that results are as inconclusive as they are. Further, with little in the way of economic laws and other subject matter considerations involved in the testing, it is questionable that the analyses are properly termed "tests of causality," according to Feigl's definition.

It is indeed surprising that, of the authors considered, only the statistician Pierce appears sensitive to the important role of economic laws or theory mentioned in the previous paragraph. Pierce (1977) writes in his concluding paragraph,

> Considering all of these problems, it is perhaps small wonder that incompatible propositions can often be "confirmed" by the same data, including in particular the proposition that a variable is not related to any of a number of other variables. If future research bears out this type of result, we might justifiably conclude that econometric [i.e., statistical] analysis is of rather limited use in ascertaining certain economic relationships. Economic theory is in such situations all the more important: since we cannot assume that the mathematical relationships contained within this theory can be established as valid statistical relationships--that is, as more valid than statistical "relationships" where a variable is related only to its own past--it is imperative that prior information be available concerning these relationships. (p. 21)

Recognizing the failure of "measurement without theory" and the failure of "theory without measurement," Pierce offers the hope that intelligent use of sophisticated economic theory and relevant statistical techniques may be successful. This approach is in line with Feigl's definition of causation and with what has been preached, if not always practiced, in the traditional econometric approach.

V. Summary and Conclusions

In the preceding sections, a philosophical definition of causation, which reflects philosophers' thinking and clarification of the concept of causation, has been reviewed and compared with several definitions of causation that have been published in the econometric literature. In addition, consideration was given to several applications of "causality tests" that have appeared in the literature. From this review and comparison of definitions of causation and analysis of causality tests, the following major conclusions have been reached:

1. The philosophical definition of causality, reviewed above, is adequate for work in econometrics and other areas of science, a conclusion considered to be fortunate, given the importance that the present writer attaches to the "unity of science" principle.
2. The philosophical definition of causality, reviewed above, is an operational definition in contrast to the Wiener-Granger "population" definition of causality, a fact that would lead some to dismiss the latter definition on methodological grounds alone.
3. Basmann's definition of causality is very close to the philosophical definition provided by Feigl. The former differs from the latter slightly in certain respects in cases in which only data relating to a single realization of a process are available.
4. The Strotz-Wold definition of causality is subsumed in Feigl's and is rather narrow. Insofar as Strotz and Wold require that the world be "truly" recursive, they are placing an a priori restriction on the forms of economic models and laws that cannot be justified on purely *deductive* methodological grounds and is not required by Feigl's, Jeffreys's, Basmann's and Simon's definitions of causality.
5. Simon's definition of causality is a formal, deductive property of models, not an inductive property involving the quality of models' predictability, a consideration embedded in Feigl's, Jeffreys's and others' definitions. By narrowing the concept of causality, Simon and others have omitted a fundamental part of what is meant by causation or causality, namely the quality of predictions. Thus, a model can be causal in Simon's sense and yet yield worthless predictions.
6. Simon's definition of causality does not require temporal asymmetry between cause and effect in chronological time. Simon's definition is in agreement with Feigl's point of view, but in conflict with the "true recursive model" view of Strotz and Wold and with views expressed by Granger.

7. The Wiener-Granger definition of causality is unusual in that in it is embedded a particular confirmatory criterion that is not very general and is inapplicable in a variety of circumstances. In contrast, Fiegl's definition does not mention any particular confirmatory procedure.

8. The Wiener-Granger definition involves a special form of predictability but no mention of economic laws. In this regard it is devoid of subject matter considerations, including subject matter theory, and thus is in conflict with others' definitions, including Feigl's, that do mention both predictability and laws.

9. In "operationalizing" the Wiener-Granger definition of causality, various a priori restrictions are imposed on the class of economic laws covered by the definition. It is concluded that it is preferable to employ a more general definition of causality, such as Feigl's, which imposes only the restriction of predictability on forms of economic laws.

10. From the review of applied "causality tests," it is concluded that results of these tests are inconclusive. The specific reasons for this conclusion can perhaps be summarized by saying that there was inadequate attention to subject matter considerations, or to put it slightly differently, the studies represent examples of measurement without much economic theory and other subject matter considerations. Where subject matter considerations were brought to bear, they were not satisfactorily integrated with the statistical analyses.

11. In the tests of causality involving linear stationary processes, a particularly extreme form of a fully recursive model is regarded as defining the condition under which "one variable causes another" in the Wiener-Granger sense. This extreme restriction on the form of models is not required by a broader definition of a causal model linking the two variables.

12. Sims's use of "forward and backward" regressions and Feige, Pearce, and Pierce's use of cross-correlations of estimated innovations involve consideration of forms of stationary single-equation models involving many, many parameters. This is in violation of the Principle of Parsimony and the Simplicity Postulate. Practically, the result of such a violation in the present instance is consideration of regressions with many free parameters, which when analyzed with limited data resulted in rather imprecise estimates and tests with low power relative to alternative hypotheses involving serious departures from independence.

13. Mechanical filtering of series can exert a substantial influence on causality tests of the kind considered above.

In summary, it can be said that an adequate definition of causality is available. Departures from this definition have produced problems, while offering little in the way of dependable and convincing results. The mechanical application of causality tests is an extreme form of "measurement without theory," perhaps motivated by the hope that application of statistical techniques without the delicate and difficult work of integrating statistical techniques and subject matter considerations will be able to produce useful and dependable results. That this hope is generally naive and misguided has been recognized by econometricians for a long time and is a reason that reference is made to laws in Feigl's definition of causation. In establishing and using these laws in econometrics, there seems to be little doubt but that economic theory, data, and other subject matter considerations as well as econometric techniques, including modern time series analysis, will all play a role. "Theory without measurement" and "measurement without theory" are extremes to be avoided.

References

Allais, M. (1966), "A Restatement of the Quantity Theory of Money," *American Economic Review*, 56: 1123-57.

Ansley, C.F. (1977), "Report on the NBER-NSF Seminar on Time Series," Graduate School of Business, University of Chicago. Mimeographed.

Basmann, R.L. (1963), "The Causal Interpretation of Non-Triangular Systems of Economic Relations," *Econometrica*, 31: 439-48.

__________(1965), "A Note on the Statistical Testability of 'Explicit Causal Chains' against the Class of 'Interdependent' Models," *Journal of the American Statistical Association*, 60: 1080-93.

Burks, A.W. (1977). *Chance, Cause, Reason: An Inquiry into the Nature of Scientific Evidence*. Chicago: University of Chicago Press.

Chetty, V.K. (1966), "Bayesian Analysis of Some Simultaneous Econometric Models." Ph.D. dissertation, Department of Economics, University of Wisconsin at Madison.

__________(1968), "Bayesian Analysis of Haavelmo's Models," *Econometrica*, 36: 582-602, reprinted in *Studies in Bayesian Econometrics and Statistics in Honor of Leonard J. Savage*, eds. S.E. Fienberg and A. Zellner. Amsterdam: North-Holland, 1975.

Feige, E.L., and Pearce, D.K. (1976), "Economically Rational Expectations: Are Innovations in the Rate of Inflation Independent of Innovations in Measures of Monetary and Fiscal Policy?" *Journal of Political Economy*, 84: 499-552.

Feigl, H. (1953), "Notes on Causality," *Readings in the Philosophy of Science*, eds. H. Feigl and M. Brodbeck. New York: Appleton-Century-Crofts, Inc.

Friedman, M. (1975), Personal communication.

Granger, C.W.J. (1969), "Investigating Causal Relations by Econometric Models and Cross-spectral Methods," *Econometrica*, 37: 424-38.

Granger, C.W.J., and Newbold, P. (1977). *Forecasting Economic Time Series.* New York: Academic Press.

Haavelmo, T. (1947), "Methods of Measuring the Marginal Propensity to Consume," *Journal of the American Statistical Association,* 42: 105-22, reprinted in *Studies in Econometric Method*, Cowles Commission Monograph No. 14, eds. W.C. Hood and T.C. Koopmans. New York: John Wiley & Sons, Inc., 1953.

Hendry, D.F. (1977), "Comments on Granger-Newbold's 'Time Series Approach to Econometric Model Building' and Sargent-Sims' 'Business Cycle Modeling Without Pretending to Have Too Much *A Priori* Economic Theory,'" *New Methods in Business Cycle Research: Proceedings from a Conference*, ed. C.A. Sims. Minneapolis: Federal Reserve Bank of Minneapolis.

Jeffreys, H. (1957). *Scientific Inference.* 2nd ed. Cambridge: University Press.

__________(1967). *Theory of Probability*. 3rd rev. ed. London: Oxford University Press.

Keynes, J.M. (1921). *A Treatise on Probability*. London: Macmillan and Co., Ltd.

Newbold, P. (1978), Personal communication.

Pierce, D.A. (1977), "Relationships–and the Lack Thereof--Between Economic Time Series, with Special Reference to Money and Interest Rates," *Journal of the American Statistical Association*, 72: 11-21.

Quenouille, M.H. (1957). *The Analysis of Multiple Time Series*. New York: Hafner Publishing Company.

Sargent, T.J. (1977), "Response to Gordon and Ando," *New Methods in Business Cycle Research: Proceedings from a Conference*, ed. C.A. Sims. Minneapolis: Federal Reserve Bank of Minneapolis.

Simon, H. (1953), "Causal Ordering and Identifiability," *Studies in Econometric Method*, Cowles Commission Monograph No. 14, eds. W.C. Hood and T.C. Koopmans. New York: John Wiley & Sons, Inc.

__________(1978), Personal communication.

Sims, C.A. (1972), "Money, Income and Causality," *American Economic Review*, 62: 540-52.

__________(1977), "Exogeneity and Causal Ordering in Macroeconomic Models," *New Methods in Business Cycle Research: Proceedings from a Conference*, ed. C.A. Sims. Minneapolis: Federal Reserve Bank of Minneapolis.

Stigler, G.J. (1949). *The Theory of Price*. New York: Macmillan Company.

Strotz, R.H. (1960), "Interdependence as a Specification Error," *Econometrica*, 28: 428-42.

Strotz, R.H., and Wold, H.O.A. (1960), "Recursive vs. Nonrecursive Systems: An Attempt at Synthesis," *Econometrica*, 28: 417-27.

Wold, H.O.A. (1960), "A Generalization of Causal Chain Models," *Econometrica*, 28: 443-63.

[4]

ECONOMETRICA

VOLUME 51 MARCH, 1983 NUMBER 2

EXOGENEITY[1]

BY ROBERT F. ENGLE, DAVID F. HENDRY, AND JEAN-FRANCOIS RICHARD

Definitions are proposed for *weak* and *strong* exogeneity in terms of the distribution of *observable* variables. The objectives of the paper are to clarify the concepts involved, isolate the essential requirements for a variable to be exogenous, and relate them to notions of predeterminedness, *strict* exogeneity and causality in order to facilitate econometric modelling. Worlds of parameter change are considered and exogeneity is related to structural invariance leading to a definition of *super* exogeneity. Throughout the paper, illustrative models are used to exposit the analysis.

1. INTRODUCTION

SINCE "EXOGENEITY" IS FUNDAMENTAL to most empirical econometric modelling, its conceptualization, its role in inference, and the testing of its validity have been the subject of extensive discussion (see inter alia, Koopmans [**21**], Orcutt [**28**], Marschak [**26**], Phillips [**29**], Sims [**38**, **39**], Geweke [**13**, **14**] and Richard [**32**]). Nevertheless, as perusal of the literature (and especially econometrics textbooks) quickly reveals, precise definitions of "exogeneity" are elusive and consequently, it is unclear exactly what is entailed for *inference* by the discovery that a certain variable is "exogenous" on any given definition. Moreover, the motivation underlying various "exogeneity" concepts has not always been stated explicitly so that their relationships to alternative notions of "causality" (see Wiener [**42**], Strotz and Wold [**40**], Granger [**16**], and Zellner [**45**]) remain ambiguous. This results in part because some definitions have been formulated for limited classes of models so that appropriate generalizations such as to nonlinear or non-Gaussian situations are not straightforward, while others are formulated in terms involving unobservable disturbances from relationships which contain unknown parameters. Whether or not such disturbances satisfy orthogonality conditions with certain observables may be a matter of construction or may be a testable hypothesis and a clear distinction between these situations is essential.

In this paper, definitions are proposed for *weak* and *strong* exogeneity in terms of the distributions of observable variables,[2] thereby explicitly relating these

[1] This paper is an abbreviated and substantially rewritten version of CORE Discussion Paper 80-38 (and U.C.S.D. Discussion Paper 81-1). This was itself an extensive revision of Warwick Discussion Paper No. 162, which was initially prepared during the 1979 Warwick Summer Workshop, with support from the Social Science Research Council. We are indebted to participants in the Workshop for useful discussions on several of the ideas developed in the paper and to Mary Morgan for historical references. We also greatly benefited from discussions with A. S. Deaton, J. P. Florens, S. Goldfeld, A. Holly, M. Mouchart, R. Quandt, C. Sims, and A. Ullah. Three anonymous referees made many constructive comments. Financial support from the Ford Foundation, the National Science Foundation, and the International Centre for Economics and Related Disciplines at the London School of Economics is gratefully acknowledged.

[2] The emphasis on observables does not preclude formulating theories in terms of unobservables (e.g., "permanent" components, expectations, disturbances, etc.), but these should be integrated out first in order to obtain an operational model to which our concepts may be applied.

concepts to the likelihood function and hence efficient estimation:[3] essentially, a variable z_t in a model is defined to be weakly exogenous for estimating a set of parameters λ if inference on λ conditional on z_t involves no loss of information. Heuristically, given that the joint density of random variables (y_t, z_t) always can be written as the product of y_t conditional on z_t times the marginal of z_t, the weak exogeneity of z_t entails that the precise specification of the latter density is irrelevant to the analysis, and, in particular that all parameters which appear in this marginal density are nuisance parameters. Such an approach builds on the important paper by Koopmans [**21**] using recently developed concepts of statistical inference (see e.g., Barndorff-Nielsen [**1**], and Florens and Mouchart [**10**]). If in addition to being weakly exogenous, z_t is *not caused* in the sense of Granger [**16**] by any of the endogenous variables in the system, then z_t is defined to be strongly exogenous.

The concept of exogeneity is then extended to the class of models where the mechanism generating z_t changes. Such changes could come about for a variety of reasons; one of the most interesting is the attempt by one agent to control the behavior of another. If all the parameters λ of the conditional model are invariant to any change in the marginal density of z_t, and z_t is weakly exogenous for λ, then z_t is said to be *super* exogenous. That is, changes in the values of z_t or its generating function will not affect the conditional relation between y_t and z_t. This aspect builds on the work of Frisch [**12**], Marschak [**26**], Hurwicz [**20**], Sims [**39**], and Richard [**32**].

The paper is organized as follows: formal definitions of weak, strong, and super exogeneity are introduced in Section 2; and, to ensure an unambiguous discussion, the familiar notions of predeterminedness, strict exogeneity, and Granger noncausality are also defined. These are then discussed in the light of several examples in Section 3. The examples illustrate the relations between the concepts in familiar models showing the importance of each part of the new definitions and showing the incompleteness of the more conventional notions. Special attention is paid to the impact of serial correlation. The analysis is then applied to potentially incomplete dynamic simultaneous equations systems in Section 4. The conclusion restates the main themes and implications of the paper.

1.1 *Notation*

Let $x_t \in R^n$ be a vector of *observable* random variables generated at time t, on which observations ($t = 1, \ldots, T$) are available. Let X_t^1 denote the $t \times n$ matrix:

$$(1) \qquad X_t^1 = (x_1, \ldots, x_t)'$$

and let X_0 represent the (possibly infinite) matrix of initial conditions. The analysis is conducted conditionally on X_0. For a discussion of marginalization

[3]Throughout the paper, the term "efficient estimation" is used as a shorthand for "conducting inference without loss of relevant information," and does not entail any claims as to e.g., the efficiency of particular estimators in small samples.

with respect to initial conditions, see Engle, Hendry, and Richard [**8**], hereafter EHR. The information available at time t is given by

$$(2)\qquad X_{t-1} = \begin{bmatrix} X_0 \\ X_{t-1}^1 \end{bmatrix}.$$

The process generating the T observations is assumed to be continuous with respect to some appropriate measure and is represented by the joint data density function $D(X_T^1 | X_0, \theta)$ where θ, in the interior of Θ, is an (identified) vector of unknown parameters. The likelihood function of θ, given the initial conditions X_0, is denoted by $L^0(\theta; X_T^1)$.

Below, $f_N^n(\cdot \mid \mu, \Sigma)$ denotes the n-dimensional normal density function with mean vector μ and covariance matrix Σ. The notation $x_t \sim IN(\mu, \Sigma)$ reads as "the vectors $x_1, \ldots, x_T$ are identically independently normally distributed with common mean vector μ and covariance matrix Σ." C_n denotes the set of symmetric positive definite matrices.

The vector x_t is partitioned into

$$(3)\qquad x_t = \begin{bmatrix} y_t \\ z_t \end{bmatrix}, \qquad y_t \in R^p, \quad z_t \in R^q, \quad p + q = n.$$

The matrices X_0, X_t^1, and X_t are partitioned conformably:

$$(4)\qquad X_0 = (Y_0 Z_0), \qquad X_t^1 = (Y_t^1 Z_t^1), \qquad X_t = (Y_t Z_t).$$

The expressions "$x_t \parallel y_t$" and "$x_t \parallel y_t | w_t$" read respectively as "x_t and y_t are independent (in probability)" and "conditionally on w_t, x_t and y_t are independent." In our framework it is implicit that all such independence statements are *conditional* on θ. The operator $\sum$ denotes a summation which starts at $i = 1$ and is over all relevant lags.

2. DEFINITIONS

Often the objective of empirical econometrics is to model how the observation x_t is generated conditionally on the past, so we factorize the joint data density as

$$(5)\qquad D(X_T^1 | X_0, \theta) = \prod_{t=1}^{T} D(x_t | X_{t-1}, \theta)$$

and focus attention on the conditional density functions $D(x_t | X_{t-1}, \theta)$. These are assumed to have a common functional form with a *finite*[4] dimensional parameter space Θ.

The following formal definitions must be introduced immediately to ensure an unambiguous discussion, but the examples presented below attempt to elucidate their content; the reader wishing a general view of the paper could proceed fairly rapidly to Section 3 and return to this section later.

[4] It is assumed that the dimensionality of Θ is sufficiently small relative to nT that it makes sense to discuss, e.g., "efficient" estimation.

2.1. *Granger Noncausality*

For the class of models defined by (5), conditioned throughout on X_0, Granger **[16]** provides a definition of noncausality which can be restated as:

DEFINITION 2.1: Y_{t-1}^1 does not Granger cause z_t with respect to X_{t-1} if and only if

$$D(z_t \mid X_{t-1}, \theta) = D(z_t \mid Z_{t-1}, Y_0, \theta), \tag{6}$$

i.e., if and only if

$$z_t \parallel Y_{t-1}^1 \mid Z_{t-1}, Y_0. \tag{7}$$

If condition (6) holds over the sample period, then the joint data density $D(X_T^1 \mid X_0, \theta)$ factorizes as

$$D(X_T^1 \mid X_0, \theta) = \left[\prod_{t=1}^{T} D(y_t \mid z_t, X_{t-1}, \theta)\right]\left[\prod_{t=1}^{T} D(z_t \mid Z_{t-1}, Y_0, \theta)\right] \tag{8}$$

where the last term is $D(Z_T^1 \mid X_0, \theta)$ and the middle term is therefore $D(Y_T^1 \mid Z_T^1, X_0, \theta)$.

Where no ambiguity is likely, condition (6) is stated below as "y does not Granger cause z." Note that the definition in Chamberlain **[3]** is the same as 2.1.

2.2. *Predeterminedness and Strict Exogeneity*

Consider a set of $g \leq n$ behavioral relationships (whose exact interpretation is discussed in Section 4 below):

$$B^* x_t + \sum C^*(i) x_{t-i} = u_t \tag{9}$$

where B^* and $\{C^*(i)\}$ are $g \times n$ matrix functions of θ, with rank $B^* = g$ almost everywhere in Θ, and u_t is the corresponding "disturbance."

The following definitions are adapted from Koopmans and Hood **[22]**—see also Christ **[4**, Chs. IV.4, VI.4] and Sims **[39]**.

DEFINITION 2.2: z_t is *predetermined* in (9) if and only if

$$z_t \parallel u_{t+i} \quad \text{for all} \quad i \geq 0. \tag{10}$$

DEFINITION 2.3: z_t is *strictly exogenous*[5] in (9) if and only if

$$z_t \parallel u_{t+i} \quad \text{for all } i. \tag{11}$$

[5] We use the term "strictly exogenous" where some authors use "exogenous" to distinguish this concept from that introduced below.

The connections between strict exogeneity and Granger noncausality have been discussed by several authors—and in particular by Sims **[39]** and Geweke **[13]**—for complete dynamic simultaneous equations models. This issue is reconsidered in Section 4. See also the discussion in Chamberlain **[3]** and Florens and Mouchart **[11]**.

2.3. *Parameters of Interest*

Often a model user is not interested in all the parameters in θ, so that his (implicit) loss function depends only on some functions of θ, say:

$$(12) \qquad f:\Theta \to \Psi; \qquad \theta \to \psi = f(\theta).$$

These functions are called *parameters of interest*. Parameters may be of interest, e.g., because they are directly related to theories the model user wishes to test concerning the structure of the economy. Equally, in seeking empirical econometric relationships which are constant over the sample period and hopefully over the forecast period, parameters which are *structurally invariant* (see Section 2.6), are typically of interest.

Since models can be parameterized in infinitely many ways, parameters of interest need not coincide with those which are chosen to characterize the data density (e.g., the mean vector and the covariance matrix in a normal framework). Consider, therefore, an arbitrary one-to-one transformation or reparameterization:

$$(13) \qquad h:\Theta \to \Lambda; \qquad \theta \to \lambda = h(\theta)$$

together with a partition of λ into (λ_1, λ_2). Let Λ_i denote the set of admissible values of λ_i. The question of whether or not the parameters of interest are *functions* of λ_1 plays an essential role in our analysis: that is, whether there exists a function ϕ,

$$(14) \qquad \phi:\Lambda_1 \to \Psi; \qquad \lambda_1 \to \psi = \phi(\lambda_1)$$

such that

$$(15) \qquad \text{for all } \lambda \in \Lambda, \qquad \psi = f\left[h^{-1}(\lambda)\right] \equiv \phi(\lambda_1).$$

When (15) holds, λ_2 is often called a *nuisance* parameter.[6]

2.4. *Sequential Cuts*

Let $x_t \in R^n$ be partitioned as in (3) and let $\lambda = (\lambda_1, \lambda_2)$ be a reparameterization as in (13). The following definition is adapted from Florens and Mouchart **[10]**

[6] The concept of *nuisance* parameter is, however, ambiguous. Whether or not a parameter is a *nuisance* parameter critically depends on which (re)parameterization is used. If, for example, $\theta = (\alpha, \beta)$ and β is the sole parameter of interest, then α is a nuisance parameter. In contrast, a reparameterization using (α, γ) where $\gamma = \beta/\alpha$ entails that β is not a function of γ alone, and so α is not a *nuisance* parameter.

who generalized the notion of cut discussed (e.g.) by Barndorff-Nielsen [**1**] to dynamic models:

DEFINITION 2.4: $[(y_t \mid z_t ; \lambda_1), (z_t ; \lambda_2)]$ operates a (classical) *sequential cut* on $D(x_t \mid X_{t-1}, \lambda)$ if and only if

$$(16) \qquad D(x_t \mid X_{t-1}, \lambda) = D(y_t \mid z_t, X_{t-1}, \lambda_1) D(z_t \mid X_{t-1}, \lambda_2)$$

where λ_1 and λ_2 are *variation free*, i.e.,

$$(17) \qquad (\lambda_1, \lambda_2) \in \Lambda_1 \times \Lambda_2 .$$

Since Λ_i denotes the set of admissible values of λ_i, condition (17) requires in effect that λ_1 and λ_2 should not be subject to "cross-restrictions," whether exact or inequality restrictions, since then the range of admissible values for λ_i would vary with λ_j $(i, j = 1, 2; j \neq i)$.

2.5. *Weak and Strong Exogeneity*

The following definitions are adapted from Richard [**32**]. As in (12), ψ denotes the parameter of interest.

DEFINITION 2.5: z_t is *weakly exogenous* over the sample period for ψ if and only if there exists a reparameterization with $\lambda = (\lambda_1, \lambda_2)$ such that

(i) ψ is a function of λ_1 (as in (15)),

(ii) $\left[(y_t \mid z_t ; \lambda_1), (z_t ; \lambda_2)\right]$ operates a sequential cut.

DEFINITION 2.6: z_t is *strongly exogenous* over the sample period for ψ if and only if it is weakly exogenous for ψ and in addition

(iii) y does not Granger cause z.

When (ii) holds, $L^0(\lambda; X_T^1)$ factorizes as in

$$(18) \qquad L^0(\lambda; X_T^1) = L_1^0(\lambda_1 ; X_T^1) L_2^0(\lambda_2 ; X_T^1),$$

where

$$(19) \qquad L_1^0(\lambda_1 ; X_T^1) = \prod_{t=1}^{T} D(y_t \mid z_t, X_{t-1}, \lambda_1),$$

$$(20) \qquad L_2^0(\lambda_2 ; X_T^1) = \prod_{t=1}^{T} D(z_t \mid X_{t-1}, \lambda_2).$$

and the two factors in (18) can be analyzed independently of each other (which, irrespective of whether or not (i) holds may considerably reduce the computational burden). If in addition (i) holds, then all the sample information concerning the parameter of interest ψ can be obtained from the partial likelihood function $L_1^0(\lambda_1; X_T^1)$. If it were known (or assumed a priori) that z_t was weakly exogenous for ψ, then the marginal process $D(z_t | X_{t-1}, \lambda_2)$ would not even need to be specified. However, tests of the weak exogeneity of z_t for ψ, as described in Section 6.1 of EHR and Engle **[6]**, evidently require that the *joint* model $D(x_t | X_{t-1}, \lambda)$ be specified.

The factorization (18)–(20) does not entail that the conditional process generating $\{y_t | z_t\}$ and the marginal process generating $\{z_t\}$ can be separated from each other, i.e., for example, that z_t can be treated as "fixed" in the conditional model $D(y_t | z_t, X_{t-1}, \lambda_1)$ since lagged values of y_t may still affect the process generating z_t.[7] Factorizing the joint data density $D(X_T^1 | X_0, \lambda)$ requires an additional assumption and this is precisely the object of Granger noncausality. When both (ii) and (iii) hold we can factorize $D(X_T^1 | X_0, \lambda)$ as in

(21) $$D(X_T^1 | X_0, \lambda) = D(Y_T^1 | Z_T^1, X_0, \lambda_1) D(Z_T^1 | X_0, \lambda_2),$$

where

(22) $$D(Y_T^1 | Z_T^1, X_0, \lambda_1) = \prod_{t=1}^{T} D(y_t | z_t, X_{t-1}, \lambda_1),$$

(23) $$D(Z_T^1 | X_0, \lambda_2) = \prod_{t=1}^{T} D(z_t | Z_{t-1}, Y_0, \lambda_2).$$

It must be stressed that the definition of Granger noncausality as given in (6) and (8), includes *no* assumption about the *parameters*. This is precisely why it must be completed by an assumption of weak exogeneity in order to entail a complete separation of the processes generating respectively $\{y_t | z_t\}$ and $\{z_t\}$.

2.6. *Structural Invariance and Super Exogeneity*

A closely related issue of statistical inference is parameter constancy. Over time, it is possible that some of the parameters of the joint distribution may change perhaps through changing tastes, technology, or institutions such as government policy making. For some classes of parameter change or "interventions" there may be parameters which remain constant and which can be estimated without difficulty even though interventions occur over the sample period. This is a familiar assumption about parameters in econometrics which is here called invariance. Just as weak exogeneity sustains conditional inference

[7] It follows that, unless y does not Granger cause z, $L_1^0(\lambda_1; X_T^1)$ is not *sensu stricto* a likelihood function, although it is often implicitly treated as such in the econometric literature, but it is a valid basis for inferences about ψ, *provided* z_t *is weakly exogenous for* ψ.

within a regime, we develop the relevant exogeneity concept for models subject to a particular class of regime changes.

DEFINITION 2.7: A parameter is *invariant* for a class of interventions if it remains constant under these interventions. A model is invariant for such interventions if all its parameters are.

DEFINITION 2.8: A conditional model is *structurally invariant* if all its parameters are invariant for any change in the distribution of the conditioning variables.[8]

Since weak exogeneity guarantees that the parameters of the conditional model and those of the marginal model are variation free, it offers a natural framework for analyzing the structural invariance of parameters of conditional models. However, by itself, weak exogeneity is neither necessary nor sufficient for structural invariance of a conditional model. Note, first, that the conditional model may be structurally invariant without its parameters providing an estimate of the parameters of interest. Conversely, weak exogeneity of the conditioning variables does not rule out the possibility that economic agents change their behavior in relation to interventions. That is, even though the parameters of interest and the nuisance parameters are variation free over any given regime, where a regime is characterized by a fixed distribution of the conditioning variables, their variations between regimes may be related. This will become clear in the examples.

The concept of structurally invariant conditional models characterizes the conditions which guarantee the appropriateness of "policy simulations" or other control exercises, since any change in the distribution of the conditioning variables has no effect on the conditional submodel and therefore on the conditional forecasts of the endogenous variables. This requirement is clearly very strong and its untested assumption has been criticized in conventional practice by Lucas [**23**] and Sargent [**35**].

To sustain conditional inference in processes subject to interventions, we define the concept of *super exogeneity*.

DEFINITION 2.9: z_t *is super exogenous* for ψ if z_t is weakly exogenous for ψ and the conditional model $D(y_t \mid z_t, X_{t-1}, \lambda_1)$ is structurally invariant.

Note that Definition 2.9 relates explicitly to *conditional* submodels: since estimable models with invariant parameters but no weakly exogenous variables are easily formulated (see Example 3.2 below), super exogeneity is a sufficient but not a necessary condition for valid inference under interventions (see e.g. the discussion of feasible policy analyses under rational expectations in Wallis [**41**] and the formulation in Sargent [**35**]).

[8] The definition can always be restricted to a specific class of distribution changes. This will implicitly be the case in the examples which are discussed in Section 3.

It is clear that any assertion concerning super exogeneity is refutable in the data for past changes in $D(z_t | X_{t-1}, \lambda_2)$ by examining the behavior of the conditional model for invariance when the parameters of the exogenous process changed. For an example of this see Hendry [**18**]. However, super exogeneity for all changes in the distribution of z_t must remain a conjecture until refuted, both because nothing precludes agents from simply changing their behavior at a certain instant and because only a limited range of interventions will have occurred in any given sample period (compare the notion of nonexcitation in Salmon and Wallis [**34**]). Such an approach is, of course, standard scientific practice. When derived from a well-articulated theory, a conditional submodel with z_t super exogenous seems to satisfy the requirement for Zellner causality of "predictability according to a law" (see Zellner [**45**]).

2.7. *Comments*

The motivation for introducing the concept of weak exogeneity is that it provides a sufficient[9] condition for conducting inference conditionally on z_t without loss of relevant sample information. Our concept is a direct extension of Koopmans' [**21**] discussion of exogeneity. He shows that an implicit static simultaneous equations system which has the properties: (a) the variables of the first block of equations do not enter the second block, (b) the disturbances between the two blocks are independent, and (c) the Jacobian of the transformation from the disturbances to the observables is nowhere zero, will have a likelihood function which factors into two components as in (18), a conditional and a marginal. The variables in the second block are labeled exogenous. Implicit in his analysis is the notion that the parameters of interest are all located in the first block and that this parameterization operates a cut. The failure to state precisely these components of the definition, leads to a lack of force in the definition as is illustrated in several of the examples in this paper. Koopmans then analyzes dynamic systems in the same framework leading to a notion of exogeneity which corresponds to our strong exogeneity and predeterminedness corresponding to that concept as defined above.

Koopmans presents sufficient conditions for the factorization of the likelihood but does not discuss the case where the factorization holds but his sufficient conditions do not. Our work therefore extends Koopmans' by making precise the assumptions about the parameters of interest and by putting the definitions squarely on the appropriate factorization of the likelihood. More recent literature has in fact stepped back from Koopmans' approach, employing definitions such as that of strict exogeneity in Section 2.2. As shown in Section 4, strict exogeneity, when applied to dynamic simultaneous equations models includes condition

[9] It is also necessary for most purposes. However, since in (14) ψ need not depend on all the elements in λ_1 it might happen that ψ and λ_2 are variation free even though λ_1 and λ_2 are not in which case neglecting the restrictions between λ_1 and λ_2 *might* entail no loss of efficiency for inference on ψ. More subtly, whether or not cuts are necessary to conduct inference based on partial models without loss of information obviously very much depends on how sample information is measured. See in particular the concepts of G- and M-ancillarity in Barndorff-Nielsen [**1**].

(iii) of Definition 2.6 together with predeterminedness; condition (ii) of Definition 2.5 is not required explicitly but, at least for just identified models, is often satisfied by construction; condition (i) of Definition 2.5 is certainly absent which, in our view, is a major lacuna[10] since, unless it holds, strict exogeneity of z_t does not ensure that there is no loss of relevant sample information when conducting inference conditionally on z_t. On the other hand, if (i) and (ii) hold, then (iii) becomes irrelevant[11] since it no longer affects inference on the parameters of interest. This does not mean that condition (iii) has no merit on its own—a model user might express specific interest in detecting causal orderings and ψ should then be defined accordingly—but simply that it is misleading to emphasize Granger noncausality when discussing exogeneity. The two concepts serve different purposes: weak exogeneity validates conducting *inference* conditional on z_t while Granger noncausality validates *forecasting* z and then forecasting y *conditional* on the future z's. As is well known, the condition that y does not Granger cause z is neither necessary nor sufficient for the weak exogeneity of z. Obviously, if estimation is required before conditional predictions are made, then strong exogeneity which covers both Granger noncausality *and* weak exogeneity becomes the relevant concept.

Note that if $[(y_t \mid z_t; \lambda_1), (z_t; \lambda_2)]$ operates a sequential cut, then the information matrix, if it exists, is block-diagonal between λ_1 and λ_2. In fact for most of the examples discussed in this paper and in EHR the condition that the information matrix be block-diagonal appears to be equivalent to the condition that the parameterization should operate a sequential cut. However, at a more general level, the finding that the information matrix is block-diagonal between two sets of parameters, one of which contains all the parameters of interest, does not entail that the likelihood function factorize as in (18). Block-diagonality of the information matrix may reflect other features of the likelihood function. Therefore, it seems difficult to discuss exogeneity by means of information matrices without explicitly referring to reparameterizations in terms of conditional and marginal submodels. Further, information matrices are often difficult to obtain analytically especially in the presence of lagged endogenous variables.

Note also that some definitions seem designed to validate specific estimation methods such as ordinary least squares within a single equation framework. For example, Phillips [**29**, Section IV] presents conditions justifying least squares estimation in dynamic systems, which if fulfilled would allow regressors to be treated as "given," despite the presence of Granger causal feedbacks. The concept of weak exogeneity is *not directly* related to validating specific estimation methods but concerns instead the conditions under which attention may be restricted to conditional submodels without loss of relevant sample information.

[10]This criticism is hardly specific to the concept of exogeneity. For example, unless there are parameters of interest, it is meaningless to require that an estimator should be consistent since it is always possible to redefine the "parameters" such that any chosen convergent estimation method yields consistent estimates thereof (see e.g., Hendry [**17**]).

[11]Evidently if one wished to test the conditions under which (ii) held then overidentifying restrictions such as the ones typically implied by Granger noncausality would affect the properties of the test.

Later selection of an *inappropriate* estimator may produce inefficiency (and inconsistency) even when weak exogeneity conditions are fulfilled.

Many existing definitions of exogeneity have been formulated in terms of orthogonality conditions between observed variables and (unobservable) disturbances in linear relationships within processes which are usually required to be Gaussian. Definitions 2.5 and 2.6 apply equally well to any joint density function and therefore encompass nonlinear and non-Gaussian processes and truncated or otherwise limited dependent variables. As such nonclassical models come into more use it is particularly important to have definitions of exogeneity which can be directly applied. See for example Gourieroux, et al. [**15**] or Maddala and Lee [**25**]. For a formulation tantamount to weak exogeneity in the context of conditional logit models, see McFadden [**24**, Section 5.1]. Exogeneity also has been discussed from the Bayesian point of view by Florens and Mouchart [**10**]. The issue then becomes whether or not the posterior density of the parameters of interest as derived from a conditional submodel coincides with that derived from the complete model. Such is the case if z_t is weakly exogenous and in addition λ_1 and λ_2 in Definition 2.5 are a priori independent. However the conditions are not necessary and it may be the case that, in the absence of a sequential cut, the prior density is such that the desired result is still achieved.

3. EXAMPLES

Many of the points made in the previous section can be illustrated with the simplest of all multivariate models, the bivariate normal. Because this is a static model, the concepts of weak and strong exogeneity coincide as do the concepts of predeterminedness and strict exogeneity. The central role of the choice of parameters of interest is seen directly.

EXAMPLE 3.1: Let the data on y_t and z_t be generated by:

$$\begin{bmatrix} y_t \\ z_t \end{bmatrix} \sim IN(\mu, \Omega), \qquad \mu = (\mu_i), \quad \Omega = (\omega_{ij}), \quad i, j = 1, 2, \tag{24}$$

with the conditional distribution of y_t given z_t:

$$y_t \mid z_t \sim IN(\alpha + \beta z_t, \sigma^2) \tag{25}$$

where $\beta = \omega_{12}/\omega_{22}$, $\alpha = \mu_1 - \beta\mu_2$, and $\sigma^2 = \omega_{11} - \omega_{12}^2/\omega_{22}$. Letting

$$u_{1t} = y_t - E(y_t \mid z_t), \qquad v_{2t} = z_t - E(z_t), \tag{26}$$

the model is correspondingly reformulated as

$$y_t = \alpha + \beta z_t + u_{1t}, \qquad u_{1t} \sim IN(0, \sigma^2), \tag{27}$$

$$z_t = \mu_2 + v_{2t}, \qquad v_{2t} \sim IN(0, \omega_{22}), \tag{28}$$

where $\text{cov}(z_t, u_{1t}) = \text{cov}(v_{2t}, u_{1t}) = 0$ by construction. The parameters of the conditional model (27) are $(\alpha, \beta, \sigma^2)$ and those of the marginal model (28) are

(μ_2, ω_{22}). They are in one-to-one correspondence with (μ, Ω) and are variation-free since, for arbitrary choices of $(\alpha, \beta, \sigma^2)$ and (μ_2, ω_{22}) in their sets of admissible values which are respectively $R^2 \times R_+$ and $R \times R_+$, μ and Ω are given by

$$(29) \qquad \mu = \begin{bmatrix} \alpha + \beta\mu_2 \\ \mu_2 \end{bmatrix}, \qquad \Omega = \begin{bmatrix} \sigma^2 + \beta^2\omega_{22} & \beta\omega_{22} \\ \beta\omega_{22} & \omega_{22} \end{bmatrix},$$

and the constraint that Ω be positive definite is automatically satisfied (see Lemma 5.1 in Drèze and Richard [5] for a generalization of this result to multivariate regression models). It follows that z_t is weakly exogenous for $(\alpha, \beta, \sigma^2)$ or for any well-defined function thereof.

However, similar reasoning applies by symmetry to the factorization

$$(30) \qquad z_t = \gamma + \delta y_t + u_{2t}, \qquad u_{2t} \sim IN(0, \tau^2),$$

$$(31) \qquad y_t = \mu_1 + v_{1t}, \qquad v_{1t} \sim IN(0, \omega_{11}),$$

where $\delta = \omega_{12}/\omega_{11}$, $\gamma = \mu_2 - \delta\mu_1$, $\tau^2 = \omega_{22} - \omega_{12}^2/\omega_{11}$, and $\text{cov}(y_t, u_{2t}) = \text{cov}(v_{1t}, u_{2t}) = 0$ by construction. Therefore, y_t is weakly exogenous for (γ, δ, τ^2) or for any well-defined function thereof. In this example the choice of parameters of interest is the sole determinant of weak exogeneity which is, therefore, not directly testable.

Next, consider the concept of predeterminedness which is here equivalent to that of strict exogeneity. Regardless of the parameters of interest, z_t is predetermined in (27) by construction and so is y_t in (30). Which variable is predetermined depends upon the form of the equation, not upon the properties of the joint density function. Until some of the parameters are assumed to be more fundamental or structural (i.e., parameters of interest), the notion of predeterminedness has no force. When δ is the parameter of interest, z_t is predetermined in equation (27) but not weakly exogenous while y_t is weakly exogenous but not predetermined. Similar results hold in more complex models where the assumptions of exogeneity can be tested.

This example also illustrates the ambiguity in Koopmans' sufficient conditions as discussed in Section 2.7 since their application leads to the conclusion that z_t is exogenous in (27) and (28) while y_t is exogenous in (30) and (31), a conclusion which seems to misrepresent Koopmans' views about exogeneity.

Now consider the concepts of structural invariance and super exogeneity. Will the parameter β in (27) be invariant to an intervention which changes the variance of z? The answer depends upon the structure of the process. If β is truly a constant parameter (because, e.g., (27) is an autonomous behavioral equation) then σ_{12} will vary with σ_{22} since, given (26), $\sigma_{12} = \beta\sigma_{22}$. Alternatively it might be σ_{12} which is the fixed constant of nature in (24) and in this case β will not be invariant to changes in σ_{22}; z_t can be weakly exogenous for β within one regime with β a derived parameter which changes between regimes. By making β the parameter of interest, most investigators are implicitly assuming that it will remain constant when the distribution of the exogenous variables changes; however, this is an assumption which may not be acceptable in the light of the Lucas [**23**] critique. Similar arguments apply to α or σ^2. Therefore, if $(\alpha, \beta, \sigma^2)$ are invariant to any changes in the distribution of z_t or, more specifically in this restricted framework, to changes in μ_2 and ω_{22}, then z_t is super exogenous for $(\alpha, \beta, \sigma^2)$. If, on the other hand, β is invariant to such changes while α and σ^2 are not, e.g., because μ_1 and ω_{11} are invariant, then z_t might be weakly exogenous for β within each regime but is not super exogenous for β since the marginal process (28) now contains valuable information on the shifts of α and σ^2 between regimes.[12] It is clear from the above argument that weak exogeneity does not imply structural invariance. It is also clear that even if β is invariant to changes in the distribution of z or in fact the conditional model (27) is structurally invariant, the parameter of interest could be γ and therefore z_t would not be weakly exogenous, and thus not super exogenous either.

Finally, since weak exogeneity explicitly requires that all relevant sample information be processed, overidentifying restrictions are bound to play an essential role in a discussion of weak exogeneity assumptions.[13] This will be discussed further in Section 4 within the framework of dynamic simultaneous equations models. Example 3.2 illustrates the role of overidentifying restrictions in a simple structure.

Example 3.2: Consider the following two-equation overidentified model:

$$y_t = z_t\beta + \epsilon_{1t}, \tag{32}$$

$$z_t = z_{t-1}\delta_1 + y_{t-1}\delta_2 + \epsilon_{2t}, \tag{33}$$

$$\begin{bmatrix} \epsilon_{1t} \\ \epsilon_{2t} \end{bmatrix} \sim IN(0, \Sigma), \qquad \Sigma = \begin{bmatrix} \sigma_{11} & \sigma_{12} \\ \sigma_{12} & \sigma_{22} \end{bmatrix}. \tag{34}$$

Equation (33) is a typical control rule for an agent attempting to control y. For example, this could be a governmental policy reaction function or a farmer's supply decision or a worker's rule for deciding whether to undertake training. These cobweb models have a long history in econometrics. The parameter of interest is assumed to be β.

[12] This illustrates the importance of incorporating in Definition 2.9 the requirement that the conditional model $D(y_t \mid z_t, X_{t-1}, \lambda_1)$ be structurally invariant even though ψ may depend only on a subvector of λ_1.

[13] An interesting example of the complexities arising from overidentification occurs if $\omega_{11} = 1$ in (24) a priori. Then the factorization (27) and (28) no longer operates a cut as a result of the overidentifying constraint $\sigma^2 + \beta^2\omega_{22} = 1$, while the factorization (30) and (31) still does. Further, β and σ^2 are well-defined functions of (γ, δ, τ^2) since $\beta = \delta/(\delta^2 + \tau^2)$ and $\sigma^2 = \tau^2/(\delta^2 + \tau^2)$ while α is not. Therefore, z_t is no longer weakly exogenous for (β, σ^2) while y_t now is! Neither of these two variables is weakly exogenous for α.

The reduced form consists of (33) and

(35) $y_t = \beta\delta_1 z_{t-1} + \beta\delta_2 y_{t-1} + v_t$

(36) $\begin{bmatrix} v_t \\ \epsilon_{2t} \end{bmatrix} \sim IN(0,\Omega), \qquad \Omega = \begin{bmatrix} \sigma_{11} + 2\beta\sigma_{12} + \beta^2\sigma_{22} & \sigma_{12} + \beta\sigma_{22} \\ \sigma_{12} + \beta\sigma_{22} & \sigma_{22} \end{bmatrix},$

and the conditional density of y_t given z_t is

(37) $D(y_t \mid z_t, X_{t-1}, \theta) = N(bz_t + c_1 z_{t-1} + c_2 y_{t-1}, \sigma^2)$ where

(38) $b = \beta + \frac{\sigma_{12}}{\sigma_{22}}, \qquad c_i = -\delta_i \frac{\sigma_{12}}{\sigma_{22}}, \qquad \sigma^2 = \sigma_{11} - \sigma_{12}^2/\sigma_{22},$

which can be written as the regression

(39) $y_t = bz_t + c_1 z_{t-1} + c_2 y_{t-1} + u_t, \qquad u_t \sim IN(0,\sigma^2).$

The condition which is of first concern is the value of the parameter σ_{12}. If $\sigma_{12} = 0$, then z_t is predetermined in (32) and is weakly exogenous for β since (β, σ_{11}) and $(\delta_1, \delta_2, \sigma_{22})$ operates a cut. Even so, for $\delta_2 \neq 0$, y Granger causes z and therefore z is not strongly exogenous, nor is it strictly exogenous. However, the important criterion for efficient estimation is weak exogeneity, not strong exogeneity, and tests for Granger causality have no bearing on either the estimability of (32), or the choice of estimator.

If σ_{12} is not zero, then z_t is not weakly exogenous for β because this parameter cannot be recovered from only the parameters b, c_1, c_2, σ^2 of the conditional distribution (37). In (32) z_t is also not predetermined; however, in (39) it is, again showing the ambiguities in this concept. Whether or not a variable is predetermined depends on which equation is checked, and is not an intrinsic property of a variable.

The preceding results remain unchanged if $\delta_2 = 0$, in which case y does not Granger cause z, yet z_t is still not weakly exogenous for β when $\sigma_{12} \neq 0$. Granger noncausality is neither necessary nor sufficient for weak exogeneity, or for that matter, for predeterminedness.

Suppose instead that b is the parameter of interest and $\delta_2 \neq 0$. Then OLS on (39) will give a consistent estimate. This however will not be an efficient estimate since the parameters should satisfy the restriction

(40) $\delta_1 c_2 = \delta_2 c_1$

and consequently joint estimation of (39) and (33) would be more efficient. The parameterization (b, c_1, c_2, σ^2), $(\delta_1, \delta_2, \sigma_{22})$ does not operate a cut because the parameter sets are not variation free so z_t is not weakly exogenous for b. If, however, $\delta_2 = 0$ so that the system becomes just identified then z_t will be weakly exogenous for b as (b, c_1, σ^2), (δ_1, σ_{22}) operates a cut. In both cases, z_t is still predetermined in (39).

Which parameter "ought" to be the parameter of interest requires further information about the behavior of the system and its possible invariants. Usually, it seems desirable to choose as parameters of interest, those parameters which are invariant to changes in the distribution of the weakly exogenous variables. Returning to the first case where β is the parameter of interest and $\sigma_{12} = 0$, the investigator might assume that (β, σ_{11}) would be invariant to changes in the distribution of z. If this were valid, z_t would be super exogenous, even though it is still Granger caused by y so it is not strongly exogenous nor strictly exogenous. Changes in the parameters of (33) or even of the distribution of z_t will not affect estimation of β nor will control of z affect the conditional relation between y_t and z_t given in (32). Conversely, if $\delta_2 = 0$, but $\sigma_{12} \neq 0$, then (b, c_1, σ^2) and (δ_1, σ_{22}) operates a cut, and z is strictly exogenous in (39) and strongly exogenous for b, yet that regression is by hypothesis not invariant to changes in either δ_1 or σ_{22}, cautioning against constructing cuts which do not isolate invariants.

The assumption of super exogeneity is testable if it is known that the parameters of the marginal distribution have changed over the sample period. A test for changes in β could be interpreted as a test for super exogeneity with respect to the particular interventions observed.

To clarify the question of structural invariance in this example, consider a derivation of the behavioral equation (32) based on the assumption that the agent chooses y to maximize his expected utility conditional on the information available to him. Let the utility function be

(41) $$U(y, z; \beta) = -(y - z\beta)^2$$

where β is a parameter which is by hypothesis completely unrelated to the distribution of z and hence is invariant to any changes in the δ's in equation (33). Allowing for a possible random error ν_t, arising from optimization, the decision rule is

(42) $$y_t = \beta z_t^e + \nu_t$$

where z_t^e represents the agent's expectation of z_t conditionally on his information set I_t. In the perfect information case where z_t is contained in I_t, $z_t^e = z_t$ and (32) follows directly from (42). Hence β is structurally invariant and the assumption that $\sigma_{12} = \mathrm{cov}(\nu_t, \epsilon_{2t}) = 0$ is sufficient for the weak exogeneity of β and, consequently, for its super exogeneity. The imperfect information case raises more subtle issues since, as argued e.g., in Hendry and Richard **[19]**, z_t^e may not coincide with the expectation of z_t as derived from (33). In this example, however, we discuss only the rational expectations formulation originally proposed by Muth **[27]** whereby it is assumed that z_t^e and $E(z_t \mid \cdot)$ in (33) coincide. Hence (32) follows from (42) and

(43) $$\epsilon_{1t} = \nu_t - \beta\epsilon_{2t}$$

so that $\sigma_{12} = \mathrm{cov}(\nu_t, \epsilon_{2t}) - \beta\sigma_{22}$. Therefore, the conventional assumption that $\mathrm{cov}(\nu_t, \epsilon_{2t}) = 0$ entails that $\sigma_{12} = -\beta\sigma_{22} \neq 0$ in which case z_t is neither weakly exogenous nor super exogenous for β even though β is invariant. On the other hand, rational expectations per se does not exclude the possibility that $\sigma_{12} = 0$ (so that z_t remains weakly exogenous for β) since, e.g.,

$$\text{(44)} \qquad \operatorname{cov}(\nu_t, \epsilon_{2t}) = \sigma_{22}\beta$$

suffices.

Under the familiar assumptions, $\operatorname{cov}(\nu_t, \epsilon_{2t}) = 0$, the conditional expectation (37), and the reduced form, (35), coincide. No current value of z belongs in the conditional expectation of y_t given (z_t, I_t). Nevertheless, z_t is not weakly exogenous for β because the parameter β cannot be recovered from the reduced form coefficients c_1 and c_2 alone. This illustrates that even when the current value fails to enter the conditional expectation, weak exogeneity need not hold.

If the c_i were the parameters of interest, then z_t would be weakly exogenous, but these reduced form parameters are not structurally invariant to changes in the δ's. The Lucas **[23]** criticism applies directly to this equation regardless of whether y Granger causes z. The derivation and the noninvariance of these parameters suggests why they should not be the parameters of interest. Once again, testing for Granger causality has little to do with the Lucas criticism or the estimability or formulation of the parameters of interest. It is still possible to estimate β efficiently, for example by estimating (32) and (33) jointly as suggested by Wallis **[41]**, but this requires specifying and estimating both equations.[14] If there is a structural shift in the parameters of the second equation, this must also be allowed for in the joint estimation. This example shows the close relationship between weak exogeneity and structural invariance and points out how models derived from rational expectations behavior may or may not have weak exogeneity and structural invariance.

EXAMPLE 3.3: This final example shows that with a slight extension of the linear Gaussian structure to include serial correlation, the concept of predeterminedness becomes even less useful.

Consider the model

$$\text{(45)} \qquad y_t = \beta z_t + u_t,$$

$$\text{(46)} \qquad u_t = \rho u_{t-1} + \epsilon_{1t},$$

$$\text{(47)} \qquad z_t = \gamma y_{t-1} + \epsilon_{2t},$$

$$\text{(48)} \qquad \begin{bmatrix} \epsilon_{1t} \\ \epsilon_{2t} \end{bmatrix} \sim IN(0, \Sigma), \qquad \Sigma = \begin{bmatrix} \sigma_{11} & \sigma_{12} \\ \sigma_{12} & \sigma_{22} \end{bmatrix}.$$

Although this model is unidentified in a rather subtle sense, this need not concern us here as all the special cases to be discussed will be identified. The issue is dealt with more fully in EHR.

[14] Depending on the model formulation, instrumental variables estimation of (say) (32) alone is sometimes fully efficient.

The conditional expectation of y_t given z_t and X_{t-1} implies the regression

(49) $$y_t = bz_t + cy_{t-1} + dz_{t-1} + \eta_t, \qquad \eta_t \sim IN(0, \sigma^2),$$

where

(50) $$b = \beta + \sigma_{12}/\sigma_{22}, \quad c = \rho - \gamma\sigma_{12}/\sigma_{22}, \quad d = -\beta\rho, \quad \sigma^2 = \sigma_{11} - \sigma_{12}^2/\sigma_{22}.$$

The covariance between z_t and u_t is given by

(51) $$\operatorname{cov}(z_t, u_t) = \left(\sigma_{12} + \sigma_{11}\frac{\gamma\rho}{1-\rho^2}\right)/(1 - \gamma\rho\beta).$$

Note first that, as indicated by (51), the condition $\sigma_{12} = 0$ is *not* sufficient for the predeterminedness of z_t in (45). However, $\sigma_{12} = 0$ is sufficient for the weak exogeneity of z_t for the parameters β and ρ, as can be seen directly from (50) where the parameters of the conditional model (49) are subject to a common factor restriction but are variation free with those of the marginal model (47). Thus, the parameters of (49) could be estimated by imposing the restrictions through some form of autoregressive maximum likelihood method. Ordinary least squares estimation of β in (45) will be inconsistent whereas autoregressive least squares will be both consistent and asymptotically efficient. This example shows the advantages of formulating definitions in terms of expectations conditional on the past.

A second interesting property of this model occurs when $\sigma_{12} \neq 0$ but $\gamma = 0$. Again (51) shows that z_t is not predetermined in (45), but surprisingly, it is weakly exogenous for β and ρ. The three regression coefficients in (49) are now a nonsingular transformation of the three unknown parameters $(\beta, \rho, \sigma_{12}/\sigma_{22})$ and these operate a cut with respect to the remaining nuisance parameter σ_{22}. *Ordinary* least squares estimation of (49) provides efficient estimates of its parameters and the maximum likelihood estimate of β is $-d/c$. Both ordinary least squares and autoregressive least squares estimation of (45) would yield inconsistent estimates of β.

The case where

(52) $$(1 - \rho^2)\sigma_{12} + \gamma\rho\sigma_{11} = 0$$

raises several important issues which are discussed in detail in EHR. In short, the condition (52) identifies the model but violates both conditions (i) and (ii) in Definition 2.5 so that z_t is not weakly exogenous for (β, ρ), neither is it for (b, c, d) in (49). In particular, the autoregressive least squares estimator of β in (45) and (46) is inconsistent even though, as a consequence of the predeterminedness of z_t in (45), the first step ordinary least squares estimators of β in (45) and ρ in (46) are consistent (but not efficient).

This concludes the discussion of the examples. It is hoped that these have shown the usefulness of the concepts of weak and strong exogeneity, structural invariance, and super exogeneity in analyzing familiar and possibly some unfamiliar situations. Further examples can be found in EHR including a truncated latent variable model based upon Maddala and Lee [**25**].

4. APPLICATION TO DYNAMIC SIMULTANEOUS EQUATIONS MODELS

In this section we shall apply our analysis to dynamic simultaneous equations models (DSEM). As this is the arena in which notions of exogeneity are most heavily used and tested, it is important to relate our concepts to conventional wisdom. It will be shown that the conventional definitions must be supplemented with several conditions for the concepts to have force. However, when these conditions are added, then in standard textbook models, predeterminedness becomes equivalent to weak exogeneity and strict exogeneity becomes equivalent to strong exogeneity. Finally, our framework helps clarify the connections between such (modified) concepts and the notions of Wold causal orderings (see Strotz and Wold [**40**]), "block recursive structures" (see Fisher [**9**]), and "exogeneity tests" as in Wu [**44**].

Following Richard [**31**, **32**] the system of equations need not be complete and thus the analysis is directly a generalization of the conventional DSEM. Assuming normality and linearity of the conditional expectations $\phi_t = E(x_t \mid X_{t-1}, \theta)$, let[15]

$$D(x_t \mid X_{t-1}, \theta) = f_N^n(x_t \mid \sum \Pi(i) x_{t-i}, \Omega) \tag{53}$$

where $\{\Pi(i)\}$ and Ω are functions of a vector of unknown parameters $\theta \in \Theta$.

Define the "innovations" or "reduced form disturbances" v_t by

$$v_t = x_t - \phi_t = x_t - \sum \Pi(i) x_{t-i}. \tag{54}$$

Then, ϕ_t being conditional on X_{t-1},

$$\operatorname{cov}(v_t, x_{t-i}) = 0 \quad \text{for all} \quad i > 0, \quad \text{and hence} \tag{55}$$

$$\operatorname{cov}(v_t, v_{t-i}) = 0 \quad \text{for all} \quad i > 0. \tag{56}$$

We define the dynamic multipliers $Q(i)$ by the recursion

$$Q(0) = I_n \quad \text{and}$$

$$Q(i) = \sum_{j=1}^{i} \Pi(j) Q(i-j), \qquad \text{for all} \quad i \geq 1, \tag{57}$$

[15] Our framework explicitly requires that the distribution of the endogenous variables be completely specified. Normality (and linearity) assumptions are introduced here because they prove algebraically convenient. Other distributional assumptions could be considered at the cost of complicating the algebra. Furthermore, there exist distributions, such as the multivariate student distribution, for which there exist no cuts. Evidently weak exogeneity can always be achieved by construction, simply by specifying independently of each other a conditional and a marginal model, but is then no longer testable. More interestingly, conditions such as the ones which are derived below could be viewed as "approximate" or "local" exogeneity conditions under more general specifications. Given the recent upsurge of nonlinear non-Gaussian models in econometrics this is clearly an area which deserves further investigation.

and note that

(58) $\operatorname{cov}(v_t, x_{t+i}) = Q(i)\Omega \qquad \text{for all} \quad i \geq 0.$

Often the specification of θ is (partially) achieved by considering sets of behavioral relationships. Such relationships can correspond to optimizing behavior given expectations about future events, allow for adaptive responses and include mechanisms for correcting previous mistakes. In our framework, where attention is focussed on the conditional densities $D(x_t | X_{t-1}, \theta)$ it is natural to specify these relationships in terms of the conditional expectations ϕ_t. Consider, therefore, a set of $g \leq n$ linear behavioral relationships of the form

(59) $B\phi_t + \sum C(i)x_{t-i} = 0$

where B and $\{C(i)\}$ are $g \times n$ matrix functions of a vector of "structural" coefficients $\delta \in \Delta$, with rank $B = g$ almost everywhere in Δ. The δ's are typically parameters of interest. We can also define a g-dimensional vector of unobservable "structural disturbances:"

(60) $\epsilon_t = Bx_t + \sum C(i)x_{t-i}$

which also satisfy, by construction, the properties (55), (56).

Let Σ denote the covariance matrix of ϵ_t. In all generality Σ is also treated as a function of δ. From (53), (54), (59), and (60) we must have $\epsilon_t = Bv_t$ and

(61) $B\Pi(i) + C(i) \equiv 0, \qquad \text{for all} \quad i \geq 0; \qquad \Sigma = B\Omega B'.$

The identities (61) define a correspondence between Δ and Θ or, equivalently, a function h from Δ to $P(\Theta)$, the set of all subsets of Θ. To any given $\delta \in \Delta$, h associates a subset of Θ which we denote by $h(\delta)$. In the rest of the paper it is assumed that: (i) δ is *identified* in the sense that

(62) $\text{for all} \quad \delta, \delta* \in \Delta, \qquad \delta \neq \delta* \rightarrow h(\delta) \cap h(\delta*) = \emptyset;$

(ii) all values in Θ are compatible with (61),

(63) $\Theta = \bigcup_{\delta \in \Delta} h(\delta),$

so that $\{h(\delta)\}$ is a partition of Θ.

Let s denote the number of nonzero columns in $\{\Pi(i)\}$ and C_n the set of $n \times n$ symmetric positive definite matrices. If $\Theta = R^{sn} \times C_n$, except for the set of zero Lebesgue measure, then the model (53) is *just identified*. It is *overidentified* if Θ is a strict subset of $R^{sn} \times C_n$.

When $g < n$, it often proves convenient to define an auxiliary parameter vector, say $\bar{\theta} \in \bar{\Theta}$ of the form $\bar{\theta} = (\delta, \theta_2)$ where θ_2 is a subvector of θ defined in such a way that $\bar{\Theta}$ and Θ are in one-to-one correspondence. If, in particular, $\{\Pi(i)\}$ and Ω are subject to no other constraints than those derived from the identities (61) as implicitly assumed in this section, then we can select for θ_2 the coefficients of $n-g$ unconstrained "reduced form" equations,[16] whereby

$$\bar{\Theta} = \Delta \times \Theta_2, \quad \text{with} \quad \Theta_2 = R^{s(n-g)} \times C_{n-g}. \tag{64}$$

The specification of many econometric models "allows for" serial correlation of the residuals, i.e., incorporates linear relationships of the form

$$B^* x_t + \sum C^*(i) x_{t-i} = u_t \sim N(0, \Phi) \tag{65}$$

where B^* and $\{C^*(i)\}$ are claimed to be parameters of interest (or well defined functions thereof) and u_t is seen as a g-dimensional "autonomous" process, subject to serial correlation. Note that if (65) is to be used to *derive* the distribution of x_t *from* that of u_t, then the system must be "complete", i.e., $g = n$.

Provided u_t has an autoregressive representation,

$$u_t = \sum R_i u_{t-i} + e_t, \quad \text{where} \quad e_t \sim IN(0, \Sigma), \tag{66}$$

then (65) can be transformed to have serially uncorrelated "errors" (the new parameterization being subject to common factor restrictions as in Sargan [37]) in which case the transformed model can be reinterpreted in terms of conditional expectations as in (53). More general specifications of u_t are not ruled out in principle, but might seriously complicate the analysis.

We can now unambiguously characterize and inter-relate the concepts of Granger noncausality, predeterminedness and strict exogeneity, as given in Definitions 2.1–2.3, for potentially overidentified and incomplete DSEM which have been transformed to have serially uncorrelated residuals. Since these concepts may apply only to a subset of the equation system (59), this is accordingly partitioned into the first $g_1 \leq p$ equations and the remaining $g_2 = g - g_1 \leq q$ equations—see e.g. Fisher [9] on the notion of block recursive structures. We partition the Π's, Q's, and Ω conformably with the variables $x_t' = (y_t' z_t')$, B conformably with the variables and the equations and the C's and Σ conformably with the equations as:

$$\Pi(i) = \begin{bmatrix} \Pi_1(i) \\ \Pi_2(i) \end{bmatrix} = \begin{bmatrix} \Pi_{11}(i) & \Pi_{12}(i) \\ \Pi_{21}(i) & \Pi_{22}(i) \end{bmatrix},$$

$$Q(i) = \begin{bmatrix} Q_1(i) \\ Q_2(i) \end{bmatrix} = \begin{bmatrix} Q_{11}(i) & Q_{12}(i) \\ Q_{21}(i) & Q_{22}(i) \end{bmatrix},$$

$$\Omega = (\Omega_1 \Omega_2) = \begin{bmatrix} \Omega_{11} & \Omega_{12} \\ \Omega_{21} & \Omega_{22} \end{bmatrix}, \quad B = \begin{bmatrix} B_1 \\ B_2 \end{bmatrix} = \begin{bmatrix} B_{11} & B_{12} \\ B_{21} & B_{22} \end{bmatrix}, \tag{67}$$

$$C(i) = \begin{bmatrix} C_1(i) \\ C_2(i) \end{bmatrix} \quad \text{and} \quad \Sigma = \begin{bmatrix} \Sigma_{11} & \Sigma_{12} \\ \Sigma_{21} & \Sigma_{22} \end{bmatrix}.$$

[16] This is current practice in the literature on so-called limited information procedures. Non-Bayesian inference procedures based on likelihood principles are invariant with respect to the choice

THEOREM 4.1: *For the class of models defined by* (53) *plus* (59): (i) y *does not Granger cause* z *if and only if*

$$Q_{21}(i) = 0, \quad \text{for all} \quad i \geq 1;$$

(ii) z_t *is predetermined in the first* g_1 *equations of* (59) *if and only if*

$$B_1\Omega_2 = 0;$$

(iii) z_t *is strictly exogenous in the first* g_1 *equations of* (59) *if and only if*

$$B_1\Omega Q_2'(i) = 0, \quad \text{for all} \quad i \geq 0.$$

(iv) *Conditions* (i) *and* (ii) *are sufficient for* (iii). *If* $g_1 = p$, *they are also necessary for* (iii).

(v) *If* $B_{21} = 0$, $\Sigma_{12} = 0$, *and rank* $B_{22} = q(= g_2)$, *then* z_t *is predetermined in the first* g_1 *equations of* (59).

PROOF: The proof follows from the Definitions 2.1–2.3 together with (57), wherefrom it can be shown by recurrence that $(\Pi_{21}(i) = 0;\, i \geq 1)$ is equivalent to $(Q_{21}(i) = 0;\, i \geq 1)$. See EHR for more details.

In order to discuss weak exogeneity the parameters of interest must be defined. In the theorems below it will be assumed that the parameters of interest are all grouped together in the first g_1 equations. Thus it is not a cavalier matter which equations are put in the first group. For example, in a control problem, the first g_1 equations might describe the behavior of the economic agents given the controlled values of z_t, while the remaining g_2 equations describe the control rules which have been operative.

Factorizing the joint density (53) also requires the introduction of an appropriate reparameterization. This is the object of Lemma 4.2 which translates into our notation results which are otherwise well-known.

LEMMA 4.2: *The joint density* (53) *factorizes into the product of the conditional density*

(68) $$D(y_t \mid z_t, X_{t-1}, \lambda_1) = f_N^p\left(y_t \mid \Delta_{12}z_t + \sum \Pi_{1.2}(i)x_{t-i}, \Omega_{11.2}\right)$$

and the marginal density

(69) $$D(z_t \mid X_{t-1}, \lambda_2) = f_N^q\left(z_t \mid \sum \Pi_2(i)x_{t-i}, \Omega_{22}\right)$$

with $\lambda_1 = (\Delta_{12}, \{\Pi_{1.2}(i)\}, \Omega_{11.2})$, $\lambda_2 = (\{\Pi_2(i)\}, \Omega_{22})$,

(70) $$\Delta_{12} = \Omega_{12}\Omega_{22}^{-1}, \quad \Omega_{11.2} = \Omega_{11} - \Omega_{12}\Omega_{22}^{-1}\Omega_{21}, \text{ and } \Pi_{1.2}(i) = \Pi_1(i) - \Delta_{12}\Pi_2(i).$$

PROOF: See e.g. Press [**30**, Sections 3.4 and 3.5].

---

of these $n - g$ reduced form equations, provided they form a nonsingular set of equations together with the g structural relationships (59). Also, in a Bayesian framework there exist prior densities on θ such that the corresponding posterior densities on δ have similar invariance properties. For details, see e.g. Drèze and Richard [**5**] for $g = 1$, or Richard [**31**] for $g > 1$.

If the model (53) is *just identified*, then λ_1 and λ_2 are variation free with respective domains of variation $\Lambda_1 = R^{p\times q} \times \{R^{p\times n}\} \times C_p$ and $\Lambda_2 = \{R^{q\times n}\} \times C_q$ and z_t is weakly exogenous for ψ if and only if ψ is a function of λ_1 only. However, in order to be operational within the framework of DSEM's, such a condition should be expressed in terms of the structural coefficients δ since these are themselves typically parameters of interest. Also, most applications involve overidentified models for which λ_1 and λ_2 are no longer variation free unless some additional conditions are satisfied. Thus, the object of Theorem 4.3 is to derive *general* conditions on δ for the weak exogeneity of z_t for ψ. By their nature, these conditions are *sufficient* and, as in Section 3, it is easy to construct examples in which they are *not necessary*. Consequently, insofar as so-called "exogeneity tests" are typically tests for such conditions, rejection on such a test does not necessarily entail that the weak exogeneity assumption is invalid (see e.g. Example 3.3 when $\sigma_{12} \neq 0$ and $\gamma = 0$).

THEOREM 4.3: *For the DSEM in* (53) *plus* (59) *consider the following conditions*:

(i) $B_1\Omega_2 = 0$,

(ii) $B_{21} = 0$,

(iii) $(B_1, \{C_1(i)\}, \Sigma_{11})$ *and* $(B_2, \{C_2(i)\}, \Sigma_{22})$ *are variation free*,

(iv) ψ *is a function of* $(B_1, \{C_1(i)\}, \Sigma_{11})$,

(v) $\Sigma_{12} = 0$,

(vi) *rank* $B_{22} = q$,

(vii) $(B_2, \{C_2(i)\}, \Sigma_{22})$ *are just identified parameters*.

The following sets of conditions are sufficient for the weak exogeneity of z_t *for* ψ:

(a) (i)(ii)(iii)(iv),

(b) (ii)(iii)(iv)(v)(vi),

(c) (i)(iii)(iv)(vii).

PROOF: The basic result (a) generalizes Theorem 3.1 in Richard **[32]** in that it also covers cases where restrictions are imposed on Σ. The proof in Richard extends to the more general case since, under (i) and (ii), the identity $\Sigma = B\Omega B'$ separates into the two identities $\Sigma_{11} = B_{11}\Omega_{11.2}B'_{11}$ and $\Sigma_{22} = B_{22}\Omega_{22}B'_{22}$. Result (b) follows from (a) together with condition (ii) and (v) in Theorem 4.1. Result (c) follows by applying (a) to a system consisting of the first g_1 behavioral relationships and g_2 *unrestricted* reduced form equations whose parameters are in one-to-one correspondence with $(B_2, \{C_2(i)\}, \Sigma_{22})$ and variation free with $(B_1, \{C_1(i)\}, \Sigma_{11})$ following conditions (vii) and (iii).

The major differences in the sufficient conditions for weak exogeneity and for predeterminedness are conditions (iii) and (iv) of Theorem 4.3, which assure the model builder that there are no cross equation restrictions to the second block of equations and that there are no interesting parameters in that block.

To show the importance of these conditions in any definition, consider a set of $g \leq p < n$ just identified behavioral relationships, as given by (59) such that $B\Omega_2 \neq 0$. As is well known (see, for example, Strotz and Wold [**40**]) the system (59) can be replaced by an observationally equivalent one in which z_t is predetermined, and hence is strictly exogenous if y does not Granger cause z. For example let

$$(71) \qquad \bar{B} = \Phi\left(I_g : -\Omega_{12}\Omega_{22}^{-1}\right),$$

$$(72) \qquad \bar{C}(i) = -\bar{B}\Pi(i), \qquad i \geq 1,$$

where Φ is an arbitrary but known $g \times g$ nonsingular matrix so that $(\bar{B}, \{\bar{C}(i)\})$ are just-identified by construction. Such transformations, with $\Phi = I_2$, have been implicitly used in the Examples 3.1–3.2. Replacing (59) by

$$(73) \qquad \bar{B}\phi_t + \sum \bar{C}(i)x_{t-i} = 0$$

leaves (53) unaffected, but now $\bar{B}\Omega_2 = 0$. Consequently, $(\bar{B}, \{\bar{C}(i)\})$ can be estimated consistently from the conditional model $D(y_t \mid z_t, X_{t-1}, \cdot)$ together with (73). These estimates would be efficient provided (59) were just-identified. However, it is essential to realize that, since $g \leq p < n$, the parameters $(B, \{C(i)\})$ are typically not functions of $(\bar{B}, \{\bar{C}(i)\})$ alone and if the former are of interest, transforming (59) to (73) does not allow valid inference conditionally on z_t.

Thus, although at first sight, in normal DSEM weak exogeneity appears to be close to the notion of a Wold causal ordering, without the concept of parameters of interest the latter lacks force since there may be no cut which separates the parameters of interest and the nuisance parameters. Nevertheless, it must be stressed that Wold and Jureen [**43**, p. 14] *explicitly* include the condition that "each equation in the system expresses a unilateral causal dependence" which, in the spirit of our use of sequential cuts, seems designed to exclude arbitrary transformations of the system (59); see also the distinction in Bentzel and Hansen [**2**] between basic and derived models.

In Wu's [**44**] analysis, where $g_1 = 1$, it is implicit that conditions (iii) and (vii) of Theorem 4.3 are satisfied in which case the condition for predeterminedness $(B_1\Omega_2 = 0)$ is indeed sufficient for the weak exogeneity of z_t for the parameters of the first behavioral equation (but not necessarily for other parameters of interest). It must be stressed, however, that if the remaining behavioral equations in the model under consideration are over-identified, then predeterminedness might no longer be sufficient on its own for the weak exogeneity of z_t. Therefore even if the conditions (iii) and (iv) of Theorem 4.3 are incorporated in the definition of predeterminedness as is sometimes implicitly done, there would remain many situations where weak exogeneity and predeterminedness would still differ. Cases (a) and (b) in Theorem 4.3 provide *sufficient* conditions which are applicable to more general cases than the one considered in Wu. Note, however, that condition (ii) in particular is not necessary and that case (c) could be made more general at the cost of some tedious notation as hinted by the following example.[17]

EXAMPLE 4.4: Consider a (complete) DSEM with $n = 3$, $p = g_1 = 1$, $q = g_2 = 2$, and

$$B = \begin{bmatrix} 1 & b_1 & 0 \\ b_2 & 1 & 0 \\ 0 & b_3 & 1 \end{bmatrix}, \qquad C(1) = \begin{bmatrix} c_1 & 0 & 0 \\ 0 & c_2 & c_3 \\ 0 & c_4 & 0 \end{bmatrix}, \qquad C(i) = 0, \qquad i > 1.$$

The b's and c's are assumed to be variation free. The condition $B_1\Omega_2 = 0$, which is equivalent to $\sigma_{12} = b_2\sigma_{11}$ and $\sigma_{13} = 0$, is sufficient for the weak exogeneity of (y_{2t}, y_{3t}) for (b_1, c_1, σ_{11}) even though $B_{21}' = (b_2 0) \neq 0$ and the third behavioral relationship is overidentified (but does not contain y_{1t}!). Note that the predeterminedness of y_{2t} in the first behavioral relationship ($\sigma_{12} = b_2\sigma_{11}$) is sufficient for the *consistency* of OLS estimation of (b_1, c_1, σ_{11}) in that relationship but not for the weak exogeneity of (y_{2t}, y_{3t})—or y_{2t} alone—for (b_1, c_1, σ_{11}). In the absence of additional restrictions such as $\sigma_{13} = 0$ a more *efficient* estimator of (b_1, c_1, σ_{11}) is obtained e.g. by FIML estimation of the complete DSEM.

Note finally from Theorem 4.1 (v) and 4.3 (b) that the standard block-recursive model is sufficient for both (block) predeterminedness and (block) weak exogeneity (again assuming the parameterization satisfies (iii) and (iv)); this may help explain its importance in the development of the theory of simultaneous equations models.

5. SUMMARY AND CONCLUSIONS

Given the pervasive role of the concept of "exogeneity" in econometrics, it is essential to uniquely characterize the implications of claims that certain variables are "exogenous" according to particular definitions. Also, it is useful to have definitions which require minimal conditions and yet are applicable to as wide a class of relevant models as possible. Consequently, general and unambiguous definitions are proposed for *weak*, *strong*, and *super* exogeneity in terms of the joint densities of observable variables and the parameters of interest in given models, thus extending and formalizing the approach in Koopmans [**21**]. "Exogeneity" assertions are usually intended to allow the analysis of one set of variables without having to specify exactly how a second related set is deter-

[17] We are grateful to A. Holly for providing us with this example and, more generally, for pointing out several shortcomings in earlier drafts of this section.

mined and such an analysis could comprise any or all of inference, forecasting, or policy. In each case, the conclusions are conditional on the validity of the relevant "exogeneity" claims (a comment germane to theoretical models also, although we only consider observable variables) and since different conditioning statements are required in these three cases, three distinct, but inter-related, concepts of exogeneity are necessary.

The joint density of the observed variables $x_t = (y_t' z_t')'$, conditional on their past, always can be factorized as the conditional density of y_t given z_t times the marginal density of z_t. If: (a) the parameters λ_1 and λ_2 of these conditional and marginal densities are not subject to cross-restrictions (i.e., there is a cut) and, (b) the parameters of interest (denoted by ψ) can be uniquely determined from the parameters of the conditional model alone (i.e., $\psi = f(\lambda_1)$), then inference concerning ψ from the joint density will be equivalent to that from the conditional density so that the latter may be used without loss of relevant information. Under such conditions, z_t is *weakly* exogenous for ψ, and for purposes of *inference* about ψ, z_t may be treated "as if" it were determined outside the (conditional) model under study, making the analysis simpler and more robust.

Conditions (a) and (b) clearly are not sufficient to treat z_t as if it were fixed in repeated samples, since the definition of weak exogeneity is unspecific about relationships between z_t and y_{t-i} for $i \geq 1$. However, if: (c) y does not Granger cause z, then the data density of $X_t^1 = (x_1, \ldots, x_t)'$ factorizes into the conditional density of Y_t^1 given Z_t^1 times the marginal of Z_t^1 and hence $\{z_t\}$ may be treated as if it were fixed. If (a), (b), and (c) are satisfied, then z_t is *strongly exogenous* for ψ and forecasts could be made conditional on fixed future z's.

Nevertheless, strong exogeneity is insufficient to sustain conditional policy analysis since (a) does not preclude the possibility that while λ_1 and λ_2 are variation free within any *given* "regime," λ_1 might vary in response to a change in λ_2 between "regimes." The additional condition that: (d) λ_1 is invariant to changes in λ_2 (or more generally the conditional distribution is invariant to any change in the marginal distribution) is required to sustain conditional *policy* experiments for fixed λ_1, and z_t is *super exogenous* for ψ if (a), (b), and (d) are satisfied (so that (c) is not necessary either).

In fact, if the generating process of the conditioning variables is susceptible to changes over either sample or forecast periods, then the failure of (d) will invalidate inference and predictions based on the assertion that λ_1 is a constant parameter, whether or not z_t includes "policy variables." In worlds where policy parameters change, false super-exogeneity assumptions are liable to produce predictive failures in conditional models (see Lucas [**23**]). Control experiments which involve changes in λ_2 must first establish the super exogeneity of z_t for ψ under the class of interventions considered; we know of no sufficient conditions for establishing such results, but a necessary condition is that the conditional model does not experience predictive failure within sample (see Hendry [**18**]).

Even in constant parameter worlds (and certainly in worlds of parameter change), the new concepts are distinct from the more familiar notions of predeterminedness and strict exogeneity. Following precise definitions of these two concepts, it is shown through examples that their formulation in terms of *unobservable* disturbances entails ambiguous implications for inference and that strict exogeneity is neither necessary nor sufficient for inference in conditional models without loss of relevant information. Moreover, models in which predeterminedness is obtained by construction need not have invariant parameters and since predeterminedness is necessary for strict exogeneity, establishing only the latter does not provide a valid basis for conditional prediction or conditional policy. The various concepts are compared and contrasted in detail in closed linear dynamic simultaneous equations systems, and the usefulness of (a) and (b) in clarifying the debate about Wold-causal-orderings is demonstrated.

It is natural to enquire about the testable implications of alternative exogeneity assumptions. Condition (d) is indirectly testable (as noted) via tests for parameter constancy, although as with all test procedures, rejection of the null does not indicate what alternative is relevant and non-rejection may simply reflect low power (so that there are advantages in specifying the regime shift process as in Richard [**32**]). Condition (c) is common to both strong and strict exogeneity notions and may be testable in the conditional model (see Sims [**38**] and Geweke [**14**]) but may also require specification of the marginal density of z_t as in Granger [**16**]. Also, predeterminedness tests have been the subject of a large literature (see inter alia Wu [**44**]).

To test weak exogeneity, the conditional and marginal densities could be embedded in a joint density function, although the choice of the latter may or may not generate testable implications. It is somewhat paradoxical to estimate the parameters of a (potentially very complicated) marginal model just to test whether or not one needed to specify that model. Moreover, misspecifications in the marginal model may induce false rejection of the null of weak exogeneity. Nevertheless, Engle [**6**, **7**] considers various weak exogeneity tests based on the Lagrange multiplier principle. Also, on a positive note, while both weak exogeneity and parameter constancy are conjectural features in a conditional modelling exercise, if the data generating process of z_t has changed, but the conditional model has not, then some credibility must attach to the latter since it was hazarded to potential rejection and survived.

Finally, we believe that the new concepts are not only general (being based explicitly on density functions and encompassing worlds of parameter change) and unambiguously characterized (thus clarifying a vital concept in econometrics) but also highlight interesting and novel aspects of familiar problems (as shown in the examples in Section 3).

University of California, San Diego,
Nuffield College, Oxford,
and
CORE, Louvain-la-Neuve, Belgium

Manuscript received November, 1979; last revision received March, 1982.

REFERENCES

[1] BARNDORFF-NIELSEN, O.: *Information and Exponential Families in Statistical Theory*. New York. John Wiley & Sons, 1978.

[2] BENTZEL, R. AND B. HANSEN: "On Recursiveness and Interdependency in Economic Models." *Review of Economic Studies*, 22(1955), 153–168.

[3] CHAMBERLAIN, G.: "The General Equivalence of Granger and Sims Causality." *Econometrica*, 50(1982), 569–582.

[4] CHRIST, C. F.: *Econometric Models and Methods*. New York: John Wiley & Sons, 1966.

[5] DRÈZE, J. H., AND J.-F. RICHARD: "Bayesian Analysis of Simultaneous Equation Systems," forthcoming in the *Handbook of Econometrics*, edited by Z. Griliches and M. Intriligator. Amsterdam: North-Holland Publishing Co.

[6] ENGLE, R. F.: "A General Approach to the Construction of Model Diagnostics Based Upon the Lagrange Multiplier Principle," University of Warwick Discussion Paper 156, UCSD Discussion Paper 79-43, 1979.

[7] ———: "Wald, Likelihood Ratio and Lagrange Multiplier Tests in Econometrics," forthcoming in *Handbook of Econometrics*, edited by Z. Griliches and M. Intriligator. Amsterdam: North-Holland Publishing Co.

[8] ENGLE, R. F., D. F. HENDRY, AND J.-F. RICHARD: "Exogeneity, Causality and Structural Invariance in Econometric Modelling," CORE Discussion Paper 80-83, UCSD Discussion Paper 81-1, 1980.

[9] FISHER, F. M.: *The Identification Problem in Econometrics*. New York: McGraw Hill, 1966.

[10] FLORENS, J.-P., AND M. MOUCHART: "Initial and Sequential Reduction of Bayesian Experiments," CORE Discussion Paper 8015, Université Catholique de Louvain, Louvain-la-Neuve, Belgium, 1980.

[11] ———: "A Note on Non-Causality," *Econometrica*, 50(1982), 583–592.

[12] FRISCH, R.: "Autonomy of Economic Relations," paper read at the Cambridge Conference of the Econometric Society, 1938.

[13] GEWEKE, J.: "Testing the Exogeneity Specification in the Complete Dynamic Simultaneous Equations Model," *Journal of Econometrics* 7(1978), 163–185.

[14] ———: "Causality, Exogeneity and Inference," Invited paper, Fourth World Congress of the Econometric Society, Aix-en Provence, 1980.

[15] GOURIEROUX, C., J.-J. LAFFONT, AND A. MONTFORT: "Disequilibrium Econometrics in Simultaneous Equations Systems," *Econometrica*, 48(1980), 75–96.

[16] GRANGER, C. W. J.: "Investigating Causal Relations by Econometric Models and Cross-Spectral Methods," *Econometrica*, 37(1969), 424–438.

[17] HENDRY, D. F.: "The Behavior of Inconsistent Instrumental Variables Estimators in Dynamic Systems with Autocorrelated Errors," *Journal of Econometrics*, 9(1979), 295–314.

[18] ———: "Predictive Failure and Econometric Modelling in Macroeconomics: The Transactions Demand for Money," in *Modelling the Economy*, ed. by P. Ormerod. London: Heinemann Educational Books, 1980.

[19] HENDRY, D. F., AND J.-F. RICHARD: "The Econometric Analysis of Economic Time Series," forthcoming in *International Statistical Review*.

[20] HURWICZ, L: "On the Structural Form of Interdependent Systems," in *Logic, Methodology and the Philosophy of Science*, ed. by E. Nagel et al. Palo Alto: Stanford University Press, 1962.

[21] KOOPMANS, T. C.: "When is an Equation System Complete for Statistical Purposes?" in *Statistical Inference in Dynamic Economic Models*, ed. by T. C. Koopmans. New York: John Wiley and Sons, 1950.

[22] KOOPMANS, T. C., AND W. C. HOOD: "The Estimation of Simultaneous Linear Economic Relationships," in *Studies in Econometric Method*, ed. by W. C. Hood and T. C. Koopmans. New Haven: Yale University Press, 1953.

[23] LUCAS, R. E., JR.: "Econometric Policy Evaluation: A Critique," in Vol. 1 of the Carnegie-Rochester Conferences on Public Policy, supplementary series to the *Journal of Monetary Economics*, ed. by K. Brunner and A. Meltzer. Amsterdam: North-Holland Publishing Company, 1976, pp. 19–46.

[24] MCFADDEN, D.: "Econometric Analysis of Discrete Data," Fisher-Schultz Lecture, European Meeting of the Econometric Society, Athens, 1979.

[25] MADDALA, G. S., AND L. F. LEE: "Recursive Models with Qualitative Endogenous Variables," *Annals of Economic and Social Measurement*, 5(1976), 525–545.

[26] Marschak, J.: "Economic Measurements for Policy and Prediction," in *Studies in Econometric Method*, ed. by W. C. Hood and T. C. Koopmans. New Haven: Yale University Press, 1953.

[27] Muth, J. F.: "Rational Expectations and the Theory of Price Movements," *Econometrica*, 29(1961), 315–335.

[28] Orcutt, G. H.: "Toward a Partial Redirection of Econometrics," *Review of Economics and Statistics*, 34(1952), 195–213.

[29] Phillips, A. W.: "Some Notes on the Estimation of Time-Forms of Reactions in Interdependent Dynamic Systems," *Economica*, 23(1956), 99–113.

[30] Press, S. J.: *Applied Multivariate Analysis*. New York: Holt, Rinehard and Winston, Inc., 1972.

[31] Richard, J.-F.: "Exogeneity, Inference and Prediction in so-called Incomplete Dynamic Simultaneous Equation Models," CORE Discussion Paper 7922, Université Catholique de Louvain, Louvain-la-Neuve, Belgium, 1979.

[32] ———: "Models with Several Regimes and Changes in Exogeneity," *Review of Economic Studies*, 47(1980), 1–20.

[33] Rothenberg, T. J.: *Efficient Estimation with A Priori Information*. Cowles Foundation Monograph 23. New Haven: Yale University Press, 1973.

[34] Salmon, M., and K. F. Wallis: "Model Validation and Forecast Comparisons: Theoretical and Practical Considerations," in *Evaluating the Reliability of Macroeconomic Models*, ed. by G. C. Chow and P. Corsi. London: Wiley, 1982.

[35] Sargent, T. J.: "Interpreting Economic Time Series," *Journal of Political Economy*, 89(1981), 213–248.

[36] Sargan, J. D.: "The Maximum Likelihood Estimation of Economic Relationships with Autoregressive Residuals," *Econometrica*, 29(1961), 414–426.

[37] ———: "Some Tests of Dynamic Specification for a Single Equation," *Econometrica*, 48(1980), 879–897.

[38] Sims, C. A.: "Money, Income and Causality," *American Economic Review*, 62(1972), 540–552.

[39] ———: "Exogeneity and Causal Ordering in Macroeconomic Models," in *New Methods in Business Cycle Research: Proceedings from a Conference*, ed. by C. A. Sims. Minneapolis: Federal Reserve Bank of Minneapolis, 1977.

[40] Strotz, R. H., and H. O. A. Wold: "Recursive Versus Non-Recursive Systems: An Attempt at a Synthesis," *Econometrica*, 28(1960), 417–421.

[41] Wallis, K. F.: "Econometric Implications of the Rational Expectations Hypothesis," *Econometrica*, 48(1980), 49–73.

[42] Wiener, N.: "The Theory of Prediction," in *Modern Mathematics for Engineers*, ed. by E. F. Beckenback. New York: McGraw-Hill, 1956.

[43] Wold, H. O. A., and L. Jureen: *Demand Analysis—A Study in Econometrics*. New York: J. Wiley & Sons, 1955.

[44] Wu, D. M.: "Alternative Tests of Independence between Stochastic Regressors and Disturbances," *Econometrica*, 41(1973), 733–750.

[45] Zellner, A.: "Causality and Econometrics," in *Three Aspects of Policy and Policymaking*, ed. by K. Brunner and A. H. Meltzer. Amsterdam: North-Holland, 1979.

[5]

Econometrica, Vol. 48, No. 1 (January, 1980)

ECONOMETRIC IMPLICATIONS OF THE RATIONAL EXPECTATIONS HYPOTHESIS

BY KENNETH F. WALLIS[1]

The implications for applied econometrics of the assumption that unobservable expectations are formed rationally in Muth's sense are examined. The statistical properties of the resulting models and their distributed lag and time series representations are described. Purely extrapolative forecasts of endogenous variables can be constructed, as alternatives to rational expectations, but are less efficient. Identification and estimation are considered: an order condition is that no more expectations variables than exogenous variables enter the model. Estimation is based on algorithms for nonlinear-in-parameters systems; other approaches are surveyed. Implications for economic policy and econometric policy evaluation are described.

1. INTRODUCTION

EXPECTATIONS VARIABLES ARE WIDELY USED in applied econometrics, since the optimizing behavior of economic agents, which empirical research endeavors to capture, depends in part on their views of the future. Directly observed expectations or anticipations are relatively rare, hence implicit forecasting schemes are used. Most commonly expectations are taken to be extrapolations, that is, weighted averages of past values of the variable under consideration. However, these "are almost surely inaccurate gauges of expectations. Consumers, workers, and businessmen . . . do read newspapers and they do know better than to base price expectations on simple extrapolation of price series alone" (Tobin [**31**, p. 14]). An alternative approach is offered by the rational expectations hypothesis of Muth [**15**], which assumes that in forming their expectations of endogenous variables, economic agents take account of the interrelationships among variables described by the appropriate economic theory. "Price movements observed and experienced do not necessarily convey information on the basis of which a rational man should alter his view of the future. When a blight destroys half the midwestern corn crop and corn prices subsequently rise, the information conveyed is that blights raise prices. No trader or farmer under these circumstances would change his view of the future of corn prices, much less of their rate of change, unless he is led to reconsider his estimate of the likelihood of blights," again quoting Tobin.

This paper examines the implications of the rational expectations hypothesis for applied econometrics, and argues that its full force has yet to be appreciated in empirical work. The discussion is quite general, proceeding in terms of the standard linear simultaneous equation system, and pays little attention to specific applications of the hypothesis, such as the "efficient markets" literature and

[1] The first version of this paper was written while I was spending a sabbatical term at the University of California, San Diego, whose kind hospitality is gratefully acknowledged. It was circulated as UCSD Department of Economics Discussion Paper No. 77-3, April 1977, and presented at, among other places, the Econometric Society European Meeting, Vienna, September 1977. The present version has benefitted from numerous comments, including those of two anonymous referees.

recent work in macroeconomic theory, both treated in the survey by Poole [**22**]. As noted by Barro and Fischer [**1**, p. 156], "it is important to distinguish the rational expectations hypothesis per se . . . from the models known as rational expectations models that have usually been constructed so that money is neutral aside from possible expectations phenomena," and the statistical implications of the former are our concern. We therefore set aside a number of topics that have arisen in theoretical models incorporating rational expectations (or "perfect foresight" in a nonstochastic context) discussed, for example, by Shiller [**29**]. Thus in the face of a model yielding multiple solutions the econometric student of recent history assumes that the system did make a choice and the data-generation process did follow a particular path. Likewise the assumptions of time invariance and an infinite past conventional in practical time series analysis leave on one side questions of learning mechanisms and the transition to rational expectations. The question of the informational requirements of rational expectations has led some to doubt the empirical applicability of these models, but this seems to be as yet unresolved: there may be specific situations in which these requirements are approximately met, but until sound empirical investigations have been carried out, this remains an open question.

Section 2 describes the statistical properties of models which incorporate the rational expectations hypothesis, showing the source and nature of the various distributed lag formulations, and comparing the predictive efficiency of rational expectations and purely extrapolative forecasts. Section 3 is concerned with the identification and estimation of such models, and fresh approaches to the estimation of complete systems and single equations are presented. The rational expectations framework is useful for considering various aspects of economic policy, as in Section 4, since it provides a model for the not uncommon sight of economic agents, having observed certain economic phenomena, anticipating the impact on the system of the government policy which they believe will be introduced in response to those phenomena. The framework used in the paper allows the force of Lucas' [**11**] criticism of conventional econometric policy evaluation to be appreciated, yet it permits a practical response to be devised, by retaining the notion of an economic structure (incorporating the rational expectations hypothesis) that is invariant to the "structure" of exogenous processes.

2. RATIONAL EXPECTATIONS MODELS

2.1. *Some Basic Properties*

Our starting point is a "classical" static model in which expected or anticipated values of certain endogenous variables are included among the inputs:

$$(2.1) \qquad \boldsymbol{B}\boldsymbol{y}_t + \boldsymbol{A}_1\boldsymbol{y}^*_{1t} + \boldsymbol{\Gamma}\boldsymbol{x}_t = \boldsymbol{u}_t.$$

The parameter matrices $\boldsymbol{B}$, $\boldsymbol{A}_1$, and $\boldsymbol{\Gamma}$ are of dimension $g \times g$, $g \times h$, and $g \times k$, respectively, and the vectors $\boldsymbol{y}_t$, $\boldsymbol{y}^*_{1t}$, $\boldsymbol{x}_t$, and $\boldsymbol{u}_t$ have g, h ($\leq g$), k, and g elements, respectively. The endogenous variables $\boldsymbol{y}_t$ and exogenous variables $\boldsymbol{x}_t$ are observable, whereas y_{1t}^* represents unobservable anticipations, formed in period $t-1$, about the values of h of the endogenous variables, which without loss of generality we take to be the first h elements of y_t.[2] All adjustments are assumed to be completed within a single period; further dynamic complications such as lagged endogenous variables or the formation of expectations about *future* values of y_{1t} are held over for the moment.

In order to proceed to empirical implementation of the model, it is necessary to add a statement concerning the formation of expectations. A common assumption in applied econometrics has been that expectations are formed purely extrapolatively, that is, based solely on the past history of the variable under consideration. The simplest example is the "adaptive expectations" hypothesis,

$$y_{it}^* - y_{i,t-1}^* = (1-\lambda)(y_{i,t-1} - y_{i,t-1}^*),$$

which implies that the current expectation is a geometrically weighted moving average of past observations,

$$y_{it}^* = (1-\lambda)\sum_{j=0}^{\infty} \lambda^j y_{i,t-1-j}, \tag{2.2}$$

although more general forms have come to be used as a result of the growing influence of the methods of time series analysis popularized by Box and Jenkins [**2**]. In contrast, the rational expectations hypothesis assumes that "expectations, since they are informed predictions of future events, are essentially the same as the predictions of the relevant economic theory" and hence depend "specifically on the structure of the relevant system describing the economy" (Muth, [**15**, p. 316]). Thus the variable y_{1t}^* is given as the expectation of y_{1t} implied by the model, conditional on information Ω_{t-1} available at time $t-1$, i.e., $y_{1t}^* = E(y_{1t}|\Omega_{t-1})$. The usual reduced form of the model (2.1) is

$$y_t = -B^{-1}A_1 y_{1t}^* - B^{-1}\Gamma x_t + B^{-1}u_t,$$

which we partition and rewrite as

$$\begin{aligned} y_{1t} &= \Pi_{11} y_{1t}^* + \Pi_{12} x_t + v_{1t}, \\ y_{2t} &= \Pi_{21} y_{1t}^* + \Pi_{22} x_t + v_{2t}. \end{aligned} \tag{2.3}$$

Taking conditional expectations in the first matrix equation gives

$$E(y_{1t}|\Omega_{t-1}) = \Pi_{11}E(y_{1t}|\Omega_{t-1}) + \Pi_{12}E(x_t|\Omega_{t-1}) + E(v_{1t}|\Omega_{t-1}).$$

Assuming that the disturbances are nonautocorrelated and that the $h \times h$ matrix $(I - \Pi_{11})$ is nonsingular, and writing $\hat{x}_t$ for $E(x_t|\Omega_{t-1})$, we obtain

$$y_{1t}^* = (I - \Pi_{11})^{-1}\Pi_{12}\hat{x}_t. \tag{2.4}$$

Thus the rational expectations are given as linear combinations of the predictions of the exogenous variables, and the relevant information on which to base these is

[2] Observable anticipations variables, such as those based on survey data, may be entered as endogenous or exogenous variables as appropriate.

the set of past values $x_{t-1}, x_{t-2}, \ldots$, assuming that the list of exogenous variables in the model is correct and complete. On substituting into (2.3) we obtain the "observable" reduced form as

$$\begin{aligned} y_{1t} &= P_{11}\hat{x}_t + P_{12}x_t + v_{1t}, \\ y_{2t} &= P_{21}\hat{x}_t + P_{22}x_t + v_{2t}, \end{aligned} \tag{2.5}$$

where

$$P = \begin{bmatrix} P_{11} & P_{12} \\ P_{21} & P_{22} \end{bmatrix} = \begin{bmatrix} \Pi_{11}(I - \Pi_{11})^{-1}\Pi_{12} & \Pi_{12} \\ \Pi_{21}(I - \Pi_{11})^{-1}\Pi_{12} & \Pi_{22} \end{bmatrix}$$

Subtracting (2.4) from (2.5) gives the error in the rational expectation as

$$y_{1t} - y_{1t}^* = \Pi_{12}(x_t - \hat{x}_t) + v_{1t}, \tag{2.6}$$

which thus depends simply on the exogenous variable forecast error and the current-period disturbances.

For certain purposes it is convenient to write the model in an alternative way, by augmenting the matrix A_1 by a $g \times (g-h)$ block of zeros and defining $A = [A_1 : 0]$. Then (2.1) becomes

$$By_t + Ay_t^* + \Gamma x_t = u_t \tag{2.7}$$

and the rational expectation is given as

$$y_t^* = -(B + A)^{-1}\Gamma\hat{x}_t. \tag{2.8}$$

There is no difficulty in defining the rational expectation of any endogenous variable, even though that expectation does not appear in the model, provided that $(B + A)$ is nonsingular, an assumption analogous to that made in deriving (2.4). The matrix P of observable reduced form coefficients is then given in terms of structural parameters as

$$P = [B^{-1}A(B + A)^{-1}\Gamma : -B^{-1}\Gamma]$$

and the counterpart to (2.6) is

$$y_t - y_t^* = -B^{-1}\Gamma(x_t - \hat{x}_t) + B^{-1}u_t. \tag{2.9}$$

To complete the stochastic specification of the model, we postulate the following vector autoregressive moving average (ARMA) model for x_t:

$$\Phi(L)x_t = \Theta(L)\varepsilon_t \tag{2.10}$$

where ε_t is a white noise process independent of u_t, and $\Phi(L)$ and $\Theta(L)$ are polynomials in the lag operator L of degree p and q, respectively, viz.

$$\Phi(L) = I + \Phi_1 L + \ldots + \Phi_p L^p, \qquad \Theta(L) = \Theta_0 + \Theta_1 L + \ldots + \Theta_q L^q.$$

It is assumed that there is no "structural" information available regarding the generation of the exogenous variables, hence (2.10) is written in reduced form, with $\boldsymbol{\Phi}_0 = \boldsymbol{I}$.[3] With respect to the moving average side, normalization can be achieved in many ways, and two possibilities used below are (a) $\boldsymbol{\Theta}_0 = \boldsymbol{I}$, $E(\boldsymbol{\varepsilon}_t\boldsymbol{\varepsilon}_t') = \boldsymbol{\Sigma}$ unrestricted, (b) $E(\boldsymbol{\varepsilon}_t\boldsymbol{\varepsilon}_t') = \text{diag}\{\sigma_{ii}\}$, $\boldsymbol{\Theta}_0$ lower triangular with unit diagonal; transfer from (a) to (b) is effected by the Choleski decomposition of $\boldsymbol{\Sigma}$. We take the "invertible" or "minimum-delay" representation in which all roots of $|\boldsymbol{\Theta}(z)| = 0$ lie outside the unit circle. The optimal[4] one-step forecasts are given by

$$(2.11) \qquad \hat{\boldsymbol{x}}_t = -\boldsymbol{\Phi}_1\boldsymbol{x}_{t-1} - \ldots - \boldsymbol{\Phi}_p\boldsymbol{x}_{t-p} + \boldsymbol{\Theta}_1\boldsymbol{\varepsilon}_{t-1} + \ldots + \boldsymbol{\Theta}_q\boldsymbol{\varepsilon}_{t-q},$$

(Granger and Newbold [**8**, Section 7.5]). Alternatively, using the infinite autoregressive representation based on the expansion

$$\boldsymbol{\Theta}(L)^{-1}\boldsymbol{\Phi}(L) = \boldsymbol{I} - \boldsymbol{\Psi}_0 L - \boldsymbol{\Psi}_1 L^2 - \ldots,$$

say, (taking the normalization $\boldsymbol{\Theta}_0 = \boldsymbol{I}$), we have

$$(2.12) \qquad \hat{\boldsymbol{x}}_t = \sum_{j=1}^{\infty} \boldsymbol{\Psi}_{j-1}\boldsymbol{x}_{t-j} = \boldsymbol{\Psi}(L)\boldsymbol{x}_{t-1},$$

where

$$\boldsymbol{\Psi}(L) = \boldsymbol{\Psi}_0 + \boldsymbol{\Psi}_1 L + \boldsymbol{\Psi}_2 L^2 + \ldots = \frac{1}{L}\boldsymbol{\Theta}(L)^{-1}\{\boldsymbol{\Theta}(L) - \boldsymbol{\Phi}(L)\}.$$

Substitution of (2.12) into the observable reduced form (2.5) yields the "final form" relations, in which each endogenous variable is given as a distributed lag function of the exogenous variables:

$$(2.13) \qquad \boldsymbol{y}_t = \boldsymbol{P}_{\cdot 2}\boldsymbol{x}_t + \boldsymbol{P}_{\cdot 1}\boldsymbol{\Psi}(L)\boldsymbol{x}_{t-1} + \boldsymbol{v}_t.$$

First note that for a given exogenous variable the shape of the lag distribution is the same in every equation, with the exception of the leading coefficient, this shape being given by the optimal forecasting weights. In practice this implication of the rational expectations hypothesis might be tested; more generally one might check the agreement between the distributed lags and the estimated time series models for the exogenous variables as an aid to the empirical specification of distributed lag functions. In any event, note that such data-based distributed lag functions give the final form equations (2.13), and not the rational expectations themselves.

Secondly it is clear that the lag distribution depends on and changes with the stochastic structure of the exogenous variables, described by Sims [**30**, p. 294] as a "negative result" of the rational expectations hypothesis: "what is called the structure in textbook treatments of simultaneous equation models can change

[3] As an alternative to (2.10) we could specify a univariate ARMA representation for each x variable, but such a specification is obtainable as a form of solution of (2.10) (see Chan and Wallis [**3**] for examples). However separate univariate analyses might be more convenient in practice, and ignoring the various restrictions and cross-correlations might not lead to much inefficiency if the exogenous variables are only weakly interconnected.

[4] Assuming that there is not a third group of variables outside the model and independent of $\boldsymbol{u}$ that nevertheless contains information useful in forecasting $\boldsymbol{x}$.

under policy changes which affect only the time path of exogenous variables", although we see in Section 4.2 that it is helpful to refine the notion of structure. If the exogenous variables have a finite-order autoregressive representation, then the distributed lag functions are similarly of finite extent. Any moving average element (i.e., $q>0$ in (2.10)) implies that the autoregressive representation and hence the distributed lag functions are of infinite extent, but if p and q are finite the lag functions can be written as a ratio of two finite lag polynomials, whereupon (2.13) has the standard transfer function or "rational" distributed lag form. Nevertheless interpretations of such lags in terms of speeds of adjustment, rates of learning and so forth are entirely out of place in the present context.

Finally, a univariate time series model for each endogenous variable can be deduced. Consider the ith equation of the observable reduced form (2.5):

$$y_{it}=\boldsymbol{\rho}_1'\hat{\boldsymbol{x}}_t+\boldsymbol{\rho}_2'\boldsymbol{x}_t+v_{it},$$

where $\boldsymbol{\rho}_1'$ and $\boldsymbol{\rho}_2'$ are the ith rows of the coefficient matrices of $\hat{\boldsymbol{x}}_t$ and $\boldsymbol{x}_t$, respectively. The model (2.10) for $\boldsymbol{x}_t$ has the infinite moving average representation

$$\boldsymbol{x}_t=\boldsymbol{\Phi}(L)^{-1}\boldsymbol{\Theta}(L)\boldsymbol{\varepsilon}_t=|\boldsymbol{\Phi}(L)|^{-1}\text{ adj }\boldsymbol{\Phi}(L)\boldsymbol{\Theta}(L)\boldsymbol{\varepsilon}_t,$$

and we take the normalization $E(\boldsymbol{\varepsilon}_t\boldsymbol{\varepsilon}_t')=\text{diag}\{\sigma_{ii}\}$. The forecast $\hat{\boldsymbol{x}}_t$ can similarly be written

$$\hat{\boldsymbol{x}}_t=\boldsymbol{Y}(L)\boldsymbol{\varepsilon}_{t-1}$$

where

$$\boldsymbol{Y}(L)=\boldsymbol{Y}_0+\boldsymbol{Y}_1L+\boldsymbol{Y}_2L^2+\ldots=\frac{1}{L}\{\boldsymbol{\Phi}(L)^{-1}\boldsymbol{\Theta}(L)-\boldsymbol{\Theta}_0\}.$$

Then on substituting and multiplying through by the scalar $|\boldsymbol{\Phi}(L)|$ we obtain

$$\begin{aligned}|\boldsymbol{\Phi}(L)|\,y_{it}&=|\boldsymbol{\Phi}(L)|\boldsymbol{\rho}_1'\boldsymbol{Y}(L)\boldsymbol{\varepsilon}_{t-1}+\boldsymbol{\rho}_2'\text{ adj }\boldsymbol{\Phi}(L)\boldsymbol{\Theta}(L)\boldsymbol{\varepsilon}_t+|\boldsymbol{\Phi}(L)|\,v_{it}\\&=\boldsymbol{\xi}'(L)\boldsymbol{\varepsilon}_t+|\boldsymbol{\Phi}(L)|v_{it},\qquad\text{say,}\end{aligned}$$

where the (finite-order) moving average operators $\boldsymbol{\xi}'(L)$ have leading coefficients $\boldsymbol{\xi}_0'=\boldsymbol{\rho}_2'\boldsymbol{\Theta}_0$. The right-hand side is a sum of $k+1$ independent moving average processes, and hence has a moving average representation in terms of a single innovation η_{it} (Granger and Morris [7]). The resulting ARMA model (taking the invertible moving average representation) can be written

$$|\boldsymbol{\Phi}(L)|y_{it}=\theta_i(L)\eta_{it}.$$

This could then form the basis of a purely extrapolative predictor y_{it}^{**}, say, whose one-step forecast error η_{it} is white noise, but the associated forecast error variance is greater than that of the rational expectation, as we now show.

The ith equation of (2.6) or (2.9) gives

$$y_{it}-y_{it}^*=\boldsymbol{\rho}_2'\boldsymbol{\Theta}_0\boldsymbol{\varepsilon}_t+v_{it}=\boldsymbol{\xi}_0'\boldsymbol{\varepsilon}_t+v_{it};$$

thus the error in the rational expectation is serially uncorrelated and uncorrelated with past values of exogenous variables, and has mean square

$$\sum_{j=1}^{k} \xi_{0j}^2\sigma_{jj} + \sigma_{v_i}^2.$$

To compare this with the mean squared error of the extrapolative predictor y_{it}^{**}, we generalize the approach of Pierce [**21**]. We have

$$\eta_{it} = \frac{|\Phi(L)|}{\theta_i(L)} y_{it} = \frac{\xi'(L)}{\theta_i(L)} \varepsilon_t + \frac{|\Phi(L)|}{\theta_i(L)} v_{it} \tag{2.14}$$

$$= \sum_{j=1}^{k} \sum_{l=0}^{\infty} w_{jl}\varepsilon_{j,t-l} + \sum_{l=0}^{\infty} w_{k+1,l} v_{i,t-l},$$

where the expansions have leading coefficients $w_{j,0}$, $j = 1, \ldots, k$, given by ξ_0', and $w_{k+1,0} = 1$. Since the ε_{jt}, $j = 1, \ldots, k$, and v_{it} are mutually uncorrelated white noise processes, we have

$$\text{var}(\eta_{it}) = \sum_{j=1}^{k} \sum_{l=0}^{\infty} w_{jl}^2\sigma_{jj} + \sum_{l=0}^{\infty} w_{k+1,l}^2\sigma_{v_i}^2$$

$$> \sum_{j=1}^{k} w_{j,0}^2\sigma_{jj} + w_{k+1,0}^2\sigma_{v_i}^2$$

$$= \sum_{j=1}^{k} \xi_{0j}^2\sigma_{jj} + \sigma_{v_i}^2 = \text{var}(y_{it} - y_{it}^*);$$

hence the error variance of the optimal extrapolative predictor is greater than that of the rational expectation.

This is discussed in the context of two simple examples by Nelson [**16, 17**], who remarks that Muth's initial example "was perhaps an unfortunate choice" since it was such a special case that the rational expectation and optimal extrapolative predictor coincided. That example was a two-equation market model, with no exogenous variables and a single autocorrelated disturbance. Muth further specialized this by taking the disturbance term to be a random walk, whereupon the rational expectation obeys the adaptive expectation model (2.2); perhaps this choice was also unfortunate, lending unwarranted support to the adaptive expectations approach. In general the prediction error in both the rational expectation and the optimal extrapolative predictor is free of autocorrelation, although the extrapolative prediction error, unlike the error in the rational expectation, is correlated with past values of the exogenous variables.

2.2. *A Simple Example*

Choosing $g = 2$, $h = k = 1$, and imposing two zero-valued parameters a priori, we have the just-identified model

$$\begin{bmatrix} 1 & \beta_{12} \\ \beta_{21} & 1 \end{bmatrix} \begin{bmatrix} y_{1t} \\ y_{2t} \end{bmatrix} + \begin{bmatrix} \alpha & 0 \\ 0 & \gamma \end{bmatrix} \begin{bmatrix} y_{1t}^* \\ x_t \end{bmatrix} = \begin{bmatrix} u_{1t} \\ u_{2t} \end{bmatrix}.$$

The usual reduced form, which cannot be implemented without an assumption about the formation of expectations, is

$$\begin{bmatrix} y_{1t} \\ y_{2t} \end{bmatrix} = \frac{1}{1-\beta_{12}\beta_{21}} \begin{bmatrix} -\alpha & \gamma\beta_{12} \\ \alpha\beta_{21} & -\gamma \end{bmatrix} \begin{bmatrix} y_{1t}^* \\ x_t \end{bmatrix} + \begin{bmatrix} v_{1t} \\ v_{2t} \end{bmatrix}$$

$$= \begin{bmatrix} \pi_{11} & \pi_{12} \\ \pi_{21} & \pi_{22} \end{bmatrix} \begin{bmatrix} y_{1t}^* \\ x_t \end{bmatrix} + \begin{bmatrix} v_{1t} \\ v_{2t} \end{bmatrix}.$$

Taking expectations in the first equation conditional on Ω_{t-1}, and assuming that the errors are free of autocorrelation, we obtain the rational expectation of y_{1t} as

$$y_{1t}^* = E(y_{1t}|\Omega_{t-1}) = \frac{\pi_{12}}{1-\pi_{11}} E(x_t|\Omega_{t-1}) = \frac{\pi_{12}}{1-\pi_{11}} \hat{x}_t,$$

where $\hat{x}_t$ is the optimal predictor of x_t based on $x_{t-1}, x_{t-2}, \ldots$. This expression can be substituted into the structural or reduced form for empirical implementation, given an appropriate specification for x_t. (Note that the effect of a "fixed regressor" assumption, in which x_t is treated as known, is to remove the identifiability of the model.)

Case (i)

$$x_t = \phi x_{t-1} + \varepsilon_t.$$

In this case the optimal predictor is $\hat{x}_t = \phi x_{t-1}$, hence the rational expectation is

$$y_{1t}^* = \frac{\pi_{12}}{1-\pi_{11}} \phi x_{t-1}$$

and the final form distributed lag relations are

$$\text{(2.15)} \quad \begin{aligned} y_{1t} &= \frac{\pi_{11}\pi_{12}\phi}{1-\pi_{11}} x_{t-1} + \pi_{12} x_t + v_{1t}, \\ y_{2t} &= \frac{\pi_{21}\pi_{12}\phi}{1-\pi_{11}} x_{t-1} + \pi_{22} x_t + v_{2t}. \end{aligned}$$

Since the model is just-identified and the rational expectation depends on a single past x value, these relations are free of restrictions.

The optimal extrapolative predictor for y_{1t} under the rational expectations hypothesis can be readily deduced. The first final form equation (2.15) is

$$y_{1t} = \pi_{12}(1+\psi L)x_t + v_{1t}, \qquad \psi = \frac{\pi_{11}\phi}{1-\pi_{11}},$$

and on substituting $x_t = \{1/(1-\phi L)\}\varepsilon_t$ and rearranging, we obtain

$$(1-\phi L)y_{1t} = \pi_{12}(1+\psi L)\varepsilon_t + (1-\phi L)v_{1t}.$$

The right-hand side is a sum of two independent first-order moving average processes, and hence has itself a first-order moving average representation, giving an ARMA(1, 1) model for y_{1t},

$$(1-\phi L)y_{1t}=(1-\theta L)\eta_t,$$

where $\theta(|\theta|<1)$ and var $(\eta_t)=\sigma_\eta^2$ are obtained in terms of $\pi_{11}, \pi_{12}, \phi, \sigma_\varepsilon^2$, and $\sigma_{v_1}^2$. (Note that the "coincidental situation" in which $\phi=-\psi$, giving a lower order ARMA model, cannot arise unless $\phi=0$.) Thus the optimal extrapolative predictor of y_{1t}, say y_{1t}^{**}, is

$$y_{1t}^{**}=\phi y_{1,t-1}-\theta\eta_{t-1},$$

with mean square error σ_η^2. The rational expectation has error

$$y_{1t}-y_{1t}^*=\pi_{12}\varepsilon_t+v_{1t}$$

with mean square $\pi_{12}^2\sigma_\varepsilon^2+\sigma_{v_1}^2$, which is smaller than σ_η^2 by the analysis of the previous section.

Case (ii)

$$x_t-x_{t-1}=\varepsilon_t-\theta\varepsilon_{t-1}, \quad |\theta|<1.$$

This is the ARIMA (0, 1, 1) model, in which the optimal predictor is given as an exponentially weighted moving average of past observations, that is

$$\hat{x}_t=(1-\theta)\sum_{j=0}^{\infty}\theta^j x_{t-1-j},$$

and

$$y_{1t}^*-\theta y_{1,t-1}^*=\frac{\pi_{12}(1-\theta)}{1-\pi_{11}}x_{t-1}.$$

The resulting distributed lag equations are of the standard Koyck form,

$$\begin{aligned} y_{1t}&=\frac{\pi_{12}}{1-\theta L}\left\{x_t-\frac{\theta-\pi_{11}}{1-\pi_{11}}x_{t-1}\right\}+v_{1t}, \\ y_{2t}&=\frac{\pi_{22}}{1-\theta L}\left[x_t-\left\{\theta-\frac{\pi_{21}\pi_{12}(1-\theta)}{\pi_{22}(1-\pi_{11})}\right\}x_{t-1}\right]+v_{2t}. \end{aligned} \tag{2.16}$$

The denominator lag polynomials are the same in the two equations, and this restriction might be imposed in estimation.

If $\theta>0$ and $0<\pi_{11}<1$ so that the distributed lag coefficients in (2.16) are positive, a "mean lag" could be calculated as $\pi_{11}/(1-\theta)$. Again, however, interpretations of this quantity in terms of a distributed lag adjustment mechanism are quite out of place—"adjustment" appears more or less "sluggish" simply as the stochastic specification of the exogenous variable (with respect to the parameter θ) changes.

In this case the pure time series model for y_1 is also ARIMA(0, 1, 1) so that the optimal extrapolative predictor is of the adaptive expectations form, but again the prediction error variance is greater than that of the rational expectation.

If in this simple model it is postulated that y_{1t}^* is generated by an adaptive expectations mechanism, as an alternative to the rational expectations hypothesis, then the distributed lag functions relating y_1 and y_2 to x are the same as (2.16), in that the same lagged variables appear with the same cross-equation restriction (but the error specification is a little different). In effect the same final form is relevant to two different models, which is always possible. Of course this correspondence does not hold for the autoregressive x of case (i), and the difference between the lag distributions (2.15) and (2.16) results simply from the different autocorrelation properties of the exogenous variable in the rational expectations context.

2.3. *Dynamic Complications*: (*a*) *Future Expectations*

We first consider how the above results are modified if the relevant expectations variables relate to a future period (or periods) as of time t. Then (2.1) becomes

$$(2.17) \qquad \boldsymbol{B}\boldsymbol{y}_t + \sum_{j=0}^{\tau} \boldsymbol{A}_{1j}\boldsymbol{y}^*_{1,t+j} + \boldsymbol{\Gamma}\boldsymbol{x}_t = \boldsymbol{u}_t$$

where τ is an "expectations horizon," and the reduced form is

$$\boldsymbol{y}_t = -\sum_{j=0}^{\tau} \boldsymbol{B}^{-1}\boldsymbol{A}_{1j}\boldsymbol{y}^*_{1,t+j} - \boldsymbol{B}^{-1}\boldsymbol{\Gamma}\boldsymbol{x}_t + \boldsymbol{B}^{-1}\boldsymbol{u}_t,$$

of which the block relating to the determination of $\boldsymbol{y}_1$ can be written

$$\boldsymbol{y}_{1t} = \sum_{j=0}^{\tau} \boldsymbol{\Pi}_{11,j}\boldsymbol{y}^*_{1,t+j} + \boldsymbol{\Pi}_{12}\boldsymbol{x}_t + \boldsymbol{v}_{1t}.$$

Taking conditional expectations, again assuming nonautocorrelated disturbances, we see that the rational expectations $\boldsymbol{y}^*_{1,t+j} = E(\boldsymbol{y}_{1,t+j} \mid \Omega_{t-1})$ satisfy

$$(\boldsymbol{I} - \boldsymbol{\Pi}_{11,0})\boldsymbol{y}^*_{1t} = \sum_{j=1}^{\tau} \boldsymbol{\Pi}_{11,j}\boldsymbol{y}^*_{1,t+j} + \boldsymbol{\Pi}_{12}E(\boldsymbol{x}_t \mid \Omega_{t-1}).$$

This is a multivariate τ-order difference equation which, if stable, yields a solution for $\boldsymbol{y}^*_{1t}$ in terms of $\hat{\boldsymbol{x}}_{t+j} = E(\boldsymbol{x}_{t+j} | \Omega_{t-1}), j = 0, 1, 2, \ldots$. Writing $\boldsymbol{C}_{1j} = (\boldsymbol{I} - \boldsymbol{\Pi}_{11,0})^{-1}\boldsymbol{\Pi}_{11,j}$, the difference equation in companion form is

$$\begin{bmatrix} \boldsymbol{y}^*_{1t} \\ \boldsymbol{y}^*_{1,t+1} \\ \vdots \\ \boldsymbol{y}^*_{1,t+\tau-1} \end{bmatrix} = \begin{bmatrix} \boldsymbol{C}_{11} & \boldsymbol{C}_{12} & \cdots & \boldsymbol{C}_{1,\tau-1} & \boldsymbol{C}_{1\tau} \\ \boldsymbol{I} & \boldsymbol{0} & \cdots & \boldsymbol{0} & \boldsymbol{0} \\ \vdots & & & \vdots & \vdots \\ \boldsymbol{0} & \boldsymbol{0} & & \boldsymbol{I} & \boldsymbol{0} \end{bmatrix} \begin{bmatrix} \boldsymbol{y}^*_{1,t+1} \\ \boldsymbol{y}^*_{1,t+2} \\ \vdots \\ \boldsymbol{y}^*_{1,t+\tau} \end{bmatrix} + \begin{bmatrix} (\boldsymbol{I} - \boldsymbol{\Pi}_{11,0})^{-1}\boldsymbol{\Pi}_{12} \\ \boldsymbol{0} \\ \vdots \\ \boldsymbol{0} \end{bmatrix} \hat{\boldsymbol{x}}_t$$

or

$$y^{\dagger}_{1,t} = Cy^{\dagger}_{1,t+1} + \chi_t.$$

The stability condition is that the eigenvalues of C have modulus less than 1, or equivalently that the characteristic equation

$$|(I - \Pi_{11,0})z^{\tau} - \Pi_{11,1}z^{\tau-1} - \ldots - \Pi_{11,\tau}| = 0$$

has roots with modulus less than 1, and if this is satisfied the solution is

$$y^{\dagger}_{1,t} = \sum_{j=0}^{\infty} C^j \chi_{t+j}.$$

The first block gives the solution for y^{*}_{1t} in terms of the predictions of *all* future values of the exogenous variables, given their past values. The remaining blocks give the same expression for $y^{*}_{1,t+j}$, $j = 1, \ldots, \tau - 1$, except that the time subscript on the x forecasts is advanced j periods; the solution for $y^{*}_{1,t+\tau}$ is obtained in the same manner. The error in the immediate rational expectation has the same form as in the model of Section 2.1,

$$\begin{aligned} y_{1t} - y^{*}_{1t} &= (\Pi_{11,0} - I)y^{*}_{1t} + \sum_{j=1}^{\tau} \Pi_{11,j} y^{*}_{1,t+j} + \Pi_{12}x_t + v_{1t} \\ &= \Pi_{12}(x_t - \hat{x}_t) + v_{1t}, \end{aligned}$$

and so is free of autocorrelation, while the future expectations variable $y^{*}_{1,t+j}$ (based on Ω_{t-1}) has an error which depends on $\varepsilon_t, \varepsilon_{t+1}, \ldots, \varepsilon_{t+j}$ together with $v_{1,t+j}$ and so exhibits autocorrelation.

The generalization of the observable reduced form (2.5) now involves all future x forecasts, and the general expression is not informative, but the final form equations are still of the same type. Using the autoregressive representation for x_t, the sequence of forecasts can be calculated recursively from the expression

$$\hat{x}_{t+l} = \sum_{j=1}^{l} \Psi_{j-1}\hat{x}_{t+l-j} + \sum_{j=0}^{\infty} \Psi_{j+l}x_{t-1-j}$$

which generalizes (2.12). If x_t has a finite autoregressive representation of order p, then each forecast $\hat{x}_{t+l}$ is a linear combination of $x_{t-1}, \ldots, x_{t-p}$ and so are the rational expectations $y^{*}_{1,t+j}$, $j = 0, \ldots, \tau$. Then the same lagged exogenous variables appear in the final form distributed lag equations as in the case in which only contemporaneous expectations variables enter the model; all that changes is their relative weights.

An illustration is obtained by advancing the expectations variable of the example of Section 2.2 by one period; thus the first reduced form equation becomes

$$y_{1t} = \pi_{11}y^{*}_{1,t+1} + \pi_{12}x_t + v_{1t}.$$

Assuming that $|\pi_{11}|<1$ the solution for the rational expectations variable is

$$(2.18) \qquad y^*_{1,t+1} = \pi_{12} \sum_{j=0}^{\infty} \pi_{11}^j \hat{x}_{t+1+j}.$$

In Case (i), where x_t obeys a first-order autoregression, we have $\hat{x}_{t+j} = \phi^{j+1} x_{t-1}$; hence the rational expectation is

$$y^*_{1,t+1} = \frac{\pi_{12}\phi^2}{1-\phi\pi_{11}} x_{t-1}$$

and the distributed lag relation is

$$y_{1t} = \pi_{12} x_t + \frac{\pi_{12}\pi_{11}\phi^2}{1-\phi\pi_{11}} x_{t-1} + v_{1t}.$$

This contains the same variables as (2.15); only the interpretation of the coefficient of x_{t-1} has changed.

In Case (ii) x_t is ARIMA(0, 1, 1) and the optimal predictor based on $x_{t-1}, x_{t-2}, \ldots$ is the same for any forecast horizon. Thus

$$y^*_{1,t+1} = \pi_{12} \sum_{j=0}^{\infty} \pi_{11}^j \left\{ (1-\theta) \sum_{i=0}^{\infty} \theta^i x_{t-1-i} \right\},$$

giving the same expression as previously, and the final form equations are identical to (2.16).

In this example, to assume that the rational expectation as of time $t+1$, rather than t, is relevant to the particular behavioral equation causes no change at all in the distributed lag relations in Case (ii); in Case (i) the form of the relation is unaltered. In general one would not expect data to be particularly informative on this question. The specification of different timing relationships amounts to the specification of different models, which may nevertheless have the same reduced or final form, and so be observationally indistinguishable. Such specification should be based on a priori institutional and information flow considerations relevant to the given context.

Different assumptions about the amount of information available when expectations are formed are clearly possible, but result in only minor modifications to the foregoing material. For example, one might include the expectational variable $y^*_{1,t+1}$ as in the above illustration, but assume that the values of the exogenous variables at time t are known when expectations are formed. Then in computing the rational expectation (2.18), the forecasts are given by $\hat{x}_{t+j} = \phi^j x_t$ in Case (i), so that $y^*_{1,t+1}$ depends only on x_t, and x_{t-1} drops out of the final form. However in Case (ii) the form of equation (2.15) remains unaltered, but the coefficients of x_t and x_{t-1} change. While McCallum [**13**] begins with such an assumption about what is known when forecasts are made, some of his empirical results lead him to suggest "that current values of exogenous variables should perhaps be excluded ... as market participants may not possess information on such values when forming expectations."

2.4. *Dynamic Complications*: (*b*) *Lagged Variables*

The second modification to the basic model is to allow lagged values of the various endogenous variables to enter, as a result of dynamic adjustment problems, timing considerations, and so forth. We use the formulation (2.7), appropriately extended, and so write

$$\boldsymbol{B}(L)\boldsymbol{y}_t + \boldsymbol{A}\boldsymbol{y}_t^* + \boldsymbol{\Gamma}(L)\boldsymbol{x}_t = \boldsymbol{u}_t, \tag{2.19}$$

where

$$\boldsymbol{B}(L) = \boldsymbol{B}_0 + \boldsymbol{B}_1(L + \ldots + \boldsymbol{B}_r L^r, \qquad \boldsymbol{\Gamma}(L) = \boldsymbol{\Gamma}_0 + \boldsymbol{\Gamma}_1 L + \ldots + \boldsymbol{\Gamma}_s L^s.$$

Taking conditional expectations and assuming nonautocorrelated disturbances as before, we obtain

$$\boldsymbol{y}_t^* = -(\boldsymbol{B}_0 + \boldsymbol{A})^{-1} E[\{\boldsymbol{\Gamma}(L)\boldsymbol{x}_t + \boldsymbol{B}_1\boldsymbol{y}_{t-1} + \ldots + \boldsymbol{B}_r\boldsymbol{y}_{t-r}\} | \Omega_{t-1}].$$

The relevant information set now includes the past values of the endogenous variables; thus the only variable in the braces which needs to be forecast is $\boldsymbol{x}_t$, and we have

$$\boldsymbol{y}_t^* = -(\boldsymbol{B}_0 + \boldsymbol{A})^{-1}\{\boldsymbol{\Gamma}_0\hat{\boldsymbol{x}}_t + \boldsymbol{\Gamma}_1\boldsymbol{x}_{t-1} + \ldots + \boldsymbol{\Gamma}_s\boldsymbol{x}_{t-s} + \boldsymbol{B}_1\boldsymbol{y}_{t-1} + \ldots + \boldsymbol{B}_r\boldsymbol{y}_{t-r}\}. \tag{2.20}$$

This modifies equation (2.8) by adding to the previous expression for $\boldsymbol{y}_t^*$ all predetermined variables in the model, appropriately weighted. Note that (2.20) is quite specific about the variables that appear; the maximum lags of variables are the same as in the structural form (2.19) and if a particular endogenous variable does not appear lagged in (2.19) then it does not appear at all in (2.20). Similarly the observable reduced form (2.5) is augmented by the same lagged variables that are introduced in (2.19). Again the error in the rational expectation depends solely on the unanticipated part of the current exogenous variables, together with the current disturbances:

$$\boldsymbol{y}_t - \boldsymbol{y}_t^* = -\boldsymbol{B}_0^{-1}\boldsymbol{\Gamma}_0(\boldsymbol{x}_t - \hat{\boldsymbol{x}}_t) + \boldsymbol{B}_0^{-1}\boldsymbol{u}_t.$$

To examine the impact of the rational expectations hypothesis on the stability of the model, we substitute the expression (2.20) for $\boldsymbol{y}_t^*$ into (2.19) and collect together the terms involving the endogenous variables. These are

$$\begin{aligned}\boldsymbol{B}(L)\boldsymbol{y}_t - \boldsymbol{A}(\boldsymbol{B}_0 + \boldsymbol{A})^{-1}\{\boldsymbol{B}_1\boldsymbol{y}_{t-1} + \ldots + \boldsymbol{B}_r\boldsymbol{y}_{t-r}\}\\ = \boldsymbol{B}_0\boldsymbol{y}_t + \boldsymbol{B}_0(\boldsymbol{B}_0 + \boldsymbol{A})^{-1}\{\boldsymbol{B}_1\boldsymbol{y}_{t-1} + \ldots + \boldsymbol{B}_r\boldsymbol{y}_{t-r}\};\end{aligned}$$

hence the model is stable provided that all roots of

$$|(\boldsymbol{B}_0 + \boldsymbol{A}) + \boldsymbol{B}_1 z + \ldots + \boldsymbol{B}_r z^r| = 0$$

lie outside the unit circle. The stability condition for the model without rational expectations depends on the roots of $|\boldsymbol{B}(z)|$, so the only change is in the constant term of the matrix polynomial. While a general description of the impact of the introduction of rational expectations on the roots of the determinantal polynomial is not possible, it is clear that for $\boldsymbol{A}$ sufficiently close to $-\boldsymbol{B}_0$, a model which appears stable if expectation formation is assumed to be exogenous can in fact be unstable.[5] On the other hand it is quite possible for a model that appears unstable according to the conventional condition to be stable under rational expectations.

3. IDENTIFICATION AND ESTIMATION

3.1. *Identification*

We first consider the basic model of Section 2.1, with structural form

$$\boldsymbol{B}\boldsymbol{y}_t + \boldsymbol{A}_1\boldsymbol{y}^*_{1t} + \boldsymbol{\Gamma}\boldsymbol{x}_t = \boldsymbol{u}_t$$

and reduced form

$$\boldsymbol{y}_{1t} = \boldsymbol{\Pi}_{11}\boldsymbol{y}^*_{1t} + \boldsymbol{\Pi}_{12}\boldsymbol{x}_t + \boldsymbol{v}_{1t},$$

$$\boldsymbol{y}_{2t} = \boldsymbol{\Pi}_{21}\boldsymbol{y}^*_{1t} + \boldsymbol{\Pi}_{22}\boldsymbol{x}_t + \boldsymbol{v}_{2t}.$$

The non-observability of $\boldsymbol{y}^*_{1t}$ is overcome by the rational expectations hypothesis

$$\boldsymbol{y}^*_{1t} = (\boldsymbol{I} - \boldsymbol{\Pi}_{11})^{-1}\boldsymbol{\Pi}_{12}\hat{\boldsymbol{x}}_t,$$

and equation (2.5) again gives the observable reduced form:

$$\boldsymbol{y}_t = \boldsymbol{P}(\hat{\boldsymbol{x}}'_t \,\vdots\, \boldsymbol{x}'_t)' + \boldsymbol{v}_t \tag{3.1}$$

where

$$\boldsymbol{P} = \begin{bmatrix} \boldsymbol{P}_{11} & \boldsymbol{P}_{12} \\ \boldsymbol{P}_{21} & \boldsymbol{P}_{22} \end{bmatrix} = \begin{bmatrix} \boldsymbol{\Pi}_{11}(\boldsymbol{I} - \boldsymbol{\Pi}_{11})^{-1}\boldsymbol{\Pi}_{12} & \boldsymbol{\Pi}_{12} \\ \boldsymbol{\Pi}_{21}(\boldsymbol{I} - \boldsymbol{\Pi}_{11})^{-1}\boldsymbol{\Pi}_{12} & \boldsymbol{\Pi}_{22} \end{bmatrix} \tag{3.2}$$

By treating $\hat{\boldsymbol{x}}_t$ as observable, this formulation incorporates the implication of the rational expectations hypothesis that lagged x values enter in a way dictated by the optimal forecasting equations corresponding to the given x structure. Other possibilities are discussed below.

It is assumed that interest lies in estimating the parameters of the structural form, and we consider the case in which the identification restrictions take the form of knowing specific elements of $\boldsymbol{B}$, $\boldsymbol{A}_1$, and $\boldsymbol{\Gamma}$. Let $\boldsymbol{\delta}$ be a column vector consisting of those elements of $\boldsymbol{B}$, $\boldsymbol{A}_1$, and $\boldsymbol{\Gamma}$ that are *not* known a priori, assumed to be r in number, and let $\boldsymbol{\rho}$ be the $2gk$-dimensional vector of the elements of $\boldsymbol{P}$. Then the condition for at least local identifiability of the structural parameters is that the matrix of first partial derivatives

$$\boldsymbol{H} = \frac{\partial \boldsymbol{\rho}}{\partial \boldsymbol{\delta}}$$

has rank r (see, for example, Rothenberg [**23**]). Using the matrix differentiation

[5] A simple illustration is obtained by modifying our example of Section 2.2 so that the lagged value of y_1, instead of the current value, appears in the second structural equation. Then the conventional stability condition, ignoring the expectations process, is $|\beta_{12}\beta_{21}| < 1$, but even if this is true the model will be unstable under rational expectations if $|1+\alpha| < |\beta_{12}\beta_{21}|$, i.e. if α is sufficiently close to -1.

conventions and theorems given by Neudecker [19], and defining $\boldsymbol{\pi} = \text{vec}(\boldsymbol{\Pi}')$, we have

$$\boldsymbol{H} = \frac{\partial \boldsymbol{\rho}}{\partial \boldsymbol{\delta}} = \frac{\partial \boldsymbol{\pi}}{\partial \boldsymbol{\delta}} \cdot \frac{\partial \boldsymbol{\rho}}{\partial \boldsymbol{\pi}}.$$

The $r \times g(h+k)$ matrix appearing as the first factor on the right-hand side arises in the usual consideration of the identification of structural parameters given $\boldsymbol{\Pi}$ (it is the transpose of Rothenberg's H_{11}) and has rank r if the conventional rank and order conditions for structure identification are satisfied. To evaluate the second factor it is convenient to form $\boldsymbol{\pi}$ by taking vec $(\boldsymbol{\Pi}'_{11})$, vec $(\boldsymbol{\Pi}'_{12}), \ldots$ in turn (and $\boldsymbol{\rho}$ likewise), then by differentiating the relations (3.2) we find that the $g(h+k) \times 2gk$ matrix $\partial \boldsymbol{\rho}/\partial \boldsymbol{\pi}$ is given as

$$\begin{bmatrix} (\boldsymbol{I}-\boldsymbol{\Pi}'_{11})^{-1} \otimes (\boldsymbol{I}-\boldsymbol{\Pi}_{11})^{-1}\boldsymbol{\Pi}_{12} & \boldsymbol{0} & (\boldsymbol{I}-\boldsymbol{\Pi}'_{11})^{-1}\boldsymbol{\Pi}'_{21} \otimes (\boldsymbol{I}-\boldsymbol{\Pi}_{11})^{-1}\boldsymbol{\Pi}_{12} & \boldsymbol{0} \\ (\boldsymbol{I}-\boldsymbol{\Pi}'_{11})^{-1}\boldsymbol{\Pi}'_{11} \otimes \boldsymbol{I}_k & \boldsymbol{I}_{hk} & (\boldsymbol{I}-\boldsymbol{\Pi}'_{11})^{-1}\boldsymbol{\Pi}'_{21} \otimes \boldsymbol{I}_k & \boldsymbol{0} \\ \boldsymbol{0} & \boldsymbol{0} & \boldsymbol{I}_{g-h} \otimes (\boldsymbol{I}-\boldsymbol{\Pi}_{11})^{-1}\boldsymbol{\Pi}_{12} & \boldsymbol{0} \\ \boldsymbol{0} & \boldsymbol{0} & \boldsymbol{0} & \boldsymbol{I}_{(g-h)k} \end{bmatrix}.$$

The condition that this matrix be of rank $g(h+k)$ is in effect a condition for the identification of the elements of $\boldsymbol{\Pi}$ given no other information but $\boldsymbol{P}$. A necessary condition is that the matrix must have at least $g(h+k)$ columns, that is $k \geqslant h$, so that there are no more expectations variables than exogenous variables in the model. To derive a rank condition for identifiability we first note that a simple permutation yields a block-triangular matrix; hence the rank of the matrix is equal to the sum of the ranks of the diagonal blocks. Recalling also that the rank of a Kronecker product is equal to the product of the ranks of the two factors, and retaining the assumption that the $h \times h$ matrix $(\boldsymbol{I}-\boldsymbol{\Pi}_{11})$ is of full rank, we obtain

$$\text{rank}\,(\partial \boldsymbol{\rho}/\partial \boldsymbol{\pi}) = gk + g\,\text{rank}\,(\boldsymbol{\Pi}_{12}).$$

Thus the rank condition for the identification of $\boldsymbol{\Pi}$ given $\boldsymbol{P}$ is rank $(\boldsymbol{P}_{12}) = h$,[6] which of course implies $h \leqslant k$.

With respect to the identification of the structural parameters given $\boldsymbol{P}$, consider first the possibility that the structure is just-identified in the usual sense. Then $r = g(h+k)$, $\boldsymbol{\Pi}$ is unrestricted, and the requirement is again rank $(\boldsymbol{P}_{12}) = h$: if $h = k$ we have an indirect least squares type of situation while if $h < k$ $\boldsymbol{P}$ is subject to restrictions. We can also consider the extent to which a "shortage" of exogenous variables (an "excess' of expectational variables, $h > k$) can be traded off against overidentifying restrictions on the structure. Suppose that there are m of these, so that $r = g(h+k) - m$. Then a necessary condition for rank $(\boldsymbol{H}) = r$ is

$$\begin{aligned} \text{rank}\,(\partial \boldsymbol{\rho}/\partial \boldsymbol{\pi}) &= gk + g\,\text{rank}\,(\boldsymbol{P}_{12}) = 2gk \\ &\geqslant g(h+k) - m = r, \end{aligned}$$

[6] For "almost all" matrices $\boldsymbol{P}_{12}$ in the usual sense (compare Malinvaud [12, Section 18.3]). However note that in the case of an overidentified structure and $h > k$, discussed below, it is not difficult to construct examples in which elements of $\boldsymbol{P}_{12}$ are identically zero.

that is,

$$m \geq g(h-k),$$

or each expectational variable over and above the number of exogenous variables should be matched by at least g overidentifying restrictions.

These results carry over to the model with lagged variables of Section 2.4 in the same way that the standard identification results carry over to dynamic models,[7] with one additional complication. This concerns the possibility that a linear identity connects the predetermined variables in the observable reduced form, which would arise, if, for example, $\boldsymbol{x}_t$ obeys a p-order autoregression with $p \leq s$ so that $\hat{\boldsymbol{x}}_t$ is a linear combination of lagged exogenous variables already in the model. To overcome this problem the forecast $\hat{\boldsymbol{x}}_t$ should be a function of past x values not present in the model. The approach does not carry over to the model with future expectations of Section 2.3 since the observable reduced form is no longer a good starting point; nevertheless an order condition of the form $h \leq k$, counting in h each separate future value of an expected variable, remains relevant.

3.2. *System Estimation*

We retain the specification for the exogenous variables given in (2.10), namely

$$\boldsymbol{\Phi}(L)\boldsymbol{x}_t = \boldsymbol{\Theta}(L)\boldsymbol{\varepsilon}_t,$$

and assume that the time series model is first estimated by an appropriate maximum likelihood procedure and that sufficient starting values are available to permit the calculation of the one-step forecasts $\hat{\boldsymbol{x}}_t$, $t = 1, \ldots, T$ (or that the sample period relevant to the basic model has been appropriately truncated). The estimation of the observable reduced form coefficients $\boldsymbol{P}$ is then a standard multivariate least squares problem. Alternatives to the treatment of the constructed x forecasts as data are discussed below.

To estimate the reduced form coefficients $\boldsymbol{\Pi}$ in the case $h \leq k$, we form a vector $\boldsymbol{\pi}$ of the $n = g(h+k)$ elements and write the observable reduced form as

$$\boldsymbol{y}_t = \boldsymbol{P}(\boldsymbol{\pi})\bar{\boldsymbol{x}}_t + \boldsymbol{v}_t \qquad (t = 1, \ldots, T),$$

where $\bar{\boldsymbol{x}}_t' = [\hat{\boldsymbol{x}}_t' \vdots \boldsymbol{x}_t']$. This is an example of the multi-equation linear model in which elements of the coefficient matrix are continuous functions of a set of parameters $\boldsymbol{\pi}$, considered by Sargan [24].[8] If $h < k$, a test of the restrictions

[7] By which is meant that if the maximum lags of variables are known, each lagged value may be treated as a separate predetermined variable when rank and order conditions are applied, and if they are not known then extensions of the standard conditions such as those given by Hatanaka [9] are needed.

[8] A simple example is the "unobservable independent variables" model of Zellner [35]. Maximum likelihood estimation of such models is considered by Goldberger [6], whose procedure amounts to a slightly different iteration than that presented below. What distinguishes the present model from "multiple-indicator, multiple-cause" models is the particular structure for the unobserved (expectations) variables implied by the rational expectations hypothesis, involving nonlinear, cross-equation parameter restrictions.

implicit in the construction of $\boldsymbol{P}(\boldsymbol{\pi})$ amounts to a test of the rational expectations hypothesis in which the maintained hypothesis simply specifies a menu of variables and not a complete structural form. Assuming that the vectors $\boldsymbol{v}_t$, $t = 1, \ldots, T$, are serially independent and normally distributed $N(\mathbf{0}, \boldsymbol{\Omega}_v)$, the first-order conditions for the concentrated likelihood function can be written

$$f_i(\boldsymbol{\pi}) = -\operatorname{tr}\left[\boldsymbol{\Omega}_v^{-1}(\boldsymbol{\pi})\left(\frac{\boldsymbol{Y}'\bar{\boldsymbol{X}}}{T} - \boldsymbol{P}(\boldsymbol{\pi})\frac{\bar{\boldsymbol{X}}'\bar{\boldsymbol{X}}}{T}\right)\frac{\partial \boldsymbol{P}'}{\partial \pi_i}\right] = 0 \qquad (i = 1, \ldots, n),$$

where $\boldsymbol{\Omega}_v(\boldsymbol{\pi}) = [\boldsymbol{Y}' - \boldsymbol{P}(\boldsymbol{\pi})\bar{\boldsymbol{X}}'][\boldsymbol{Y} - \bar{\boldsymbol{X}}\boldsymbol{P}'(\boldsymbol{\pi})]/T$ and the $T \times g$ and $T \times 2k$ data matrices $\boldsymbol{Y}, \bar{\boldsymbol{X}}$ are given by $\boldsymbol{Y}' = [y_1 \vdots \ldots \vdots y_T]$, $\bar{\boldsymbol{X}}' = [\bar{x}_1 \vdots \ldots \vdots \bar{x}_T]$. Sargan describes the following gradient maximization procedure, which has been found to work well in practice. Writing $\boldsymbol{\pi}_\kappa$ for the value of $\boldsymbol{\pi}$ at the κth iteration and $\Delta\pi_j = \pi_{j,\kappa+1} - \pi_{j,\kappa}$, the iteration is

$$\sum_{j=1}^{n} L_{ij}(\boldsymbol{\pi}_\kappa)\Delta\pi_j + \lambda f_i(\boldsymbol{\pi}_\kappa) = 0 \qquad (i = 1, \ldots, n),$$

where

$$L_{ij}(\boldsymbol{\pi}) = \operatorname{tr}\left[\boldsymbol{\Omega}_v^{-1}(\boldsymbol{\pi})\frac{\partial \boldsymbol{P}}{\partial \pi_j}\left(\frac{\bar{\boldsymbol{X}}'\bar{\boldsymbol{X}}}{T}\right)\frac{\partial \boldsymbol{P}'}{\partial \pi_i}\right].$$

For structural estimation it is convenient notationally to use the square matrix $\boldsymbol{A}$ and write the model as in (2.7), viz.

$$\boldsymbol{B}\boldsymbol{y}_t + \boldsymbol{A}\boldsymbol{y}_t^* + \boldsymbol{\Gamma}\boldsymbol{x}_t = \boldsymbol{u}_t.$$

It is assumed that this structural form satisfies the identification conditions discussed above. The rational expectation of $\boldsymbol{y}_t$ is given by (2.8) and the system in terms of observable variables is

$$\boldsymbol{B}\boldsymbol{y}_t - \boldsymbol{A}(\boldsymbol{B}+\boldsymbol{A})^{-1}\boldsymbol{\Gamma}\hat{\boldsymbol{x}}_t + \boldsymbol{\Gamma}\boldsymbol{x}_t = \boldsymbol{u}_t \qquad (t = 1, \ldots, T). \tag{3.3}$$

Placing the unknown elements of the matrices $\boldsymbol{B}$, $\boldsymbol{A}$, and $\boldsymbol{\Gamma}$ into a vector $\boldsymbol{\delta}$ the model can be written compactly as

$$\boldsymbol{\Lambda}(\boldsymbol{\delta})\boldsymbol{z}_t = \boldsymbol{u}_t$$

where $\boldsymbol{z}_t' = [\boldsymbol{y}_t' \vdots \hat{\boldsymbol{x}}_t' \vdots \boldsymbol{x}_t']$ and $\boldsymbol{\Lambda}(\boldsymbol{\delta}) = [\boldsymbol{B} \vdots -\boldsymbol{A}(\boldsymbol{B}+\boldsymbol{A})^{-1}\boldsymbol{\Gamma} \vdots \boldsymbol{\Gamma}]$. This is again a form considered by Sargan [24], although slightly simpler than his general case since our endogenous variable coefficient matrix involves no nonlinearities. Assuming that the vectors $\boldsymbol{u}_t$, $t = 1, \ldots, T$, are serially independent and normally distributed $N(\mathbf{0}, \boldsymbol{\Omega}_u)$, the log-likelihood function concentrated with respect to $\boldsymbol{\Omega}_u$ is

$$T \log|\det \boldsymbol{B}| - \tfrac{1}{2}T \log\det[\boldsymbol{\Lambda}(\boldsymbol{\delta})\boldsymbol{Z}'\boldsymbol{Z}\boldsymbol{\Lambda}'(\boldsymbol{\delta})],$$

where $\boldsymbol{Z} = [\boldsymbol{Y} \vdots \bar{\boldsymbol{X}}]$ is the $T \times (g + 2k)$ data matrix. Differentiating with respect to δ_i gives the first-order condition

$$T \operatorname{tr}\left[(\boldsymbol{B}')^{-1}\frac{\partial \boldsymbol{B}}{\partial \delta_i}\right] - T \operatorname{tr}\left[\boldsymbol{\Omega}_u^{-1}(\boldsymbol{\delta})\,\boldsymbol{\Lambda}(\boldsymbol{\delta})\left(\frac{Z'Z}{T}\right)\frac{\partial \boldsymbol{\Lambda}'}{\partial \delta_i}\right] = 0$$

where $\boldsymbol{\Omega}_u(\boldsymbol{\delta}) = \boldsymbol{\Lambda}(\boldsymbol{\delta})(\boldsymbol{Z}'\boldsymbol{Z}/T)\boldsymbol{\Lambda}'(\boldsymbol{\delta})$. This can also be written

$$-T\,\mathrm{tr}\left[\boldsymbol{\Omega}_u^{-1}(\boldsymbol{\delta})\,\boldsymbol{\Lambda}(\boldsymbol{\delta})\left(\frac{\boldsymbol{Z}'\hat{\boldsymbol{Z}}}{T}\right)\frac{\partial\boldsymbol{\Lambda}'}{\partial\delta_i}\right]=0$$

where $\hat{\boldsymbol{Z}} = [\hat{\boldsymbol{Y}} \,\vdots\, \bar{\boldsymbol{X}}]$ and $\boldsymbol{B}\hat{\boldsymbol{Y}}' = \boldsymbol{A}(\boldsymbol{B}+\boldsymbol{A})^{-1}\boldsymbol{\Gamma}\hat{\boldsymbol{X}}' - \boldsymbol{\Gamma}\boldsymbol{X}'$.

Experience in solving FIML problems of this kind through a variety of numerical optimization procedures is described by Sargan and Sylwestrowicz [**25**]. The computer program includes a subroutine which differentiates analytically rational functions $\lambda_{ij}(\boldsymbol{\delta})$ of any order; alternatively in the present context the elements of $\partial\boldsymbol{\Lambda}'/\partial\delta_i$ can be obtained from matrix derivatives given, for example, by Dwyer [**4**].

The use of the constructed $\hat{x}$ series as data treats the parameters of the exogenous process as given, but if this is not correct the estimated variance-covariance matrix of the model's parameter estimates obtained at the final iteration will be subject to a common error in two-step-type procedures, namely that of treating as known in the second step a parameter that has in fact been estimated in the first step. To avoid this the parameters of the model and the exogenous process may be estimated jointly, by substituting in (3.1) or (3.3) the expression (2.11) for $\hat{\boldsymbol{x}}_t$ and adjoining the vector ARMA model (2.10), then estimating the $(g+k)$-equation system by an appropriate algorithm as already discussed. (Separate estimates of the x process and the model as described above would provide convenient starting values for this joint estimation.) This also achieves fully efficient estimates, since exploiting the parameter restrictions between the x process and the y process gives an improvement despite the independence of $\boldsymbol{\varepsilon}_t$ and $\boldsymbol{u}_t$ (or $\boldsymbol{v}_t$).

The methods of this section are applicable to models containing lagged variables, while the method of the previous paragraph is applicable to models containing future expectations variables provided that the parameter restrictions resulting from the dependence of the rational expectations on the predictions of all future values of the exogenous variables and the dependence in turn of such predictions on past values can be conveniently expressed. For example, to estimate the parameters of our simple example as amended in Section 2.3, with rational expectation given by (2.18) and autoregressive x, the following three-equation system would be estimated:

$$y_{1t}+\beta_{12}y_{2t}-\frac{\alpha\gamma\beta_{12}\phi^2}{1-\beta_{12}\beta_{21}-\alpha\phi}x_{t-1}=u_{1t},$$

$$\beta_{21}y_{1t}+y_{2t}+\gamma x_t=u_{2t},$$

$$x_t=\phi x_{t-1}+\varepsilon_t.$$

3.3. *Limited-Information Methods*

Under the limited-information heading we include single-equation estimation methods and other procedures that make less than the maximum possible use of the restrictions implied by the rational expectations hypothesis: some of these procedures will be seen to be applicable to complete systems.

First, we assume that interest centers on estimating the parameters of the first equation of the structural form, namely

$$\boldsymbol{\beta}_1\boldsymbol{y}_t+\boldsymbol{\alpha}_1\boldsymbol{y}_t^*+\boldsymbol{\gamma}_1\boldsymbol{x}_t=u_{1t}, \tag{3.4}$$

where $\boldsymbol{\beta}_1$, $\boldsymbol{\alpha}_1$, and $\boldsymbol{\gamma}_1$ are the first rows of $\boldsymbol{B}$, $\boldsymbol{A}$, and $\boldsymbol{\Gamma}$, respectively, and together contain no more than $h+k$ unknown elements. The rational expectations variables are given by

$$\boldsymbol{y}_t^*=-(\boldsymbol{B}+\boldsymbol{A})^{-1}\boldsymbol{\Gamma}\hat{\boldsymbol{x}}_t \quad \text{or} \quad \boldsymbol{y}_{1t}^*=(\boldsymbol{I}-\boldsymbol{\Pi}_{11})^{-1}\boldsymbol{\Pi}_{12}\hat{\boldsymbol{x}}_t, \tag{3.5}$$

but in the absence of knowledge of the remainder of the system it is not possible to specify the weights with which the elements of $\hat{\boldsymbol{x}}_t$ appear. However, substituting $\boldsymbol{x}_t=\hat{\boldsymbol{x}}_t+\boldsymbol{\varepsilon}_t$ into the observable reduced form gives

$$\begin{aligned}\boldsymbol{y}_{1t}&=\boldsymbol{\Pi}_{11}(\boldsymbol{I}-\boldsymbol{\Pi}_{11})^{-1}\boldsymbol{\Pi}_{12}\hat{\boldsymbol{x}}_t+\boldsymbol{\Pi}_{12}(\hat{\boldsymbol{x}}_t+\boldsymbol{\varepsilon}_t)+\boldsymbol{v}_{1t}\\&=(\boldsymbol{I}-\boldsymbol{\Pi}_{11})^{-1}\boldsymbol{\Pi}_{12}\hat{\boldsymbol{x}}_t+(\boldsymbol{\Pi}_{12}\boldsymbol{\varepsilon}_t+\boldsymbol{v}_{1t}),\end{aligned} \tag{3.6}$$

hence a set of h least squares regressions of the elements of $\boldsymbol{y}_{1t}$ on $\hat{\boldsymbol{x}}_t$ yields consistent estimates of the coefficients in (3.5). Again, if it is unrealistic to treat the $\hat{x}$ series as given, the expression (2.11) may be substituted for $\hat{\boldsymbol{x}}_t$ in (3.6), which may then be estimated jointly with the vector ARMA model (2.10). The resulting regression estimates $\hat{\boldsymbol{y}}_{1t}^*$ can then be substituted into (3.4), and treated as predetermined variables. If (3.4) is to be estimated by two-stage least squares, then the first stage comprises estimation of certain equations of the reduced form (2.3), where once more $\hat{\boldsymbol{y}}_{1t}^*$ replaces $\boldsymbol{y}_{1t}^*$. The error $\boldsymbol{y}_{1t}^*-\hat{\boldsymbol{y}}_{1t}^*$ comprises coefficient estimation error, which in turn involves the disturbances $\boldsymbol{\varepsilon}_t$ and $\boldsymbol{v}_{1t}$, but this does not deny the consistency of the final parameter estimates, by an argument analogous to the standard proof of consistency of 2SLS.

Although this procedure is based on consistent estimates of the rational expectation coefficients, it does not provide a test of the rational expectations hypothesis, since having estimated but a single structural equation or reduced form equation the restrictions on the rational expectations coefficients cannot be checked. A restriction that has been imposed so far is that past information on the exogenous variables is used optimally. This can be relaxed by replacing $\hat{\boldsymbol{x}}_t$ in (3.6) by past values of $\boldsymbol{x}_t$, and no longer estimating jointly with the x process.[9] If the correct distributed lag formulations are employed, as given by the forecasting equations, then estimation using past x values will provide a better fit than that based on calculated $\hat{x}$ values or subject to restrictions, though the difference will not be significant if the optimality hypothesis is correct. In practice one would expect the distributed lag specifications to be determined empirically, nevertheless the agreement (or lack thereof) with the forecasting equations determined by separate time series analyses of the exogenous variables could then be checked.

[9] Such regression-based proxies for the expectations variables are employed by Sargent [26, 27].

Although such regression-based proxies incorporate neither the rational expectations coefficient restrictions nor those implied by optimal forecasting of exogenous variables, they are consistent with the model to the extent that the correct (and complete) set of exogenous variables is employed.

Possibly as a result of Muth's initial special case, one might consider the use of extrapolative forecasts of endogenous variables. It is then necessary to heed Nelson's [**18**] warning that a purely extrapolative predictor is an inadequate proxy for a rational expectations variable. As shown in Section 2.1, a univariate ARMA representation for each endogenous variable can always be derived, providing a purely extrapolative predictor y_{it}^{**}, and the one-step forecast error $\eta_{it} = y_{it} - y_{it}^{**}$ can be written, from (2.14), as

$$\eta_{it} = \left\{ \sum_{j=1}^{k} \xi_{0j}\varepsilon_{jt} + v_{it} \right\} + \left\{ \sum_{j=1}^{k} \sum_{l=1}^{\infty} w_{jl}\varepsilon_{j,t-l} + \sum_{l=1}^{\infty} w_{k+1,l}v_{i,t-l} \right\}. \tag{3.7}$$

The first expression in braces is equal to $y_{it} - y_{it}^*$, hence the second expression in braces represents the difference between the rational expectation and extrapolative prediction of y_{it}. This term is added to the disturbance term in (3.4) when y_{it}^{**} is substituted for y_{it}^*, and through its correlation with the exogenous variables removes the consistency of conventional estimators applied to (3.4). This argument applies equally to a reduced form equation. In the event that (3.4) contains more than one endogenous variable, fewer than $g-1$ zero restrictions being imposed on $\boldsymbol{\beta}_1$, instrumental variable or 2SLS procedures are further invalidated by the replacement of y_{it}^* by y_{it}^{**}, as Nelson points out, since the potential instruments (exogenous variables) are now correlated with the composite disturbance term.

McCallum's [**14**] answer to these difficulties is to use as a proxy for the expectations variable y_{it}^* not y_{it}^{**} but the actual value y_{it}, and then to use y_{it}^{**} as the associated instrumental variable. Substituting y_{it} for y_{it}^* augments the disturbance term by the first expression in braces in (3.7), but this is not correlated with y_{it}^{**}, which is thereby a valid instrument. It *is* correlated with $\boldsymbol{x}_t$, however, so further instruments are required and McCallum proposes the use of lagged exogenous variables $\boldsymbol{x}_{t-1}$. Note however that the applicability of this procedure is limited to equations which do not simultaneously contain an endogenous variable and its own rational expectation. This difficulty does not arise in McCallum's discussion of Nelson's example, in which y_{2t}^* but not y_{2t} appears in the equation for y_{1t}. However the substitution might still cause loss of identification, as when the Nelson-McCallum example is regarded as the first equation of the following just-identified two-equation system:

$$\begin{bmatrix} 1 & 0 \\ \beta & 1 \end{bmatrix} \begin{bmatrix} y_{1t} \\ y_{2t} \end{bmatrix} + \begin{bmatrix} \alpha & \gamma_1 \\ 0 & \gamma_2 \end{bmatrix} \begin{bmatrix} y_{2t}^* \\ x_t \end{bmatrix} = \begin{bmatrix} u_{1t} \\ u_{2t} \end{bmatrix}.$$

Clearly the use of actual values as proxies for rational expectations is not restricted to single equations (but may be subject to further identifiability problems in larger systems), and can also be applied when future expectations enter the model, as in

McCallum's [**13**] empirical work. In effect the only information about the rational expectation now being employed is that it is unbiased, but its further properties clearly influence the choice of instrumental variables. As a consequence of the result on comparative forecast variance given in Section 2.1, the rational expectation is a more efficient instrumental variable than the extrapolative predictor, and although it cannot be fully implemented in this limited information context, taking account of its dependence on the past values of specific variables (and possibly with those past values entering in a specific way) when constructing instruments could be expected to lead to an improvement.

4. ECONOMIC POLICY

4.1. *The Effects of Policy Variables*

We now extend the exogenous variable specification to include the possibility that certain variables are policy instruments under the control of economic policy makers. Writing

$$x_t = G(\Omega_{t-1}) + \varepsilon_t, \tag{4.1}$$

where Ω_{t-1} denotes information about the values of *all* variables available as of time $t-1$, allows such policy instruments to be determined by feedback control rules, possibly with a superimposed random element. The relation

$$y_t - y_t^* = -B^{-1}\Gamma(x_t - \hat{x}_t) + B^{-1}u_t \tag{4.2}$$

holds for the basic model of Section 2.1 and its subsequent extensions, and states that only unanticipated movements in exogenous variables (or disturbances) cause endogenous variables to diverge from their previously expected values. Thus if the public has the same information as the policy maker including knowledge of $G(\cdot)$, so that $\hat{x}_t = G(\Omega_{t-1})$, then there is no choice of $G(\cdot)$, i.e. no feedback rule, that permits the policy maker to offset expected movements in endogenous ("target") variables. Of course the policy in general affects the actual realized values of the endogenous variables, but the effect is fully anticipated unless the policy contains surprise or random elements, ε_t. From (2.8) and (2.9) we have

$$y_t = -(B + A)^{-1}\Gamma G(\Omega_{t-1}) - B^{-1}\Gamma\varepsilon_t + v_t. \tag{4.3}$$

The conventional view that for example under fixed exchange rates a devaluation must be sprung as a surprise, and that perfect foresight would frustrate the policy, is then presumably based on the relative signs and magnitudes of coefficients of ε_t and $G(\Omega_{t-1})$ in (4.3).

Special cases arise when for key endogenous variables the coefficients of certain policy variables $G(\cdot)$ are zero, as in macroeconomic models constructed so that output is independent of the particular deterministic money supply rule in effect, such as that of Sargent and Wallace [**28**]. A feature of such models is behavioral relations giving one endogenous variable (output, employment) in terms of the forecast errors in another (prices, wages); compare also the aggregate supply function of Lucas [**10**], and note that the restriction that the variables y_{jt} and y^*_{jt} enter a given equation with coefficients that are equal but opposite in sign can clearly be tested following estimation as in Section 3. In the present framework suppose that we can rearrange equations and variables so that in the first g_1 structural equations the last g_2 variables y_{2t} and y^*_{2t} either appear with equal and opposite coefficients or do not appear at all ($g_1+g_2=g$). Then $(\boldsymbol{B}+\boldsymbol{A})$ is block-lower-triangular and so is its inverse. If given policy instruments do not appear in these g_1 equations, the corresponding elements of $\boldsymbol{\Gamma}$ being zero (as is true of the Lucas–Sargent–Wallace models), then the systematic part of policy has no effect on the first g_1 endogenous variables, since the relevant elements of $(\boldsymbol{B}+\boldsymbol{A})^{-1}\boldsymbol{\Gamma}$ in (4.3) are zero.[10]

4.2. *Econometric Policy Evaluation*

The conventional approach to the quantitative evaluation of alternative economic policies is to take an estimated macroeconometric model and examine the implied behavior of the endogenous variables under alternative specifications of the future values of policy instruments (exogenous variables).[11] Lucas [**11**] criticizes such comparisons of alternative policy rules on the grounds that the "structure" of econometric models is not invariant to changes in policy. The elements of such models are behavioral relationships derived from optimal decision rules of economic agents, which are based in part on the agents' views of the future movements of relevant variables. Changes in the nature of these movements cause changes in the optimal decision rules, hence "any change in policy will systematically alter the structure of econometric models" (Lucas [**11**, p. 41]). This criticism also applies to ex post analysis of the effectiveness of an actual policy, where the procedure is first to estimate a model using data for periods when the policy was not in operation and then to compare its predictions for the periods when the policy was applied with either the actual outcomes or the predictions of a model estimated for the policy period. For such comparisons to be meaningful, it is necessary to assume that the nature of the economic system's response is unaltered when substantially different movements in key variables occur, movements which are such as to cause the policy makers to act.[12]

[10] The reassertion of the potential of monetary policy to stabilize fluctuations in output and employment by Phelps and Taylor [**20**] rests on a model in which firms "set their prices and wage rates *1 period in advance* of the period over which they will apply, hence before the central bank decides on the money supply for that (latter) period;" thus the policymakers have a larger information set available to them. Likewise, Fischer's [**5**] model in which labor contracts are made for *two* periods at a time also admits monetary policy effects on the short-run behavior of output. As discussed in Section 2.3, data are unlikely to be informative about the details of such timing relationships, so that when these models are implemented empirically, it will be necessary to give careful prior consideration to the relevant institutional and informational arrangements and decision sequences.

[11] Descriptions of the general procedure and its applications are contained in my survey article and lecture course (Wallis [**32**, **34**]), but pay no attention to the criticism to be discussed below.

[12] Such endogenization of policy may invalidate tests of structural change across policy regimes, since a division of a sample period into policy regimes is not arbitrary but is related to the behavior of key variables (Wallis [**33**]).

In the linear model context used throughout this paper, the force of the Lucas criticism and the nature of a practical response can be seen by comparing the approaches of Sections 2 and 3. The basic model of Section 2.1 demonstrates the source of the distributed lag function relating endogenous to exogenous variables and the fact that the stochastic structure of the exogenous variables determines the nature of the distributed lag. Any change in the behavior of the exogenous variables perceived by economic agents changes these distributed lags, hence "old" lag functions do not provide an appropriate description of behavior in response to "new" exogenous shocks. However the focus of attention in estimation is the system (2.1) (or (2.17) or (2.19)), which is taken to represent the optimal decision rules of economic agents prior to the insertion of specific forecasting procedures, and the structure incorporating the rational expectations hypothesis *is* invariant to changes in the behavior of exogenous variables, since the parameters of say (3.1) or (3.3) do not depend on such behavior. To carry out policy evaluation in this framework it is then necessary to postulate a new x process and associated forecasts, and evaluate its impact on the endogenous variables using the estimated structure.

The difficulty in the usual approach is that data-based distributed lags confuse two separate aspects, namely economic optimization procedures and forecasting procedures, and the effect of a required change in the latter on the lag function cannot be perceived without separating the two components. Distinguishing an underlying economic structure, albeit one incorporating the rational expectations hypothesis, from a forecasting scheme relevant for particular exogenous or policy processes and changing when they do, then permits policy evaluation to proceed. In effect, keeping the "structure" of exogenous processes separate from the economic structure allows the traditional view of econometric policy evaluation to be reasserted. Moreover the cases we have considered amount to those of prediction under unchanged structure, providing the simpler case in which knowledge of the reduced form but not the structural form is usually held to be sufficient.

University of Warwick

Manuscript received May, 1977; final revision received January, 1979.

REFERENCES

[1] BARRO, R. J., AND S. FISCHER: "Recent Developments in Monetary Theory," *Journal of Monetary Economics*, 2 (1976), 133–167.

[2] BOX, G. E. P., AND G. M. JENKINS: *Time Series Analysis, Forecasting and Control.* San Francisco: Holden-Day, 1970.

[3] CHAN, W.-Y. T., AND K. F. WALLIS: "Multiple Time Series Modelling: Another Look at the Mink-Muskrat Interaction," *Applied Statistics*, 27 (1978), 168–175.

[4] DWYER, P. S.: "Some Applications of Matrix Derivatives in Multivariate Analysis," *Journal of the American Statistical Association*, 62 (1967), 607–625.

[5] FISCHER, S.: "Long-term Contracts, Rational Expectations, and the Optimal Money Supply Rule," *Journal of Political Economy*, 85 (1977), 191–205.

[6] GOLDBERGER, A. S.: Maximum-likelihood Estimation of Regressions Containing Unobservable Independent Variables," *International Economic Review*, 13 (1972), 1–15.

[7] GRANGER, C. W. J., AND M. J. MORRIS: "Time Series Modelling and Interpretation," *Journal of the Royal Statistical Society* A, 139 (1976), 246–257.

[8] GRANGER, C. W. J., AND P. NEWBOLD: *Forecasting Economic Time Series*. New York: Academic Press, 1977.

[9] HATANAKA, M.: "On the Global Identification of the Dynamic Simultaneous Equations Model with Stationary Disturbances," *International Economic Review*, 16 (1975), 545–554.

[10] LUCAS, R. E. JR: "Econometric Testing of the Natural Rate Hypothesis," in *The Econometrics of Price Determination Conference*, ed. by O. Eckstein. Washington, DC: Federal Reserve System, 1972, pp. 50–59.

[11] ———: "Econometric Policy Evaluation: A Critique," in *The Phillips Curve and Labor Markets*, ed. by K. Brunner and A. H. Meltzer. Amsterdam: North-Holland, 1976, pp. 19–46. (Carnegie-Rochester Conference Series on Public Policy No. 1, supplement to the *Journal of Monetary Economics*, January, 1976.)

[12] MALINVAUD, E.: *Statistical Methods of Econometrics*, 2nd ed. Amsterdam: North-Holland, 1970.

[13] MCCALLUM, B. T.: "Rational Expectations and the Natural Rate Hypothesis: Some Consistent Estimates," *Econometrica*, 44 (1976), 43–52.

[14] ———: Rational Expectations and the Estimation of Econometric Models: An Alternative Procedure," *International Economic Review*, 17 (1976), 484–490.

[15] MUTH, J. F.: "Rational Expectations and the Theory of Price Movements," *Econometrica*, 29 (1961), 315–335.

[16] NELSON, C. R.: "Time Series Forecasting and Economic Models," unpublished paper, University of Chicago, 1969.

[17]———: "Rational Expectations and the Predictive Efficiency of Economic Models," *Journal of Business*, 48 (1975), 331–343.

[18] ———: "Rational Expectations and the Estimation of Econometric Models," *International Economic Review*, 16 (1975), 555–561.

[19] NEUDECKER, H.: "Some Theorems on Matrix Differentiation with Special Reference to Kronecker Matrix Products," *Journal of the American Statistical Association*, 64 (1969), 953–963.

[20] PHELPS, E. S., AND J. B. TAYLOR: "Stabilizing Power of Monetary Policy under Rational Expectations," *Journal of Political Economy*, 85 (1977), 163–190.

[21] PIERCE, D. A.: "Forecasting in Dynamic Models with Stochastic Regressors," *Journal of Econometrics*, 3 (1975), 349–374.

[22] POOLE, W.: "Rational Expectations in the Macro Model," *Brookings Papers on Economic Activity*, 1976, 463–505.

[23] ROTHENBERG, T. J.: *Efficient Estimation with A Priori Information*. New Haven: Yale University Press, 1973. (Cowles Foundation Monograph 23.)

[24] SARGAN, J. D.: "The Identification and Estimation of Sets of Simultaneous Stochastic Equations," unpublished paper, London School of Economics, 1972.

[25] SARGAN, J. D., AND J. D. SYLWESTROWICZ: "A Comparison of Alternative Methods of Numerical Optimisation in Estimating Simultaneous Equation Econometric Models," unpublished paper, London School of Economics, 1976.

[26] SARGENT, T. J.: "Rational Expectations, the Real Rate of Interest, and the Natural Rate of Unemployment," *Brookings Papers on Economic Activity*, 1973, 429–472.

[27] ———: "A Classical Macroeconometric Model for the United States," *Journal of Political Economy*, 84 (1976), 207–237.

[28] SARGENT, T. J., AND N. WALLACE: " 'Rational' Expectations, the Optimal Monetary Instrument, and the Optimal Money Supply Rule," *Journal of Political Economy*, 83 (1975), 241–254.

[29] SHILLER, R. J.: "Rational Expectations and the Dynamic Structure of Macroeconomic Models," *Journal of Monetary Economics*, 4 (1978), 1–44.

[30] SIMS, C. A.: "Distributed Lags," in *Frontiers of Quantitative Economics*, Vol. II, ed. by M. D. Intriligator and D. A. Kendrick. Amsterdam: North-Holland, 1974, pp. 289–332.

[31] TOBIN, J.: "The Wage-Price Mechanism: Overview of the Conference," in *The Econometrics of Price Determination Conference*, ed. by O. Eckstein. Washington, D.C.: Federal Reserve System, 1972, pp, 5–15.

[32] WALLIS, K. F.: "Some Recent Developments in Applied Econometrics: Dynamic Models and Simultaneous Equation Systems," *Journal of Economic Literature*, 7 (1969), 771–796.

[33] ———: "Wages, Prices and Incomes Policies: Some Comments," *Economica*, 38 (1971), 304–310. Reprinted in *Incomes Policy and Inflation*, ed. by M. Parkin and M. T. Sumner, Manchester: Manchester University Press, 1972.

[34] ———: *Topics in Applied Econometrics.* Oxford: Basil Blackwell, 1973.

[35] ZELLNER, A.: "Estimation of Regression Relationships Containing Unobservable Independent Variables," *International Economic Review*, 11 (1970), 441–454.

Part II
State Space Models and the Kalman Filter

[6]

A New Approach to Linear Filtering and Prediction Problems[1]

R. E. KALMAN

Research Institute for Advanced Study,[2]
Baltimore, Md.

The classical filtering and prediction problem is re-examined using the Bode-Shannon representation of random processes and the "state-transition" method of analysis of dynamic systems. New results are:

(1) The formulation and methods of solution of the problem apply without modification to stationary and nonstationary statistics and to growing-memory and infinite-memory filters.

(2) A nonlinear difference (or differential) equation is derived for the covariance matrix of the optimal estimation error. From the solution of this equation the coefficients of the difference (or differential) equation of the optimal linear filter are obtained without further calculations.

(3) The filtering problem is shown to be the dual of the noise-free regulator problem.

The new method developed here is applied to two well-known problems, confirming and extending earlier results.

The discussion is largely self-contained and proceeds from first principles; basic concepts of the theory of random processes are reviewed in the Appendix.

Introduction

An important class of theoretical and practical problems in communication and control is of a statistical nature. Such problems are: (i) Prediction of random signals; (ii) separation of random signals from random noise; (iii) detection of signals of known form (pulses, sinusoids) in the presence of random noise.

In his pioneering work, Wiener [1][3] showed that problems (i) and (ii) lead to the so-called Wiener-Hopf integral equation; he also gave a method (spectral factorization) for the solution of this integral equation in the practically important special case of stationary statistics and rational spectra.

Many extensions and generalizations followed Wiener's basic work. Zadeh and Ragazzini solved the finite-memory case [2]. Concurrently and independently of Bode and Shannon [3], they also gave a simplified method [2] of solution. Booton discussed the nonstationary Wiener-Hopf equation [4]. These results are now in standard texts [5-6]. A somewhat different approach along these main lines has been given recently by Darlington [7]. For extensions to sampled signals, see, e.g., Franklin [8], Lees [9]. Another approach based on the eigenfunctions of the Wiener-Hopf equation (which applies also to nonstationary problems whereas the preceding methods in general don't), has been pioneered by Davis [10] and applied by many others, e.g., Shinbrot [11], Blum [12], Pugachev [13], Solodovnikov [14].

In all these works, the objective is to obtain the specification of a linear dynamic system (Wiener filter) which accomplishes the prediction, separation, or detection of a random signal.[4]

[1] This research was supported in part by the U. S. Air Force Office of Scientific Research under Contract AF 49 (638)-382.

[2] 7212 Bellona Ave.

[3] Numbers in brackets designate References at end of paper.

[4] Of course, in general these tasks may be done better by nonlinear filters. At present, however, little or nothing is known about how to obtain (both theoretically and practically) these nonlinear filters.

Contributed by the Instruments and Regulators Division and presented at the Instruments and Regulators Conference, March 29–April 2, 1959, of The American Society of Mechanical Engineers.

Note: Statements and opinions advanced in papers are to be understood as individual expressions of their authors and not those of the Society. Manuscript received at ASME Headquarters, February 24, 1959. Paper No. 59—IRD-11.

Present methods for solving the Wiener problem are subject to a number of limitations which seriously curtail their practical usefulness:

(1) The optimal filter is specified by its impulse response. It is not a simple task to synthesize the filter from such data.

(2) Numerical determination of the optimal impulse response is often quite involved and poorly suited to machine computation. The situation gets rapidly worse with increasing complexity of the problem.

(3) Important generalizations (e.g., growing-memory filters, nonstationary prediction) require new derivations, frequently of considerable difficulty to the nonspecialist.

(4) The mathematics of the derivations are not transparent. Fundamental assumptions and their consequences tend to be obscured.

This paper introduces a new look at this whole assemblage of problems, sidestepping the difficulties just mentioned. The following are the highlights of the paper:

(5) *Optimal Estimates and Orthogonal Projections.* The Wiener problem is approached from the point of view of conditional distributions and expectations. In this way, basic facts of the Wiener theory are quickly obtained; the scope of the results and the fundamental assumptions appear clearly. It is seen that all statistical calculations and results are based on first and second order averages; no other statistical data are needed. Thus difficulty (4) is eliminated. This method is well known in probability theory (see pp. 75–78 and 148–155 of Doob [15] and pp. 455–464 of Loève [16]) but has not yet been used extensively in engineering.

(6) *Models for Random Processes.* Following, in particular, Bode and Shannon [3], arbitrary random signals are represented (up to second order average statistical properties) as the output of a linear dynamic system excited by independent or uncorrelated random signals ("white noise"). This is a standard trick in the engineering applications of the Wiener theory [2–7]. The approach taken here differs from the conventional one only in the way in which linear dynamic systems are described. We shall emphasize the concepts of *state* and *state transition;* in other words, linear systems will be specified by systems of first-order difference (or differential) equations. This point of view is

natural and also necessary in order to take advantage of the simplifications mentioned under (5).

(7) *Solution of the Wiener Problem.* With the state-transition method, a single derivation covers a large variety of problems: growing and infinite memory filters, stationary and nonstationary statistics, etc.; difficulty (3) disappears. Having guessed the "state" of the estimation (i.e., filtering or prediction) problem correctly, one is led to a nonlinear difference (or differential) equation for the covariance matrix of the optimal estimation error. This is vaguely analogous to the Wiener-Hopf equation. Solution of the equation for the covariance matrix starts at the time t_0 when the first observation is taken; at each later time t the solution of the equation represents the covariance of the optimal prediction error given observations in the interval (t_0, t). From the covariance matrix at time t we obtain at once, without further calculations, the coefficients (in general, time-varying) characterizing the optimal linear filter.

(8) *The Dual Problem.* The new formulation of the Wiener problem brings it into contact with the growing new theory of control systems based on the "state" point of view [17–24]. It turns out, *surprisingly*, that the Wiener problem is the *dual* of the noise-free optimal regulator problem, which has been solved previously by the author, using the state-transition method to great advantage [18, 23, 24]. The mathematical background of the two problems is identical—this has been suspected all along, but until now the analogies have never been made explicit.

(9) *Applications.* The power of the new method is most apparent in theoretical investigations and in numerical answers to complex practical problems. In the latter case, it is best to resort to machine computation. Examples of this type will be discussed later. To provide some feel for applications, two standard examples from nonstationary prediction are included; in these cases the solution of the nonlinear difference equation mentioned under (7) above can be obtained even in closed form.

For easy reference, the main results are displayed in the form of theorems. Only Theorems 3 and 4 are original. The next section and the Appendix serve mainly to review well-known material in a form suitable for the present purposes.

Notation Conventions

Throughout the paper, we shall deal mainly with *discrete* (or *sampled*) dynamic systems; in other words, signals will be observed at equally spaced points in time (*sampling instants*). By suitable choice of the time scale, the constant intervals between successive sampling instants (*sampling periods*) may be chosen as unity. Thus variables referring to time, such as t, t_0, τ, T will always be integers. The restriction to discrete dynamic systems is not at all essential (at least from the engineering point of view); by using the discreteness, however, we can keep the mathematics rigorous and yet elementary. Vectors will be denoted by small bold-face letters: $\mathbf{a}$, $\mathbf{b}$, . . ., $\mathbf{u}$, $\mathbf{x}$, $\mathbf{y}$, . . . A *vector* or more precisely an *n-vector* is a set of n numbers $x_1, \ldots x_n$; the x_i are the *co-ordinates* or *components* of the vector $\mathbf{x}$.

Matrices will be denoted by capital bold-face letters: $\mathbf{A}$, $\mathbf{B}$, $\mathbf{Q}$, $\mathbf{\Phi}$, $\mathbf{\Psi}$, . . .; they are $m \times n$ arrays of elements a_{ij}, b_{ij}, q_{ij}, . . . The *transpose* (interchanging rows and columns) of a matrix will be denoted by the prime. In manipulating formulas, it will be convenient to regard a vector as a matrix with a single column.

Using the conventional definition of matrix multiplication, we write the *scalar product* of two n-vectors $\mathbf{x}$, $\mathbf{y}$ as

$$\mathbf{x}'\mathbf{y} = \sum_{i=1}^{n} x_i y_i = \mathbf{y}'\mathbf{x}$$

The scalar product is clearly a scalar, i.e., not a vector, quantity.

Similarly, the *quadratic form* associated with the $n \times n$ matrix $\mathbf{Q}$ is

$$\mathbf{x}'\mathbf{Q}\mathbf{x} = \sum_{i,j=1}^{n} x_i q_{ij} x_j$$

We define the expression $\mathbf{x}\mathbf{y}'$ where $\mathbf{x}$ is an m-vector and $\mathbf{y}$ is an n-vector to be the $m \times n$ matrix with elements $x_i y_j$.

We write $E(\mathbf{x}) = E\mathbf{x}$ for the expected value of the random vector $\mathbf{x}$ (see Appendix). It is usually convenient to omit the brackets after E. This does not result in confusion in simple cases since constants and the operator E commute. Thus $E\mathbf{x}\mathbf{y}'$ = matrix with elements $E(x_i y_j)$; $E\mathbf{x}E\mathbf{y}'$ = matrix with elements $E(x_i)E(y_j)$.

For ease of reference, a list of the principal symbols used is given below.

Optimal Estimates

- t time in general; present time.
- t_0 time at which observations start.
- $x_1(t)$, $x_2(t)$ basic random variables.
- $y(t)$ observed random variable.
- $x_1^*(t_1|t)$ optimal estimate of $x_1(t_1)$ given $y(t_0), \ldots, y(t)$.
- L loss function (nonrandom function of its argument).
- ϵ estimation error (random variable).

Orthogonal Projections

- $\mathcal{Y}(t)$ linear manifold generated by the random variables $y(t_0), \ldots, y(t)$.
- $\bar{x}(t_1|t)$ orthogonal projection of $x(t_1)$ on $\mathcal{Y}(t)$.
- $\tilde{x}(t_1|t)$ component of $x(t_1)$ orthogonal to $\mathcal{Y}(t)$.

Models for Random Processes

- $\mathbf{\Phi}(t+1; t)$ transition matrix
- $\mathbf{Q}(t)$ covariance of random excitation

Solution of the Wiener Problem

- $\mathbf{x}(t)$ basic random variable.
- $\mathbf{y}(t)$ observed random variable.
- $\mathcal{Y}(t)$ linear manifold generated by $\mathbf{y}(t_0), \ldots, \mathbf{y}(t)$.
- $\mathcal{Z}(t)$ linear manifold generated by $\tilde{\mathbf{y}}(t|t-1)$.
- $\mathbf{x}^*(t_1|t)$ optimal estimate of $\mathbf{x}(t_1)$ given $\mathcal{Y}(t)$.
- $\tilde{\mathbf{x}}(t_1|t)$ error in optimal estimate of $\mathbf{x}(t_1)$ given $\mathcal{Y}(t)$.

Optimal Estimates

To have a concrete description of the type of problems to be studied, consider the following situation. We are given signal $x_1(t)$ and noise $x_2(t)$. Only the sum $y(t) = x_1(t) + x_2(t)$ can be observed. Suppose we have observed and know exactly the values of $y(t_0), \ldots, y(t)$. What can we infer from this knowledge in regard to the (unobservable) value of the signal at $t = t_1$, where t_1 may be less than, equal to, or greater than t? If $t_1 < t$, this is a *data-smoothing* (*interpolation*) problem. If $t_1 = t$, this is called *filtering*. If $t_1 > t$, we have a *prediction* problem. Since our treatment will be general enough to include these and similar problems, we shall use hereafter the collective term *estimation*.

As was pointed out by Wiener [1], the natural setting of the estimation problem belongs to the realm of probability theory and statistics. Thus signal, noise, and their sum will be random variables, and consequently they may be regarded as random processes. From the probabilistic description of the random processes we can determine the probability with which a particular sample of the signal and noise will occur. For any given set of measured values $\eta(t_0), \ldots, \eta(t)$ of the random variable $y(t)$ one can then also determine, in principle, the probability of simultaneous occurrence of various values $\xi_1(t)$ of the random variable $x_1(t_1)$. This is the conditional probability distribution function

$$Pr[x_1(t_1) \leqq \xi_1 | y(t_0) = \eta(t_0), \ldots, y(t) = \eta(t)] = F(\xi_1) \quad (1)$$

Evidently, $F(\xi_1)$ represents all the information which the measurement of the random variables $y(t_0), \ldots, y(t)$ has conveyed about the random variable $x_1(t_1)$. Any statistical estimate of the random variable $x_1(t_1)$ will be some function of this distribution and therefore a (nonrandom) function of the random variables $y(t_0), \ldots, y(t)$. This statistical estimate is denoted by $X_1(t_1|t)$, or by just $X_1(t_1)$ or X_1 when the set of observed random variables or the time at which the estimate is required are clear from context.

Suppose now that X_1 is given as a fixed function of the random variables $y(t_0), \ldots, y(t)$. Then X_1 is itself a random variable and its actual value is known whenever the actual values of $y(t_0), \ldots, y(t)$ are known. In general, the actual value of $X_1(t_1)$ will be different from the (unknown) actual value of $x_1(t_1)$. To arrive at a rational way of determining X_1, it is natural to assign a *penalty* or *loss* for incorrect estimates. Clearly, the loss should be a (i) positive, (ii) nondecreasing function of the *estimation error* $\epsilon = x_1(t_1) - X_1(t_1)$. Thus we define a *loss function* by

$$L(0) = 0$$

$$L(\epsilon_2) \geqq L(\epsilon_1) \geqq 0 \quad \text{when} \quad \epsilon_2 \geqq \epsilon_1 \geqq 0 \qquad (2)$$

$$L(\epsilon) = L(-\epsilon)$$

Some common examples of loss functions are: $L(\epsilon) = a\epsilon^2, a\epsilon^4, a|\epsilon|, a[1 - \exp(-\epsilon^2)]$, etc., where a is a positive constant.

One (but by no means the only) natural way of choosing the random variable X_1 is to require that this choice should minimize the average loss or risk

$$E\{L[x_1(t_1) - X_1(t_1)]\} = E[E\{L[x(t_1) - X_1(t_1)]|y(t_0), \ldots, y(t)\}] \quad (3)$$

Since the first expectation on the right-hand side of (3) does not depend on the choice of X_1 but only on $y(t_0), \ldots, y(t)$, it is clear that minimizing (3) is equivalent to minimizing

$$E\{L[x_1(t_1) - X_1(t_1)]|y(t_0), \ldots, y(t)\} \qquad (4)$$

Under just slight additional assumptions, optimal estimates can be characterized in a simple way.

Theorem 1. *Assume that L is of type* (2) *and that the conditional distribution function* $F(\xi)$ *defined by* (1) *is:*

(*A*) *symmetric about the mean* $\bar{\xi}$:

$$F(\xi - \bar{\xi}) = 1 - F(\bar{\xi} - \xi)$$

(*B*) *convex for* $\xi \leqq \bar{\xi}$:

$$F(\lambda\xi_1 + (1 - \lambda)\xi_2) \leqq \lambda F(\xi_1) + (1 - \lambda)F(\xi_2)$$

for all $\xi_1, \xi_2 \leqq \bar{\xi}$ *and* $0 \leqq \lambda \leqq 1$

Then the random variable $x_1^*(t_1|t)$ *which minimizes the average loss* (3) *is the conditional expectation*

$$x_1^*(t_1|t) = E[x_1(t_1)|y(t_0), \ldots, y(t)] \qquad (5)$$

Proof: As pointed out recently by Sherman [25], this theorem follows immediately from a well-known lemma in probability theory.

Corollary. *If the random processes* $\{x_1(t)\}$, $\{x_2(t)\}$, *and* $\{y(t)\}$ *are gaussian, Theorem 1 holds.*

Proof: By Theorem 5, (*A*) (see Appendix), conditional distributions on a gaussian random process are gaussian. Hence the requirements of Theorem 1 are always satisfied.

In the control systems literature, this theorem appears sometimes in a form which is more restrictive in one way and more general in another way:

Theorem 1-a. *If* $L(\epsilon) = \epsilon^2$, *then Theorem 1 is true without assumptions* (*A*) *and* (*B*).

Proof: Expand the conditional expectation (4):

$$E[x_1^2(t_1)|y(t_0), \ldots, y(t)] - 2X_1(t_1)E[x_1(t_1)|y(t_0), \ldots, y(t)] + X_1^2(t_1)$$

and differentiate with respect to $X_1(t_1)$. This is not a completely rigorous argument; for a simple rigorous proof see Doob [15], pp. 77–78.

Remarks: (*a*) As far as the author is aware, it is not known what is the most general class of random processes $\{x_1(t)\}$, $\{x_2(t)\}$ for which the conditional distribution function satisfies the requirements of Theorem 1.

(*b*) Aside from the note of Sherman, Theorem 1 apparently has never been stated explicitly in the control systems literature. In fact, one finds many statements to the effect that loss functions of the general type (2) cannot be conveniently handled mathematically.

(*c*) In the sequel, we shall be dealing mainly with vector-valued random variables. In that case, the estimation problem is stated as: Given a vector-valued random process $\{\mathbf{x}(t)\}$ and observed random variables $\mathbf{y}(t_0), \ldots, \mathbf{y}(t)$, where $\mathbf{y}(t) = \mathbf{M}\mathbf{x}(t)$ ($\mathbf{M}$ being a singular matrix; in other words, not all co-ordinates of $\mathbf{x}(t)$ can be observed), find an estimate $\mathbf{X}(t_1)$ which minimizes the expected loss $E[L(\|\mathbf{x}(t_1) - \mathbf{X}(t_1)\|)]$, $\|\ \|$ being the norm of a vector.

Theorem 1 remains true in the vector case also, provided we require that the conditional distribution function of the n co-ordinates of the vector $\mathbf{x}(t_1)$,

$$Pr[x_1(t_1) \leqq \xi_1, \ldots, x_n(t_1) \leqq \xi_n|\mathbf{y}(t_0), \ldots, \mathbf{y}(t)] = F(\xi_1, \ldots, \xi_n)$$

be symmetric with respect to the n variables $\xi_1 - \bar{\xi}_1, \ldots, \xi_n - \bar{\xi}_n$ and convex in the region where all of these variables are negative.

Orthogonal Projections

The explicit calculation of the optimal estimate as a function of the observed variables is, in general, impossible. There is an important exception: The processes $\{x_1(t)\}$, $\{x_2(t)\}$ are gaussian.

On the other hand, if we attempt to get an optimal estimate under the restriction $L(\epsilon) = \epsilon^2$ and the additional requirement that the estimate be a linear function of the observed random variables, we get an estimate which is identical with the optimal estimate in the gaussian case, without the assumption of linearity or quadratic loss function. This shows that results obtainable by linear estimation can be bettered by nonlinear estimation only when (i) the random processes are nongaussian and even then (in view of Theorem 5, (*C*)) only (ii) by considering at least third-order probability distribution functions.

In the special cases just mentioned, the explicit solution of the estimation problem is most easily understood with the help of a geometric picture. This is the subject of the present section.

Consider the (real-valued) random variables $y(t_0), \ldots, y(t)$. The set of all linear combinations of these random variables with real coefficients

$$\sum_{i=t_0}^{t} a_i y(i) \qquad (6)$$

forms a *vector space* (*linear manifold*) which we denote by $\mathcal{Y}(t)$. We regard, abstractly, any expression of the form (6) as "point" or "vector" in $\mathcal{Y}(t)$; this use of the word "vector" should not be confused, of course, with "vector-valued" random variables, etc. Since we do not want to fix the value of t (i.e., the total number of possible observations), $\mathcal{Y}(t)$ should be regarded as a finite-dimensional subspace of the space of all possible observations.

Given any two vectors u, v in $\mathcal{Y}(t)$ (i.e., random variables expressible in the form (6)), we say that u and v are *orthogonal* if $Euv = 0$. Using the Schmidt orthogonalization procedure, as described for instance by Doob [15], p. 151, or by Loève [16], p. 459, it is easy to select an *orthonormal basis* in $\mathcal{Y}(t)$. By this is meant a set of vectors $e_{t_0}, \ldots, e_t$ in $\mathcal{Y}(t)$ such that any vector in $\mathcal{Y}(t)$ can be expressed as a unique linear combination of $e_{t_0}, \ldots, e_t$ and

$$Ee_ie_j = \delta_{ij} = \left.\begin{array}{ll} 1 & \text{if } i = j \\ 0 & \text{if } i \neq j \end{array}\right\} (i, j = t_0, \ldots, t) \qquad (7)$$

Thus any vector $\bar{x}$ in $\mathcal{Y}(t)$ is given by

$$\bar{x} = \sum_{i=t_0}^{t} a_ie_i$$

and so the coefficients a_i can be immediately determined with the aid of (7):

$$E\bar{x}e_j = E\left(\sum_{i=t_0}^{t} a_ie_i\right)e_j = \sum_{i=t_0}^{t} a_iEe_ie_j = \sum_{i=t_0}^{t} a_i\delta_{ij} = a_j \qquad (8)$$

It follows further that any random variable x (not necessarily in $\mathcal{Y}(t)$) can be uniquely decomposed into two parts: a part $\bar{x}$ in $\mathcal{Y}(t)$ and a part $\tilde{x}$ orthogonal to $\mathcal{Y}(t)$ (i.e., orthogonal to every vector in $\mathcal{Y}(t)$). In fact, we can write

$$x = \bar{x} + \tilde{x} = \sum_{i=t_0}^{t} (Exe_i)e_i + \tilde{x} \qquad (9)$$

Thus $\bar{x}$ is uniquely determined by equation (9) and is obviously a vector in $\mathcal{Y}(t)$. Therefore $\tilde{x}$ is also uniquely determined; it remains to check that it is orthogonal to $\mathcal{Y}(t)$:

$$E\tilde{x}e_i = E(x - \bar{x})e_i = Exe_i - E\bar{x}e_i$$

Now the co-ordinates of $\bar{x}$ with respect to the basis $e_{t_0}, \ldots, e_t$ are given either in the form $E\bar{x}e_i$ (as in (8)) or in the form Exe_i (as in (9)). Since the co-ordinates are unique, $Exe_i = E\bar{x}e_i$ ($i = t_0, \ldots, t$); hence $E\tilde{x}e_i = 0$ and $\tilde{x}$ is orthogonal to every base vector e_i and therefore to $\mathcal{Y}(t)$. We call $\bar{x}$ the *orthogonal projection* of x on $\mathcal{Y}(t)$.

There is another way in which the orthogonal projection can be characterized: $\bar{x}$ is that vector in $\mathcal{Y}(t)$ (i.e., that *linear* function of the random variables $y(t_0), \ldots, y(t)$) which minimizes the quadratic loss function. In fact, if $\bar{w}$ is any other vector in $\mathcal{Y}(t)$, we have

$$E(x - \bar{w})^2 = E(\tilde{x} + \bar{x} - \bar{w})^2 = E[(x - \bar{x}) + (\bar{x} - \bar{w})]^2$$

Since $\tilde{x}$ is orthogonal to every vector in $\mathcal{Y}(t)$ and in particular to $\bar{x} - \bar{w}$ we have

$$E(x - \bar{w})^2 = E(x - \bar{x})^2 + E(\bar{x} - \bar{w})^2 \geq E(x - \bar{x})^2 \qquad (10)$$

This shows that, if $\bar{w}$ also minimizes the quadratic loss, we must have $E(\bar{x} - \bar{w})^2 = 0$ which means that the random variables $\bar{x}$ and $\bar{w}$ are equal (except possibly for a set of events whose probability is zero).

These results may be summarized as follows:

Theorem 2. *Let $\{x(t)\}$, $\{y(t)\}$ random processes with zero mean (i.e., $Ex(t) = Ey(t) = 0$ for all t). We observe $y(t_0), \ldots, y(t)$. If either*

(A) the random processes $\{x(t)\}$, $\{y(t)\}$ are gaussian; or

(B) the optimal estimate is restricted to be a linear function of the observed random variables and $L(\epsilon) = \epsilon^2$;

then

$$x^*(t_1|t) = \textit{optimal estimate of } x(t_1) \textit{ given } y(t_0), \ldots, y(t)$$
$$= \textit{orthogonal projection } \bar{x}(t_1|t) \textit{ of } x(t_1) \textit{ on } \mathcal{Y}(t). \qquad (11)$$

These results are well-known though not easily accessible in the control systems literature. See Doob [15], pp. 75–78, or Pugachev [26]. It is sometimes convenient to denote the orthogonal projection by

$$\bar{x}(t_1|t) \equiv x^*(t_1|t) = \hat{E}[x(t_1)|\mathcal{Y}(t)]$$

The notation $\hat{E}$ is motivated by part (*b*) of the theorem: If the stochastic processes in question are gaussian, then orthogonal projection is actually identical with conditional expectation.

Proof. (*A*) This is a direct consequence of the remarks in connection with (10).

(*B*) Since $x(t)$, $y(t)$ are random variables with zero mean, it is clear from formula (9) that the orthogonal part $\tilde{x}(t_1|t)$ of $x(t_1)$ with respect to the linear manifold $\mathcal{Y}(t)$ is also a random variable with zero mean. Orthogonal random variables with zero mean are uncorrelated; if they are also gaussian then (by Theorem 5 (*B*)) they are independent. Thus

$$\begin{aligned} 0 = E\tilde{x}(t_1|t) &= E[\tilde{x}(t_1|t)|y(t_0), \ldots, y(t)] \\ &= E[x(t_1) - \bar{x}(t_1|t)|y(t_0), \ldots, y(t)] \\ &= E[x(t_1)|y(t_0), \ldots, y(t)] - \bar{x}(t_1|t) = 0 \end{aligned}$$

Remarks. (*d*) A rigorous formulation of the contents of this section as $t \to \infty$ requires some elementary notions from the theory of Hilbert space. See Doob [15] and Loève [16].

(*e*) The physical interpretation of Theorem 2 is largely a matter of taste. If we are not worried about the assumption of gaussianness, part (*A*) shows that the orthogonal projection is the optimal estimate for all reasonable loss functions. If we do worry about gaussianness, even if we are resigned to consider only linear estimates, we know that orthogonal projections are *not* the optimal estimate for many reasonable loss functions. Since in practice it is difficult to ascertain to what degree of approximation a random process of physical origin is gaussian, it is hard to decide whether Theorem 2 has very broad or very limited significance.

(*f*) Theorem 2 is immediately generalized for the case of vector-valued random variables. In fact, we define the linear manifold $\mathcal{Y}(t)$ generated by $\mathbf{y}(t_0), \ldots, \mathbf{y}(t)$ to be the set of all linear combinations

$$\sum_{i=t_0}^{t} \sum_{j=1}^{m} a_{ij}y_j(i)$$

of all m co-ordinates of each of the random vectors $\mathbf{y}(t_0), \ldots, \mathbf{y}(t)$. The rest of the story proceeds as before.

(*g*) Theorem 2 states in effect that the optimal estimate under conditions (*A*) or (*B*) is a linear combination of all previous observations. In other words, the optimal estimate can be regarded as the output of a linear filter, with the input being the actually occurring values of the observable random variables; Theorem 2 gives a way of computing the impulse response of the optimal filter. As pointed out before, knowledge of this impulse response is not a complete solution of the problem; for this reason, no explicit formulas for the calculation of the impulse response will be given.

Models for Random Processes

In dealing with physical phenomena, it is not sufficient to give an empirical description but one must have also some idea of the underlying causes. Without being able to separate in some sense causes and effects, i.e., without the assumption of causality, one can hardly hope for useful results.

It is a fairly generally accepted fact that primary macroscopic sources of random phenomena are independent gaussian processes.[5] A well-known example is the noise voltage produced in a resistor due to thermal agitation. In most cases, *observed* random phenomena are not describable by independent random variables. The statistical dependence (correlation) between random signals observed at different times is usually explained by the presence of a dynamic system between the primary random source and the observer. *Thus a random function of time may be thought of as the output of a dynamic system excited by an independent gaussian random process.*

An important property of gaussian random signals is that they remain gaussian after passing through a linear system (Theorem 5(*A*)). Assuming independent gaussian primary random sources, if the observed random signal is also gaussian, we may assume that the dynamic system between the observer and the primary source is *linear*. This conclusion may be forced on us also because of lack of detailed knowledge of the statistical properties of the observed random signal: Given any random process with known first and second-order averages, we can find a gaussian random process with the same properties (Theorem 5(*C*)). Thus gaussian distributions and linear dynamics are natural, mutually plausible assumptions particularly when the statistical data are scant.

How is a dynamic system (linear or nonlinear) described? The fundamental concept is the notion of the *state*. By this is meant, intuitively, some quantitative information (a set of numbers, a function, etc.) which is the least amount of data one has to know about the past behavior of the system in order to predict its future behavior. The dynamics is then described in terms of *state transitions*, i.e., one must specify how one state is transformed into another as time passes.

A *linear* dynamic system may be described in general by the vector differential equation

$$\left.\begin{aligned} d\mathbf{x}/dt &= \mathsf{F}(t)\mathbf{x} + \mathsf{D}(t)\mathbf{u}(t) \\ \text{and} \qquad & \\ \mathbf{y}(t) &= \mathsf{M}(t)\mathbf{x}(t) \end{aligned}\right\} \qquad (12)$$

where $\mathbf{x}$ is an n-vector, the *state* of the system (the components x_i of $\mathbf{x}$ are called *state variables*); $\mathbf{u}(t)$ is an m-vector ($m \leqq n$) representing the *inputs* to the system; $\mathsf{F}(t)$ and $\mathsf{D}(t)$ are $n \times n$, respectively, $n \times m$ matrices. If all coefficients of $\mathsf{F}(t)$, $\mathsf{D}(t)$, $\mathsf{M}(t)$ are constants, we say that the dynamic system (12) is *time-invariant* or *stationary*. Finally, $\mathbf{y}(t)$ is a p-vector denoting the outputs of the system; $\mathsf{M}(t)$ is an $n \times p$ matrix; $p \leqq n$.

The physical interpretation of (12) has been discussed in detail elsewhere [18, 20, 23]. A look at the block diagram in Fig. 1 may be helpful. This is not an ordinary but a matrix block diagram (as revealed by the fat lines indicating signal flow). The integrator in Fig. 1 actually stands for n integrators such that the output of each is a state variable; $\mathsf{F}(t)$ indicates how the outputs of the integrators are fed back to the inputs of the integrators. Thus $f_{ij}(t)$ is the coefficient with which the output of the jth integrator is fed back to the input of the ith integrator. It is not hard to relate this formalism to more conventional methods of linear system analysis.

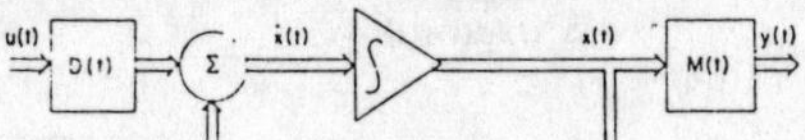

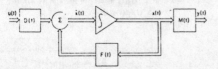

Fig. 1 Matrix block diagram of the general linear continuous-dynamic system

If we assume that the system (12) is stationary and that $\mathbf{u}(t)$ is constant during each sampling period, that is

$$\mathbf{u}(t + \tau) = \mathbf{u}(t); \ 0 \leqq \tau < 1, \quad t = 0, 1, \ldots \qquad (13)$$

then (12) can be readily transformed into the more convenient discrete form

$$\mathbf{x}(t + 1) = \mathbf{\Phi}(1)\mathbf{x}(t) + \mathbf{\Delta}(1)\mathbf{u}(t); \ t = 0, 1, \ldots$$

where [18, 20]

$$\mathbf{\Phi}(1) = \exp \mathsf{F} = \sum_{i=0}^{\infty} \mathsf{F}^i/i! \quad (\mathsf{F}^0 = \text{unit matrix})$$

and

$$\mathbf{\Delta}(1) = \left(\int_0^1 \exp \mathsf{F}\tau d\tau\right) \mathsf{D}$$

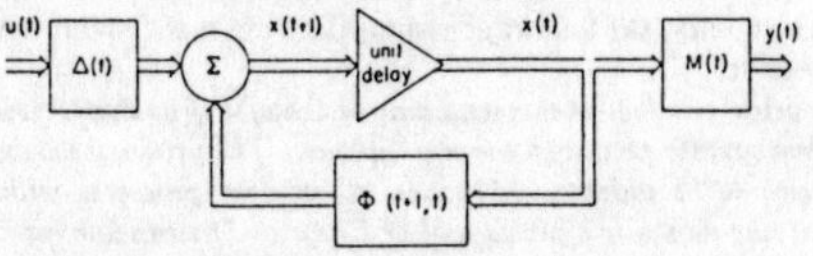

Fig. 2 Matrix block diagram of the general linear discrete-dynamic system

See Fig. 2. One could also express *exp* $\mathsf{F}\tau$ in closed form using Laplace transform methods [18, 20, 22, 24]. If $\mathbf{u}(t)$ satisfies (13) but the system (12) is nonstationary, we can write analogously

$$\left.\begin{aligned} \mathbf{x}(t + 1) &= \mathbf{\Phi}(t + 1; \ t) + \mathbf{\Delta}(t)\mathbf{u}(t) \\ \mathbf{y}(t) &= \mathsf{M}(t)\mathbf{x}(t) \end{aligned}\right\} \ t = 0, 1, \ldots \qquad (14)$$

but of course now $\mathbf{\Phi}(t + 1; \ t)$, $\mathbf{\Delta}(t)$ cannot be expressed in general in closed form. Equations of type (14) are encountered frequently also in the study of complicated sampled-data systems [22]. See Fig. 2.

$\mathbf{\Phi}(t + 1; \ t)$ is the *transition matrix* of the system (12) or (14). The notation $\mathbf{\Phi}(t_2; \ t_1)$ (t_2, t_1 = integers) indicates transition from time t_1 to time t_2. Evidently $\mathbf{\Phi}(t; \ t) = \mathsf{I}$ = unit matrix. If the system (12) is stationary then $\mathbf{\Phi}(t + 1; \ t) = \mathbf{\Phi}(t + 1 - t) = \mathbf{\Phi}(1)$ = const. Note also the product rule: $\mathbf{\Phi}(t; \ s)\mathbf{\Phi}(s; \ r) = \mathbf{\Phi}(t; \ r)$ and the inverse rule $\mathbf{\Phi}^{-1}(t; \ s) = \mathbf{\Phi}(s; \ t)$, where t, s, r are integers. In a stationary system, $\mathbf{\Phi}(t; \ \tau) = \exp \mathsf{F}(t - \tau)$.

As a result of the preceding discussion, we shall represent random phenomena by the model

$$\mathbf{x}(t + 1) = \mathbf{\Phi}(t + 1; \ t)\mathbf{x}(t) + \mathbf{u}(t) \qquad (15)$$

where $\{\mathbf{u}(t)\}$ is a vector-valued, independent, gaussian random process, with zero mean, which is completely described by (in view of Theorem 5(*C*))

$$Eu(t) = 0 \text{ for all } t;$$

$$Eu(t)\mathbf{u}'(s) = 0 \quad \text{if} \quad t \neq s$$

$$Eu(t)\mathbf{u}'(t) = \mathsf{G}(t).$$

Of course (Theorem 5(*A*)), $\mathbf{x}(t)$ is then also a gaussian random process with zero mean, but it is no longer independent. In fact, if we consider (15) in the steady state (assuming it is a stable system), in other words, if we neglect the initial state $\mathbf{x}(t_0)$, then

[5] The probability distributions will be gaussian because macroscopic random effects may be thought of as the superposition of very many microscopic random effects; under very general conditions, such aggregate effects tend to be gaussian, regardless of the statistical properties of the microscopic effects. The assumption of independence in this context is motivated by the fact that microscopic phenomena tend to take place much more rapidly than macroscopic phenomena; thus primary random sources would appear to be independent on a macroscopic time scale.

$$\mathbf{x}(t) = \sum_{r=-\infty}^{t-1} \mathbf{\Phi}(t;\ r+1)\mathbf{u}(r).$$

Therefore if $t \geqq s$ we have

$$E\mathbf{x}(t)\mathbf{x}'(s) = \sum_{r=-\infty}^{s-1} \mathbf{\Phi}(t;\ r+1)\mathbf{Q}(r)\mathbf{\Phi}'(s;\ r+1).$$

Thus if we assume a linear dynamic model and know the statistical properties of the gaussian random excitation, it is easy to find the corresponding statistical properties of the gaussian random process $\{\mathbf{x}(t)\}$.

In real life, however, the situation is usually reversed. One is given the covariance matrix $E\mathbf{x}(t)\mathbf{x}'(s)$ (or rather, one attempts to estimate the matrix from limited statistical data) and the problem is to get (15) and the statistical properties of $\mathbf{u}(t)$. This is a subtle and presently largely unsolved problem in experimentation and data reduction. As in the vast majority of the engineering literature on the Wiener problem, we shall find it convenient to start with the model (15) and regard the problem of obtaining the model itself as a separate question. To be sure, the two problems *should* be optimized jointly if possible; the author is not aware, however, of any study of the *joint* optimization problem.

In summary, the following assumptions are made about random processes:

Physical random phenomena may be thought of as due to primary random sources exciting dynamic systems. The primary sources are assumed to be independent gaussian random processes with zero mean; the dynamic systems will be linear. The random processes are therefore described by models such as (15). The question of how the numbers specifying the model are obtained from experimental data will not be considered.

Solution of the Wiener Problem

Let us now define the principal problem of the paper.

Problem I. *Consider the dynamic model*

$$\mathbf{x}(t+1) = \mathbf{\Phi}(t+1;\ t)\mathbf{x}(t) + \mathbf{u}(t) \tag{16}$$

$$\mathbf{y}(t) = \mathbf{M}(t)\mathbf{x}(t) \tag{17}$$

where $\mathbf{u}(t)$ is an independent gaussian random process of n-vectors with zero mean, $\mathbf{x}(t)$ is an n-vector, $\mathbf{y}(t)$ is a p-vector ($p \leqq n$), $\mathbf{\Phi}(t+1;\ t)$, $\mathbf{M}(t)$ are $n \times n$, resp. $p \times n$, matrices whose elements are nonrandom functions of time.

Given the observed values of $\mathbf{y}(t_0), \ldots, \mathbf{y}(t)$ find an estimate $\mathbf{x}^*(t_1|t)$ of $\mathbf{x}(t_1)$ which minimizes the expected loss. (See Fig. 2, where $\mathbf{\Delta}(t) = \mathbf{I}$.)

This problem includes as a special case the problems of filtering, prediction, and data smoothing mentioned earlier. It includes also the problem of reconstructing all the state variables of a linear dynamic system from noisy observations of some of the state variables ($p < n!$).

From Theorem 2-*a* we know that the solution of Problem I is simply the orthogonal projection of $\mathbf{x}(t_1)$ on the linear manifold $\mathcal{Y}(t)$ generated by the observed random variables. As remarked in the Introduction, this is to be accomplished by means of a linear (not necessarily stationary!) dynamic system of the general form (14). With this in mind, we proceed as follows.

Assume that $\mathbf{y}(t_0), \ldots, \mathbf{y}(t-1)$ have been measured, i.e., that $\mathcal{Y}(t-1)$ is known. Next, at time t, the random variable $\mathbf{y}(t)$ is measured. As before let $\tilde{\mathbf{y}}(t|t-1)$ be the component of $\mathbf{y}(t)$ orthogonal to $\mathcal{Y}(t-1)$. If $\tilde{\mathbf{y}}(t|t-1) \equiv 0$, which means that the values of all components of this random vector are zero for almost every possible event, then $\mathcal{Y}(t)$ is obviously the same as $\mathcal{Y}(t-1)$ and therefore the measurement of $\mathbf{y}(t)$ does not convey any additional information. This is not likely to happen in a physically meaningful situation. In any case, $\tilde{\mathbf{y}}(t|t-1)$ generates a linear manifold (possibly 0) which we denote by $\mathcal{Z}(t)$. By definition, $\mathcal{Y}(t-1)$ and $\mathcal{Z}(t)$ taken together are the same manifold as $\mathcal{Y}(t)$, and every vector in $\mathcal{Z}(t)$ is orthogonal to every vector in $\mathcal{Y}(t-1)$.

Assuming by induction that $\mathbf{x}^*(t_1 - 1|t-1)$ is known, we can write:

$$\begin{aligned}\mathbf{x}^*(t_1|t) &= \hat{E}[\mathbf{x}(t_1)|\mathcal{Y}(t)] = \hat{E}[\mathbf{x}(t_1)|\mathcal{Y}(t-1)] + \hat{E}[\mathbf{x}(t_1)|\mathcal{Z}(t)] \\ &= \mathbf{\Phi}(t+1;\ t)\mathbf{x}^*(t_1 - 1|t-1) + \hat{E}[\mathbf{u}(t_1 - 1)|\mathcal{Y}(t-1)] \\ &\qquad + \hat{E}[\mathbf{x}(t_1)|\mathcal{Z}(t)]\end{aligned} \tag{18}$$

where the last line is obtained using (16).

Let $t_1 = t + s$, where s is any integer. If $s \geqq 0$, then $\mathbf{u}(t_1 - 1)$ is independent of $\mathcal{Y}(t-1)$. This is because $\mathbf{u}(t_1 - 1) = \mathbf{u}(t + s - 1)$ is then independent of $\mathbf{u}(t-2), \mathbf{u}(t-3), \ldots$ and therefore by (16–17), independent of $\mathbf{y}(t_0), \ldots, \mathbf{y}(t-1)$, hence independent of $\mathcal{Y}(t-1)$. Since, for all t, $\mathbf{u}(t_0)$ has zero mean by assumption, it follows that $\mathbf{u}(t_1 - 1)$ ($s \geqq 0$) is orthogonal to $\mathcal{Y}(t-1)$. Thus if $s \geqq 0$, the second term on the right-hand side of (18) vanishes; if $s < 0$, considerable complications result in evaluating this term. We shall consider only the case $t_1 \geqq t$. Furthermore, it will suffice to consider in detail only the case $t_1 = t + 1$ since the other cases can be easily reduced to this one.

The last term in (18) must be a linear operation on the random variable $\tilde{\mathbf{y}}(t|t-1)$:

$$\hat{E}[\mathbf{x}(t+1)\,|\,\mathcal{Z}(t)] = \mathbf{\Delta}^*(t)\tilde{\mathbf{y}}(t\,|\,t-1) \tag{19}$$

where $\mathbf{\Delta}^*(t)$ is an $n \times p$ matrix, and the star refers to "optimal filtering."

The component of $\mathbf{y}(t)$ lying in $\mathcal{Y}(t-1)$ is $\bar{\mathbf{y}}(t|t-1) = \mathbf{M}(t)\mathbf{x}^*(t|t-1)$. Hence

$$\tilde{\mathbf{y}}(t|t-1) = \mathbf{y}(t) - \bar{\mathbf{y}}(t|t-1) = \mathbf{y}(t) - \mathbf{M}(t)\mathbf{x}^*(t|t-1) \tag{20}$$

Combining (18–20) (see Fig. 3) we obtain

$$\mathbf{x}^*(t+1|t) = \mathbf{\Phi}^*(t+1;\ t)\mathbf{x}^*(t|t-1) + \mathbf{\Delta}^*(t)\mathbf{y}(t) \tag{21}$$

where

$$\mathbf{\Phi}^*(t+1;\ t) = \mathbf{\Phi}(t+1;\ t) - \mathbf{\Delta}^*(t)\mathbf{M}(t) \tag{22}$$

Thus optimal estimation is performed by a linear dynamic system of the same form as (14). The state of the estimator is the previous estimate, the input is the last measured value of the observable random variable $\mathbf{y}(t)$, the transition matrix is given by (22). Notice that physical realization of the optimal filter requires only (*i*) the model of the random process (*ii*) the operator $\mathbf{\Delta}^*(t)$.

The estimation error is also governed by a linear dynamic system. In fact,

$$\begin{aligned}\tilde{\mathbf{x}}(t+1|t) &= \mathbf{x}(t+1) - \mathbf{x}^*(t+1|t) \\ &= \mathbf{\Phi}(t+1;\ t)\mathbf{x}(t) + \mathbf{u}(t) - \mathbf{\Phi}^*(t+1;\ t)\mathbf{x}^*(t|t-1) \\ &\qquad - \mathbf{\Delta}^*(t)\mathbf{M}(t)\mathbf{x}(t)\end{aligned}$$

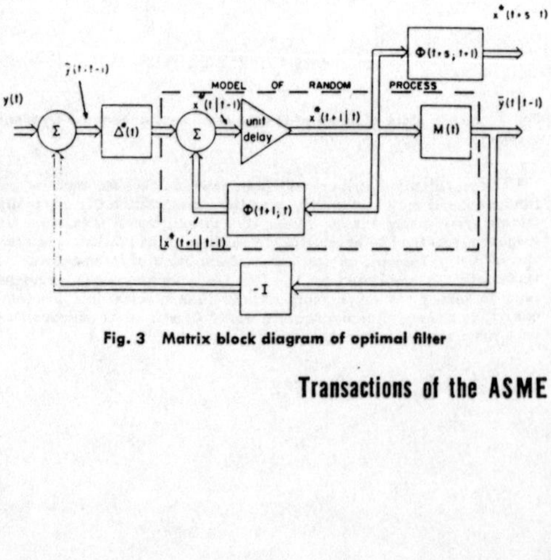

Fig. 3 Matrix block diagram of optimal filter

$$= \mathbf{\Phi}^*(t+1;\; t)\tilde{\mathbf{x}}(t|t-1) + \mathbf{u}(t) \qquad (23)$$

Thus $\mathbf{\Phi}^*$ is also the transition matrix of the linear dynamic system governing the error.

From (23) we obtain at once a recursion relation for the covariance matrix $\mathbf{P}^*(t)$ of the optimal error $\tilde{\mathbf{x}}(t|t-1)$. Noting that $\mathbf{u}(t)$ is independent of $\mathbf{x}(t)$ and therefore of $\tilde{\mathbf{x}}(t|t-1)$, we get

$$\mathbf{P}^*(t+1) = E\tilde{\mathbf{x}}(t+1|t)\tilde{\mathbf{x}}'(t+1|t)$$
$$= \mathbf{\Phi}^*(t+1;\; t)E\tilde{\mathbf{x}}(t|t-1)\tilde{\mathbf{x}}'(t|t-1)\mathbf{\Phi}^{*\prime}(t+1;\; t) + \mathbf{Q}(t)$$
$$= \mathbf{\Phi}^*(t+1;\; t)E\tilde{\mathbf{x}}(t|t-1)\tilde{\mathbf{x}}'(t|t-1)\mathbf{\Phi}'(t+1;\; t) + \mathbf{Q}(t)$$
$$= \mathbf{\Phi}^*(t+1;\; t)\mathbf{P}^*(t)\mathbf{\Phi}'(t+1;\; t) + \mathbf{Q}(t) \qquad (24)$$

where $\mathbf{Q}(t) = E\mathbf{u}(t)\mathbf{u}'(t)$.

There remains the problem of obtaining an explicit formula for $\mathbf{\Delta}^*$ (and thus also for $\mathbf{\Phi}^*$). Since,

$$\tilde{\mathbf{x}}(t+1|\mathcal{Z}(t)) = \mathbf{x}(t+1) - \hat{E}[\mathbf{x}(t+1)|\mathcal{Z}(t)]$$

is orthogonal to $\tilde{\mathbf{y}}(t|t-1)$, it follows by (19) that

$$0 = E[\mathbf{x}(t+1) - \mathbf{\Delta}^*(t)\tilde{\mathbf{y}}(t|t-1)]\tilde{\mathbf{y}}'(t|t-1)$$
$$= E\mathbf{x}(t+1)\tilde{\mathbf{y}}'(t|t-1) - \mathbf{\Delta}^*(t)E\tilde{\mathbf{y}}(t|t-1)\tilde{\mathbf{y}}'(t|t-1).$$

Noting that $\tilde{\mathbf{x}}(t+1|t-1)$ is orthogonal to $\mathcal{Z}(t)$, the definition of $\mathbf{P}(t)$ given earlier, and (17), it follows further

$$0 = E\tilde{\mathbf{x}}(t+1|t-1)\tilde{\mathbf{y}}'(t|t-1) - \mathbf{\Delta}^*(t)\mathbf{M}(t)\mathbf{P}^*(t)\mathbf{M}'(t)$$
$$= E[\mathbf{\Phi}(t+1;\; t)\tilde{\mathbf{x}}(t|t-1) + \mathbf{u}(t|t-1)]\tilde{\mathbf{x}}'(t|t-1)\mathbf{M}'(t)$$
$$- \mathbf{\Delta}^*(t)\mathbf{M}(t)\mathbf{P}^*(t)\mathbf{M}'(t).$$

Finally, since $\mathbf{u}(t)$ is independent of $\mathbf{x}(t)$,

$$0 = \mathbf{\Phi}(t+1;\; t)\mathbf{P}^*(t)\mathbf{M}'(t) - \mathbf{\Delta}^*(t)\mathbf{M}(t)\mathbf{P}^*(t)\mathbf{M}'(t).$$

Now the matrix $\mathbf{M}(t)\mathbf{P}^*(t)\mathbf{M}'(t)$ will be positive definite and hence invertible whenever $\mathbf{P}^*(t)$ is positive definite, provided that none of the rows of $\mathbf{M}(t)$ are linearly dependent at any time, in other words, that none of the observed scalar random variables $y_1(t)$, . . ., $y_m(t)$ is a linear combination of the others. Under these circumstances we get finally:

$$\mathbf{\Delta}^*(t) = \mathbf{\Phi}(t+1;\; t)\mathbf{P}^*(t)\mathbf{M}'(t)[\mathbf{M}(t)\mathbf{P}^*(t)\mathbf{M}'(t)]^{-1} \qquad (25)$$

Since observations start at t_0, $\tilde{\mathbf{x}}(t_0|t_0-1) = \mathbf{x}(t_0)$; to begin the iterative evaluation of $\mathbf{P}^*(t)$ by means of equation (24), we must obviously specify $\mathbf{P}^*(t_0) = E\mathbf{x}(t_0)\mathbf{x}'(t_0)$. Assuming this matrix is positive definite, equation (25) then yields $\mathbf{\Delta}^*(t_0)$; equation (22) $\mathbf{\Phi}^*(t_0+1;\; t_0)$, and equation (24) $\mathbf{P}^*(t_0+1)$, completing the cycle. If now $\mathbf{Q}(t)$ is positive definite, then all the $\mathbf{P}^*(t)$ will be positive definite and the requirements in deriving (25) will be satisfied at each step.

Now we remove the restriction that $t_1 = t + 1$. Since $\mathbf{u}(t)$ is orthogonal to $\mathcal{Y}(t)$, we have

$$\mathbf{x}^*(t+1|t) = \hat{E}[\mathbf{\Phi}(t+1;\; t)\mathbf{x}(t) + \mathbf{u}(t)|\mathcal{Y}(t)] = \mathbf{\Phi}(t+1;\; t)\mathbf{x}^*(t|t)$$

Hence if $\mathbf{\Phi}(t+1;\; t)$ has an inverse $\mathbf{\Phi}(t;\; t+1)$ (which is always the case when $\mathbf{\Phi}$ is the transition matrix of a dynamic system describable by a differential equation) we have

$$\mathbf{x}^*(t|t) = \mathbf{\Phi}(t;\; t+1)\mathbf{x}^*(t+1|t)$$

If $t_1 \geqq t+1$, we first observe by repeated application of (16) that

$$\mathbf{x}(t+s) = \mathbf{\Phi}(t+s;\; t+1)\mathbf{x}(t+1)$$
$$+ \sum_{r1}^{s-1} \mathbf{\Phi}(t+s;\; t+r)\mathbf{u}(t+r) \qquad (s \geqq 1)$$

Since $\mathbf{u}(t+s-1)$, . . ., $\mathbf{u}(t+1)$ are all orthogonal to $\mathcal{Y}(t)$,

$$\mathbf{x}^*(t+s|t) = \hat{E}[\mathbf{x}(t+s)|\mathcal{Y}(t)]$$
$$= \hat{E}[\mathbf{\Phi}(t+s;\; t+1)\mathbf{x}(t+1)\,|\mathcal{Y}(t)]$$
$$= \mathbf{\Phi}(t+s;\; t+1)\mathbf{x}^*(t+1|t) \qquad (s \geqq 1)$$

If $s < 0$, the results are similar, but $\mathbf{x}^*(t-s|t)$ will have $(1-s)(n-p)$ co-ordinates.

The results of this section may be summarized as follows:

Theorem 3. (*Solution of the Wiener Problem*)

Consider Problem I. The optimal estimate $\mathbf{x}^*(t+1|t)$ *of* $\mathbf{x}(t+1)$ *given* $\mathbf{y}(t_0)$, . . ., $\mathbf{y}(t)$ *is generated by the linear dynamic system*

$$\mathbf{x}^*(t+1|t) = \mathbf{\Phi}^*(t+1;\; t)\mathbf{x}^*(t|t-1) + \mathbf{\Delta}^*(t)\mathbf{y}(t) \qquad (21)$$

The estimation error is given by

$$\tilde{\mathbf{x}}(t+1|t) = \mathbf{\Phi}^*(t+1;\; t)\tilde{\mathbf{x}}(t|t-1) + \mathbf{u}(t) \qquad (23)$$

The covariance matrix of the estimation error is

$$\text{cov}\ \tilde{\mathbf{x}}(t|t-1) = E\tilde{\mathbf{x}}(t|t-1)\tilde{\mathbf{x}}'(t|t-1) = \mathbf{P}^*(t) \qquad (26)$$

The expected quadratic loss is

$$\sum_{i=1}^{n} E\tilde{x}_i^2(t|t-1) = \text{trace}\ \mathbf{P}^*(t) \qquad (27)$$

The matrices $\mathbf{\Delta}^*(t)$, $\mathbf{\Phi}^*(t+1;\; t)$, $\mathbf{P}^*(t)$ *are generated by the recursion relations*

$$\left.\begin{aligned} &\mathbf{\Delta}^*(t) = \mathbf{\Phi}(t+1;\; t)\mathbf{P}^*(t)\mathbf{M}'(t)[\mathbf{M}(t)\mathbf{P}^*(t)\mathbf{M}'(t)]^{-1} && (28)\\ &\mathbf{\Phi}^*(t+1;\; t) = \mathbf{\Phi}(t+1;\; t) - \mathbf{\Delta}^*(t)\mathbf{M}(t) && (29)\\ &\mathbf{P}^*(t+1) = \mathbf{\Phi}^*(t+1;\; t)\mathbf{P}^*(t)\mathbf{\Phi}'(t+1;\; t) + \mathbf{Q}(t) && (30)\end{aligned}\right\} t \geqq t_0$$

In order to carry out the iterations, one must specify the covariance $\mathbf{P}^*(t_0)$ *of* $\mathbf{x}(t_0)$ *and the covariance* $\mathbf{Q}(t)$ *of* $\mathbf{u}(t)$. *Finally, for any* $s \geqq 0$, *if* $\mathbf{\Phi}$ *is invertible*

$$\mathbf{x}^*(t+s|t) = \mathbf{\Phi}(t+s;\; t+1)\mathbf{x}^*(t+1|t)$$
$$= \mathbf{\Phi}(t+s;\; t+1)\mathbf{\Phi}^*(t+1;\; t)\mathbf{\Phi}(t;\; t+s-1)$$
$$\times\, \mathbf{x}^*(t+s-1|t-1)$$
$$+ \mathbf{\Phi}(t+s;\; t+1)\mathbf{\Delta}^*(t)\mathbf{y}(t) \qquad (31)$$

so that the estimate $\mathbf{x}^*(t+s|t)$ $(s \geqq 0)$ *is also given by a linear dynamic system of the type* (21).

Remarks. (*h*) Eliminating $\mathbf{\Delta}^*$ and $\mathbf{\Phi}^*$ from (28–30), a nonlinear difference equation is obtained for $\mathbf{P}^*(t)$:

$$\mathbf{P}^*(t+1) = \mathbf{\Phi}(t+1;\; t)\{\mathbf{P}^*(t) - \mathbf{P}^*(t)\mathbf{M}'(t)[\mathbf{M}(t)\mathbf{P}^*(t)\mathbf{M}'(t)]^{-1}$$
$$\times\, \mathbf{P}^*(t)\mathbf{M}(t)\}\mathbf{\Phi}'(t+1;\; t) + \mathbf{Q}(t) \qquad (t \geqq t_0) \qquad (32)$$

This equation is linear only if $\mathbf{M}(t)$ is invertible but then the problem is trivial since all components of the random vector $\mathbf{x}(t)$ are observable $\mathbf{P}^*(t+1) = \mathbf{Q}(t)$. Observe that equation (32) plays a role in the present theory analogous to that of the Wiener-Hopf equation in the conventional theory.

Once $\mathbf{P}^*(t)$ has been computed via (32) starting at $t = t_0$, the explicit specification of the optimal linear filter is immediately available from formulas (29–30). Of course, the solution of Equation (32), or of its differential-equation equivalent, is a much simpler task than solution of the Wiener-Hopf equation.

(*i*) The results stated in Theorem 3 do not resolve completely Problem I. Little has been said, for instance, about the physical significance of the assumptions needed to obtain equation (25), the convergence and stability of the nonlinear difference equation (32), the stability of the optimal filter (21), etc. This can actually be done in a completely satisfactory way, but must be left to a future paper. In this connection, the principal guide and tool turns out to be the duality theorem mentioned briefly in the next section. See [29].

(*j*) By letting the sampling period (equal to one so far) approach zero, the method can be used to obtain the specification of a differential equation for the optimal filter. To do this, i.e., to pass from equation (14) to equation (12), requires computing the logarithm $\mathbf{F}^*$ of the matrix $\mathbf{\Phi}^*$. But this can be done only if $\mathbf{\Phi}^*$ is nonsingular—which is easily seen *not* to be the case. This is because it is sufficient for the optimal filter to have $n - p$ state variables, rather than n, as the formalism of equation (22) would seem to imply. By appropriate modifications, therefore, equation (22) can be reduced to an equivalent set of only $n - p$ equations whose transition matrix is nonsingular. Details of this type will be covered in later publications.

(*k*) The dynamic system (21) is, in general, nonstationary. This is due to two things: (1) The time dependence of $\mathbf{\Phi}(t+1;t)$ and $\mathbf{M}(t)$; (2) the fact that the estimation starts at $t = t_0$ and improves as more data are accumulated. If $\mathbf{\Phi}$, $\mathbf{M}$ are constants, it can be shown that (21) becomes a stationary dynamic system in the limit $t \to \infty$. This is the case treated by the classical Wiener theory.

(*l*) It is noteworthy that the derivations given are not affected by the nonstationarity of the model for $\mathbf{x}(t)$ or the finiteness of available data. In fact, as far as the author is aware, the only explicit recursion relations given before for the growing-memory filter are due to Blum [12]. However, his results are much more complicated than ours.

(*m*) By inspection of Fig. 3 we see that the optimal filter is a feedback system, and that the signal after the first summer is white noise since $\tilde{\mathbf{y}}(t|t-1)$ is obviously an orthogonal random process. This corresponds to some well-known results in Wiener filtering, see, e.g., Smith [28], Chapter 6, Fig. 6-4. However, this is apparently the first *rigorous* proof that every Wiener filter is realizable by means of a feedback system. Moreover, it will be shown in another paper that such a filter is always *stable*, under very mild assumptions on the model (16-17). See [29].

The Dual Problem

Let us now consider another problem which is conceptually very different from optimal estimation, namely, the noise-free regulator problem. In the simplest cases, this is:

Problem II. *Consider the dynamic system*

$$\mathbf{x}(t+1) = \hat{\mathbf{\Phi}}(t+1;\, t)\mathbf{x}(t) + \hat{\mathbf{M}}(t)\mathbf{u}(t) \qquad (33)$$

where $\mathbf{x}(t)$ is an n-vector, $\mathbf{u}(t)$ is an m-vector ($m \leqq n$), $\hat{\mathbf{\Phi}}$, $\hat{\mathbf{M}}$ are $n \times n$ resp. $n \times m$ matrices whose elements are nonrandom functions of time. Given any state $\mathbf{x}(t)$ at time t, we are to find a sequence $\mathbf{u}(t), \ldots, \mathbf{u}(T)$ of control vectors which minimizes the performance index

$$V[\mathbf{x}(t)] = \sum_{\tau=t}^{T+1} \mathbf{x}'(\tau)\mathbf{Q}(\tau)\mathbf{x}(\tau)$$

where $\hat{\mathbf{Q}}(t)$ is a positive definite matrix whose elements are nonrandom functions of time. See Fig. 2, where $\mathbf{\Delta} = \hat{\mathbf{M}}$ and $\mathbf{M} = \mathbf{I}$.

Probabilistic considerations play no part in Problem II; it is implicitly assumed that every state variable can be measured exactly at each instant $t, t+1, \ldots, T$. It is customary to call $T \geqq t$ the *terminal time* (it may be infinity).

The first general solution of the noise-free regulator problem is due to the author [18]. The main result is that the optimal control vectors $\mathbf{u}^*(t)$ are nonstationary linear functions of $\mathbf{x}(t)$. After a change in notation, the formulas of the Appendix, Reference [18] (see also Reference [23]) are as follows:

$$\mathbf{u}^*(t) = -\hat{\mathbf{\Delta}}^*(t)\mathbf{x}(t) \qquad (34)$$

Under optimal control as given by (34), the "closed-loop" equations for the system are (see Fig. 4)

$$\mathbf{x}(t+1) = \hat{\mathbf{\Phi}}^*(t+1;\, t)\mathbf{x}(t)$$

and the minimum performance index at time t is given by

$$V^*[\mathbf{x}(t)] = \mathbf{x}'(t)\mathbf{P}^*(t-1)\mathbf{x}(t)$$

The matrices $\hat{\mathbf{\Delta}}^*(t)$, $\hat{\mathbf{\Phi}}^*(t+1;\, t)$, $\hat{\mathbf{P}}^*(t)$ are determined by the recursion relations:

$$\left.\begin{aligned} \hat{\mathbf{\Delta}}^*(t) &= [\hat{\mathbf{M}}'(t)\hat{\mathbf{P}}^*(t)\hat{\mathbf{M}}(t)]^{-1}\hat{\mathbf{M}}'(t)\hat{\mathbf{P}}^*(t)\hat{\mathbf{\Phi}}(t+1;\, t) & (35)\\ \hat{\mathbf{\Phi}}^*(t+1;\, t) &= \hat{\mathbf{\Phi}}(t+1;\, t) - \hat{\mathbf{M}}(t)\hat{\mathbf{\Delta}}^*(t) & (36)\\ \hat{\mathbf{P}}^*(t-1) &= \hat{\mathbf{\Phi}}'(t+1;t)\hat{\mathbf{P}}^*(t)\hat{\mathbf{\Phi}}^*(t+1;\, t) + \hat{\mathbf{Q}}(t) & (37) \end{aligned}\right\} t \leqq T$$

Initially we must set $\hat{\mathbf{P}}^*(T) = \hat{\mathbf{Q}}(T+1)$.

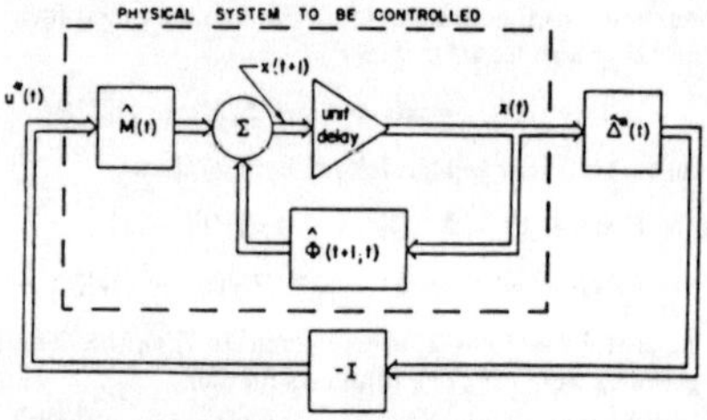

Fig. 4 Matrix block diagram of optimal controller

Comparing equations (35-37) with (28-30) and Fig. 3 with Fig. 4 we notice some interesting things which are expressed precisely by

Theorem 4. (*Duality Theorem*) *Problem I and Problem II are duals of each other in the following sense:*

Let $\tau \geqq 0$. Replace every matrix $\mathbf{X}(t) = \mathbf{X}(t_0 + \tau)$ in (28-30) by $\hat{\mathbf{X}}'(t) = \hat{\mathbf{X}}'(T - \tau)$. Then one has (35-37). Conversely, replace every matrix $\hat{\mathbf{X}}(T - \tau)$ in (35-37) by $\mathbf{X}'(t_0 + \tau)$. Then one has (28-30).

Proof. Carry out the substitutions. For ease of reference, the dualities between the two problems are given in detail in Table 1.

Table 1

	Problem I	Problem II
1	$\mathbf{x}(t)$ (unobservable) state variables of random process.	$\mathbf{x}(t)$ (observable) state variables of plant to be regulated.
2	$\mathbf{y}(t)$ observed random variables.	$\mathbf{u}(t)$ control variables.
3	t_0 first observation.	T last control action.
4	$\mathbf{\Phi}(t_0+\tau+1;\, t_0+\tau)$ transition matrix.	$\hat{\mathbf{\Phi}}(T-\tau+1;\, T-\tau)$ transition matrix.
5	$\mathbf{P}^*(t_0+\tau)$ covariance of optimized estimation error.	$\hat{\mathbf{P}}^*(T-\tau)$ matrix of quadratic form for performance index under optimal regulation.
6	$\mathbf{\Delta}^*(t_0+\tau)$ weighting of observation for optimal estimation.	$\hat{\mathbf{\Delta}}^*(T-\tau)$ weighting of state for optimal control.
7	$\mathbf{\Phi}^*(t_0+\tau+1;\, t_0+\tau)$ transition matrix for optimal estimation error.	$\hat{\mathbf{\Phi}}^*(T-\tau+1;\, T-\tau)$ transition matrix under optimal regulation.
8	$\mathbf{M}(t_0+\tau)$ effect of state on observation.	$\hat{\mathbf{M}}(T-\tau)$ effect of control vectors on state.
9	$\mathbf{Q}(t_0+\tau)$ covariance of random excitation.	$\hat{\mathbf{Q}}(T-\tau)$ matrix of quadratic form defining error criterion.

Remarks. (*n*) The *mathematical* significance of the duality between Problem I and Problem II is that both problems reduce to the solution of the Wiener-Hopf-like equation (32).

(*o*) The *physical* significance of the duality is intriguing. Why are observations and control dual quantities?

Recent research [29] has shown that the essence of the Duality Theorem lies in the duality of constraints at the output (represented by the matrix $\hat{\mathbf{M}}(t)$ in Problem I) and constraints at the input (represented by the matrix $\hat{\mathbf{M}}(t)$ in Problem II).

(p) Applications of Wiener's methods to the solution of noise-free regulator problem have been known for a long time; see the recent textbook of Newton, Gould, and Kaiser [27]. However, the connections between the two problems, and in particular the duality, have apparently never been stated precisely before.

(q) The duality theorem offers a powerful tool for developing more deeply the theory (as opposed to the computation) of Wiener filters, as mentioned in Remark (i). This will be published elsewhere [29].

Applications

The power of the new approach to the Wiener problem, as expressed by Theorem 3, is most obvious when the data of the problem are given in numerical form. In that case, one simply performs the numerical computations required by (28–30). Results of such calculations, in some cases of practical engineering interest, will be published elsewhere.

When the answers are desired in closed analytic form, the iterations (28–30) may lead to very unwieldy expressions. In a few cases, $\boldsymbol{\Delta}^*$ and $\boldsymbol{\Phi}^*$ can be put into "closed form." Without discussing here how (if at all) such closed forms can be obtained, we now give two examples indicative of the type of results to be expected.

Example 1. Consider the problem mentioned under "Optimal Estimates." Let $x_1(t)$ be the signal and $x_2(t)$ the noise. We assume the model:

$$x_1(t+1) = \phi_{11}(t+1;\, t)x_1(t) + u_1(t)$$

$$x_2(t+1) = u_2(t)$$

$$y_1(t) = x_1(t) + x_2(t)$$

The specific data for which we desire a solution of the estimation problem are as follows:

1 $t_1 = t + 1$; $t_0 = 0$
2 $Ex_1^2(0) = 0$, i.e., $x_1(0) = 0$
3 $Eu_1^2(t) = a^2$, $Eu^2_2(t) = b^2$, $Eu_1(t)u_2(t) = 0$ (for all t)
4 $\phi_{11}(t+1;\, t) = \phi_{11} = \text{const.}$

A simple calculation shows that the following matrices satisfy the difference equations (28–30), for all $t \geqq t_0$:

$$\boldsymbol{\Delta}^*(t) = \begin{bmatrix} \phi_{11}C(t) \\ 0 \end{bmatrix}$$

$$\boldsymbol{\Phi}^*(t+1;\, t) = \begin{bmatrix} \phi_{11}[1 - C(t)] & 0 \\ 0 & 0 \end{bmatrix}$$

$$\mathbf{P}^*(t+1) = \begin{bmatrix} a^2 + \phi_{11}^2b^2C(t) & 0 \\ 0 & b^2 \end{bmatrix}$$

where $$C(t+1) = 1 - \frac{b^2}{a^2 + b^2 + \phi_{11}^2b^2C(t)} \quad t \geqq 0 \qquad (38)$$

Since it was assumed that $x_1(0) = 0$, neither $x_1(1)$ nor $x_2(1)$ can be predicted from the measurement of $y_1(0)$. Hence the measurement at time $t = 0$ is useless, which shows that we should set $C(0) = 0$. This fact, with the iterations (38), completely determines the function $C(t)$. The nonlinear difference equation (38) plays the role of the Wiener-Hopf equation.

If $b^2/a^2 \ll 1$, then $C(t) \cong 1$ which is essentially pure prediction. If $b^2/a^2 \gg 1$, then $C(t) \cong 0$, and we depend mainly on $x_1^*(t|t-1)$ for the estimation of $x_1^*(t+1|t)$ and assign only very small weight to the measurement $y_1(t)$; this is what one would expect when the measured data are very noisy.

In any case, $x_2^*(t|t-1) = 0$ at all times; one cannot predict independent noise! This means that ϕ^*_{12} can be set equal to zero. The optimal predictor is a first-order dynamic system. See Remark (j).

To find the stationary Wiener filter, let $t = \infty$ on both sides of (38), solve the resulting quadratic equation in $C(\infty)$, etc.

Example 2. A number of particles leave the origin at time $t_0 = 0$ with random velocities; after $t = 0$, each particle moves with a constant (unknown) velocity. Suppose that the position of one of these particles is measured, the data being contaminated by stationary, additive, correlated noise. What is the optimal estimate of the position and velocity of the particle at the time of the last measurement?

Let $x_1(t)$ be the position and $x_2(t)$ the velocity of the particle; $x_3(t)$ is the noise. The problem is then represented by the model,

$$x_1(t+1) = x_1(t) + x_2(t)$$

$$x_2(t+1) = x_2(t)$$

$$x_3(t+1) = \phi_{33}(t+1;\, t)x_3(t) + u_3(t)$$

$$y_1(t) = x_1(t) + x_3(t)$$

and the additional conditions

1 $t_1 = t$; $t_0 = 0$
2 $Ex_1^2(0) = Ex_2(0) = 0$, $Ex_2^2(0) = a^2 > 0$;
3 $Eu_3(t) = 0$, $Eu_3^2(t) = b^2$.
4 $\phi_{33}(t+1;\, t) = \phi_{33} = \text{const.}$

According to Theorem 3, $\mathbf{x}^*(t|t)$ is calculated using the dynamic system (31).

First we solve the problem of predicting the position and velocity of the particle one step ahead. Simple considerations show that

$$\mathbf{P}^*(1) = \begin{bmatrix} a^2 & a^2 & 0 \\ a^2 & a^2 & 0 \\ 0 & 0 & b^2 \end{bmatrix} \quad \text{and} \quad \boldsymbol{\Delta}^*(0) = \begin{bmatrix} 0 \\ 0 \\ 1 \end{bmatrix}$$

It is then easy to check by substitution into equations (28–30) that

$$\mathbf{P}^*(t) = \frac{b^2}{C_1(t-1)} \times \begin{bmatrix} t^2 & t & -\phi_{33}t(t-1) \\ t & 1 & -\phi_{33}(t-1) \\ -\phi_{33}t(t-1) & -\phi_{33}(t-1) & \phi_{33}^2(t-1)^2 + C_1(t-1) \end{bmatrix}$$

is the correct expression for the covariance matrix of the prediction error $\tilde{\mathbf{x}}(t|t-1)$ for all $t \geqq 1$, provided that we define

$$C_1(0) = b^2/a^2$$
$$C_1(t) = C_1(t-1) + [t - \phi_{33}(t-1)]^2,\ t \geqq 1$$

It is interesting to note that the results just obtained are valid also when ϕ_{33} depends on t. This is true also in Example 1. In conventional treatments of such problems there *seems* to be an essential difference between the cases of stationary and nonstationary noise. This misleading impression created by the conventional theory is due to the very special *methods* used in solving the Wiener-Hopf equation.

Introducing the abbreviation

$$C_2(0) = 0$$
$$C_2(t) = t - \phi_{33}(t-1),\ t \geqq 1$$

and observing that

$$\text{cov}\ \tilde{\mathbf{x}}(t+1|t) = \mathbf{P}^*(t+1) = \boldsymbol{\Phi}(t+1;\, t)[\text{cov}\ \tilde{\mathbf{x}}(t|t)]\boldsymbol{\Phi}'(t+1;\, t) + \mathbf{Q}(t)$$

the matrices occurring in equation (31) and the covariance matrix of $\tilde{\mathbf{x}}(t|t)$ are found after simple calculations. We have, for all $t \geqq 0$,

$$\mathbf{\Phi}(t;\, t+1)\mathbf{\Delta}^*(t) = \frac{1}{C_1(t)}\begin{bmatrix} tC_2(t) \\ C_2(t) \\ C_1(t) - tC_2(t) \end{bmatrix}$$

$$\mathbf{\Phi}(t;\, t+1)\mathbf{\Phi}^*(t+1;\, t)\mathbf{\Phi}(t+1;\, t)$$

$$= \frac{1}{C_1(t)}\begin{bmatrix} C_1(t) - tC_2(t) & C_1(t) - tC_3(t) & -\phi_{33}tC_2(t) \\ -C_2(t) & C_1(t) - C_2(t) & -\phi_{33}C_2(t) \\ -C_1(t) + tC_2(t) & -C_1(t) + tC_2(t) & +\phi_{33}tC_2(t) \end{bmatrix}$$

and

$$\text{cov}\ \tilde{\mathbf{x}}(t|t) = E\tilde{\mathbf{x}}(t|t)\tilde{\mathbf{x}}'(t|t) = \frac{b^2}{C_1(t)}\begin{bmatrix} t^2 & t & -t^2 \\ t & 1 & -t \\ -t^2 & -t & t^2 \end{bmatrix}$$

To gain some insight into the behavior of this system, let us examine the limiting case $t \to \infty$ of a large number of observations. Then $C_1(t)$ obeys approximately the differential equation

$$dC_1(t)/dt \cong C_2^2(t) \qquad (t \gg 1)$$

from which we find

$$C_1(t) \cong (1 - \phi_{33})^2 t^3/3 + \phi_{33}(1 - \phi_{33})t^2 + \phi_{33}^2 t + b^2/a^2 \qquad (t \gg 1) \quad (39)$$

Using (39), we get further

$$\mathbf{\Phi}^{-1}\mathbf{\Phi}^*\mathbf{\Phi} \cong \begin{bmatrix} 1 & 1 & 0 \\ 0 & 1 & 0 \\ -1 & -1 & 0 \end{bmatrix} \text{ and } \mathbf{\Phi}^{-1}\mathbf{\Delta}^* \cong \begin{bmatrix} 0 \\ 0 \\ 1 \end{bmatrix} \qquad (t \gg 1)$$

Thus as the number of observations becomes large, we depend almost exclusively on $x_1^*(t|t)$ and $x_2^*(t|t)$ to estimate $x_1^*(t+1|t+1)$ and $x_2^*(t+1|t+1)$. Current observations are used almost exclusively to estimate the noise

$$x_3^*(t|t) \cong y_1(t) - x_1^*(t|t) \qquad (t \gg 1)$$

One would of course expect something like this since the problem is analogous to fitting a straight line to an increasing number of points.

As a second check on the reasonableness of the results given, observe that the case $t \gg 1$ is essentially the same as prediction based on continuous observations. Setting $\phi_{33} = 0$, we have

$$E\tilde{x}_1^2(t|t) \cong \frac{a^2b^2t^2}{b^2 + a^2t^3/3} \qquad (t \gg 1;\ \phi_{33} = 0)$$

which is identical with the result obtained by Shinbrot [11], Example 1, and Solodovnikov [14], Example 2, in their treatment of the Wiener problem in the finite-length, continuous-data case, using an approach entirely different from ours.

Conclusions

This paper formulates and solves the Wiener problem from the "state" point of view. On the one hand, this leads to a very general treatment including cases which cause difficulties when attacked by other methods. On the other hand, the Wiener problem is shown to be closely connected with other problems in the theory of control. Much remains to be done to exploit these connections.

References

1 N. Wiener, "The Extrapolation, Interpolation and Smoothing of Stationary Time Series," John Wiley & Sons, Inc., New York, N. Y., 1949.

2 L. A. Zadeh and J. R. Ragazzini, "An Extension of Wiener's Theory of Prediction," *Journal of Applied Physics*, vol. 21, 1950, pp. 645–655.

3 H. W. Bode and C. E. Shannon, "A Simplified Derivation of Linear Least-Squares Smoothing and Prediction Theory," *Proceedings IRE*, vol. 38, 1950, pp. 417–425.

4 R. C. Booton, "An Optimization Theory for Time-Varying Linear Systems With Nonstationary Statistical Inputs," *Proceedings IRE*, vol. 40, 1952, pp. 977–981.

5 J. H. Laning and R. H. Battin, "Random Processes in Automatic Control," McGraw-Hill Book Company, Inc., New York, N.Y., 1956.

6 W. B. Davenport, Jr., and W. L. Root, "An Introduction to the Theory of Random Signals and Noise," McGraw-Hill Book Company, Inc., New York, N. Y., 1958.

7 S. Darlington, "Linear Least-Squares Smoothing and Prediction, With Applications," *Bell System Tech. Journal*, vol. 37, 1958, pp. 1221–1294.

8 G. Franklin, "The Optimum Synthesis of Sampled-Data Systems," Doctoral dissertation, Dept. of Elect. Engr., Columbia University, 1955.

9 A. B. Lees, "Interpolation and Extrapolation of Sampled Data," *Trans. IRE Prof. Group on Information Theory*, IT-2, 1956, pp. 173–175.

10 R. C. Davis, "On the Theory of Prediction of Nonstationary Stochastic Processes," *Journal of Applied Physics*, vol. 23, 1952, pp. 1047–1053.

11 M. Shinbrot, "Optimization of Time-Varying Linear Systems With Nonstationary Inputs," Trans. ASME, vol. 80, 1958, pp. 457–462.

12 M. Blum, "Recursion Formulas for Growing Memory Digital Filters," *Trans. IRE Prof. Group on Information Theory*, IT-4, 1958, pp. 24–30.

13 V. S. Pugachev, "The Use of Canonical Expansions of Random Functions in Determining an Optimum Linear System," *Automatics and Remote Control* (USSR), vol. 17, 1956, pp. 489–499; translation pp. 545–556.

14 V. V. Solodovnikov and A. M. Batkov, "On the Theory of Self-Optimizing Systems (in German and Russian)," Proc. Heidelberg Conference on Automatic Control, 1956, pp. 308–323.

15 J. L. Doob, "Stochastic Processes," John Wiley & Sons, Inc., New York, N. Y., 1955.

16 M. Loève, "Probability Theory," Van Nostrand Company, Inc., New York, N. Y., 1955.

17 R. E. Bellman, I. Glicksberg, and O. A. Gross, "Some Aspects of the Mathematical Theory of Control Processes," RAND Report R-313, 1958, 244 pp.

18 R. E. Kalman and R. W. Koepcke, "Optimal Synthesis of Linear Sampling Control Systems Using Generalized Performance Indexes," Trans. ASME, vol. 80, 1958, pp. 1820–1826.

19 J. E. Bertram, "Effect of Quantization in Sampled-Feedback Systems," *Trans. AIEE*, vol. 77, II, 1958, pp. 177–182.

20 R. E. Kalman and J. E. Bertram, "General Synthesis Procedure for Computer Control of Single and Multi-Loop Linear Systems," *Trans. AIEE*, vol. 77, II, 1958, pp. 602–609.

21 C. W. Merriam, III, "A Class of Optimum Control Systems," *Journal of the Franklin Institute*, vol. 267, 1959, pp. 267–281.

22 R. E. Kalman and J. E. Bertram, "A Unified Approach to the Theory of Sampling Systems," *Journal of the Franklin Institute*, vol. 267, 1959, pp. 405–436.

23 R. E. Kalman and R. W. Koepcke, "The Role of Digital Computers in the Dynamic Optimization of Chemical Reactors," Proc. Western Joint Computer Conference, 1959, pp. 107–116.

24 R. E. Kalman, "Dynamic Optimization of Linear Control Systems, I. Theory," to appear.

25 S. Sherman, "Non-Mean-Square Error Criteria," *Trans. IRE Prof. Group on Information Theory*, IT-4, 1958, pp. 125–126.

26 V. S. Pugachev, "On a Possible General Solution of the Problem of Determining Optimum Dynamic Systems," *Automatics and Remote Control* (USSR), vol. 17, 1956, pp. 585–589.

27 G. C. Newton, Jr., L. A. Gould, and J. F. Kaiser, "Analytical Design of Linear Feedback Controls," John Wiley & Sons, Inc., New York, N. Y., 1957.

28 O. J. M. Smith, "Feedback Control Systems," McGraw-Hill Book Company, Inc., New York, N. Y., 1958.

29 R. E. Kalman, "On the General Theory of Control Systems," Proceedings First International Conference on Automatic Control, Moscow, USSR, 1960.

APPENDIX

RANDOM PROCESSES: BASIC CONCEPTS

For convenience of the reader, we review here some elementary definitions and facts about probability and random processes. Everything is presented with the utmost possible simplicity; for greater depth and breadth, consult Laning and Battin [5] or Doob [15].

A *random variable* is a function whose values depend on the outcome of a chance event. The *values* of a random variable may be any convenient mathematical entities; real or complex numbers, vectors, etc. For simplicity, we shall consider here only real-valued random variables, but this is no real restriction. Random variables will be denoted by $x, y, \ldots$ and their values by $\xi, \eta, \ldots$. Sums, products, and functions of random variables are also random variables.

A random variable x can be explicitly defined by stating the probability that x is less than or equal to some real constant ξ. This is expressed symbolically by writing

$$Pr(x \leqq \xi) = F_x(\xi); \; F_x(-\infty) = 0, \; F_x(+\infty) = 1$$

$F_x(\xi)$ is called the *probability distribution function* of the random variable x. When $F_x(\xi)$ is differentiable with respect to ξ, then $f_x(\xi) = dF_x(\xi)/d\xi$ is called the *probability density function* of x.

The *expected value* (*mathematical expectation, statistical average, ensemble average, mean*, etc., are commonly used synonyms) of any nonrandom function $g(x)$ of a random variable x is defined by

$$Eg(x) = E[g(x)] = \int_{-\infty}^{\infty} g(\xi)dF_x(\xi) = \int_{-\infty}^{\infty} g(\xi)f_x(\xi)d\xi \quad (40)$$

As indicated, it is often convenient to omit the brackets after the symbol E. A sequence of random variables (finite or infinite)

$$\{x(t)\} = \ldots, x(-1), x(0), x(1), \ldots \quad (41)$$

is called a *discrete* (or *discrete-parameter*) *random* (or *stochastic*) *process*. One particular set of observed values of the random process (41)

$$\ldots, \xi(-1), \xi(0), \xi(1), \ldots$$

is called a *realization* (or a *sample function*) of the process. Intuitively, a random process is simply a set of random variables which are indexed in such a way as to bring the notion of time into the picture.

A random process is *uncorrelated* if

$$Ex(t)x(s) = Ex(t)Ex(s) \quad (t \neq s)$$

If, furthermore,

$$Ex(t)x(s) = 0 \quad (t \neq s)$$

then the random process is *orthogonal*. Any uncorrelated random process can be changed into orthogonal random process by replacing $x(t)$ by $x'(t) = x(t) - Ex(t)$ since then

$$Ex'(t)x'(s) = E[x(t) - Ex(t)]\cdot[x(s) - Ex(s)] = Ex(t)x(s) - Ex(t)Ex(s) = 0$$

It is useful to remember that, if a random process is orthogonal, then

$$E[x(t_1) + x(t_2) + \ldots]^2 = Ex^2(t_1) + Ex^2(t_2) + \ldots \; (t_1 \neq t_2 \neq \ldots)$$

If $\mathbf{x}$ is a vector-valued random variable with components $x_1, \ldots, x_n$ (which are of course random variables), the matrix

$$[E(x_i - Ex_i)(x_j - Ex_j)] = E(\mathbf{x} - E\mathbf{x})(\mathbf{x}' - E\mathbf{x}') = \text{cov } \mathbf{x} \quad (42)$$

is called the *covariance matrix* of x.

A random process may be specified explicitly by stating the probability of simultaneous occurrence of any finite number of events of the type

$x(t_1) \leqq \xi_1, \ldots, x(t_n) \leqq \xi_n; \; (t_1 \neq \ldots \neq t_n)$, i.e.,

$$Pr[(x(t_1) \leqq \xi_1, \ldots, x(t_n) \leqq \xi_n)] = F_{x(t_1), \ldots, x(t_n)}(\xi_1, \ldots, \xi_n) \quad (43)$$

where $F_{x(t_1), \ldots, x(t_n)}$ is called the *joint probability distribution function* of the random variables $x(t_1), \ldots, x(t_n)$. The *joint probability density function* is then

$$f_{x(t_1), \ldots, x(t_n)}(\xi_1, \ldots, \xi_n) = \partial^n F_{x(t_1), \ldots, x(t_n)}/\partial\xi_1, \ldots, \partial\xi_n$$

provided the required derivatives exist. The expected value $Eg[x(t_1), \ldots, x(t_n)]$ of any nonrandom function of n random variables is defined by an n-fold integral analogous to (40).

A random process is *independent* if for any finite $t_1 \neq \ldots \neq t_n$, (43) is equal to the product of the first-order distributions

$$Pr[x(t_1) \leqq \xi_1] \ldots Pr[x(t_n) \leqq \xi_n]$$

If a set of random variables is independent, then they are obviously also uncorrelated. The converse is not true in general. For a set of more than 2 random variables to be independent, it is not sufficient that any pair of random variables be independent.

Frequently it is of interest to consider the probability distribution of a random variable $x(t_{n+1})$ of a random process given the actual values $\xi(t_1), \ldots, \xi(t_n)$ with which the random variables $x(t_1), \ldots, x(t_n)$ have occurred. This is denoted by

$$Pr[x(t_{n+1}) \leqq \xi_{n+1}|x(t_1) = \xi_1, \ldots, x(t_n) = \xi_n] = \frac{\int_{-\infty}^{\xi_{n+1}} f_{x(t_1), \ldots, x(t_{n+1})}(\xi_1, \ldots, \xi_{n+1})d\xi_{n+1}}{f_{x(t_1), \ldots, x(t_n)}(\xi_1, \ldots, \xi_n)} \quad (44)$$

which is called the *conditional probability distribution function* of $x(t_{n+1})$ given $x(t_1), \ldots, x(t_n)$. The *conditional expectation*

$$E\{g[x(t_{n+1})]|x(t_1), \ldots, x(t_n)\}$$

is defined analogously to (40). The conditional expectation is a random variable; it follows that

$$E[E\{g[x(t_{n+1})]|x(t_1), \ldots, x(t_n)\}] = E\{g[x(t_{n+1})]\}$$

In all cases of interest in this paper, integrals of the type (40) or (44) need never be evaluated explicitly; only the *concept* of the expected value is needed.

A random variable x is *gaussian* (or *normally distributed*) if

$$f_x(\xi) = \frac{1}{[2\pi E(x - Ex)^2]^{1/2}} \exp\left[-\frac{1}{2}\frac{(\xi - Ex)^2}{E(x - Ex)^2}\right]$$

which is the well-known bell-shaped curve. Similarly, a random vector $\mathbf{x}$ is *gaussian* if

$$f_x(\xi) = \frac{1}{(2\pi)^{n/2}(\det \mathbf{C})^{1/2}} \exp\left[-\frac{1}{2}(\xi - E\mathbf{x})'\mathbf{C}^{-1}(\xi - E\mathbf{x})\right]$$

where $\mathbf{C}^{-1}$ is the inverse of the covariance matrix (42) of $\mathbf{x}$. A *gaussian random process* is defined similarly.

The importance of gaussian random variables and processes is largely due to the following facts:

Theorem 5. (*A*) *Linear functions (and therefore conditional expectations) on a gaussian random process are gaussian random variables.*

(*B*) *Orthogonal gaussian random variables are independent.*

(*C*) *Given any random process with means $Ex(t)$ and covariances $Ex(t)x(s)$, there exists a unique gaussian random process with the same means and covariances.*

[7]

Understanding the Kalman Filter

RICHARD J. MEINHOLD and NOZER D. SINGPURWALLA*

This is an expository article. Here we show how the successfully used Kalman filter, popular with control engineers and other scientists, can be easily understood by statisticians if we use a Bayesian formulation and some well-known results in multivariate statistics. We also give a simple example illustrating the use of the Kalman filter for quality control work.

KEY WORDS: Bayesian inference; Box-Jenkins models; Forecasting; Exponential smoothing; Multivariate normal distribution; Time series.

1. INTRODUCTION

The Kalman filter (KF) commonly employed by control engineers and other physical scientists has been successfully used in such diverse areas as the processing of signals in aerospace tracking and underwater sonar, and the statistical control of quality. More recently, it has also been used in some nonengineering applications such as short-term forecasting and the analysis of life lengths from dose-response experiments. Unfortunately, much of the published literature on the KF is in the engineering journals (including the original development, in Kalman 1960 and Kalman and Bucy 1961), and uses a language, notation, and style that is alien to statisticians. Consequently, many practitioners of statistics are not aware of the simplicity of this useful methodology. However, the model, the notions, and the techniques of Kalman filtering are potentially of great interest to statisticians owing to their similarity to linear models of regression and time series analysis, and because of their great utility in applications.

In actuality, the KF may be easily understood by the statistician if it is cast as a problem in Bayesian inference and we employ some well-known elementary results in multivariate statistics. This feature was evidently first published by Harrison and Stevens (1971, 1976), who were primarily interested in Bayesian forecasting. However, the particular result presented by them is in a nontutorial manner, with emphasis placed on the implementation of the KF. Our aim, on the other hand, is to provide an exposition of the key notions of the approach in a single source, laying out its derivation in a few easy steps, filling in some clarifying technical details, giving an example, and giving an interpretation of results. A more mathematical discussion of the KF emphasizing the stochastic differential equation approach is given by Wegman (1982). We feel that once it is demystified, the KF will be used more often by applied statisticians.

2. THE KALMAN FILTER MODEL: MOTIVATION AND APPLICATIONS

Let $Y_t, Y_{t-1}, \ldots, Y_1$, the data (which may be either scalars or vectors), denote the observed values of a variable of interest at times $t, t-1, \ldots, 1$. We assume that Y_t depends on an unobservable quantity θ_t, known as the *state of nature*. Our aim is to make inferences about θ_t, which may be either a scalar or a vector and whose dimension is independent of the dimension of Y_t. The relationship between Y_t and θ_t is linear and is specified by the *observation equation*

$$Y_t = F_t\theta_t + v_t, \quad (2.1)$$

where F_t is a known quantity. The *observation error* v_t is assumed to be normally distributed with mean zero and a known variance V_t, denoted as $v_t \sim N(0, V_t)$.

The essential difference between the KF and the conventional linear model representation is that in the former, the state of nature—analogous to the regression coefficients of the latter—is not assumed to be a constant but may change with time. This dynamic feature is incorporated via the *system equation*, wherein

$$\theta_t = G_t\theta_{t-1} + w_t, \quad (2.2)$$

G_t being a known quantity, and the *system equation error* $w_t \sim N(0, W_t)$, with W_t known. Since there are many physical systems for which the state of nature θ_t changes over time according to a relationship prescribed by engineering or scientific principles, the ability to include a knowledge of the system behavior in the statistical model is an apparent source of attractiveness of the KF. Note that the relationships (2.1) and (2.2) specified through F_t and G_t may or may not change with time, as is also true of the variances V_t and W_t; we have subscripted these here for the sake of generality.

In addition to the usual linear model assumptions regarding the error terms, we also postulate that v_t is independent of w_t; while extension to the case of dependency is straightforward, there is no need in this article to do so.

2.1 Some Applications

To look at how the KF model might be employed in practice, we consider a simplified version of the frequently referenced example of tracking a satellite's orbit around the earth. The unknown state of nature θ_t

*Richard J. Meinhold is a graduate student, and Nozer D. Singpurwalla is Professor of Operations Research and Statistics at George Washington University, Washington, D.C. 20052. The work of the second author was supported in part by the Office of Naval Research Contract N00014-77-C-0263 and by the U.S. Army Research Office under Grant DAAG-29-80-C-0067 with George Washington University.

could be the position and speed of the satellite at time t, with respect to a spherical coordinate system with origin at the center of the earth. These quantities cannot be measured directly. Instead, from tracking stations around the earth, we may obtain measurements of distance to the satellite and the accompanying angles of measurement; these are the Y_t's. The principles of geometry, mapping Y_t into θ_t, would be incorporated in F_t, while v_t would reflect the measurement error; G_t would prescribe how the position and speed change in time according to the physical laws governing orbiting bodies, while w_t would allow for deviations from these laws owing to such factors as nonuniformity of the earth's gravitational field, and so on.

A less complicated situation is considered by Phadke (1981) in the context of statistical quality control. Here the observation Y_t is a simple (approximately normal) transform of the number of defectives observed in a sample obtained at time t, while $\theta_{1,t}$ and $\theta_{2,t}$ represent, respectively, the true defective index of the process and the drift of this index. We then have as the observation equation

$$Y_t = \theta_{1,t} + v_t,$$

and as the system equations

$$\theta_{1,t} = \theta_{2,t} + w_{1,t}$$

$$\theta_{2,t} = \theta_{2,t-1} + w_{2,t}.$$

In vector notation, this system of equations becomes

$$\boldsymbol{\theta}_t = G\boldsymbol{\theta}_{t-1} + \mathbf{U}_t,$$

where

$$\boldsymbol{\theta}_t = \begin{bmatrix}\theta_{1,t}\\ \theta_{2,t}\end{bmatrix} \quad \text{and} \quad \mathbf{U}_t = \begin{bmatrix}1 & 1\\ 0 & 1\end{bmatrix}\begin{bmatrix}w_{1,t}\\ w_{2,t}\end{bmatrix};$$

$$G = \begin{bmatrix}0 & 1\\ 0 & 1\end{bmatrix}$$

does not change with time.

If we examine $Y_t - Y_{t-1}$ for this model, we observe that, under the assumption of constant variances, namely, $V_t = V$ and $W_t = W$, the autocorrelation structure of this difference is identical to that of an *ARIMA* (0,1,1) process in the sense of Box and Jenkins (1970). Although such a correspondence is sometimes easily discernible, we should in general not, because of the discrepancies in the philosophies and methodologies involved, consider the two approaches to be equivalent.

3. THE RECURSIVE ESTIMATION PROCEDURE

The term "Kalman filter" or "Kalman filtering" refers to a recursive procedure for inference about the state of nature θ_t. The key notion here is that given the data $\mathbf{Y}_t = (Y_t, \ldots, Y_1)$, inference about θ_t can be carried out through a direct application of Bayes's theorem:

$$\text{Prob\{State of Nature | Data\}}$$
$$\propto \text{Prob\{Data | State of Nature\}} \times \text{Prob\{State of Nature\}}, \qquad (3.1)$$

which can also be written as

$$P(\theta_t \mid \mathbf{Y}_t) \propto P(Y_t \mid \theta_t, \mathbf{Y}_{t-1}) \times P(\theta_t \mid \mathbf{Y}_{t-1}), \qquad (3.2)$$

where the notation $P(A \mid B)$ denotes the probability of occurrence of event A given that (or conditional on) event B has occurred. Note that the expression on the left side of (3.2) denotes the *posterior distribution* for θ at time t, whereas the first and second expressions on the right side denote the *likelihood* and the *prior distribution* for θ, respectively.

The recursive procedure can best be explained if we focus attention on time point $t-1$, $t = 1,2,\ldots,$ and the observed data until then, $\mathbf{Y}_{t-1} = (Y_{t-1}, Y_{t-2}, \ldots, Y_1)$. In what follows, we use matrix manipulations in allowing for Y and/or θ to be vectors, without explicitly noting them as such.

At $t-1$, our state of knowledge about θ_{t-1} is embodied in the following probability statement for θ_{t-1}:

$$(\theta_{t-1} \mid \mathbf{Y}_{t-1}) \sim N(\hat{\theta}_{t-1}, \Sigma_{t-1}), \qquad (3.3)$$

where $\hat{\theta}_{t-1}$ and Σ_{t-1} are the expectation and the variance of $(\theta_{t-1} \mid \mathbf{Y}_{t-1})$. In effect, (3.3) represents the posterior distribution of θ_{t-1}; its evolution will become clear in the subsequent text.

It is helpful to remark here that the recursive procedure is started off at time 0 by choosing $\hat{\theta}_0$ and Σ_0 to be our best guesses about the mean and the variance of θ_0, respectively.

We now look forward to time t, but in two stages:

1. prior to observing Y_t, and
2. after observing Y_t.

Stage 1. Prior to observing Y_t, our best choice for θ_t is governed by the system equation (2.2) and is given as $G_t\theta_{t-1} + w_t$. Since θ_{t-1} is described by (3.3), our state of knowledge about θ_t is embodied in the probability statement

$$(\theta_t \mid \mathbf{Y}_{t-1}) \sim N(G_t\hat{\theta}_{t-1},\ R_t = G_t\Sigma_{t-1}G_t' + W_t); \qquad (3.4)$$

this is our prior distribution.

In obtaining (3.4), which represents our prior for θ_t in the next cycle of (3.2), we used the well-known result that for any constant C

$$X \sim N(\mu, \Sigma) \Rightarrow CX \sim N(C\mu, C\Sigma C'),$$

where C' denotes the transpose of C.

Stage 2. On observing Y_t, our goal is to compute the posterior of θ_t using (3.2). However, to do this, we need to know the likelihood $\mathcal{L}(\theta_t \mid Y_t)$, or equivalently $P(Y_t \mid \theta_t, \mathbf{Y}_{t-1})$, the determination of which is undertaken via the following arguments.

Let e_t denote the *error* in predicting Y_t from the point $t-1$; thus

$$e_t = Y_t - \hat{Y}_t = Y_t - F_tG_t\hat{\theta}_{t-1}. \qquad (3.5)$$

Since F_t, G_t, and $\hat{\theta}_{t-1}$ are all known, observing Y_t is equivalent to observing e_t. Thus (3.2) can be rewritten as

$$P(\theta_t \mid Y_t, \mathbf{Y}_{t-1}) = P(\theta_t \mid e_t, \mathbf{Y}_{t-1}) \propto P(e_t \mid \theta_t, \mathbf{Y}_{t-1}) \times P(\theta_t \mid \mathbf{Y}_{t-1}), \quad (3.6)$$

with $P(e_t \mid \theta_t, \mathbf{Y}_{t-1})$ being the likelihood.

Using the fact that $Y_t = F_t\theta_t + v_t$, (3.5) can be written as $e_t = F_t(\theta_t - G_t\hat{\theta}_{t-1}) + v_t$, so that $E(e_t \mid \theta_t, \mathbf{Y}_{t-1}) = F_t(\theta_t - G_t\hat{\theta}_{t-1})$.

Since $v_t \sim N(0, V_t)$, it follows that the likelihood is described by

$$(e_t \mid \theta_t, \mathbf{Y}_{t-1}) \sim N(F_t(\theta_t - G_t\hat{\theta}_{t-1}), V_t). \quad (3.7)$$

We can now use Bayes's theorem (Eq. (3.6)) to obtain

$$P(\theta_t \mid Y_t, \mathbf{Y}_{t-1}) = \frac{P(e_t \mid \theta_t, \mathbf{Y}_{t-1}) \times P(\theta_t \mid \mathbf{Y}_{t-1})}{\int_{\text{all } \theta_t} P(e_t, \theta_t \mid \mathbf{Y}_{t-1}) d\theta_t}, \quad (3.8)$$

and this best describes our state of knowledge about θ_t at time t. Once $P(\theta_t \mid Y_t, \mathbf{Y}_{t-1})$ is computed, we can go back to (3.3) for the next cycle of the recursive procedure. In the next section, we show that the posterior distribution of (3.8) is of the form presented in (3.3).

4. DETERMINATION OF THE POSTERIOR DISTRIBUTION

The tedious effort required to obtain $P(\theta_t \mid \mathbf{Y}_t)$ using (3.8) can be avoided if we make use of the following well-known result in multivariate statistics (Anderson 1958, pp. 28–29), and some standard properties of the normal distribution.

Let X_1 and X_2 have a bivariate normal distribution with means μ_1 and μ_2, respectively, and a covariance matrix

$$\begin{pmatrix} \Sigma_{11} & \Sigma_{12} \\ \Sigma_{21} & \Sigma_{22} \end{pmatrix};$$

we denote this by

$$\begin{pmatrix} X_1 \\ X_2 \end{pmatrix} \sim N\left[\begin{pmatrix} \mu_1 \\ \mu_2 \end{pmatrix}, \begin{pmatrix} \Sigma_{11} & \Sigma_{12} \\ \Sigma_{21} & \Sigma_{22} \end{pmatrix}\right]. \quad (4.1)$$

When (4.1) holds, the conditional distribution of X_1 given X_2 is described by

$$(X_1 \mid X_2 = x_2) \sim N(\mu_1 + \Sigma_{12}\Sigma_{22}^{-1}(x_2 - \mu_2), \Sigma_{11} - \Sigma_{12}\Sigma_{22}^{-1}\Sigma_{21}). \quad (4.2)$$

The quantity $\mu_1 + \Sigma_{12}\Sigma_{22}^{-1}(x_2 - \mu_2)$ is called the *regression function*, and $\Sigma_{12}\Sigma_{22}^{-1}$ is referred to as the *coefficient of the least squares regression of X_1 on x_2*.

As a converse to the relationship (4.1) implies (4.2), we have the result that whenever (4.2) holds, and when $X_2 \sim N(\mu_2, \Sigma_{22})$, then (4.1) will hold; we will use this converse relationship.

For our situation, we suppress the conditioning variables $\mathbf{Y}_{t-1}$ and let X_1 correspond to e_t, and X_2 correspond to θ_t; we denote this correspondence by $X_1 \Leftrightarrow e_t$ and $X_2 \Leftrightarrow \theta_t$. Since $(\theta_t \mid \mathbf{Y}_{t-1}) \sim N(G_t\hat{\theta}_{t-1}, R_t)$ (see (3.4)), we note that

$$\mu_2 \Leftrightarrow G_t\hat{\theta}_{t-1}$$

and

$$\Sigma_{22} \Leftrightarrow R_t.$$

If in (4.2) we replace X_1, X_2, μ_2, and Σ_{22} by e_t, θ_t, $G_t\hat{\theta}_{t-1}$, and R_t, respectively, and recall the result that $(e_t \mid \theta_t, \mathbf{Y}_{t-1}) \sim N(F_t(\theta_t - G_t\hat{\theta}_{t-1}), V_t)$ (Eq. (3.7)), then

$$\mu_1 + \Sigma_{12}R_t^{-1}(\theta_t - G_t\hat{\theta}_{t-1}) \Leftrightarrow F_t(\theta_t - G_t\hat{\theta}_{t-1}),$$

so that $\mu_1 \Leftrightarrow 0$ and $\Sigma_{12} \Leftrightarrow F_tR_t$; similarly,

$$\Sigma_{11} - \Sigma_{12}\Sigma_{22}^{-1}\Sigma_{21} = \Sigma_{11} - F_tR_tF_t' \Leftrightarrow V_t,$$

so that $\Sigma_{11} \Leftrightarrow V_t + F_tR_tF_t'$.

We now invoke the converse relation mentioned previously to conclude that the joint distribution of θ_t and e_t, given $\mathbf{Y}_{t-1}$, can be described as

$$\left[\begin{pmatrix} \theta_t \\ e_t \end{pmatrix} \middle| \mathbf{Y}_{t-1}\right] \sim N\left[\begin{pmatrix} G_t\hat{\theta}_{t-1} \\ 0 \end{pmatrix}, \begin{pmatrix} R_t & R_tF_t' \\ F_tR_t & V_t + F_tR_tF_t' \end{pmatrix}\right]. \quad (4.3)$$

Making e_t the conditioning variable and identifying (4.3) with (4.1), we obtain via (4.2) the result that

$$(\theta_t \mid e_t, \mathbf{Y}_{t-1}) \sim N[G_t\hat{\theta}_{t-1} + R_tF_t'(V_t + F_tR_tF_t')^{-1}e_t, \; R_t - R_tF_t'(V_t + F_tR_tF_t')^{-1}F_tR_t]. \quad (4.4)$$

This is the desired posterior distribution. We now summarize to highlight the elements of the recursive procedure.

After time $t-1$, we had a posterior distribution for θ_{t-1} with mean $\hat{\theta}_{t-1}$ and variance Σ_{t-1} (Eq. (3.3)). Forming a prior for θ_t with mean $G_t\hat{\theta}_{t-1}$ and variance $R_t = G_t\Sigma_{t-1}G_t' + W_t$ (Eq. (3.4)) and evaluating a likelihood given $e_t = Y_t - F_tG_t\hat{\theta}_{t-1}$ (Eq. (3.5)), we arrive at the posterior density for θ_t; this has mean

$$\hat{\theta}_t = G_t\hat{\theta}_{t-1} + R_tF_t'(V_t + F_tR_tF_t')^{-1}e_t \quad (4.5)$$

and variance

$$\Sigma_t = R_t - R_tF_t'(V_t + F_tR_tF_t')^{-1}F_tR_t. \quad (4.6)$$

We now continue through the next cycle of the process.

5. INTERPRETATION OF RESULTS AND CONCLUDING REMARKS

If we look at (4.4) for obtaining some additional insight into the workings of the Kalman filter, we note that the mean of the posterior distribution of $(\theta_t \mid e_t, \mathbf{Y}_{t-1})$ is indeed the regression function of θ_t on e_t. The mean (regression function) is the sum of two quantities $G_t\hat{\theta}_{t-1}$, and a multiple of the *one step ahead forecast error* e_t.

We first remark that $G_t\hat{\theta}_{t-1}$ is the mean of the prior distribution of θ_t (see (3.4)), and by comparing (4.3) and (4.4) to (4.1) and (4.2) we verify that the multiplier of e_t, $R_tF_t'(V_t + F_tR_tF_t')^{-1}$, is the coefficient of the least squares regression of θ_t on e_t (conditional on $\mathbf{Y}_{t-1}$). Thus one way to view Kalman filtering is to think of it as an updating procedure that consists of forming a preliminary (prior) guess about the state of nature and then adding a correction to this guess, the correction being determined by how well the guess has performed in predicting the next observation.

Second, we should clarify the meaning of regressing θ_t on e_t since this pair constitutes but a single observation and the regression relationship is not estimated in the familiar way. Rather, we recall the usual framework of sequential Bayesian estimation, wherein a new posterior distribution arises with each successive piece of data. At time zero, the regression of θ_1 on e_1 is determined entirely by our prior specifications. On receiving the first observation, the value of e_1 is mapped into $\hat{\theta}_1$ through this function, which is then replaced by a new regression relation based on $\hat{\theta}_1$, F_1, G_1, V_1, and W_1. This in turn is used to map e_2 into $\hat{\theta}_2$, and so on as the process continues in the usual Bayesian prior/posterior iterative manner; see Figure 1. Thus Kalman filtering can also be viewed as the evolution of a series of regression functions of θ_t on e_t, at times $0, 1, \ldots, t-1, t$, each having a potentially different intercept and regression coefficient; the evolution stems from a learning process involving all the data.

The original development of the Kalman filter approach was motivated by the updating feature just described, and its derivation followed via the least squares estimation theory. The Bayesian formulation described here yields the same result in an elegant manner and additionally provides the attractive feature of enabling inference about θ_t through a probability distribution rather than just a point estimate.

6. ILLUSTRATIVE EXAMPLES

6.1 The Steady Model

We consider two examples to illustrate the preceding mechanism and its performance.

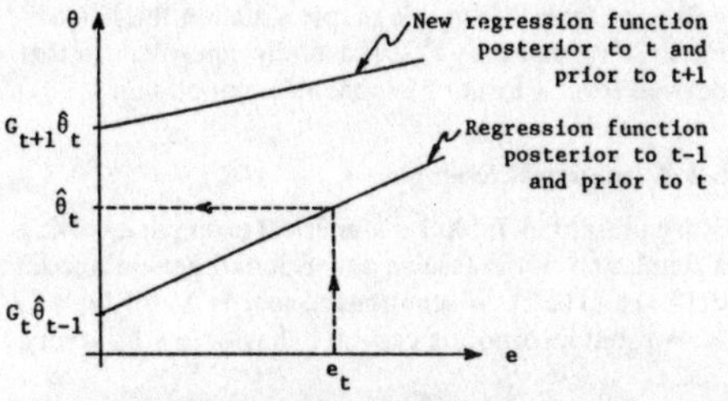

Figure 1. Regression of θ_t on e_t

We first return to the quality control model of Section 2.1, simplified by the removal of the drift parameter. This yields

$$Y_t = \theta_t + v_t \text{ (Obs. Eqn.)}$$

and (6.1)

$$\theta_t = \theta_{t-1} + w_t \text{ (Sys. Eqn.)}.$$

This is a simplest possible nontrivial KF model (sometimes referred to in the forecasting literature as the steady model); it also corresponds, in the sense of possessing the same autocorrelation structure (assuming constant variances), to a class of *ARIMA* (0, 1, 1) models of Box and Jenkins (1970). In this situation, $F_t \equiv G_t \equiv 1$; if we further specified that $\Sigma_0 = 1$, $V_t \equiv 2$, $W_t \equiv 1$, we can easily demonstrate inductively that $R_t = G_t\Sigma_{t-1}G_t' + W_t \equiv 2$, and from (4.6), $\Sigma_t \equiv 1$. In (4.5), then, our recursive relationship becomes

$$\hat{\theta}_t = \hat{\theta}_{t-1} + \tfrac{1}{2}(Y_t - \hat{\theta}_{t-1})$$
$$= \tfrac{1}{2}(Y_t + \hat{\theta}_{t-1})$$
$$= \sum_{j=0}^{t-1} (\tfrac{1}{2})^{j+1} Y_{t-j} + (\tfrac{1}{2})^t \hat{\theta}_0. \quad (6.2)$$

Table 1. A Simulation of the Process Described in Section (6.2)

t	$v_t \sim N(0, 2)$	$w_t \sim N(0, 1)$	F_t	$\theta_t = G_t\theta_{t-1} + w_t$	$Y_t = F_t\theta_t + v_t$	$\hat{\theta}_t$	Σ_t
0				− .353		4.183	1
1	− .376	.887	1.3	1.063	1.007	− .619	.608
2	.023	−1.021	.8	− .489	− .368	− .350	.842
3	− .898	−1.207	.9	− .962	−1.764	− .527	.812
4	1.645	.150	1.1	− .331	1.281	.338	.696
5	− .701	− .329	1.2	− .163	− .897	− .434	.636
6	− .257	.448	1.0	.366	.109	− .097	.734
7	−1.766	.403	1.1	.220	−1.524	− .550	.690
8	−1.551	−1.069	.9	− .959	−2.414	−1.050	.795
9	.443	.186	.9	.666	1.042	.732	.807
10	.300	− .267	1.0	.066	.366	.366	.751
11	− .745	.406	1.2	.373	− .297	− .213	.640
12	−1.175	− .789	.8	− .602	−1.657	− .638	.846
13	1.281	.386	1.1	.687	2.037	.967	.699
14	−1.017	− .753	.7	− .409	−1.304	− .041	.912
15	− .991	− .120	.9	.085	− .915	− .324	.820
16	.861	.524	1.0	.566	1.427	.436	.752
17	−1.047	.224	1.3	− .059	−1.124	− .542	.593
18	.076	− .356	1.1	− .386	− .348	− .290	.678
19	2.498	− .907	1.2	− .714	1.641	.704	.635
20	1.482	− .881	.9	−1.238	.368	.370	.789
21	−1.683	.023	.7	.642	−1.234	− .543	.926
22	1.072	.632	.6	.953	1.644	.275	1.008
23	− .684	− .314	1.1	− .791	−1.554	− .687	.712
24	− .580	− .217	1.0	− .612	−1.192	− .658	.741
25	−1.894	1.927	.9	2.233	.116	.264	.801

We see then that in this simple situation the KF estimator of θ_t, and thus Y_{t+1}, is actually equivalent to that derived from a form of exponential smoothing.

6.2 A Numerical Example

We present in Table 1 a numerical example involving a simulation of the (scalar-dimensional) general model of (2.1) and (2.2). We continue to specify $\Sigma_0 = 1$, $V_t \equiv 2$, $W_t \equiv 1$, but incorporate cyclical behavior in θ_t by setting

$$G_t = \frac{1}{2}\sin\left(\frac{\pi}{2}[2t+1]\right) = (-1)^t/2,$$

while F_t is in the nature of the familiar independent variable of ordinary regression. This situation clearly cannot be contained in any class of the *ARIMA* family; instead it is analogous, if not equivalent, to the transfer function model approach of Box and Jenkins (1970).

Starting with a value for θ_0, the disturbances v_t and w_t were generated from a table of random normal variates and used in turn to produce, via the system and observation equations, the processes $\{\theta_t\}$ and $\{Y_t\}$, of which only the latter would ordinarily be visible. A "bad guess" value of $\hat{\theta}_0$ was chosen; as can be seen in Figure 2, where the actual values of θ_t and their estimates $\hat{\theta}_t$ are plotted, the effect of this error is short-lived. The reader may find it conducive to a better understanding of the model to work through several iterations of the recursive procedure.

[*Received October 1981. Revised July 1982.*]

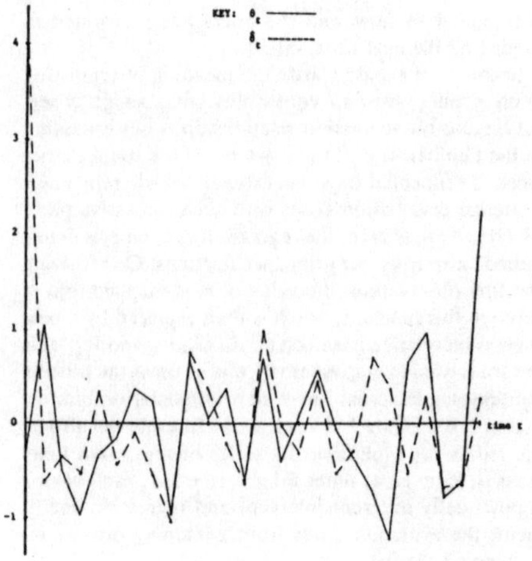

Figure 2. A Plot of the Simulated Values of θ_t, the State of Nature at Time t, and Their Estimated Values $\hat{\theta}_t$ Via the Kalman Filter

REFERENCES

ANDERSON, T.W. (1958), *An Introduction to Multivariate Statistical Analysis*, New York: John Wiley.

BOX, G.E.P., and JENKINS, G.M. (1970), *Time Series Analysis, Forecasting and Control*, San Francisco: Holden-Day.

HARRISON, P.J., and STEVENS, C.F. (1971), "A Bayesian Approach to Short-Term Forecasting," *Operations Research Quarterly*, 22, 341–362.

——— (1976), "Bayesian Forecasting (with discussion)," *Journal of the Royal Statistical Society*, Ser. B, 38, 205–247.

KALMAN, R.E. (1960), "A New Approach to Linear Filtering and Prediction Problems," *Journal of Basic Engineering*, 82, 34–45.

KALMAN, R.E., and BUCY, R.S. (1961), "New Results in Linear Filtering and Prediction Theory," *Journal of Basic Engineering*, 83, 95–108.

PHADKE, M.S. (1981), "Quality Audit Using Adaptive Kalman Filtering," *ASQC Quality Congress Transactions—San Francisco*, 1045–1052.

WEGMAN, E.J. (1982), "Kalman Filtering," in *Encyclopedia of Statistics*, eds. Norman Johnson and Samuel Kotz, New York: John Wiley.

[8]

Linear Dynamic Recursive Estimation from the Viewpoint of Regression Analysis

D. B. DUNCAN and S. D. HORN*

A large class of useful multivariate recursive time series models and estimation methods has appeared in the engineering literature. Despite the interest and utility which this recursive work has when viewed as an extension of regression analysis, little of it has reached statisticians working in regression. To overcome this we (a) present the relevant random-β regression theory as a natural extension of conventional fixed-β regression theory and (b) derive the optimal recursive estimators in terms of the extended regression theory for a typical form of the recursive model. This also opens the way for further developments in recursive estimation, which are more tractable in the regression approach and will be presented in future papers.

1. INTRODUCTION

A very useful class of multivariate time series models and estimation methods has been developed in the engineering literature (by Kalman [5, 6] and others) under titles such as *linear dynamic recursive filtering and prediction*. These are useful for all sorts of problems varying from missile trajectory estimation to estimating and predicting the condition of a critically ill medical patient.

Despite a basic closeness which this work has to classical regression theory and despite its high utility for providing simple solutions to otherwise difficult extensions of regression problems, little of this work has come to the attention of the average statistician working in regression theory. We feel this lack of communication is due to the fact that the new theory has not been developed as a direct extension of regression theory, but instead from a different, though elegant, point of view of wide sense conditional probability theory (e.g., [3]).

In an effort to overcome this communications block we show how a typical form of linear dynamic recursive estimation can be developed as a natural extension of regression theory. To do this, we must present first a wide sense random-β regression theory of considerable interest in its own right. Some of these ideas have appeared previously in the statistical literature (e.g., [2], [4], [7], [9]).

The Kalman time series models are expressed in terms of two recursive equations. A typical form for a p-variate time series $y_1, \cdots, y_n$ consists of (1) an observation equation: $y_t = X_t\beta_t + \varepsilon_t$ for times $t=1, \cdots, n$ and (2) a dynamic regression coefficients transition equation: $\beta_t = T_t\beta_{t-1} + u_t$, $t=2, \cdots, n$, starting with $\beta_1 = \mu_1 + u_1$ at $t=1$ where μ_1 is a known prior mean for β_1. Each observation equation is of the familiar regression form in which the regression coefficient vector $\beta_t(r\times 1)$ is called the *state* at time t, $X_t(p\times r)$ is a known matrix of regressors, and $\varepsilon_t(p\times 1)$ is a vector of random errors.

The dynamic state transition equation $\beta_t = T_t\beta_{t-1} + u_t$ is new to conventional fixed-β regression theory and expresses the state β_t as a known linear transformation $T_t(r\times r)$ of the previous state β_{t-1} plus a vector $u_t(r\times 1)$ of random errors.

The linear operation on β_{t-1} and the introduction of randomness are what give β_t its *linear dynamic* aspect. A situation where this is of particular value, e.g., is in the modelling of a "trajectory" (interpreted broadly as any smooth time function) in which the parameters describing the trajectory at time t depend on those at time $t-1$.

The dynamic state transition equations, the starting equation $\beta_1 = \mu_1 + u_1$, and assumptions about the error vectors u_t, $t=1, \cdots, n$ provide a prior model for the complete vector β of all the regression coefficients or state elements concerned.

As in conventional regression theory, the assumptions made about the error vectors ε_t and u_t are of one of two forms. In the stronger form, the *Gaussian* assumptions, all the error vectors have zero expectations, all are uncorrelated with one another, and all have known variance-covariance matrices $Q_t = \text{var}(u_t)$ and $R_t = \text{var}(\varepsilon_t)$ for all t. Each error vector has the multivariate normal (Gaussian) distribution, $u_t \sim N(0, Q_t)$ and $\varepsilon_t \sim N(0, R_t)$. In the weaker form, the *wide-sense* assumptions, no distributional assumptions are made except the same ones specifying the first and second moments. We denote these by $u_t \sim WS(0, Q_t)$ and $\varepsilon_t \sim WS(0, R_t)$. In the Gaussian case, of course, all the error vectors are independent.

The following specializations reduce the new dynamic model to the conventional fixed-β regression model $y = X\beta + \varepsilon$: (1) The state transition equation $\beta_t = T_t\beta_{t-1} + u_t$ is now the trivial identity transformation (i.e., $T_t \equiv I$ and $u_t \equiv 0 \leftrightarrow Q_t \equiv 0$) and β_1 is fixed and unknown. This is the only vector of regression coefficients involved, so the need for the subscript is removed. Thus we may write $\beta_t = \beta_1 = \beta$ for all t. (2) The tth observation equation

* D.B. Duncan is professor and S.D. Horn is assistant professor, both with the Departments of Biostatistics and Mathematical Sciences, Johns Hopkins University. Research was sponsored by the Air Force Office of Scientific Research, Air Force Systems Command, USAF, under contract number F44620-70-C-0066. Technical Report No. 162 of the Department of Statistics; Publication No. 478 of the Department of Biostatistics.

© Journal of the American Statistical Association
December 1972, Volume 67, Number 340
Theory and Methods Section

$y_t = X_t\beta_t + \varepsilon_t$ is univariate $p=1$ and represents the tth row $y_t = x_t'\beta + \varepsilon_t$ of the conventional model $y = X\beta + \varepsilon$ where $y_t(1\times 1)$ is the tth element of y, $x_t' = X_t(1\times r)$ is the tth row of X, etc.

The most important advantage of the new work is the *increased versatility* of the dynamic model, i.e., the enlarged range of real and important problems involving univariate or multivariate ($p \geq 1$) non-stationary time series with which it can cope.

Another advantage is the *simplicity* of the recursive methods for the efficient handling of the optimal estimation of extremely large numbers of parameters. A sequence of very simple recursive solutions replaces the direct simultaneous solution for all of the β parameters involved. In a typical form of these methods, filtering, an optimal estimator b_t of β_t is obtained recursively as a linear combination of the previous estimator b_{t-1} and of y_t, the response vector at time t. The recursive filtering equations simultaneously provide the variance-covariance matrix $S_t = \text{var}(b_t - \beta_t)$ of the estimator. Both equations have been developed in an updating form which is useful especially in programmed computing (cf. (3.5a) and (3.5b)).

It is well known from the engineering literature that under the wide sense error assumptions the filter estimator b_t for β_t is optimal in the sense of being the minimum mean square linear estimator based on all the data $\mu_1, y_1, \cdots, y_t$ up through time t. Under the Gaussian assumptions it is the minimum mean square estimator. Variations of the updating equations give similarly optimal estimators $b_{t|s}$ of β_t based on all the data $\mu_1, y_1, \cdots, y_s$ up through time s, for varying values of s and t. Of special interest are the estimators $b_{t|n}$ which are optimal based on all the data.

Despite its advantages as a natural extension of conventional regression theory, the engineering approach has so far been little understood or used by the conventional regression analyst, perhaps due partly to the unfamiliarity of the notation and terms in the engineering literature. But more importantly, the neglect is due to a confusion caused by the use, in its development, of a theory in which the names are the same as in conventional regression theory but the roles are different. Specifically, the central objective in both cases is to estimate β, the entire vector of regression coefficients involved. Speaking in terms of vector space projections, as Kalman does, the conventional regressionist approaches this problem by projecting an observation y vector onto a linear vector space spanned by the columns of an X matrix, i.e., by "fitting a regression $\hat{y}$ of y on X." The optimal estimates b of β are then found as the coefficients of the orthogonal projection $\hat{y}$ so obtained, i.e., the coefficients of X in the equation for $\hat{y}$. The Kalman [6] approach, on the other hand, makes use of the fact that β_t is now a random variable. By a suitable redefinition of the vector space terms involved, the optimal estimate *itself* is found directly as an orthogonal projection $b_{t|s}$ of β_t on a vector space spanned by the vectors $\mu_1, y_1, \cdots, y_s$ of the data involved. In regression terms, this is "fitting a regression of β_t on $\mu_1, y_1, \cdots, y_s$." The normal equations for doing this are based on the *expected* first and second moments of the variables involved.

The purpose of the present paper is to overcome the communications block by: (1) explaining the new dynamic models and methods in the terms and notation of conventional regression theory, and (2) deriving the optimality of the recursive estimators in terms of a natural random-β extension of the conventional fixed-β regression theory.

The random-β regression theory approach should serve as a two-way communications bridge; a bridge by which the conventional regressionist can move to an easier understanding of the more direct derivation of recursive estimators, and by which the engineer can move to an easier understanding of the relevance to his problems of many valuable results in regression theory. Apart from these objectives, the random-β extensions of fixed-β regression theory, e.g., the extended Gauss-Markov theorem, are of considerable interest in themselves, and of potential value for a wide class of applications.

2. A WIDE-SENSE RANDOM-β REGRESSION THEORY

In this section we extend well-known definitions and theorems of fixed-β regression theory in a natural way to form a random-β regression theory required for a simple regression development of the Kalman recursive equations.

2.1 The Model

The model can be written in the familiar fixed-β regression form

$$y = X\beta + \varepsilon \quad \text{where} \quad \varepsilon \sim WS(0, \Sigma) \tag{2.1}$$

except that β now is random and may be written in a similar style as

$$\beta = \mu + u \quad \text{where} \quad u \sim WS(0, \Sigma_0) \tag{2.2}$$

and u is uncorrelated with ε. The notation $z \sim WS(\mu, \Sigma)$, as used in the introduction, indicates the wide sense model that z has any distribution with mean μ and variance Σ.

The dimensions and properties of the vectors and matrices involved are:

- y is an $n\times 1$ vector of random variables or observations on same,
- X is an $n\times r$ matrix of known regressors,
- β is an $r\times 1$ vector of unknown parameters (regression coefficients),
- ε is an $n\times 1$ vector of observation errors,
- μ is an $r\times 1$ known prior mean for β,
- u is an $r\times 1$ vector of prior errors,
- $\Sigma(n\times n)$ and $\Sigma_0(r\times r)$ are variance matrices both of which are known except possibly for a scale factor σ^2.

The Condensed Model. By writing

$$\tilde{y} = \tilde{X}\beta + \tilde{\varepsilon} \tag{2.3}$$

for

$$\begin{bmatrix} \mu \\ y \end{bmatrix} = \begin{bmatrix} I \\ X \end{bmatrix} \beta + \begin{bmatrix} -u \\ \varepsilon \end{bmatrix}$$

the whole model, (2.1) and (2.2) above, may be written more briefly as

$$(\tilde{y} - \tilde{X}\beta) \sim WS(0, \tilde{\Sigma}) \qquad (2.4)$$

where

$$\tilde{\Sigma} = \begin{bmatrix} \Sigma_\beta & 0 \\ 0 & \Sigma \end{bmatrix} \qquad (2.5)$$

with dimensions $\tilde{y}(\tilde{n}\times 1)$, $\tilde{X}(\tilde{n}\times r)$, $\tilde{\Sigma}(\tilde{n}\times\tilde{n})$, $\tilde{n}\equiv r+n$.

It is precisely this condensation that allows us to extend the familiar fixed-β regression theory to the random-β case with a minimum of new techniques needed to prove the required results.

In fixed-β theory an important estimator is the WLSE (weighted least squares estimator) of β. The natural extension of this in random-β theory is:

Definition 2.2: Weighted Least Squares Estimator. The vector $b(r\times 1)$ is the WLSE of β if

$$(\tilde{y} - \tilde{X}\hat{\beta})'\tilde{\Sigma}^{-1}(\tilde{y} - \tilde{X}\hat{\beta}) \qquad (2.6)$$

is minimized when $\hat{\beta} = b$.

Theorem 2.3: Normal Equations. The WLSE of β is given by the solution of the Normal Equations

$$(\tilde{X}'\tilde{\Sigma}^{-1}\tilde{X})b = \tilde{X}'\tilde{\Sigma}^{-1}\tilde{y}. \qquad (2.7)$$

Proof: The quadratic form (2.6) to be minimized has the same form as that in fixed-β theory where it is known that the minimum is given by the solution of (2.7).

By substitution the estimator b given by (2.7) is seen to be the familiar weighted combination:

$$b = V[\Sigma_\beta^{-1}\mu + X'\Sigma^{-1}y] \qquad (2.8)$$

where

$$V = [\Sigma_\beta^{-1} + X'\Sigma^{-1}X]^{-1} \qquad (2.9)$$

The distribution of the WLSE b of β in wide-sense fixed-β theory is known to be $b\sim WS(\beta,(X'\Sigma^{-1}X)^{-1})$. Note that it is this fixed-β estimator weighted inversely by its variance which gives the $X'\Sigma^{-1}y$ term in (2.8). Intuitively, in the random-β case interest is centered on the distribution of $b-\beta$, since this difference tells how well a random β is being estimated.

Lemma 2.4: Wide-Sense Distribution of $b-\beta$. Given that

$$(\tilde{y} - \tilde{X}\beta) \sim WS(0, \tilde{\Sigma})$$

and

$$b = (\tilde{X}'\tilde{\Sigma}^{-1}\tilde{X})^{-1}\tilde{X}'\tilde{\Sigma}^{-1}\tilde{y}$$

then

(1) $(b - \beta) \sim WS(0, (\tilde{X}'\tilde{\Sigma}^{-1}\tilde{X})^{-1})$

(2) $E(b - \beta)(\tilde{y} - \tilde{X}b)' = 0$, and

(3) $E(b - \beta)\tilde{y}' = 0$.

Proof: We first note that

$$\begin{aligned}(b - \beta) &= (\tilde{X}'\tilde{\Sigma}^{-1}\tilde{X})^{-1}\tilde{X}'\tilde{\Sigma}^{-1}(\tilde{y} - \tilde{X}\beta) \\ &= (\tilde{X}'\tilde{\Sigma}^{-1}\tilde{X})^{-1}\tilde{X}\tilde{\Sigma}^{-1}\tilde{\varepsilon};\end{aligned} \qquad (2.10)$$

$$\begin{aligned}(\tilde{y} - \tilde{X}b) &= [I - \tilde{X}(\tilde{X}'\tilde{\Sigma}^{-1}\tilde{X})^{-1}\tilde{X}'\tilde{\Sigma}^{-1}]\tilde{y} \\ &= [I - \tilde{X}(\tilde{X}'\tilde{\Sigma}^{-1}\tilde{X})^{-1}\tilde{X}'\tilde{\Sigma}^{-1}](\tilde{X}\beta + \tilde{\varepsilon}) \\ &= [I - \tilde{X}(\tilde{X}'\tilde{\Sigma}^{-1}\tilde{X})^{-1}\tilde{X}'\tilde{\Sigma}^{-1}]\tilde{\varepsilon}.\end{aligned} \qquad (2.11)$$

Results (1) and (2) follow directly.

From (2.1) and (2.2)

$$y = X\beta + \varepsilon = X\mu + Xu + \varepsilon. \qquad (2.12)$$

From (2.10) and (2.12) we get

$$\begin{aligned}E(b-\beta)y' &= (\tilde{X}'\tilde{\Sigma}^{-1}\tilde{X})^{-1}\tilde{X}'\tilde{\Sigma}^{-1} \\ &\quad \cdot E\left\{\begin{bmatrix} -u \\ \varepsilon \end{bmatrix}\mu'X' + \begin{bmatrix} -u \\ \varepsilon \end{bmatrix}(u'X'+\varepsilon')\right\} \\ &= 0 + (\tilde{X}'\tilde{\Sigma}^{-1}\tilde{X})^{-1}(-\Sigma_\beta^{-1}\Sigma_\beta X' + X'\Sigma^{-1}\Sigma) = 0.\end{aligned}$$

Since $E(b-\beta)\mu' = 0$ also, result (3) follows.

Definitions 2.5: An estimator $\hat{\gamma}(q\times 1)$ of any $q\times 1$ linear vector function $\gamma = C\beta$ of β is

1. *linear* if it is linear in $\tilde{y}$, i.e., if $\hat{\gamma} = A\tilde{y} = A_1\mu + A_2 y$, where A, A_1 and A_2 are $q\times\tilde{n}, q\times r$ and $q\times n$ respectively;
2. *unconditionally unbiased* (*u-unbiased*) if $E(\hat{\gamma} - \gamma) = 0$;
3. *minimum mean square* if $E(\hat{\gamma}_i - \gamma_i)^2$ is minimized for each $i = 1, \cdots, q$;
4. *minimum variance* if var $(\hat{\gamma}_i - \gamma_i)$ is minimized for each $i = 1, \cdots, q$;
5. *the MVLUE* (minimum variance linear *u*-unbiased estimator) if for every $\hat{\gamma}_i$ no other estimator has equal or smaller variance in the class of all linear *u*-unbiased estimators of γ_i, $i = 1, \cdots, q$;
6. *the MMSLE* (minimum mean square linear estimator) if for every $\hat{\gamma}_i$ no other estimator has equal or smaller mean square in the class of all linear estimators of γ_i, $i = 1, \cdots, q$.

Because a linear estimator $\hat{\gamma}$ is linear in μ as well as y we get the following useful result in the random-β case.

Lemma 2.6: Equivalence of the MVLUE and the MMSLE. Given that $(\tilde{y} - \tilde{X}\beta)\sim WS(0, \tilde{\Sigma})$, the MVLUE of any linear vector function $\gamma = C\beta$ of β is the MMSLE of γ.

Proof: Suppose $\mu \neq 0$. Let $\hat{\gamma}$ be linear, i.e., $\hat{\gamma} = A_1\mu + A_2 y$, and consider

$$E(\hat{\gamma}_i - \gamma_i)^2 = [E(\hat{\gamma}_i - \gamma_i)]^2 + \text{var}(\hat{\gamma}_i - \gamma_i) \quad \text{for } i = 1, \cdots, q. \qquad (2.13)$$

Since A_1 and μ are non-random, the var$(\hat{\gamma}_i - \gamma_i)$ does not depend on A_1 (or μ) for $i=1, \cdots, q$ and we can minimize the right-hand side of (2.13) in two steps:

1. Choose A_2 to minimize var $(\hat{\gamma}_i - \gamma_i)$ for $i=1, \cdots, q$, and then
2. choose A_1 (which will be a function of A_2) so as to make the bias $E(\hat{\gamma}_i - \gamma_i) = 0$ for $i=1, \cdots, q$.

From Step 2 it follows that the MMSLE is u-unbiased and thus the MVLUE is the MMSLE of γ. If $\mu=0$ then $E(\hat{\gamma}-\gamma)=0$ and we see immediately from (2.13) that the MVLUE is the MMSLE of γ.

We are now ready to prove the natural random-β extension of the Gauss-Markov theorem. We prove the theorem by a well-known style like that of Bose [1] which ascribes a property that may be called "wide-sense sufficiency" to the right-hand side of the normal equations for estimating any linear vector function $\gamma = C\beta$ of β.

Theorem 2.7: The Extended Gauss-Markov Theorem. Given that $(\tilde{y}-\tilde{X}\beta) \sim WS(0, \tilde{\Sigma})$, an estimator $\hat{\gamma}(q\times 1)$ is the MMSLE based on $\tilde{y}$ of any linear vector function $\gamma = C\beta$ of β if and only if

(1) $\hat{\gamma}$ is a u-unbiased estimator of γ

and

(2) $\hat{\gamma}$ is a linear vector function

$$\hat{\gamma} = Mg$$

of the right-hand side $g = (\tilde{X}'\tilde{\Sigma}^{-1}\tilde{y})$ of the normal equations (2.7) where M is $q\times r$.

Proof: We show that $\hat{\gamma}$ is the unique MVLUE of γ. From Lemma 2.6 it follows that $\hat{\gamma}$ is the unique MMSLE of γ. To show the sufficiency of (1) and (2) let

$$\gamma^* = A\tilde{y}$$

be any other linear u-unbiased estimator of γ. Then

$$E(\gamma^*) = E(\gamma) = E(\hat{\gamma}),$$

from which it follows that

$$A\tilde{X}\mu = C\mu = M\tilde{X}'\tilde{\Sigma}^{-1}\tilde{X}\mu. \tag{2.14}$$

Since (2.14) is an identity in μ we have

$$(A\tilde{X} - M\tilde{X}'\tilde{\Sigma}^{-1}\tilde{X}) = 0, \tag{2.15}$$

$$(A\tilde{X} - C) = 0, \tag{2.16}$$

and

$$(M\tilde{X}'\tilde{\Sigma}^{-1}\tilde{X} - C) = 0. \tag{2.17}$$

Now

$$\begin{aligned} \text{var}[\gamma^* - \gamma] &= \text{var}[A\tilde{y} - C\beta] \\ &= \text{var}[A(\tilde{X}\beta + \tilde{\epsilon}) - C\beta] \\ &= \text{var}[A\tilde{X}\mu + A\tilde{X}u + A\tilde{\epsilon} - C\mu - Cu] \\ &= \text{var}[(A\tilde{X} - C)u + A\tilde{\epsilon}] \\ &= A\tilde{\Sigma}A'. \quad \text{(using (2.16))} \end{aligned}$$

Similarly

$$\begin{aligned} \text{var}[\hat{\gamma} - \gamma] &= \text{var}[M\tilde{X}'\tilde{\Sigma}^{-1}\tilde{y} - C\beta] \\ &= \text{var}[M\tilde{X}'\tilde{\Sigma}^{-1}(\tilde{X}\beta + \tilde{\epsilon}) - C\beta] \\ &= \text{var}[M\tilde{X}'\tilde{\Sigma}^{-1}(\tilde{X}\mu + \tilde{X}u + \tilde{\epsilon}) - C\mu - Cu] \\ &= \text{var}[(M\tilde{X}'\tilde{\Sigma}^{-1}\tilde{X} - C)u + M\tilde{X}'\tilde{\Sigma}^{-1}\tilde{\epsilon}] \\ &= M\tilde{X}'\tilde{\Sigma}^{-1}\tilde{\Sigma}\tilde{\Sigma}^{-1}\tilde{X}M' = M\tilde{X}'\tilde{\Sigma}^{-1}\tilde{X}M'. \end{aligned}$$

(using (2.17))

Write

$$\begin{aligned} &\text{var}[\gamma^* - \gamma] \\ &= [A - M\tilde{X}'\tilde{\Sigma}^{-1} + M\tilde{X}'\tilde{\Sigma}^{-1}]\tilde{\Sigma}[A' - \tilde{\Sigma}^{-1}\tilde{X}M' + \tilde{\Sigma}^{-1}\tilde{X}M'] \\ &= [A - M\tilde{X}'\tilde{\Sigma}^{-1}]\tilde{\Sigma}[A' - \tilde{\Sigma}^{-1}\tilde{X}M'] \qquad (2.18) \\ &\quad + 2[A - M\tilde{X}'\tilde{\Sigma}^{-1}]\tilde{X}M' + M\tilde{X}'\tilde{\Sigma}^{-1}\tilde{X}M' \\ &= \text{non-negative quadratic form} + 0 + \text{var}[\hat{\gamma} - \gamma] \end{aligned}$$

(using (2.15))

Since the diagonal elements of a non-negative quadratic form are non-negative,

$$\text{var}[\gamma_i^* - \gamma_i] \geq \text{var}[\hat{\gamma}_i - \gamma_i] \qquad i = 1, \cdots, q.$$

Thus $\hat{\gamma}$ is a MVLUE of γ. Uniqueness follows from (2.18), for if $\text{var}[\gamma^* - \gamma] = \text{var}[\hat{\gamma} - \gamma]$ it is necessary that $A = M\tilde{X}'\tilde{\Sigma}^{-1}$ and hence that $\gamma^* = \hat{\gamma}$. This establishes the sufficiency of conditions (1) and (2). Their necessity follows from Lemma 2.6 for (1) and a similar proof by contradiction for (2).

2.8 Corollary: The MMSLE of Random β. Given that

$$(\tilde{y} - \tilde{X}\beta) \sim WS(0, \tilde{\Sigma})$$

then

$$b = (\tilde{X}'\tilde{\Sigma}^{-1}\tilde{X})^{-1}\tilde{X}'\tilde{\Sigma}^{-1}\tilde{y}$$

is the MMSLE of β based on $\tilde{y}$.

Proof: Note that (1) $E(b-\beta)=0$ from Lemma 2.4, and (2) $b = Mg$ where $g = \tilde{X}'\tilde{\Sigma}^{-1}\tilde{y}$, the right-hand side of the normal equations (2.7), and $M = (\tilde{X}'\tilde{\Sigma}^{-1}\tilde{X})^{-1}$. The desired conclusion follows from the Extended Gauss-Markov Theorem 2.7.

In Section 3 we shall review briefly a typical Kalman-type dynamic model discussed in the introduction and present the optimal estimators. In Section 4 we shall show how these optimal estimators may be derived from the random-β regression theory given above.

3. LINEAR DYNAMIC RECURSIVE ESTIMATION

3.1 The Model

A typical form of a linear dynamic model [5, 6] for a p-variate time series $y_1, \cdots, y_n$ is given by the recursive equations (using regression-like notation) as:

$$\beta_t = T_t\beta_{t-1} + u_t \tag{3.1}$$

$$y_t = X_t\beta_t + \epsilon_t \tag{3.2}$$

where

$$\begin{bmatrix} u_t \\ \varepsilon_t \end{bmatrix} \sim WS\left(\begin{bmatrix} 0 \\ 0 \end{bmatrix}, \begin{bmatrix} Q_t & 0 \\ 0 & R_t \end{bmatrix}\right). \quad (3.3)$$

for $t=1, \cdots, n$. The starting equation for β_t may be written

$$\beta_1 = \mu_1 + u_1 \quad (3.4)$$

where μ_1 is assumed known. All the error vectors are uncorrelated between times. Equation (3.1) expresses the unknown state $\beta_t(r\times 1)$ as a known linear transformation of the previous state β_{t-1} plus a vector u_t of random errors. As mentioned before, it is the linear dynamic state transition equation (3.1) in the parameters β_t which is new to conventional regression theory and gives the model so much of its versatility.

3.2 The Recursive Estimation Equation

In the engineering literature it is shown [5, 6] that the MMSLE b_t of β_t based on all the data $\mu_1, y_1, \cdots, y_t$ up through time t is given by the recursive *updating* equations:

$$b_t = b_{t|t-1} + S_{t|t-1}X_t' D_t^{-1}(y_t - X_t b_{t|t-1}) \quad (3.5a)$$

and

$$S_t = S_{t|t-1} - S_{t|t-1}X_t' D_t^{-1}X_t S_{t|t-1} \quad (3.5b)$$

where

$b_{1|0} = \mu_1$; $S_{1|0} = Q_1$;

$b_{t|t-1} = T_t b_{t-1}$; $S_{t|t-1} = T_t S_{t-1} T_t' + Q_t$; $\quad t=2, \cdots, n$

$D_t = R_t + X_t S_{t|t-1} X_t'$ $\quad t=1, \cdots, n$.

It is also shown that

$$(b_t - \beta_t) \sim WS(0, S_t) \quad (3.6)$$

and that

$$E(b_t - \beta_t)\tilde{y}_t' = 0 \quad (3.7)$$

where

$$\tilde{y}_t = (\mu_1', y_1', \cdots, y_t')'.$$

Kalman [6] derives these results from the point of view of wide-sense conditional distributions and expectations as described, e.g., in [3]. In this approach b_t is obtained as an orthogonal projection of β_t on a linear manifold spanned by the elements of $\tilde{y}_t$. As mentioned previously, this is the same as fitting a regression of β_t on the elements of $\tilde{y}_t$ using *expected* first and second moments in the normal equations involved. Result (3.7) represents the special form of orthogonality so obtained, and the fact that $E(b_t-\beta_t)^2$ is minimized follows at the same time.

Another method of deriving similar stronger results is by the Bayesian approach under the Gaussian assumptions given in Section 1. The estimator b_t in (3.5a) is readily shown to be the posterior mean for β_t given $\tilde{y}_t$ and is thus the Bayes estimator under squared error loss or, in other words, the MMSE for β_t. For a complete discussion see [8].

The updating equations (3.5) are equivalent to the more intuitive recursive weighting equations [cf. (2.8) and (2.9)]:

$$b_t = S_t[S_{t|t-1}^{-1} b_{t|t-1} + X_t' R_t^{-1} y_t] \quad (3.8a)$$

and

$$S_t = [S_{t|t-1}^{-1} + X_t' R_t^{-1} X_t]^{-1}. \quad (3.8b)$$

Usually equations (3.5) are more convenient than the weighting equations (3.8) for computing, especially in the common cases $p<r$. The equivalence of equations (3.5) and (3.8) follows from the following two well-known lemmas.

Lemma 3.3: If $S=[M^{-1}+X'R^{-1}X]^{-1}$

then

$$S = M - MX'D^{-1}XM$$

where M is $r\times r$, R is $p\times p$, X is $p\times r$, and $D=R+XMX'$.

Proof: The result follows from showing that

$$\begin{aligned}
&[M^{-1} + X'R^{-1}X][M - MX'D^{-1}XM] \\
&= I - X'D^{-1}XM + X'R^{-1}XM - X'R^{-1}XMX'D^{-1}XM \\
&= I + [-X'D^{-1} + X'R^{-1} - X'R^{-1}XMX'D^{-1}]XM \\
&= I + X'R^{-1}[-RD^{-1} + I - XMX'D^{-1}]XM \\
&= I + X'R^{-1}[I - DD^{-1}]XM = I.
\end{aligned}$$

Lemma 3.4: If $b_1 = S[M^{-1}b_0 + X'R^{-1}y]$

then

$$b_1 = b_0 + MX'D^{-1}[y - \hat{y}]$$

where

M is $r\times r$, b_0 is $r\times 1$, X is $p\times r$, R is $p\times p$, y is $p\times 1$, $D=R+XMX'$, $\hat{y}=Xb_0$, and $S=[M^{-1}+X'R^{-1}X]^{-1}$.

Proof: Using the previous lemma we see that

$$\begin{aligned}
b_1 &= [M - MX'D^{-1}XM][M^{-1}b_0 + X'R^{-1}y] \\
&= b_0 + MX'[R^{-1}y - D^{-1}Xb_0 - D^{-1}XMX'R^{-1}y] \\
&= b_0 + MX'D^{-1}[(D - XMX')R^{-1}y - Xb_0] \\
&= b_0 + MX'D^{-1}[y - \hat{y}].
\end{aligned}$$

4. REGRESSION APPROACH DERIVATION

Using the random-β regression theory developed in Section 2, we derive the distribution of $b_t-\beta_t$ with b_t expressed in the intuitive weighting form (3.8a) and show directly that this b_t is the MMSLE of β_t based on all the data $\tilde{y}_t=[\mu_1', y_1', \cdots, y_t']'$ up through time t. Since equation (3.8a) is equivalent to equation (3.5a) we have an indirect derivation of the Kalman updating optimal estimator and its distribution.

Lemma 4.1: The distribution of $b_t-\beta_t$. Given the model described in equations (3.1) through (3.4), the recursive weighting equations (3.8a) and (3.8b) give b_t and S_t

such that

$$(b_t - \beta_t) \sim WS(0, S_t), \quad t = 1, \cdots, n. \quad (4.1)$$

Proof: To prove this inductively, suppose the result (4.1) is true for time $t-1$. Then from

$$b_{t|t-1} - \beta_t = T_t b_{t-1} - T_t \beta_{t-1} - u_t = T_t(b_{t-1} - \beta_{t-1}) - u_t$$

we have

$$(b_{t|t-1} - \beta_t) \sim WS(0, S_{t|t-1}). \quad (4.2)$$

Now letting

$$y_t^\dagger = X_t^\dagger \beta_t + \varepsilon_t^\dagger$$

represent

$$\begin{bmatrix} b_{t|t-1} \\ y_t \end{bmatrix} = \begin{bmatrix} I \\ X_t \end{bmatrix} \beta_t + \begin{bmatrix} b_{t|t-1} - \beta_t \\ \varepsilon_t \end{bmatrix} \quad (4.3)$$

we have, from (4.2)

$$(y_t^\dagger - X_t^\dagger \beta_t) \sim WS\left(0, \begin{bmatrix} S_{t|t-1} & 0 \\ 0 & R_t \end{bmatrix}\right). \quad (4.4)$$

Using (4.4) and the distribution Lemma 2.4(1) it is seen that the recursive weighting equations (3.8a) and (3.8b) give b_t and S_t such that $(b_t - \beta_t) \sim WS(0, S_t)$. This completes the induction step.

From the initial equations $b_{1|0} = \mu_1$ and $S_{1|0} = Q_1$, the premise (4.2) is satisfied at time $t=1$. Hence the Lemma is true at $t=1$ and therefore by induction at the successive times $t=2, 3, \cdots, n$.

From model (4.4) above, the Extended Gauss-Markov Theorem 2.7 tells us that b_t is the MMSLE of β_t based on $b_{t|t-1}$ and y_t. It remains to be shown that b_t is MMSLE of β_t based on all the data $\tilde{y}_t$ up through time t. We show this in the following theorem.

Theorem 4.2: The Optimality of b_t. Given the recursive model described in equations (3.1) through (3.4), the recursive estimating equations (3.8a) and (3.8b) give the MMSLE b_t of β_t based on all the data $\mu_1, y_1, \cdots, y_t$ up through time t.

Proof: Write the recursive dynamic model (3.1) through (3.4) in the regression form

$$y_t^* = X_t^* \beta_t^* + \varepsilon_t^* \quad (4.5)$$

to represent

$$\begin{bmatrix} u_1 \\ y_1 \\ 0 \\ y_2 \\ \vdots \\ 0 \\ y_t \end{bmatrix} = \begin{bmatrix} I & 0 & 0 & \cdots & 0 \\ X_1 & 0 & 0 & \cdots & 0 \\ -T_2 & I & 0 & \cdots & 0 \\ 0 & X_2 & 0 & \cdots & 0 \\ \vdots & & & & \\ 0 & \cdots 0 & -T_t & & I \\ 0 & \cdots 0 & 0 & & X_t \end{bmatrix} \begin{bmatrix} \beta_1 \\ \beta_2 \\ \vdots \\ \beta_{t-1} \\ \beta_t \end{bmatrix} + \begin{bmatrix} -u_1 \\ \varepsilon_1 \\ -u_2 \\ \varepsilon_2 \\ \vdots \\ -u_t \\ \varepsilon_t \end{bmatrix}$$

where the third row partition, for example, comes from rewriting

$$\beta_2 = T_2 \beta_1 + u_2$$

as

$$0 = \beta_2 - T_2 \beta_1 - u_2.$$

Let

$$R_t^* \equiv \text{var}(\varepsilon_t^*).$$

Note that the right hand side of the normal equations for (4.5) is

$$g_t^* = X_t^{*\prime} R_t^{*-1} y_t^*$$

which reduces to

$$g_t^* = \begin{bmatrix} X_{t-1}^{*\prime} R_{t-1}^{-1*} y_{t-1}^* \\ X_t' R_t^{-1} y_t \end{bmatrix},$$

and that b_t is a linear function of g_t^*.

Since b_t is a linear function of the right-hand side of the normal equations for (4.5) and b_t is u-unbiased from Lemma 4.1, we conclude from the Extended Gauss-Markov Theorem that b_t is MMSLE of β_t based on all the data y_t^* and therefore $\tilde{y}_t$. This then establishes the optimality of b_t from the point of view of regressing y_t^* on X_t^*.

We have shown that b_t is also the MMSLE of β_t based on $b_{t|t-1}$ and y_t. In addition to the statistic g_t^*, the statistics $b_{t|t-1}$ and y_t may well be called wide-sense sufficient statistics for estimating any linear function $\gamma = C\beta$ of β just as $X'\Sigma^{-1}y$ is the complete and sufficient statistic for the fixed-β model $y = X\beta + \varepsilon$ where $\varepsilon \sim N(0, \Sigma)$.

We show the final property (3.7) in the following lemma.

Lemma 4.3: Given the conditions of Theorem 4.2,

$$E(b_t - \beta_t)\tilde{y}_t' = 0. \quad (4.6)$$

Proof: Using Lemma 2.4(3) in model (4.5)

$$E(b_t - \beta_t) y_t^{*\prime} = 0$$

and (4.6) follows from this.

5. CONCLUDING REMARKS

The conventional regressionist will have found our approach to the Kalman recursive results in Section 4 more natural since we derived them from the regression point of view. One of the keys to our approach is the fact that the recursive dynamic model (3.1) to (3.4) may be written in the form $y_t^* = X_t^* \beta_t^* + \varepsilon_t^*$, (4.5). We plan to show in future articles that this opens the way for the application of regression techniques to new problems arising in recursive estimation, e.g., the problem of estimating the R_t and Q_t variance matrices.

Before closing, it should be noted that Kalman's recursive estimation theory is considerably more general than the form discussed in this article. The more general problem is to find an optimal estimator b_t based on all the data $\tilde{y}_s$ up through time s: If $s<t$, $s=t$, or $s>t$, this is, respectively, a problem of 'prediction,' 'filtering,' or 'smoothing'. If the errors are assumed Gaussian, stronger results can be obtained, e.g., that b_t is minimum mean square in the class of all (and not just linear) estimators.

For brevity we have dealt with only one single, but important, case of filtering under the wide-sense error assumptions. However, this illustrates a method for deriving similar results in the more general cases.

[*Received November 1971. Revised May 1972.*]

REFERENCES

[1] Bose, R.C., personal communication, 1956.

[2] Burnett, Thomas D. and Guthrie, Donald, "Estimation of Stationary Stochastic Regression Parameters," *Journal of the American Statistical Association*, 65 (December 1970), 1547–53.

[3] Doob, J.L., *Stochastic Processes*, New York: John Wiley and Sons, Inc., 1953.

[4] Hartigan, J.A., "Linear Bayesian Methods," *Journal of the Royal Statistical Society*, Ser. B, 31 (No. 3, 1969), 446–54.

[5] Kalman, R.E., "New Methods in Wiener Filtering Theory," in J.L. Bodanoff and F. Kozin, eds., *Proceedings of the First Symposium on Engineering Applications of Random Function Theory and Probability*, New York: John Wiley and Sons, Inc., 1963, 270–388.

[6] ———, "A New Approach to Linear Filtering and Prediction Problems," *Transactions ASME Journal of Basic Engineering*, 82 (March 1960), 35–45.

[7] Rao, C. Radhakrishna, *Linear Statistical Inference and its Applications*, New York: John Wiley and Sons, Inc., 1965, 192–3.

[8] Sage, Andrew P., *Optimum Systems Control*, Englewood Cliffs, N.J.: Prentice-Hall, Inc., 1968, 265–75.

[9] Sorenson, H.W., "Kalman Filtering Techniques," in C.T. Leondis, ed., *Advances in Control Systems*, 3, New York: Academic Press, 1966, 219–92.

[9]

Evaluation of Likelihood Functions for Gaussian Signals

FRED C. SCHWEPPE, MEMBER, IEEE

Abstract—State variable techniques are used to derive new expressions for the likelihood function for Gaussian signals corrupted by additive Gaussian noise. The continuous time case is obtained as a limit of the discrete time case. The likelihood function is expressed in terms of the conditional expectation of the signal given only past and present observations, multipliers, and integrators (adders). Thus, the likelihood function can be generated in real time using a physically realizable system. Time-varying finite-dimensional Markov models are also discussed as they lead to a direct mechanization for the required conditional expectation. A simple example of a multipath communication system is discussed and an explicit mechanization indicated.

I. Introduction

THE STATISTICAL theory of detection and parameter estimation for Gaussian stochastic signals observed in the presence of additive Gaussian noise has received much attention in recent years (for example, see [1]-[7]). Multipath communication systems and fluctuating radar targets have provided stimulus for such investigations. The theory of optimum procedures is well advanced in the sense that theorems on singular cases are available and integral equations whose solutions give optimum systems are well known. However, from a practical point of view, the existing theory has several shortcomings. Except for very special cases, the integral equations are hard to solve and usually difficult to implement. For example, many procedures involve a physically unrealizable operation, as they require the conditional expectation of the signal given all the observations, both past and future. We employ state variable concepts to derive the optimum formulas in a form which performs correlations between the observed quantities and the conditional expectation of the signal given only the past and present observations. Thus, the system is physically realizable without storing the observations, and can work in real time. In addition, we illustrate how the difficulties of solving integral equations are circumvented by modeling the stochastic processes in terms of state variables, that is, as finite-dimensional Markov processes. This results in optimum systems specified by differential or difference equations which can be directly implemented. We first investigate the

Manuscript received April 2, 1964; revised July 16, 1964.
The author is with the Lincoln Laboratory, Massachusetts Institute of Technology, Lexington, Mass. (Operated with support from the U. S. Air Force.)

discrete time case and then obtain the continuous time case as a limiting operation.

In general, scalars are denoted by lower case letters, with or without subscripts. Vectors are bold face letters, with or without subscripts. Matrices are denoted by captial letters. Exceptions to these rules are so indicated in the text. All vectors are column vectors. Transpose is indicated by a prime. "| |" denotes the determinant and "tr" the trace of a matrix. The observations are always denoted by z. We use the same symbol for both a random variable and a sample of the random variable, and rely on the text to furnish the necessary distinction. All random variables are Gaussian with zero mean.

A copy of Magill [8] was received after completion of this paper. His report [8] is similar in many respects to our discussion on the discrete time case, and appropriate discussions have been inserted into the text.

II. Problem Statement

Assume the α-dimensional vector time function, $\mathbf{z}(t)$, is observed over the time interval $0 \le t \le T$, where $\mathbf{z}(t)$ is of the form

$$\mathbf{z}(t : \mathbf{q}) = \mathbf{s}(t : \mathbf{q}_1) + \mathbf{r}(t : \mathbf{q}_2) \quad 0 \le t \le T \tag{1}$$

where $\mathbf{s}(t : \mathbf{q}_1)$ and $\mathbf{r}(t : \mathbf{q}_2)$ are independent α-dimensional stochastic processes whose statistical behavior is assumed to be completely known except possibly for the values of a finite number of parameters which are the elements of $\mathbf{q}_j$. The vector $\mathbf{q}$ contains the elements of both $\mathbf{q}_1$ and $\mathbf{q}_2$. If no $\mathbf{q}$ dependence is indicated as in

$$\mathbf{z}(t) = \mathbf{s}(t) + \mathbf{r}(t) \tag{2}$$

then the values of the parameters are assumed known. The discrete time version of (1) is

$$\mathbf{z}(n\Delta : \mathbf{q}) = \mathbf{s}(n\Delta : \mathbf{q}_1) + \mathbf{r}(n\Delta : \mathbf{q}_2) \quad n = 1, \cdots, N \tag{3}$$

where

$$\Delta = T/N \tag{4}$$

We call $\mathbf{s}(t)$ or $\mathbf{s}(n\Delta)$ the signal process and $\mathbf{r}(t)$ or $\mathbf{r}(n\Delta)$ the noise process.

Consider first the discrete time case. Let $f[\mathbf{z}(\Delta), \cdots, \mathbf{z}(N\Delta)]$ denote the probability density of the random vectors $\mathbf{z}(\Delta), \cdots, \mathbf{z}(N\Delta)$. Define

$$\lambda(n) = \log f[\mathbf{z}(\Delta), \cdots, \mathbf{z}(n\Delta)] \tag{5}$$

as the likelihood function. The presence of unknown parameters as in (1) is indicated by writing $\lambda(n : \mathbf{q})$. We now briefly review the role of the likelihood function in parameter estimation, signal detection, and decoding. The resulting systems are often called optimum. Helstron [1] and Wilks [9] are among two of many applicable references.

If unknown parameters exist, a basic problem is to estimate them. For example, when a radar is tracking a fluctuating target, the slant range is to be estimated. The maximum-likelihood method of parameter estimation chooses as the estimate of $\mathbf{q}$ the value that maximizes $\lambda(N : \mathbf{q})$. Another basic problem is that of signal detection. Given $\mathbf{z}(n\Delta)$, $n = 1, \cdots, N$, we want to decide whether or not the signal $\mathbf{s}(n\Delta)$ is present. The statistical theory of hypothesis testing provides a basis for this decision. Let H_1 be the hypothesis that the signal is present and H_2 be the hypothesis that no signal is present. If there are no unknown parameters,

$$\begin{aligned} H_1 &: \mathbf{z}(n\Delta) = \mathbf{s}(n\Delta) + \mathbf{r}(n\Delta) \\ H_2 &: \mathbf{z}(n\Delta) = \mathbf{r}(n\Delta) \end{aligned} \tag{6}$$

Define f_j, $j = 1, 2$ as the probability density of $\mathbf{z}(\Delta), \cdots, \mathbf{z}(N\Delta)$ when H_j is true and $\lambda_j(N)$ as the corresponding likelihood function. Then a decision between H_1 and H_2 can be based on the value of

$$\theta(N) = \log \frac{f_1}{f_2} = \lambda_1(N) - \lambda_2(N) \tag{7}$$

where $\theta(N)$ is the (logarithm of the) likelihood ratio. If $\theta(N)$ exceeds some chosen threshold, H_1 is accepted; otherwise, H_2 is accepted. If unknown parameters exist, the λ_j of (7) are evaluated for the maximum-likelihood estimate of $\mathbf{q}$ under the assumption H_j is true. The basic signal detection problem generalizes directly to the case of deciding which of M possible signals is present, i.e., decoding. Such a decision can be performed using an array of hypothesis tests similar to (7) to test the hypothesis the jth signal is present vs. the hypothesis the kth signal is present. The above review illustrates why the evaluation of $\lambda(N)$ under the assumption the statistics of $\mathbf{z}(n\Delta)$, $n = 1, \cdots, N$ are completely known is the basic mechanization problem for a very wide range of discrete time situations. In parameter estimation, we evaluate $\lambda(N)$ for all possible values of $\mathbf{q}$; in signal detection, for both hypotheses; in decoding, for all possible signal combinations; etc.

The continuous time case can be obtained from the discrete model by letting $N \to \infty$ with T fixed. Since the limit of $\lambda(N)$ usually does not exist, we work with the likelihood ratio, $\theta(N)$, of (7), but $\theta(N)$ can be used for parameter estimation as well as detection by changing the hypotheses H_j. As an example, assume the distribution of the noise $\mathbf{r}(n\Delta)$ is completely known and the unknown parameters $\mathbf{q}$ affect only the signal $\mathbf{s}(n\Delta)$. Then if we make the hypotheses

$$\begin{aligned} H_1 &: \mathbf{z}(n\Delta) : \mathbf{q}) = \mathbf{s}(n\Delta : \mathbf{q}) + \mathbf{r}(n\Delta) \\ H_2 &: \mathbf{z}(n\Delta) = \mathbf{r}(n\Delta) \end{aligned} \tag{8}$$

the value of $\mathbf{q}$ which maximizes $\theta(N : \mathbf{q})$ is a maximum likelihood estimate where

$$\theta(N : \mathbf{q}) = \lambda_1(N : \mathbf{q}) - \lambda_2(N) \tag{9}$$

Therefore, the same arguments made with respect to $\lambda(N)$ also apply to $\theta(N)$; that is, the mechanization of

$\theta(N)$ for a completely specified H_1 and H_2 forms the basis for a wide variety of actual problems.

To simplify further developments, we confine ourselves to investigations of $\lambda(N)$ in the discrete time case and the limit of $\theta(N)$ in the continuous time case. Although somewhat confusing, we call both $\lambda(N)$ and $\theta(N)$ likelihood functions. Obviously, $\theta(N)$ could also be employed for discrete time, but it is conceptually clearer to work with $\lambda(N)$. The incorporation of the basic mechanizations into complete parameter estimation, detection, or decoding systems is left as an exercise for the reader, which may or may not be simple.

It should also be mentioned that our restriction to zero-mean stochastic processes is not really essential. A known deterministic component is handled by subtraction. A deterministic component with unknown parameters requires conceptually, at least, only a simple extension of our results.

At various points in our developments, we use discrete time and continuous time vector white noise processes which are defined as follows: If $\mathbf{v}(n\Delta)/\Delta$ is vector discrete white noise,

$$E[\mathbf{v}(n\Delta)\mathbf{v}'(m\Delta)] = \begin{cases} 0 & n \neq m \\ \Delta I & n = m \end{cases}$$

where I is the unit matrix. If $\mathbf{v}(t)$ is vector continuous white noise,

$$E[\mathbf{v}(t)\mathbf{v}'(\tau)] = \delta(t-\tau)I$$

where $\delta(t-\tau)$ is the Dirac delta function.

III. Discrete Time

We investigate the likelihood function $\lambda(N)$ as defined by (5). In an attempt to gain perspective, we discuss two "classical" solutions before introducing the state variable approach. The sequence of α-dimensional vector observations, $\mathbf{z}(k\Delta)$, $k = 1, \cdots, N$ can be considered one $N\alpha$-dimensional vector observation defined by

$$\mathbf{z}_N = \mathbf{s}_N + \mathbf{r}_N \tag{10}$$

where $\mathbf{s}_N$ and $\mathbf{r}_N$ are $N\alpha$-dimensional, random vectors with covariance matrices

$$\Psi_s = E(\mathbf{s}_N\mathbf{s}_N') \tag{11}$$

$$\Psi_r = E(\mathbf{r}_N\mathbf{r}_N') \tag{12}$$

Since $\mathbf{s}_N$ and $\mathbf{r}_N$ are assumed independent, $\mathbf{z}_N$ is a random vector with

$$\Psi_z = E(\mathbf{z}_N\mathbf{z}_N') = \Psi_s + \Psi_r \tag{13}$$

Thus, from the Gaussian, zero mean assumption, the likelihood function of (5) is

$$2\lambda(N) = -\log(2\pi)^N \,|\Psi_z| - \mathbf{z}_N'\Psi_z^{-1}\mathbf{z}_N \tag{14}$$

One classical approach to evaluating (14) is a change of variables based on the eigenfunctions of Ψ_z. Let J be the $N\alpha$ by $N\alpha$ matrix formed by the eigenfunctions of Ψ_z such that

$$J'\Psi_z J = D \tag{15}$$

where D is a diagonal matrix whose elements, d_{kk}, are the eigenvalues of Ψ_z. If

$$\tilde{\mathbf{z}}_N = J\mathbf{z}_N \tag{16}$$

then

$$2\lambda(N) = -\log\left[(2\pi)^N \prod_{k=1}^{N\alpha} d_{kk}\right] - \sum_{k=1}^{N\alpha} \frac{\tilde{z}_k^2}{d_{kk}} \tag{17}$$

where the $\tilde{z}_k$ are the elements of $\tilde{\mathbf{z}}_N$. The transformation of (16) changes $\mathbf{z}_N$ into a vector of independent random variables, each with variance d_{kk}. This approach corresponds to the Karhunen-Loève expansion used in the continuous time case.

The second classical approach to evaluating (14), uses the matrix identity

$$(\Psi_s + \Psi_r)^{-1} = \Psi_r^{-1} - \Psi_r^{-1}(\Psi_s^{-1} + \Psi_r^{-1})^{-1}\Psi_r^{-1} \tag{18}$$

combined with the equation for $\hat{\mathbf{s}}_N$, the conditional expectation of $\mathbf{s}_N$ given $\mathbf{z}_N$, which is

$$\hat{\mathbf{s}}_N = E(\mathbf{s}_N/\mathbf{z}_N) = (\Psi_s^{-1} + \Psi_r^{-1})^{-1}\Psi_r^{-1}\mathbf{z}_N \tag{19}$$

Equation (19), has been derived in many forms by many authors (see, for example, Kailath [5]). Combining (13), (18), and (19)) gives

$$\mathbf{z}_N'\Psi_z^{-1}\mathbf{z}_N = \mathbf{z}_N'\Psi_r^{-1}\mathbf{z}_N - \mathbf{z}_N'\Psi_r^{-1}\hat{\mathbf{s}}_N \tag{20}$$

Equation (20) leads to the "cross-correlation" implementation, which also has a continuous time analog.

Now let us discuss the state variable approach which is the heart of this paper. We consider $\lambda(n)$ as a function of time and write $\lambda(n)$ in terms of $\lambda(n-1)$. By the definition of conditional probability,

$$f(\mathbf{z}_n) = f(\mathbf{z}_{n-1})f(\mathbf{z}(n\Delta)/\mathbf{z}_{n-1}) \tag{21}$$

where $f(\mathbf{z}(n\Delta)/\mathbf{z}_{n-1})$ is the conditional probability density of $\mathbf{z}(n\Delta)$ given $\mathbf{z}(k\Delta)$, $k = 1, \cdots, n-1$. Thus

$$\lambda(n) = \lambda(n-1) + \log f(\mathbf{z}(n\Delta)/\mathbf{z}_{N-1}) \tag{22}$$

Let $\hat{\mathbf{z}}(n\Delta/n-1)$ denote the conditional expectation of $\mathbf{z}(n\Delta)$ given $\mathbf{z}_{n-1}$; that is,

$$\hat{\mathbf{z}}(n\Delta/n-1) = E[\mathbf{z}(n\Delta)/\mathbf{z}_{n-1}]$$

Define further

$$\mathbf{q}(n) = \mathbf{z}(n\Delta) - \hat{\mathbf{z}}(n\Delta/n-1) \tag{23}$$

and

$$\Sigma_z(n/n-1) = E[\mathbf{q}(n)\mathbf{q}'(n)] \tag{24}$$

Then, from (22) and the Gaussian assumption,

$$2[\lambda(n) - \lambda(n-1)] = -\log 2\pi \mid \Sigma_s(n/n-1) \mid - q'(n)\Sigma_s^{-1}(n/n-1)q(n) \qquad (25)$$

or

$$2[\lambda(N)] = -\sum_{k=1}^{N} \log 2\pi \mid \Sigma_s(k/k-1) \mid - \sum_{k=1}^{N} q'(k)\Sigma_s^{-1}(k/k-1)q(k) \qquad (26)$$

where $q(1) = z(\Delta)$.

Now consider the relationship between (26) and the two classical approaches. By the projection theorem (Loève [10] is one of many references),

$$E[q(k)q'(j)] = 0 \quad k \neq j$$

Thus, the change of variables from $z(k\Delta)k = 1, \cdots, N$ to $q(k\Delta)$, $k = 1, \cdots, N$ is analogous to the eigenfunction transformation of (16) in that the observations, $z(k\Delta)$, $k = 1, \cdots, N$ are transformed into a sequence of independent random vectors (variables).[1]

To compare (26) with the cross-correlation approach of (20), assume the noise is white, i.e., $\Psi_r = I$, and that $z(n\Delta)$ is a scalar, $z(n\Delta)$. Let $\hat{s}(k\Delta/N)k = 1, \cdots$, denote the elements of $\hat{s}_N$. Then (20) gives

$$z_N'\Psi_s^{-1}z_N = \sum_{k=1}^{N} z(k\Delta)[z(k\Delta) - \hat{s}(k\Delta/N)] \qquad (27)$$

From the white noise assumption

$$\hat{z}(n\Delta/n-1) = \hat{s}(n\Delta/n-1)$$

and (26) gives

$$z_N'\Psi_s^{-1}z_N = \sum_{k=1}^{N} \frac{[z(k\Delta) - \hat{s}(k\Delta/k-1)]^2}{\Sigma_s(k/k-1)} \qquad (28)$$

Equation (25) is a difference equation driven by $\hat{z}(n\Delta/n-1)$ and $\Sigma_s(n/n-1)$. $\Sigma_s(n/n-1)$ is a deterministic quantity, and since $z(n\Delta)$ is a Gaussian process, $\hat{z}(n\Delta/n-1)$ is given by a linear operation on the $z(k\Delta)$, $k = 1, \cdots, n-1$. The necessary equations for $\hat{z}(n\Delta/n-1)$ and $\Sigma_s(n/n-1)$ are given in Appendix I for the case of a finite-dimensional Markov signal and white noise. For this case, a complete mechanization of $\lambda(N)$ can be implemented on a digital computer in real time, and the storage requirements do not increase with N.

Results analogous to (25) and (26) are also given in Magill [8] for the scalar case.

IV. Continuous Time

The continuous time case is obtained by taking the limit of the likelihood function, $\theta(N)$, as $N \to \infty$ with fixed T. We have two hypotheses,

[1] Equation (23) can be considered a Gram-Schmidt orthogonalization procedure.

H_1 : z_N has probability distribution $f_1(z_N)$

H_2 : z_N has probability distribution $f_2(z_N)$

and

$$\theta(N) = \log \frac{f_1(z_N)}{f_2(z_N)} \qquad (29)$$

where, as in Section III, z_n is the vector containing $z(\Delta), \cdots, z(n\Delta)$. We define $\hat{z}_j(n\Delta/n-1)$ as the conditional expectation of $\hat{z}(n\Delta)$ given z_{n-1} under the assumption hypothesis H_j is true. Thus

$$\hat{z}_j(n\Delta/n-1) = E_j[z(n\Delta)/z_{n-1}] \quad j = 1, 2 \qquad (30)$$

and similarly

$$q_j(n) = z(n\Delta) - \hat{z}_j(n\Delta/n-1) \quad j = 1, 2 \qquad (31)$$

$$\Sigma_{s,j}(n/n-1) = E_j[q_j(n)q_j'(n)] \quad j = 1, 2 \qquad (32)$$

where E_j denotes expectation under hypothesis j. Then by direct analogy with (21) through (26) we have from the Gaussian assumption

$$2[\theta(n) - \theta(n-1)] = -\log \frac{\mid \Sigma_{s,1}(n/n-1) \mid}{\mid \Sigma_{s,2}(n/n-1) \mid} - q_1'(n)\Sigma_{s,1}^{-1}(n/n-1)q_1(n) + q_2'(n)\Sigma_{s,2}^{-1}(n/n-1)q_2(n) \qquad (33)$$

The limiting behavior of $\theta(N)$ as $N \to \infty$ depends on the explicit hypothesis. Singular cases can arise [3]. To circumvent such complications, we investigate the limit of $\theta(N)$ as $N \to \infty$ only for the special case

$$H_1 : z(n\Delta) = s_1(n\Delta) + \frac{C(n\Delta)}{\Delta} v(n\Delta)$$
$$H_2 : z(n\Delta) = s_2(n\Delta) + \frac{C(n\Delta)}{\Delta} v(n\Delta) \qquad (34)$$

where $v(n\Delta)/\Delta$ is discrete white noise and where the $s_j(n\Delta)$ do not contain any white noise. This model is obviously not as general as (1) but fortunately (34) encompasses most problems of interest. For example, Section V uses (34) to consider a problem in which the observation noise is actually the sum of two independent processes, one white and the other correlated.

Define

$$\hat{s}_j(n\Delta/n-1) = E_j(s_j(n\Delta)/z_{n-1}) \quad j = 1, 2 \qquad (35)$$

as the conditional expectation under hypothesis j of $s_j(n\Delta)$ given the observations up to time $n-1$. From (34), we note that

$$\hat{z}_j(n\Delta/n-1) = \hat{s}_j(n\Delta/n-1) \quad j = 1, 2$$

and thus

$$q_j(n\Delta) = z(n\Delta) - \hat{s}_j(n\Delta/n-1) \quad j = 1, 2 \qquad (36)$$

$$\Sigma_{s,j}(n/n-1) = \Sigma_{s,j}(n/n-1) + \frac{Q(n\Delta)}{\Delta} \quad j = 1, 2 \qquad (37)$$

where $Q(n\Delta) = C(n\Delta)C'(n\Delta)$ and

$$\Sigma_{\cdot,j}(n/n-1) = E_j\{[\hat{s}_j(n\Delta/n-1) - s_j(n\Delta)][\hat{s}_j(n\Delta/n-1) - s_j(n\Delta)]'\} \quad j = 1, 2 \tag{38}$$

For the model of (34), (33) becomes

$$2\theta(N) = \mu_1(N) + \mu_2(N) \tag{39}$$

where

$$\mu_1(N) = -\sum_{k=1}^{N} \log \frac{\left|\Sigma_{\cdot,1}(k/k-1) + \frac{Q(k\Delta)}{\Delta}\right|}{\left|\Sigma_{\cdot,2}(k/k-1) + \frac{Q(k\Delta)}{\Delta}\right|} \tag{40}$$

and

$$\mu_2(N) = -\sum_{k=1}^{N} q_1'(k\Delta/k-1)\left[\Sigma_{\cdot,1}(k/k-1) + \frac{Q(k\Delta)}{\Delta}\right]^{-1} q_1(k\Delta/k-1) + \sum_{k=1}^{N} q_2'(k\Delta/k-1)\left[\Sigma_{\cdot,2}(k/k-1) + \frac{Q(k\Delta)}{\Delta}\right]^{-1} q_2(k\Delta/k-1) \tag{41}$$

The limit as $N \to \infty$ presents a problem as the limit of discrete white noise does not exist in either reality or most mathematical senses. In practice, the white noise model is used for a random process with a spectrum that is flat over some finite range of interest; and although a system may be designed under a continuous white noise assumption, it obviously does not process continuous white noise. Therefore, we adopt the following philosophy for our limiting operation: $\theta(N)$ of (39) is a nonlinear operation on a set of numbers, $z(\Delta), \cdots, z(N\Delta)$ where $z(k\Delta)$ is the value of $z(t)$ for $t = k\Delta$ and we evaluate the limit under the assumption $z(t)$ is a well-behaved function. Our analysis is formal rather than rigorous as we do not explicitly state the conditions which are required for the existence of the limit.

Define $\hat{s}_j(t/t)$ as the limit of $\hat{s}_j(n\Delta/n-1)$ and $\Sigma_{\cdot,j}(t/t)$ as the limit of $\Sigma_{\cdot,j}(n/n-1)$ as $N \to \infty$. Now consider $\mu_1(N)$ of (40). Matrix manipulation gives

$$\mu_1(N) = -\sum_{k=1}^{N} \log |I + \Delta\{[\Sigma_{\cdot,1}(k/k-1) - \Sigma_{\cdot,2}(k/k-1)][I + \Delta Q^{-1}(k\Delta)\Sigma_{\cdot,2}(k/k-1)]^{-1}Q^{-1}(k\Delta)\}| \tag{42}$$

For small Δ

$$|I + \Delta F| \approx 1 + \Delta trF$$

$$\log(1 + \Delta trF) \approx \Delta trF$$

Thus, for large N and small Δ, (42) gives

$$\mu_1(N) \approx -\sum_{k=1}^{N} \Delta tr\{[\Sigma_{\cdot,1}(k/k-1) - \Sigma_{\cdot,2}(k/k-1)]Q^{-1}(k\Delta)\} \tag{43}$$

or in the limit

$$\mu_1(T) = -\int_0^T tr\{[\Sigma_{\cdot,1}(t/t) - \Sigma_{\cdot,2}(t/t)]Q^{-1}(t)\}\, dt \tag{44}$$

Now consider $\mu_2(N)$ as given by (41). From our assumption that $z(t)$ is well behaved,

$$\mu_2(N) \to \mu_2(T) = \int_0^T \{-q_1'(t)Q^{-1}(t)q_1(t) + q_2'(t)Q^{-1}(t)q_2(t)\}\, dt \tag{45}$$

where

$$q_j(t) = z(t) - \hat{s}_j(t/t) \quad j = 1, 2 \tag{46}$$

Equations (39), (44), and (45) can be combined to give $\theta(T)$. Using (46), the resulting expression is

$$2\theta(T) = -\int_0^T tr\{[\Sigma_{\cdot,1}(t/t) - \Sigma_{\cdot,2}(t/t)]Q^{-1}(t)\}\, dt + \int_0^T \{2z'(t)Q^{-1}(t)[\hat{s}_1(t/t) - \hat{s}_2(t/t)] - \hat{s}_2'(t/t)Q^{-1}(t)\hat{s}_2(t/t) + \hat{s}_1'(t/t)Q^{-1}(t)\hat{s}_1(t/t)\}\, dt \tag{47}$$

From the Gaussian assumption, $\hat{s}_j(t/t)$ is a linear operation on the observations,

$$\hat{s}_j(t/t) = \int_0^t K_j(t, \tau)z(\tau)\, d\tau \quad j = 1, 2 \tag{48}$$

where $K_j(t, \tau)$ is the appropriate matrix weighting function. For a Markov model, Appendix I provides explicit differential equations for $\hat{s}_j(t/t)$ and $\Sigma_{\cdot,j}(t/t)$ so that (48) and, hence, (47) can be directly mechanized.

In the special case of detecting the presence of a signal s, the hypotheses are

$$H_1 : z(n\Delta) = s(n\Delta) + \frac{C(n\Delta)v(n\Delta)}{\Delta}$$
$$H_2 : z(n\Delta) = \frac{C(n\Delta)v(n\Delta)}{\Delta} \tag{49}$$

The corresponding likelihood function is obtained from (47) by setting $\Sigma_{\cdot,2}(t/t) = 0$ and $\hat{s}_2(t/t) = 0$. When a scalar observation is made, Q, $\Sigma_\cdot$, z and $\hat{s}$ are all scalar and thus for the detection problem we have from (47),

$$2\theta(T) = \int_0^T \left[-\frac{\Sigma_\cdot(t/t)}{Q(t)} + \frac{2z(t)\hat{s}(t/t)}{Q(t)} - \frac{\hat{s}^2(t/t)}{Q(t)}\right] dt \tag{50}$$

We demonstrate in Appendix II how the nondeterministic part of (50) can also be derived using integral equations.

In this paper, we handle the difficulties associated with the nonexistence of continuous white noise by assuming $z(t)$ is a well-behaved function. However, during our original investigations, we also considered the limiting operation for the $z(n\Delta)$ explicitly given by (34) so that $z(n\Delta)$ actually approaches a process containing continuous white noise. This analysis resulted in additional nonrandom term (a bias). However, our limit actually gives an expression for $\hat{s}(t/t)$, (48), in which the upper limit of integration is not t but $t-$. If continuous white noise is "actually" present, a change from $t-$ to t introduces still another bias term which cancels out the first, leaving once again (47). This other analysis is mentioned to point out once again some of the mathematical difficulties which can arise when using a white noise model.

V. Example

We now discuss an example which could correspond to a low-pass version of a multipath communication system or a fluctuating radar target. The model is as follows: A known waveform, $x(t)$, is transmitted either over the communication channel or towards the radar target. The receiver then observes

$$z(t) = s(t) + r(t) \quad 0 \leq t \leq T$$

where

$$s(t) = \sum_{i=1}^{3} x(t - \tau_i)y_i(t)$$

The τ_i are three different time delays, corresponding to the various communication paths or to the finite size of the radar target. The $y_i(t)$ are independent, first-order Markov processes defined by

$$\frac{dy_j(t)}{dt} = a_j y_j(t) + b_j u_j(t) \quad j = 1, 2, 3$$

where the $u_j(t)$ are independent white noise processes. The observation noise, $r(t)$, is independent of the signal and is given by

$$r(t) = cv(t) + r_1(t)$$

where $v(t)$ is white noise and $r_1(t)$ is a second-order Markov process defined by

$$\frac{d}{dt}\begin{bmatrix} r_1(t) \\ r_2(t) \end{bmatrix} = \begin{bmatrix} 0 & 1 \\ a_{r_1} & a_{r_2} \end{bmatrix}\begin{bmatrix} r_1(t) \\ r_2(t) \end{bmatrix} + \begin{bmatrix} 0 \\ b_r \end{bmatrix} u_r(t)$$

where $u_r(t)$ is white noise, independent of the $u_j(t)$ and $v(t)$. If we define

$$\mathbf{w}(t) = \begin{bmatrix} y_1(t) \\ y_2(t) \\ y_3(t) \\ r_1(t) \\ r_2(t) \end{bmatrix}$$

$$A(t) = \begin{bmatrix} a_1 & 0 & 0 & 0 & 0 \\ 0 & a_2 & 0 & 0 & 0 \\ 0 & 0 & a_3 & 0 & 0 \\ 0 & 0 & 0 & 0 & 1 \\ 0 & 0 & 0 & a_{r_1} & a_{r_2} \end{bmatrix}$$

$$B(t) = \begin{bmatrix} b_1 & 0 & 0 & 0 \\ 0 & b_2 & 0 & 0 \\ 0 & 0 & b_3 & 0 \\ 0 & 0 & 0 & 0 \\ 0 & 0 & 0 & b_r \end{bmatrix}$$

$$\mathbf{u}(t) = \begin{bmatrix} u_1(t) \\ u_2(t) \\ u_3(t) \\ u_r(t) \end{bmatrix}$$

$$H'(t) = \begin{bmatrix} x(t-\tau_1) \\ x(t-\tau_2) \\ x(t-\tau_3) \\ 1 \\ 0 \end{bmatrix}$$

our model can be written as

$$\frac{d}{dt}\mathbf{w}(t) = A(t)\mathbf{w}(t) + B(t)\mathbf{u}(t)$$

$$\bar{s}(t) = s(t) + r_1(t) = H(t)\mathbf{w}(t)$$

$$z(t) = \bar{s}(t) + cv(t)$$

This is a special case of the model discussed in Appendix I. Extensions to M time delays and higher order Markov models for the $y_i(t)$ and $r_1(t)$ should be obvious. Extension to statistical dependence between the $y_i(t)$ can be obtained by "filling in" the $A(t)$ and $B(t)$ matrices. A high-frequency band-pass model can be obtained from a 2-dimensional observation, $\mathbf{z}(t)$, each component corresponding to one of the quadrature components.

Our example illustrates the type of unknown parameters which may occur in practice. The time delays τ are obvious candidates. If the signal power or noise power is uncertain, the b's or c can be considered unknown parameters. Unknown a_i correspond to channels with uncertain time constants. The ideas summarized in Section II enable us to discuss systems to estimate the values of such unknown parameters. However, for this example we are content to consider only the detection problem of deciding whether $s(t)$ is actually present. Thus, we have two hypotheses:

$$H_1 : z(t) = s(t) + r(t)$$

$$H_2 : z(t) = r(t)$$

If we make the following associations with the $s_1(t)$ and $s_2(t)$ of Section IV,

$$s_1(t) : s(t) + r_1(t)$$

$$s_2(t) : r_1(t)$$

then the likelihood ratio, $\theta(T)$, to be used for detection is given by (47). Appendix I gives the necessary equations for evaluating $\Sigma_{*,i}(t/t)$ and $\hat{s}_i(t/t)$.

To carry the detection problem further, we simplify it to the case of only one time delay and observation noise that is completely white; that is, $r_1(t)$ is not present.

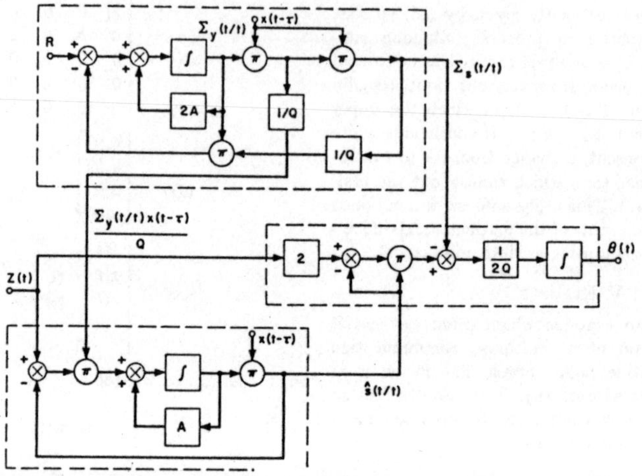

Fig. 1. Sample mechanization.

Thus

$$z(t) = s(t) + cv(t)$$
$$s(t) = x(t - \tau)y(t)$$
$$\frac{dy(t)}{dt} = Ay(t) + bu(t)$$

where $v(t)$ and $u(t)$ are independent white noise processes and A is a scalar. Define the scalars

$$c^2 = Q$$
$$b^2 = R$$

For this special case

$$y(t) = w(t)$$

and therefore using (63)

$$\frac{d\hat{y}(t/t)}{dt} = A\hat{y}(t/t) + \frac{\Sigma_y(t/t)x(t-\tau)}{Q}[z(t) - x(t-\tau)\hat{y}(t/t)] \qquad (51)$$

where from (64)

$$\frac{d\Sigma_y(t/t)}{dt} = 2A\Sigma_y(t/t) + R - \frac{\Sigma_y^2(t/t)x^2(t-\tau)}{Q} \qquad (52)$$

From (65) and (66)

$$\hat{s}(t/t) = x(t-\tau)\hat{y}(t/t) \qquad (53)$$
$$\Sigma_s(t/t) = x^2(t-\tau)\Sigma_y(t/t) \qquad (54)$$

Figure 1 shows, in block diagram form, a possible system for mechanizing $\theta(t)$ as defined by (50) combined with (51) through (54). The figure is illustrative, not necessarily efficient. The following conventions are used:

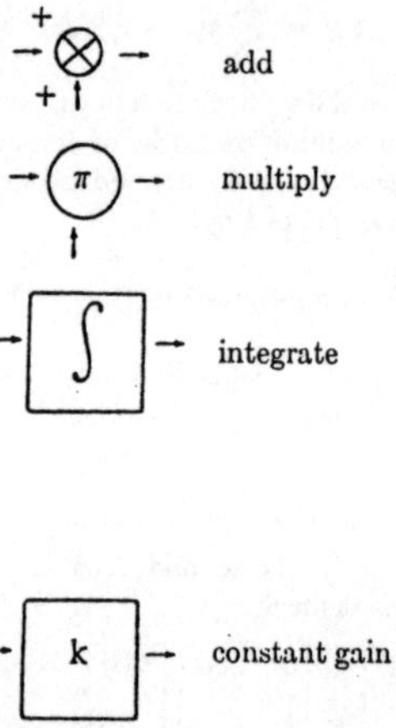

Figure 1 is subdivided into its three main operations. The upper main block generates the necessary time-varying coefficients, (52) and (54). Since it is entirely deterministic, its outputs can be stored before the actual data processing begins if desired. The lower main block is the filter, (51) and (53), while the third main block is (50), whose output is $\theta(t)$.

VI. Summary and Extensions

The basic idea underlying this paper is simplicity itself. We merely consider the likelihood function as a state variable and write equations for its evolution in time. However, the result is extremely valuable as it involves only physically realizable operations. The practical implications are magnified when the Markov model of Appendix I used for the likelihood function is then completely specified by a system of difference or differential equations which are ready for implementation for real time operation with no growing storage requirements. Section V provides an example of a complete system. As discussed in Section II, the mechanization of the likelihood function forms the basis for a wide variety of detection, decoding, and parameter estimation problems. Since the likelihood function is evaluated dynamically in time, sequential decision problems without a fixed observation interval are automatically included.

There are areas of extension other than the obvious ones of mathematical rigor and of a model without white noise for the continuous time case. In the case of deterministic signals, a variety of iterative techniques have been developed for parameter estimation. Initial investigations indicate that some of these techniques are also applicable to stochastic signals with the case of low SNR being especially promising. Although we investigated only the Gaussian case, the state variable concept is not explicitly tied to a Gaussian assumption. Although not yet attempted, there is reason to believe similar results can be obtained for the non-Gaussian case, in particular, for the Poisson process. Iterative parameter estimation and non-Gaussian signals form two explicit extensions. However, the state variable concept is part of the rapidly developing field of modern control (system) theory. Thus, if we consider our basic theme to be the application of modern control techniques to communication and radar problems, the scope of possible extensions is almost unbounded. Schweppe [11] is another example of such exploitation which combines Pontryagin's Maximum Principle with the state variable concept in order to design optimum signals.

Appendix I

Markov Model

The likelihood function was derived in terms of a differential or difference equation driven by certain covariance matrices and conditional expectations. Since these covariances and conditional expectations must also be calculated, we now list without proof some pertinent results which have appeared in the literature. The basic model is a combination of Markov processes and white noise. There are various references to this material. References [12], [13], and [14] contain the original derivations of the equations in the general form we present them. The reader who is familiar with the Weiner-Hopf integral equation approach to filtering Gaussian processes may find [12] most suitable. Schweppe [15] contains one of many alternate derivations.

The model and equations to follow are closely related to our derivations for the likelihood function as both employ state variable concepts and result in systems defined in terms of difference or differential equations. In fact our derivation was motivated by the analysis done on the Markov model. Of course, in the main text we make no Markov assumptions and, thus, in theory, it is not essential. However, it appears to be the only approach which yields practical results for the nonstationary problems which must be solved.

Consider first the basic model. We observe $\mathbf{z}$, which is the sum of the signal $\mathbf{s}$ and the noise $\mathbf{r}$. The continuous time model is

$$\mathbf{r}(t) = C(t)\mathbf{v}(t)$$

$$\frac{d}{dt}\mathbf{w}(t) = A(t)\mathbf{w}(t) + B(t)\mathbf{u}(t)$$

$$\mathbf{s}(t) = H(t)\mathbf{w}(t)$$

where

$A(t)$ is a $\gamma \times \gamma$ matrix

$B(t)$ is a $\gamma \times \beta$ matrix

$C(t)$ is a $\alpha \times \alpha$ matrix

$H(t)$ is a $\alpha \times \gamma$ matrix

$\mathbf{v}(t)$ is α-dimensional vector white noise

$\mathbf{u}(t)$ is β-dimensional vector white noise

$\mathbf{u}(t)$ and $\mathbf{v}(t)$ are mutually independent

$\mathbf{w}(t)$ is a γ-dimensional vector Markov process

$$\gamma \geq \alpha$$

In direct analogy, the discrete time model is

$$\mathbf{r}(n\Delta) = \frac{C(n\Delta)}{\Delta}\mathbf{v}(n\Delta)$$

$$\mathbf{w}(n\Delta) = G(n\Delta)\mathbf{w}(n\Delta - \Delta) + B(n\Delta)\mathbf{u}(n\Delta)$$

where

$$G(n\Delta) = I + \Delta A(n\Delta)$$

$$\mathbf{s}(n\Delta) = H(n\Delta)\mathbf{w}(n\Delta)$$

Define the conditional expectation of a random vector $\mathbf{x}(t)$ or $\mathbf{x}(n\Delta)$, given $\mathbf{z}(\tau)$, $0 \leq \tau \leq t$ or $\mathbf{z}(k\Delta)$, $k = 1, \cdots, m$ by $\hat{\mathbf{x}}(t/t)$ or $\hat{\mathbf{x}}(n\Delta/m)$. Define the covariance matrix of $[\mathbf{x}(t) - \hat{\mathbf{x}}(t/t)]$ by $\Sigma_x(t/t)$ and that of $[\mathbf{x}(n\Delta) - \hat{\mathbf{x}}(n\Delta/m)]$ by $\Sigma_x(n/m)$.

The following formulas can then be derived for the discrete time case. Let

$$Q(n\Delta) = C(n\Delta)C'(n\Delta)$$

$$R(n\Delta) = B(n\Delta)B'(n\Delta)$$

Then

$$\hat{\mathbf{w}}(n\Delta/n) = [I - \Delta\Sigma_w(n/n)H'(n)Q^{-1}(n\Delta)H(n\Delta)]\hat{\mathbf{w}}(n\Delta/n - 1) + \Delta\Sigma_w(n/n)H'(n\Delta)Q^{-1}(n\Delta)\mathbf{z}(n\Delta) \quad (55)$$

$$\hat{w}(n\Delta/n-1) = G(n\Delta)\hat{w}(n\Delta - \Delta/n-1) \quad (56)$$

$$\Sigma_w(n/n) = \Sigma_w(n/n-1) - \Sigma_w(n/n-1)H'(n\Delta)[\Delta Q(n\Delta) + H(n\Delta)\Sigma_w(n/n-1)H'(n\Delta)]^{-1}H(n\Delta)\Sigma_w(n/n-1) \quad (57)$$

$$\Sigma_w(n/n-1) = G(n\Delta)\Sigma_w(n-1/n-1)G'(n\Delta) + \Delta R(n\Delta) \quad (58)$$

$$\hat{s}(n\Delta/n-1) = H(n\Delta)\hat{w}(n\Delta/n-1) \quad (59)$$

$$\Sigma_s(n/n-1) = H(n\Delta)\Sigma_w(n/n-1)H'(n\Delta) \quad (60)$$

$$\hat{z}(n\Delta/n-1) = \hat{s}(n\Delta/n-1) \quad (61)$$

$$\Sigma_z(n/n-1) = \Sigma_s(n/n-1) + \frac{Q(n\Delta)}{\Delta} \quad (62)$$

Equations (55)–(58) can be written in various forms (see Schweppe [15]), and in some cases the alternative forms may be easier to mechanize.

The continuous time case can be found from the discrete by letting $N \to \infty$ where $\Delta = T/N$ with T fixed. The results are

$$\frac{d}{dt}\hat{w}(t/t) = A(t)\hat{w}(t/t) + \Sigma_w(t/t)H'(t)Q^{-1}(t)[z(t) - H(t)\hat{w}(t/t)] \quad (63)$$

$$\frac{d\Sigma_w(t/t)}{dt} = A(t)\Sigma_w(t/t) + \Sigma_w(t/t)A'(t) + R(t) - \Sigma_w(t/t)H'(t)Q^{-1}(t)H(t)\Sigma_w(t/t) \quad (64)$$

$$\hat{s}(t/t) = H(t)\hat{w}(t/t) \quad (65)$$

$$\Sigma_s(t/t) = H(t)\Sigma_w(t/t)H'(t) \quad (66)$$

Magill [8] derives equivalent discrete time formulas for the case of scalar observations using, however, a basic model without white observation noise, that is

$$z(n\Delta) = s(n\Delta)$$

Letting $Q(n\Delta) \to 0$ in (55) through (62) gives this case; our case can also be obtained from Magill's equations [8]. Magill also discusses other problems such as interpolation.

Appendix II

An Integral Equation Derivation

Since the state variable approach is not yet prevalent in the communication and radar literature, we rederive certain of our results using the more common integral equation formulation. We again employ the assumption of Section IV that, although the system equations are derived from a white noise model, the actual system input, $z(t)$, is a well-behaved process.

Consider the detection problem of Section IV and, in particular, the special case of a scalar observation, (50). Assume $Q(t) = 1$. If we ignore the deterministic portion of (50), our test statistic is

$$2\theta(t) = \int_0^t [2z(\tau)\hat{s}(\tau/\tau) - \hat{s}^2(\tau/\tau)]\, d\tau \quad (67)$$

evaluated for $t = T$.

Now consider the integral equation approach.[2] For the same problem as (67),

$$2\theta(t) = \int_0^t \int_0^t z(r)z(\tau)h(r, \tau : t)\, dr\, d\tau \quad (68)$$

where $h(r, \tau : t)$ is a solution of the integral equation

$$h(r, \tau : t) + \int_0^t \Phi(r, \sigma)h(\sigma, \tau : t)\, d\sigma = \Phi(r, \tau) \quad (69)$$

where $\Phi(r, \tau)$ is the covariance function of the signal, $s(t)$. The kernel $h(r, \tau : t)$ has the property that

$$\hat{s}(t/t) = \int_0^t h(\sigma, t : t)z(\sigma)d\sigma = \int_0^t h(t, \sigma : t)z(\sigma)d\sigma \quad (70)$$

that is, $h(\sigma, t : t)$ is the scalar version of $K(\sigma, t)$ of (48). From (68) and (70)

$$\frac{d}{dt}2\theta(t) = 2z(t)\hat{s}(t/t) + \int_0^t \int_0^t \frac{\partial}{\partial t}h(r, \tau : t)z(r)z(\tau)\, d\tau\, dr \quad (71)$$

This differentiation is valid for most covariance functions, $\Phi(r, \tau)$, of practical interest. We now write

$$\frac{\partial h}{\partial t}(r, \tau : t) = -h(r, t : t)h(t, \tau : t) + g(r, \tau : t) \quad (72)$$

and then show $g(r, \tau : t) = 0$. (This result is also derived in Siegert [16].) Differentiating (69) with respect to t gives

$$\frac{\partial h}{\partial t}(r, \tau : t) + \Phi(r, t)h(t, \tau : t) + \int_0^t \Phi(r, \sigma)\frac{\partial}{\partial t}h(\sigma, \tau : t)\, d\sigma = 0 \quad (73)$$

Substituting (72) into (73) gives

$$-h(r, t : t)h(t, \tau : t) + \Phi(r, t)h(t, \tau : t) - \int_0^t \Phi(r, \sigma)h(\sigma, t : t)h(t, \tau : t)\, d\sigma + g(r, \tau : t) + \int_0^t \Phi(r, \sigma)g(\sigma, \tau : t)\, d\sigma = 0 \quad (74)$$

Using (69) for $\tau = t$, (74) reduces to

$$g(r, \tau : t) + \int_0^t \Phi(r, \sigma)g(\sigma, \tau : t)\, d\sigma = 0 \quad (75)$$

which implies

$$g(r, \tau : t) \equiv 0 \quad (76)$$

[2] Helstrom [1], ch. II, sec. 2 is followed here.

Substituting (76) into (72) and then (72) into (71), gives with the help of (70),

$$\frac{d20(t)}{dt} = 2z(t)\hat{s}(t/t) - \hat{s}^2(t/t)$$

which is the same as (67).

Acknowledgment

The author wishes to thank Dr. R. Price of the M. I. T. Lincoln Lab., for his help and suggestions; discussions with him helped to germinate the ideas in this work. Gratitude is also expressed to Dr. E. Hofstetter, also of the Lincoln Lab., whose critical evaluation of the results led to a revision of Section IV.

References

[1] Helstron, C. W., *Statistical theory of signal detection*, Pergamon Press, New York, N. Y., 1960.
[2] Price, R., Optimum detection of random signals in noise with application to scatter-multipath communications, *IRE Trans. on Information Theory*, vol. IT-2, pp. 125–135, Dec 1956.
[3] Rosenblatt, M., Ed., *Proceedings of the symposium on time series analysis*, John Wiley & Sons, Inc., New York, N. Y., 1963.
[4] Grenander, U., Stochastic processes and statistical inference, *Arkiv. for Mat.*, vol. 1, p. 295, 1950.
[5] Kailath, T., Optimum receivers for randomly varying channels, in *Information Theory*, Butterworth and Co., London, England, pp. 190–122, 1960.
[6] Middleton, D., On the detection of stochastic signals in additive normal noise, pt. 1, *IRE Trans. on Information Theory*, vol. IT-3, pp. 86–121, Jun 1957.
[7] Kailath, T., Correlation detection of signals perturbed by a random channel, *IRE Trans. on Information Theory*, vol. IT-6, pp. 361–366, Jun 1960.
[8] Magill, D. T., Optimal adaptive estimation of sampled stochastic processes, Tech. Rept. No. 6302-3, Stanford Electronics Labs., Stanford University, Stanford, Calif., Dec 1963.
[9] Wilks, S. L., *Mathematical statistics*, John Wiley & Sons, Inc., New York, N. Y., 1962.
[10] Loève, M., *Probability theory*, D. Van Nostrand Co., Princeton, N. J., 1955.
[11] Schweppe, F. C., Optimization of signals, Tech. Rept. No. 1964-4, M.I.T. Lincoln Lab., Lexington, Mass., Jan 1964. Also, presented at the Internat'l Conf. on Microwaves, Circuit Theory, and Information Theory, Tokyo, Japan, Sep 7, 1964.
[12] Kalman, R. E., and R. S. Bucy, New results in linear filtering and prediction theory, Tech. Rept. No. TR-61-1, RIAS, Baltimore, Md., Nov 1960.
[13] Kalman, R. E., New methods and results in linear prediction and filtering theory, Tech. Rept. No. TR-61-1, RIAS, Baltimore, Md., Nov 1960.
[14] ——, A new approach to linear filtering and prediction problems, *J. Basic Engrg., ASME Trans.*, vol. 82D, pp. 35–45, 1960.
[15] Schweppe, F. C., An introduction to estimation theory for time varying systems, Tech. Rept. No. 22G-15(U), M.I.T. Lincoln Lab., Lexington, Mass., Sep 1963.
[16] Siegert, A. F., A systematic approach to a class of problems in the theory of noise and other random phenomena, pt. II, *IRE Trans. on Information Theory*, vol. IT-3, pp. 38–43, Mar 1957.

The Annals of Statistics
1991, Vol. 19, No. 2, 1073–1083

THE DIFFUSE KALMAN FILTER[1]

BY PIET DE JONG

University of British Columbia

The Kalman recursion for state space models is extended to allow for likelihood evaluation and minimum mean square estimation given states with an arbitrarily large covariance matrix. The extension is computationally minor. Application is made to likelihood evaluation, state estimation, prediction and smoothing.

1. Introduction. This paper deals with likelihood evaluation and minimum mean square error prediction given observations generated by a state space model with a diffuse initial state. A state is said to be diffuse if its covariance matrix is arbitrarily large. Diffuse initial states arise in the context of parameter uncertainty and model nonstationarity as illustrated later.

To deal with a diffuse initial state in the state space model, Schweppe (1973) and Harvey and Phillips (1979) propose initiating the Kalman filter with a very large covariance matrix. This poses numerical problems and does not answer the question of the existence of diffuse constructs. A variant of the Kalman filter, called the information filter, has also been proposed. However, as Ansley and Kohn [(1985), page 1298] point out, the information filter breaks down in many important cases and can be numerically inefficient. Harvey and Pierse (1984) and Harvey (1990) propose initiating the Kalman filter with regression type estimates based on an initial stretch of the data. These estimates may be cumbersome to construct and questions of existence are not dealt with. Pole and West (1989) deal with diffuse initial states in a Bayesian setting. In a sequence of papers, Ansley and Kohn (1985), Kohn and Ansley (1986, 1987a, 1987b) develop, discuss and advocate the use of a modified form of the Kalman filter to allow for diffuse states. This paper presents alternate modifications with the following merits:

1. *Computational*. The modified filter is a computationally trivial extension of the ordinary Kalman filter, turning the two existing vector recursions into matrix recursions and the addition of a matrix recursion. No extra matrix inversions are required.
2. *Analytic*. Proofs are general and direct. Necessary and sufficient conditions for the existence of diffuse constructs are in terms of extended filter quantities.

Received August 1987; revised March 1990.
[1]Research supported by a grant from ZWO, the Dutch agency for the support of pure scientific research and the National Science and Engineering Research Council of Canada.
AMS 1980 subject classifications. Primary 62M15; secondary 62M20, 60G35.
Key words and phrases. State space, Kalman filter, smoothing, diffuse, nonstationarity, likelihood.

Special cases of the methods used in this paper have been alluded to in Rosenberg (1973), Wecker and Ansley (1983) and Kohn and Ansley (1985, 1987a), as discussed later.

The program of this paper is as follows. The next section introduces the state space model (SSM), examples and the Kalman filter (KF). Section 3 discusses likelihood evaluation and introduces the diffuse Kalman filter (DKF). Section 4 deals with the diffuse likelihood. Section 5 goes on to consider diffuse prediction. Diffuse smoothing is dealt with in Section 6.

2. The state space model and the Kalman filter. Throughout this article capital letters denote nonrandom matrices. Lower case letters denote column vectors. The notation $\gamma \sim (c, \sigma^2 C)$ indicates γ is a random vector with expectation $E(\gamma) = c$ and covariance matrix $\mathrm{Cov}(\gamma) = \sigma^2 C$. Expectations and covariances are always unconditional.

If A and B have identical column dimension, then $(A; B) \equiv (A', B')'$. Thus $(y_1; y_2; \dots; y_n)$ is the stack of the column vectors $y_1, y_2, \dots, y_n$. The notation $y^{\#}$ indicates the number of components in y while A^{-} denotes the Moore–Penrose generalized inverse of A.

DEFINITION 2.1. The state space model (SSM). Random vector $y = (y_1; y_2; \dots; y_n)$ is said to be generated by a state space model, denoted $y \leftarrow$ SSM, if for $1 \le t \le n$, $y_t = X_t\beta + Z_t\alpha_t + G_t u_t$, where for $0 \le t \le n$, $\alpha_{t+1} = W_t\beta + T_t\alpha_t + H_t u_t$ and

(i) $(u_0; u_1; \dots; u_n) \sim (0, \sigma^2 I)$ with $\sigma^2 > 0$,
(ii) $\alpha_0 = 0$ and $\beta = b + B\gamma$, where $\gamma \sim (c, \sigma^2 C)$, b is fixed and B has full column rank,
(iii) γ and $(u_0; u_1; \dots; u_n)$ are uncorrelated,
(iv) C is nonsingular unless $C = 0$; $\mathrm{Cov}(y)$ is nonsingular if $C = 0$.

This article deals with state space methods when γ is diffuse. Random vector γ is said to be diffuse, denoted $C \to \infty$, if C^{-1} converges to a zero matrix in the Euclidean norm. Diffuse random vectors arise in two ways. First, to model parameter uncertainty and second, diffuseness arises when a nonstationary model is assumed to have applied since time immemorial. The next example illustrates matters.

EXAMPLE 2.1. Suppose for scalar y_t, $(y_{t+1} - x'_{t+1}\delta) = a(y_t - x'_t\delta) + u_t$, where the $u_t \sim (0, \sigma^2)$ are serially uncorrelated. Special cases of this model are the regression model ($a = 0$), the autoregressive model of order 1 ($x_t = 1$), the random walk ($\delta = 0$, $a = 1$), white noise ($\delta = 0$, $a = 0$), the regression model with random walk disturbances ($a = 1$) and the random walk with drift ($a = 1$, $x_{t+1} - x_t = 1$). A SSM formulation is to take for $t \ge 1$, $Z_t = 1$, $G_t = 0$, $W_t = 0$, $T_t = a$ and $H_t = 1$. Table 1 indicates alternative specifications for the remaining quantities. For the last three cases reported in Table 1, γ is identified with, respectively, δ, $y_0 - x_0'\delta$ and $(\delta; y_0 - x_0'\delta)$. The entries $1/\sqrt{1-a^2}$ in the column for H_0 are derived assuming the model has applied since time immemorial. This is a standard assumption in practical time series modelling leading to parameter parsimony since no new parameters have to be introduced to model initial conditions.

THEOREM 2.1. *If* $y \leftarrow SSM$, *then* $y = X\beta + \varepsilon$, *where*

$$X = [X_1 + Z_1W_0; X_2 + Z_2(W_1 + T_1W_0); \ldots; \\ X_n + Z_n\{W_{n-1} + T_{n-1}W_{n-2} + \cdots + (T_{n-1} \cdots T_1)W_0\}]$$

and $\varepsilon \sim (0, \sigma^2\Sigma)$ *with* Σ *nonsingular and* $\mathrm{Cov}(\beta, \varepsilon) = 0$.

The proof is direct. In terms of this notation, $\mathrm{Cov}(y) = \sigma^2\{(XB)C(XB)' + \Sigma\}$ and in particular, $\sigma^2\Sigma$ is the covariance matrix of y assuming $C = 0$, or in other words, the residual covariance matrix of y given γ. Note that Σ has a complicated but specialized structure as induced by the SSM.

Well-known constructs and results used in this article include the following. Suppose x is a random vector. Then a predictor of x using y is defined as $a + Ay$, where a and A are chosen such that the diagonal entries of $\mathrm{Cov}(x - a - Ay)$ are minimum. If $\hat{x}$ is the predictor of x using y, then define $\mathrm{mse}(\hat{x}) \equiv \mathrm{Cov}(x - \hat{x})$.

The Kalman filter (KF) computes predictors in the context of the SSM when $C = 0$. In particular the KF is the recursion

$$\begin{aligned} &e_t = y_t - X_t\beta - Z_ta_t, \qquad D_t = Z_tP_tZ_t' + G_tG_t', \\ (2.1) \qquad &K_t = (T_tP_tZ_t' + H_tG_t')D_t^{-1}, \qquad a_{t+1} = W_t\beta + T_ta_t + K_te_t, \\ &P_{t+1} = (T_t - K_tZ_t)P_tT_t' + (H_t - K_tG_t)H_t', \end{aligned}$$

with starting conditions $a_1 = W_0\beta$, $P_1 = H_0H_0'$. Here a_t is the predictor of α_t using $(y_1; y_2; \ldots; y_{t-1})$ and $\mathrm{mse}(a_t) = \sigma^2P_t$. Also e_t is the error of predicting y_t using $(y_1; y_2; \ldots; y_{t-1})$, $E(e_t) = 0$, $\mathrm{Cov}(e_t) = \sigma^2D_t$ and for $t \neq s$, $\mathrm{Cov}(e_t, e_s) = 0$. It is assumed the D_t are nonsingular, a condition guaranteed by Definition 2.1 (iv); proofs are in Anderson and Moore (1979).

3. Evaluation of the likelihood with the diffuse Kalman filter. Suppose $y \leftarrow$ SSM, γ is fixed ($C = 0$) and y is normally distributed. From Theorem 2.1, $y = X(b + B\gamma) + \varepsilon$ and hence $\mathrm{Cov}(y) = \mathrm{Cov}(\varepsilon) = \sigma^2\Sigma$. The log of the likelihood based on y is, apart from a constant,

$$\begin{aligned} \lambda(y) &= -\tfrac{1}{2}\{\ln|\sigma^2\Sigma| + (y - X\beta)'\Sigma^{-1}(y - X\beta)/\sigma^2\} \\ &= -\tfrac{1}{2}\{y^{\#}\ln(\sigma^2) + \ln|\Sigma| + (q - 2s'\gamma + \gamma'S\gamma)/\sigma^2\}, \end{aligned}$$

where

$$S = (XB)'\Sigma^{-1}(XB), \qquad s = (XB)'\Sigma^{-1}(y - Xb),$$
$$q = (y - Xb)'\Sigma^{-1}(y - Xb).$$

The maximum likelihood estimators (mle's) of γ and σ^2 are, respectively,

$$\hat{\gamma} = S^{-1}s, \qquad \hat{\sigma}^2 = (q - s'S^{-1}s)/y^{\#},$$

where it is assumed that S is nonsingular. Substituting $\hat{\gamma}$ and $\hat{\sigma}^2$ back into $\lambda(y)$ yields the (γ, σ^2)-maximized log-likelihood $-\frac{1}{2}[y^{\#}\{\ln(\hat{\sigma}^2)\} + \ln|\Sigma|]$.

The expressions for S, s, q and $|\Sigma|$ as indicated before are not computationally practical. However, a viable approach to calculating these quantities is to employ the KF (2.1). This method was first proposed by Schweppe (1965) and extended upon by Rosenberg (1973). The next development indicates further extensions and is stated in terms of the following notation.

DEFINITION 3.1. The diffuse Kalman filter (DKF). The DKF is the KF (2.1) with the equations for e_t and a_{t+1}, respectively, replaced by

$$E_t = (X_t B, y_t - X_t b) - Z_t A_t, \qquad A_{t+1} = W_t(-B, b) + T_t A_t + K_t E_t,$$

with starting condition $A_1 = W_0(-B, b)$. Also the following recursion is added: $Q_{t+1} = Q_t + E_t' D_t^{-1} E_t$, where $Q_1 = 0$.

THEOREM 3.1. *Suppose $y \leftarrow SSM$, γ is fixed, y is normally distributed and the DKF is applied. Then $Q_{n+1} = \{(S, s); (s', q)\}$. If S is nonsingular, then the mle's of γ and σ^2 are $\hat{\gamma} = S^{-1}s$ and $\hat{\sigma}^2 = (q - s'S^{-1}s)/y^{\#}$, respectively. The (γ, σ^2)-maximized log-likelihood is $-\frac{1}{2}[y^{\#}\{\ln(\hat{\sigma}^2)\} + \sum_{t=1}^{n} \ln|D_t|]$.*

PROOF. Suppose $e = (e_1; e_2; \ldots; e_n)$, where the e_t are as defined in (2.1). Then for some matrices K and L, $e = Ky - L\beta$. In particular, K is zero above the main diagonal and has all ones on the diagonal implying $|K| = 1$. Since $E(e) = 0$, it follows that $KX\beta = L\beta$ for all β and hence $KX = L$ and $e = K(y - X\beta)$. Furthermore, Cov(e) is block-diagonal with blocks $D_1, D_2, \ldots, D_n$ as given in (2.1) and hence $K\Sigma K' = D = \text{diag}(D_1, D_2, \ldots, D_n)$, $\Sigma^{-1} = K'D^{-1}K$ and

$$\ln|\Sigma| = \ln|D_1| + \ln|D_2| + \cdots + \ln|D_n|,$$
$$S = (KXB)'D^{-1}(KXB), \qquad s = (KXB)'D^{-1}K(y - Xb),$$
$$q = \{K(y - Xb)\}'D^{-1}K(y - Xb).$$

Now suppose β in (2.1) is replaced by b to yield $f = (f_1; f_2; \ldots; f_n)$ instead of e. Then $f = K(y - Xb)$. If $F = KXB$, then the columns of F can be computed in the same way as f, except that y is replaced by zero and b by the corresponding columns of $-B$. In terms of this notation, $S = F'D^{-1}F$, $s = F'D^{-1}f$ and $q = f'D^{-1}f$. It is clear that $E_t = (F_t, f_t)$, where $(F_1; F_2; \ldots; F_n) = F$. Hence Q_{n+1} is as asserted. □

The DKF can thus be used for likelihood evaluation when $C = 0$. Further uses are outlined later. These are similar to the uses of the Ansley and Kohn [(1985), page 1297] algorithm. However, the DKF is simple and efficient compared to the Ansley and Kohn (1985) algorithm: no factorizations are

TABLE 1
Alternative initial conditions

Alternative	X_t	W_0	b	B	c	C	H_0
δ known, $\|a\| < 1$	x_t'	0	δ	I	0	0	$1/\sqrt{1-a^2}$
δ diffuse, $\|a\| < 1$	x_t'	0	0	I	0	∞	$1/\sqrt{1-a^2}$
δ known, $\|a\| \geq 1$	$(x_t', 0)$	$(0, a)$	$(\delta; 0)$	$(0; 1)$	0	∞	1
δ diffuse, $\|a\| \geq 1$	$(x_t', 0)$	$(0, a)$	$(0; 0)$	I	0	∞	1

required and attendant proofs are short, direct and more general [e.g., Assumption 2.5(i) of Ansley and Kohn (1985) is not needed]. Rosenberg [(1973), page 410] has suggested a special case of the DKF for likelihood maximization when $C = 0$. Wecker and Ansley (1983) and Kohn and Ansley (1985) also make Rosenberg's (1973) suggestion. A square root version of the DKF is discussed in de Jong (1990).

EXAMPLE 2.1 (continued). Suppose $a = 0$ and suppose δ is regarded as diffuse. Then Q_t accumulates the squares and cross products and $Q_{n+1} = (X, y)'(X, y)$. Theorem 3.1 in this case specializes to the usual regression results. Alternatively, supposed $|a| \geq 1$ and the specification of the last row of Table 1. Detailed calculations show for $t \geq 1$, $E_t = (x_t' - ax_{t-1}', 0, y_t - ay_{t-1})$, $D_t = 1$ except that $E_1 = (x_1', a, y_1)$. Thus the symmetric matrix Q is

$$Q = \begin{bmatrix} x_1x_1' + \sum_{t=2}^{n} (x_t - ax_{t-1})(x_t - ax_{t-1})' & & \\ ax_1' & a^2 & \\ y_1x_1' + \sum_{t=2}^{n} (y_t - ay_{t-1})(x_t - ax_{t-1})' & ay_1 & y_1^2 + \sum_{t=2}^{n} (y_t - ay_{t-1})^2 \end{bmatrix}$$

and the mle of δ is

$$\hat{\delta} = \left\{ \sum_{t=2}^{n} (x_t - ax_{t-1})(x_t - ax_{t-1})' \right\}^{-1} \left\{ \sum_{t=2}^{n} (x_t - ax_{t-1})(y_t - ay_{t-1}) \right\},$$

while the mle of $y_0 - x_0'\delta$ is $(y_1 - x_1'\hat{\delta})/a$. Further, the mle of σ^2 is

$$\hat{\sigma}^2 = n^{-1} \sum_{t=2}^{n} \left\{ (y_t - ay_{t-1}) - (x_t - ax_{t-1})'\hat{\delta} \right\}^2$$

and the (δ, σ^2)-maximized log-likelihood is $-\frac{1}{2}n\{\ln(\hat{\sigma}^2)\}$. In the special case of a random walk with drift ($a = 1$, $x_{t+1} - x_t = 1$), the mle's of δ, $y_0 - x_0'\delta$ and

σ^2 reduce to

$$\frac{y_n - y_1}{n-1}, \qquad \frac{ny_1 - y_n}{n-1}, \qquad \frac{1}{n}\left\{\sum_{t=2}^{n}(y_t - y_{t-1})^2 - \frac{(y_n - y_1)^2}{n-1}\right\}.$$

4. The diffuse likelihood. The next result generalizes Theorem 3.1 to the case where γ is random. The result sets the stage for a consideration of the diffuse likelihood.

THEOREM 4.1. *Suppose $y \leftarrow$ SSM and $(\gamma; y)$ is normally distributed. Further suppose the DKF is applied and S is nonsingular. Then the mle of c is $\hat{\gamma} = S^{-1}s$, with covariance matrix $\sigma^2 S^{-1}$. The mle of σ^2 is $\hat{\sigma}^2 = (q - s'S^{-1}s)/y^{\#}$, while the mle of C is zero. The log-likelihood $\lambda(y)$ maximized with respect to c, σ^2 and C is* $-\frac{1}{2}[y^{\#}\{\ln(\hat{\sigma}^2)\} + \Sigma_{t=1}^{n} \ln|D_t|]$.

PROOF. Write, for example, $\lambda(y|\gamma)$ as the conditional log-likelihood of y given γ. Then $\gamma(y) = \lambda(\gamma) + \lambda(y|\gamma) - \lambda(\gamma|y)$ and $-2\lambda(y)$ thus equals

$$\begin{aligned}
&\ln|\sigma^2 C| + (\gamma - c)'C^{-1}(\gamma - c)/\sigma^2 + \ln|\sigma^2\Sigma| \\
&\quad + (y - Xb - XB\gamma)'\Sigma^{-1}(y - Xb - XB\gamma)/\sigma^2 \\
&\quad - \ln\left|\sigma^2(C^{-1} + S)^{-1}\right| - \left\{\gamma - (C^{-1} + S)^{-1}(s + C^{-1}c)\right\}' \\
&\qquad\qquad \times (C^{-1} + S)\left\{\gamma - (C^{-1} + S)^{-1}(s + C^{-1}c)\right\}/\sigma^2
\end{aligned}$$

Expanding the various terms and simplifying, shows $\lambda(y)$ equals

$$\begin{aligned}
&-\frac{1}{2}\Big[\ln|C| + \ln|C^{-1} + S| + \ln|\sigma^2\Sigma| \\
(4.1)\qquad &\quad + \left\{q + c'C^{-1}c - (C^{-1}c + s)'(S + C^{-1})^{-1}(C^{-1}c + s)\right\}/\sigma^2\Big].
\end{aligned}$$

Maximizing with respect to c yields the first assertion of the theorem. Substituting $c = S^{-1}s$ into (4.1) shows that the c-maximized log-likelihood is $-\frac{1}{2}\{\ln|I + CS| + \ln|\sigma^2\Sigma| + (q - s'S^{-1}s)/\sigma^2\}$ and hence the mle's of σ^2 and C are as asserted. Substituting the mle's of σ^2 and C into c-maximized log-likelihood yields the (c, σ^2, C)-maximized log-likelihood as asserted. □

Thus $\hat{\gamma} = S^{-1}s$ is the mle of c for every σ^2 and C, while the mle's of σ^2 and C are maximizers in the c-maximized likelihood. Furthermore, as $C \to \infty$, both $\hat{\gamma}$ and $\hat{\sigma}^2$ stay fixed. The next theorem considers the behaviour of $\lambda(y)$ as $C \to \infty$. The theorem expands a result of de Jong (1988) and shows the role of the DKF.

THEOREM 4.2. *Suppose $y \leftarrow SSM$ and $(\gamma; y)$ is normally distributed. Further, suppose the DKF is applied and S is nonsingular. Then as $C \to \infty$, $\lambda(y) + \frac{1}{2}\ln|C|$ converges to*

$$(4.2)\qquad -\frac{1}{2}\left[y^{\#}\{\ln(\sigma^2)\} + \ln|S| + \sum_{t=1}^{n}\ln|D_t| + (q - s'S^{-1}s)/\sigma^2\right].$$

Moreover (4.2) *is a log-likelihood based on Ny, where N has rank $y^{\#} - \gamma^{\#}$, $\mathrm{Cov}(Ny, \gamma) = 0$ and $\ln|\mathrm{Cov}(Ny)|$ equals the first three terms in* (4.2). *The log-likelihood* (4.2) *maximized with respect to σ^2 equals*

$$(4.3)\qquad -\frac{1}{2}\left[y^{\#}\{\ln(\hat{\sigma}^2)\} + \ln|S| + \sum_{t=1}^{n}\ln|D_t|\right].$$

PROOF. Consider $\lambda(y)$ as given in (4.1). Add $\frac{1}{2}\ln|C|$ and let $C \to \infty$ to show $\lambda(y) + \frac{1}{2}\ln|C|$ converges to (4.2).

For the second part of the theorem, let N be any matrix of full row rank such that the row space of N coincides with the row space of M, where $M = I - (XB)\{(XB)'\Sigma^{-1}(XB)\}^{-1}(XB)'\Sigma^{-1}$. Then $NXB = 0$, $E(Ny) = NXb$, $\mathrm{Cov}(Ny) = \sigma^2 N\Sigma N'$ and

$$\begin{aligned} q - s'S^{-1}s &= (y - Xb)'\Sigma^{-1}M(y - Xb) = (y - Xb)'M'\Sigma^{-1}M(y - Xb) \\ &= \{M(y - Xb)\}'M'\Sigma^{-1}M\{M(y - Xb)\} \\ &= \{N(y - Xb)\}'(N\Sigma N')^{-1}\{N(y - Xb)\}. \end{aligned}$$

Thus the likelihood based on Ny agrees with (4.2) if $\ln|\mathrm{Cov}(Ny)|$ is as specified. Expression (4.3) is arrived at by substituting $\hat{\sigma}^2$ for σ^2 in (4.2). □

Theorem 4.2 implies that (4.2) is a proper log-likelihood, called the diffuse log-likelihood. Since $\mathrm{Cov}(Ny, \gamma) = 0$, the diffuse log-likelihood is a likelihood based on those aspects of y invariant to γ. Note that the diffuse log-likelihood differs from the (c, C, σ^2)-maximized log-likelihood only with respect to the term $\frac{1}{2}\ln|S|$.

EXAMPLE 2.1 (continued). Assume the specification given in the last line of Table 1. Then $|S| = a^2|\Sigma_{t=2}^{n}(x_t - ax_{t-1})(x_t - ax_{t-1})'|$ and the diffuse log-likelihood maximized with respect to σ^2 is

$$n\{\ln(\hat{\sigma}^2)\} + a^2\left|\sum_{t=2}^{n}(x_t - ax_{t-1})(x_t - ax_{t-1})'\right|.$$

5. Diffuse prediction. The DKF can be used to compute diffuse predictors of α_t and y_t in the context of the SSM. These are predictors constructed under the assumption that $y \leftarrow$ SSM with $C \to \infty$. For $1 \le t \le n + 1$, let $\hat{\gamma}_t$, $\hat{\alpha}_t$ and $\hat{y}_t$ denote the predictors of γ, α_t and y_t using $(y_1; y_2; \dots; y_{t-1})$. Note that if $C = 0$, then $\hat{\gamma}_t = c$, $\mathrm{mse}(\hat{\gamma}_t) = 0$, $\hat{\alpha}_t = a_t$ and $\hat{y}_t = X_t\beta + Z_t a_t$, where a_t is as given in the KF (2.1). The case where $C \neq 0$ is treated in the next theorem which uses the notation $Q_t \equiv \{(S_t, s_t); (s_t', q_t)\}$, where q_t is scalar.

THEOREM 5.1. *Suppose $y \leftarrow SSM$, where $C \neq 0$ and the DKF is applied. Let $A_{t\gamma}$ and $E_{t\gamma}$ denote all but the last columns of A_t and E_t. Then*

$$\hat{\gamma}_t = (S_t + C^{-1})^{-1}(C^{-1}c + s_t), \qquad \text{mse}(\hat{\gamma}_t) = \sigma^2(S_t + C)^{-1},$$
$$\hat{\alpha}_t = A_t(-\hat{\gamma}_t; 1), \qquad \text{mse}(\hat{\alpha}_t) = \sigma^2 P_t + A_{t\gamma}\,\text{mse}(\hat{\gamma}_t)\,A_{t\gamma}',$$
$$y_t - \hat{y}_t = E_t(-\hat{\gamma}_t; 1), \qquad \text{mse}(\hat{y}_t) = \sigma^2 D_t + E_{t\gamma}\,\text{mse}(\hat{\gamma}_t)\,E_{t\gamma}'.$$

PROOF. Without loss of generality, assume $t = n + 1$. The predictor of γ not using y is c with mse matrix $\sigma^2 C$. By Theorem 2.1, $y = Xb + XB\gamma + \varepsilon$, where $\varepsilon \sim (0, \sigma^2\Sigma)$. Using a well-known result, the predictor of γ using y is thus

$$\{(XB)'\Sigma^{-1}(XB) + C^{-1}\}^{-1}\{C^{-1}c + (XB)'\Sigma^{-1}(y - Xb)\}$$
$$= (S + C^{-1})^{-1}(C^{-1}c + s),$$

with mse matrix $\sigma^2(S + C^{-1})^{-1}$. Hence $\hat{\gamma}_t$ and mse($\hat{\gamma}_t$) are as asserted.

Now consider predicting α_t using $(y_1; y_2; \dots; y_{t-1})$. This is equivalent to first predicting α_t using $(\gamma; y_1; y_2; \dots; y_{t-1})$, and then predicting this predictor using $(y_1; y_2; \dots; y_{t-1})$. The first mentioned predictor is a_t given in (2.1). However from the DKF,

$$A_{t+1}(-\gamma; 1) = [W_t(-B, b) + T_t A_t + K_t\{(X_t B, y_t - X_t b) - Z_t A_t\}](-\gamma; 1)$$
$$= W_t\beta + T_t A_t(-\gamma; 1) + K_t\{y_t - X_t\beta - A_t(-\gamma; 1)\},$$

with starting condition $A_1(-\gamma; 1) = W_0\beta$. Thus $A_t(-\gamma; 1)$ satisfies the same recursion and starting condition as a_t and hence $a_t = A_t(-\gamma; 1)$. Thus $\hat{\alpha}_t = A_t(-\hat{\gamma}_t; 1)$ as required. The formula for mse($\hat{\alpha}_t$) follows from

$$\text{mse}(\hat{\alpha}_t) = \text{Cov}(\alpha_t - a_t + a_t - \hat{\alpha}_t) = \text{Cov}(\alpha_t - a_t) + \text{Cov}(a_t - \hat{\alpha}_t)$$
$$= \sigma^2 P_t + \text{Cov}\{A_t(\hat{\gamma}_t - \gamma; 0)\},$$

where the second equality results from the fact that $\alpha_t - a_t$ is a prediction error using the random vector $(\gamma; y_1; y_2, \dots, y_{t-1})$ and both a_t and $\hat{\alpha}_t$ are based on this random vector. The expressions for $\hat{y}_t$ and mse($\hat{y}_t$) are proved similarly. □

Now suppose in the formula for $\hat{\gamma}_t$, c is replaced by its mle $S_t^{-1}s_t$. Then $\hat{\gamma}_t$ reduces to $S_t^{-1}s_t$. This evidently is also the limit of $\hat{\gamma}_t$ as $C \to \infty$. Thus the diffuse predictor of γ based on $(y_1; y_2, \dots, y_{t-1})$ coincides with the predictor of γ replacing c by its mle. Similar statements apply to $\hat{\alpha}_t$ and $\hat{y}_t$. Thus replacing c by its mle is tantamount to treating γ as random with an arbitarily large covariance matrix. A formal statement is contained in Theorem 5.2, the proof of which follows directly from Theorem 5.1.

THEOREM 5.2. *Suppose* $y \leftarrow$ *SSM and* $1 \le t \le n+1$. *If* S_t *is nonsingular, then as* $C \to \infty$, $\hat{\gamma}_t \to S_t^{-1}s_t$ *and* $\text{mse}(\hat{\gamma}_t) \to \sigma^2 S_t^{-1}$. *If the rows of* $A_{t\gamma}$ *are in the row space of* S_t, *then as* $C \to \infty$, $\hat{\alpha}_t \to A_t(-S_t^- s_t; 1)$ *and* $\text{mse}(\hat{\alpha}_t) \to \sigma^2(P_t + A_{t\gamma}S_t^- A'_{t\gamma})$. *If the rows of* $E_{t\gamma}$ *are in the row space of* S_t, *then as* $C \to \infty$, $\hat{y}_t \to \{X_t(-B, b) + Z_t A_t\}(-S_t^- s_t; 1)$ *and* $\text{mse}(\hat{y}_t) \to \sigma^2(D_t + E_{t\gamma}S_t^- E'_{t\gamma})$.

A special case of this result is displayed in Rosenberg (1973). Kohn and Ansley [(1987a), page 45], in the context of spline smoothing, show that their modified filter for computing limiting predictors yields the same results as the approach taken in Wecker and Ansley (1983) which is that of Rosenberg (1973). Kohn and Ansley [(1987a), page 45] go on to conclude that the Rosenberg (1973) approach is numerically inefficient. A comparison of the DKF and the Ansley and Kohn [(1985), page 1297] filter shows that this is not so.

Like the Ansley and Kohn filter, the DKF can be collapsed to the ordinary Kalman filter after a few iterations. This combines the ideas of this section and Section 4. Initially, suppose γ corresponds to purely initial conditions (as in the third row of Table 1) and hence for $1 \le t \le n$, $X_t\beta = 0$ and $W_t\beta = 0$. Suppose m is the first integer such that S_m is nonsingular. Consider

$$\lambda(y) + \tfrac{1}{2}\ln|C| = \{\lambda(y_1, y_2, \dots, y_{m-1}) + \tfrac{1}{2}\ln|C|\} + \lambda(y_m, \dots, y_n | y_1, \dots, y_{m-1}),$$

where $\lambda(y_m, \dots, y_n | y_1, \dots, y_{m-1})$ is the conditional log-likelihood based on $(y_m; \dots; y_n)$ conditioning on $(y_1; \dots; y_{m-1})$. As $C \to \infty$, the term in curly brackets converges to

$$-\frac{1}{2}\left[(y_1; \dots; y_{m-1})^{\#}\ln(\sigma^2) + \ln|S_m| + \sum_{t=1}^{m-1}\ln|D_t| + (q_m - s'_m S_m^{-1}s_m)/\sigma^2\right],$$

while $\lambda(y_m, \dots, y_n | y_1, \dots, y_{m-1})$ converges to the log-likelihood based on $(y_m; \dots; y_n)$ generated by a SSM with initial conditions

$$E(\alpha_m) = A_m(-S_m^{-1}s_m; 1), \qquad \text{Cov}(\alpha_m) = \sigma^2\left(P_m + A_{m\gamma}S_m^{-1}A'_{m\gamma}\right).$$

Thus, if KF is initialized at $t = m$ with $E(\alpha_m)$ and $\text{Cov}(\alpha_m)$ as given, then as $C \to \infty$,

$$\lambda(y) + \tfrac{1}{2}\ln|C| \to -\frac{1}{2}\left[y^{\#}\ln(\sigma^2) + \ln|S_m| + \sum_{t=1}^{n}\ln|D_t| + q_n/\sigma^2\right],$$

where $q_n = q_m - s'_m S_m^{-1}s_m + \sum_{t=m}^{n} e'_t D_t^{-1} e_t$. The KF as initialized also directly yields the limits of $\hat{\alpha}_t$ and $\text{mse}(\hat{\alpha}_t)$, $m < t \le n$ as $C \to \infty$. If $X_t\beta \ne 0$ or $W_t\beta \ne 0$ for some $1 \le t \le n$, then the state vector for $m \le t \le n$ is taken to be $(\alpha_t; \gamma)$ and the DKF can be collapsed to the KF based on the SSM employing the augmented state vector.

6. Diffuse smoothing. Smoothing refers to predicting the state α_t, $1 \leq t \leq n$, using the entire observation vector y where $y \rightarrow$ SSM. Smoothing can be based on the recursion

$$(6.1) \qquad N_{t-1} = Z_t' D_t^{-1} E_t + L_t' N_t, \qquad R_{t-1} = Z_t' D_t^{-1} Z_t + L_t' R_t L_t,$$

where $N_n = 0$, $R_n = 0$ and for $1 \leq t \leq n$, $L_t = T_t - K_t Z_t$, and all other quantities are defined as in the DKF.

THEOREM 6.1. *Suppose $y \leftarrow$ SSM, where $C \neq 0$ and the DKF is applied followed by the recursion* (6.1). *For $1 \leq t \leq n = 1$, suppose $\tilde{\alpha}_t$ denotes the predictor of α_t using y. Then*

$$\tilde{\alpha}_t = (A_t + P_t N_{t-1})(-\hat{\gamma}_{n+1}; 1),$$

$$\text{mse}(\tilde{\alpha}_t) = \sigma^2(P_t - P_t R_{t-1} P_t) + N_{t-1,\gamma}\, \text{mse}(\hat{\gamma}_{n+1}) N'_{t-1,\gamma},$$

where $N_{t-1,\gamma}$ denotes all but the last column of $A_t + P_t N_{t-1}$ and $\hat{\gamma}_{n=1}$ and mse$(\hat{\gamma}_{n+1})$ *are as given in Theorem* 5.1 *with $t = n + 1$. Furthermore, as $C \rightarrow \infty$ and provided $N_{t-1,\gamma}$ is in the row space of S_{n+1}, $\tilde{\alpha}_t$ and* mse$(\tilde{\alpha}_t)$ *converge to the previous expressions with $\hat{\gamma}_{n+1}$ replaced by $S_{n+1}^{-} s_{n+1}$ and* mse$(\hat{\gamma}_{n+1})$ *replaced by $\sigma^2 S_{n+1}^{-}$.*

PROOF. From de Jong (1989), if $r_{t-1} = Z_t' D_t^{-1} e_t + K_t' r_t$ with $r_n = 0$ and e_t as in (2.1), then the predictor of α_t and associated mse matrix using $(\gamma; y)$ are respectively, $a_t + P_t r_{t-1}$ and $\sigma^2(P_t - P_t R_{t-1} P_t)$. Now

$$N_{t-1}(-\gamma; 1) = \left(Z_t' D_t^{-1} E_t + L_t' N_t\right)(-\gamma; 1) = Z_t' D_t^{-1} e_t + L_t' N_t(-\gamma; 1),$$

with starting condition $N_n(-\gamma; 1) = 0$. Thus $N_{t-1}(-\gamma; 1) = r_{t-1}$ and the predictor of α_t using $(\gamma; y)$ is $(A_t + P_t N_{t-1})(-\gamma; 1)$, which implies $\tilde{\alpha}_t$ and mse$(\tilde{\alpha}_t)$ are as asserted. The limiting expressions as $C \rightarrow \infty$ are arrived at by letting $C \rightarrow \infty$ in the expressions for $\hat{\gamma}_{n+1}$ and mse$(\hat{\gamma}_{n+1})$. □

Using the results in de Jong (1989), expressions analogous to those in Theorem 6.1 can also be derived for predictors of the signal $X_t\beta + Z_t\alpha_t$ using y or $X_t\beta + Z_t\alpha_t$ and α_t using $(y_1; \ldots; y_{t-1}; y_{t+1}; \ldots; y_n)$. Furthermore, the results can be generalized to derive cross covariances of the form, for example, Cov$(\alpha_t - \tilde{\alpha}_t, \alpha_s - \tilde{\alpha}_s)$, $t \neq s$ and fixed point and fixed lag smoothing algorithms for the case $C \rightarrow \infty$.

EXAMPLE 2.1 (continued). Consider the specification as in the last row of Table 1. Then $N_{t-1} = E_t$ and $R_{t-1} = 1$. Thus as $C \rightarrow \infty$, $\tilde{\alpha}_t \rightarrow y_t - x_t'\hat{\delta}$, where $\hat{\delta} = S_{n+1}^{-1} s_{n+1}$.

Acknowledgments. I am indebted to Andrew Harvey and anonymous referees for helpful comments.

REFERENCES

ANDERSON, B. D. O. and MOORE, J. B. (1979). *Optimal Filtering*. Prentice-Hall, Englewood Cliffs, N.J.

ANSLEY, C. F. and KOHN, R. (1985). Estimation, filtering and smoothing in state space models with incompletely specified initial conditions. *Ann. Statist.* **13** 1286–1316.

DE JONG, P. (1988). The likelihood for a state space model. *Biometrika* **75** 165–169.

DE JONG, P. (1989). Smoothing and interpolation with the state space model. *J. Amer. Statist. Assoc.* **84** 1085–1088.

DE JONG, P. (1991). Stable algorithms for the state space model. *J. Time Ser. Anal*. To appear.

HARVEY, A. C. (1990). *Forecasting, structural time series models, and the Kalman filter*. Cambridge Univ. Press.

HARVEY, A. C. and PHILLIPS, G. D. A. (1979). Maximum likelihood estimation of regression models with autoregressive-moving average disturbances. *Biometrika* **66** 49–58.

HARVEY, A. C. and PIERSE, R. G. (1984). Estimating missing observations in economic time series. *J. Amer. Statist. Assoc.* **79** 125–131.

KOHN, R. and ANSLEY C. F. (1985). Efficient estimation and prediction in time series regression models. *Biometrika* **72** 694–697.

KOHN, R. and ANSLEY C. F. (1986). Estimation, prediction, and interpolation for ARIMA models with missing data. *J. Amer. Statist. Assoc.* **81** 751–761.

KOHN, R. and ANSLEY C. F. (1987a). A new algorithm for spline smoothing based on smoothing a stochastic process. *SIAM J. Scientific Statist. Comput.* **8** 33–48.

KOHN, R. and ANSLEY C. F. (1987b). Signal extraction for finite nonstationary time series. *Biometrika* **74** 411–421.

POLE, A. and WEST M. (1989). Reference analysis for the DLM. *J. Time Ser. Anal.* **10** 131–147.

ROSENBERG, B. (1973). The analysis of a cross section of time series by stochastically convergent parameter regression. *Ann. Social Economic Measurement* **2** 399–428.

SCHWEPPE, F. C. (1965). Evaluation of likelihood functions for Gaussian signals. *IEEE Trans. Inform. Theory* **11** 61–70.

SCHWEPPE, F. C. (1973). *Uncertain Dynamic Systems*. Prentice-Hall, Englewood Cliffs, N.J.

WECKER, W. and ANSLEY, C. F. (1983). The signal extraction approach to nonlinear regression and spline smoothing. *J. Amer. Statist. Assoc.* **78** 81–89.

FACULTY OF COMMERCE AND BUSINESS ADMINISTRATION
UNIVERSITY OF BRITISH COLUMBIA
VANCOUVER, B.C. V6T 1Y8
CANADA

[11]

Annals of Economic and Social Measurement, 2/4, 1973

RANDOM COEFFICIENTS MODELS

THE ANALYSIS OF A CROSS SECTION OF TIME SERIES BY STOCHASTICALLY CONVERGENT PARAMETER REGRESSION[1]

BY BARR ROSENBERG

This paper develops a "convergent-parameter" regression model for a cross section of time series. Cross-sectional diversity in the regression parameters results from sequential random increments to the individual parameters. These random walks are subordinated to a continual tendency for individual parameters to converge to the population norm. The model implies stationary cross-sectional parameter dispersion, with nonconstant but serially correlated individual parameters. Maximum likelihood and Bayesian estimation methods are derived for the model. An approximation that makes the computations feasible is evaluated and found to be satisfactorily efficient. The estimators are compared with ordinary least squares.

I. THE "CONVERGENT PARAMETER" MODEL

A. Consider the familiar cross-section, time-series regression problem, where an endogenous variable y and exogenous variables $x_1, \ldots, x_k$ are observed for each of N individuals, $n = 1, \ldots, N$ in each of T time periods, $t = 1, \ldots, T$. The regression parameters $b_1, \ldots, b_k$ are the partial derivatives of the endogenous with respect to the exogenous variables. The parameter vector $\mathbf{b}_{nt} = (b_{1nt} : \ldots : b_{knt})'$ specific to individual n in period t is determined by the behavior and environment of that individual at that date. In most economic applications, it is unreasonable to expect these parameters to be the same for all individuals in all periods.

A variety of cross section, time series regression models have previously introduced stochastic variation in individual parameters. The most widely known methods are extensions of the analysis of covariance: shifts in the intercept term are associated with each individual ("individual effects") and with each time period ("time effects"). Sometimes these shifts in the intercept are introduced as dummy variables, or equivalently, as stochastic terms with diffuse prior distributions (Hildreth (1949, 1950), Hoch (1962), Wilks (1943: 195–200)). In other applications, these shifts are treated as stochastic terms with proper prior distributions, or "error components" (Wallace and Hussain (1969)). Serial correlation in individual disturbances may be superimposed upon these models (Parks (1967)). However, this class of models has the deficiency of postulating that regression parameters other than the intercept are identical for all individuals in all periods.

Where regression parameters do vary, an estimator assuming constant parameters has two important defects. First, the estimator is inefficient and the associated sampling theory is invalid, usually leading to downward-biased estimates of error variance. Second, when the pattern of parameter variation is of interest in

[1] The bulk of this research, reported in "Varying Parameter Regression in the Analysis of a Cross Section of Time Series," IBER Working Paper No. IP 165, 1969 (revised 1973), was completed under NSF Grant GS 2102, aided by subsidized funds of the Computer Center, University of California, Berkeley. The research was completed under NSF Grant GS 3306. The resourceful assistance of Daryl Carlson, and the indomitable work of Mrs. Ellen McGibbon in preparing various stages of the manuscript, are gratefully acknowledged.

its own right, a constant parameter model is totally incapable of shedding light on this aspect of the economic process.

Two models have introduced more general parameter variation. In Swamy's work, individual parameters are randomly dispersed across the population, but are constant over time (1970, 1971). In Hsiao's recent paper (1973), regression parameters are the sums of "individual effects" and "time effects," so that the model extends to the regression parameters the methods previously applied to the intercept term alone. These two approaches are appealing. However, they do not allow the individual parameters to vary independently of the rest of the population. If individual parameters do vary stochastically, these methods cannot track the individual parameter vectors nor model the stochastic variations.

B. What pattern of parameter variation can be expected in a cross section of economic decision units? There are certainly tendencies for different individuals' parameters to be alike. Social interaction within a population tends to preserve similarity among individuals playing the same role. When conformity is highly valued, or when the role of a deviate is, for any reason, difficult, individuals will tend to converge in behavior and in environment toward group norms, or toward subgroup norms if a deviant subgroup coalesces. Under competition, individuals will strive for profitable differentiation from the population, but as soon as such differentiation is achieved, competitive responses by others will tend to offset it. Uniformity may be enforced by institutional devices, such as trade organizations, or may result from interdependent individual responses to similar environments, as, for example, in loosely organized groups such as consumers.

On the other hand, within a group of individuals, each being somewhat different in innate characteristics and in environment, freedom of action will facilitate continual developments which are in opposition to, or at least independent of, the converging trends. These independent events will be a source of diversity which, when balanced against the conforming forces, may preserve a relatively stable degree of differentiation in the population. Individual characteristics will be different, but will not remain constant over time. The differences may behave as if subjected to sequential random increments and as if continually converging toward zero from the position randomly arrived at. Individual differences will then be serially correlated but nonconstant.

To fix ideas, it may be helpful to consider an example. In analyzing the returns to stockholders, it is useful to write for each stock in a universe of N stocks and for each holding period within a sequence of T holding periods:

$$r_{nt} = b_{0nt} + b_{1nt} r_{Mt} + b_{2nt} f_{2t} + \dots + b_{k-1,nt} f_{k-1,t} + u_{nt},$$
$$n = 1, \dots, N, \quad t = 1, \dots, T$$

where r_{nt} is the (excess) return on stock n over holding period t, r_{Mt} is the (excess) return on a stock market index in period t, and the f_{it}, $i = 2, \dots, k - 1$, are other major economic or social factors which influence the returns on securities. The coefficient b_1, widely known in finance as the stock's "beta," is a partial derivative with respect to return on the index. The "beta" and the other coefficients are important in the theory and practice of investment management, since they determine the risk of a diversified portfolio (see, for example, Sharpe (1970)). The "beta," in particular, has been widely studied empirically. It has been shown that "beta," for any security, is serially correlated but nonconstant. A possible stochastic model for "beta" is:

$$b_{nt} = (1 - \phi)\bar{b}_n + \phi b_{n,t-1} + \varepsilon_{nt}.$$

The autoregressive parameter ϕ induces serial correlation, the term $(1 - \phi)$ implements a tendency to converge toward a normal value $\bar{b}_n$, and the serially independent random increments ε introduce stochastic variation over time. The characteristics of this process have been studied by Rosenberg and Ohlson (1973). The results support the model, and, in particular, show significant nonconstancy in beta and confirm the tendency of beta to converge toward a normal value $\bar{b}_n$.

This paper is concerned with the case where the normal value is a population norm common to several individuals. Every individual parameter vector is regarded as the sum of a population mean parameter vector and an individual difference, with the latter tending to converge toward zero.

Each individual difference is assumed to converge at the same rate and to be subject to random shocks of the same variance. This is clearly an oversimplification as a model of many economic processes. For example, in a study of competition in the computer industry, one would suspect that the tendency of IBM to converge toward the group norm would differ from other firms. Also, in many populations, individuals fall naturally into subgroups, so that a two-level hierarchy, in which individuals converge toward subgroup norms and subgroups may or may not converge toward the population norm, may be more appropriate. Nevertheless, the simple convergence structure is used here for several reasons.

One reason is heuristic: although the computational difficulty of the estimation problem does not increase as the convergence patterns become more complex, the notation becomes more painful. A second reason is one of operational usefulness. When the stochastic parameter process is known a priori, as it may be when the process determining behavioral modifications is well understood, it is quite possible to operate in the fully general framework. However, when the parameter process is to be estimated from the data, a simple structure must be postulated. The simplification that all individual parameters have convergence and stochastic-shift characteristics which are identical and unchanging over time is analogous to the traditional regression assumption that all parameters are identical, in that it asserts a similarity across the population which is necessary to develop an operationally feasible method. However, while the assumption of fixed parameters was originally thought to be needed before computations could be carried out at all, here the simplifying assumption is imposed, not by computational necessity, but by the experimenter's ignorance as to the exact nature of the parameter process.

There may also be events which induce simultaneous shifts in all of the individual parameters. It will be assumed that the effects of these constitute a series of serially independent communal increments occurring in all parameter vectors.

The individual parameter vector may contain both parameters which vary across the population ("cross-varying parameters") and parameters which are the same for all individuals in any time period ("cross-fixed parameters"). Accordingly, each k-element individual parameter vector is partitioned as $\mathbf{b}_{nt} = (\mathbf{c}_t' : \mathbf{a}_{nt}')'$, where $\mathbf{c}_t$ is a (possibly empty) κ-element subvector of cross-fixed parameters and $\mathbf{a}_{nt}$ is a

λ-element subvector of cross-varying parameters, with $k = \kappa + \lambda$. The explanatory variables $x_1, \ldots, x_k$ are partitioned correspondingly, with $w_1, \ldots, w_\kappa$, the explanatory variables having cross-fixed coefficients, and $z_1, \ldots, z_\lambda$, the explanatory variables having cross-varying coefficients. Let $\bar{\mathbf{b}}_t \equiv \begin{pmatrix} \mathbf{c}_t \\ \bar{\mathbf{a}}_t \end{pmatrix} \equiv \sum_{n=1}^{N} \mathbf{b}_{nt}/N$ be the population mean parameter vector.

The convergent parameter regression structure then takes the form:

$$(1) \qquad y_{nt} = \sum_{i=1}^{\kappa} w_{int}c_{it} + \sum_{j=1}^{\lambda} z_{jnt}a_{jnt} + u_{nt} \qquad t = 1, \ldots, T, n = 1, \ldots, N$$

$$E(u_{nt}) = 0 \qquad E(u_{ms}u_{nt}) = \delta_{st}\sigma^2(\delta_{mn}R_n + R_G)$$

or in vector notation,

$$y_{nt} = (\mathbf{w}'_{nt} : \mathbf{z}'_{nt})\begin{pmatrix} \mathbf{c}_t \\ \mathbf{a}_{nt} \end{pmatrix} + u_{nt} = \mathbf{x}'_{nt}\mathbf{b}_{nt} + u_{nt}.$$

Parameter Transition Relations:

$$(2) \qquad \mathbf{c}_{t+1} = \mathbf{c}_t + \boldsymbol{\gamma}_t \qquad t = 1, \ldots, T - 1$$

and

$$(3) \qquad \mathbf{a}_{n,t+1} = \bar{\mathbf{a}}_t + \boldsymbol{\Delta}_\phi(\mathbf{a}_{nt} - \bar{\mathbf{a}}_t) + \boldsymbol{\eta}_{nt} \qquad t = 1, \ldots, T - 1, n = 1, \ldots, N$$

where $\quad E(\boldsymbol{\gamma}_t) = 0 \qquad E(\boldsymbol{\gamma}_s\boldsymbol{\gamma}'_t) = \delta_{st}\sigma^2\mathbf{Q}_c$

$$E(\boldsymbol{\eta}_{nt}) = 0 \qquad E(\boldsymbol{\eta}_{ms}\boldsymbol{\eta}'_{nt}) = \delta_{st}\sigma^2(\delta_{mn}\mathbf{Q}_a + \mathbf{Q}_G)$$

and $\quad E(u_{ms}\boldsymbol{\gamma}'_t) = 0 \qquad E(u_{ms}\boldsymbol{\eta}'_{nt}) = 0 \qquad E(\boldsymbol{\gamma}_s\boldsymbol{\eta}'_{nt}) = \delta_{st}\sigma^2\mathbf{Q}_{ca}.$

Here, δ_{ij} is the Kronecker delta equal to 1 if $i = j$, equal to zero otherwise. The disturbances are assumed to be serially uncorrelated, and to be composed of a communal disturbance with variance $\sigma^2 R_G \geq 0$, and uncorrelated individual terms with possibly heteroscedastic variances $\sigma^2 R_n$, $n = 1, \ldots, N$, with $R_n > 0$ for all n. The cross-fixed parameter vector is subject to serially uncorrelated increments having mean zero and variance matrix $\sigma^2\mathbf{Q}_c$. The convergence matrix $\boldsymbol{\Delta}_\phi$ is diagonal with diagonal entries ϕ_i, $0 \leq \phi_i < 1$, for $i = 1, \ldots, \lambda$. These diagonal entries are "convergence rates," in that ϕ_j is the proportion of the individual divergence $a_{jnt} - \bar{a}_{jt}$ which survives to period $t + 1$. The cross-varying parameter vectors are subject to serially uncorrelated individual parameter shifts. Each shift is the sum of a communal component with zero mean and variance matrix $\sigma^2\mathbf{Q}_G$ and an individual component with zero mean and variance matrix $\sigma^2\mathbf{Q}_a$. The disturbances are uncorrelated with the parameter process. The contemporaneous covariance between the cross-fixed parameter shift vector and any individual cross-varying parameter shift vector, or, equivalently, the covariance between the cross-fixed parameter shift and the communal component of the cross-varying parameter shifts, is $\sigma^2\mathbf{Q}_{ca}$. The variance matrices of parameter shifts may be positive semi-definite, permitting some parameters to remain fixed over time. All stochastic terms are assumed to be independent of the exogenous variables.

C. It is important for some purposes to view all individual parameter vectors as components of a single "grand parameter vector" $\boldsymbol{\beta}_t = (\mathbf{c}' : \mathbf{a}'_1 : \ldots : \mathbf{a}'_N)'_t$, with dimension $K = N\lambda + \kappa$. All the individual regressions in each period make up a single regression for the grand parameter vector

$$(4) \qquad \begin{pmatrix} y_1\\ y_2\\ \vdots\\ y_N\end{pmatrix}_t = \begin{pmatrix} \mathbf{w}'_1 & \mathbf{z}'_1 & & \\ \mathbf{w}'_2 & & \mathbf{z}'_2 & \mathbf{0} \\ \vdots & \mathbf{0} & & \ddots \\ \mathbf{w}'_N & & & \mathbf{z}'_N\end{pmatrix}_t \begin{pmatrix}\mathbf{c}\\ \mathbf{a}_1\\ \vdots\\ \mathbf{a}_N\end{pmatrix}_t + \begin{pmatrix}u_1\\ \vdots \\ u_N\end{pmatrix}_t \qquad t = 1,\dots,T$$

or

$$\mathbf{y}_t = \mathbf{X}_t\boldsymbol{\beta}_t + \mathbf{u}_t, \qquad E[\mathbf{u}_t\mathbf{u}'_t] = \sigma^2\mathbf{R},$$

$$\mathbf{R} = \begin{pmatrix} R_1 + R_G & R_G & \cdots & R_G \\ R_G & R_2 + R_G & \cdots & R_G \\ \vdots & \vdots & & \vdots \\ R_G & \cdots \quad R_G & \cdots & R_N + R_G \end{pmatrix} = \begin{pmatrix} R_1 & & \mathbf{0} \\ & \ddots & \\ \mathbf{0} & & R_N \end{pmatrix} + R_G\boldsymbol{\iota}\boldsymbol{\iota}',$$

where $\boldsymbol{\iota}$ denotes a vector of units. The parameter transition relations coalesce similarly into a single transition relation

$$(5) \qquad \begin{pmatrix}\mathbf{c}\\ \mathbf{a}_1\\ \mathbf{a}_2\\ \vdots\\ \mathbf{a}_N\end{pmatrix}_{t+1} = \begin{pmatrix} \mathbf{I} & \mathbf{0} & \mathbf{0} & \cdots & \mathbf{0} \\ \mathbf{0} & \Delta_\phi + \frac{(\mathbf{I} - \Delta_\phi)}{N} & \frac{(\mathbf{I} - \Delta_\phi)}{N} & \cdots & \frac{(\mathbf{I} - \Delta_\phi)}{N} \\ \mathbf{0} & \frac{(\mathbf{I} - \Delta_\phi)}{N} & \Delta_\phi + \frac{(\mathbf{I} - \Delta_\phi)}{N} & \cdots & \frac{(\mathbf{I} - \Delta_\phi)}{N} \\ \vdots & \vdots & \vdots & \ddots & \vdots \\ \mathbf{0} & \frac{(\mathbf{I} - \Delta_\phi)}{N} & \frac{(\mathbf{I} - \Delta_\phi)}{N} & \cdots & \Delta_\phi + \frac{(\mathbf{I} - \Delta_\phi)}{N} \end{pmatrix} \times \begin{pmatrix}\mathbf{c}\\ \mathbf{a}_1\\ \mathbf{a}_2\\ \vdots\\ \mathbf{a}_N\end{pmatrix}_t + \begin{pmatrix}\boldsymbol{\gamma}\\ \boldsymbol{\eta}_1\\ \boldsymbol{\eta}_2\\ \vdots\\ \boldsymbol{\eta}_N\end{pmatrix}_t$$

or

$$\boldsymbol{\beta}_{t+1} = \boldsymbol{\Phi}\boldsymbol{\beta}_t + \mathbf{d}_t, \qquad E[\mathbf{d}_t\mathbf{d}'_t] = \sigma^2\mathbf{Q}$$

where

$$\mathbf{Q} = \begin{pmatrix} \mathbf{Q}_c & \mathbf{Q}_{ca} & \mathbf{Q}_{ca} & \cdots & \mathbf{Q}_{ca} \\ \mathbf{Q}'_{ca} & \mathbf{Q}_a + \mathbf{Q}_G & \mathbf{Q}_G & \cdots & \mathbf{Q}_G \\ \mathbf{Q}'_{ca} & \mathbf{Q}_G & \mathbf{Q}_a + \mathbf{Q}_G & \cdots & \mathbf{Q}_G \\ \vdots & \vdots & \vdots & \ddots & \vdots \\ \mathbf{Q}'_{ca} & \mathbf{Q}_G & \mathbf{Q}_G & & \mathbf{Q}_a + \mathbf{Q}_G \end{pmatrix}$$

D. One important property of the convergent parameter model is the stationary cross-sectional parameter dispersion which it generates. If the cross section of the individual parameter vectors is examined in any one period, for any individual n,

$$\mathbf{a}_{n,t+1} - \bar{\mathbf{a}}_{t+1} = \boldsymbol{\Delta}_{\phi}(\mathbf{a}_{nt} - \bar{\mathbf{a}}_t) + \boldsymbol{\eta}_{nt} - \bar{\boldsymbol{\eta}}_t. \tag{6}$$

Since parameter shifts between periods t and $t + 1$ are uncorrelated with the parameters in period t,

$$E[(\mathbf{a}_{n,t+1} - \bar{\mathbf{a}}_{t+1})(\mathbf{a}_{n,t+1} - \bar{\mathbf{a}}_{t+1})'] = \boldsymbol{\Delta}_{\phi} E[(\mathbf{a}_{nt} - \bar{\mathbf{a}}_t)(\mathbf{a}_{nt} - \bar{\mathbf{a}}_t)']\boldsymbol{\Delta}_{\phi}' + \frac{N-1}{N}(\sigma^2 \mathbf{Q}_a) \tag{7}$$

and for $m \neq n$

$$E[(a_{m,t+1} - \bar{\mathbf{a}}_{t+1})(\mathbf{a}_{n,t+1} - \bar{\mathbf{a}}_{t+1})'] = \boldsymbol{\Delta}_{\phi} E[(\mathbf{a}_{mt} - \bar{\mathbf{a}}_t)(\mathbf{a}_{nt} - \bar{\mathbf{a}}_t)']\boldsymbol{\Delta}_{\phi}' - \frac{1}{N}(\sigma^2 \mathbf{Q}_a). \tag{8}$$

Since $\boldsymbol{\Delta}_{\phi}$ is diagonal, the stationary solutions to these difference equations are easily found to be:

$$\{E[(\mathbf{a}_{nt} - \bar{\mathbf{a}}_t)(\mathbf{a}_{nt} - \bar{\mathbf{a}}_t)']\}_{ij} = \frac{N-1}{N} \frac{\sigma^2 \{\mathbf{Q}_a\}_{ij}}{1 - \phi_i \phi_j} \tag{9}$$

$$\{E[(\mathbf{a}_{mt} - \bar{\mathbf{a}}_t)(\mathbf{a}_{nt} - \bar{\mathbf{a}}_t)']\}_{ij} = \frac{-1}{N} \frac{\sigma^2 \{\mathbf{Q}_a\}_{ij}}{1 - \phi_i \phi_j} \quad \text{for } m \neq n \tag{10}$$

where $\{\mathbf{A}\}_{ij}$ denotes element (i, j) in the matrix $\mathbf{A}$. Since the eigenvalues of $\boldsymbol{\Delta}_{\phi}$ are smaller than one, this is, indeed, the stationary joint distribution of the cross-varying parameter vectors about their sample mean in any single time period. Notice that the dispersion about the sample mean is identical to that in a sample of vectors drawn independently from a multivariate population with variance matrix $\sigma^2 \boldsymbol{\Omega}$ given by

$$\omega_{ij} \equiv \{\boldsymbol{\Omega}\}_{ij} = \frac{\{\mathbf{Q}_a\}_{ij}}{1 - \phi_i \phi_j}. \tag{11}$$

Thus, in any single cross section, the individual cross-varying parameter vectors in a convergent-parameter structure are distributed as if randomly drawn from a population with dispersion matrix $\sigma^2 \boldsymbol{\Omega}$. Cross-sectional regressions of this kind, often called random or randomly dispersed parameter regressions, have been studied previously (Rao (1965), Swamy (1970), Rosenberg (1973a)).

The parameter interrelationships in the convergent-parameter model are diagrammed in two ways in Figure 1. In both diagrams, a link between vectors denotes a transition relation. Figure 1a exhibits the interrelationships among individual parameter vectors. At the top of the diagram is a representation of the stationary joint distribution of the individual parameter vectors in the initial period. The vector $\mathbf{b}_0$ is brought in as the mean of the hypothetical multivariate population from which the initial parameter vectors are drawn.

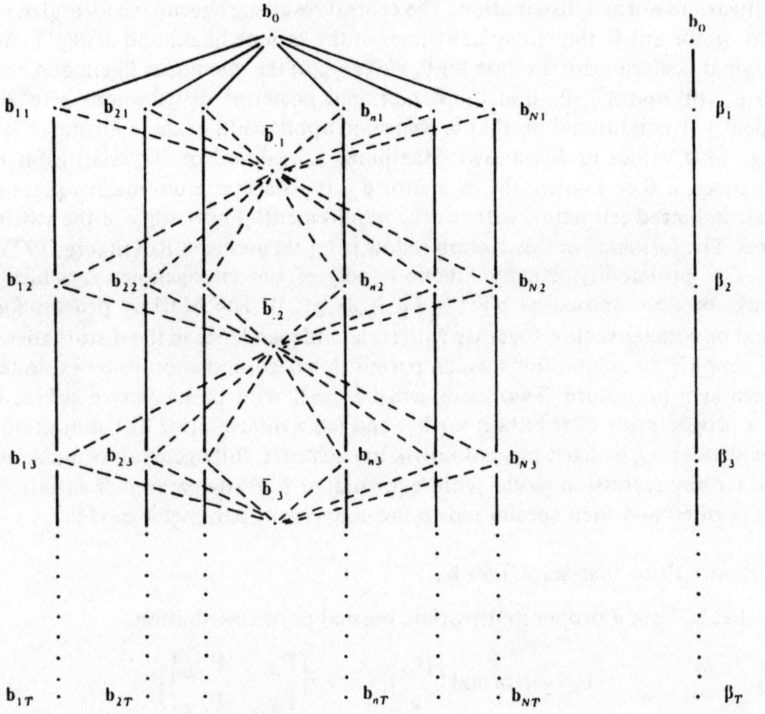

Figure 1a Figure 1b

In the transitions between successive periods in Figure 1a, the solid lines denote the contributions of the individual parameter vectors to their own subsequent values, and the broken lines denote the contribution of the sample mean to the subsequent values of the individual vectors.

Figure 1b shows the elementary structure of the serially independent transitions between successive grand parameter vectors. The grand regression is a Markovian or sequential parameter regression problem in that the grand parameter vector obeys a first order Markov process.

II. Estimation in the Convergent Parameter Model

Let $\boldsymbol{\theta}$ denote the vector of parameters in the stochastic specification, including the second moments of the stochastic terms $R_1, \ldots, R_N, R_G, Q_c, Q_{ca}, Q_a, Q_G$ and the convergence rates $\phi_1, \ldots, \phi_\lambda$, but excluding the scale parameter σ^2. Let R_θ denote the admissible region of parameter values, which may be constrained by a priori information as well as nonnegativity and symmetry conditions on the second moments. Let $\mathbf{y}^s = (\mathbf{y}_1' : \ldots : \mathbf{y}_s')'$ denote the vector of all observations through period s.

In this section, Maximum Likelihood and Bayesian methods for estimating $\boldsymbol{\theta}, \sigma^2$, and $\boldsymbol{\beta}_T$ are developed under the assumption that all stochastic terms follow a multivariate normal distribution. The central results are recursive formulae which yield: (i) for any $\boldsymbol{\theta}$, the numerical values of the sample likelihood $\mathscr{L}(\boldsymbol{\theta}|\mathbf{y}^T)$ and the marginal posterior distribution for $\boldsymbol{\theta}$, $p''(\boldsymbol{\theta}|\mathbf{y}^T)$; (ii) the maximum likelihood estimators $\hat{\boldsymbol{\beta}}_{T|T}(\boldsymbol{\theta})$ and $\hat{\sigma}^2_{ML}(\boldsymbol{\theta})$, and the conditional posterior distributions $p''(\sigma^2|\boldsymbol{\theta}, y^T)$, $p''(\boldsymbol{\beta}_T|\boldsymbol{\theta}, \mathbf{y}^T)$, conditional on that $\boldsymbol{\theta}$. Repeated application of these formulae, over a range of $\boldsymbol{\theta}$ values in R_θ, allows Maximum Likelihood or Bayesian estimation. Moreover, if $\boldsymbol{\theta}$ be known, the estimator $\hat{\boldsymbol{\beta}}_{T|T}(\boldsymbol{\theta})$ is a minimum mean square error linear unbiased estimator, without the requirement of normality in the stochastic terms. The formulae in this section follow from theorems in Rosenberg (1973b).

The probability density function (pdf) of the endogenous variables may always be decomposed as $p(\mathbf{y}^T) = \prod_{t=1}^T p(\mathbf{y}_t|\mathbf{y}^{t-1})$. The Markov process for the grand parameter vector, together with serial independence in the disturbances, are key simplifying assumptions which permit this decomposition to be exploited by a recursive procedure. Two cases will be dealt with in successive subsections: (A) a proper prior distribution for $\mathbf{b}_0$; and (B) a diffuse prior distribution for $\mathbf{b}_0$, or equivalently, $\mathbf{b}_0$ fixed but unknown. In each case, fully general formulae which hold for any regression model with sequential or Markov parameter variation will be exhibited and then specialized to the convergent parameter model.

A. Proper Prior Distribution for $\mathbf{b}_0$

Let $\mathbf{b}_0$ have a proper multivariate normal prior distribution

$$\text{(12)} \qquad \mathbf{b}_0 \sim \text{Normal}\left(\begin{pmatrix}\bar{\mathbf{c}}_0\\ \bar{\mathbf{a}}_0\end{pmatrix}, \quad \sigma^2\begin{pmatrix}\mathbf{P}_{0.c} & \mathbf{P}_{0.ca}\\ \mathbf{P}'_{0.ca} & \mathbf{P}_{0.a}\end{pmatrix}\right)$$

independently of all other stochastic terms. Then all regression parameters and endogenous variables follow a joint proper multivariate normal pdf, and it is easily shown that

$$\text{(13)} \quad p(\mathbf{y}^T|\sigma, \boldsymbol{\theta}) = \prod_{t=1}^{T} (2\pi\sigma^2)^{-(N/2)}|\mathbf{F}_t(\boldsymbol{\theta})|^{-1/2} \exp\left\{-\frac{1}{2\sigma^2}\|\mathbf{y}_t - \mathbf{X}_t\boldsymbol{\mu}_{t|t-1}(\boldsymbol{\theta})\|_{\mathbf{F}_t(\boldsymbol{\theta})^{-1}}\right\},$$

where

$$\sigma^2\mathbf{F}_t(\boldsymbol{\theta}) \equiv \text{var}\,[\mathbf{y}_t|\sigma, \boldsymbol{\theta}, \mathbf{y}^{t-1}] = \sigma^2(\mathbf{X}_t\mathbf{M}_{t|t-1}(\boldsymbol{\theta})\mathbf{X}'_t + \mathbf{R}),$$

and where, in general,

$$\boldsymbol{\mu}_{r|s}(\boldsymbol{\theta}) \equiv E[\boldsymbol{\beta}_r|\boldsymbol{\theta}, \mathbf{y}^s], \qquad \sigma^2\mathbf{M}_{r|s}(\boldsymbol{\theta}) \equiv \text{var}\,[\boldsymbol{\beta}_r|\sigma, \boldsymbol{\theta}, \mathbf{y}^s].$$

The notation $\|\mathbf{e}\|_{\mathbf{A}}$ denotes the norm $\mathbf{e}'\mathbf{A}\mathbf{e}$. The subscript $r|s$ denotes an estimator or distribution for an item in period r, conditional on regression information up to and including period s.

Therefore, when $\boldsymbol{\mu}(\boldsymbol{\theta})$ and $\mathbf{F}(\boldsymbol{\theta})$ are computed by the recursive formulae provided below, the sample likelihood is

$$\text{(14)} \qquad \mathscr{L}(\sigma, \boldsymbol{\theta}\,|\mathbf{y}^T) = (2\pi\sigma^2)^{-TN/2}\left(\prod_{t=1}^{T}\zeta_t(\boldsymbol{\theta})\right)^{-1/2} \exp\left\{-\frac{TNs^2(\boldsymbol{\theta})}{2\sigma^2}\right\},$$

where

$$\zeta_t(\boldsymbol{\theta}) = |F_t(\boldsymbol{\theta})|, \qquad \upsilon_t(\boldsymbol{\theta}) = \|\mathbf{y}_t - \mathbf{X}_t\boldsymbol{\mu}_{t|t-1}(\boldsymbol{\theta})\|_{\mathbf{F}_t^{-1}(\boldsymbol{\theta})}, \qquad s^2(\boldsymbol{\theta}) = \frac{\sum_{t=1}^T \upsilon_t(\boldsymbol{\theta})}{TN}.$$

Also, from the joint normal distribution of $\mathbf{y}^T$ and $\boldsymbol{\beta}_T$,

$$p(\boldsymbol{\beta}_T|\sigma,\boldsymbol{\theta},y^T) = (2\pi\sigma^2)^{-(K/2)}|\mathbf{M}_{T|T}(\boldsymbol{\theta})|^{-1/2} \times \exp\left\{-\frac{1}{2\sigma^2}\|\boldsymbol{\beta}_T - \boldsymbol{\mu}(\boldsymbol{\theta})_{T|T}\|_{\mathbf{M}_{T|T}(\boldsymbol{\theta})^{-1}}\right\}. \tag{15}$$

These formulae provide the basis for Maximum Likelihood and Bayesian estimation.

A.1. *Maximum Likelihood Estimation*

The maximum value of the natural log of the likelihood function (14), for any $\boldsymbol{\theta}$, is

$$l(\boldsymbol{\theta}|\mathbf{y}^T) \equiv \max_{\sigma^2} \ln \mathscr{L}(\sigma,\boldsymbol{\theta}|\mathbf{y}^T) = -\frac{1}{2}\left(TN\left(\ln\left(\frac{2\pi}{TN}\right)+1\right) + TN\ln(TNs^2(\boldsymbol{\theta})) + \sum_{t=1}^{T}\ln\zeta_t(\boldsymbol{\theta})\right). \tag{16}$$

The maximum likelihood estimators of σ^2 and $\boldsymbol{\beta}_T$, conditional on $\boldsymbol{\theta}$, are

$$\hat{\sigma}^2_{ML}(\boldsymbol{\theta}) = s^2(\boldsymbol{\theta}), \qquad \hat{\boldsymbol{\beta}}_{T|T}(\boldsymbol{\theta}) = \boldsymbol{\mu}_{T|T}(\boldsymbol{\theta}). \tag{17}$$

For maximum likelihood estimation, it is necessary to search R_θ for that $\boldsymbol{\theta}$, $\hat{\boldsymbol{\theta}}_{ML}$, which maximizes the log likelihood function (16). The maximum likelihood estimators of σ^2 and $\boldsymbol{\beta}_T$ are then $\hat{\sigma}^2_{ML}(\hat{\boldsymbol{\theta}}_{ML})$ and $\hat{\boldsymbol{\beta}}_{T|T}(\hat{\boldsymbol{\theta}}_{ML})$.

A.2. *Bayesian Estimation*

Let $p'(\boldsymbol{\theta})$ be a possibly diffuse prior pdf for $\boldsymbol{\theta}$, and let $p'(\sigma) \propto 1/\sigma$ be a diffuse prior for σ, following Zellner (1971 : Ch. 2). Then the posterior pdf for $\boldsymbol{\beta}_T, \sigma, \boldsymbol{\theta}$, is

$$p''(\boldsymbol{\beta}_T,\sigma,\boldsymbol{\theta}) = p(\boldsymbol{\beta}_T|\sigma,\boldsymbol{\theta},\mathbf{y}^T)p''(\sigma,\boldsymbol{\theta}), \tag{18}$$

where the conditional pdf for $\boldsymbol{\beta}_T$ is given in (15), and the marginal posterior pdf for σ and $\boldsymbol{\theta}$ is, from (14),

$$p''(\sigma,\boldsymbol{\theta}) \propto \mathscr{L}(\sigma,\boldsymbol{\theta}|\mathbf{y}^T)p'(\sigma)p'(\boldsymbol{\theta}) \propto \sigma^{-(TN+1)}p'(\boldsymbol{\theta})\left(\prod_{t=1}^{T}\zeta_t(\boldsymbol{\theta})\right)^{-1/2}\exp\left\{-\frac{TNs^2(\boldsymbol{\theta})}{2\sigma^2}\right\}. \tag{19}$$

This may be decomposed into the marginal posterior pdf for $\boldsymbol{\theta}$,

$$p''(\boldsymbol{\theta}) = \int_{R_\sigma} p''(\sigma,\boldsymbol{\theta})\,d\sigma \propto p'(\boldsymbol{\theta})\left(\prod_{t=1}^{T}\zeta_t(\boldsymbol{\theta})\right)^{-1/2}(s^2(\boldsymbol{\theta}))^{-TN/2}, \tag{20}$$

and the conditional posterior pdf for σ,

$$p''(\sigma|\boldsymbol{\theta}) \propto \sigma^{-(NT+1)}\exp\left\{-\frac{TNs^2(\boldsymbol{\theta})}{2\sigma^2}\right\}. \tag{21}$$

Let $\overline{\sigma^2}(\boldsymbol{\theta})$ be the conditional posterior mean of σ^2, $\overline{\sigma^2}(\boldsymbol{\theta}) = TNs^2(\boldsymbol{\theta})/(TN-2)$.

The conditional posterior pdf for $\boldsymbol{\beta}_T$ is multivariate Student t:

(22) $p''(\boldsymbol{\beta}_T|\boldsymbol{\theta}) \propto |s^2(\boldsymbol{\theta})\mathbf{M}_{T|T}(\boldsymbol{\theta})|^{-1/2}(TN + \|\boldsymbol{\beta}_T - \boldsymbol{\mu}(\boldsymbol{\theta})_{T|T}\|_{(s^2(\boldsymbol{\theta})\mathbf{M}_{T|T}(\boldsymbol{\theta}))^{-1}})^{-(NT+K)/2}$,

Hence, the moments of the marginal posterior pdf are

$$(23)\quad \begin{cases} \breve{\boldsymbol{\beta}}_{T|T} \equiv E[\boldsymbol{\beta}_T|\mathbf{y}^T] = \displaystyle\int_{R_\theta} \boldsymbol{\mu}_{T|T}(\boldsymbol{\theta}))p''(\boldsymbol{\theta})\, d\boldsymbol{\theta}. \\ \breve{\mathbf{M}}_{T|T} \equiv \text{var}\,[\boldsymbol{\beta}_T|\mathbf{y}^T] \\ \quad = \displaystyle\int_{R_\theta} (\overline{\sigma^2}(\boldsymbol{\theta})\mathbf{M}_{T|T}(\boldsymbol{\theta}) + (\boldsymbol{\mu}_{T|T}(\boldsymbol{\theta}) - \breve{\boldsymbol{\beta}}_{T|T})(\boldsymbol{\mu}'_{T|T}(\boldsymbol{\theta}) - \breve{\boldsymbol{\beta}}_{T|T}')p''(\boldsymbol{\theta})\, d\boldsymbol{\theta}. \end{cases}$$

Thus, the posterior pdfs for $\boldsymbol{\beta}_T$ and σ, conditional on $\boldsymbol{\theta}$, are available in analytical form, so that Bayesian estimation may be carried out by numerical integration, with respect to $p''(\boldsymbol{\theta})$, over R_θ.

A.3. The Recursive Formulae

The required recursive formulae are well known in the applied physical sciences, and are often referred to as the Kalman-Bucy filter. (See, for example, Aoki (1967), Ho and Lee (1964), Kalman (1960), and Kalman and Bucy (1961).) For the special case of the convergent parameter regression model, the predictive pdf for the grand parameter vector in the initial period follows from the prior pdf(12) for $\mathbf{b}_0$ and the stationary dispersion of the individual parameter vectors (11):

$$(24a)\quad \boldsymbol{\mu}_{1|0} = \begin{pmatrix} \bar{\mathbf{c}}_0 \\ \bar{\mathbf{a}}_0 \\ \vdots \\ \bar{\mathbf{a}}_0 \end{pmatrix}, \quad \mathbf{M}_{1|0}(\boldsymbol{\theta}) =$$

$$\begin{pmatrix} \mathbf{P}_{0,c} & \mathbf{P}_{0,ca} & \mathbf{P}_{0,ca} & \cdots & \mathbf{P}_{0,ca} \\ \mathbf{P}'_{0,ca} & \mathbf{P}_{0,a} + \boldsymbol{\Omega}(\boldsymbol{\theta}) & \mathbf{P}_{0,a} & \cdots & \mathbf{P}_{0,a} \\ \mathbf{P}'_{0,ca} & \mathbf{P}_{0,a} & \mathbf{P}_{0,a} + \boldsymbol{\Omega}(\boldsymbol{\theta}) & \cdots & \mathbf{P}_{0,a} \\ \vdots & \vdots & \vdots & & \vdots \\ \mathbf{P}'_{0,ca} & \mathbf{P}_{0,a} & \mathbf{P}_{0,a} & \cdots & \mathbf{P}_{0,a} + \boldsymbol{\Omega}(\boldsymbol{\theta}) \end{pmatrix}$$

In a later period t, suppose that the regression information through period $t-1$ has been exploited to yield the posterior moments $\boldsymbol{\mu}_{t-1|t-1}(\boldsymbol{\theta})$ and $\sigma^2\mathbf{M}_{t-1|t-1}(\boldsymbol{\theta})$. Then the conditional predictive pdf for the parameters in period t, has moments given by the

Parameter Extrapolation Formulae:

$$(24b)\quad \boldsymbol{\mu}_{t|t-1}(\boldsymbol{\theta}) = \boldsymbol{\Phi}(\boldsymbol{\theta})\boldsymbol{\mu}_{t-1|t-1}(\boldsymbol{\theta})$$

$$(24c)\quad \mathbf{M}_{t|t-1}(\boldsymbol{\theta}) = \boldsymbol{\Phi}(\boldsymbol{\theta})\mathbf{M}_{t-1|t-1}(\boldsymbol{\theta})\boldsymbol{\Phi}'(\boldsymbol{\theta}) + \mathbf{Q}(\boldsymbol{\theta})$$

The predictive pdf for the parameters (24a) or (24b,c) implies a predictive pdf for the endogenous variables in that period.

Forecasting Formulae

(24e) $\mathbf{e}_t(\boldsymbol{\theta}) \equiv \mathbf{y}_t - E(\mathbf{y}_t|\boldsymbol{\theta}, \mathbf{y}^{t-1}) = \mathbf{y}_t - \mathbf{X}_t\boldsymbol{\mu}_{t|t-1}(\boldsymbol{\theta})$

(24f) $\mathbf{F}_t(\boldsymbol{\theta}) \equiv \frac{1}{\sigma^2}\operatorname{var}(\mathbf{e}_t|\sigma, \theta, \mathbf{y}^{t-1}) = \mathbf{X}_t\mathbf{M}_{t|t-1}(\boldsymbol{\theta})\mathbf{X}_t' + \mathbf{R}(\boldsymbol{\theta})$

(24g) $\mathbf{L}_t(\boldsymbol{\theta}) \equiv \frac{1}{\sigma^2}\operatorname{cov}(\boldsymbol{\beta}_t - \boldsymbol{\mu}_{t|t-1}(\boldsymbol{\theta}), \mathbf{e}_t(\boldsymbol{\theta})|\sigma, \boldsymbol{\theta}, \mathbf{y}^{t-1}) = \mathbf{M}_{t|t-1}(\boldsymbol{\theta})\mathbf{X}_t'$

(24h) $v_t(\boldsymbol{\theta}) = \mathbf{e}_t'(\boldsymbol{\theta})\mathbf{F}_t^{-1}(\boldsymbol{\theta})\mathbf{e}_t(\boldsymbol{\theta})$

(24i) $\zeta_t(\boldsymbol{\theta}) = |\mathbf{F}_t(\boldsymbol{\theta})|.$

Finally, the observations on the endogenous variables in period t are incorporated into a revised conditional pdf, given by the

Revision Formulae

(24m) $\mathbf{K}_t(\boldsymbol{\theta}) = \mathbf{L}_t(\boldsymbol{\theta})\mathbf{F}_t^{-1}(\boldsymbol{\theta})$

(24n) $\boldsymbol{\mu}_{t|t}(\boldsymbol{\theta}) = \boldsymbol{\mu}_{t|t-1}(\boldsymbol{\theta}) + \mathbf{K}_t(\boldsymbol{\theta})\mathbf{e}_t(\boldsymbol{\theta})$

(24o) $\mathbf{M}_{t|t}(\boldsymbol{\theta}) = \mathbf{M}_{t|t-1}(\boldsymbol{\theta}) - \mathbf{L}_t(\boldsymbol{\theta})\mathbf{F}_t^{-1}(\boldsymbol{\theta})\mathbf{L}_t'(\boldsymbol{\theta}) = (\mathbf{I} - \mathbf{K}_t(\boldsymbol{\theta})\mathbf{X}_t)\mathbf{M}_{t|t-1}(\boldsymbol{\theta}).$

B. No Prior Distribution for $\mathbf{b}_0$

Where no prior distribution for $\mathbf{b}_0$ exists (or, equivalently, where $\mathbf{b}_0$ is a fixed but unknown vector from the classical viewpoint), a "starting problem" exists. This problem proved to be quite troublesome. Indeed, the solution proposed in Aoki (1967) was erroneous, because it was based on false "identities" for generalized matrix inverses (p. 80). Fortunately, there is a straightforward solution to the problem. It may be shown (Rosenberg (1973b)) that the pdf for $\boldsymbol{\beta}_s$, conditional on $\mathbf{y}^t, \boldsymbol{\theta}, \sigma^2$, and $\mathbf{b}_0$, is of the form

(25) $p(\boldsymbol{\beta}_s|\mathbf{b}_0, \sigma, \boldsymbol{\theta}, \mathbf{y}^t) = \text{Normal}\,(\boldsymbol{\xi}_{s|t}(\mathbf{b}_0, \boldsymbol{\theta}), \sigma^2\mathbf{M}^*_{s|t}(\boldsymbol{\theta})),$

where the mean value is linear in $\mathbf{b}_0$,

$$\boldsymbol{\xi}_{s|t}(\mathbf{b}_0, \boldsymbol{\theta}) \equiv E[\mathbf{b}_s|\mathbf{b}_0, \boldsymbol{\theta}, \mathbf{y}^t] \equiv \boldsymbol{\mu}^*_{s|t}(\boldsymbol{\theta}) + \boldsymbol{\Xi}_{s|t}(\boldsymbol{\theta})\mathbf{b}_0.$$

It follows that

(26) $$p(\mathbf{y}^T|\mathbf{b}_0, \sigma, \boldsymbol{\theta}) = \prod_{t=1}^{T} (2\pi\sigma^2)^{-N/2}|\mathbf{F}_t^*(\boldsymbol{\theta})|^{-1/2}$$
$$\times \exp\left\{-\frac{1}{2\sigma^2}\|\mathbf{y}_t - \mathbf{X}_t\boldsymbol{\mu}^*_{t|t-1}(\boldsymbol{\theta}) - \mathbf{X}_t\boldsymbol{\Xi}_{t|t-1}(\boldsymbol{\theta})\mathbf{b}_0\|_{\mathbf{F}_t^*(\boldsymbol{\theta})^{-1}}\right\}.$$

where

$$\mathbf{F}_t^*(\boldsymbol{\theta}) \equiv \frac{1}{\sigma^2}\operatorname{var}[\mathbf{y}_t|\mathbf{b}_0, \sigma, \boldsymbol{\theta}, \mathbf{y}^{t-1}] = \mathbf{X}_t\mathbf{M}^*_{t|t-1}(\boldsymbol{\theta})\mathbf{X}_t' + \mathbf{R}(\boldsymbol{\theta}).$$

This is formally equivalent to the pdf in a regression with regressands $\mathbf{e}_t^*(\boldsymbol{\theta})$, regressor matrices $\boldsymbol{\Upsilon}_t(\boldsymbol{\theta})$, and with $\mathbf{b}_0$ the unknown parameter vector, where

$$\mathbf{e}_t^*(\boldsymbol{\theta}) = \mathbf{y}_t - \mathbf{X}_t\boldsymbol{\mu}^*_{t|t-1}(\boldsymbol{\theta}), \qquad \boldsymbol{\Upsilon}_t(\boldsymbol{\theta}) = \mathbf{X}_t\boldsymbol{\Xi}_{t|t-1}(\boldsymbol{\theta}).$$

In analogy with the familiar linear regression, it may be shown that

$$(27)\qquad \mathscr{L}(\mathbf{b}_0, \sigma, \boldsymbol{\theta}|\mathbf{y}^T) = (2\pi\sigma^2)^{-TN/2}\left(\prod_{t=1}^{T} \zeta_t^*(\boldsymbol{\theta})\right)^{-1/2} \exp\left\{-\frac{1}{2\sigma^2}((TN-k)s^2(\boldsymbol{\theta}) + \|\mathbf{b}_0 - \hat{\mathbf{b}}_0(\boldsymbol{\theta})\|_{\mathbf{W}_0(\boldsymbol{\theta})})\right\},$$

where

$$(28)\qquad \hat{\mathbf{b}}_0(\boldsymbol{\theta}) = \left(\sum_{t=1}^{T} \mathbf{H}_t^*(\boldsymbol{\theta})\right)^{-1} \sum_{t=1}^{T} \mathbf{h}_t^*(\boldsymbol{\theta}), \qquad \mathbf{W}_0(\boldsymbol{\theta}) = \left(\sum_{t=1}^{T} \mathbf{H}_t^*(\boldsymbol{\theta})\right)^{-1},$$

$$s^2(\boldsymbol{\theta}) = \frac{\sum_{t=1}^{T} \|\mathbf{e}_t^*(\boldsymbol{\theta}) - \boldsymbol{\Upsilon}_t(\boldsymbol{\theta})\hat{\mathbf{b}}_0(\boldsymbol{\theta})\|_{\mathbf{F}_t^*(\boldsymbol{\theta})^{-1}}}{TN-k} = \frac{\sum_{t=1}^{T} v_t^*(\boldsymbol{\theta}) - \hat{\mathbf{b}}_0' \sum_{t=1}^{T} \mathbf{h}_t^*(\boldsymbol{\theta})}{TN-k},$$

and where, for each t,

$$v_t^*(\boldsymbol{\theta}) = \mathbf{e}_t^*(\boldsymbol{\theta})'\mathbf{F}_t^{*-1}(\boldsymbol{\theta})\mathbf{e}_t^*(\boldsymbol{\theta}), \qquad \mathbf{H}_t^*(\boldsymbol{\theta}) = \boldsymbol{\Upsilon}_t'(\boldsymbol{\theta})\mathbf{F}_t^{*-1}(\boldsymbol{\theta})\boldsymbol{\Upsilon}_t(\boldsymbol{\theta})$$

$$\zeta_t^*(\boldsymbol{\theta}) = |\mathbf{F}_t^*(\boldsymbol{\theta})|, \qquad \mathbf{h}_t^*(\boldsymbol{\theta}) = \boldsymbol{\Upsilon}_t'(\boldsymbol{\theta})\mathbf{F}_t^{*-1}(\boldsymbol{\theta})\mathbf{e}_t^*(\boldsymbol{\theta}).$$

B.1. Maximum Likelihood Estimation

From (27), the maximum value of the natural log of the likelihood function, for any $\boldsymbol{\theta}$, is

$$(29)\qquad l(\boldsymbol{\theta}|\mathbf{y}^T) \equiv \max_{\sigma,\mathbf{b}_0} \ln \mathscr{L}(\sigma, \boldsymbol{\theta}, \mathbf{b}_0|\mathbf{y}^T) = -\frac{1}{2}\left(TN\left(\ln\left(\frac{2\pi}{TN}\right) + 1\right) + TN\ln((TN-k)s^2(\boldsymbol{\theta})) + \sum_{t=1}^{T} \ln \zeta_t^*(\boldsymbol{\theta})\right).$$

The Maximum Likelihood estimator of $\mathbf{b}_0$, conditional on $\boldsymbol{\theta}$, is $\hat{\mathbf{b}}_0(\boldsymbol{\theta})$ given in (28). The Maximum Likelihood estimators for σ^2 and $\boldsymbol{\beta}_T$, conditional on $\boldsymbol{\theta}$, are

$$(30)\qquad \hat{\sigma}^2_{ML}(\boldsymbol{\theta}) = \frac{(TN-k)}{TN}s^2(\boldsymbol{\theta}), \qquad \hat{\boldsymbol{\beta}}_{T|T}(\boldsymbol{\theta}) = \boldsymbol{\mu}^*_{T|T}(\boldsymbol{\theta}) + \boldsymbol{\Xi}_{T|T}(\boldsymbol{\theta})\hat{\mathbf{b}}_0(\boldsymbol{\theta}).$$

As in A.1 above, the unconditional Maximum Likelihood estimators are $\hat{\boldsymbol{\theta}}_{ML}$, $\hat{\mathbf{b}}_0(\hat{\boldsymbol{\theta}}_{ML})$, $\hat{\sigma}^2_{ML}(\hat{\boldsymbol{\theta}}_{ML})$, and $\hat{\boldsymbol{\beta}}_{T|T}(\hat{\boldsymbol{\theta}}_{ML})$, where $\hat{\boldsymbol{\theta}}_{ML}$ maximizes (29) over $R_{\boldsymbol{\theta}}$.

B.2. Bayesian Estimation

Assume the same prior densities for $\boldsymbol{\theta}$ and σ as in A.2, above. The posterior pdf for all parameters is

$$(31)\qquad p''(\boldsymbol{\beta}_T, \mathbf{b}_0, \sigma, \boldsymbol{\theta}) = p(\boldsymbol{\beta}_T|\mathbf{b}_0, \sigma, \boldsymbol{\theta}, \mathbf{y}^T)p''(\mathbf{b}_0, \sigma, \boldsymbol{\theta}).$$

The conditional pdf for $\boldsymbol{\beta}_T$ is given in (25). The marginal posterior pdf for the other parameters is

$$(32)\qquad p''(\mathbf{b}_0, \sigma, \boldsymbol{\theta}) = p(\mathbf{b}_0, \sigma, \boldsymbol{\theta}|\mathbf{y}^T)p'(\sigma)p'(\boldsymbol{\theta})$$

$$\propto \sigma^{-(TN+1)}p'(\boldsymbol{\theta})\left(\prod_{t=1}^{T} \zeta_t^*(\boldsymbol{\theta})\right)^{-1/2} \exp\left\{-\frac{1}{2\sigma^2}((TN-k)s^2(\boldsymbol{\theta}) + \|\mathbf{b}_0 - \hat{\mathbf{b}}_0(\boldsymbol{\theta})\|_{\mathbf{W}_0(\boldsymbol{\theta})})\right\}.$$

Integrating with respect to $\mathbf{b}_0$ and σ, the marginal posterior pdf for $\boldsymbol{\theta}$ is found to be

(33) $$p''(\boldsymbol{\theta}) \propto p'(\boldsymbol{\theta})\left(\prod_{t=1}^{T} \zeta_t^*(\boldsymbol{\theta})\right)^{-1/2} |\mathbf{W}_0(\boldsymbol{\theta})|^{1/2}(s^2(\boldsymbol{\theta}))^{-(TN-k)/2}.$$

The conditional posterior pdf for σ is

(34) $$p''(\sigma|\boldsymbol{\theta}) \propto \sigma^{-(NT+1-k)} \exp\left\{-\frac{(TN-k)s^2(\boldsymbol{\theta})}{2\sigma^2}\right\}.$$

The mean is $\overline{\sigma^2}(\boldsymbol{\theta}) = [(TN-k)s^2(\boldsymbol{\theta})/(TN-k-2)]$. The conditional posterior pdf for $\boldsymbol{\beta}_T$ is again multivariate Student t:

(35) $$p''(\boldsymbol{\beta}_T|\boldsymbol{\theta}) \propto |s^2(\boldsymbol{\theta})\mathbf{M}_{T|T}(\boldsymbol{\theta})|^{-1/2} \times (TN-k+\|\boldsymbol{\beta}_T-\boldsymbol{\mu}_{T|T}(\boldsymbol{\theta})\|_{(s^2(\boldsymbol{\theta})\mathbf{M}_{T|T}(\boldsymbol{\theta}))^{-1}})^{-(TN-k+K)/2},$$

where

(36) $$\boldsymbol{\mu}_{T|T}(\boldsymbol{\theta}) = \boldsymbol{\mu}^*_{T|T}(\boldsymbol{\theta}) + \boldsymbol{\Xi}_{T|T}(\boldsymbol{\theta})\hat{\mathbf{b}}_0(\boldsymbol{\theta}),$$
$$\mathbf{M}_{T|T}(\boldsymbol{\theta}) = \mathbf{M}^*_{T|T}(\boldsymbol{\theta}) + \boldsymbol{\Xi}_{T|T}(\boldsymbol{\theta})\mathbf{W}_0(\boldsymbol{\theta})\boldsymbol{\Xi}'_{T|T}(\boldsymbol{\theta}).$$

The moments of the marginal posterior pdf of $\boldsymbol{\beta}_T$ are again given by formula (23).

B.3. The Recursive Formulae

The recursive formulae are closely related to those in the previous case. The initial conditions are somewhat changed.

Initial Conditions:

(37a) $$\boldsymbol{\mu}^*_{1|0}(\boldsymbol{\theta}) = 0, \qquad \boldsymbol{\Xi}_{1|0}(\boldsymbol{\theta}) = \begin{pmatrix} \mathbf{I} & \mathbf{0} \\ \mathbf{0} & \mathbf{I} \\ \mathbf{0} & \mathbf{I} \\ \vdots & \vdots \\ \mathbf{0} & \mathbf{I} \end{pmatrix}$$

$$\mathbf{M}_{1|0}(\boldsymbol{\theta}) = \begin{pmatrix} \mathbf{0} & \mathbf{0} & \mathbf{0} & \cdots & \mathbf{0} \\ \mathbf{0} & \boldsymbol{\Omega}(\boldsymbol{\theta}) & \mathbf{0} & \cdots & \mathbf{0} \\ \mathbf{0} & \mathbf{0} & \boldsymbol{\Omega}(\boldsymbol{\theta}) & \cdots & \mathbf{0} \\ \vdots & & & & \vdots \\ \mathbf{0} & \mathbf{0} & \mathbf{0} & \cdots & \boldsymbol{\Omega}(\boldsymbol{\theta}) \end{pmatrix}.$$

All other formulae in the previous list (24b, ..., 24o) carry over to the present case, with the variables $\boldsymbol{\mu}$, $\mathbf{M}$, $\mathbf{e}$, $\mathbf{F}$, υ, ζ, $\mathbf{L}$, $\mathbf{K}$ having a superscript *. In addition, the following formulae are inserted in the list in alphabetical order:

Parameter Extrapolation:

(37d) $$\boldsymbol{\Xi}_{t|t-1}(\boldsymbol{\theta}) = \boldsymbol{\Phi}(\boldsymbol{\theta})\boldsymbol{\Xi}_{t-1|t-1}(\boldsymbol{\theta})$$

Forecasting:

(37j) $$\Upsilon_t(\theta) = \mathbf{X}_t \Xi_{t|t-1}(\theta)$$

(37k) $$\mathbf{h}_t^*(\theta) = \Upsilon_t'(\theta)\mathbf{F}_t^{*-1}(\theta)\mathbf{e}_t^*(\theta)$$

(37l) $$\mathbf{H}_t^*(\theta) = \Upsilon_t'(\theta)\mathbf{F}_t^{*-1}(\theta)\Upsilon_t(\theta)$$

Revision:

(37p) $$\Xi_{t|t}(\theta) = \Xi_{t|t-1}(\theta) - \mathbf{K}_t^*(\theta)\Upsilon_t(\theta) = (\mathbf{I} - \mathbf{K}_t^*(\theta)\mathbf{X}_t)\Xi_{t|t-1}(\theta).$$

C. Both Maximum Likelihood and Bayesian estimation require an efficient means of searching R_θ. It is sometimes convenient to transform the parameters to a vector θ^* such that the admissible region for the transformed parameters, R_{θ^*}, coincides with Euclidean space. For instance, the variance matrices are required to be positive semi-definite symmetric. This constraint may be imposed by expressing each matrix as the product of a lower-triangular matrix with its transpose, for instance, $\mathbf{Q}_b = \mathbf{TT}'$. Searching the space of unconstrained lower-triangular matrices T is equivalent to searching the space of positive semi-definite symmetric matrices $\mathbf{Q}_b$, and the constraints are removed from the transformed problem. Similarly, for the convergence rates ϕ_i, a convenient transformation is $\phi_i = d_i^2/(1 + d_i^2)$, since the admissable range $0 \leq \phi_i < 1$ is equivalent to the range $-\infty < d_i < \infty$. However, note that in both cases $-\theta^*$ and θ^* yield identical values for θ, and also that $\partial\theta/\partial\theta^*|_{\theta^*=0} = \mathbf{0}$, so that attention must be given to avoiding the spurious local extremum at $\theta^* = \mathbf{0}$.

A good initial estimate of the stochastic specification is also helpful. The following algorithm provides an initial estimate when the sample size is large:

(i) First, under the temporary simplifying assumption that parameters are not dispersed across the population, estimates of the mean parameters in every period, $\bar{\bar{\mathbf{b}}}_1, \ldots, \bar{\bar{\mathbf{b}}}_T$, are generated. If the population mean is assumed to be essentially unchanging over time, ($\mathbf{Q}_c = \mathbf{Q}_{ca} = \mathbf{Q}_G = \mathbf{0}$), this is done by ordinary least squares. Otherwise, the population mean changes sequentially over time according to a Markov process with incremental variance

$$\sigma^2 \begin{pmatrix} \mathbf{Q}_c : & \mathbf{Q}_{ca} \\ \mathbf{Q}_{ca}' : \mathbf{Q}_G + & \dfrac{\mathbf{Q}_a}{N} \end{pmatrix}.$$

This variance, together with the realized values of the population mean parameters, may be estimated by an application of the previous formulae to this simpler sequential model. The communal disturbance variance $\sigma^2 R_G$ may also be estimated at this stage.

(ii) If the sample size is large, the residuals about these sample mean parameter estimates will approximate the contributions of the parameter dispersion and the disturbances,

$$\bar{e}_{nt} = y_{nt} - \mathbf{x}_{nt}'\bar{\bar{\mathbf{b}}}_t \simeq y_{nt} - \mathbf{x}_{nt}'\bar{\mathbf{b}}_t = \mathbf{z}_{nt}'(\mathbf{a}_{nt} - \bar{\mathbf{a}}_t) + u_{nt}.$$

Therefore,

(38) $$E[\bar{e}_{nt}^2] \simeq g_0 + \sum_{i=1}^{\lambda}\sum_{j=i}^{\lambda} g_{ij} z_{int} z_{jnt} \qquad n = 1, \ldots, N \quad t = 1, \ldots, T$$

where

$$g_0 = \sigma^2(1 + R_G), \qquad g_{ii} = \sigma^2\omega_{ii}, \quad \text{and} \quad g_{ij} = 2\sigma^2\omega_{ij} \quad \text{for } j > i.$$

(Note that, for simplicity, R_n is assumed here to equal unity for all n.) Also, for any time lag τ,

$$(39) \quad E[\hat{e}_{nt}\hat{e}_{n,t-\tau}] \simeq \sum_{i=1}^{\lambda}\sum_{j=1}^{\lambda} g_{\tau ij} z_{int} z_{jn,t-\tau} \qquad n = 1,\ldots,N \quad t = \tau + 1,\ldots,T$$

where

$$g_{\tau ij} = \sigma^2\omega_{ij}\phi_i^\tau.$$

If (38) is treated as a regression equation, with the squared residuals regressed on the cross products of the explanatory variables, then estimates of $g_0, g_1, \ldots, g_{1\lambda}, \ldots, g_{\lambda\lambda}$ and, hence, of σ^2 and $\mathbf{\Omega}$ are obtained. Similarly, for each time lag τ, a regression of the lagged products of the residuals on the lagged products of the explanatory variables of form (39) provides estimates of $\sigma^2\mathbf{\Delta}_\phi^\tau\mathbf{\Omega}$.

The various g's are nonlinear functions of the underlying parameters $\mathbf{\Delta}_\phi$ and $\mathbf{Q}_a$. The estimates $\hat{g}_{\tau ij}$ may be examined for their implications about the pattern of parameter variation, and initial estimates of the underlying parameters may be obtained by inspection or, if necessary, by nonlinear regression of the various $\hat{g}_{\tau ij}$ onto $\mathbf{\Delta}_\phi$ and $\mathbf{Q}_a$.

D. *Minimum Mean Square Error Linear Estimation*

Suppose that $\boldsymbol{\theta}$ is known. Let a minimum mean square linear unbiased estimator be defined as follows:

(i) An estimator $\boldsymbol{\beta}_{T|T}$ is linear unbiased iff it is a linear function of $\mathbf{y}^T$ such that $E[\boldsymbol{\beta}_{T|T}|\boldsymbol{\theta}] = E[\boldsymbol{\beta}_T|\boldsymbol{\theta}]$.

(ii) The minimum mean square error linear unbiased estimator $\hat{\boldsymbol{\beta}}_{T|T}$ is defined by the condition that for every linear combination of the parameters, $\boldsymbol{\alpha}'\boldsymbol{\beta}_T$, and for every linear unbiased estimator $\boldsymbol{\beta}_{T|T}$, $E[(\boldsymbol{\alpha}'\hat{\boldsymbol{\beta}}_{T|T} - \boldsymbol{\alpha}'\boldsymbol{\beta}_T)^2|\boldsymbol{\theta}] \leq E[(\boldsymbol{\alpha}'\boldsymbol{\beta}_{T|T} - \boldsymbol{\alpha}'\boldsymbol{\beta}_T)^2|\boldsymbol{\theta}]$

Then it may be shown (Rosenberg (1973b)) that the estimators $\hat{\boldsymbol{\beta}}_{T|T}(\boldsymbol{\theta})$ derived in Sections II.A.2. and II.B.2. are minimum mean square error linear unbiased estimators, with mean square error matrices $\sigma^2\mathbf{M}_{T|T}(\boldsymbol{\theta})$. Also, $s^2(\boldsymbol{\theta})$ is an unbiased estimator of σ^2. These properties do not require that the stochastic terms be normally distributed.

III. Approximate Formulae

The number of arithmetic operations in the recursive formulae increases as $N^3\lambda^2$, and the number of entries in $\mathbf{M}$ increases as $N^2\lambda^2$. Consequently, the exact method requires excessive computer time and storage when N is large. Fortunately, a natural simplifying approximation eliminates these problems.

The parameter covariance matrix $\sigma^2\mathbf{M}$ may be partitioned as

$$\sigma^2\mathbf{M}_{s|t} \equiv E\left[\begin{pmatrix}\hat{\mathbf{c}}_{s|t}-\mathbf{c}_s\\ \hat{\mathbf{a}}_{1s|t}-\mathbf{a}_{1s}\\ \cdot\\ \cdot\\ \cdot\\ \hat{\mathbf{a}}_{Ns|t}-\mathbf{a}_{Ns}\end{pmatrix}\begin{pmatrix}\hat{\mathbf{c}}_{s|t}-\mathbf{c}_s\\ \hat{\mathbf{a}}_{1s|t}-\mathbf{a}_{1s}\\ \cdot\\ \cdot\\ \cdot\\ \hat{\mathbf{a}}_{Ns|t}-\mathbf{a}_{Ns}\end{pmatrix}'\right] \equiv \sigma^2\begin{bmatrix}\mathbf{C} & \mathbf{D}_1 & \mathbf{D}_2 & \cdots & \mathbf{D}_N\\ \mathbf{D}'_1 & \mathbf{A}_{11} & \mathbf{A}_{12} & \cdots & \mathbf{A}_{1N}\\ \mathbf{D}'_2 & \mathbf{A}_{21} & \mathbf{A}_{22} & \cdots & \mathbf{A}_{2N}\\ \vdots & & & & \vdots\\ \mathbf{D}'_N & \mathbf{A}_{N1} & \mathbf{A}_{N2} & \cdots & \mathbf{A}_{NN}\end{bmatrix}_{s|t}$$

Throughout the recursive procedure, the largest part of the covariance between the parameters of different individuals arises from the common influence of the population mean. As a consequence, the matrices $\sigma^2\mathbf{A}_{mn}$, $m \neq n$, giving the covariance between the mth and nth individual parameter vectors, are similar for all pairs of individuals, as are the matrices $\mathbf{D}_n$ for all individuals. Accordingly, the following approximation suggests itself:

$$\tilde{\mathbf{M}} = \begin{pmatrix}\tilde{\mathbf{C}} & \tilde{\mathbf{D}} & \tilde{\mathbf{D}} & \cdots & \tilde{\mathbf{D}}\\ \tilde{\mathbf{D}}' & \tilde{\mathbf{A}}_G + \tilde{\mathbf{A}}_1 & \tilde{\mathbf{A}}_G & \cdots & \tilde{\mathbf{A}}_G\\ \tilde{\mathbf{D}}' & \tilde{\mathbf{A}}_G & \tilde{\mathbf{A}}_G + \tilde{\mathbf{A}}_2 & \cdots & \tilde{\mathbf{A}}_G\\ \vdots & \vdots & & \vdots & \\ \tilde{\mathbf{D}}' & \tilde{\mathbf{A}}_G & \tilde{\mathbf{A}}_G & \cdots & \tilde{\mathbf{A}}_G + \tilde{\mathbf{A}}_N\end{pmatrix}. \tag{40}$$

Here

$$\sigma^2\tilde{\mathbf{A}}_G = \sigma^2\left(\frac{\sum_{\substack{m,n=1\\ m\neq n}}^{N}\mathbf{A}_{mn}}{N(N-1)}\right)$$

is the average interindividual covariance,

$$\sigma^2\tilde{\mathbf{D}} = \sigma^2\left(\frac{\sum_{n=1}^{N}\mathbf{D}_n}{N}\right)$$

is the average covariance between cross-fixed parameters and individual cross-varying parameters, and the matrices $\sigma^2\tilde{\mathbf{A}}_n = \sigma^2(\mathbf{A}_{nn} - \tilde{\mathbf{A}}_G)$, $n = 1, \ldots, N$ are the excess of intra-individual over average interindividual covariance. The superscript tilde denotes an approximation to a statistic.

The simplifying approximation reduces the number of distinct entries in $\mathbf{M}$ to order $\lambda^2 N$ and the number of arithmetic operations to order $k^2 N$. Estimation for a given $\boldsymbol{\theta}$ then requires the same order of magnitude of storage and computations as would be required by ordinary regressions for all individuals in the population, in which similarities across individuals would be in no way exploited.

In this section, the recursive formulae resulting from this approximation are given in terms of the individual parameters. These formulae, the exact recursive formulae, and the formulae for another approximation were derived in detail in (Rosenberg (1973c)), but only the approximation that was found to be preferable will be reported here. To simplify the presentation, the notation $(\boldsymbol{\theta})$ and the subscript t on the variables $\mathbf{y}$, $\mathbf{e}$, $\mathbf{X}$, $\mathbf{Z}$, $\mathbf{W}$, $\mathbf{F}$, $\mathbf{K}$, $\mathbf{L}$, $\boldsymbol{\Upsilon}$ will be omitted where no confusion can result.

A. Approximate Recursive Formulae

The initial conditions (24a) and (37a) both satisfy the approximation exactly, and may be used in the forms already given.

Parameter Extrapolation

Suppose that for some t, $\tilde{\mathbf{M}}_{t-1|t-1}$ satisfies the approximation (40). Then the parameter extrapolation formulae are

$$\text{b}\begin{cases}\tilde{\mathbf{c}}_{t|t-1} = \tilde{\mathbf{c}}_{t-1|t-1} \\ \tilde{\mathbf{a}}_{n,t|t-1} = \boldsymbol{\Delta}_\phi \tilde{\mathbf{a}}_{n,t-1|t-1} + (\mathbf{I} - \boldsymbol{\Delta}_\phi)\bar{\tilde{\mathbf{a}}}_{t-1|t-1} \qquad n = 1, \ldots, N\end{cases}$$

$$\text{c}\begin{cases}\tilde{\mathbf{C}}_{t|t-1} = \tilde{\mathbf{C}}_{t-1|t-1} + \mathbf{Q}_c \\ \tilde{\mathbf{D}}_{t|t-1} = \tilde{\mathbf{D}}_{t-1|t-1} + \mathbf{Q}_{ca} \\ \tilde{\mathbf{A}}_{G,t|t-1} = \tilde{\mathbf{A}}_{G,t-1|t-1} + \mathbf{Q}_G + \dfrac{\bar{\bar{\mathbf{A}}}_{t-1|t-1} - \boldsymbol{\Delta}_\phi \bar{\bar{\mathbf{A}}}_{t-1|t-1}\boldsymbol{\Delta}_\phi}{N} \\ \tilde{\mathbf{A}}_{n,t|t-1} = \boldsymbol{\Delta}_\phi \tilde{\mathbf{A}}_{n,t-1|t-1}\boldsymbol{\Delta}_\phi + \mathbf{Q}_a \\ \quad + \dfrac{\boldsymbol{\Delta}_\phi(\bar{\mathbf{A}}_{n,t-1|t-1} - \bar{\bar{\mathbf{A}}}_{t-1|t-1})(\mathbf{I} - \boldsymbol{\Delta}_\phi) + (\mathbf{I} - \boldsymbol{\Delta}_\phi)(\bar{\mathbf{A}}_{n,t-1|t-1} - \bar{\bar{\mathbf{A}}}_{t-1|t-1})\boldsymbol{\Delta}_\phi}{N} \\ \qquad n = 1, \ldots, N\end{cases}$$

$$\text{d}\begin{cases}\tilde{\boldsymbol{\Xi}}_{c,t|t-1} = \tilde{\boldsymbol{\Xi}}_{c,t-1|t-1} \\ \tilde{\boldsymbol{\Xi}}_{n,t|t-1} = \boldsymbol{\Delta}_\phi \tilde{\boldsymbol{\Xi}}_{n,t-1|t-1} + (\mathbf{I} - \boldsymbol{\Delta}_\phi)\bar{\tilde{\boldsymbol{\Xi}}}_{t-1|t-1} \qquad n = 1, \ldots, N\end{cases}$$

where $\tilde{\boldsymbol{\mu}}$ and $\tilde{\boldsymbol{\Xi}}$ have been partitioned as

$$\tilde{\boldsymbol{\mu}} = \begin{pmatrix}\tilde{\mathbf{c}} \\ \tilde{\mathbf{a}}_1 \\ \vdots \\ \tilde{\mathbf{a}}_N\end{pmatrix} \qquad \tilde{\boldsymbol{\Xi}} = \begin{pmatrix}\tilde{\boldsymbol{\Xi}}_c \\ \tilde{\boldsymbol{\Xi}}_1 \\ \vdots \\ \tilde{\boldsymbol{\Xi}}_N\end{pmatrix}$$

and where the bar denotes an average over $n = 1, \ldots, N$, e.g.,

$$\bar{\tilde{\mathbf{a}}}_{t-1|t-1} = \frac{\sum_{m=1}^{N} \tilde{\mathbf{a}}_{m,t-1|t-1}}{N}.$$

Note that if $\mathbf{M}_{t-1|t-1}$ satisfies the approximation, then $\mathbf{M}_{t|t-1}$ also exactly satisfies it.

Forecasting

The forecast error vector is

$$\text{e}\left\{\mathbf{e} = \mathbf{y} - \mathbf{X}\tilde{\boldsymbol{\beta}}_{t|t-1} = \begin{pmatrix} y_1 - (\mathbf{w}'_1 : \mathbf{z}'_1)\begin{pmatrix}\tilde{\mathbf{c}} \\ \tilde{\mathbf{a}}_1\end{pmatrix}_{t|t-1} \\ \vdots \\ y_N - (\mathbf{w}'_N : \mathbf{z}'_N)\begin{pmatrix}\tilde{\mathbf{c}} \\ \tilde{\mathbf{a}}_N\end{pmatrix}_{t|t-1}\end{pmatrix} \equiv \begin{pmatrix}e_1 \\ \vdots \\ e_N\end{pmatrix}\right.$$

When $\mathbf{M}_{t-1|t-1}$ satisfies the approximation (40), $\mathbf{F}$ simplifies to

$$\mathbf{F} = \begin{pmatrix} \mathbf{w}_1' & \mathbf{z}_1' \\ \vdots & \vdots \\ \mathbf{w}_N' & \mathbf{z}_N' \end{pmatrix} \begin{pmatrix} \bar{\mathbf{C}} & \bar{\mathbf{D}} \\ \bar{\mathbf{D}}' & \bar{\mathbf{A}}_G \end{pmatrix}_{t|t-1} \begin{pmatrix} \mathbf{w}_1 & \cdots & \mathbf{w}_N \\ \mathbf{z}_1 & \cdots & \mathbf{z}_N \end{pmatrix} + R_G \mathbf{u}' + \begin{pmatrix} f_1 & & 0 \\ & \ddots & \\ 0 & & f_N \end{pmatrix},$$

where

$$f_n = \mathbf{z}_n' \mathbf{A}_{n,t|t-1} \mathbf{z}_n + R_n, \qquad n = 1, \ldots, N,$$

and where $\mathbf{\iota}$ is again a vector of units.

When the communal disturbance variance R_G is zero, the middle term vanishes. Otherwise, it may be adjoined to the first term:

$$\left\{\mathbf{F} = \begin{pmatrix} \mathbf{w}_1' & \mathbf{z}_1'[1] \\ \vdots & \\ \mathbf{w}_N' & \mathbf{z}_N'[1] \end{pmatrix} \begin{pmatrix} \mathbf{C} & \mathbf{D} & [0] \\ \mathbf{D}' & \mathbf{A}_G & [0] \\ [0] & [0] & [R_G] \end{pmatrix}_{t|t-1} \begin{pmatrix} \mathbf{w}_1 & \cdots & \mathbf{w}_N \\ \mathbf{z}_1 & \cdots & \mathbf{z}_N \\ [1] & \cdots & [1] \end{pmatrix} + \begin{pmatrix} f_1 & & 0 \\ & \ddots & \\ 0 & & f_N \end{pmatrix}\right. \quad f$$

$$\equiv \mathbf{\Psi} \mathbf{P}_{t|t-1} \mathbf{\Psi}' + \mathbf{\Delta}_f.$$

Let $\psi_n = (\mathbf{w}_n' : \mathbf{z}_n' : [1])'$ denote the nth column of $\mathbf{\Psi}'$. Here the communal disturbance changes status from a component of the disturbances with variance $\sigma^2 R_G$ to a cross-fixed parameter, with a coefficient vector of units, having forecast value of zero and forecast error variance of $\sigma^2 R_G$. Square brackets enclose terms which appear only when this artifice is in use. k [or $k + 1$] dimensional matrices such as $\mathbf{P}$ will be partitioned in the self-explanatory notation:

$$\mathbf{P} = \begin{pmatrix} \mathbf{P}_c \\ \mathbf{P}_a \\ [\mathbf{P}_u] \end{pmatrix} = \begin{pmatrix} \mathbf{P}_{cc} & \mathbf{P}_{ca} & [P_{cu}] \\ \mathbf{P}_{ac} & \mathbf{P}_{aa} & [P_{au}] \\ [P_{uc} & [P_{ua}] & [P_{uu}] \end{pmatrix}.$$

When $\mathbf{M}_{t-1|t-1}$ satisfies the approximation, $\mathbf{L}$ simplifies to

$$\left\{\mathbf{L} = \begin{pmatrix} \bar{\mathbf{C}} & \bar{\mathbf{D}} \\ \bar{\mathbf{D}}' & \bar{\mathbf{A}}_G \\ \vdots & \\ \bar{\mathbf{D}}' & \bar{\mathbf{A}}_G \end{pmatrix}_{t|t-1} \begin{pmatrix} \mathbf{w}_1 & \cdots & \mathbf{w}_N \\ \mathbf{z}_1 & \cdots & \mathbf{z}_N \end{pmatrix} + \begin{pmatrix} \mathbf{0} & \cdots & \mathbf{0} \\ \bar{\mathbf{A}}_{1,t|t-1}\mathbf{z}_1 & & \\ \mathbf{0} & \ddots & \mathbf{0} \\ & & \bar{\mathbf{A}}_{N,t|t-1}\mathbf{z}_N \end{pmatrix}\right. \quad g$$

$$= \begin{pmatrix} \mathbf{P}_c \\ \mathbf{P}_a \\ \vdots \\ \mathbf{P}_a \end{pmatrix} \mathbf{\Psi}' + \begin{pmatrix} \mathbf{0} & \mathbf{0} & \cdots & \mathbf{0} \\ \lambda_1 & \mathbf{0} & & \mathbf{0} \\ & & \ddots & \\ \mathbf{0} & \mathbf{0} & & \lambda_N \end{pmatrix}$$

where $\lambda_n = \bar{\mathbf{A}}_{n,t|t-1} \mathbf{z}_n$.

The inversion of $\mathbf{F}$ can be simplified by the matrix inversion identity

$$\mathbf{F}^{-1} = \mathbf{\Delta}_f^{-1} - \mathbf{\Delta}_f^{-1} \mathbf{\Psi} (\mathbf{\Psi}' \mathbf{\Delta}_f^{-1} \mathbf{\Psi} + \mathbf{P}^{-1})^{-1} \mathbf{\Psi}' \mathbf{\Delta}_f^{-1}. \tag{41}$$

The matrix $\mathbf{\Psi}' \mathbf{\Delta}_f^{-1} \mathbf{\Psi} = \sum_{n=1}^{N} (\psi_n \psi_n' / f_n)$, which has the form of a precision matrix, will be denoted by $\mathbf{H}$. Let $\mathbf{S} = (\mathbf{\Psi}'\Delta_f^{-1}\mathbf{\Psi} + \mathbf{P}^{-1})^{-1} = (\mathbf{H} + \mathbf{P}^{-1})^{-1}$. Also, let $\mathbf{h} = \mathbf{\Psi}'\Delta_f^{-1}\mathbf{e} = \sum_{n=1}^{N}(\psi_n e_n/f_n)$. Then the residual sum of squares is

$$(h)\left\{\quad \upsilon_t = \mathbf{e}'\mathbf{F}^{-1}\mathbf{e} = \mathbf{e}'\Delta_f^{-1}\mathbf{e} - \mathbf{e}'\Delta_f^{-1}\mathbf{\Psi}\mathbf{S}\mathbf{\Psi}'\Delta_f^{-1}\mathbf{e} = \sum_{n=1}^{N}\frac{e_n^2}{f_n} - \mathbf{h}'\mathbf{S}\mathbf{h}.\right.$$

The determinant of $\mathbf{F}$ is given by the determinantal identity

$$|\mathbf{F}| = |\Delta_f + \mathbf{\Psi}\mathbf{P}\mathbf{\Psi}'| = |\Delta_f|\cdot|\mathbf{P}|\cdot|\mathbf{P}^{-1} + \mathbf{\Psi}'\Delta_f^{-1}\mathbf{\Psi}| \tag{42}$$

which yields

$$(i)\left\{\quad \zeta_t = \left(\prod_{n=1}^{N} f_n\right)\cdot|\mathbf{P}|\cdot|\mathbf{S}^{-1}|.\right.$$

Whether or not $\mathbf{M}_{t-1|t-1}$ satisfies the approximation, Υ is given by

$$(j)\left\{\quad \Upsilon = \mathbf{X}_t\Xi_{t|t-1} = \begin{pmatrix} \mathbf{w}_1'\Xi_{c,t|t-1} & + & \mathbf{z}_1'\Xi_{1,t|t-1} \\ & \vdots & \\ \mathbf{w}_N'\Xi_{c,t|t-1} & + & \mathbf{z}_N'\Xi_{N,t|t-1} \end{pmatrix} \equiv \begin{pmatrix} \Upsilon_1' \\ \vdots \\ \Upsilon_N' \end{pmatrix}.\right.$$

Therefore,

$$(k)\left\{\quad \mathbf{h}_t^* = \Upsilon'\mathbf{F}^{-1}\mathbf{e} = \sum_{n=1}^{N}\Upsilon_n\left(\frac{e_n - \psi_n'\mathbf{S}\mathbf{h}}{f_n}\right)\right.$$

$$(l)\left\{\quad \mathbf{H}_t^* = \Upsilon'\mathbf{F}^{-1}\Upsilon = \sum_{n=1}^{N}\frac{\Upsilon_n\Upsilon_n'}{f_n} - \left(\sum_{n=1}^{N}\frac{\Upsilon_n\psi_n'}{f_n}\right)\mathbf{S}\left(\sum_{n=1}^{N}\frac{\Upsilon_n\psi_n'}{f_n}\right)'.\right.$$

Revision

The first term of $\mathbf{L}$, when post-multiplied by $\mathbf{F}^{-1}$, assumes the simple form

$$\begin{pmatrix}\mathbf{P}_c\\ \mathbf{P}_a\end{pmatrix}\mathbf{\Psi}'(\Delta_f^{-1} - \Delta_f^{-1}\mathbf{\Psi}(\mathbf{H} + \mathbf{P}^{-1})^{-1}\mathbf{\Psi}'\Delta_f^{-1}) = \begin{pmatrix}\mathbf{P}_c\\ \mathbf{P}_a\end{pmatrix}(\mathbf{I} - \mathbf{H}(\mathbf{H} + \mathbf{P}^{-1})^{-1})\mathbf{\Psi}'\Delta_f^{-1}$$

$$= \begin{pmatrix}\mathbf{P}_c\\ \mathbf{P}_a\end{pmatrix}(\mathbf{P}^{-1}(\mathbf{H} + \mathbf{P}^{-1})^{-1})\mathbf{\Psi}'\Delta_f^{-1} = (\mathbf{I}:[0])\mathbf{S}\mathbf{\Psi}'\Delta_f^{-1}.$$

The revision matrix $\mathbf{K}$ may therefore be written:

$$m\left\{\quad \mathbf{K} = \begin{pmatrix} \mathbf{I} & \mathbf{0} & [0] \\ \mathbf{0} & \mathbf{I} & [0] \\ & \vdots & \\ \mathbf{0} & \mathbf{I} & [0] \end{pmatrix}\mathbf{S}\mathbf{\Psi}'\Delta_f^{-1} + \begin{pmatrix} \mathbf{0} & \mathbf{0} & \dots & \mathbf{0} \\ \lambda_1 & \mathbf{0} & \dots & \mathbf{0} \\ \vdots & & & \\ \mathbf{0} & \mathbf{0} & \dots & \lambda_N \end{pmatrix}(\Delta_f^{-1} - \Delta_f^{-1}\mathbf{\Psi}\mathbf{S}\mathbf{\Psi}'\Delta_f^{-1}).\right.$$

Row-by-row evaluation of the revision equation for $\boldsymbol{\beta}$ yields

$$n\left\{\begin{aligned} \tilde{\mathbf{c}}_{t|t} &= \tilde{\mathbf{c}}_{t|t-1} + \mathbf{S}_c\mathbf{h} \\ \tilde{\mathbf{a}}_{n,t|t} &= \tilde{\mathbf{a}}_{n,t|t-1} + \mathbf{S}_a\mathbf{h} + \lambda_n\left(\frac{e_n - \psi_n'\mathbf{S}\mathbf{h}}{f_n}\right) \qquad n = 1,\dots,N. \end{aligned}\right.$$

Thus, a communal revision equal to **Sh** is made. Each cross-varying parameter estimate vector is further incremented by a multiple of the corresponding vector $\boldsymbol{\lambda}$.[1]

For revision of **M**, it is necessary to evaluate the term $-\mathbf{LF}^{-1}\mathbf{L}'$. After substitution of the expressions for $\mathbf{F}^{-1}$ and $\mathbf{L}$, use of the equality $\mathbf{P} - \mathbf{SHP} = (\mathbf{I} - \mathbf{SH})\mathbf{P} = \mathbf{SP}^{-1}\mathbf{P} = \mathbf{S}$ in partitioned form yields the revision formulae for the various components of the matrix:

$$o\left\{ \quad \bar{\mathbf{C}}_{t|t} = \mathbf{S}_{cc} \right.$$

$$(43) \quad \mathbf{D}_{n.t|t} = \mathbf{S}_{ca} - \mathbf{S}_c \frac{\boldsymbol{\psi}_n \boldsymbol{\lambda}_n'}{f_n}, \qquad n = 1, \ldots, N$$

$$(44) \quad \mathbf{A}_{mn.t|t} = \mathbf{S}_{aa} + \delta_{mn}\left(\bar{\mathbf{A}}_{m.t|t-1} - \frac{\boldsymbol{\lambda}_m \boldsymbol{\lambda}_m'}{f_m}\right) + \frac{\boldsymbol{\lambda}_m \boldsymbol{\psi}_m' \mathbf{S} \boldsymbol{\psi}_n \boldsymbol{\lambda}_n'}{f_m^2} - \frac{\boldsymbol{\lambda}_m \boldsymbol{\psi}_m' \mathbf{S}_a'}{f_m} - \frac{\mathbf{S}_a \boldsymbol{\psi}_n \boldsymbol{\lambda}_n'}{f_n}, \qquad m = 1, \ldots, N \quad n = 1, \ldots, N.$$

From these formulae, it is apparent that **S** gives the variance in an individual estimate stemming from the communal sources of error *after* the new regression information has been incorporated.

The revised interindividual covariances (43), (44) are not identical unless $\mathbf{x}_{nt}$, $t = 1, \ldots T$ and R_n are the same for all individuals. Hence, if the regressors and disturbance variances are identical for all n, so that **M** satisfies (40) without adjustment, the "approximate" formulae in this section coincide with the true recursive formulae. When this is not the case, in order to preserve the simplifying conditions of the approximation, it is natural to force the interindividual covariances to equal their averages. This arbitrary adjustment is the sole cause of inefficiency in the approximation. The average values are:

$$o\left\{ \begin{aligned} \bar{\mathbf{D}}_{t|t} &= \frac{\sum_{n=1}^N \mathbf{D}_{n.t|t}}{N} = \mathbf{S}_{ca} - \mathbf{S}_c\left(\frac{\sum_{n=1}^N (\boldsymbol{\psi}_n \boldsymbol{\lambda}_n'/f_n)}{N}\right) \\ \bar{\mathbf{A}}_{G.t|t} &= \frac{\sum_{\substack{m,n=1 \\ m \neq n}}^N \mathbf{A}_{mn.t|t}}{N(N-1)} = \mathbf{S}_{aa} - \mathbf{S}_a\left(\frac{\sum_{n=1}^N (\boldsymbol{\psi}_n \boldsymbol{\lambda}_n'/f_n)}{N}\right) \\ &\quad - \left(\mathbf{S}_a\left(\frac{\sum_{n=1}^N (\boldsymbol{\psi}_n \boldsymbol{\lambda}_n'/f_n)}{N}\right)\right)' + \frac{\sum_{\substack{m,n=1 \\ m \neq n}}^N (\boldsymbol{\lambda}_m \boldsymbol{\psi}_m' \mathbf{S} \boldsymbol{\psi}_n \boldsymbol{\lambda}_n'/f_m f_n)}{N(N-1)}. \end{aligned} \right.$$

[1]Note that the factor multiplying $\boldsymbol{\lambda}$ is equal to that part of the forecast error not explained by the communal parameter revision, divided by the individual increment to forecast error variance. Thus, one part of the forecast error, $\boldsymbol{\psi}_n'\mathbf{Sh}$, is attributed to an error in estimating the population mean parameter vector; a proportion of the communally unexplained forecast error, equal to $\mathbf{z}_n'\boldsymbol{\lambda}_n/f_n$, is attributed to an error in estimating the individual cross-varying parameters; and the balance of the communally unexplained error, the proportion $1 - (\mathbf{z}_n'\boldsymbol{\lambda}_n/f_n) = R_n/f_n$, remains as a residual after revision of the parameter estimates. The communally unexplained forecast error is therefore divided between error in forecasting individual parameters and the individual disturbance in proportion to the contributions of these sources of error to prediction error variance.

For computational purposes, the last term can be simplified:

$$\frac{\sum_{\substack{m,n=1\\ m\neq n}}^{N} (\lambda_m \psi_m' \mathbf{S} \psi_n \lambda_n' / f_m f_n)}{N(N-1)} = \frac{N}{N-1}\left(\frac{\sum_{n=1}^{N} (\lambda_n \psi_n' / f_n)}{N}\right) \mathbf{S} \left(\frac{\sum_{n=1}^{N} (\lambda_n \psi_n' / f_n)}{N}\right)' - \frac{\sum_{n=1}^{N} (\lambda_n \psi_n' \mathbf{S} \psi_n \lambda_n' / f_n^2)}{N(N-1)}.$$

The intra-individual variance increments are then set to be exact.

$$\tilde{\mathbf{A}}_{n,t|t} = \mathbf{A}_{nn,t|t} - \tilde{\mathbf{A}}_{G,t|t} \qquad n = 1, \ldots, N.$$

When N is small, an "increment" $\tilde{\mathbf{A}}_{n,t|t}$ may occasionally fail to be positive definite in the first few periods of the sample, because the previous data for that individual have provided more information about an individual parameter than all sample data have provided about the sample mean. In this event, the approximated matrix $\tilde{\mathbf{M}}$ is not positive definite, and the method can break down. During the recursive algorithm, difficulties arise only when f_n is nonpositive in the following period $t+1$, in which case the negative eigenvalues of $\tilde{\mathbf{A}}_{n,t|t}$ can be retrospectively adjusted to equal 0. After completion of the algorithm, the individual increments $\tilde{\mathbf{A}}_{n,T|T}$ can be checked for nonpositive eigenvalues, but this check is probably unnecessary, since nonpositive eigenvalues were never encountered in more than 150 simulations with $N = 10$, 20, or 40 at times $T = 10$, 15, or 20.

B. An Approximation to the Distribution of $\boldsymbol{\beta}_T$

In Maximum Likelihood estimation, the asymptotic approximate distribution for $\hat{\boldsymbol{\beta}}_{T|T}(\boldsymbol{\theta}_{ML})$ is normal $(\boldsymbol{\beta}_T, \hat{\sigma}^2_{ML}(\boldsymbol{\theta}_{ML})\mathbf{M}_{T|T}(\boldsymbol{\theta}_{ML}))$. In order for this distribution to be tractable, $\mathbf{M}_{T|T}$ may be approximated by $\tilde{\mathbf{M}}_{T|T}$, so that the variance matrix for $\boldsymbol{\beta}$ will satisfy (40). In Bayesian estimation, where $\boldsymbol{\beta}_{T|T}$ has the second moment given in (23), the numerical integration is facilitated by the use of $\tilde{\mathbf{M}}_{T|T}$ and by the further approximation:

$$\boldsymbol{\mu}_{T|T}(\boldsymbol{\theta}) - \breve{\boldsymbol{\beta}}_{T|T} \simeq \begin{pmatrix} \hat{\mathbf{c}}_{T|T}(\boldsymbol{\theta}) - \breve{\mathbf{c}}_{T|T} \\ \hat{\bar{\mathbf{a}}}_{T|T}(\boldsymbol{\theta}) - \breve{\bar{\mathbf{a}}}_{T|T} \\ \vdots \\ \hat{\bar{\mathbf{a}}}_{T|T}(\boldsymbol{\theta}) - \breve{\bar{\mathbf{a}}}_{T|T} \end{pmatrix} \quad \text{for all } \boldsymbol{\theta}. \tag{45}$$

After this simplification, the integrand satisfies (40), and hence $\tilde{\mathbf{M}}_{T|T}$ will satisfy (40) as well.

Statistical inference in the presence of a distribution with variance matrix $\tilde{\mathbf{M}}$ satisfying (40) requires evaluation of $|\tilde{\mathbf{M}}|$, and of the term

$$q = \begin{pmatrix} \tilde{\mathbf{c}} - \mathbf{c}^0 \\ \tilde{\mathbf{a}}_1 - \mathbf{a}_1^0 \\ \tilde{\mathbf{a}}_2 - \mathbf{a}_2^0 \\ \vdots \\ \tilde{\mathbf{a}}_N - \mathbf{a}_N^0 \end{pmatrix}' \tilde{\mathbf{M}}^{-1} \begin{pmatrix} \tilde{\mathbf{c}} - c^0 \\ \tilde{\mathbf{a}}_1 - \mathbf{a}_1^0 \\ \tilde{\mathbf{a}}_2 - \mathbf{a}_2^0 \\ \vdots \\ \tilde{\mathbf{a}}_N - \mathbf{a}_N^0 \end{pmatrix}.$$

By an application of the determinantal identity (42),

$$|\tilde{\mathbf{M}}| = \left| \begin{pmatrix} \tilde{\mathbf{C}} & & & & \\ & \mathbf{A}_1 & & 0 & \\ & & \mathbf{A}_2 & & \\ & 0 & & \ddots & \\ & & & & \tilde{\mathbf{A}}_N \end{pmatrix} + \begin{pmatrix} \mathbf{I} & 0 \\ 0 & \mathbf{I} \\ 0 & \mathbf{I} \\ \vdots & \\ 0 & \mathbf{I} \end{pmatrix} \begin{pmatrix} 0 & \tilde{\mathbf{D}} \\ \tilde{\mathbf{D}}' & \tilde{\mathbf{A}}_G \end{pmatrix} \begin{pmatrix} \mathbf{I} & 0 & 0 \cdot 0 \\ 0 & \mathbf{I} & \mathbf{I} \cdot \mathbf{I} \end{pmatrix} \right| \tag{46}$$

$$= \begin{vmatrix} \tilde{\mathbf{C}} & \tilde{\mathbf{D}} \\ \tilde{\mathbf{D}}' & \tilde{\mathbf{A}}_G + \left(\sum_{n=1}^{N} \tilde{\mathbf{A}}_n^{-1} \right)^{-1} \end{vmatrix} \cdot \left| \sum_{n=1}^{N} \tilde{\mathbf{A}}_n^{-1} \right| \cdot \prod_{n=1}^{N} |\tilde{\mathbf{A}}_n|.$$

An application of the matrix inversion identity (41) yields a rank k formula for $\tilde{\mathbf{M}}^{-1}$. After some matrix manipulations, an expression for the statistic q may be derived in terms of the matrix

$$\Lambda = \left(\sum_{n=1}^{N} \tilde{\mathbf{A}}_n^{-1} + (\tilde{\mathbf{A}}_G - \tilde{\mathbf{D}}'\tilde{\mathbf{C}}^{-1}\tilde{\mathbf{D}})^{-1} \right):$$

$$q = \|\tilde{\mathbf{c}} - \mathbf{c}^0\|_{[\mathbf{C}^{-1}]} + \sum_{n=1}^{N} \|\tilde{\mathbf{a}}_n - \mathbf{a}_n^0 - \tilde{\mathbf{D}}'\tilde{\mathbf{C}}^{-1}(\tilde{\mathbf{c}} - \mathbf{c}^0)\|_{[\mathbf{A}_n^{-1}]} \tag{47}$$

$$- \left\| \sum_{n=1}^{N} \tilde{\mathbf{A}}_n^{-1}(\tilde{\mathbf{a}}_n - \mathbf{a}_n^0 - \tilde{\mathbf{D}}'\tilde{\mathbf{C}}^{-1}(\tilde{\mathbf{c}} - \mathbf{c}^0)) \right\|_{[\Lambda^{-1}]}.$$

IV. The Statistical Efficiency and Validity of the Approximation

In this section, the properties of the approximation (hereafter referred to as A.I), conditional on $\boldsymbol{\theta}$ being correctly specified, will be analyzed. Upon examination of the recursive formulae that make up A.I, it may be seen to yield a linear unbiased estimator that is inefficient as a result of the simplifications in step (o). Recursive formulae for the *true* mean square error matrix of $\tilde{\boldsymbol{\beta}}_{T|T}$, as opposed to the approximation $\tilde{\mathbf{M}}$, may be derived. Then, for any $\boldsymbol{\theta}$, and for any set of explanatory variables $\mathbf{X}$, the exact properties of A.I may be computed, and two questions may be answered:

(i) How much larger is the mean square error of A.I than that of the exact, fully efficient method?

(ii) How valid is the approximated mean square error matrix $\tilde{\mathbf{M}}_{T|T}$ as an estimate of the true mean square error matrix for the approximate estimator, and how accurate is the approximated likelihood?

In addition, the properties of A.I may be compared with those of Ordinary Least Squares (OLS). These calculations, for a variety of convergent parameter regression structures $(\boldsymbol{\theta}, \mathbf{X})$, are reported in detail in Rosenberg (1973c, Sec. 5). The broad outlines will be summarized here.

A. Convergent Parameter Structures To Be Analyzed

Under the simplifying assumption that the cross-fixed parameters are constant over time and that the individual disturbance variances $R_n = R$ are identical for all n, a convergent parameter structure is specified by:

(i) the explanatory variables, $\mathbf{X}$
(ii) the communal disturbance variance, $\sigma^2 R_G$
(iii) the communal parameter shift variance, $\sigma^2 \mathbf{Q}_G$
(iv) the individual parameter shift variance, $\sigma^2 \mathbf{Q}_a$
(v) the convergence rates for parameters, $\phi_1, \ldots, \phi_\lambda$.

In selecting a set of representative structures among the infinite variety of options, the first problem is to construct the explanatory variables. The performance of the approximation is easily seen to be invariant to a linear transformation on the explanatory variables and a simultaneous inverse transformation on the parameter process. Accordingly, the explanatory variables can be normalized to have mean zero and variance unity, with inclusion of a constant being optional, provided that effects of changing scale are introduced through the parameter process. The correlation structure of the explanatory variables may be specified by four parameters, $\mathbf{X}(\rho_T, \rho_0, \rho_V, \rho_I)$, as follows:

$$\operatorname{corr}(x_{int}, x_{jmt}) = \begin{Bmatrix} \rho_0 \\ \rho_0 + \rho_V \\ \rho_0 + \rho_I \end{Bmatrix} \quad \text{for} \quad \begin{cases} i \neq j, & m \neq n \\ i = j, & m \neq n \\ i \neq j, & m = n \end{cases}$$

$$\operatorname{corr}(x_{int}, x_{jm,t-s}) = \rho_T^s \operatorname{corr}(x_{int}, x_{jmt}).$$

Thus, ρ_0 is the correlation between different variables for different individuals in the same period, ρ_V is the increment to this when the same variable is observed for different individuals, ρ_I is the increment when two different variables are observed for the same individual, and ρ_T is the attenuating factor for serial correlation. A set of pseudo-random, normally distributed explanatory variables obeying this correlation is easily constructed. In specifying $\boldsymbol{\theta}$, the covariances between parameter shifts for different parameters can be assumed to be zero, since variations in correlation are introduced in $\mathbf{X}$.

For each specification of $\mathbf{X}$, any combination of the remaining options—R_G, $\mathbf{Q}_G$, $\mathbf{Q}_a$, and Δ_ϕ—may be selected. The stochastic specification can be summarized by two statistics: the average convergence rate, $\bar{\phi} = \sum_{i=1}^{\lambda} \phi_i/\lambda$, and the approximate proportion of variance due to parameter dispersion, $\bar{f} = \boldsymbol{\iota}'\boldsymbol{\Omega}\boldsymbol{\iota}/(\boldsymbol{\iota}'\boldsymbol{\Omega}\boldsymbol{\iota} + R + R_G)$. The first statistic captures the degree of serial memory in the parameter dispersion, and the second expresses the importance of parameter dispersion as a source of noise in the system.

In Rosenberg (1973c), efficiency and validity measures were computed for 166 structures. In all of these, κ and λ were set to 3. Cross-section sizes of $N = 10, 20, 40$ were tried, with 40 being the largest feasible cross section because efficiency evaluation requires calculations increasing as N^3. The performance of the approximation was evaluated after each five time periods through to a maximum of thirty time periods, and it was found to stabilize within fifteen periods. Accordingly, all results are based on evaluations after fifteen or more periods.

Fifty-one widely varied structures were tried first in an effort to discover which of the parameters in the specification most influenced efficiency. Then fifty-one additional structures were studied to analyze the effects of extreme values in the more influential parameters. Finally, a study of sixty-four structures was carried out to compare A.I with OLS, again for extreme values of the influential parameters. In these last structures, communal parameter shift variance $\sigma^2 Q_G$ was set to zero, so that the inefficiency observed in OLS would be due solely to nonresponsiveness to parameter dispersion.

The most important conclusions based on results in all the structures are summarized below. Also, detailed results for the last 64 structures are reported by grouping the results according to the presence or absence of serial correlation in **X**, and by eight pairs of values for the two summary statistics $\bar{\phi}$ and $\bar{f}$. In this way, the 64 structures are segregated into 16 groups, and the results will be summarized by the worst value for each group. This simplification hides the systematic effects of variations other than serial correlation that were made in **X**, but since these effects are small relative to the effect of serial correlation, the summary tables do give an accurate representation of the performance of the approximation.

B. The Statistical Efficiency of the Approximation

Each measure of efficiency will be reported as a percentage inefficiency, i.e., as $100(z_a/z_e - 1)$, where z_a is a mean square error measure for the method under analysis, and z_e is the same measure for the exact method. Perhaps the most interesting single measure of efficiency is the kth root of the determinant of the mean square error matrix (the "generalized mean square error") for the population mean parameter vector. The pattern of inefficiency is summarized in Table 1.

The inefficiency of A.I is far less than the inefficiency of OLS, but inefficiency does increase as serial correlation in **X** increases. Detailed analysis of mean square estimation errors for the separate parameters shows that almost all inefficiency in A.I arises in estimating the cross-fixed parameters. The maximal inefficiency of A.I. for a cross-fixed parameter is 95 percent, whereas the maximal inefficiency for a cross-varying parameter is only 2.5 percent. (OLS reaches 258 percent inefficiency for a cross-varying parameter.) In a large sample, the mean square error in cross-fixed parameters, even when inflated by substantial inefficiency, is very small relative to the mean square error in cross-varying parameters. For this

TABLE 1

MAXIMUM PERCENTAGE INEFFICIENCY IN GENERALIZED MEAN SQUARE ERROR FOR THE POPULATION MEAN PARAMETER VECTOR

(16 Groupings from 64 Different Specifications, with $N = 20$, $T = 15$)

Serial Correlation in X		Stochastic Specifications							
		$\bar{\phi} = 0.600$ $\bar{f} = 0.957$	0.833 0.977	0.600 0.938	0.833 0.972	0.800 0.963	0.517 0.938	0.800 0.971	0.517 0.980
$\rho_T = 0$	A.I	07	17	06	16	13	06	14	12
	OLS	232	392	269	378	338	234	368	536
$\rho_T = 0.6$ or $\rho_T = 0.9$	A.I	10	26	09	25	36	20	38	34
	OLS	317	546	269	510	363	267	369	644

reason, if the criterion of performance is taken as the arithmetic average of the eigenvalues of the mean square error matrix (rather than the geometric average implied by the generalized variance), A.I performs extremely well, with a maximum inefficiency of less than 5 percent versus over 200 percent for OLS.

The following influences of the parameters in the stochastic specification emerge:

(a) As N increases, the inefficiency of A.I tends to decrease.

(b) As ϕ increases for any parameter, inefficiency increases for that parameter, and as $\bar{\phi}$ increases for a regression, inefficiency increases for that regression.

(c) As $\bar{f}$ increases for a regression, inefficiency increases.

(d) As the communal parameter shift variance $\mathbf{Q}_G$ increases, inefficiency decreases.

(e) The variance of the communal disturbance, R_G, has little effect.

(f) With regard to the structure of the explanatory variables, the presence of a constant has little effect, the presence of serial correlation increases inefficiency, the presence of correlation across variables for the same individual has little effect, and correlation of the variables across individuals reduces inefficiency. The last is to be expected, since if the correlation rises to one, the approximation becomes exact and hence perfectly efficient.

Comparison of forecasting efficiency provides another important test of the approximation. Consider forecast errors for single dependent variables ($e_{nT} = y_{nT} - \mathbf{x}'_{nT}\hat{\mathbf{b}}_{n,T|T-1}$, $n = 1, \ldots, N$) and for the population aggregate ($e_{.T} = \sum_n y_{nT} - \sum_n \mathbf{x}'_{nT}\hat{\mathbf{b}}_{n,T|T-1}$). The sources of error are the unpredictable disturbances and parameter shifts in period T, and the estimation error for the parameters in period $T - 1$. Differences across methods in mean square estimation error in period $T - 1$ therefore determine differences in the mean square forecast error. Moreover, since the explanatory variables are generated by a stationary stochastic process, the mean square forecast error weighs the efficiency of estimating various dimensions of the parameter vectors by the expected magnitude of the components of the explanatory variables corresponding to these dimensions.

For A.I, two possible forecasting procedures are available: to forecast each individual by the estimated parameters for that individual (Method I), or to forecast all individuals by the population mean parameter estimate (Method M). Method M should be less efficient, since it discards the disaggregated parameter estimates. For OLS with fixed parameters, these two methods coincide.

The criterion of forecasting performance for the single dependent variables is the sum of the mean square errors in the individual forecasts:

$$S_I = \sum_{n=1}^{N} E[(y_{nT} - \mathbf{x}'_{nT}\hat{\mathbf{b}}_{n,T|T-1})^2], \qquad S_M = \sum_{n=1}^{N} E[(y_{nT} - \mathbf{x}'_{nT}\hat{\bar{\mathbf{b}}}_{T|T-1})^2],$$

where the subscripts indicate the use of individual or population mean parameter estimates. For the aggregate forecast, the criterion is the mean square error:

$$A_I = E\left[\left(\sum_{n=1}^{N} y_{nT} - \sum_{n=1}^{N} \mathbf{x}'_{nT}\hat{\mathbf{b}}_{nT|T-1}\right)^2\right],$$

$$A_M = E\left[\left(\sum_{n=1}^{N} y_{nT} - \left(\sum_{n=1}^{N} \mathbf{x}'_{nT}\right)\hat{\bar{\mathbf{b}}}_{T|T-1}\right)^2\right].$$

TABLE 2

MAXIMUM PERCENT INEFFICIENCY IN SUM OF MEAN SQUARE ERRORS IN INDIVIDUAL FORECASTS
(16 Groupings from 64 Different Specifications, with $N = 20$, $T = 15$)

Specification			Using the Individual Parameter Forecasts (S_I)	Using the Forecast Population Mean Parameters (S_M)	
			A.I	A.I	OLS
$\rho_T = 0$	$\bar{\phi} = 0.600$	0.957	1	39	53
	0.833	0.977	1	138	131
	0.600	0.938	0	29	43
	0.833	0.972	0	156	149
	0.800	0.963	1	97	117
	0.517	0.938	1	45	53
	0.800	0.971	0	78	118
	0.517	0.980	1	189	212
$\rho_T = 0.6$ or $\rho_T = 0.9$	$\bar{\phi} = 0.600$	$\bar{f} = 0.957$	1	76	71
	0.833	0.977	0	155	184
	0.600	0.938	0	56	55
	0.833	0.972	0	166	199
	0.800	0.963	0	115	131
	0.517	0.938	0	76	62
	0.800	0.971	0	141	130
	0.517	0.980	0	338	233

TABLE 3

MAXIMUM PERCENT INEFFICIENCY IN MEAN SQUARE ERROR IN FORECASTING THE AGGREGATE
(16 Groupings from 64 Different Specifications, with $N = 20$, $T = 15$)

Specification			Using the Individual Parameter Forecasts (A_I)	Using the Forecast Population Mean Parameters (A_M)	
			A.I	A.I	OLS
$\rho_T = 0$	$\bar{\phi} = 0.600$	$\bar{f} = 0.957$	1	85	148
	0.833	0.977	3	28	170
	0.600	0.938	1	51	153
	0.833	0.972	3	8	183
	0.800	0.963	4	15	255
	0.517	0.938	4	44	278
	0.800	0.971	2	56	234
	0.517	0.980	14	228	326
$\rho_T = 0.6$ or $\rho_T = 0.9$	$\bar{\phi} = 0.600$	$\bar{f} = 0.957$	1	50	112
	0.833	0.977	3	60	182
	0.600	0.938	1	29	105
	0.833	0.972	2	71	205
	0.800	0.963	1	139	148
	0.517	0.938	1	5	79
	0.800	0.971	1	10	131
	0.517	0.980	0	12	210

In Tables 2 and 3, maximal percentage inefficiences of A.I and OLS are compared. A.I is almost perfectly efficient in forecasting the individual dependent variables but suffers a percentage inefficiency of up to 14 percent in forecasting the aggregate, due to relatively greater inefficiency in estimating the cross-fixed parameters. OLS has a percentage inefficiency of more than 200 percent in many cases. Notice that the results are dependent upon the $(\mathbf{X}, \mathbf{0})$ specifications chosen, but that for each specification, the results are the exact theoretical values, not the output of some sampling experiment.

C. Validity of Approximated Mean Square Error and Goodness of Fit

Let $\tilde{\sigma}^2$ denote $s^2(\mathbf{0})$ from A.I or from OLS, and let $\hat{\sigma}^2$ denote $s^2(\mathbf{0})$ from the Exact Method. Let $\tilde{l}$ and l denote the approximate and exact log likelihoods of the true structure, and let l_{FP} denote the exact log likelihood of the fixed-parameter structure.

In order to validate the approximated mean square error yielded by A.I or OLS, the statistics

$$V_n = \sqrt[k]{\frac{|\text{approximated mean square error matrix for } \tilde{\mathbf{b}}_n|}{|\text{true mean square error matrix for } \tilde{\mathbf{b}}_n|}} \quad \text{for } n = 1, \ldots, N$$

and

$$V_\cdot = \sqrt[k]{\frac{|\text{approximated mean square error matrix for } \tilde{\bar{\mathbf{b}}}|}{|\text{true mean square error matrix for } \tilde{\bar{\mathbf{b}}}|}}$$

are computed. The generalized mean square error ratios V_n are relatively constant across the population, so their value is summarized by the arithmetic mean $\bar{V} = \sum_{n=1}^{N} V_n/N$. The effect of estimation error in σ^2, which is omitted in these ratios, is introduced by computation of the additional ratios $(\tilde{\sigma}^2/\hat{\sigma}^2)V_\cdot$ and $((\tilde{\sigma}^2/\hat{\sigma}^2)\bar{V})$. The ratio $(\tilde{\sigma}^2/\hat{\sigma}^2)$ and the difference in log likelihoods are also computed. If A.I were exact, all ratios would be equal to their ideal value of unity, and the difference in log likelihood would be zero.

The results show a clear pattern. The validity of the approximation increases with N in more than 95 percent of the cases, an extremely encouraging property since sample sizes will be much larger in applications. Moreover, as the sample size doubles from $N = 20$ to $N = 40$, the difference $l - \tilde{l}$ declines in almost all cases, although the magnitude of l typically doubles. Thus, the proportional error in l declines more rapidly than $1/N$. If these results persist in large samples, the approximated log likelihood should be virtually perfect.

The values of the statistics that deviated most from the ideal values are given in Table 4 for the sixty-four structures already reported. The approximation is everywhere more valid than OLS. Moreover, the error in the approximated log likelihood is nowhere more than one-twentieth of the difference between the approximated log likelihood for the convergent-parameter structure and the log likelihood of the fixed-parameter structure. Hence, the approximated log likelihood reliably rejects the fixed-parameter model despite the small sample size.

TABLE 4
APPROXIMATED VERSUS TRUE PROPERTIES OF A.I AND OLS: MOST DEVIANT CASES
$N = 20\ T = 15$[a]

		$\bar{V}$	$V.$	$\frac{\tilde{\sigma}^2}{\hat{\sigma}^2}\bar{V}$	$\frac{\tilde{\sigma}^2}{\hat{\sigma}^2}V.$	$\frac{\tilde{\sigma}^2}{\hat{\sigma}^2}$	$l - l$ or $l_{FP} - l$
Ideal Values		1.0	1.0	1.0	1.0	1.0	0.0
$\rho_T = 0$	A.I	1.025	1.028	1.043	1.039	1.032	8.5
	OLS	0.002	0.007	0.069	0.239	64.66	−369.4
$\rho_T = 0.6$ or $\rho_T = 0.9$	A.I	0.493	0.446	0.499	0.451	1.027	8.9
	OLS	0.001	0.003	0.048	0.117	67.91	−269.6

[a] For OLS, the values computed under the erroneous assumption of fixed parameters are compared to the true properties of OLS. The difference in log likelihoods is an exception: the figure is the (exact) log likelihood of fixed parameters minus the exact log likelihood of the true structure.

Throughout the results, A.I appears to be entirely valid when the explanatory variables are serially independent, but to understate the estimation error variance when the explanatory variables are serially correlated. In the most severe case, one with serial correlation of 0.9, the approximated mean square error falls to 45 percent of the true value. This is a serious defect, in view of the prevalence of serial correlation in economic variables. It will have to be taken into account in applications. Fortunately, the degree of understatement decreases with N and, in large samples, the downward bias may be small. It is interesting to note that the approximated sampling properties of OLS are far worse. In fact, the estimated generalized mean square error of OLS falls below one-twentieth of the true value for individual parameters and below one-ninth of the true value for the population mean parameters. These deficiencies highlight the dangers of using the fixed-parameter assumption where it is inappropriate.

In summary, the approximation is highly efficient in estimating the cross-varying parameters and satisfactorily efficient in estimating the cross-fixed parameters, and the approximated likelihood can apparently be used with confidence. The only defect of the approximation that must be taken into account is understatement of the mean square error in the case of serially correlated explanatory variables. Subject to this caution, the approximation may be substituted into the recursive formulae of Section II. The results also imply that the method is sharply superior to ordinary least squares—in terms of efficiency and in terms of validity of sampling theory—when parameter dispersion is present. These results are overly favorable to the method, since $\boldsymbol{\theta}$ is presumed known, whereas, in fact, it must be estimated. However, the very large difference in sample log likelihood between the true structure and the fixed-parameter structure suggests that, if $\boldsymbol{\theta}$ were estimated by maximum approximated likelihood, then the estimated structure would be relatively close to the true structure. Hence, much of the gain in efficiency due to recognition of parameter variation would be achieved. Moreover, the very large sample sizes in many cross-section, time-series applications promise excellent estimates of $\boldsymbol{\theta}$, and therefore full exploitation of the potential efficiency of the method—provided, of course, that the model permits an appropriate description of the true parameter process.

Finally, notice that the computations involved in the method are feasible: the calculations required to evaluate a single stochastic specification with $N = 40$ were equivalent to repeating the approximation more than 500 times, enough iterations for Maximum Likelihood estimation or Bayesian estimation with $\boldsymbol{\theta}$ of reasonable dimension.

V. Conclusion

There are numerous extensions of the method that need not be added to an already lengthy paper. "Smoothed" estimates of parameter vectors $\boldsymbol{\beta}_t$ for $t < T$ may be computed by modifications of the recursive formulae derived here (see, e.g., Rosenberg (1973b)). A more complex model, where individual parameters converge to subgroup norms, which in turn may converge to the population norm, is relatively easy to implement. An underlying population mean, which serves as the norm for convergence in place of the sample mean in every period, may be added to the model if variations in the sample mean are not desired to affect the convergence pattern. Nonconstant variances or convergence rates, which differ across individuals or over time as functions of known characteristics of the individual or time period may be easily introduced, and the parameters specifying these functions may be adjoined to $\boldsymbol{\theta}$ without changing the estimation approach.

To summarize, a model of parameter variation in a cross section of time series was presented, in which individual parameters obey random walks subordinated to a tendency to converge toward the population norm. The model involves an intuitively plausible dynamic model of the determinants of individual diversity, and it is consistent with the empirical observation that, in some cross sections of time series, individual parameters vary relative to one another as if subjected to sequential random increments, but that cross-sectional parameter dispersion nevertheless remains roughly constant. Next, a computationally feasible method for Maximum Likelihood or Bayesian estimation of the parameters specifying the stochastic structure, as well as of the individual regression parameters themselves, was derived. The approximation involved in these computations was validated, subject to the one defect of understating mean square error when explanatory variables are serially correlated. The method was shown to be superior to Ordinary Least Squares in the presence of stochastic parameter variation of the type conjectured.

University of California, Berkeley

Bibliography

Aoki, Masanao (1967), *Optimization of Stochastic Systems*, New York: Academic Press.

Balestra, P. and Nerlove, M. (1966), "Pooling Cross-Section and Time Series Data in the Estimation of a Dynamic Model: The Demand for Natural Gas," *Econometrica*, 34 (July), 585–612.

Chetty, V. K. (1968), "Pooling of Time Series and Cross Section Data," *Econometrica*, 36 (April), 279–290.

Hildreth, Clifford (1949), "Preliminary Considerations Regarding Time Series and/or Cross-Section Studies," Cowles Commission Discussion Paper No. 333.

———. (1950), "Combining Cross Section and Time Series Data," Cowles Commission Discussion Paper No. 347.

Ho, Y. C. and Lee, R. C. K. (1964), "A Bayesian Approach to Problems in Stochastic Estimation and Control," *IEEE Transactions on Automatic Control*. AC-9, pp. 333–339.
Hoch, Irving (1962), "Estimation of Production Function Parameters Combining Time-Series and Cross-Section Data," *Econometrica*. 30 (January), 34–53.
Hsiao, Cheng (1973), "Statistical Inference for a Model with Both Random Cross-Sectional and Time Effects," Technical Report No. 83, Stanford, Calif.: Institute for Mathematical Studies in the Social Sciences, Stanford University.
Kalman, R. E. (1960), "A New Approach to Linear Filtering and Prediction Problems," Transactions of ASME, Series D, *Journal of Basic Engineering*, 82, pp. 35–45.
Kalman, R. E. and Bucy, R. S. (1961), "New Results in Linear Filtering and Prediction Theory," Transactions of ASME, Series D, *Journal of Basic Engineering*, 83, pp. 95–108.
Kuh, E. (1959), "The Validity of Cross-Sectionally Estimated Behavioral Equations in Time Series Applications," *Econometrica*, 27 (April), 197–214.
Kuh, E. and Meyer, J. R. (1957), "How Extraneous Are Extraneous Estimates?" *Review of Economics and Statistics*, 39 (November), 380–393.
Mundlak, Yair (1963), "Estimation of Production and Behavioral Functions from a Combination of Cross-Section and Time-Series Data," *Measurement in Economics*. Edited by Carl F. Christ, *et al.* Stanford, Calif.: Stanford University Press.
Nerlove, Marc (1965), *Estimation and Identification of Cobb-Douglas Production Functions*, Chicago: Rand McNally & Co.
———. (1968), "Further Evidence on the Estimation of Dynamic Economic Relations from a Time Series of Cross-Sections," Cowles Commission Discussion Paper No. 257.
Parks, Richard W. (1967), "Efficient Estimation of a System of Regression Equations When Disturbances Are Both Serially and Contemporaneously Correlated," *JASA*, 62 (June), 500–509.
Rao, C. R. (1965), "The Theory of Least Squares When the Parameters Are Stochastic," *Biometrika*, 52, pp. 447–458.
Rosenberg, Barr (1973a), "Linear Regression with Randomly Dispersed Parameters," *Biometrika*, 60, pp. 65–72.
———. (1973b), "Estimation in the General Linear Stochastic Parameter Model," Research Report. Cambridge, Mass: National Bureau of Economic Research, Computer Research Center.
———. (1973c), "Varying Parameter Regression in the Analysis of a Cross Section of Time Series," Working Paper No. IP 165. Berkeley: Institute of Business and Economic Research, University of California.
Sharpe, William F. (1970), *Portfolio Theory and Capital Markets*, New York: McGraw Hill Book Company.
Swamy, P. A. V. B. (1970), "Efficient Inference in a Random Coefficient Regression Model," *Econometrica*, 38, pp. 311–323.
———. (1971), *Statistical Inference in Random Coefficient Regression Models*, Berlin-Heidelberg-New York: Springer-Verlag.
Telser, Lester (1964), "Iterative Estimation of a Set of Linear Regression Equations," *JASA*, 59 (September), 845–862.
Wallace, T. D. and Hussain, Ashiq (1969), "The Use of Error Components Models in Combining Cross Section with Time Series Data," *Econometrica*, 3 (January), 37.1, 55–72.
Wilks, S. S. (1943), *Mathematical Statistics*, Princeton, N.J.: Princeton University Press.
Zellner, Arnold (1962), "An Efficient Method of Estimating Seemingly Unrelated Relations and Tests for Aggregation Bias," *JASA*, 57 (June), 348–367.
———. (1971), *An Introduction to Bayesian Inference in Econometrics*, New York: John Wiley & Sons.

[12]

Techniques for Testing the Constancy of Regression Relationships over Time

By R. L. Brown, J. Durbin and J. M. Evans

Central Statistical Office · *London School of Economics and Political Science* · *Central Statistical Office*

[Read before the Royal Statistical Society at a meeting organized by the Research Section on Wednesday, December 4th, 1974, Professor R. L. Plackett in the Chair]

Summary

Methods for studying the stability over time of regression relationships are considered. Recursive residuals, defined to be uncorrelated with zero means and constant variance, are introduced and tests based on the cusum and cusum of squares of recursive residuals are developed. Further techniques based on moving regressions, in which the regression model is fitted from a segment of data which is moved along the series, and on regression models whose coefficients are polynomials in time are studied. The Quandt log-likelihood ratio statistic is considered. Emphasis is placed on the use of graphical methods. The techniques proposed have been embodied in a comprehensive computer program, TIMVAR. Use of the techniques is illustrated by applying them to three sets of data.

Keywords: CUSUM; REGRESSION RESIDUALS; RECURSIVE RESIDUALS

1. Introduction

This paper describes and exemplifies a set of techniques for detecting departures from constancy of regression relationships over time when regression analysis is applied to time-series data. All the techniques described have been embodied in a computer program, TIMVAR. Enquiries about the availability of this program should be addressed to the Computer Development for Statistics Unit of the Central Statistical Office. A "User's Guide" to the program (Evans, 1973) is available from the Central Statistical Office. In what follows, the name TIMVAR will be used indifferently to describe either the set of methods used or the computer program written to implement them.

The theory underlying the paper was developed jointly by Brown and Durbin who gave a preliminary account of it in Brown and Durbin (1968). The original version of the program was written by C. E. Rogers and later work on it was done by R. P. Bayes and Evans. Mr Brown unfortunately died in 1972 so the actual writing of the paper was done by Durbin and Evans who accept full responsibility for the final version. However, since they have made substantial use of material left by Mr Brown they feel that he should be regarded as a co-author of the paper.

Regression analysis of time-series data is usually based on the assumption that the regression relationship is constant over time. In some applications, particularly in the social and economic fields, the validity of this assumption is open to question, and it is often desirable to examine it critically, particularly if the model is to be used for forecasting.

TIMVAR includes formal significance tests but its philosophy is basically that of data analysis as expounded by Tukey (1962). Essentially, the techniques are designed to bring out departures from constancy in a graphic way instead of parametrizing particular types of departure in advance and then developing formal significance tests intended to have high power against these particular alternatives. From this point of view the significance tests suggested should be regarded as yardsticks for the interpretation of data rather than leading to hard and fast decisions.

The problem we consider is a special case of a general class of problems concerned with the detection of changes of model structure over time, but we shall not attempt to review here the extensive literature dealing with the whole range of problems. Apart from citing references which have specific relevance to our own treatment we merely call attention to two papers of special importance, those of Chernoff and Zacks (1964) and Hinkley (1972).

The next section begins by specifying the basic regression model and the null hypothesis under consideration. It goes on to show how this hypothesis can be investigated by constructing plots of cumulative sums and sums of squares of the so-called recursive residuals. These are the standardized residuals from the regression of each observation y_t, the regression coefficients being calculated from the observations $y_1, ..., y_{t-1}$ for $t = k+1, ..., T$, where k is the number of regressors and T is the number of observations. It is shown that on the null hypothesis the recursive residuals are uncorrelated with zero mean and constant variance and are therefore independent under the normality assumption. Suitable formulae for carrying out the recursive calculations in a highly economical way are presented.

Other methods of transforming least-squares residuals to independent $N(0, \sigma^2)$ variables have been given by several authors including Theil (1965, 1968) and Durbin (1970). However, the recursive residuals seem preferable for detecting the change of model over time since until a change takes place the recursive residuals behave exactly as on the null hypothesis. When the change does occur, one hopes that signs of it will soon be apparent. With the other methods one would normally expect the effects of the change to be spread over the full set of transformed residuals.

In section 2.5 further techniques based on plotting the coefficients obtained by fitting the model to a segment of n successive observations and moving this segment along the series are presented. The plots are supplemented by a homogeneity test based on the analysis of variance. Section 2.6 considers the fitting and testing of time-trending regressions in which each coefficient is represented as a polynomial in time. The final technique considered is the plotting of Quandt's log-likelihood ratio statistic, intended to detect the single time-point, if any, at which there is a discontinuous change from one constant set of regression parameters to another.

In Section 3 the techniques developed are applied to three sets of real data taken from the field of economics. These examples illustrate how TIMVAR can be used in the model-building process to investigate the stability of models over time. The first example refers to data from the Post Office on the growth in the number of local telephone calls, the second uses data from the International Monetary Fund on the demand for money and the third deals with a model for forecasting manpower requirements using data provided by the Civil Service Department. Section 4 outlines the structure of the TIMVAR program and indicates the options available.

2. THE TECHNIQUES PROPOSED

2.1. *The Regression Model under Study*

The basic regression model we consider is

$$y_t = \mathbf{x}_t' \boldsymbol{\beta}_t + u_t, \quad t = 1, ..., T, \tag{1}$$

where at time t, y_t is the observation on the dependent variable and $\mathbf{x}_t$ is the column vector of observations on k regressors. The first regressor, x_{1t}, will be taken to equal unity for all values of t if the model contains a constant. The other regressors are assumed to be non-stochastic so auto-regressive models are excluded from consideration. The column vector of parameters, $\boldsymbol{\beta}_t$, is written with the subscript t to indicate that it may vary with time. We assume that the error terms, u_t, are independent and normally distributed with means zero and variances σ_t^2, $t = 1, ..., T$. The hypothesis of constancy over time, which will be denoted by H_0, is

$$\boldsymbol{\beta}_1 = \boldsymbol{\beta}_2 = ... = \boldsymbol{\beta}_T = \boldsymbol{\beta},$$
$$\sigma_1^2 = \sigma_2^2 = ... = \sigma_T^2 = \sigma^2.$$

We shall be more concerned with detecting differences among the $\boldsymbol{\beta}$'s than among the σ's though we do give a procedure which permits the investigation of variance changes. We have not considered the effects of serial correlation in the u's on the performance of the tests proposed.

It is natural to look at residuals to investigate departures from model specification, and a variety of procedures for doing this have been proposed in the literature (see, for example, Anscombe, 1961; Anscombe and Tukey, 1963). However, experience has shown that in the present situation the plot of the ordinary least-squares residuals, or the plot of their squares, against time is not a very sensitive indicator of small or gradual changes in the $\boldsymbol{\beta}$'s. In this respect the problem resembles that of detecting changes in the mean in industrial quality control for which the cumulative sum or cusum technique, introduced by Page (1954) and discussed further by Barnard (1959) and by Woodward and Goldsmith (1964), has been found to be a more effective tool for detecting small changes than the ordinary control chart in some circumstances.

This suggests that instead of plotting out the individual least-squares residuals z_t the cusums $Z_r = \hat{\sigma}^{-1} \sum_1^r z_t$, $r = 1, ..., T$, should be plotted, where we have divided by the estimated standard deviation $\hat{\sigma}$ to eliminate the irrelevant scale factor. The difficulty about this suggestion is that there seems no way of assessing the significance of the departure of the observed graph of Z_r against r from the mean-value line $E(Z_r) = 0$. The intractability of the problem arises from the fact that in general the covariance function $E(Z_r Z_s)$ does not reduce to a form that is manageable by standard Gaussian process techniques (cf. Mehr and McFadden, 1965). For instance, for the simple case of regression on a linear time trend with zero intercept, the covariance function is asymptotically $r - 3r^2 s^2/4T^3$ $(r < s)$, which is an unmanageable form.

An alternative is to consider the standardized cusum of squares, $\hat{\sigma}^{-2} \sum_1^r z_t^2$. Although more tractable, this is still difficult to deal with. Instead of considering it we prefer to make the transformation to recursive residuals given in the following section which enables us to treat the problem in terms of standardized cusums and cusums of squares of independent $N(0, \sigma^2)$ variables.

2.2. *The Recursive Residuals and their Properties*

Assuming H_0 to be true, let $\mathbf{b}_r$ be the least-squares estimate of $\boldsymbol{\beta}$ based on the first r observations, i.e. $\mathbf{b}_r = (\mathbf{X}_r' \mathbf{X}_r)^{-1} \mathbf{X}_r' \mathbf{Y}_r$ where the matrix $\mathbf{X}_r' \mathbf{X}_r$ is assumed to be non-singular, and let

$$w_r = \frac{y_r - \mathbf{x}_r' \mathbf{b}_{r-1}}{\sqrt{(1 + \mathbf{x}_r'(\mathbf{X}_{r-1}' \mathbf{X}_{r-1})^{-1} \mathbf{x}_r)}}, \quad r = k+1, ..., T, \tag{2}$$

where $\mathbf{X}_{r-1}' = [\mathbf{x}_1, ..., \mathbf{x}_{r-1}]$ and $\mathbf{Y}_r' = [y_1, ..., y_r]$.

Lemma 1. Under H_0, $w_{k+1}, \ldots, w_T$ are independent, $N(0, \sigma^2)$.

Proof. The unbiasedness of w_r is obvious and the assertion $V(w_r) = \sigma^2$ follows immediately from the independence of y_r and b_{r-1}. Also,

$$w_r = \left(u_r - \mathbf{x}_r'(\mathbf{X}_{r-1}'\mathbf{X}_{r-1})^{-1}\sum_{j=1}^{r-1}\mathbf{x}_j u_j\right)(1+\mathbf{x}_r'(\mathbf{X}_{r-1}'\mathbf{X}_{r-1})^{-1}\mathbf{x}_r)^{-\frac{1}{2}}.$$

Since each w_r is a linear combination of the normal variates u_j, the w_j's are jointly normally distributed. Now

$$E\left[\left\{u_r - \mathbf{x}_r'(\mathbf{X}_{r-1}'\mathbf{X}_{r-1})^{-1}\sum_{j=1}^{r-1}\mathbf{x}_j u_j\right\}\left\{u_s - \mathbf{x}_s'(\mathbf{X}_{s-1}'\mathbf{X}_{s-1})^{-1}\sum_{j=1}^{s-1}\mathbf{x}_j u_j\right\}\right]$$

$$= \sigma^2[0-0-\mathbf{x}_s'(\mathbf{X}_{s-1}'\mathbf{X}_{s-1})\mathbf{x}_r + \mathbf{x}_r'(\mathbf{X}_{r-1}'\mathbf{X}_{r-1})^{-1}(\mathbf{X}_{r-1}'\mathbf{X}_{r-1})(\mathbf{X}_{s-1}'\mathbf{X}_{s-1})^{-1}\mathbf{x}_s'] = 0 \quad (r<s).$$

It follows that $w_{k+1}, \ldots, w_T$ are uncorrelated and are therefore independent in view of their joint normality. The transformation from the u_r's to the w_r's is a generalized form of the Helmert transformation (Kendall and Stuart, 1969, p. 250).

Let S_r be the residual sum of squares after fitting the model to the first r observations assuming H_0 true, i.e. $S_r = (\mathbf{Y}_r - \mathbf{X}_r\mathbf{b}_r)'(\mathbf{Y}_r - \mathbf{X}_r\mathbf{b}_r)$.

Lemma 2.

$$(\mathbf{X}_r'\mathbf{X}_r)^{-1} = (\mathbf{X}_{r-1}'\mathbf{X}_{r-1})^{-1} - \frac{(\mathbf{X}_{r-1}'\mathbf{X}_{r-1})^{-1}\mathbf{x}_r\mathbf{x}_r'(\mathbf{X}_{r-1}'\mathbf{X}_{r-1})^{-1}}{1+\mathbf{x}_r'(\mathbf{X}_{r-1}'\mathbf{X}_{r-1})^{-1}\mathbf{x}_r}, \tag{3}$$

$$\mathbf{b}_r = \mathbf{b}_{r-1} + (\mathbf{X}_r'\mathbf{X}_r)^{-1}\mathbf{x}_r(\mathbf{y}_r - \mathbf{x}_r'\mathbf{b}_{r-1}), \tag{4}$$

$$S_r = S_{r-1} + w_r^2, \quad r = k+1, \ldots, T. \tag{5}$$

The relation (3) was given by Plackett (1950) and Bartlett (1951). It is used in the program to avoid having to invert the matrix $(\mathbf{X}_r'\mathbf{X}_r)$ directly at each stage of the calculations. It is proved by multiplying the left-hand side by $\mathbf{X}_r'\mathbf{X}_r$ and the right-hand side by $\mathbf{X}_{r-1}'\mathbf{X}_{r-1} + \mathbf{x}_r\mathbf{x}_r' = \mathbf{X}_r'\mathbf{X}_r$.

Proof of (4). Since b_r is the least-squares estimate it satisfies

$$\mathbf{X}_r'\mathbf{X}_r\mathbf{b}_r = \mathbf{X}_r'\mathbf{Y}_r = \mathbf{X}_{r-1}'\mathbf{Y}_{r-1} + \mathbf{x}_r y_r = \mathbf{X}_{r-1}'\mathbf{X}_{r-1}\mathbf{b}_{r-1} + \mathbf{x}_r y_r$$
$$= \mathbf{X}_r'\mathbf{X}_r\mathbf{b}_{r-1} + \mathbf{x}_r(y_r - \mathbf{x}_r'\mathbf{b}_{r-1}).$$

Proof of (5).

$$S_r = (\mathbf{Y}_r - \mathbf{X}_r\mathbf{b}_r)'(\mathbf{Y}_r - \mathbf{X}_r\mathbf{b}_r)$$
$$= (\mathbf{Y}_r - \mathbf{X}_r\mathbf{b}_{r-1})'(\mathbf{Y}_r - \mathbf{X}_r\mathbf{b}_{r-1}) - (\mathbf{b}_r - \mathbf{b}_{r-1})'\mathbf{X}_r'\mathbf{X}_r(\mathbf{b}_r - \mathbf{b}_{r-1})$$
$$= S_{r-1} + (y_r - \mathbf{x}_r'\mathbf{b}_{r-1})^2 - \mathbf{x}_r'(\mathbf{X}_r'\mathbf{X}_r)^{-1}\mathbf{x}_r(y_r - \mathbf{x}_r'\mathbf{b}_{r-1})^2$$

which gives (5) on substituting for $(\mathbf{X}'\mathbf{X}_r)^{-1}$ from (3).

An alternative proof of (3), (4) and (5) may be derived from the results of Heyadat and Robson (1970) since their quantities f_r are multiples of our quantities w_r. Note that w_r is the standardized prediction error of y_r when predicted from $y_1, \ldots, y_{r-1}$.

A situation arising frequently in practice is one where the regression model contains a constant and one of the regressor variables is itself constant for the first r_1 observations, where $r_1 \geq k$. Even though, in this case, the recursive residuals cannot be calculated from direct application of (2) above because of multicollinearity, it is possible to derive them in the following manner. The basic idea is to drop the initially constant regressor (which must be supplied to the program last) at the beginning of the recursions, reducing the number of regressors to $k-1$. Then recursive residuals $w_k^0, \ldots, w_{r_1}^0$ are derived from estimates $\mathbf{b}_{k-1}^0, \ldots, \mathbf{b}_{r_1-1}^0$ of the regressor vector $\boldsymbol{\beta}^0$, the ^{0} denoting the fact that only $k-1$ regressors have been used. (The first component of each of these estimates will of course be an estimate of $(\beta_1+\beta_k d)$ where d is the initial value of the last regressor.) When the last regressor has changed it is brought into the regression and recursive residuals are calculated from then on by formula (2). If, for $r = k+1, \ldots, r_1$, w_r is defined to be w_{r-1}^0 then we again have a set of $T-k$ values $w_{k+1}, \ldots, w_r$, which may be shown to be independent $N(0, \sigma^2)$ as before. When the kth regressor is brought into the regression the extra degree of freedom absorbed means that there is no increase in the residual sum of squares, i.e. $S_{r_1+1} = S_{r_1}^0$; moreover, apart from the constant term, the first $k-1$ components of $\mathbf{b}_{r_1+1}$ are equal to the corresponding components of $\mathbf{b}_{r_1}^0$. Having made the transition from $k-1$ to k regressors, the recursion proceeds as in the standard case.

2.3. *The Cusum Test*

If $\boldsymbol{\beta}_t$ is constant up to time $t = t_0$ and differs from this constant value from then on, the w_r's will have zero means for r up to t_0 but in general will have non-zero means subsequently. This suggests examination of plots intended to reveal departures of the means of the w_r's from zero as one travels along the series through time.

The first plot we consider is the plot of the cusum quantity

$$W_r = \frac{1}{\hat{\sigma}} \sum_{k+1}^{r} w_j,$$

against r for $r = k+1, \ldots, T$, where $\hat{\sigma}$ denotes the estimated standard deviation determined by $\hat{\sigma}^2 = S_T/(T-k)$. We require a method of testing the significance of the departure of the sample path of W_r from its mean value line $E(W_r) = 0$. A suitable procedure is to find a pair of lines lying symmetrically above and below the line $W_r = 0$ such that the probability of crossing one or both lines is α, the required significance level.

From the properties of the w_r's, under H_0 the sequence $W_{k+1}, \ldots, W_r$ is a sequence of approximately normal variables such that

$$E(W_r) = 0, \quad V(W_r) = r-k \quad \text{and} \quad C(W_r, W_s) = \min(r, s) - k,$$

to a good approximation. To derive the test, W_r is approximated by the continuous Gaussian process $\{Z_t, k \leqslant t \leqslant T\}$ with these mean and covariance functions. This is in fact the Brownian motion process starting from zero at time $t = k$. The form of straight line to choose was decided in two stages. The standard deviation of Z_t is $\sqrt{(t-k)}$. Consequently, if we wished to find a curve such that under H_0 the probability that the sample path lies above the curve at any point between $t = k$ and $t = T$ is constant, we should choose curves of the form $\pm\lambda\sqrt{(t-k)}$ where λ is constant. However, since we wish to limit ourselves to straight lines, the crossing probability cannot be constant for all t and the procedure adopted is to choose the family of lines tangent to the curves $\pm\lambda\sqrt{(t-k)}$ at the points halfway between $t = k$ and $t = T$. This leads to the family of pairs of straight lines through the points $\{k, \pm a\sqrt{(T-k)}\}$, $\{T, \pm 3a\sqrt{(T-k)}\}$, where a is the parameter. For any given line in this family, the probability that the point (r, W_r) lies outside the line is a maximum for r halfway between $r = k$ and $r = T$. We want to find a member of this family such that the probability that a sample path Z_t crosses it is $\frac{1}{2}\alpha$. Known results in Brownian motion theory give for the probability that a sample path Z_t crosses the line $y = d+c(t-k)$ for some t in (k, T) the value

$$Q\left(\frac{d+c(T-k)}{\sqrt{(T-k)}}\right)+\exp(-2dc)\,Q\left(\frac{d-c(T-k)}{\sqrt{(T-k)}}\right),$$

where

$$Q(z) = \frac{1}{\sqrt{(2\pi)}}\int_z^\infty \exp(-\tfrac{1}{2}u^2)\,du$$

(see, for example, Durbin, 1971, Lemma 3). Substituting $d = a\sqrt{(T-k)}$ and $c = 2a/\sqrt{(T-k)}$ we obtain the equation

$$Q(3a)+\exp(-4a^2)(1-Q(a)) = \tfrac{1}{2}\alpha,$$

to be solved for a.

It has been assumed that the probability that W_r crosses both lines is negligible, which will be justifiable for values of α normally used for significance testing, say 0·1 or less. Useful pairs of values of a and α are

$$\alpha = 0{\cdot}01, \quad a = 1{\cdot}143,$$
$$\alpha = 0{\cdot}05, \quad a = 0{\cdot}948,$$
$$\alpha = 0{\cdot}10, \quad a = 0{\cdot}850.$$

From the standpoint of data analysis, the function of these lines is to provide a yard-stick against which to assess the observed behaviour of the sample path, though of course they can be used to provide a formal test of significance by rejecting if the sample path travels outside the region between the lines.

2.4. *The Cusum of Squares Test*

This test uses the squared recursive residuals, w_r^2, and is based on the plot of the quantities

$$s_r = \left(\sum_{j=k+1}^{r} w_j^2\right)\bigg/\left(\sum_{j=k+1}^{T} w_j^2\right) = S_r/S_T, \quad r = k+1, \ldots, T.$$

The test provides a useful complement to the cusum test, particularly when the departure from constancy of the $\boldsymbol{\beta}_t$'s is haphazard rather than systematic. On H_0, s_r may be shown to have a beta distribution with mean $(r-k)/(T-k)$. This suggests drawing a pair of lines $s_r = \pm c_0+(r-k)/(T-k)$ on the diagram parallel to the mean-value line such that the probability that the sample path crosses one or both lines is α, the required significance level.

To find the significance values, c_0, it is convenient to consider first the case when $T-k$ is even. Then the joint distribution of the $\frac{1}{2}(T-k)-1$ statistics $s_{k+2}, s_{k+4}, \ldots, s_{T-2}$ is the same as that of an ordered sample of $\frac{1}{2}(T-k)-1$ independent observations from the uniform (0, 1) distribution. This may be shown by writing

$$n = \tfrac{1}{2}(T-k)-1 \quad \text{and} \quad z_j = (w_{k+2j}^2+w_{k+2j-1}^2)/2\sigma^2, \quad j = 1, \ldots, n+1.$$

Then the z_j's are independent, exponentially distributed random variables with mean one. If Z is the sum of the z_j's we have

$$s_{k+2j} = (z_1+\ldots+z_j)/Z, \quad j = 1, \ldots, n.$$

The required result follows by transforming the variables $z_1, \ldots, z_{n+1}$ to give the joint distribution of $s_{k+2}, \ldots, s_{T-2}$, Z and then integrating out Z.

The distribution of an ordered sample of independent observations from the uniform (0, 1) distribution plays an important part in the theory of non-parametric statistics, and the distribution of each of the statistics c^+ and c^-, defined by

$$c^+ = \max_{j=1,\ldots,m-1} (s_{k+2j} - j/m), \quad c^- = \max_{j=1,\ldots,m-1} (j/m - s_{k+2j})$$

where $m = \frac{1}{2}(T-k)$, can be recognized as being equivalent to that of Pyke's (1959) modified Kolmogorov–Smirnov statistic, C_n^+, with $n = m-1$. The statistics c^+ and c^- are the maximum positive and negative deviations respectively of the set of statistics $(s_{k+2}, \ldots, s_{T-2})$ from their mean-value line.

A table of significance values of the quantity C_n^+ for $n = m-1$ is given by Durbin (1969) (Table 1, p. 4). The procedure suggested for the cusum of squares test is to take these values as approximations to the significance values of

$$c_1^+ = \max_{i=1,\ldots,T-k-1} \left(s_{k+i} - \frac{i}{T-k}\right) \quad \text{and} \quad c_1^- = \max_{i=1,\ldots,T-k-1} \left(\frac{i}{T-k} - s_{k+i}\right),$$

which are the maximum positive and negative deviations of the whole set of s_r's from the mean-value line. For the value of the significance level, α, normally chosen, say 0·1 or less, the probability of crossing both lines is negligible, so that given a significance level α, to find the value of c_0 we may take the value obtained by entering the table at $n = \frac{1}{2}(T-k)-1$ and $\frac{1}{2}\alpha$. If $T-k$ is odd the procedure suggested is to interpolate linearly between the values for $n = \frac{1}{2}(T-k) - \frac{3}{2}$ and $n = \frac{1}{2}(T-k) - \frac{1}{2}$. Monte Carlo runs made by M. C. Hutchison have shown that this test gives significant results more often than the exact test would give, but that the discrepancy is very small when $(T-k)$ exceeds 30.

It may sometimes be appropriate to consider a one-sided test. For example, if it is assumed that $\boldsymbol{\beta}_t = \boldsymbol{\beta}^*$ for $t \leqslant r$ and $\boldsymbol{\beta}_t = \boldsymbol{\beta}^{**} \neq \boldsymbol{\beta}^*$ for $t > r$ while $\sigma_t^2 = \sigma^2$ for all t, then $E(w_t^2) = \sigma^2$ for $t \leqslant r$ and $E(w_t^2) > \sigma^2$ for $t > r$. One would therefore expect the departure from the null hypothesis to be indicated by a tendency for the sample path s_r to lie below the mean value line, and would therefore use a one-sided test. For this purpose, one would take the significance value of c_0 corresponding to significance level α, not $\frac{1}{2}\alpha$. However, whether the two- or one-sided situations are envisaged we ourselves prefer to regard the lines constructed in this way as yardsticks against which to assess the observed sample path rather than providing formal tests of significance.

If the two plots described above do indicate departures from constancy it may be useful to examine plots of the components of $\mathbf{b}_r$ against time to try to identify the source. Further, to help locate the point of change it is often informative to look at the set of plots which are obtained by running the analysis backwards through time as well as forwards.

2.5. *Moving Regressions*

Another useful way of investigating the time-variation of $\boldsymbol{\beta}_t$ is to fit the regression on a short segment of n successive observations and to move this segment along the series. The graphs of the resulting coefficients against time provide further evidence of departures from constancy. In addition, the estimated residual variance may be computed and plotted to investigate the constancy of σ^2.

The quantities required for each new segment are computed by first adding a new observation to the segment just dealt with using formulae (3)–(5) and then allowing for the effect of dropping an observation from the beginning by means of the following analogues of (3)–(5):

$$(\tilde{X}_n' \tilde{X}_n)^{-1} = (X_{n+1}' X_{n+1})^{-1} + (X_{n+1}' X_{n+1})^{-1} x_1 x_1' (X_{n+1}')^{-1} / (1 - x_1'(X_{n+1}' X_{n+1})^{-1} x_1),$$

$$\tilde{b}_n = b_{n+1} - (\tilde{X}_n' \tilde{X}_n)^{-1} x_1 (y_1 - x_1' b_{n+1}),$$

$$\tilde{S}_n = S_{n+1} - (y_1 - x_1' \tilde{b}_n)^2 / (1 + x_1'(\tilde{X}_n \tilde{X}_n)^{-1} x_1),$$

where $\tilde{X}_n, \tilde{b}_n, \tilde{S}_n$ are the values of the regressor matrix, the coefficient vector and the residual sum of squares based on observations from $t = 2$ to $n+1$. For simplicity of notation we have given the formulae for the first update only but the further formulae are, of course, similar. Proofs are similar to those of (3)–(5).

A significance test for constancy based on this approach, called by us the homogeneity test, is derived from the results of regressions based on non-overlapping time segments, using the analysis of variance. The time segments used by the program, for a moving regression of length n, are $(1, n)$, $((n+1), 2n)$, ..., $((p-2)n+1, (p-1)n)$, $((p-1)n+1, T)$, where p is the integral part of T/n, and the variance ratio considered, called by us the homogeneity statistic, is

$$\frac{(T-kp)}{(kp-k)} \frac{S(1,T) - \{S(1,n) + S(n+1,2n) + \ldots + S(pn-2n+1, pn-n) + S(pn-n+1,T)\}}{\{S(1,n) + S(n+1,2n) + \ldots + S(pn-n+1,T)\}},$$

where $S(r,s)$ is the residual sum of squares from the regression calculated from observations from $t = r$ to s inclusive. This is equivalent to the usual "between groups over within groups" ratio of mean squares and under H_0 is distributed as $F(kp-k, T-kp)$.

The TIMVAR program also calculates the quantity M_1, the mean square prediction error one period ahead. This is defined as

$$M_1 = \sum_{m=n+1}^{T} \{y_m - x_m' b(m-n, m-1)\}^2 / (T-n),$$

where the vector $b(m-n, m-1)$ is the estimate of the vector of regression coefficients from the time segment $(m-n, m-1)$. When calculated for moving regressions of several different lengths its minimum value gives a useful criterion for the length of record to use when predicting one period ahead. Also calculated are M_2, defined by

$$M_2 = \sum_{m=1}^{T-n} \{y_m - x_m' b(m+1, m+n)\}^2 / (T-n),$$

which is equivalent to M_1 calculated from a moving regression passed in the reverse direction, and M the sum of M_1 and M_2. Of these M_1 will normally be the most useful. Finally, M_3 is calculated. This is $\sum_{m=n_1+n}^{T} (y_m - x_m' b(m-n, m-1))^2 / (T-n_1)$ where n_1 is the maximum length of regression considered. This fulfils the same function as M_1, except that the different regression lengths are now compared over the same part of the record, namely that from n_1 to T.

2.6. *Time-trending Regressions*

This technique introduces time variation into the regression model explicitly by allowing the regression coefficients to become polynomials in time. To determine whether this extended model will produce a significantly better fit than one based on constancy, and further to determine what degree of polynomial should be employed, the program calculates the sum of squares removed by each of the following nested hypotheses:

$$(0):\quad y_t = \mathbf{x}_t' \boldsymbol{\beta}_{(0)} + \varepsilon_t$$
$$(1):\quad y_t = \mathbf{x}_t'(\boldsymbol{\beta}_{(0)} + \boldsymbol{\beta}_{(1)} t) + \varepsilon_t$$
$$\vdots \qquad \vdots \qquad \vdots$$
$$(e):\quad y_t = \mathbf{x}_t'(\boldsymbol{\beta}_{(0)} + \boldsymbol{\beta}_{(1)} t + \ldots + \boldsymbol{\beta}_{(e)} t^e) + \varepsilon_t.$$

The $\boldsymbol{\beta}$'s are all vectors of length k, and e is a positive integer specified by the user.

Comparison of the mean-square increase in the explained variation with an estimate of the error variance gives a test for determining whether each model gives a significantly better fit than the one before. This estimate of the error variance may be derived from either the residual sum of squares from the model in the next higher degree in t or from the residual sum of square of the full model (e) and so two F-ratios are calculated, one for each estimate.

2.7. *Quandt's Log-likelihood Ratio Technique*

This technique, described in two papers by Quandt (1958, 1960), is appropriate when it is believed that the regression relationship may have changed abruptly at an unknown time point $t = r$ from one constant relationship specified by $\boldsymbol{\beta}^{(1)}$, σ_1^2, to another constant relationship specified by $\boldsymbol{\beta}^{(2)}$, σ_2^2. For each r from $r = k+1$ to $r = T-k-1$ the program computes and plots

$$\lambda_r = \log_{10}\left(\frac{\text{max likelihood of the observations given } H_0}{\text{max likelihood of the observations given } H_1}\right),$$

where H_1 is the hypothesis that the observations in the time segments $(1, \ldots, r)$ and $(r+1, \ldots, T)$ come from two different regressions. This is the standard likelihood ratio statistic for deciding between the two hypotheses H_0 and H_1, and it is easy to show that

$$\lambda_r = \tfrac{1}{2} r \log \hat{\sigma}_1^2 + \tfrac{1}{2}(T-r) \log \hat{\sigma}_2^2 - \tfrac{1}{2} T \log \hat{\sigma}^2,$$

where $\hat{\sigma}_1^2$, $\hat{\sigma}_2^2$ and $\hat{\sigma}^2$ are the ratios of the residual sums of squares to number of observations when the regression is fitted to the first r observations, the remaining $T-r$ observations and the whole set of T observations, respectively. The estimate of the point at which the switch from one relationship to another has occurred is then the value of r at which λ_r attains its minimum. Unfortunately, no test has yet been devised for min λ_r since its distribution on H_0 is unknown. However, the behaviour of the graph of λ_r against r sheds light on the stability of the regression and in particular indicates whether changes have occurred as an abrupt transition or gradually.

3. EXAMPLES OF THE APPLICATION OF TIMVAR

In this section we present three examples which illustrate the use of TIMVAR techniques. The first and third examples reveal evidence of change while the second does not. The graphs have been chosen to illustrate different kinds of TIMVAR output but in each case the graphs shown are only a small fraction of the total output available.

Example 1. This example was made available by the Statistics and Business Research Department of the Post Office. As part of a wider study of posts and telecommunications described in Turner (1973), a regression model was developed to explain growth in the number of local telephone calls (i.e. the differences between the numbers of calls in consecutive years) in terms of a linear model involving a constant and four independent variables. These four variables, which were used in first difference forms, were a measure of economic activity, the number of residential telephones, the "real" price of local calls and the "real" price of residential telephones. (The deflator used to arrive at the "real" prices was the retail price index.) The data ran from 1950/51 to 1971/72, but it had been felt that the estimates of the number of local calls and hence of local call growth were subject to some uncertainty after 1964/65; however, the 1971/72 figure was thought to be reliable. In order to use this model as part of a larger model, reliable estimates for the growth of local calls were required for the whole period. Thus it was important that the stability of the relationship over time should be investigated.

Figs 1–4 give respectively the plots of the least-squares residuals, the cusum of least-squares residuals, the cusum of recursive residuals and the cusum of squares of

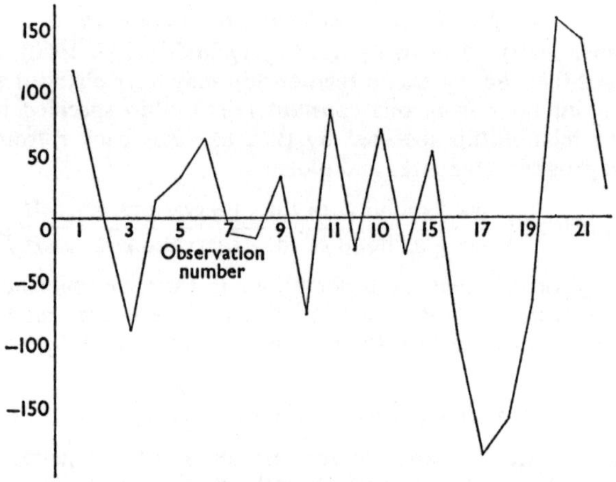

FIG. 1. *Example* 1: Ordinary least-square residuals.

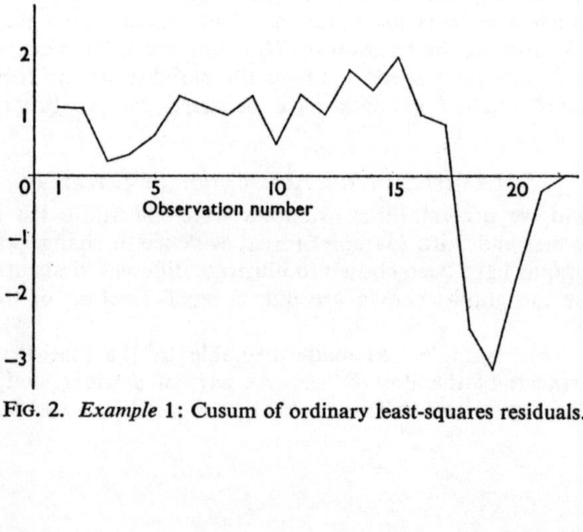

FIG. 2. *Example* 1: Cusum of ordinary least-squares residuals.

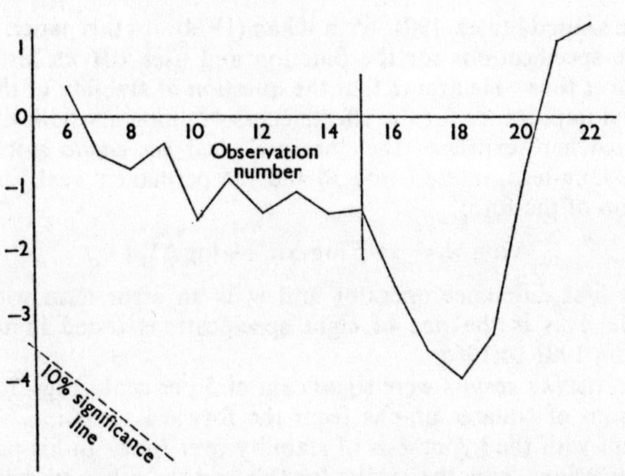

FIG. 3. *Example* 1: Cusum of recursive residuals, forward recursion.

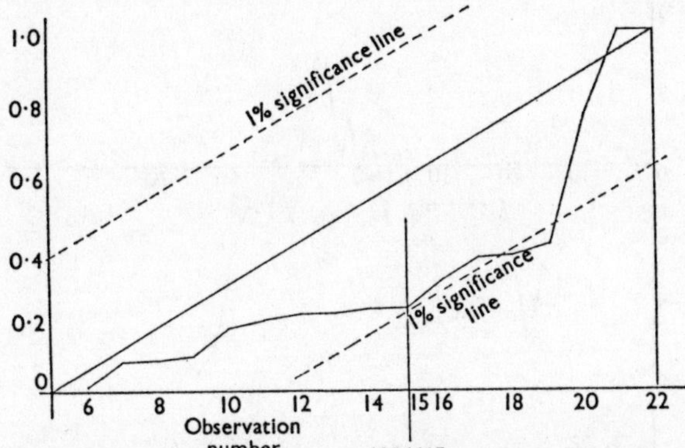

FIG. 4. *Example* 1: Cusum of squares of recursive residuals, forward recursion.

least-squares residuals. These plots provide increasing indication of evidence of instability after 1964/65, 1 per cent significance being attained in Fig. 4. The fact that significance is achieved by the cusum of squares plot but not by the cusum of recursive residuals suggests that instability may be due to a shift in residual variance than to shifts in values of regression coefficients. However, examination of the plots of coefficients and residual variance estimated from moving regressions showed that the instability was due to local changes in the regression coefficients and not to changes in variance. The model shows no sign of instability in the years up to 1964/65 and it was further found that a forecast of the 1971/72 figure from the model fitted to the data up to 1964/65 was very close to the actual 1971/72 estimate, which had been accepted as reliable. In the circumstances it was decided to ignore the suspect estimates between 1964/65 and 1971/72, to use the model fitted from the remaining data to provide the explanatory equation required and to replace the discarded data by forecasts derived from it.

Example 2. The second example, using data made available by Dr M. S. Khan of the International Monetary Fund, is based on a study of the demand for money function for the United States, 1901–65 in Khan (1974). In this paper, Khan considers several possible specifications for the function and uses TIMVAR tests to investigate their stability over time. He argues that the question of stability of the function over time is of crucial importance for the effectiveness of monetary policy. The particular model considered here expresses the "narrow" real *per capita* stock of money M_t in terms of the long-term interest rate R_t and the permanent real *per capita* income Y_t in an equation of the form

$$\Delta \log M_t = \alpha + \beta \log \Delta R_t + \gamma \log \Delta Y_t + w_t,$$

where Δ is the first difference operator and w_t is an error term with the property $w_t \sim \text{NID}(0, \sigma_w^2)$. This is the one of eight specifications tested in the paper using annual data from 1901 to 1965.

None of the TIMVAR results were significant at 5 per cent. Figs 5 and 6 show the cusum and cusum of squares graphs from the forward recursion. The results are clearly consistent with the hypothesis of stability over time. In his paper Khan goes on to draw conclusions from the results for this and the other model specifications.

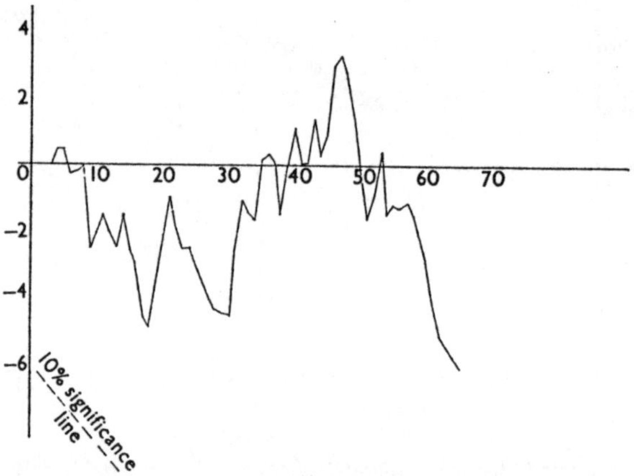

FIG. 5. *Example* 2: Cusum of recursive residuals, forward recursion.

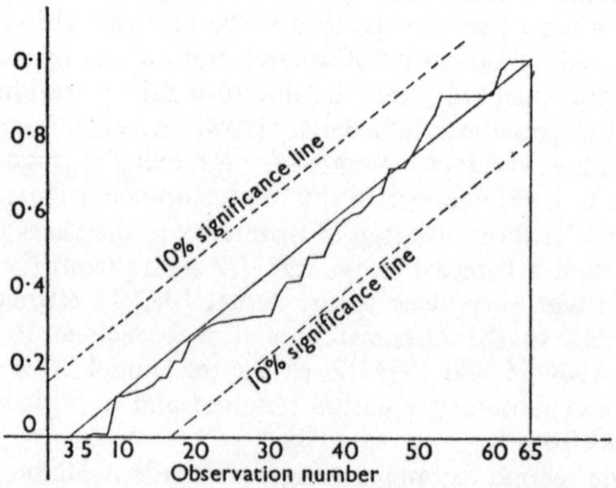

FIG. 6. *Example* 2: Cusum of squares of recursive residuals, forward recursion.

Example 3. This example uses data provided by the Civil Service Department and is concerned with the staff requirement S_t of an organization expressed as a function of workloads of 9 different categories. The example is studied in detail in Cameron and Nash (1974) and uses quarterly data from the first period of 1960 to the third quarter of 1970 (43 observations). Cameron and Nash found that the 9 workload categories were highly intercorrelated so they employed factor analysis to reduce them to three uncorrelated factors F_1, F_2, F_3. They then fitted the regression model:

$$S_t = \beta_0 + \sum_{j=1}^{3} \beta_j F_{jt} + e_t,$$

where e_t is a disturbance term.

Forward and backward cusum and cusum squared recursive residuals plots showed strong evidence of instability. Fig. 7 gives the graph of Quandt's log likelihood ratio and this indicates clearly that an abrupt change took place just after the 27th quarter.

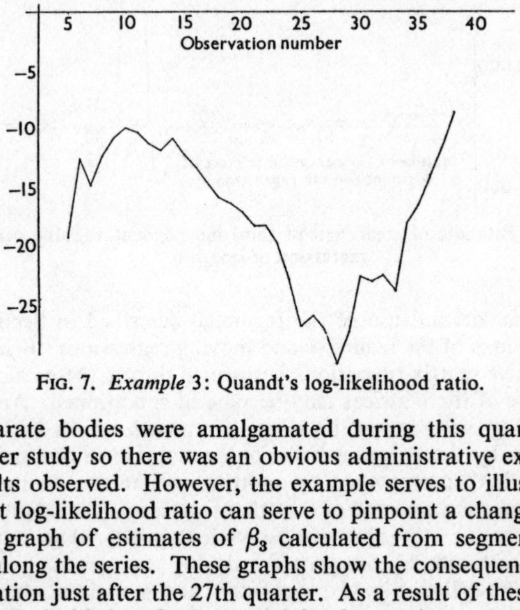

FIG. 7. *Example* 3: Quandt's log-likelihood ratio.

In fact two separate bodies were amalgamated during this quarter to form the organization under study so there was an obvious administrative explanation in this case for the results observed. However, the example serves to illustrate the way in which the Quandt log-likelihood ratio can serve to pinpoint a change in the relation. Fig. 8 gives the graph of estimates of β_3 calculated from segments of length six quarters moved along the series. These graphs show the consequences of the abrupt change in the relation just after the 27th quarter. As a result of these and other tests Cameron and Nash decided to fit the model for forecasting purposes from the last 14 observations only.

4. THE TIMVAR PROGRAM

The TIMVAR program was written to calculate all the results necessary for the tests and techniques described in the paper and to produce a considerable amount of graphical output to aid the interpretation of the results. Any or all of the following results are available:

(a) The standard regression. The analysis of variance over the whole time span and the DW statistic. Tables and plots of the residuals and regression estimates.

(b) The results of the time-trending regressions (see Section 2.6).
(c) The results of the recursive regressions, both forward and backward, giving tables and plots of the successive regression estimates, the recursive residuals and their cusums, and the test statistics (see Sections 2.2, 2.3, 2.4).
(d) The values of Quandt's log-likelihood ratio (see Section 2.7).
(e) The results of the moving regressions for each specified length giving tables and plots of the successive regression estimates, mean square errors, the quantities M_1, M_2, M and M_3, and the statistic for the homogeneity test (see Section 2.5).

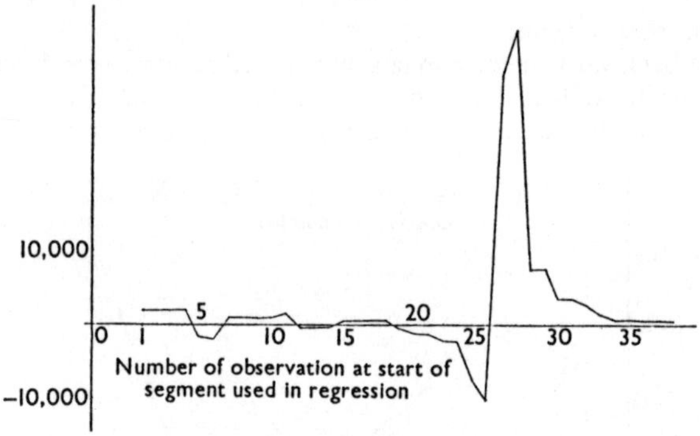

FIG. 8. *Example* 3: Estimate of coefficient of third independent variable derived from moving regression of length 6.

The program makes full use of the formulae described in Sections 2.2 and 2.5 during the calculations of the recursive and moving regressions. Because of the large number of successive matrix operations performed during these calculations there is a danger that some of the matrices may become ill-conditioned. Any such tendency is usually reduced by subtracting the means from each of the variables and this is done automatically by the program if the model contains a constant. The value of the constant term is then recovered by another mechanism. In the case where the model contains a constant and one of the other regressors is constant at the beginning or end of the record for a number of observations greater than k, this regressor, if supplied last, is dealt with by the program during the recursive regressions in the manner described in Section 2.2. If it is constant at the start only it can be dealt with in a similar fashion during the moving regressions. The extension to the case where two or more regressors are constant at the beginning or end of the record has not been programmed.

REFERENCES

ANSCOMBE, F. J. (1961). Examination of residuals. *Proc. 4th Berkeley Symp. Math. Statist. Prob.*, **1**, 1–36.

ANSCOMBE, F. J. and TUKEY, J. W. (1963). The examination and analysis of residuals. *Technometrics*, **5**, 141–160.

BARNARD, G. A. (1959). Control charts and stochastic processes. *J. R. Statist. Soc.* B, **21**, 239–271.

BARTLETT, M. S. (1951). An inverse matrix adjustment arising in discriminant analysis. *Ann. Math. Statist.*, **22**, 107–111.

Brown, R. L. and Durbin, J. (1968). Methods of investigating whether a regression relationship is constant over time. *Selected Statistical Papers, European Meeting*, Mathematical Centre Tracts No. 26, Amsterdam.

Cameron, M. H. and Nash, J. E. (1974). On forecasting the manpower requirements of an organization with homogeneous workloads. *J. R. Statist. Soc.* A, **137**, 200–218.

Chernoff, H. and Zacks, S. (1964). Estimating the current mean of a normal distribution which is subjected to changes in time. *Ann. Math. Statist.*, **35**, 999–1018.

Durbin, J. (1969). Tests for serial correlation in regression analysis based on the periodogram of least squares residuals. *Biometrika*, **56**, 1–15.

—— (1970). An alternative to the bound test for testing serial correlation in least-squares regression. *Econometrica*, **38**, 422–429.

—— (1971). Boundary-crossing probabilities for the Brownian motion and Poisson processes and techniques for computing the power of the Kolmogorov–Smirnov test. *J. Appl. Prob.*, **8**, 431–453.

Evans, J. M. (1973). User's Guide to TIMVAR. Research Exercise Note 10/73 of the Central Statistical Office.

Heyadat, A. and Robson, D. S. (1970). Independent stepwise residuals for testing homoscedasticity. *J. Amer. Statist. Ass.*, **65**, 1573–1581.

Hinkley, D. V. (1972). Time-ordered classification. *Biometrika*, **59**, 509–523.

Kendall, M. G. and Stuart, A. (1969). *The Advanced Theory of Statistics*, Vol. I, 3rd ed. London: Griffin.

Khan, M. S. (1974). The stability of the demand for money function in the United States, 1901–65. *J. Polit. Econ.* **82**, 1205–1219.

Mehr, C. B. and McFadden, J. A. (1965). Certain properties of Gaussian processes and their first passage times. *J. R. Statist. Soc. B*, **27**, 505–522.

Page, E. S. (1954). Continuous inspection schemes. *Biometrika*, **41**, 100–114.

Plackett, R. L. (1950). Some theorems in least squares. *Biometrika*, **37**, 149–157.

Pyke, R. (1959). The supremum and the infimum of the Poisson process. *Ann. Math. Statist.*, **30**, 569–576.

Quandt, R. E. (1958). The estimation of the parameters of a linear regression system obeying two separate regimes. *J. Amer. Statist. Ass.*, **53**, 873–880.

—— (1960). Tests of the hypothesis that a linear regression system obeys two separate regimes. *J. Amer. Statist. Ass.*, **55**, 324–330.

Theil, H. (1965). The analysis of disturbances in regression analysis. *J. Amer. Statist. Ass.*, **60**, 1067–1079.

—— (1968). A simplification of the BLUS procedure for analysing regression disturbances. *J. Amer. Statist. Ass.*, **63**, 242–251.

Tukey, J. W. (1962). The future of data analysis. *Ann. Math. Statist.*, **33**, 1–67.

Turner, W. M. (1973). A critical reappraisal of the interaction of posts and telecommunications. Report No. 29. Statistics and Business Research Department, Post Office.

Woodward, R. H. and Goldsmith, P. L. (1964). *Cumulative Sum Techniques.* Monograph No. 3, ICI Series on Mathematical and Statistical Techniques for Industry, Edinburgh: Oliver & Boyd.

Discussion of the Paper by Dr Brown, Professor Durbin and Mr Evans

Professor D. R. Cox (Imperial College): This is an important and interesting paper; it deals with a common practical problem, gives valuable new methods and their theory and concludes with cogent illustrations.

My comments concern two theoretical aspects of the paper. First there is the efficiency of the procedures in idealized situations which, notwithstanding the remarks in Section 1 of the paper, seems of some interest in understanding the applicability of the methods. I shall deal only with the very simplest situation, in particular where the fitted model contains just a constant term, so that the recursive residuals are defined by the standard Helmert transformation and are

$$\frac{y_2-y_1}{\sqrt{2}},\ \frac{2y_3-y_2-y_1}{\sqrt{6}},\ \ldots.$$

Suppose further that $E(y_i)=\mu\ (i=1,\ldots,m)$, $E(y_{m+j})=\mu+\delta\ (j=1,\ldots,n)$.

[13]

TECHNOMETRICS©, VOL. 22, NO. 3, AUGUST 1980

Maximum Likelihood Fitting of ARMA Models to Time Series With Missing Observations

Richard H. Jones
Department of Biometrics
University of Colorado School of Medicine
Denver, CO 80262

The method of calculating the exact likelihood function of a stationary autoregressive moving average (ARMA) time series based on Akaike's Markovian representation and using Kalman recursive estimation is reviewed. This state space approach involves matrices and vectors with dimensions equal to Max $(p, q + 1)$ where p is the order of the autoregression and q is the order of the moving average, rather than matrices with dimensions equal to the number of observations. A key to the calculation of the exact likelihood function is the proper calculation of the initial state covariance matrix. The inclusion of observational error into the model is discussed as is the extension to missing observations. The use of a nonlinear optimization program gives the maximum likelihood estimates of the parameters and allows for model identification based on Akaike's Information Criterion (AIC). An example is presented fitting models to western United States drought data.

KEY WORDS

Time series analysis
Missing observations
Fitting ARMA models
State space
Maximum likelihood

1. INTRODUCTION

Approximate maximum likelihood estimates of the parameters of an autoregressive, moving average (ARMA) process have received much attention in the last decade (see, for example, Box and Jenkins, 1970). Galbraith and Galbraith (1974) have derived the exact inverse of the covariance matrix of an ARMA process and Newbold (1974) has derived the exact likelihood function. This work was recently extended by Ali (1977), Akaike (1978), and Harvey and Phillips (1979).

The use of *state space* methodology in stochastic processes has been used quite extensively in recent years. Kailath's (1970) innovation approach is fundamental in developing this concept and pointing out the broad range of applications. Mehra (1974) and Caines and Rissanen (1974) used Kalman recursive estimation to calculate the exact likelihood of an ARMA process. Akaike's (1973, 1974, 1975) Markovian representation provides a minimal state space representation for recursive calculation of the likelihood function for a Gaussian ARMA process for given values of the parameters. Nonlinear optimization programs can then be used to obtain maximum likelihood estimates of the parameters. In this paper, the recursive calculation procedure is extended to include the cases of missing observations and observational error. An extension to unequally spaced data is given in Jones (1980).

Received November 1978; revised October 1979

A stationary time series observed with error has a different covariance function and spectral density than the actual time series. If the observational errors are uncorrelated with constant variance, the errors appear as an increase in the covariance at lag zero, and as the addition of a constant to the spectral density. When fitting an autoregressive, moving average (ARMA) model, if the order of the moving average (q) is less than the order of the autoregression (p), observational error increases the order of the moving average to p (Box and Jenkins, 1970, Appendix A4.4). Therefore, if q is less than $p - 1$, modeling observational error directly may give a more parsimonious representation.

2. MARKOVIAN REPRESENTATION

The use of a Markovian representation summarizes the information in the past and present observations, needed to predict the future, in the best estimate of the current state vector. The difference between the next available observation and the prediction from the best estimate of the current state is orthogonal to earlier observations (see Kalman, 1960). For a Gaussian process this provides a simple recursive method for calculating the likelihood function with or without missing observations. The likelihood function is then used to obtain maximum likelihood estimates of the autoregressive coefficients, moving average coefficients and variances of the random input process and observational error. In this section, the derivation of the Markovian representation is presented since this is not readily available in other references.

The autoregressive moving average model of order p, q with zero mean can be written

$$x_t = \sum_{k=1}^{p} \alpha_k x_{t-k} + \epsilon_t + \sum_{k=1}^{q} \beta_k \epsilon_{t-k} \tag{2.1}$$

where the ϵ_t are the uncorrelated random plant noise or shocks with variance σ^2. For stationarity and invertibility of the moving average, the roots of

$$\left.\begin{aligned} 1 - \sum_{k=1}^{p} \alpha_k z^k &= 0 \\ \text{and} \qquad & \\ 1 + \sum_{k=1}^{q} \beta_k z^k &= 0 \end{aligned}\right\} \tag{2.2}$$

are assumed to be outside the unit circle.

Akaike's Markovian representation for this process defines the state of the process as a column vector of length

$$m = \text{Max}\,(p, q + 1), \tag{2.3}$$

$$Z(t) = \begin{bmatrix} x(t \mid t) \\ x(t+1 \mid t) \\ \vdots \\ x(t+m-1 \mid t) \end{bmatrix} \tag{2.4}$$

where $x(t + j \mid t)$ denotes the projection of x_{t+j} on the values of the times series up to time t, i.e. the j-step prediction, or $E\{x(t + j) \mid x(s), s \leq t\}$; $x(t \mid t)$ is simply the value of the process at time t,

$$x(t \mid t) = x_t. \tag{2.5}$$

The one-step prediction is

$$x(t + 1 \mid t) = \sum_{k=1}^{p} \alpha_k x_{t+1-k} + \sum_{k=1}^{q} \beta_k \epsilon_{t+1-k}. \tag{2.6}$$

The j-step prediction uses the previous predictions in the autoregressive part,

$$x(t + j \mid t) = \sum_{k=1}^{j-1} \alpha_k x(t + j - k \mid t) + \sum_{k=j}^{p} \alpha_k x_{t+j-k} + \sum_{k=j}^{q} \beta_k \epsilon_{t+j-k}, \tag{2.7}$$

where the various summations are eliminated if the indices are not in the proper range. Similarly,

$$x(t + j \mid t + 1) = \sum_{k=1}^{j-2} \alpha_k x(t + j - k \mid t + 1) + \sum_{k=j-1}^{p} \alpha_k x_{t+j-k} + \sum_{k=j-1}^{q} \beta_k \epsilon_{t+j-k}. \tag{2.8}$$

From (2.7) and (2.8),

$$x(t + j \mid t + 1) - x(t + j \mid t) = \sum_{k=1}^{j-1} \alpha_k [x(t + j - k \mid t + 1) - x(t + j - k \mid t)] + \beta_{j-1} \epsilon_{t+1}. \tag{2.9}$$

This equation gives a recursion involving only the random input at time $t + 1$. Let

$$x(t + j \mid t + 1) - x(t + j \mid t) = g_j \epsilon_{t+1}, \tag{2.10}$$

then

$$x(t + j \mid t + 1) = x(t + j \mid t) + \left[\beta_{j-1} + \sum_{k=1}^{j-1} \alpha_k g_{j-k}\right] \epsilon_{t+1} \tag{2.11}$$

or

$$x(t + j \mid t + 1) = x(t + j \mid t) + g_j \epsilon_{t+1} \tag{2.12}$$

where the g's are generated by the recursion

$$g_1 = 1$$

$$g_j = \beta_{j-1} + \sum_{k=1}^{j-1} \alpha_k g_{j-k} \tag{2.13}$$

where $\beta_j = 0$ for $j > q$.

The final element in the state vector can be written

$$x(t + m \mid t + 1) = \sum_{k=1}^{p} \alpha_k x(t + m - k \mid t) + g_m \epsilon_{t+1}. \tag{2.14}$$

A matrix formulation of these equations is known as the *equation of state*;

$$\begin{bmatrix} x(t+1 \mid t+1) \\ x(t+2 \mid t+1) \\ \vdots \\ x(t+m \mid t+1) \end{bmatrix} = \begin{bmatrix} 0 & 1 & 0 & \cdots & 0 \\ 0 & 0 & 1 & \cdots & 0 \\ & & \vdots & & \\ \alpha_m & & \cdots & \alpha_2 & \alpha_1 \end{bmatrix} \times \begin{bmatrix} x(t \mid t) \\ x(t+1 \mid t) \\ \vdots \\ x(t+m-1 \mid t) \end{bmatrix} + \begin{bmatrix} 1 \\ g_2 \\ \vdots \\ g_m \end{bmatrix} \epsilon_{t+1} \tag{2.15}$$

where $\alpha_i = 0$ for $i > p$. In matrix notation

$$\mathbf{Z}(t + 1) = \mathbf{F}\mathbf{Z}(t) + \mathbf{G}\epsilon\,(t + 1) \tag{2.16}$$

so that $\mathbf{Z}(t)$ is a vector-valued Markov process and $\mathbf{F}$ is an m by m state transition matrix containing ones on the superdiagonal to shift the positions of the state elements, and containing the autoregressive parameters in the last row. The elements of the G vector are calculated from the autoregressive and moving average parameters.

The second equation in the state space representation of the process is the observational equation

$$y(t) = [1, 0 \cdots 0] \begin{bmatrix} x(t \mid t) \\ x(t+1 \mid t) \\ \vdots \\ x(t+m-1 \mid t) \end{bmatrix} + v(t), \tag{2.17}$$

or

$$y(t) = \mathbf{H}\, \mathbf{Z}(t) + v(t).$$

Here the observation $y(t)$ consists of a linear combination of the state vector, but the linear combination simply picks off the first element. The term $v(t)$ is a random variable denoting observational error which is uncorrelated at different times, uncorrelated with the ϵ's and with mean zero and variance

$$R = E[v(t)]^2. \tag{2.18}$$

3. EVALUATION OF THE LIKELIHOOD FUNCTION

Assuming that the errors are normally distributed, for given values of the autoregressive and moving average parameters, the likelihood function can be calculated using Kalman recursive estimation. This procedure starts by specifying the initial state vector, $\mathbf{Z}(0 \mid 0)$. This notation indicates the estimate of the state at time zero given data up to time zero, i.e. the estimate of the state at time zero before any data are collected. For a mean zero process, this will be a vector of zeros. It is also necessary to specify the covariance matrix of this vector, $\mathbf{P}(0 \mid 0)$; the equations for generating this matrix will be given in the next section.

The recursion first calculates a one-step prediction from equation (2.16),

$$\mathbf{Z}(t+1 \mid t) = \mathbf{F}\, \mathbf{Z}(t \mid t), \tag{3.1}$$

where $\mathbf{Z}(t+j \mid t)$ denotes the projection of $\mathbf{Z}(t+j)$ on the observations up to time t, i.e. $E\{Z(t+j) \mid y(s), s \le t\}$. The covariance matrix of this prediction is (from 2.15)

$$\mathbf{P}(t+1 \mid t) = \mathbf{F}\, \mathbf{P}(t \mid t)\, \mathbf{F}' + \sigma^2 \mathbf{G}\mathbf{G}', \tag{3.2}$$

where $'$ denotes the transposed vector or matrix. The predicted value of the next observation is

$$y(t+1 \mid t) = \mathbf{H}\, \mathbf{Z}(t+1 \mid t) = x(t+1 \mid t). \tag{3.3}$$

Using the next observation, the state vector estimate is updated:

$$\mathbf{Z}(t+1 \mid t+1) = \mathbf{Z}(t+1 \mid t) + \mathbf{\Delta}(t+1)\,[y(t+1) - y(t+1 \mid t)] \tag{3.4}$$

where

$$\Delta(t+1) = \mathbf{P}(t+1 \mid t) \cdot \mathbf{H}'[\mathbf{H}\, \mathbf{P}(t+1 \mid t)\mathbf{H}' + R]^{-1}. \tag{3.5}$$

Note that $\mathbf{P}(t+1 \mid t)\mathbf{H}'$ is the first column of $\mathbf{P}(t+1 \mid t)$, and

$$\mathbf{H}\, \mathbf{P}(t+1 \mid t)\, \mathbf{H}' = P_{11}(t+1 \mid t) \tag{3.6}$$

is the upper left-hand element of the $\mathbf{P}(t+1 \mid t)$ matrix. Finally, the covariance matrix of the updated state is

$$\mathbf{P}(t+1 \mid t+1) = \mathbf{P}(t+1 \mid t) - \mathbf{\Delta}(t+1)\, \mathbf{H}\, \mathbf{P}(t+1 \mid t). \tag{3.7}$$

In Kalman's theory the quantity

$$\tilde{y}(t+1) = y(t+1) - y(t+1 \mid t) \tag{3.8}$$

in equation (3.4) is the component of the observation at time $t+1$, $y(t+1)$, which is orthogonal to the previous observations, the innovation, and this orthogonal component has variance

$$\mathbf{H}\, \mathbf{P}(t+1 \mid t)\mathbf{H}' + R. \tag{3.9}$$

For the ARMA model considered here, this is

$$\mathbf{V}(t+1) = P_{11}(t+1 \mid t) + R, \tag{3.10}$$

the one-step prediction error variance of the process at time $t+1$ plus the observational error variance. If the errors are Gaussian, the likelihood for n observations of the zero mean process, $x_1, \cdots x_n$, is

$$L = \prod_{i=1}^{n} (2\pi V_i)^{-1/2} \exp(-\tilde{y}_i^2/2V_i). \tag{3.11}$$

Dropping the constant 2π, -2 ln likelihood is

$$l = \sum_{i=1}^{n} [\ln V_i + \tilde{y}_i^2/V_i]. \tag{3.12}$$

The variance σ^2 can be removed from the nonlinear estimation problem by dividing R by σ^2. The observational error variance then is replaced by the ratio of the observational error variance to σ^2. In the recursions, since all variances have the same scale factor, $\mathbf{P}(t+1 \mid t)$ and $\mathbf{P}(t+1 \mid t+1)$ are replaced by $\sigma^2\mathbf{P}(t+1 \mid t)$ and $\sigma^2\mathbf{P}(t+1 \mid t+1)$, and -2 ln likelihood becomes

$$l = \sum_{i=1}^{n} [\ln \sigma^2 V_i + \tilde{y}_i^2/\sigma^2 V_i]. \tag{3.13}$$

Differentiating this with respect to σ^2 and equating to zero gives

$$\sigma^2 = \frac{1}{n} \sum_{i=1}^{n} \tilde{y}_i^2/V_i \tag{3.14}$$

and substituting into (3.13) and dropping constants gives

$$l = \sum_{i=1}^{n} \ln V_i + n \ln \sum_{i=1}^{n} \tilde{y}_i^2/V_i, \qquad (3.15)$$

the function to be minimized with respect to the remaining parameters, $\alpha_1, \cdots, \alpha_p, \beta_1, \cdots, \beta_q$, and R. Note that σ^2 has been eliminated and is calculated after the minimization from (3.14).

4. THE INITIAL STATE COVARIANCE MATRIX

The initial state vector is a vector of zeros

$$\mathbf{X}(0 \mid 0) = [0, 0 \cdots 0]' \qquad (4.1)$$

representing knowledge of the state before the first observation. The initial state covariance matrix can be calculated by a method due to Akaike (1978). The method begins by first calculating the cross covariances between the process and the errors, γ_k. When normalized so that $\gamma_0 = 1$, these are the impulse responses used by Akaike. Since the errors are uncorrelated with the past of the process, these cross covariances satisfy the following recursion,

$$\gamma_0 = E\{x_t \epsilon_t\} = \sigma^2,$$

$$\gamma_k = E\{x_{t+k} \epsilon_t\}$$

$$= E\left\{\left[\sum_{j=1}^{p} \alpha_j x_{t+k-j} + \sum_{j=0}^{q} \beta_j \epsilon_{t+k-j}\right] \epsilon_t\right\}$$

$$= \sigma^2 \beta_k + \sum_{j=1}^{p} \alpha_j \gamma_{k-j}, \qquad k > 0 \qquad (4.2)$$

where

$$\gamma_k = 0 \quad \text{if} \quad k < 0. \qquad (4.3)$$

Normalizing γ_k by dividing by σ^2, the g's in equation (2.12) are the same as the γ's in equation (4.2) shifted by one, i.e.

$$g_k = \gamma_{k-1}. \qquad (4.4)$$

The impulse responses appear in the G vector and are used to calculate the initial state covariance matrix. They are also the coefficients of the one-sided moving average representation of the process

$$x_t = \sum_{k=0}^{\infty} \gamma_k \epsilon_{t-k} \qquad (4.5)$$

where

$$\gamma_0 = 1.$$

For $j \geq 0$, the elements of the state vector can be represented as

$$x(t + j|t) = \sum_{k=0}^{\infty} \gamma_{j+k} \epsilon_{t-k}, \qquad (4.6)$$

and for $j > 0$

$$x_{t+j} = \sum_{k=-j}^{-1} \gamma_{j+k} \epsilon_{t-k} + x(t + j|t). \qquad (4.7)$$

Now, for $j \geq 0$, since the ϵ's are uncorrelated with past x's,

$$E\{x_t x_{t+j}\} = E\{x(t|t)x(t + j|t)\}$$

and for $j \geq i > 0$,

$$E\{x_{t+i} x_{t+j}\} = \sigma^2 \sum_{k=0}^{i-1} \gamma_k \gamma_{k+j-i} + E\{x(t + i|t)x(t + j|t)\}. \qquad (4.8)$$

On the left-hand side of this equation are the covariances of the process. On the right-hand side are the covariances of the state vector which need to be calculated. The covariances satisfy, for $k \geq 0$,

$$C_k = E\{x_{t+k} x_t\} = E\left\{\left[\sum_{j=1}^{p} \alpha_j x_{t+k-j} + \sum_{j=0}^{q} \beta_j \epsilon_{t+k-j}\right] x_t\right\}$$

$$= \sum_{j=1}^{p} \alpha_j C_{k-j} + \sum_{j=k}^{q} \beta_j \gamma_{j-k} \qquad (4.9)$$

where $\beta_0 = 1$.

From (4.2) the normalized cross covariances can be calculated recursively:

$$\gamma_0 = 1$$
$$\gamma_1 = \alpha_1 \gamma_0 + \beta_1$$
$$\gamma_2 = \alpha_1 \gamma_1 + \alpha_2 \gamma_0 + \beta_2$$
$$\gamma_3 = \alpha_1 \gamma_2 + \alpha_2 \gamma_1 + \alpha_3 \gamma_0 + \beta_3$$
$$\vdots \qquad (4.10)$$

From (4.9), the covariances can then be calculated by solving a system of linear equations:

$$C_0 = \alpha_1 C_1 + \alpha_2 C_2 + \cdots + \alpha_p C_p + \gamma_0 + \beta_1 \gamma_1 + \beta_2 \gamma_2 + \cdots$$

$$C_1 = \alpha_1 C_0 + \alpha_2 C_{-1} + \cdots + \alpha_p C_{1-p} + \beta_1 \gamma_0 + \beta_2 \gamma_1 + \cdots$$

$$\vdots$$

$$C_p = \alpha_1 C_{p-1} + \alpha_2 C_{p-2} + \cdots + \alpha_p C_0 + \beta_p \gamma_0 + \beta_{p+1} \gamma_1 + \cdots. \qquad (4.11)$$

These equations can be rearranged to give a set of $p + 1$ linear equations to solve for $C_0, C_1, \cdots, C_p$ in terms the α's, β's and γ's. If $q > p$, the remaining covariances necessary to calculate the state covariance matrix are C_{p+1} to C_q and can be calculated from (4.9). The initial state covariance matrix can then be calculated from (4.8) after dividing by σ^2,

$$P_{0j}(0|0) = C(j)$$

and for $j \geq i > 0$,

$$P_{ij}(0|0) = C(j-i) - \sum_{k=0}^{i-1} \gamma_k \gamma_{k+j-i}. \qquad (4.12)$$

5. MISSING OBSERVATIONS

If an observation, $y(t+1)$, is missing, the recursion proceeds through equations (3.1)–(3.3) noting as shown in equations (3.13)–(3.15) that σ^2 can be set equal to one and estimated later. Equations (3.4)–(3.7) are replaced by

$$\mathbf{Z}(t+1|t+1) = \mathbf{Z}(t+1|t) \qquad (5.1)$$

and

$$\mathbf{P}(t+1|t+1) = \mathbf{P}(t+1|t). \qquad (5.2)$$

The corresponding term in equation (3.15) for the accumulation of -2 ln likelihood is skipped.

This procedure works for any number of observations missing in a row, and has been programmed by inserting a missing value code in place of an actual observation to determine whether part of the recursion is skipped. If a large block of data is missing, the information about the past contained in the state vector slowly fades away, i.e. $\mathbf{Z}(t+j|t)$ approaches the zero vector as $j \to \infty$ and $\mathbf{P}(t+j|t) \to \mathbf{P}(0|0)$, the initial state covariance matrix. Therefore, running the recursion across a large block of missing data is equivalent to restarting the recursion at the other end.

6. REPARAMETERIZING FOR STABILITY

In the maximum likelihood estimation of the parameters of the ARMA time series with or without observational error, the stability criterion of equation (2.2) can be guaranteed by reparameterizing in terms of the partial autoregressive coefficients, a_k, where the a's are constrained to be in the open interval $(-1,1)$ by the transformation

$$a_k = [1 - \exp(-u_k)]/[1 + \exp(-u_k)]. \qquad (6.1)$$

The α's can then be calculated by the well-known Levinson (1947)–Durbin (1960) recursion, for $j = 1, \cdots, p$,

$$\alpha_j^{(j)} = a_j,$$

and for $j > 1$,

$$\alpha_k^{(j)} = \alpha_k^{(j-1)} - a_j \alpha_{j-k}^{(j-1)}, \text{ for } k = 1, 2, \cdots, j-1. \qquad (6.2)$$

The autoregressive coefficients in the model are

$$\alpha_k = \alpha_k^{(p)}.$$

Similarly, for invertibility, partial moving average coefficients could be used and transformed as

$$b_k = [1 - \exp(-w_k)]/[1 + \exp(-w_k)], \qquad (6.3)$$

and the β's calculated from

$$\beta_j^{(j)} = b_j \qquad (6.4)$$

$$\beta_k^{(j)} = \beta_k^{(j-1)} + b_j \beta_{j-k}^{(j-1)}, \; k = 1, 2, \cdots, j-1,$$

where

$$\beta_k = \beta_k^{(p)}.$$

If observational error is included in the model, the transformation

$$R = s^2 \text{ or } R = e^s$$

will insure a nonnegative estimate of the observational error variance.

The nonlinear optimization is now carried out with respect to

$$u_k, \; k = 1, \cdots, p$$

$$w_k, \; k = 1, \cdots, q$$

and s, and the α's and β's calculated by (6.1)–(6.4).

7. EXAMPLE

An example of maximum likelihood ARMA model fitting with observational error has been calculated from data supplied to the author by J. Murray Mitchell from the National Oceanographic and Atmospheric Administration. The data are yearly areas of western United States with the Palmer wetness index less than -1 (indicating drought) as reconstructed from tree ring data. Various models were fitted to the data with autoregressive orders up to three, moving average orders zero and one, and with and without observational error. Models were compared using chi-square tests based on changes in -2 ln likelihood and by Akaike's Information Criterion (AIC) (see for example, Jones, 1974). The result of various fits are shown in Table 1.

The model selected as best based on the minimum AIC,

$$\text{AIC} = -2 \ln \text{likelihood} + 2 \text{ (no. of fitted parameters)}, \qquad (7.1)$$

is a first-order autoregression with observational error. This is equivalent to a model with $p = 1$, $q = 1$ and no observational error. A first-order autoregression is sometimes referred to as "red noise." The observational error is "white noise," so the sum of the two has been called "pink noise."

A visual comparison of goodness of fit of the

TABLE 1—*Maximum likelihood fitting of ARMA models to western United States drought data reconstructed from tree rings.*

Autoregression Order	Moving Average Order	Observational Error?	-2 Ln Likelihood	AIC
1	0	No	2653.3	2655.3
1	0	Yes	2648.0	2652.0*
0	1	No	2655.9	2657.9
2	0	No	2649.2	2653.2
2	0	Yes	2647.8	2653.8
3	0	No	2647.5	2653.5
3	0	Yes	2647.5	2655.5

* Selected as best model.

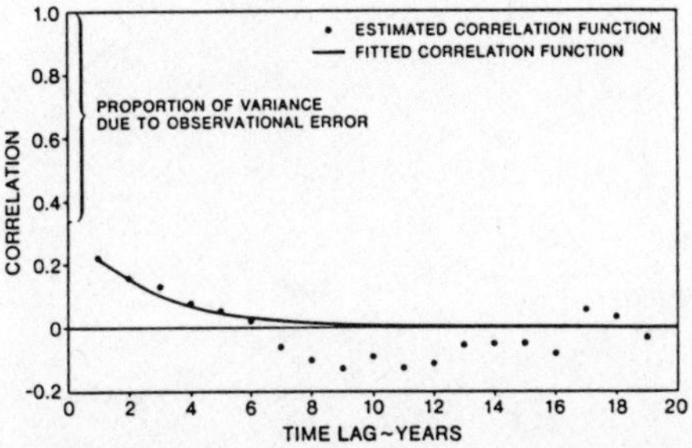

FIGURE 1. Estimated correlation function of western United States drought data from 271 yearly observations, and correlation function from fitted first order autoregression with observational error (pink noise).

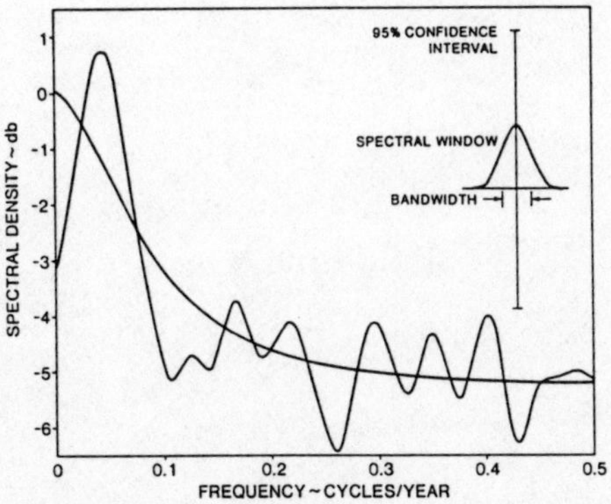

FIGURE 2. Estimated spectral density of western United States drought data from 271 yearly observations using Parzen's spectral window with 24.5 degrees of freedom (wiggly line) and spectral density from fitted first order autoregression with observational error (pink noise).

model can be made by comparing the correlation function and spectral density of the fitted model with the estimated correlation function and spectral density. The correlation function of the fitted model can be calculated as in Section 4 for lags up to Max (p, q), and extended to higher lags from

$$R_k = \sum_{j=1}^{p} \alpha_j R_{k-j}. \tag{7.2}$$

The spectral density of the fitted model is

$$s(f) = hR + h\sigma^2 \left| \left[\sum_{k=0}^{q} \beta_k e^{2\pi ikhf} \right] \Big/ \left[1 - \sum_{k=1}^{p} \alpha_k e^{2\pi ikhf} \right] \right|^2, \tag{7.3}$$

for $0 \le f \le 1/2h$, where h is the sampling interval. The fitted and estimated covariance function and spectral density are shown in Figures 1 and 2.

8. CONCLUSION

Fitting ARMA models to stationary time series which have observational error and missing observations is not difficult when using Akaike's Markovian representation and Kalman's recursive estimation. Model identification is possible using standard statistical tests based on changes in −2 ln likelihood or Akaike's Information Criterion (AIC). Since it is possible to calculate the covariance function and spectral density from the estimated parameters, visual comparisons of goodness of fit are also possible. A FORTRAN 77 listing of subroutines for generating the exact likelihood is available from the author.

REFERENCES

AKAIKE, H. (1973). Maximum likelihood identification of Gaussian autoregressive moving average models. *Biometrika, 60,* 255–265.

AKAIKE, H. (1974). Markovian representation of stochastic processes and its application to the analysis of autoregressive moving average processes. *Annals of the Institute of Statistical Mathematics, 26*, 363–387.

AKAIKE, H. (1975). Markovian representation of stochastic processes by canonical variables. *SIAM J. Control, 13*, 162–173.

AKAIKE, H. (1978). Covariance matrix computation of the state variable of a stationary Gaussian process. Research Memorandum No. 139, The Institute of Statistical Mathematics, Tokyo.

ALI, M. M. (1977). Analysis of autoregressive-moving average models: Estimation and prediction. *Biometrika, 64*, 535–545.

BOX, G. E. P. and Jenkins, G. M. (1970). *Time Series Analysis Forecasting and Control.* San Francisco: Holden-Day.

CAINES, P. E. and RISSANEN, J. (1974). Maximum likelihood estimation of parameters in multivariate Gaussian stochastic processes. *IEEE Transactions on Information Theory, IT-20*, 102–104.

DURBIN, J. (1960). The fitting of time series models. *Review of the International Institute of Statistics, 28*, 233–244.

GALBRAITH, R. F. and GALBRAITH, J. I. (1974). On the inverses of some patterned matrices arising in the theory of stationary time series. *J. Appl. Prob., 11*, 63–71.

HARVEY, C. C. and PHILLIPS, G. D. (1979). Maximum likelihood estimation of regression models with autoregressive-moving average disturbances. *Biometrika, 66*, 49–58.

JONES, R. H. (1974). Identification and autoregressive spectrum estimation. *IEEE Transactions on Automatic Control, AC-19*, 894–897.

JONES, R. H. (1980). Fitting a continuous time autoregression to discrete data. In *Applied Time Series Analysis II*, ed. by D. F. Findley (in press). New York: Academic Press.

KAILATH, T. (1970). The innovations approach to detection and estimation theory. *Proceedings of the IEEE, 58*, 680–695.

KALMAN, R. E. (1960). A new approach to linear filtering and prediction problems. *Trans. ASME, J. Basic Engineering, 82*, 34–35.

LEVINSON, N. (1947). The Wiener RMS error criterion in filter design and prediction. *J. Mathematical Physics, 25*, 261–278.

MEHRA, R. K. (1974). Identification in control econometrics; similarities and differences. *Annals of Economics and Social Measurement, 3*, 21–47.

NEWBOLD, P. (1974). The exact likelihood function for a mixed autoregressive-moving average process. *Biometrika, 61*, 423–426.

Part III
Non-Linear and Non-Gaussian Models

[14]

Econometrica, Vol. 50, No. 4 (July, 1982)

AUTOREGRESSIVE CONDITIONAL HETEROSCEDASTICITY WITH ESTIMATES OF THE VARIANCE OF UNITED KINGDOM INFLATION[1]

BY ROBERT F. ENGLE

Traditional econometric models assume a constant one-period forecast variance. To generalize this implausible assumption, a new class of stochastic processes called autoregressive conditional heteroscedastic (ARCH) processes are introduced in this paper. These are mean zero, serially uncorrelated processes with nonconstant variances conditional on the past, but constant unconditional variances. For such processes, the recent past gives information about the one-period forecast variance.

A regression model is then introduced with disturbances following an ARCH process. Maximum likelihood estimators are described and a simple scoring iteration formulated. Ordinary least squares maintains its optimality properties in this set-up, but maximum likelihood is more efficient. The relative efficiency is calculated and can be infinite. To test whether the disturbances follow an ARCH process, the Lagrange multiplier procedure is employed. The test is based simply on the autocorrelation of the squared OLS residuals.

This model is used to estimate the means and variances of inflation in the U.K. The ARCH effect is found to be significant and the estimated variances increase substantially during the chaotic seventies.

1. INTRODUCTION

IF A RANDOM VARIABLE y_t is drawn from the conditional density function $f(y_t \mid y_{t-1})$, the forecast of today's value based upon the past information, under standard assumptions, is simply $E(y_t \mid y_{t-1})$, which depends upon the value of the conditioning variable y_{t-1}. The variance of this one-period forecast is given by $V(y_t \mid y_{t-1})$. Such an expression recognizes that the conditional forecast variance depends upon past information and may therefore be a random variable. For conventional econometric models, however, the conditional variance does not depend upon y_{t-1}. This paper will propose a class of models where the variance does depend upon the past and will argue for their usefulness in economics. Estimation methods, tests for the presence of such models, and an empirical example will be presented.

Consider initially the first-order autoregression

$$y_t = \gamma y_{t-1} + \epsilon_t$$

where ϵ is white noise with $V(\epsilon) = \sigma^2$. The conditional mean of y_t is γy_{t-1} while the unconditional mean is zero. Clearly, the vast improvement in forecasts due to time-series models stems from the use of the conditional mean. The conditional

[1]This paper was written while the author was visiting the London School of Economics. He benefited greatly from many stimulating conversations with David Hendry and helpful suggestions by Denis Sargan and Andrew Harvey. Special thanks are due Frank Srba who carried out the computations. Further insightful comments are due to Clive Granger, Tom Rothenberg, Edmond Malinvaud, Jean-Francois Richard, Wayne Fuller, and two anonymous referees. The research was supported by NSF SOC 78-09476 and The International Centre for Economics and Related Disciplines. All errors remain the author's responsibility.

variance of y_t is σ^2 while the unconditional variance is $\sigma^2/1-\gamma^2$. For real processes one might expect better forecast intervals if additional information from the past were allowed to affect the forecast variance; a more general class of models seems desirable.

The standard approach of heteroscedasticity is to introduce an exogenous variable x_t which predicts the variance. With a known zero mean, the model might be

$$y_t = \epsilon_t x_{t-1}$$

where again $V(\epsilon) = \sigma^2$. The variance of y_t is simply $\sigma^2 x_{t-1}^2$ and, therefore, the forecast interval depends upon the evolution of an exogenous variable. This standard solution to the problem seems unsatisfactory, as it requires a specification of the causes of the changing variance, rather than recognizing that both conditional means and variances may jointly evolve over time. Perhaps because of this difficulty, heteroscedasticity corrections are rarely considered in time-series data.

A model which allows the conditional variance to depend on the past realization of the series is the bilinear model described by Granger and Andersen [13]. A simple case is

$$y_t = \epsilon_t y_{t-1}.$$

The conditional variance is now $\sigma^2 y_{t-1}^2$. However, the unconditional variance is either zero or infinity, which makes this an unattractive formulation, although slight generalizations avoid this problem.

A preferable model is

$$y_t = \epsilon_t h_t^{1/2},$$

$$h_t = \alpha_0 + \alpha_1 y_{t-1}^2,$$

with $V(\epsilon_t) = 1$. This is an example of what will be called an autoregressive conditional heteroscedasticity (ARCH) model. It is not exactly a bilinear model, but is very close to one. Adding the assumption of normality, it can be more directly expressed in terms of ψ_t, the information set available at time t. Using conditional densities,

$$y_t \mid \psi_{t-1} \sim N(0, h_t), \tag{1}$$

$$h_t = \alpha_0 + \alpha_1 y_{t-1}^2. \tag{2}$$

The variance function can be expressed more generally as

$$h_t = h(y_{t-1}, y_{t-2}, \ldots, y_{t-p}, \alpha) \tag{3}$$

where p is the order of the ARCH process and α is a vector of unknown parameters.

The ARCH regression model is obtained by assuming that the mean of y_t is given as $x_t\beta$, a linear combination of lagged endogenous and exogenous variables included in the information set ψ_{t-1} with β a vector of unknown parameters. Formally,

$$y_t \mid \psi_{t-1} \sim N(x_t\beta, h_t),$$

$$h_t = h(\epsilon_{t-1}, \epsilon_{t-2}, \ldots, \epsilon_{t-p}, \alpha), \tag{4}$$

$$\epsilon_t = y_t - x_t\beta.$$

The variance function can be further generalized to include current and lagged x's as these also enter the information set. The h function then becomes

$$h_t = h(\epsilon_{t-1}, \ldots, \epsilon_{t-p}, x_t, x_{t-1}, \ldots, x_{t-p}, \alpha) \tag{5}$$

or simply

$$h_t = h(\psi_{t-1}, \alpha).$$

This generalization will not be treated in this paper, but represents a simple extension of the results. In particular, if the h function factors into

$$h_t = h_\epsilon(\epsilon_{t-1}, \ldots, \epsilon_{t-p}, \alpha) h_x(x_t, \ldots, x_{t-p}),$$

the two types of heteroscedasticity can be dealt with sequentially by first correcting for the x component and then fitting the ARCH model on the transformed data.

The ARCH regression model in (4) has a variety of characteristics which make it attractive for econometric applications. Econometric forecasters have found that their ability to predict the future varies from one period to another. McNees [17, p. 52] suggests that, "the inherent uncertainty or randomness associated with different forecast periods seems to vary widely over time." He also documents that, "large and small errors tend to cluster together (in contiguous time periods)." This analysis immediately suggests the usefulness of the ARCH model where the underlying forecast variance may change over time and is predicted by past forecast errors. The results presented by McNees also show some serial correlation during the episodes of large variance.

A second example is found in monetary theory and the theory of finance. By the simplest assumptions, portfolios of financial assets are held as functions of the expected means and variances of the rates of return. Any shifts in asset demand must be associated with changes in expected means and variances of the rates of return. If the mean is assumed to follow a standard regression or time-series model, the variance is immediately constrained to be constant over time. The use of an exogenous variable to explain changes in variance is usually not appropriate.

A third interpretation is that the ARCH regression model is an approximation to a more complex regression which has non-ARCH disturbances. The ARCH specification might then be picking up the effect of variables omitted from the estimated model. The existence of an ARCH effect would be interpreted as evidence of misspecification, either by omitted variables or through structural change. If this is the case, ARCH may be a better approximation to reality than making standard assumptions about the disturbances, but trying to find the omitted variable or determine the nature of the structural change would be even better.

Empirical work using time-series data frequently adopts *ad hoc* methods to measure (and allow) shifts in the variance over time. For example, Klein [15] obtains estimates of variance by constructing the five-period moving variance about the ten-period moving mean of annual inflation rates. Others, such as Khan [**14**], resort to the notion of "variability" rather than variance, and use the absolute value of the first difference of the inflation rate. Engle [**10**] compares these with the ARCH estimates for U.S. data.

2. THE LIKELIHOOD FUNCTION

Suppose y_t is generated by an ARCH process described in equations (1) and (3). The properties of this process can easily be determined by repeated application of the relation $Ex = E(Ex \mid \psi))$. The mean of y_t is zero and all autocovariances are zero. The unconditional variance is given by $\sigma_t^2 = Ey_t^2 = Eh_t$. For many functions h and values of α, the variance is independent of t. Under such conditions, y_t is covariance stationary; a set of sufficient conditions for this is derived below.

Although the process defined by (1) and (3) has all observations conditionally normally distributed, the vector of y is not jointly normally distributed. The joint density is the product of all the conditional densities and, therefore, the log likelihood is the sum of the conditional normal log likelihoods corresponding to (1) and (3). Let l be the average log likelihood and l_t be the log likelihood of the tth observation and T the sample size. Then

$$l = \frac{1}{T}\sum_{t=1}^{T} l_t, \tag{6}$$
$$l_t = -\tfrac{1}{2}\log h_t - \tfrac{1}{2} y_t^2 / h_t,$$

apart from some constants in the likelihood.

To estimate the unknown parameters α, this likelihood function can be maximized. The first-order conditions are

$$\frac{\partial l_t}{\partial \alpha} = \frac{1}{2h_t}\frac{\partial h_t}{\partial \alpha}\left(\frac{y_t^2}{h_t} - 1\right) \tag{7}$$

and the Hessian is

$$\frac{\partial^2 l_t}{\partial\alpha\partial\alpha'} = -\frac{1}{2h_t^2}\frac{\partial h_t}{\partial\alpha}\frac{\partial h_t}{\partial\alpha'}\left(\frac{y_t^2}{h_t}\right) + \left[\frac{y_t^2}{h_t} - 1\right]\frac{\partial}{\partial\alpha'}\left[\frac{1}{2h_t}\frac{\partial h_t}{\partial\alpha}\right]. \tag{8}$$

The conditional expectation of the second term, given ψ_{t-m-1}, is zero, and of the last factor in the first, is just one. Hence, the information matrix, which is simply the negative expectation of the Hessian averaged over all observations, becomes

$$\mathcal{I}_{\alpha\alpha} = \sum_t \frac{1}{2T} E\left[\frac{1}{h_t^2}\frac{\partial h_t}{\partial\alpha'}\frac{\partial h_t}{\partial\alpha'}\right] \tag{9}$$

which is consistently estimated by

$$\hat{\mathcal{I}}_{\alpha\alpha} = \frac{1}{T}\sum_t\left[\frac{1}{2h_t^2}\frac{\partial h_t}{\partial\alpha}\frac{\partial h_t}{\partial\alpha'}\right]. \tag{10}$$

If the h function is pth order linear (in the squares), so that it can be written as

$$h_t = \alpha_0 + \alpha_1 y_{t-1}^2 + \cdots + \alpha_p y_{t-p}^2, \tag{11}$$

then the information matrix and gradient have a particularly simple form. Let $z_t = (1, y_{t-1}^2, \ldots, y_{t-p}^2)$ and $\alpha' = (\alpha_0, \alpha_1, \cdots, \alpha_p)$ so that (11) can be rewritten as

$$h_t = z_t\alpha. \tag{12}$$

The gradient then becomes simply

$$\frac{\partial l}{\partial\alpha} = \frac{1}{2h_t} z_t\left(\frac{y_t^2}{h_t} - 1\right) \tag{13}$$

and the estimate of the information matrix

$$\hat{\mathcal{I}}_{\alpha\alpha} = \frac{1}{2T}\sum_t (z_t' z_t / h_t^2). \tag{14}$$

3. DISTRIBUTION OF THE FIRST-ORDER LINEAR ARCH PROCESS

The simplest and often very useful ARCH model is the first-order linear model given by (1) and (2). A large observation for y will lead to a large variance for the next period's distribution, but the memory is confined to one period. If $\alpha_1 = 0$, of course y will be Gaussian white noise and if it is a positive number, successive observations will be dependent through higher-order moments. As shown below, if α_1 is too large, the variance of the process will be infinite.

To determine the conditions for the process to be stationary and to find the marginal distribution of the y's, a recursive argument is required. The odd moments are immediately seen to be zero by symmetry and the even moments are computed using the following theorem. In all cases it is assumed that the process begins indefinitely far in the past with $2r$ finite initial moments.

THEOREM 1: *For integer r, the 2rth moment of a first-order linear ARCH process with $\alpha_0 > 0$, $\alpha_1 \geq 0$, exists if, and only if,*

$$\alpha_1^r \prod_{j=1}^{r} (2j-1) < 1.$$

A constructive expression for the moments is given in the proof.

PROOF: See Appendix.

The theorem is easily used to find the second and fourth moments of a first-order process. Letting $w_t = (y_t^4, y_t^2)'$,

$$E(w_t \mid \psi_{t-1}) = \begin{pmatrix} 3\alpha_0^2 \\ \alpha_0 \end{pmatrix} + \begin{pmatrix} 3\alpha_1^2 & 6\alpha_0\alpha_1 \\ 0 & \alpha_1 \end{pmatrix} w_{t-1}.$$

The condition for the variance to be finite is simply that $\alpha_1 < 1$, while to have a finite fourth moment it is also required that $3\alpha_1^2 < 1$. If these conditions are met, the moments can be computed from (A4) as

$$E(w_t) = \begin{bmatrix} \left[\dfrac{3\alpha_0^2}{(1-\alpha_1)^2}\right]\left[\dfrac{1-\alpha_1^2}{1-3\alpha_1^2}\right] \\ \dfrac{\alpha_0}{1-\alpha_1} \end{bmatrix}. \tag{15}$$

The lower element is the unconditional variance, while the upper product gives the fourth moment. The first expression in square brackets is three times the squared variance. For $\alpha_1 \neq 0$, the second term is strictly greater than one implying a fourth moment greater than that of a normal random variable.

The first-order ARCH process generates data with fatter tails than the normal density. Many statistical procedures have been designed to be robust to large errors, but to the author's knowledge, none of this literature has made use of the fact that temporal clustering of outliers can be used to predict their occurrence and minimize their effects. This is exactly the approach taken by the ARCH model.

4. GENERAL ARCH PROCESSES

The conditions for a first-order linear ARCH process to have a finite variance and, therefore, to be covariance stationary can directly be generalized for pth-order processes.

THEOREM 2: *The pth-order linear ARCH processes, with* $\alpha_0 > 0, \alpha_1, \ldots, \alpha_p \geq 0$, *is covariance stationary if, and only if, the associated characteristic equation has all roots outside the unit circle. The stationary variance is given by* $E(y_t^2) = \alpha_0/(1 - \sum_{j=1}^{p} \alpha_j)$.

PROOF: See Appendix.

Although the pth-order linear model is a convenient specification, it is likely that other formulations of the variance model may be more appropriate for particular applications. Two simple alternatives are the exponential and absolute value forms:

(16) $$h_t = \exp(\alpha_0 + \alpha_1 y_{t-1}^2),$$

(17) $$h_t = \alpha_0 + \alpha_1 |y_{t-1}|.$$

These provide an interesting contrast. The exponential form has the advantage that the variance is positive for all values of alpha, but it is not difficult to show that data generated from such a model have infinite variance for any value of $\alpha_1 \neq 0$. The implications of this deserve further study. The absolute value form requires both parameters to be positive, but can be shown to have finite variance for any parameter values.

In order to find estimation results which are more general than the linear model, general conditions on the variance model will be formulated and shown to be implied for the linear process.

Let ξ_t be a $p \times 1$ random vector drawn from the sample space Ξ, which has elements $\xi_t' = (\xi_{t-1}, \ldots, \xi_{t-p})$. For any ξ_t, let ξ_t^* be identical, except that the mth element has been multiplied by -1, where m lies between 1 and p.

DEFINITION: The ARCH process defined by (1) and (3) is *symmetric* if

(a) $h(\xi_t) = h(\xi_t^*)$ for any m and $\xi_t \epsilon \Xi$,

(b) $\partial h(\xi_t)/\partial \alpha_i = \partial h(\xi_t^*)/\partial \alpha_i$ for any m, i and $\xi_t \epsilon \Xi$,

(c) $\partial h(\xi_t)/\partial \xi_{t-m} = -\partial h(\xi_t^*)/\partial \xi_{t-m}$ for any m and $\xi_t \epsilon \Xi$.

All the functions described have been symmetric. This condition is the main distinction between mean and variance models.

Another characterization of general ARCH models is in terms of regularity conditions.

DEFINITION: The ARCH model defined by (1) and (3) is *regular* if

(a) $\min h(\xi_t) \geq \delta$ for some $\delta > 0$ and $\xi_t \epsilon \Xi$,

(b) $E(|\partial h(\xi_t)/\partial \alpha_i||\partial h(\xi_t)/\partial \xi_{t-m}||\psi_{t-m-1})$ exists for all i, m, t.

The first portion of the definition is very important and easy to check, as it requires the variance always to be positive. This eliminates, for example, the log-log autoregression. The second portion is difficult to check in some cases, yet should generally be true if the process is stationary with bounded derivatives, since conditional expectations are finite if unconditional ones are. Condition (b) is a sufficient condition for the existence of some expectations of the Hessian used in Theorem 4. Presumably weaker conditions could be found.

THEOREM 3: *The pth-order linear ARCH model satisfies the regularity conditions, if $\alpha_0 > 0$ and $\alpha_1, \ldots, \alpha_p \geq 0$.*

PROOF: See Appendix.

In the estimation portion of the paper, a very substantial simplification results if the ARCH process is symmetric and regular.

5. ARCH REGRESSION MODELS

If the ARCH random variables discussed thus far have a non-zero mean, which can be expressed as a linear combination of exogenous and lagged dependent variables, then a regression framework is appropriate, and the model can be written as in (4) or (5). An alternative interpretation for the model is that the disturbances in a linear regression follow an ARCH process.

In the pth-order linear case, the specification and likelihood are given by

$$\begin{aligned} & y_t \mid \psi_{t-1} \sim N(x_t\beta, h_t), \\ & h_t = \alpha_0 + \alpha_1\epsilon_{t-1}^2 + \cdots + \alpha_p\epsilon_{t-p}^2, \\ (18) \quad & \epsilon_t = y_t - x_t\beta, \\ & l = \frac{1}{T}\sum_{t=1}^{T} l_t, \\ & l_t = -\tfrac{1}{2}\log h_t - \tfrac{1}{2}\epsilon_t^2/h_t, \end{aligned}$$

where x_t may include lagged dependent and exogenous variables and an irrelevant constant has been omitted from the likelihood. This likelihood function can be maximized with respect to the unknown parameters α and β. Attractive methods for computing such an estimate and its properties are discussed below.

Under the assumptions in (18), the ordinary least squares estimator of β is still consistent as x and ϵ are uncorrelated through the definition of the regression as a conditional expectation. If the x's can be treated as fixed constants then the least squares standard errors will be correct; however, if there are lagged dependent variables in x_t, the standard errors as conventionally computed will not be consistent, since the squares of the disturbances will be correlated with squares of the x's. This is an extension of White's **[18]** argument on heteroscedasticity and it suggests that using his alternative form for the covariance matrix would give a consistent estimate of the least-squares standard errors.

If the regressors include no lagged dependent variables and the process is stationary, then letting y and x be the $T \times 1$ and $T \times K$ vector and matrix of dependent and independent variables, respectively,

$$
\begin{aligned}
&E(y \mid x) = x\beta, \\
(19)\qquad & \\
&\operatorname{Var}(y \mid x) = \sigma^2 I,
\end{aligned}
$$

and the Gauss–Markov assumptions are statisfied. Ordinary least squares is the best linear unbiased estimator for the model in (18) and the variance estimates are unbiased and consistent. However, maximum likelihood is different and consequently asymptotically superior; ordinary least squares does not achieve the Cramer–Rao bound. The maximum-likelihood estimator is nonlinear and is more efficient than OLS by an amount calculated in Section 6.

The maximum likelihood estimator is found by solving the first order conditions. The derivative with respect to β is

$$
(20)\qquad \frac{\partial l_t}{\partial \beta} = \frac{\epsilon_t x_t'}{h_t} + \frac{1}{2h_t}\frac{\partial h_t}{\partial \beta}\left(\frac{\epsilon_t^2}{h_t} - 1\right).
$$

The first term is the familiar first-order condition for an exogenous heteroscedastic correction; the second term results because h_t is also a function of the β's, as in Amemiya **[1]**. Substituting the linear variance function gives

$$
(21)\qquad \frac{\partial l}{\partial \beta} = \frac{1}{T}\sum\left[\frac{\epsilon_t x_t'}{h_t} - \frac{1}{h_t}\left(\frac{\epsilon_t^2}{h_t} - 1\right)\sum_j \alpha_j \epsilon_{t-j} x_{t-j}'\right],
$$

which can be rewritten approximately by collecting terms in x and ϵ as

$$
\begin{aligned}
(22)\qquad \frac{\partial l}{\partial \beta} &= \frac{1}{T}\sum_t x_t'\epsilon_t\left[h_t^{-1} - \sum_{j=1}^{p} \alpha_j h_{t+j}^{-2}\left(\epsilon_{t+j}^2 - h_{t+j}\right)\right] \\
&\equiv \frac{1}{T}\sum_t x_t'\epsilon_t s_t.
\end{aligned}
$$

The Hessian is

$$
\begin{aligned}
\frac{\partial^2 l_t}{\partial \beta \partial \beta'} &= -\frac{x_t' x_t}{h_t} - \frac{1}{2h_t^2}\frac{\partial h_t}{\partial \beta}\frac{\partial h_t}{\partial \beta'}\left(\frac{\epsilon_t^2}{h_t}\right) \\
&\quad - \frac{2\epsilon_t x_t'}{h_t^2}\frac{\partial h_t}{\partial \beta} + \left(\frac{\epsilon_t^2}{h_t} - 1\right)\frac{\partial}{\partial \beta'}\left[\frac{1}{2h_t}\frac{\partial h_t}{\partial \beta}\right].
\end{aligned}
$$

Taking conditional expectations of the Hessian, the last two terms vanish because h_t is entirely a function of the past. Similarly, ϵ_t^2/h_t becomes one, since it is the only current value in the second term. Notice that these results hold regardless of whether x_t includes lagged-dependent variables. The information matrix is the average over all t of the expected value of the conditional expectation and is, therefore, given by

$$\mathcal{I}_{\beta\beta} = \frac{1}{T}\sum_t E\left[E\left(\frac{\partial^2 l_t}{\partial\beta\,\partial\beta'} \mid \psi_{t-1}\right)\right] \tag{23}$$

$$= \frac{1}{T}\sum_t E\left[\frac{x_t'x_t}{h_t} + \frac{1}{2h_t^2}\frac{\partial h_t}{\partial\beta}\frac{\partial h_t}{\partial\beta'}\right].$$

For the pth order linear ARCH regression this is consistently estimated by

$$\hat{\mathcal{I}}_{\beta\beta} = \frac{1}{T}\sum\left[\frac{x_t'x_t}{h_t} + 2\sum_j \alpha_j^2 \frac{\epsilon_{t-j}^2}{h_t^2} x_{t-j}'x_{t-j}\right]. \tag{24}$$

By gathering terms in $x_t'x_t$, (24) can be rewritten, except for end effects, as

$$\hat{\mathcal{I}}_{\beta\beta} = \frac{1}{T}\sum_t x_t'x_t\left[h_t^{-1} + 2\epsilon_t^2\sum_{j=1}^{p}\alpha_j^2 h_{t+j}^{-2}\right] \tag{25}$$

$$\equiv \frac{1}{T}\sum_t x_t'x_t r_t^2.$$

In a similar fashion, the off-diagonal blocks of the information matrix can be expressed as:

$$\mathcal{I}_{\alpha\beta} = \frac{1}{T}\sum_t E\left(\frac{1}{2h_t^2}\frac{\partial h_t}{\partial\alpha}\frac{\partial h_t}{\partial\beta'}\right). \tag{26}$$

The important result to be shown in Theorem 4 below is that this off-diagonal block is zero. The implications are far-reaching in that estimation of α and β can be undertaken separately without asymptotic loss of efficiency and their variances can be calculated separately.

THEOREM 4: *If an ARCH regression model is symmetric and regular, then* $\mathcal{I}_{\alpha\beta} = 0$.

PROOF: See Appendix.

6. ESTIMATION OF THE ARCH REGRESSION MODEL

Because of the block diagonality of the information matrix, the estimation of α and β can be considered separately without loss of asymptotic efficiency.

Furthermore, either can be estimated with full efficiency based only on a consistent estimate of the other. See, for example, Cox and Hinkley [6, p. 308]. The procedure recommended here is to initially estimate β by ordinary least squares, and obtain the residuals. From these residuals, an efficient estimate of α can be constructed, and based upon these $\hat{\alpha}$ estimates, efficient estimates of β are found. The iterations are calculated using the scoring algorithm. Each step for a parameter vector ϕ produces estimates ϕ^{i+1} based on ϕ^i according to

$$(27) \qquad \phi^{i+1} = \phi^i + \left[\hat{\mathfrak{I}}^i_{\phi\phi}\right]^{-1} \frac{1}{T} \sum_t \frac{\partial l_t^i}{\partial \phi},$$

where $\hat{\mathfrak{I}}^i$ and $\partial l_t^i / \partial \phi$ are evaluated at ϕ^i. The advantage of this algorithm is partly that it requires only first derivatives of the likelihood function in this case and partly that it uses the statistical properties of the problem to tailor the algorithm to this application.

For the pth-order linear model, the scoring step for α can be rewritten by substituting (12), (13), and (14) into (27) and interpreting y_t^2 as the residuals e_t^2. The iteration is simply

$$(28) \qquad \alpha^{i+1} = \alpha^i + (\tilde{z}'\tilde{z})^{-1}\tilde{z}'f^i$$

where

$$\tilde{z}_t = \left(1, e_{t-1}^2, \ldots, e_{t-p}^2\right)/h_t^i,$$

$$\tilde{z}' = (\tilde{z}'_1, \ldots, \tilde{z}'_T),$$

$$f_t^i = (e_t^2 - h_t^i)/h_t^i,$$

$$f^{i\prime} = (f_1^i, \ldots, f_T^i).$$

In these expressions, e_t is the residual from iteration i, h_t^i is the estimated conditional variance, and α^i is the estimate of the vector of unknown parameters from iteration i. Each step is, therefore, easily constructed from a least-squares regression on transformed variables. The variance-covariance matrix of the parameters is consistently estimated by the inverse of the estimate of the information matrix divided by T, which is simply $2(\tilde{z}'\tilde{z})^{-1}$. This differs slightly from $\hat{\sigma}^2(\tilde{z}'\tilde{z})^{-1}$ computed by the auxiliary regression. Asymptotically, $\hat{\sigma}^2 = 2$, if the distributional assumptions are correct, but it is not clear which formulation is better in practice.

The parameters in α must satisfy some nonnegativity conditions and some stationarity conditions. These could be imposed via penalty functions or the parameters could be estimated and checked for conformity. The latter approach is used here, although a perhaps useful reformulation of the model might employ squares to impose the nonnegativity constraints directly:

$$(29) \qquad h_t = \alpha_0^2 + \alpha_1^2\epsilon_{t-1}^2 + \cdots + \alpha_p^2\epsilon_{t-p}^2.$$

Convergence for such an iteration can be formulated in many ways. Following Belsley [3], a simple criterion is the gradient around the inverse Hessian. For a parameter vector, ϕ, this is

$$\theta = \frac{\partial l'}{\partial \phi}\left(\frac{\partial^2 l}{\partial \phi \partial \phi'}\right)^{-1}\frac{\partial l}{\partial \phi}. \tag{30}$$

Using θ as the convergence criterion is attractive, as it provides a natural normalization and as it is interpretable as the remainder term in a Taylor-series expansion about the estimated maximum. In any case, substituting the gradient and estimated information matrix in (30), $\theta = R^2$ of the auxiliary regression.

For a given estimate of α, a scoring step can be computed to improve the estimate of beta. The scoring algorithm for β is

$$\beta^{i+1} = \beta^i + \left[\hat{\mathcal{I}}_{\beta\beta}\right]^{-1}\frac{\partial l^i}{\partial \beta}. \tag{31}$$

Defining $\tilde{x}_t = x_t r_t$ and $\tilde{e}_t = e_t s_t / r_t$ with $\tilde{x}$ and $\tilde{e}$ as the corresponding matrix and vector, (31) can be rewritten using (22) and (24) and e_t for the estimate of ϵ_t on the ith iteration, as

$$\beta^{i+1} = \beta^i + (\tilde{x}'\tilde{x})^{-1}\tilde{x}'\tilde{e}. \tag{32}$$

Thus, an ordinary least-squares program can again perform the scoring iteration, and $(\tilde{x}'\tilde{x})^{-1}$ from this calculation will be the final variance-covariance matrix of the maximum likelihood estimates of β.

Under the conditions of Crowder's [7] theorem for martingales, it can be established that the maximum likelihood estimators $\hat{\alpha}$ and $\hat{\beta}$ are asymptotically normally distributed with limiting distribution

$$\begin{aligned} &\sqrt{T}(\hat{\alpha} - \alpha) \xrightarrow{D} N(0, \mathcal{I}_{\alpha\alpha}^{-1}), \\ &\sqrt{T}(\hat{\beta} - \beta) \xrightarrow{D} N(0, \mathcal{I}_{\beta\beta}^{-1}). \end{aligned} \tag{33}$$

7. GAINS IN EFFICIENCY FROM MAXIMUM LIKELIHOOD ESTIMATION

The gain in efficiency from using the maximum-likelihood estimation rather than OLS has been asserted above. In this section, the gains are calculated for a special case. Consider the linear stationary ARCH model with $p = 1$ and all x_t exogenous. This is the case where the Gauss–Markov theorem applies and OLS has a variance matrix $\sigma^2(x'x)^{-1} = E\epsilon_t^2(\sum_t x_t' x_t)^{-1}$. The stationary variance is $\sigma^2 = \alpha_0/(1 - \alpha_1)$.

The information matrix for this case becomes, from (25),

$$E\left[\sum_t x_t' x_t (h_t^{-1} + 2\epsilon_t^2 \alpha_1^2 / h_{t+1}^2)\right].$$

With x exogenous, the expectation is only necessary over the scale factor. Because the disturbance process is stationary, the variance-covariance matrix is proportional to that for OLS and the relative efficiency depends only upon the scale factors. The relative efficiency of MLE to OLS is, therefore,

$$R = E(h_t^{-1} + 2\epsilon_t^2\alpha_1^2/h_{t+1}^2)\sigma^2.$$

Now substitute $h_t = \alpha_0 + \alpha_1\epsilon_{t-1}^2$, $\sigma^2 = \alpha_0/1 - \alpha_1$, and $\gamma = \alpha_1/1 - \alpha_1$. Recognizing that ϵ_{t-1}^2 and ϵ_t^2 have the same density, define for each

$$u = \epsilon\sqrt{(1-\alpha_1)/\alpha_0}\,.$$

The expression for the relative efficiency becomes

$$R = E\left(\frac{1+\gamma}{1+\gamma u^2}\right) + 2\gamma^2 E\frac{u^2}{(1+\gamma u^2)^2}, \tag{34}$$

where u has variance one and mean zero. From Jensen's inequality, the expected value of a reciprocal exceeds the reciprocal of the expected value and, therefore, the first term is greater than unity. The second is positive, so there is a gain in efficiency whenever $\gamma \neq 0$. Eu^{-2} is infinite because u^2 is conditionally chi squared with one degree of freedom. Thus, the limit of the relative efficiency goes to infinity with γ:

$$\lim_{\gamma\to\infty} R \to \infty.$$

For α_1 close to unity, the gain in efficiency from using a maximum likelihood estimator may be very large.

8. TESTING FOR ARCH DISTURBANCES

In the linear regression model, with or without lagged-dependent variables, OLS is the appropriate procedure if the disturbances are not conditionally heteroscedastic. Because the ARCH model requires iterative procedures, it may be desirable to test whether it is appropriate before going to the effort to estimate it. The Lagrange multiplier test procedure is ideal for this as in many similar cases. See, for example, Breusch and Pagan [**4, 5**], Godfrey [**12**], and Engle [**9**].

Under the null hypothesis, $\alpha_1 = \alpha_2 \cdots = \alpha_p = 0$. The test is based upon the score under the null and the information matrix under the null. Consider the ARCH model with $h_t = h(z_t\alpha)$, where h is some differentiable function which, therefore, includes both the linear and exponential cases as well as lots of others and $z_t = (1, e_{t-1}^2, \ldots, e_{t-p}^2)$ where e_t are the ordinary least squares residuals. Under the null, h_t is a constant denoted h^0. Writing $\partial h_t/\partial\alpha = h'z_t'$, where h' is the scalar derivative of h, the score and information can be written as

$$\left.\frac{\partial l}{\partial \alpha}\right|_0 = \frac{h'}{2h^0}\sum_t z_t'\left(\frac{e_t^2}{h^0}-1\right) = \frac{h^{0\prime}}{2h^0}z'f^0,$$

$$\mathcal{I}^0_{\alpha\alpha} = \frac{1}{2}\left(\frac{h^{0\prime}}{h^0}\right)^2 Ez'z,$$

and, therefore, the LM test statistic can be consistently estimated by

(35) $\xi^* = \frac{1}{2}f^{0\prime}z(z'z)^{-1}z'f^0$

where $z' = (z_1', \ldots, z_T')$, f^0 is the column vector of

$$\left(\frac{e_t^2}{h^0}-1\right).$$

This is the form used by Breusch and Pagan **[4]** and Godfrey **[12]** for testing for heteroscedasticity. As they point out, all reference to the h function has disappeared and, thus, the test is the same for any h which is a function only of $z_t\alpha$.

In this problem, the expectation required in the information matrix could be evaluated quite simply under the null; this could have superior finite sample performance. A second simplification, which is appropriate for this model as well as the heteroscedasticity model, is to note that plim $f^{0\prime}f^0/T = 2$ because normality has already been assumed. Thus, an asymptotically equivalent statistic would be

(36) $\xi = Tf^{0\prime}z(z'z)^{-1}z'f^0/f^{0\prime}f^0 = TR^2$

where R^2 is the squared multiple correlation between f^0 and z. Since adding a constant and multiplying by a scalar will not change the R^2 of a regression, this is also the R^2 of the regression of e_t^2 on an intercept and p lagged values of e_t^2. The statistic will be asymptotically distributed as chi square with p degrees of freedom when the null hypothesis is true.

The test procedure is to run the OLS regression and save the residuals. Regress the squared residuals on a constant and p lags and test TR^2 as a χ_p^2. This will be an asymptotically locally most powerful test, a characterization it shares with likelihood ratio and Wald tests. The same test has been proposed by Granger and Anderson **[13]** to test for higher moments in bilinear time series.

9. ESTIMATION OF THE VARIANCE OF INFLATION

Economic theory frequently suggests that economic agents respond not only to the mean, but also to higher moments of economic random variables. In financial theory, the variance as well as the mean of the rate of return are determinants of portfolio decisions. In macroeconomics, Lucas **[16]**, for example, argues that the variance of inflation is a determinant of the response to various shocks. Furthermore, the variance of inflation may be of independent interest as it is the unanticipated component which is responsible for the bulk of the welfare loss due to inflation. Friedman [11] also argues that, as high inflation will generally be associated with high variability of inflation, the statistical relationship between inflation and unemployment should have a positive slope, not a negative one as in the traditional Phillips curve.

Measuring the variance of inflation over time has presented problems to various researchers. Khan [14] has used the absolute value of the first difference of inflation while Klein [15] has used a moving variance around a moving mean. Each of these approaches makes very simple assumptions about the mean of the distribution, which are inconsistent with conventional econometric approaches. The ARCH method allows a conventional regression specification for the mean function, with a variance which is permitted to change stochastically over the sample period. For a comparison of several measures for U.S. data, see Engle [10].

A conventional price equation was estimated using British data from 1958-II through 1977-II. It was assumed that price inflation followed wage increases; thus the model is a restricted transfer function.

Letting $\dot{p}$ be the first difference of the log of the quarterly consumer price index and w be the log of the quarterly index of manual wage rates, the model chosen after some experimentation was

$$\dot{p} = \beta_1\dot{p}_{-1} + \beta_2\dot{p}_{-4} + \beta_3\dot{p}_{-5} + \beta_4(p - w)_{-1} + \beta_5. \tag{37}$$

The model has typical seasonal behavior with the first, fourth, and fifth lags of the first difference. The lagged value of the real wage is the error correction mechanism of Davidson, et al. [8], which restricts the lag weights to give a constant real wage in the long run. As this is a reduced form, the current wage rate cannot enter.

The least squares estimates of this model are given in Table I. The fit is quite good, with less than 1 per cent standard error of forecast, and all t statistics greater than 3. Notice that $\dot{p}_{-4}$ and $\dot{p}_{-5}$ have equal and opposite signs, suggesting that it is the acceleration of inflation one year ago which explains much of the short-run behavior in prices.

TABLE I

ORDINARY LEAST SQUARES (36)[a]

Variable	$\dot{p}_{-1}$	$\dot{p}_{-4}$	$\dot{p}_{-5}$	$(p-w)_{-1}$	Const.	α_0 ($\times 10^{-6}$)	α_1
Coeff.	0.334	0.408	−0.404	−0.0559	0.0257	89	0
St. Err.	0.103	0.110	0.114	0.0136	0.00572		
t Stat.	3.25	3.72	3.55	4.12	4.49		

[a] Dependent variable $p = \log(P) - \log(P_{-1})$ where P is quarterly U.K. consumer price index. $w = \log(W)$ where W is the U.K. index of manual wage rates. Sample period 1958-II to 1977-II.

To establish the reliability of the model by conventional criteria, it was tested for serial correlation and for coefficient restrictions. Godfrey's [**12**] Lagrange multiplier test, for serial correlation up to sixth order, yields a chi-squared statistic with 6 degrees of freedom of 4.53, which is not significant, and the square of Durbin's h is 0.57. Only the 9th autocorrelation of the least squares residuals exceeds two asymptotic standard errors and, thus, the hypothesis of white noise disturbances can be accepted. The model was compared with an unrestricted regression, including all lagged p and w from one quarter through six. The asymptotic F statistic was 2.04, which is not significant at the 5 per cent level. When (37) was tested for the exclusion of w_{-1} through w_{-6}, the statistic was 2.34, which is barely significant at the 5 per cent but not the 2.5 per cent level. The only variable which enters significantly in either of these regressions is w_{-6} and it seems unattractive to include this alone.

The Lagrange multiplier test for a first-order linear ARCH effect for the model in (37) was not significant. However, testing for a fourth-order linear ARCH process, the chi-squared statistic with 4 degrees of freedom was 15.2, which is highly significant. Assuming that agents discount past residuals, a linearly declining set of weights was formulated to give the model

$$h_t = \alpha_0 + \alpha_1(0.4\epsilon_{t-1}^2 + 0.3\epsilon_{t-2}^2 + 0.2\epsilon_{t-3}^2 + 0.1\epsilon_{t-4}^2) \tag{38}$$

which is used in the balance of the paper. A two-parameter variance function was chosen because it was suspected that the nonnegativity and stationarity constraints on the α's would be hard to satisfy in an unrestricted model. The chi-squared test for $\alpha_1 = 0$ in (38) was 6.1, which has one degree of freedom.

One step of the scoring algorithm was employed to estimate model (37) and (38). The scoring step on α was performed first and then, using the new efficient $\hat{\alpha}$, the algorithm obtains in one step, efficient estimates of β. These are given in Table II. The procedure was also iterated to convergence by doing three steps on α, followed by three steps on β, followed by three more steps on α, and so forth. Convergence, within 0.1 per cent of the final value, occurred after two sets of α and β steps. These results are given in Table III.

The maximum likelihood estimates differ from the least squares effects primarily in decreasing the sizes of the short-run dynamic coefficients and increasing

TABLE II
MAXIMUM LIKELIHOOD ESTIMATES OF ARCH MODEL (36) (37)
ONE-STEP SCORING ESTIMATES[a]

Variable	$\dot{p}_{-1}$	$\dot{p}_{-4}$	$\dot{p}_{-5}$	$(p-w)_{-1}$	Const.	$\alpha_0\ (\times 10^{-6})$	α_1
Coeff.	0.210	0.270	− 0.334	− 0.0697	0.0321	19	0.846
St. Err.	0.110	0.094	0.109	0.0117	0.00498	14	0.243
t Stat.	1.90	2.86	3.06	5.98	6.44	1.32	3.49

[a] Dependent variable $p = \log(P) - \log(P_{-1})$ where P is quarterly U.K. consumer price index. $w = \log(W)$ where W is the U.K. index of manual wage rates. Sample period 1958-II to 1977-II.

TABLE III
MAXIMUM LIKELIHOOD ESTIMATES OF ARCH MODEL (36) (37)
ITERATED ESTIMATES[a]

Variables	$\dot{p}_{-1}$	$\dot{p}_{-4}$	$\dot{p}_{-5}$	$(p-w)_{-1}$	Const.	$\alpha_0\,(\times 10^{-6})$	α_1
Coeff.	0.162	0.264	−0.325	−0.0707	0.0328	14	0.955
St. Err.	0.108	0.0892	0.0987	0.0115	0.00491	8.5	0.298
t Stat.	1.50	2.96	3.29	6.17	6.67	1.56	3.20

[a] Dependent variable $\dot{p} = \log(P) - \log(P_{-1})$ where P is quarterly U.K. consumer price index. $w = \log(W)$ where W is the U.K. index of manual wage rates. Sample period 1958-II to 1977-II.

the coefficient on the long run, as incorporated in the error correction mechanism. The acceleration term is not so clearly implied as in the least squares estimates. These seem reasonable results, since much of the inflationary dynamics are estimated by a period of very severe inflation in the middle seventies. This, however, is also the period of the largest forecast errors and, hence, the maximum likelihood estimator will discount these observations. By the end of the sample period, inflationary levels were rather modest and one might expect that the maximum likelihood estimates would provide a better forecasting equation.

The standard errors for ordinary least squares are generally greater than for maximum likelihood. The least squares standard errors are 15 per cent to 25 per cent greater, with one exception where the standard error actually falls by 5 per cent to 7 per cent. As mentioned earlier, however, the least squares estimates are biased when there are lagged dependent variables. The Wald test for $\alpha_1 = 0$ is also significant.

The final estimates of h_t are the one-step-ahead forecast variances. For the one-step scoring estimator, these vary from 23×10^{-6} to 481×10^{-6}. That is, the forecast standard deviation ranges from 0.5 per cent to 2.2 per cent, which is more than a factor of 4. The average of the h_t, since 1974, is 230×10^{-6}, as compared with 42×10^{-6} during the last four years of the sixties. Thus, the standard deviation of inflation increased from 0.6 per cent to 1.5 per cent over a few years, as the economy moved from the rather predictable sixties into the chaotic seventies.

In order to determine whether the confidence intervals arising from the ARCH model were superior to the least squares model, the outliers were examined. The expected number of residuals exceeding two (conditional) standard deviations is 3.5. For ordinary least squares, there were 5 while ARCH produced 3. For least squares these occurred in '74-I, '75-I, '75-II, '75-IV, and '76-II; they all occur within three years of each other and, in fact, three of them are in the same year. For the ARCH model, they are much more spread out and only one of the least squares points remains an outlier, although the others are still large. Examining the observations exceeding one standard deviation shows similar effects. In the seventies, there were 13 OLS and 12 ARCH residuals outside one sigma, which are both above the expected value of 9. In the sixties, there were 6 for OLS, 10 for ARCH and an expected number of 12. Thus, the number of outliers for ordinary least squares is reasonable; however, the timing of their occurrence is far from random. The ARCH model comes closer to truly random residuals after standardizing for their conditional distributions.

This example illustrates the usefulness of the ARCH model for improving the performance of a least squares model and for obtaining more realistic forecast variances.

University of California, San Diego

Manuscript received July, 1979; final revision received July, 1981.

APPENDIX

PROOF OF THEOREM 1: Let

$$w_t' = (y_t^{2r}, y_t^{2(r-1)}, \dots, y_t^2). \tag{A2}$$

First, it is shown that there is an upper triangular $r \times r$ matrix A and $r \times 1$ vector b such that

$$E(w_t \mid \psi_{t-1}) = b + Aw_{t-1}. \tag{A2}$$

For any zero-mean normal random variable u, with variance σ^2,

$$E(u^{2r}) = \sigma^{2r} \prod_{j=1}^{r} (2j-1).$$

Because the conditional distribution of y is normal

$$E(y_t^{2m} \mid \psi_{t-1}) = h_t^{2m} \prod_{j=1}^{m} (2j-1) \tag{A3}$$

$$= (\alpha_1 y_{t-1}^2 + \alpha_0)^m \prod_{j=1}^{m} (2j-1).$$

Expanding this expression establishes that the moment is a linear combination of w_{t-1}. Furthermore, only powers of y less than or equal to $2m$ are required; therefore, A in (A2) is upper triangular.

Now

$$E(w_t \mid \psi_{t-2}) = b + A(b + Aw_{t-2})$$

or in general

$$E(w_t \mid \psi_{t-k}) = (\mathcal{I} + A + A^2 + \dots + A^{k-1})b + A^k w_{t-k}.$$

Because the series starts indefinitely far in the past with $2r$ finite moments, the limit as k goes to infinity exists if, and only if, all the eigenvalues of A lie within the unit circle.

The limit can be written as

$$\lim_{k \to \infty} E(w_t \mid \psi_{t-k}) = (I - A)^{-1} b,$$

which does not depend upon the conditioning variables and does not depend upon t. Hence, this is an expression for the stationary moments of the unconditional distribution of y.

$$E(w_t) = (I - A)^{-1} b. \tag{A4}$$

It remains only to establish that the condition in the theorem is necessary and sufficient to have all eigenvalues lie within the unit circle. As the matrix has already been shown to be upper triangular, the diagonal elements are the eigenvalues. From (A3), it is seen that the diagonal elements are simply

$$\alpha_1^m \prod_{j=1}^{m} (2j-1) = \prod_{j=1}^{m} \alpha_1(2j-1) \equiv \theta_m$$

for $m = 1, \ldots, r$. If θ_r exceeds or equals unity, the eigenvalues do not lie in the unit circle. It must also be shown that if $\theta_r < 1$, then $\theta_m < 1$ for all $m < r$. Notice that θ_m is a product of m factors which are monotonically increasing. If the mth factor is greater than one, then θ_{m-1} will necessarily be smaller than θ_m. If the mth factor is less than one, all the other factors must also be less than one and, therefore, θ_{m-1} must also have all factors less than one and have a value less than one. This establishes that a necessary and sufficient condition for all diagonal elements to be less than one is that $\theta_r < 1$, which is the statement in the theorem. *Q.E.D.*

PROOF OF THEOREM 2: Let

$$w_t' = \left(y_t^2, y_{t-1}^2, \ldots, y_{t-p}^2\right).$$

Then in terms of the companion matrix A,

$$E(w_t \mid \psi_{t-1}) = b + Aw_{t-1} \tag{A5}$$

where $b' = (\alpha_0, 0, \ldots, 0)$ and

$$A = \begin{bmatrix} \alpha_1 & \alpha_2 & \cdots & \alpha_p & 0 \\ 1 & 0 & \cdots & 0 & 0 \\ 0 & 1 & \cdots & 0 & 0 \\ 0 & 0 & \cdots & 1 & 0 \end{bmatrix}.$$

Taking successive expectations

$$E(w_t \mid \psi_{t-k}) = (I + A + A^2 + \cdots + A^{k-1})b + A^k w_{t-k}.$$

Because the series starts indefinitely far in the past with finite variance, if, and only if, all eigenvalues lie within the unit circle, the limit exists and is given by

$$\lim_{k\to\infty} E(w_t \mid \psi_{t-k}) = (I - A)^{-1}b. \tag{A6}$$

As this does not depend upon initial conditions or on t, this vector is the common variance for all t. As is well known in time series analysis, this condition is equivalent to the condition that all the roots of the characteristic equation, formed from the α's, lie outside the unit circle. See Anderson [2, p. 177]. Finally, the limit of the first element can be rewritten as

$$Ey_t^2 = \alpha_0 \Big/ \left(1 - \sum_{j=1}^{p} \alpha_j\right). \tag{A7}$$

Q.E.D.

PROOF OF THEOREM 3: Clearly, under the conditions, $h(\xi_t) \geq \alpha_0 > 0$, establishing part (a). Let

$$\begin{aligned}\phi_{i,m,t} &= E(|\partial h(\xi_t)/\partial\alpha_i|\partial h(\xi_t)/\partial\xi_{t-m} \mid \psi_{t-m-1}) \\ &= 2\alpha_m E(|\xi_{t-i}|^2 |\xi_{t-m}| \psi_{t-m-1}).\end{aligned}$$

Now there are three cases; $i > m$, $i = m$, and $i < m$. If $i > m$, then $\xi_{t-i} \in \psi_{t-m-1}$ and the conditional expectation of $|\xi_{t-m}|$ is finite, because the conditional density is normal. If $i = m$, then the expectation becomes $E(|\xi_{t-m}|^3 \mid \psi_{t-m-1})$. Again, because the conditional density is normal, all moments exist including the expectation of the third power of the absolute value. If $i < m$, the expectation is taken in two parts, first with respect to $t-i-1$:

$$\phi_{i,m,t} = 2\alpha_m E\{|\xi_{t-m}| E(\xi_{t-i}^2 \mid \psi_{t-i-1}) \mid \psi_{t-m-1}\}$$

$$= 2\alpha_m E\left\{|\xi_{t-m}|\alpha_0 + \sum_{j=1}^{p} \alpha_j \xi_{t-i-j}^2)\mid \psi_{t-m-1}\right\}$$

$$= 2\alpha_m \alpha_0 E\{\xi_{t-m} \mid \psi_{t-m-1}\} + \sum_{j=1}^{p} \alpha_j \phi_{i+j,m,t}.$$

In the final expression, the initial index on ϕ is larger and, therefore, may fall into either of the preceding cases, which, therefore, establishes the existence of the term. If there remain terms with $i+j<m$, the recursion can be repeated. As all lags are finite, an expression for $\phi_{i,m,t}$ can be written as a constant times the third absolute moment of ξ_{t-m} conditional on ψ_{t-m-1}, plus another constant times the first absolute moment. As these are both conditionally normal, and as the constants must be finite as they have a finite number of terms, the second part of the regularity condition has been established.

Q.E.D.

To establish Theorem 4, a careful symmetry argument is required, beginning with the following lemma.

LEMMA: *Let u and v be any two random variables. $E(g(u,v)\mid v)$ will be an anti-symmetric function of v if g is anti-symmetric in v, the conditional density of $u \mid v$ is symmetric in v, and the expectation exists.*

PROOF:

$$E(g(u,-v)\mid -v) = -E(g(u,v)\mid -v) \quad \text{because } g \text{ is anti-symmetric in } v$$

$$= -E(g(u,v)\mid v) \quad \text{because the conditional density is symmetric.}$$

Q.E.D.

PROOF OF THEOREM 4: The i,j element of $I_{\alpha\beta}$ is given by

$$(I_{\alpha\beta})_{ij} = \frac{1}{2T}\sum_t E\left(\frac{1}{h_t^2}\frac{\partial h_t}{\partial \alpha_i}\frac{\partial h_t}{\partial \beta_j}\right)$$

$$= -\frac{1}{2T}\sum_t \sum_{m=1}^{p} E\left[\frac{1}{h_t^2}\frac{\partial h_t}{\partial \alpha_i}\frac{\partial h_t}{\partial \epsilon_{t-m}} x_{jt-m}\right] \quad \text{by the chain rule.}$$

If the expectation of the term in square brackets, conditional on ψ_{t-m-1}, is zero for all i, j, t, m, then the theorem is proven.

$$E\left(\frac{1}{h_t^2}\frac{\partial h_t}{\partial \alpha_i}\frac{\partial h_t}{\partial \epsilon_{t-m}} x_{jt-m} \mid \psi_{t-m-1}\right) = x_{jt-m} E\left(\frac{1}{h_t^2}\frac{\partial h_t}{\partial \alpha_i}\frac{\partial h_t}{\partial \epsilon_{t-m}} \mid \psi_{t-m-1}\right)$$

because x_{jt-m} is either exogenous or it is a lagged dependent variable, in which case it is included in ψ_{t-m-1}.

$$\left|E\left(\frac{1}{h_t^2}\frac{\partial h_t}{\partial \alpha_i}\frac{\partial h_t}{\partial \epsilon_{t-m}} \mid \psi_{t-m-1}\right)\right| \le E\left(\frac{1}{h_t^2}\left|\frac{\partial h_t}{\partial \alpha_i}\right|\left|\frac{\partial h_t}{\partial \epsilon_{t-m}}\right| \mid \psi_{t-m-1}\right)$$

$$\le \frac{1}{\delta^2} E\left(\left|\frac{\partial h_t}{\partial \alpha_i}\right|\left|\frac{\partial h_t}{\partial \epsilon_{t-m}}\right| \mid \psi_{t-m-1}\right)$$

by part (a) of the regularity conditions and this integral is finite by part (b) of the condition. Hence, each term is finite. Now take the expectation in two steps, first with respect to ψ_{t-m}. This must therefore also be finite.

$$E\left(\frac{1}{h_t^2}\frac{\partial h_t}{\partial \alpha_i}\frac{\partial h_t}{\partial \epsilon_{t-m}} \mid \psi_{t-m}\right) \equiv g(\epsilon_{t-m}).$$

By the symmetry assumption, h_t^{-1} is symmetric in ϵ_{t-m}, $\partial h_t/\partial \epsilon_{t-m}$ is anti-symmetric. Therefore, the whole expression is anti-symmetric in ϵ_{t-m}, which is part of the conditioning set ψ_{t-m}. Because h is symmetric, the conditional density must be symmetric in ϵ_{t-m} and the lemma can be invoked to show that $g(\epsilon_{t-m})$ is anti-symmetric.

Finally, taking expectations of g conditional on ψ_{t-m-1} gives zero, because the density of ϵ_{t-m} conditional on the past is a symmetric (normal) density and the theorem is established. *Q.E.D.*

REFERENCES

[1] AMEMIYA, T.: "Regression Analysis when the Variance of the Dependent Variable is Proportional to the Square of Its Expectation," *Journal of the American Statistical Association*, 68(1973), 928–934.

[2] ANDERSON, T. W.: *The Statistical Analysis of Time Series*. New York: John Wiley and Sons, 1958.

[3] BELSLEY, DAVID: "On the Efficient Computation of Non-Linear Full-Information Maximum Likelihood Estimator," paper presented to the European Meetings of the Econometric Society, Athens, 1979.

[4] BREUSCH, T. S., AND A. R. PAGAN: "A Simple Test for Heteroscedasticity and Random Coefficient Variation," *Econometrica*, 46(1978), 1287–1294.

[5] ———: "The Lagrange Multiplier Test and Its Applications to Model Specification," *Review of Economic Studies*, 47(1980), 239–254.

[6] COX, D. R., AND D. V. HINKLEY: *Theoretical Statistics*. London: Chapman and Hall, 1974.

[7] CROWDER, M. J.: "Maximum Likelihood Estimation for Dependent Observations," *Journal of the Royal Statistical Society*, Series B, 38(1976), 45–53.

[8] DAVIDSON, J. E. H., D. F. HENDRY, F. SRBA, AND S. YEO: "Econometric Modelling of the Aggregate Time-Series Relationship Between Consumers' Expenditure and Income in the United Kingdom," *The Economic Journal*, 88(1978), 661–691.

[9] ENGLE, R. F.: "A General Approach to the Construction of Model Diagnostics Based upon the Lagrange Multiplier Principle," University of California, San Diego Discussion Paper 79-43, 1979.

[10] ———: "Estimates of the Variance of U.S. Inflation Based on the ARCH Model," University of California, San Diego Discussion Paper 80-14, 1980.

[11] FRIEDMAN, MILTON: "Nobel Lecture: Inflation and Unemployment," *Journal of Political Economy*, 85(1977), 451–472.

[12] GODFREY, L. G.: "Testing Against General Autoregressive and Moving Average Error Models When the Regressors Include Lagged Dependent Variables," *Econometrica*, 46(1978), 1293–1302.

[13] GRANGER, C. W. J., AND A. ANDERSEN: *An Introduction to Bilinear Time-Series Models*. Göttingen: Vandenhoeck and Ruprecht, 1978.

[14] KHAN, M. S.: "The Variability of Expectations in Hyperinflations," *Journal of Political Economy*, 85(1977), 817–827.

[15] KLEIN, B.: "The Demand for Quality-Adjusted Cash Balances: Price Uncertainty in the U.S. Demand for Money Function," *Journal of Political Economy*, 85(1977), 692–715.

[16] LUCAS, R. E., JR.: "Some International Evidence on Output-Inflation Tradeoffs," *American Economic Review*, 63(1973), 326–334.

[17] MCNEES, S. S.: "The Forecasting Record for the 1970's," *New England Economic Review*, September/October 1979, 33–53.

[18] WHITE, H.: "A Heteroscedasticity Consistent Covariance Matrix Estimator and a Direct Test for Heteroscedasticity," *Econometrica*, 48(1980), 817–838.

[15]

Journal of Econometrics 31 (1986) 307–327. North-Holland

GENERALIZED AUTOREGRESSIVE CONDITIONAL HETEROSKEDASTICITY

Tim BOLLERSLEV *

University of California at San Diego, La Jolla, CA 92093, USA
Institute of Economics, University of Aarhus, Denmark

Received May 1985, final version received February 1986

A natural generalization of the ARCH (Autoregressive Conditional Heteroskedastic) process introduced in Engle (1982) to allow for past conditional variances in the current conditional variance equation is proposed. Stationarity conditions and autocorrelation structure for this new class of parametric models are derived. Maximum likelihood estimation and testing are also considered. Finally an empirical example relating to the uncertainty of the inflation rate is presented.

1. Introduction

While conventional time series and econometric models operate under an assumption of constant variance, the ARCH (Autoregressive Conditional Heteroskedastic) process introduced in Engle (1982) allows the conditional variance to change over time as a function of past errors leaving the unconditional variance constant.

This type of model behavior has already proven useful in modelling several different economic phenomena. In Engle (1982), Engle (1983) and Engle and Kraft (1983), models for the inflation rate are constructed recognizing that the uncertainty of inflation tends to change over time. In Coulson and Robins (1985) the estimated inflation volatility is related to some key macroeconomic variables. Models for the term structure using an estimate of the conditional variance as a proxy for the risk premium are given in Engle, Lilien and Robins (1985). The same idea is applied to the foreign exchange market in Domowitz and Hakkio (1985). In Weiss (1984) ARMA models with ARCH errors are found to be successful in modelling thirteen different U.S. macroeconomic time series. Common to most of the above applications however, is the introduction of a rather arbitrary linear declining lag structure in the condi-

*I am grateful to David Hendry and Rob Engle for introducing me to this new idea, and to Rob Engle for many helpful discussions. I would also like to thank Sastry Pantula for suggesting the alternative parameterization, two anonymous referees for useful comments, and Kirsten Stentoft for typing the manuscript. The usual disclaimer applies.

tional variance equation to take account of the long memory typically found in empirical work, since estimating a totally free lag distribution often will lead to violation of the non-negativity constraints.

In this paper a new, more general class of processes, GARCH (Generalized Autoregressive Conditional Heteroskedastic), is introduced, allowing for a much more flexible lag structure. The extension of the ARCH process to the GARCH process bears much resemblance to the extension of the standard time series AR process to the general ARMA process and, as is argued below, permits a more parsimonious description in many situations.

The paper proceeds as follows. In section 2 the new class of processes is formally presented and conditions for their wide-sense stationarity are derived. The simple GARCH(1,1) process is considered in some detail in section 3. It is well established, that the autocorrelation and partial autocorrelation functions are useful tools in identifying and checking time series behavior of the ARMA form in the conditional mean. Similarly the autocorrelations and partial autocorrelations for the squared process may prove helpful in identifying and checking GARCH behavior in the conditional variance equation. This is the theme in section 4. In section 5 maximum likelihood estimation of the linear regression model with GARCH errors is briefly discussed, and it is seen that the asymptotic independence between the estimates of the mean and the variance parameters carries over from the ARCH regression model. Some test results are presented in section 6. As in the ARMA analogue, cf. Godfrey (1978), a general test for the presence of GARCH is not feasible. Section 7 contains an empirical example explaining the uncertainty of the inflation rate. It is argued that a simple GARCH model provides a marginally better fit and a more plausible learning mechanism than the ARCH model with an eighth-order linear declining lag structure as in Engle and Kraft (1983).

2. The GARCH(p,q) process

The ARCH process introduced by Engle (1982) explicitly recognizes the difference between the unconditional and the conditional variance allowing the latter to change over time as a function of past errors. The statistical properties of this new parametric class of models has been studied further in Weiss (1982) and in a recent paper by Milhøj (1984).

In empirical applications of the ARCH model a relatively long lag in the conditional variance equation is often called for, and to avoid problems with negative variance parameter estimates a fixed lag structure is typically imposed, cf. Engle (1982), Engle (1983) and Engle and Kraft (1983). In this light it seems of immediate practical interest to extend the ARCH class of models to allow for both a longer memory and a more flexible lag structure.

Let ε_t denote a real-valued discrete-time stochastic process, and ψ_t the information set (σ-field) of all information through time t. The GARCH(p,q)

process (Generalized Autoregressive Conditional Heteroskedasticity) is then given by[1]

$$\varepsilon_t|\psi_{t-1} \sim \mathrm{N}(0, h_t), \tag{1}$$

$$\begin{aligned} h_t &= \alpha_0 + \sum_{i=1}^{q} \alpha_i \varepsilon_{t-i}^2 + \sum_{i=1}^{p} \beta_i h_{t-i} \\ &= \alpha_0 + A(L)\varepsilon_t^2 + B(L)h_t, \end{aligned} \tag{2}$$

where

$$p \geq 0, \qquad q > 0$$

$$\alpha_0 > 0, \qquad \alpha_i \geq 0, \quad i = 1, \ldots, q,$$

$$\beta_i \geq 0, \qquad i = 1, \ldots, p.$$

For $p = 0$ the process reduces to the ARCH(q) process, and for $p = q = 0$ ε_t is simply white noise. In the ARCH(q) process the conditional variance is specified as a linear function of past sample variances only, whereas the GARCH(p, q) process allows lagged conditional variances to enter as well. This corresponds to some sort of adaptive learning mechanism.

The GARCH(p, q) regression model is obtained by letting the ε_t's be innovations in a linear regression,

$$\varepsilon_t = y_t - x_t'b, \tag{3}$$

where y_t is the dependent variable, x_t a vector of explanatory variables, and b a vector of unknown parameters. This model is studied in some detail in section 5.

If all the roots of $1 - B(z) = 0$ lie outside the unit circle, (2) can be rewritten as a distributed lag of past ε_t^2's,

$$\begin{aligned} h_t &= \alpha_0(1 - B(1))^{-1} + A(L)(1 - B(L))^{-1}\varepsilon_t^2 \\ &= \alpha_0\left(1 - \sum_{i=1}^{p} \beta_i\right)^{-1} + \sum_{i=1}^{\infty} \delta_i \varepsilon_{t-i}^2, \end{aligned} \tag{4}$$

which together with (1) may be seen as an infinite-dimensional ARCH(∞) process. The δ_i's are found from the power series expansion of $D(L) =$

[1]We follow Engle (1982) in assuming the conditional distribution to be normal, but of course other distributions could be applied as well. Instead of ε_{t-i}^2 in eq. (2) the absolute value of ε_{t-i} may be more appropriate in some applications; cf. McCulloch (1983).

$A(L)(1-B(L))^{-1}$,

$$\begin{aligned}\delta_i &= \alpha_i + \sum_{j=1}^{n} \beta_j \delta_{i-j}, \qquad i = 1,\dots,q, \\ &= \sum_{j=1}^{n} \beta_j \delta_{i-j}, \qquad i = q+1,\dots,\end{aligned} \tag{5}$$

where $n = \min\{p, i-1\}$. It follows, that if $B(1) < 1$, δ_i will be decreasing for i greater than $m = \max\{p, q\}$. Thus if $D(1) < 1$, the GARCH(p, q) process can be approximated to any degree of accuracy by a stationary ARCH(Q) for a sufficiently large value of Q. But as in the ARMA analogue, the GARCH process might possibly be justified through a Wald's decomposition type of arguments as a more parsimonious description.

From the theory on finite-dimensional ARCH(q) processes it is to be expected that $D(1) < 1$, or equivalently $A(1) + B(1) < 1$, suffices for wide-sense stationarity; cf. Milhøj (1984). This is indeed the case.

Theorem 1. The GARCH(p, q) process as defined in (1) and (2) is wide-sense stationary with $\mathrm{E}(\varepsilon_t) = 0$, $\mathrm{var}(\varepsilon_t) = \alpha_0(1 - A(1) - B(1))^{-1}$ *and* $\mathrm{cov}(\varepsilon_t, \varepsilon_s) = 0$ *for* $t \neq s$ *if and only if* $A(1) + B(1) < 1$.

Proof. See appendix.

As pointed out by Sastry Pantula and an anonymous referee, an equivalent representation of the GARCH(p, q) process is given by

$$\varepsilon_t^2 = \alpha_0 + \sum_{i=1}^{q} \alpha_i \varepsilon_{t-i}^2 + \sum_{j=1}^{p} \beta_j \varepsilon_{t-j}^2 - \sum_{j=1}^{p} \beta_j \nu_{t-j} + \nu_t, \tag{6}$$

and

$$\nu_t = \varepsilon_t^2 - h_t = \left(\eta_t^2 - 1\right) h_t, \tag{7}$$

where

$$\eta_t \overset{\text{i.i.d.}}{\sim} \mathrm{N}(0,1).$$

Note, by definition ν_t is serially uncorrelated with mean zero. Therefore, the GARCH(p, q) process can be interpreted as an autoregressive moving average process in ε_t^2 of orders $m = \max\{p, q\}$ and p, respectively. Although a parameterization along the lines of (6) might be more meaningful from a theoretical time series point of view, (1) and (2) are easier to work with in practice.

3. The GARCH(1, 1) process

The simplest but often very useful GARCH process is of course the GARCH(1, 1) process given by (1) and

$$h_t = \alpha_0 \alpha_1 \varepsilon_{t-1}^2 + \beta_1 h_{t-1}, \qquad \alpha_0 > 0, \quad \alpha_1 \geq 0, \quad \beta_1 \geq 0. \tag{8}$$

From Theorem 1, $\alpha_1 + \beta_1 < 1$ suffices for wide-sense stationarity, and in general we have:[2]

Theorem 2. For the GARCH(1, 1) process given by (1) and (6) a necessary and sufficient condition for existence of the $2m$th *moment is*

$$\mu(\alpha_1, \beta_1, m) = \sum_{j=0}^{m} \binom{m}{j} a_j \alpha_1^j \beta_1^{m-j} < 1, \tag{9}$$

where

$$a_0 = 1, \quad a_j = \prod_{i=1}^{j} (2j-1), \qquad j = 1, \ldots. \tag{10}$$

The $2m$th *moment can be expressed by the recursive formula*

$$\mathrm{E}(\varepsilon_t^{2m}) = a_m \left[\sum_{n=0}^{m-1} a_n^{-1} \mathrm{E}(\varepsilon_t^{2n}) \alpha_0^{m-n} \binom{m}{m-n} \mu(\alpha_1, \beta_1, n) \right]$$

$$\times [1 - \mu(\alpha_1, \beta_1, m)]^{-1}. \tag{11}$$

Proof. See appendix.

The conditions for existence of the first twelve moments are illustrated in fig. 1.

It follows by symmetry that if the $2m$th moment exists, $\mathrm{E}(\varepsilon_t^{2m-1}) = 0$.

For $\beta_1 = 0$, (9) reduces to the well-known condition for the ARCH(1) process, $a_m \alpha_1^m < 1$; cf. Engle (1982). Thus if $\alpha_1 > (a_m)^{-1/m}$ in the ARCH(1) process, the $2m$th moment does not exist, whereas even if $\sum_{i=1}^{\infty} \delta_i = \alpha_1 (1 - \beta_1)^{-1} > (a_m)^{-1/m}$ in the GARCH(1, 1) process, the $2m$th moment might very well exist because of the longer memory in this process.

In the GARCH(1, 1) process the mean lag in the conditional variance equation is given by

$$\zeta = \sum_{i=1}^{\infty} i\delta_i \bigg/ \sum_{i=1}^{\infty} \delta_i = (1 - \beta_1)^{-1},$$

[2] As in Engle (1982) we assume for simplicity that the process starts indefinitely far in the past with $2m$ finite initial moments.

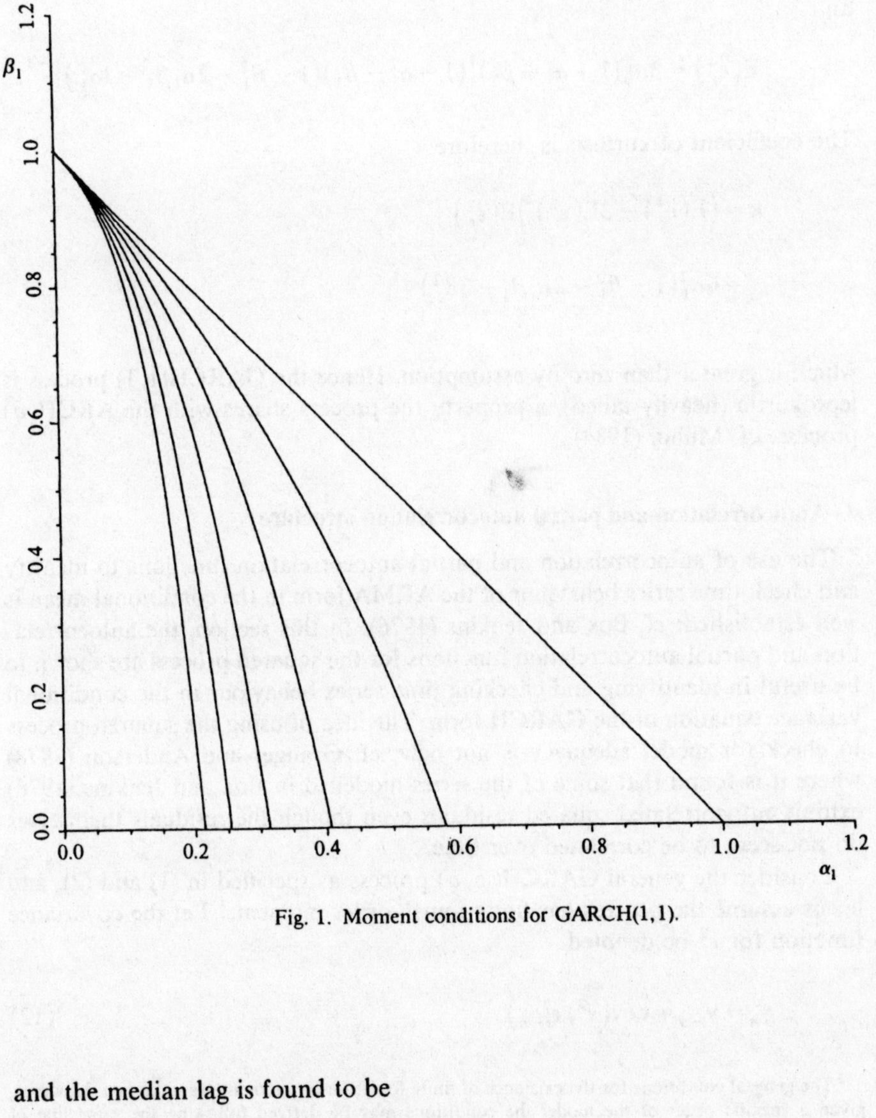

Fig. 1. Moment conditions for GARCH(1,1).

and the median lag is found to be

$$\nu = -\log 2/\log \beta_1,$$

where $\sum_{i=1}^{\nu}\delta_i/\sum_{i=1}^{\infty}\delta_i = \frac{1}{2}$ and the δ_i's are defined in (5); cf. Harvey (1982).

If $3\alpha_1^2 + 2\alpha_1\beta_1 + \beta_1^2 < 1$, the fourth-order moment exists and by Theorem 2

$$\mathrm{E}(\varepsilon_t^2) = \alpha_0(1 - \alpha_1 - \beta_1)^{-1},$$

and

$$\mathrm{E}(\varepsilon_t^4) = 3\alpha_0^2(1+\alpha_1+\beta_1)\left[(1-\alpha_1-\beta_1)(1-\beta_1^2-2\alpha_1\beta_1-3\alpha_1^2)\right]^{-1}.$$

The coefficient of kurtosis is therefore

$$\begin{aligned}\kappa &= \left(\mathrm{E}(\varepsilon_t^4) - 3\mathrm{E}(\varepsilon_t^2)^2\right)\mathrm{E}(\varepsilon_t^2)^{-2} \\ &= 6\alpha_1^2(1-\beta_1^2-2\alpha_1\beta_1-3\alpha_1^2)^{-1},\end{aligned}$$

which is greater than zero by assumption. Hence the GARCH(1,1) process is leptokurtic (heavily tailed), a property the process shares with the ARCH(q) process; cf. Milhøj (1984).

4. Autocorrelation and partial autocorrelation structure

The use of autocorrelation and partial autocorrelation functions to identify and check time series behaviour of the ARMA form in the conditional mean is well established; cf. Box and Jenkins (1976). In this section, the autocorrelation and partial autocorrelation functions for the squared process are shown to be useful in identifying and checking time series behaviour in the conditional variance equation of the GARCH form. The idea of using the squared process to check for model adequacy is not new; cf. Granger and Anderson (1978) where it is found that some of the series modelled in Box and Jenkins (1976) exhibit autocorrelated squared residuals even though the residuals themselves do not seem to be correlated over time.

Consider the general GARCH(p, q) process as specified in (1) and (2), and let us assume the process has finite fourth-order moment.[3] Let the covariance function for ε_t^2 be denoted

$$\gamma_n = \gamma_{-n} = \mathrm{cov}(\varepsilon_t^2, \varepsilon_{t-n}^2). \tag{12}$$

[3] The general conditions for the existence of finite fourth-order moment are unknown. However, given a specific order of the model the conditions may be derived following the same line of arguments as lead to Theorem 2 for the GARCH(1,1) process. For instance the necessary and sufficient condition for the GARCH(1,2) process is found to be

$$\alpha_2 + 3\alpha_1^2 + 3\alpha_2^2 + \beta_1^2 + 2\alpha_1\beta_1 - 3\alpha_2^3 + 3\alpha_1^2\alpha_2 + 6\alpha_1\alpha_2\beta_1 + \alpha_2\beta_1^2 < 1,$$

and for the GARCH(2,1) the condition is

$$\beta_2 + 3\alpha_1^2 + \beta_1^2 + \beta_2^2 + 2\alpha_1\beta_1 - \beta_2^3 - \alpha_1^2\beta_2 + 2\alpha_1\beta_1\beta_2 + \beta_1^2\beta_2 < 1.$$

In Milhøj (1984) the condition for the ARCH(q) process is derived and expressed in terms of the inverse of a $q \times q$ matrix, $3\varphi'(I-\phi)^{-1}\varphi < 1$, where $\varphi' = (\alpha_1, \ldots, \alpha_q)$, $\phi_{ij} = \varphi_{i+j} + \varphi_{i-j}$, $i, j = 1, \ldots, q$, and $\varphi_k = 0$ for $k \le 0$ and $k > q$.

It follows then immediately from (6) and (7) that

$$\gamma_n = \sum_{i=1}^{q} \alpha_i \gamma_{n-i} + \sum_{i=1}^{p} \beta_i \gamma_{n-i}$$
$$= \sum_{i=1}^{m} \varphi_i \gamma_{n-i}, \qquad n \geq p+1, \tag{13}$$

where $m = \max\{p, q\}$,

$$\varphi_i = \alpha_i + \beta_i, \qquad i = 1, \ldots, q,$$

$\alpha_i \equiv 0$ for $i > q$ and $\beta_i \equiv 0$ for $i > p$. From (13) we get the following analogue to the Yule–Walker equations:

$$\rho_n = \gamma_n \gamma_0^{-1} = \sum_{i=1}^{m} \varphi_i \rho_{n-i}, \qquad n \geq p+1. \tag{14}$$

Thus, the first p autocorrelations for ε_t^2 depend 'directly' on the parameters $\alpha_1, \ldots, \alpha_q$, $\beta_1, \ldots, \beta_p$, but given $\rho_p, \ldots, \rho_{p+1-m}$ the above difference equation uniquely determines the autocorrelations at higher lags. This is similar to the result for the autocorrelations for an ARMA(m, p) process; cf. Box and Jenkins (1976). Note also, that (14) depends on the parameters $\alpha_1, \ldots, \alpha_q$, $\beta_1, \ldots, \beta_p$ only through $\varphi_1, \ldots, \varphi_m$.

Let ϕ_{kk} denote the kth partial autocorrelation for ε_t^2 found by solving the set of k equations in the k unknown $\phi_{k1}, \ldots, \phi_{kk}$:

$$\rho_n = \sum_{i=1}^{k} \phi_{ki} \rho_{n-i}, \qquad n = 1, \ldots, k. \tag{15}$$

By (14) ϕ_{kk} cuts off after lag q for an ARCH(q) process

$$\phi_{kk} \neq 0, \qquad k \leq q,$$
$$= 0, \qquad k > q. \tag{16}$$

This is identical to the behaviour of the partial autocorrelation function for an AR(q) process. Also from (14) and well-known results in the time series literature, the partial autocorrelation function for ε_t^2 for a GARCH(p, q) process is in general non-zero but dies out; see Granger and Newbold (1977).

In practice, of course, the ρ_n's and ϕ_{kk}'s will be unknown. However, the sample analogue, say $\hat{\rho}_n$, yields a consistent estimate for ρ_n, and ϕ_{kk} is consistently estimated by the kth coefficient, say $\hat{\phi}_{kk}$, in a kth-order autoregression for ε_t^2; see Granger and Newbold (1977). These estimates together with their asymptotic variance under the null of no GARCH $1/T$ [cf. Weiss (1984) and McLeod and Li (1983)] can be used in the preliminary identification stage, and are also useful for diagnostic checking.

5. Estimation of the GARCH regression model

In this section we consider maximum likelihood estimation of the GARCH regression model (1), (2), (3). Because the results are quite similar to those for the ARCH regression model, our discussion will be very schematic.

Let $z_t' = (1, \varepsilon_{t-1}^2, \dots, \varepsilon_{t-q}^2, h_{t-1}, \dots, h_{t-p})$, $\omega' = (\alpha_0, \alpha_1, \dots, \alpha_q, \beta_1, \dots, \beta_p)$ and $\theta \in \Theta$, where $\theta = (b', w')$ and Θ is a compact subspace of a Euclidean space such that ε_t possesses finite second moments. Denote the true parameters by θ_0, where $\theta_0 \in \operatorname{int} \Theta$. We may then rewrite the model as

$$\begin{aligned} \varepsilon_t &= y_t - x_t' b, \\ \varepsilon_t | \psi_{t-1} &\sim \mathrm{N}(0, h_t), \\ h_t &= z_t' \omega. \end{aligned} \tag{17}$$

The log likelihood function for a sample of T observations is apart from some constant,[4]

$$\begin{aligned} L_T(\theta) &= T^{-1} \sum_{t=1}^{T} l_t(\theta), \\ l_t(\theta) &= -\tfrac{1}{2} \log h_t - \tfrac{1}{2} \varepsilon_t^2 h_t^{-1}. \end{aligned} \tag{18}$$

Differentiating with respect to the variance parameter yields

$$\frac{\partial l_t}{\partial \omega} = \tfrac{1}{2} h_t^{-1} \frac{\partial h_t}{\partial \omega} \left(\frac{\varepsilon_t^2}{h_t} - 1 \right), \tag{19}$$

$$\frac{\partial^2 l_t}{\partial \omega\, \partial \omega'} = \left(\frac{\varepsilon_t^2}{h_t} - 1 \right) \frac{\partial}{\partial \omega'} \left[\tfrac{1}{2} h_t^{-1} \frac{\partial h_t}{\partial \omega} \right] - \tfrac{1}{2} h_t^{-2} \frac{\partial h_t}{\partial \omega} \frac{\partial h_t}{\partial \omega'} \frac{\varepsilon_t^2}{h_t}, \tag{20}$$

[4] For simplicity we are conditioning on the pre-sample values. This does of course not affect the asymptotic results; cf. Weiss (1982).

where

$$\frac{\partial h_t}{\partial \omega} = z_t + \sum_{i=1}^{p} \beta_i \frac{\partial h_{t-i}}{\partial \omega}. \tag{21}$$

The only difference from Engle (1982) is the inclusion of the recursive part in (21).[5] Note, $B(1) < 1$ guarantees that (21) is stable. Since the conditional expectation of the first term in (20) is zero, the part of Fisher's information matrix corresponding to ω is consistently estimated by the sample analogue of the last term in (20) which involves first derivatives only.

Differentiating with respect to the mean parameters yields

$$\frac{\partial l_t}{\partial b} = \varepsilon_t x_t h_t^{-1} + \tfrac{1}{2} h_t \frac{\partial h_t}{\partial b}\left(\frac{\varepsilon_t^2}{h_t} - 1\right), \tag{22}$$

$$\frac{\partial^2 l_t}{\partial b\, \partial b'} = -h_t^{-1} x_t x_t' - \tfrac{1}{2} h_t^{-2} \frac{\partial h_t}{\partial b} \frac{\partial h_t}{\partial b'}\left(\frac{\varepsilon_t^2}{h_t}\right)$$
$$- 2 h_t^{-2} \varepsilon_t x_t \frac{\partial h_t}{\partial b} + \left(\frac{\varepsilon_t^2}{h_t} - 1\right) \frac{\partial}{\partial b'}\left[\tfrac{1}{2} h_t^{-1} \frac{\partial h_t}{\partial b}\right], \tag{23}$$

where

$$\frac{\partial h_t}{\partial b} = -2 \sum_{j=1}^{q} \alpha_j x_{t-j} \varepsilon_{t-j} + \sum_{j=1}^{p} \beta_j \frac{\partial h_{t-j}}{\partial b}. \tag{24}$$

Again the single difference from the ARCH(q) regression model is the inclusion of the recursive part in (24). A consistent estimate of the part of the information matrix corresponding to b is given by the sample analogue of the first two terms in (23) but with $\varepsilon_t^2 h_t^{-1}$ in the second term replaced by its expected value of one. This estimate will also involve first derivatives only.

Finally, the elements in the off-diagonal block in the information matrix may be shown to be zero. Because of this asymptotic independence ω can be estimated without loss of asymptotic efficiency based on a consistent estimate of b, and vice versa.

To obtain maximum likelihood estimates, and second-order efficiency, an iterative procedure is called for. For the ARCH(q) regression model the method of scoring could be expressed in terms of a simple auxiliary regression, but the recursive terms in (21) and (24) complicate this procedure. Instead the

[5] To start up the recursion we need pre-sample estimates for h_t and ε_t^2, $t \leq 0$. A natural choice is the sample analogue $T^{-1}\sum_{t=1}^{T}\varepsilon_t^2$.

Berndt, Hall, Hall and Hausman (1974) algorithm turns out to be convenient. Let $\theta^{(i)}$ denote the parameter estimates after the ith iteration. $\theta^{(i+1)}$ is then calculated from

$$\theta^{(i+1)} = \theta^{(i)} + \lambda_i \left(\sum_{t=1}^{T} \frac{\partial l_t}{\partial \theta} \frac{\partial l_t}{\partial \theta'} \right)^{-1} \sum_{t=1}^{T} \frac{\partial l_t}{\partial \theta},$$

where $\partial l_t / \partial \theta$ is evaluated at $\theta^{(i)}$, and λ_i is a variable step length chosen to maximize the likelihood function in the given direction. Note, the direction vector is easily calculated from a least squares regression of a $T \times 1$ vector of ones on $\partial l_t / \partial \theta$. Also, the iterations for $\omega^{(i)}$ and $b^{(i)}$ may be carried out separately because of the block diagonality in the information matrix.

From Weiss (1982) it follows that the maximum likelihood estimate $\hat{\theta}_T$ is strongly consistent for θ_0 and asymptotically normal with mean θ_0 and covariance matrix $\mathscr{F}^{-1} = -\mathrm{E}(\partial^2 l_t / \partial \theta \partial \theta')^{-1}$. However, $\mathscr{F} = F$, where $F = \mathrm{E}((\partial l_t / \partial \theta)(\partial l_t / \partial \theta'))$, and a consistent estimate of the asymptotic covariance matrix is therefore given by $T^{-1}(\sum_{t=1}^{T}(\partial l_t / \partial \theta)(\partial l_t / \partial \theta'))^{-1}$ from the last BHHH iteration.

Replacing (1) with the weaker set of assumptions

$$\begin{aligned} &\mathrm{E}(\varepsilon_t | \psi_{t-1}) = 0, \\ &\mathrm{E}(\varepsilon_t^2 h_t^{-1} | \psi_{t-1}) = 1, \qquad (25) \\ &\mathrm{E}(\varepsilon_t^4 h_t^{-2} | \psi_{t-1}) \leq M < \infty, \end{aligned}$$

$\hat{\theta}_T$ is still strongly consistent for θ_0 and asymptotically normal with mean θ_0 but with covariance matrix $\mathscr{F}^{-1} F \mathscr{F}^{-1}$; see Weiss (1982) and White (1982). Of course, if the true conditional distribution is normal, $F = \mathscr{F}$ and therefore $\mathscr{F}^{-1} F \mathscr{F}^{-1} = \mathscr{F}^{-1}$.

6. Testing for GARCH

Because of the complication involved in estimating a GARCH process, it seems of interest to have a formal test for the presence of GARCH instead of just relying on the more informal tools developed in section 4.

Consider the GARCH(p, q) regression model (17). As in Engle and Kraft (1983) let us partition the conditional variance equation

$$h_t = z_t' \omega = z_{1t}' \omega_1 + z_{2t}' \omega_2. \qquad (26)$$

The Lagrange multiplier test statistic for H_0: $\omega_2 = 0$ is then given by[6]

$$\xi^*_{LM} = \tfrac{1}{2} f_0' Z_0 (Z_0' Z_0)^{-1} Z_0' f_0, \tag{27}$$

where

$$f_0 = (\varepsilon_1^2 h_1^{-1} - 1, \ldots, \varepsilon_T^2 h_T^{-1} - 1)',$$

$$Z_0 = \left(h_1 \frac{\partial h_1}{\partial \omega}, \ldots, h_T \frac{\partial h_T}{\partial \omega} \right)', \tag{28}$$

and both are evaluated under H_0. When H_0 is true, ξ^*_{LM} is asymptotically chi-square with r, the number of elements in ω_2, degrees of freedom. This test differs slightly from the standard results, Breusch and Pagan (1978), in that $\partial h_t / \partial \omega$ does not simplify when the conditional variance equation contains lagged conditional variances; cf. eq. (21).

It is well known that by normality an asymptotically equivalent test statistic is

$$\xi_{LM} = T \cdot R^2,$$

where R^2 is the squared multiple correlation coefficient between f_0 and Z_0. From section 5 this corresponds to $T \cdot R^2$ from the OLS regression in the first BHHH iteration for the general model starting at the maximum likelihood estimates under H_0.

The alternative as represented by z_{2t} needs some consideration. Straightforward calculations show that under the null of white noise, $Z_0' Z_0$ is singular if both $p > 0$ and $q > 0$, and therefore a general test for GARCH(p, q) is not feasible. In fact if the null is an ARCH(q) process, $Z_0' Z_0$ is singular for GARCH($r_1, q + r_2$) alternatives, where $r_1 > 0$ and $r_2 > 0$. It is also interesting to note that for an ARCH(q) null, the LM test for GARCH(r, q) and ARCH($q + r$) alternatives coincide. This is similar to the results in Godfrey (1978), where it is shown that the LM tests for AR(p) and MA(q) errors in a linear regression model coincide and that the test procedures break down when a full ARMA(p, q) model is considered. These test results are, of course, not peculiar to the LM test, but concern the Likelihood Ratio and the Wald tests as well. A formal proof of the above statements can be constructed along the same lines as in Godfrey (1978, 1981).

[6] Note, because of the block diagonality in the information matrix in the GARCH regression model, the same test applies in this more general context.

7. Empirical example

The uncertainty of inflation is an unobservable economic variable of major importance, and within the ARCH framework several different models have already been constructed; see Engle (1982), Engle (1983) and Engle and Kraft (1983). We will here concentrate on the model in Engle and Kraft (1983) where the rate of growth in the implicit GNP deflator in the U.S. is explained in terms of its own past.

Let $\pi_t = 100 \cdot \ln(GD_t/GD_{t-1})$ where GD_t is the implicit price deflator for GNP.[7] Standard univariate time series methods lead to identification of the following model for π_t:

$$\pi_t = \underset{(0.080)}{0.240} + \underset{(0.083)}{0.552}\pi_{t-1} + \underset{(0.089)}{0.177}\pi_{t-2} + \underset{(0.090)}{0.232}\pi_{t-3} - \underset{(0.080)}{0.209}\pi_{t-4} + \varepsilon_t,$$

$$h_t = \underset{(0.034)}{0.282}. \tag{29}$$

The model is estimated on quarterly data from 1948.2 to 1983.4, i.e., a total of 143 observations, using ordinary least squares, with OLS standard errors in parentheses.[8] The model is stationary, and none of the first ten autocorrelations or partial autocorrelations for ε_t are significant at the 5% level. However, looking at the autocorrelations for ε_t^2 it turns out that the 1st, 3rd, 7th, 9th and 10th all exceed two asymptotic standard errors. Similar results hold for the partial autocorrelations for ε_t^2. The LM test for ARCH(1), ARCH(4) and ARCH(8) are also highly significant at any reasonable level.

This leads Engle and Kraft (1983) to suggest the following specification:

$$\pi_t = \underset{(0.059)}{0.138} + \underset{(0.081)}{0.423}\pi_{t-1} + \underset{(0.108)}{0.222}\pi_{t-2} + \underset{(0.078)}{0.377}\pi_{t-3} - \underset{(0.104)}{0.175}\pi_{t-4} + \varepsilon_t,$$

$$h_t = \underset{(0.033)}{0.058} + \underset{(0.265)}{0.802} \sum_{i=1}^{8} (9-i)/36\varepsilon_{t-i}^2. \tag{30}$$

The estimates are maximum likelihood with heteroskedastic consistent standard errors in parentheses; see section 5. The choice of the eighth-order linear declining lag structure is rather ad hoc, but motivated by the long memory in the conditional variance equation. The order of the lag polynomial may be viewed as an additional parameter in the conditional variance equation. From

[7] The values of GD_t are taken from the Citibank Economic Database and U.S. Department of Commerce, *Survey of Current Business*, Vol. 64, no. 9, September 1984.

[8] Note, in Engle and Kraft (1983) the estimation period is 1948.2 to 1980.3 accounting for the small differences in the estimation results.

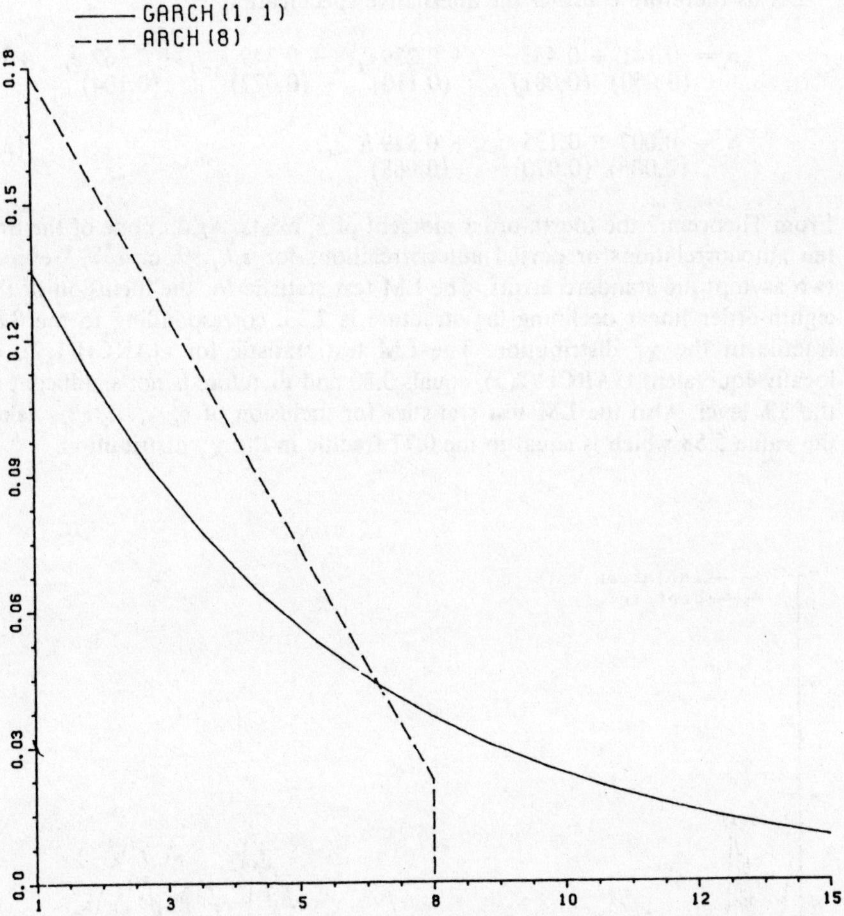

Fig. 2. Lag distribution.

Milhøj (1984) the condition for existence of the fourth-order moment of ε_t is just met.[9] None of the first ten autocorrelations or partial autocorrelations for $\varepsilon_t h_t^{-1/2}$ or $\varepsilon_t^2 h_t^{-1}$ exceed $2/\sqrt{143}$. The LM test statistics for the linear restriction takes the value 8.87, corresponding to the 0.74 fractile in the χ_7^2 distribution. However, the LM test statistic for the inclusion of h_{t-1} in the conditional variance equation is 4.57, which is significant at the 5% level.

[9] The condition as discussed in footnote 3 takes the value 0.989 for 0.802.

Let us therefore consider the alternative specification

$$\underset{}{\pi_t} = \underset{(0.060)}{0.141} + \underset{(0.081)}{0.433}\pi_{t-1} + \underset{(0.110)}{0.229}\pi_{t-2} + \underset{(0.077)}{0.349}\pi_{t-3} - \underset{(0.104)}{0.162}\pi_{t-4} + \varepsilon_t,$$

$$h_t = \underset{(0.006)}{0.007} + \underset{(0.070)}{0.135}\varepsilon^2_{t-1} + \underset{(0.068)}{0.829}h_{t-1}. \tag{31}$$

From Theorem 2 the fourth-order moment of ε_t exists. Again none of the first ten autocorrelations or partial autocorrelations for $\varepsilon_t h_t^{-1/2}$ or $\varepsilon_t^2 h_t^{-1}$ exceed two asymptotic standard errors. The LM test statistic for the inclusion of the eighth-order linear declining lag structure is 2.33, corresponding to the 0.87 fractile in the χ_1^2 distribution. The LM test statistic for GARCH(1,2), or locally equivalent GARCH(2,1), equals 3.80 and therefore is not significant at the 5% level. Also the LM test statistics for inclusion of $\varepsilon^2_{t-2}, \ldots, \varepsilon^2_{t-5}$ takes the value 5.58 which is equal to the 0.77 fractile in the χ_4^2 distribution.

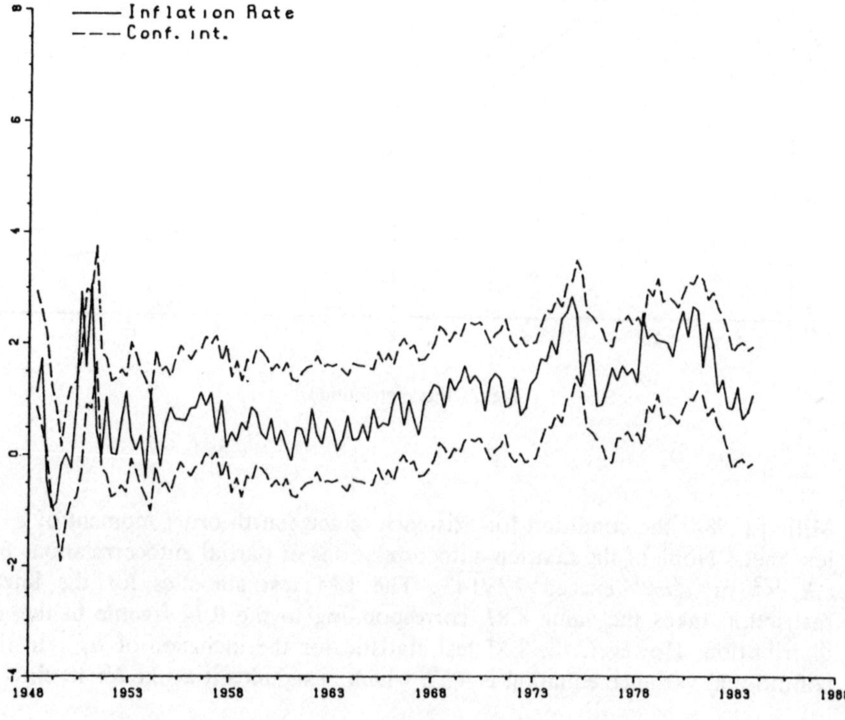

Fig. 3. 95% confidence intervals for OLS.

It is also interesting to note that the sample coefficient of kurtosis for $\varepsilon_t h_t^{-1/2}$ from model (31) equals 3.81, which differs from the 'normal' value of 3.00 by slightly less than two asymptotic standard errors, $2\sqrt{24/T} \simeq 0.82$. For models (29) and (30) the coefficient of kurtosis equals 6.90 and 4.07, respectively. The sample coefficient of skewness for $\varepsilon_t h_t^{-1/2}$ from each of the three models, -0.13, 0.18 and 0.11, are all within one asymptotic standard error, $\sqrt{6/T} \simeq 0.20$.

The mean and median lag in the conditional variance equation in (31) are estimated to be 5.848 and 3.696, respectively [cf. section 3], whereas in (30) the mean lag is forced to $3\frac{1}{3}$ and the median lag to $2\frac{1}{2}$. Furthermore, the lag structure in the GARCH(1,1) model can be rationalized by some sort of adaptive learning mechanism. See also fig. 2, where the two different lag shapes are illustrated. In this light it seems that not only does the GARCH(1,1) model provide a slightly better fit than the ARCH(8) model in Engle and Kraft (1983), but it also exhibits a more reasonable lag structure.

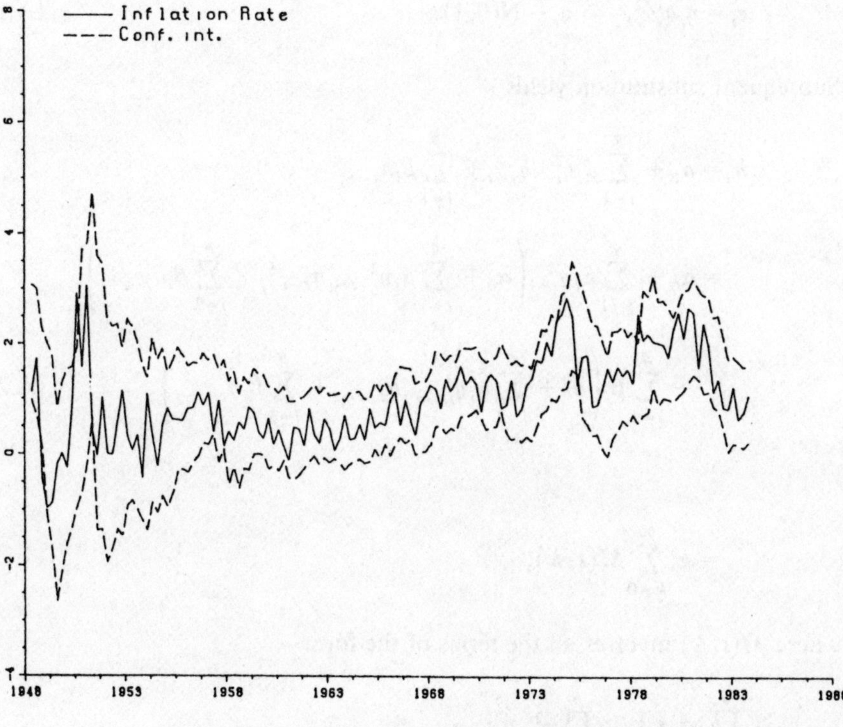

Fig. 4. 95% confidence intervals for GARCH(1,1).

In figs. 3 and 4 the actual inflation rate, π_t, is graphed together with 95% asymptotic confidence intervals for the one-step-ahead forecast errors for the two models (29) and (31). From the late forties until the mid-fifties the inflation rate was very volatile and hard to predict. This is reflected in the wide confidence intervals for the GARCH model. The sixties and early seventies, however, were characterized by a stable and predictable inflation rate, and the OLS confidence interval seems much too wide. Starting with the second oil crises in 1974 there is a slight increase in the uncertainty of the inflation rate, although it does not compare in magnitude to the uncertainty at the beginning of the sample period.

Appendix

A.1. Proof of Theorem 1

The basic idea of the proof follows that of Theorem 1 in Milhøj (1984). By definition

$$\varepsilon_t = \eta_t h_t^{1/2}, \qquad \eta_t \overset{\text{iid}}{\sim} \mathrm{N}(0,1). \tag{A.1}$$

Subsequent substitution yields

$$\begin{aligned} h_t &= \alpha_0 + \sum_{i=1}^{q} \alpha_i \eta_{t-i}^2 h_{t-i} + \sum_{i=1}^{p} \beta_i h_{t-i} \\ &= \alpha_0 + \sum_{j=1}^{q} \alpha_j \eta_{t-j}^2 \left(\alpha_0 + \sum_{i=1}^{q} \alpha_i \eta_{t-i-j}^2 h_{t-i-j} + \sum_{i=1}^{p} \beta_i h_{t-i-j} \right) \\ &\quad + \sum_{j=1}^{p} \beta_j \left(\alpha_0 + \sum_{i=1}^{q} \alpha_i \eta_{t-i-j}^2 h_{t-i-j} + \sum_{i=1}^{p} \beta_i h_{t-i-j} \right) \qquad \text{(A.2)} \\ &\;\;\vdots \\ &= \alpha_0 \sum_{k=0}^{\infty} M(t,k), \end{aligned}$$

where $M(t,k)$ involves all the terms of the form

$$\prod_{i=1}^{q} \alpha_i^{a_i} \prod_{j=1}^{p} \beta_j^{b_j} \prod_{l=1}^{n} \eta_{t-s_l}^2,$$

for

$$\sum_{i=1}^{q} a_i + \sum_{j=1}^{p} b_j = k, \qquad \sum_{i=1}^{q} a_i = n,$$

and

$$1 \leq S_1 < S_2 < \cdots < S_n \leq \max\{kq, (k-1)q + p\}.$$

Thus,

$$M(t,0) = 1,$$

$$M(t,1) = \sum_{i=1}^{q} \alpha_i \eta_{t-i}^2 + \sum_{i=1}^{p} \beta_i,$$

$$M(t,2) = \sum_{j=1}^{q} \alpha_j \eta_{t-j}^2 \left(\sum_{i=1}^{q} \alpha_i \eta_{t-i-j}^2 + \sum_{i=1}^{p} \beta_i \right)$$

$$+ \sum_{j=1}^{p} \beta_j \left(\sum_{i=1}^{q} \alpha_i \eta_{t-i-j}^2 + \sum_{i=1}^{p} \beta_i \right),$$

and in general

$$M(t, k+1) = \sum_{i=1}^{q} \alpha_i \eta_{t-i}^2 M(t-i, k) + \sum_{i=1}^{p} \beta_i M(t-i, k). \tag{A.3}$$

Since η_t^2 is i.i.d., the moments of $M(t,k)$ do not depend on t, and in particular

$$\mathrm{E}(M(t,k)) = \mathrm{E}(M(s,k)) \quad \text{for all } k, t, s, \tag{A.4}$$

From (A.3) and (A.4) we get

$$\mathrm{E}(M(t,k+1)) = \left(\sum_{i=1}^{q} \alpha_i + \sum_{i=1}^{p} \beta_i \right) \mathrm{E}(M(t,k))$$

$$\vdots$$

$$= \left(\sum_{i=1}^{q} \alpha_i + \sum_{i=1}^{p} \beta_i \right)^{k+1} \mathrm{E}(M(t,0)) \tag{A.5}$$

$$= \left(\sum_{i=1}^{q} \alpha_i + \sum_{i=1}^{p} \beta_i \right)^{k+1}.$$

Finally by (A.1), (A.2) and (A.5),

$$\begin{aligned}\mathrm{E}(\varepsilon_t^2) &= \alpha_0 \mathrm{E}\left(\sum_{k=0}^{\infty} M(t,k)\right) \\ &= \alpha_0 \sum_{k=0}^{\infty} \mathrm{E}(M(t,k)) \\ &= \alpha_0 \left(1 - \sum_{i=1}^{q} \alpha_i - \sum_{i=1}^{p} \beta_i\right)^{-1},\end{aligned} \tag{A.6}$$

if and only if

$$\sum_{i=1}^{q} \alpha_i + \sum_{i=1}^{p} \beta_i < 1,$$

and ε_t^2 converges almost surely.

$\mathrm{E}(\varepsilon_t) = 0$ and $\mathrm{cov}(\varepsilon_t, \varepsilon_s) = 0$ for $t \neq s$ follows immediately by symmetry.

A.2. Proof of Theorem 2

By normality

$$\mathrm{E}(\varepsilon_t^{2m}) = a_m \mathrm{E}(h_t^m), \tag{A.7}$$

where a_m is defined in (10). The binomial formula yields

$$\begin{aligned}h_t^m &= \left(\alpha_0 + \alpha_1 \varepsilon_{t-1}^2 + \beta_1 h_{t-1}\right)^m \\ &= \sum_{n=0}^{m} \binom{m}{n} \alpha_0^{m-n} \sum_{j=0}^{n} \binom{n}{j} \alpha_1^j \beta_1^{n-j} \varepsilon_{t-1}^{2j} h_{t-1}^{n-j}.\end{aligned}$$

Because

$$\mathrm{E}(\varepsilon_{t-1}^{2j} h_{t-1}^{n-j} | \psi_{t-2}) = a_j h_{t-1}^n,$$

we have

$$\mathrm{E}(h_t^m | \psi_{t-2}) = \sum_{n=0}^{m} h_{t-1}^n \binom{m}{n} \alpha_0^{m-n} \sum_{j=0}^{n} \binom{n}{j} a_j \alpha_1^j \beta_1^{n-j}. \tag{A.8}$$

Let $w_t = (h_t^m, h_t^{m-1}, \dots, h_t)'$, then by (A.8)

$$\mathrm{E}(w_t | \psi_{t-2}) = d + C w_{t-1}, \tag{A.9}$$

where C is an $m \times m$ upper triangular matrix with diagonal elements.

$$\mu(\alpha_1, \beta_1, i) = \sum_{j=0}^{i} \binom{i}{j} a_j \alpha_1^j \beta_1^{i-j}, \qquad i = 1, \ldots, m. \tag{A.10}$$

Substituting in (A.9) yields

$$\mathrm{E}(w_t | \psi_{t-k-1}) = (I + C + C^2 + \cdots + C^{k-1})d + C^k w_{t-k}.$$

Since the process is assumed to start indefinitely far in the past with finite $2m$ moments, the limit as k goes to infinity exists and does not depend on t if and only if all the eigenvalues of C lie inside the unit circle,

$$\lim_{k \to \infty} \mathrm{E}(w_t | \psi_{t-k-1}) = (I - C)^{-1} d = \mathrm{E}(w_t).$$

Because C is upper triangular, the eigenvalues are equal to the diagonal elements as given in (A.10). Tedious, but rather straightforward calculations show that $\mu(\alpha_1, \beta_1, i) < 1$ implies $\mu(\alpha_1, \beta_1, i-1) < 1$ for $\alpha_1 + \beta_1 \leq 1$, and $\mu(\alpha, \beta_1, m) < 1$ suffices for the $2m$th moment to exist; cf. fig. 1.

Finally (11) follows from (A.7) and (A.8) by rearranging terms.

References

Berndt, E.K., B.H. Hall, R.E. Hall and J.A. Hausman, 1974, Estimation inference in nonlinear structural models, Annals of Economic and Social Measurement, no. 4, 653–665.

Box, G.E.P. and J.M. Jenkins, 1976, Time series analysis: Forecasting and control (Holden-Day, San Francisco, CA).

Breusch, T.S. and A.R. Pagan, 1978, A simple test for heteroskedastic city and random coefficient variation, Econometrica 46, 1287–1294.

Coulson, N.E. and R.P. Robins, 1985, Aggregate economic activity and the variance of inflation: Another look, Economics Letters 17, 71–75.

Domowitz, I. and C.S. Hakkio, 1985, Conditional variance and the risk premium in the foreign exchange market, Journal of International Economics 19, 47–66.

Engle, R.F., 1982, Autoregressive conditional heteroskedasticity with estimates of the variance of U.K. inflation, Econometrica 50, 987–1008.

Engle, R.F., 1983, Estimates of the variance of U.S. inflation based on the ARCH model, Journal of Money Credit and Banking 15, 286–301.

Engle, R.F. and D. Kraft, 1983, Multiperiod forecast error variances of inflation estimated from ARCH models, in: A. Zellner, ed., Applied time series analysis of economic data (Bureau of the Census, Washington, DC) 293–302.

Engle, R.F., D. Lilien and R. Robins, 1985, Estimation of time varying risk premiums in the term structure, Discussion paper 85-17 (University of California, San Diego, CA).

Garbade, K., 1977, Two methods for examining the stability of regression coefficients, Journal of the American Statistical Association 72, 54–63.

Godfrey, L.J., 1978, Testing against general autoregressive and moving average error models when the regressors include lagged dependent variables, Econometrica 46, 1293–1302.

Godfrey, L.J., 1981, On the invariance of the Lagrange multiplier test with respect to certain changes in the alternative hypothesis, Econometrica 49, 1443–1455.

Granger, C.W.J. and A.P. Andersen, 1978, An introduction to bilinear time series models (Vandenhoeck and Ruprecht, Göttingen).
Granger, C.W.J. and P. Newbold, 1977, Forecasting economic time series (Academic Press, New York).
Harvey, A.C., 1982, The econometric analysis of time series (Philip Allen, Oxford).
McCulloch, J.H., 1983, Interest-risk sensitive deposit insurance premia: Adaptive conditional heteroscedastic estimates, Discussion paper, June (Ohio State University, Columbus, OH).
McLeod, A.J. and W.K. Li, 1900, Diagnostic checking ARMA time series models using squared-residual autocorrelations, Journal of Time Series Analysis 4, 269–273.
Milhøj, A., 1984, The moment structure of ARCH processes, Research report 94 (Institute of Statistics, University of Copenhagen, Copenhagen).
Weiss, A.A., 1982, Asymptotic theory for ARCH models: Stability, estimation and testing, Discussion paper 82-36 (University of California, San Diego, CA).
Weiss, A.A., 1984, ARMA models with ARCH errors, Journal of Time Series Analysis 5, 129–143.
White, H., 1982, Maximum likelihood estimation of misspecified models, Econometrica 50, 1–25.

[16]

Econometrica, Vol. 57, No. 2 (March, 1989), 357–384

A NEW APPROACH TO THE ECONOMIC ANALYSIS OF NONSTATIONARY TIME SERIES AND THE BUSINESS CYCLE

BY JAMES D. HAMILTON[1]

This paper proposes a very tractable approach to modeling changes in regime. The parameters of an autoregression are viewed as the outcome of a discrete-state Markov process. For example, the mean growth rate of a nonstationary series may be subject to occasional, discrete shifts.

The econometrician is presumed not to observe these shifts directly, but instead must draw probabilistic inference about whether and when they may have occurred based on the observed behavior of the series. The paper presents an algorithm for drawing such probabilistic inference in the form of a nonlinear iterative filter. The filter also permits estimation of population parameters by the method of maximum likelihood and provides the foundation for forecasting future values of the series.

An empirical application of this technique to postwar U.S. real GNP suggests that the periodic shift from a positive growth rate to a negative growth rate is a recurrent feature of the U.S. business cycle, and indeed could be used as an objective criterion for defining and measuring economic recessions. The estimated parameter values suggest that a typical economic recession is associated with a 3% permanent drop in the level of GNP.

KEYWORDS: Switching regression, segmentation, nonstationary, business cycle, nonlinear filtering, regime changes.

1. INTRODUCTION AND SUMMARY

A NUMBER OF RECENT STUDIES have sought to characterize the nature of the long term trend in GNP and its relation to the business cycle. Researchers such as Beveridge and Nelson (1981), Nelson and Plosser (1982), and Campbell and Mankiw (1987a, b) explored this question using ARIMA models or ARMA processes around a deterministic trend. Others, such as Harvey (1985), Watson (1986), and Clark (1987) based their analyses on linear unobserved components models. A third approach employs the co-integrated specification of Engle and Granger (1987), whose relevance for business cycle research is examined in a fascinating paper by King, Plosser, Stock, and Watson (1987).

These approaches are based on the assumption that first differences of the log of GNP follow a linear stationary process; that is, in all of the above studies, optimal forecasts of variables are assumed to be a linear function of their lagged values. In this paper I suggest a modest alternative to these currently popular approaches to nonstationarity, exploring the consequences of specifying that first differences of the observed series follow a nonlinear stationary process rather than a linear stationary process. A variety of parameterizations for characterizing nonlinear dynamics have recently been proposed, and there has now accumulated

[1] I am indebted to John Cochrane, Angus Deaton, Robert Engle, Marjorie Flavin, Kevin Hassett, and anonymous referees for comments on earlier drafts of this paper. This material is based upon work supported by the National Science Foundation under Grant No. SES-8720731. The Government has certain rights to this material.

abundant evidence that departures from linearity are an important feature of many key macro series. Studies establishing such nonlinearities include the bispectral analysis of Hinich and Patterson (1985), documentation of business cycle asymmetries by Neftci (1984) and Sichel (1987), the ARCH-M model of Engle, Lilien, and Robins (1987), Stock's (1987) time transformation, chaos models (Brock and Sayers, 1988), Gallant and Tauchen's (1987) "seminonparametric" approach to modeling dynamics, and Quah's (1987) "clinging" process.

The nonlinearities with which my paper is concerned arise if the process is subject to discrete shifts in regime—episodes across which the dynamic behavior of the series is markedly different. My basic approach is to use Goldfeld and Quandt's (1973) Markov switching regression to characterize changes in the parameters of an autoregressive process. For example, the economy may either be in a fast growth or slow growth phase, with the switch between the two governed by the outcome of a Markov process. Building upon ideas developed by Cosslett and Lee (1985), a nonlinear filter and smoother are presented for uncovering optimal statistical estimates of the state of the economy based on observations of output. As in the Kalman filter, one is using the time path of an observed series to draw inference about an unobserved state variable. But whereas the Kalman filter is a linear algorithm for generating estimates of a continuous unobserved state vector, the filter and smoother in this paper provide nonlinear inference about a discrete-valued unobserved state vector.

A very similar stochastic specification has also been explored by Aoki (1967, p. 131), Tong (1983, p. 62), and Sclove (1983), though the statistical approach of these researchers was quite different from the one suggested here. Aoki discussed control of such systems but did not develop the estimation algorithm presented in this paper. Tong treated the shifts in regime as directly observable, whereas the core of my paper addresses optimal probabilistic inference about such shifts based on the observed behavior of GNP. Sclove calculated what the likelihood function would have been if the regimes were observable, and then assumed that the actual historical regimes were those that would make this joint likelihood of GNP along with unobserved regimes as big as possible. My approach, by contrast, is to solve for the actual marginal likelihood function for GNP, maximize this likelihood function with respect to population parameters, and then use these parameters and the data to draw the optimal statistical inference about the unobserved regimes.

My algorithm might also be viewed as formalizing the statistical identification of "turning points" of a time series. Modern treatments by Wecker (1979), Neftci (1982), and Diebold and Rudebusch (1987) provide references to some of the earlier work and interest on this question. Wecker discussed optimal forecasts of an "indicator function" (e.g., $z_t = 1$ if both $y_{t-1} < y_t$ and $y_t > y_{t+1}$). Wecker's indicator is imposed more or less arbitrarily on an otherwise linear process; in my specification, by contrast, the "turning point" is a structural event that is inherent in the data-generating process. Neftci (1982) analyzed the case where (1) only the most recent turning point influences the density function for current observations, and (2) there is known to be a possibility of at most one turning point observed during a given interval (t_1, t_2). These assumptions could also be imposed as a special case of the general framework studied here, generating Neftci's algorithm for dating turning points as a special case of the basic filter used in this study.

The filter also has a clear analog in the analysis of Liptser and Shiryayev (1977), who developed a nonlinear continuous-time filter for a similar problem.[2] The discrete-time filter developed here has three distinct advantages over their treatment. First, if one used Liptser and Shiryayev's formula (which is only strictly valid for continuous time) to approximate discrete changes over short intervals of time, in principle one could end up generating a probability outside the unit interval. By contrast, all probabilities generated by the filter and smoother proposed in this paper are exact, and so lie in $[0,1]$ by construction. Second, a natural byproduct of the discrete-time filter used here is evaluation of the sample likelihood, permitting ready estimation and hypothesis testing about the system's parameters. Third, the specification adopted in this paper fits in neatly as a complement to conventional time series tools and techniques; for example, present value calculations turn out to be quite straightforward.

My approach could also be viewed as a natural extension of Neftci's (1984) analysis of U.S. unemployment data. In Neftci's specification, the economy is said to be in state 1 whenever unemployment is rising and in state 2 whenever unemployment is falling, with transitions between these two states modeled as the outcome of a second-order Markov process. In my paper, by contrast, the unobserved state is only one of many influences governing the dynamic process followed by output, so that even when the economy is in the "fast growth" state, output in principle might be observed to decrease.

The paper applies the technique to postwar U.S. data on real GNP. One possible outcome of maximum likelihood estimation of parameters might have been the identification of long-term trends in the U.S. economy, separating periods with faster growth from those with slower growth. In fact, this is not what was found. Instead, the best empirical fit to the data is obtained when the growth states of the Markov process are associated in a very direct way with the business cycle. A positive growth rate is associated with normal times, and a negative growth rate associated with recessions. Indeed, the best statistical estimates of which quarters were historically characterized by negative growth states for the U.S. economy are remarkably similar to NBER dating of business cycles, and could be used as an alternative objective algorithm for dating business cycles. The results complement the findings by Nelson and Plosser (1982) and Campbell and Mankiw (1987a, b), who concluded that business cycles are associated with a large permanent effect on the long run level of output. The estimates also provide empirical support for the proposition that the dynamics of recessions are qualitatively distinct from those of normal times in a clear statistical sense, and reinforce Neftci's (1984) and Sichel's (1987) evidence on the asymmetry of U.S. business cycles.

[2]See Liptser and Shiryayev (1977, Theorem (9.1), p. 333).

The plan of the paper is as follows. Section 2 specifies the basic model of trend explored in the paper, and compares it with an ARIMA model with normally distributed innovations. Section 3 characterizes the optimal forecast of the future level of a series generated by such a trend. Section 4 presents one example of how this nonlinear trend might interact with a linear process to generate data, and discusses maximum likelihood estimation and inference about the unobserved state for this case. Section 5 applies the technique to postwar U.S. data on real GNP. Section 6 explores the implications for defining and measuring business cycles, and provides a comparison of alternative approaches. Section 7 presents diagnostics comparing the model with the standard ARIMA specification, while Section 8 addresses the long-term consequences of an economic recession. Brief conclusions are offered in Section 9.

2. A MARKOV MODEL OF TREND

Let n_t denote the trend component of a particular time series $\tilde{y}_t$. I will say that n_t obeys a *Markov trend in levels* if

(2.1) $$n_t = \alpha_1 \cdot s_t + \alpha_0 + n_{t-1}$$

where $s_t = 0$ or 1 denotes the unobserved state of the system.[3] I assume that the transition between states is governed by a first-order Markov process:

(2.2) $$\begin{aligned} &\text{Prob}[S_t = 1 | S_{t-1} = 1] = p, \\ &\text{Prob}[S_t = 0 | S_{t-1} = 1] = 1 - p, \\ &\text{Prob}[S_t = 0 | S_{t-1} = 0] = q, \\ &\text{Prob}[S_t = 1 | S_{t-1} = 0] = 1 - q. \end{aligned}$$

Generalization to a higher-order process and to more than two states is discussed below.

I will describe $\hat{n}_t \equiv \exp(n_t)$ as exhibiting a *Markov trend in logs*.

The stochastic process for S_t (equation 2.2) is strictly stationary, and admits the following AR(1) representation:

(2.3) $$s_t = (1 - q) + \lambda s_{t-1} + v_t,$$

(2.4) $$\lambda \equiv -1 + p + q,$$

where conditional on $S_{t-1} = 1$,

$$\begin{aligned} V_t &= (1 - p) && \text{with probability } p, \\ V_t &= -p && \text{with probability } 1 - p, \end{aligned}$$

conditional on $S_{t-1} = 0$,

$$\begin{aligned} V_t &= -(1 - q) && \text{with probability } q, \\ V_t &= q && \text{with probability } 1 - q. \end{aligned}$$

[3]I adopt the usual notational convention that for discrete-valued variables, capital letters denote the random variable and small letters a particular realization. Both interpretations of course apply to equations such as (2.1), in which I will use small letters by convention.

On the basis of representation (2.3), then, one can view (2.1) as a special case of a standard ARIMA model, albeit with a somewhat unusual probability distribution of the innovation sequence $\{V_t\}$. It is therefore useful to describe in some detail the differences between (2.3) and an AR(1) process driven by normally distributed innovations.

Before doing so, however, note some of the essential properties of (2.3). From (2.3) and the fact that $E_0 V_t = 0$ for all $t > 0$, we see

$$(2.5) \qquad E_0 S_t = \frac{(1-q)(1-\lambda^t)}{(1-\lambda)} + \lambda^t E_0 S_0$$

where E_0 denotes the expectation conditional on information available at date zero (which need not include observation of s_0). Observing that $E_0 S_t$ can be interpreted as the probability that $S_t = 1$ given information available at time zero (denoted $P_0[S_t = 1]$), (2.5) can be rewritten

$$(2.6) \qquad P_0[S_t = 1] = \pi + \lambda^t(\pi_0 - \pi)$$

where

$$(2.7) \qquad \pi \equiv (1-q)/(1-p+1-q),$$
$$\pi_0 \equiv P_0[S_0 = 1].$$

Asymptotically, then, the conditional probability converges to the limiting unconditional probability given by

$$P[S_t = 1] = \pi.$$

As in the case of an ARIMA process with normally distributed innovations, the error term V_t in equation (2.3) is uncorrelated with lagged values of S_t,

$$E[V_t | S_{t-j} = 1] = E[V_t | S_{t-j} = 0] = 0 \qquad \text{for} \quad j = 1, 2, \ldots.$$

In contrast to the normal case, however, V_t is not statistically independent of lagged values of S_t, e.g.,

$$E[V_t^2 | S_{t-1} = 1] = p(1-p),$$
$$E[V_t^2 | S_{t-1} = 0] = q(1-q).$$

The latter property makes an important difference when noise is added to the system. For example, in the model that I will fit to data, I assume that the state s_t is not observed directly, but instead is one of many factors influencing an observed series. To appreciate the difference that arises in this case between (2.1) and an ARIMA model with normal innovations, consider the simplest possible example:

$$(2.8) \qquad y_t = s_t + \varepsilon_t.$$

Here y_t is a stationary process (perhaps the first difference of $\tilde{y}_t$) and $\varepsilon_t \sim N(0, \sigma_\varepsilon^2)$ is an i.i.d. series independent of V_{t-j} for all j. Applying $(1 - \lambda L)$ where L is the lag operator ($L^j x_t = x_{t-j}$) to (2.8),

(2.9) $$y_t - \lambda y_{t-1} = (1-q) + v_t + \varepsilon_t - \lambda\varepsilon_{t-1}.$$

The error term on the right-hand side of (2.9) admits an MA(1) representation,

$$v_t + \varepsilon_t - \lambda\varepsilon_{t-1} = u_t - \theta u_{t-1},$$

or

(2.10) $$u_t = v_t + \theta v_{t-1} + \theta^2 v_{t-2} + \theta^3 v_{t-3} + \cdots + \varepsilon_t + (\theta - \lambda)\varepsilon_{t-1} + (\theta-\lambda)\theta\varepsilon_{t-2} + (\theta-\lambda)\theta^2\varepsilon_{t-3} + \cdots$$

where θ is the value less than one in absolute value that, along with σ_u^2, satisfies

(2.11) $$(1+\theta^2)\sigma_u^2 = (1+\lambda^2)\sigma_\varepsilon^2 + \sigma_v^2$$

(2.12) $$-\theta\sigma_u^2 = -\lambda\sigma_\varepsilon^2,$$

where

(2.13) $$\sigma_v^2 = E(V_t^2) = p(1-p)\pi + q(1-q)(1-\pi).$$

As in the case of V_t, the innovation U_t is uncorrelated with U_{t-j} for $j > 0$, but is not independent. An earlier version of this paper illustrated the relevance of this point by way of example, showing that while $E[U_t(U_{t-1} - \theta U_{t-2})] = 0$, it nonetheless is the case that

$$E\left[U_t(U_{t-1} - \theta U_{t-2})^2\right] = \theta\left(\frac{(1-p)(1-q)(p-q)}{(1-\lambda)}\right)\left(\frac{\theta\lambda^2 - 2\lambda - 1}{1-\theta\lambda}\right),$$

in general not zero. What this means in practical terms is that while one could use the ARMA(1, 1) representation

$$y_t - \lambda y_{t-1} = (1-q) + u_t - \theta u_{t-1}$$

as a basis for forecasting y_{t+j} as a linear function of $y_t, y_{t-1}, \ldots$, these forecasts are not optimal; nonlinear forecasts that exploit the serial dependence of the white noise series U_t are superior.[4] From (2.6), these optimal forecasts are given by

$$E_t y_{t+j} = \pi + \lambda^j \cdot \{P[S_t = 1 | y_t, y_{t-1}, \ldots] - \pi\}$$

where $P[S_t = 1 | y_t, y_{t-1}, \ldots]$ is the nonlinear function of $y_t, y_{t-1}, \ldots$ to be presented in Section 4.

Thus, the essential differences between the specification (2.1) and a standard ARIMA model with normal innovations are twofold. First, (2.1) specifies that the growth rate $n_t - n_{t-1}$ need not change every period, but rather only does so in response to occasional, discrete events. Second, when added to a linear normal process, (2.1) generates a nonlinear process for the observed series for which,

[4]See Granger (1983) on this general issue.

while an ARIMA representation exists, it does not generate optimal forecasts of the future value of the series.

3. FORECASTING AND PRESENT VALUE CALCULATIONS

3.1. *Markov Trend in Levels*

Let i_t denote the cumulative number of "ones" since time zero,

$$i_t \equiv s_1 + s_2 + \cdots + s_t,$$

so from (2.1),

$$n_t = n_0 + \alpha_1 i_t + \alpha_0 t. \tag{3.1}$$

Recall from (2.6) that

$$E\{S_t | \text{Prob}[S_0 = 1] = \pi_0\} = \pi + \lambda^t(\pi_0 - \pi) \tag{3.2}$$

and so from (3.1),

$$\begin{aligned} E_0\{N_t | E_0[N_0] = n_0, \text{Prob}[S_0 = 1] = \pi_0\} &= n_0 + \alpha_1\left[\pi t + \sum_{\tau=1}^{t} \lambda^\tau(\pi_0 - \pi)\right] + \alpha_0 t \\ &= n_0 + [\alpha_1\pi + \alpha_0]t + [\alpha_1\lambda(1 - \lambda^t)/(1 - \lambda)][\pi_0 - \pi]. \end{aligned} \tag{3.3}$$

The limiting growth rate as $t \to \infty$ is seen from (3.3) to be independent of information about the state of the system at date 0:

$$\lim_{t\to\infty} E[(N_{t+1} - N_t) | n_0, \pi_0] = \alpha_1\pi + \alpha_0.$$

Intuitively, we know from equation (2.6) that for large t the economy will be in state 1 with probability π, in which case the growth rate would be $\alpha_1 + \alpha_0$, whereas the economy will be in state 0 with probability $1 - \pi$, in which case the growth rate would be α_0; hence the expected growth rate is $\alpha_1\pi + \alpha_0$. Furthermore, if one had no useful information about the state of the system at date 0, $\pi_0 = \pi$ and (3.3) implies that this limiting growth rate would be the basis for constructing forecasts of N_t for all finite t. On the other hand, if one did have useful information that, say, $\pi_0 > \pi$, then for $\alpha_1\lambda > 0$, $E[N_t | P_0(S_0 = 1) = \pi_0]$ would be systematically larger than $E[N_t | P_0(S_0 = 1) = \pi]$ for all t, with the difference growing with t as the term $(1 - \lambda^t)$ goes to unity. In particular, if we compare certain knowledge that $S_0 = 1$ ($\pi_0 = 1$) with certain knowledge that $S_0 = 0$ ($\pi_0 = 0$), we see

$$\lim_{t\to\infty} \{E[N_t | S_0 = 1] - E[N_t | S_0 = 0]\} = \alpha_1\lambda/(1 - \lambda). \tag{3.4}$$

So, while information about the state of the economy at date 0 has no effect on the long run growth rate $(N_{t+1} - N_t)$, it does exert a permanent effect on the level N_t.[5]

[5]An analogous result of course characterizes a standard ARIMA($p, 1, q$) process. See Beveridge and Nelson (1981, p. 155).

The discounted present value can also be evaluated from (3.3):

$$(3.5)\qquad E\left\{\sum_{t=0}^{\infty}\beta^t N_t|n_0,\pi_0\right\}=\frac{n_0}{(1-\beta)}+\alpha_1\left[\frac{\beta(1-q)}{(1-\beta)^2(1-\beta\lambda)}+\frac{\beta\lambda\pi_0}{(1-\beta)(1-\beta\lambda)}\right]+\frac{\alpha_0\beta}{(1-\beta)^2}.$$

3.2. *Markov Trend in Logs*

Here I characterize forecasts of future values of a series that follows a Markov trend in logs by exploiting a simple vector recursion in expected values.

Let $P_\tau[A, B]$ denote the probability that events A and B will occur together, conditional on information available at τ. Note that the following recursion,

$$(3.6)\qquad P_0[I_t=i,\ S_t=1]=p\cdot P_0[I_{t-1}=i-1,\ S_{t-1}=1]+(1-q)\cdot P_0[I_{t-1}=i-1,\ S_{t-1}=0],$$

holds for $t=1,2,\ldots$ and $i=1,2,\ldots,t$. For $i=0$ we of course have

$$(3.7)\qquad P_0[I_t=0,\ S_t=1]=0$$

holding for $t=1,2,\ldots$. Similarly, the recursion

$$(3.8)\qquad P_0[I_t=i,\ S_t=0]=(1-p)\cdot P_0[I_{t-1}=i,\ S_{t-1}=1]+q\cdot P_0[I_{t-1}=i,\ S_{t-1}=0],$$

holds for $t=1,2,\ldots$ and $i=0,1,\ldots,t-1$, with

$$(3.9)\qquad P_0[I_t=t,\ S_t=0]=0$$

for $t=1,2,\ldots$.

Let $\hat{\alpha}_1\equiv\exp(\alpha_1)$ and $\hat{\alpha}_0\equiv\exp(\alpha_0)$. Multiplying equation (3.6) by $\hat{\alpha}_1^i\hat{\alpha}_0^t$, summing for $i=1,2,\ldots,t$, and using (3.7) yields

$$(3.10)\qquad \sum_{i=0}^{t}\hat{\alpha}_1^i\hat{\alpha}_0^t\cdot P_0[I_t=i,\ S_t=1]=[\hat{\alpha}_1\hat{\alpha}_0 p]\cdot\sum_{j=0}^{t-1}\hat{\alpha}_1^j\hat{\alpha}_0^{t-1}\cdot P_0[I_{t-1}=j,\ S_{t-1}=1]+[\hat{\alpha}_1\hat{\alpha}_0(1-q)]\cdot\sum_{j=0}^{t-1}\hat{\alpha}_1^j\hat{\alpha}_0^{t-1}\cdot P_0[I_{t-1}=j,\ S_{t-1}=0].$$

Similarly, multiplying (3.8) by $\hat{\alpha}_1^i\hat{\alpha}_0^t$, summing for $i=0,1,\ldots,t-1$, and using

(3.9) gives

$$(3.11)\qquad \sum_{i=0}^{t} \hat{\alpha}_1^i \hat{\alpha}_0^t \cdot P_0[I_t = i,\ S_t = 0]$$

$$= [(1-p)\hat{\alpha}_0] \cdot \sum_{j=0}^{t-1} \hat{\alpha}_1^j \hat{\alpha}_0^{t-1} \cdot P_0[I_{t-1} = j,\ S_{t-1} = 1]$$

$$+ [q\hat{\alpha}_0] \cdot \sum_{j=0}^{t-1} \hat{\alpha}_1^j \hat{\alpha}_0^{t-1} \cdot P_0[I_{t-1} = j,\ S_{t-1} = 0].$$

Define

$$(3.12)\qquad M_0(t,s) = \sum_{i=0}^{t} \hat{\alpha}_1^i \hat{\alpha}_0^t \cdot P_0[I_t = i,\ S_t = s]$$

for $s = 0, 1$ and write (3.10) and (3.11) as

$$\begin{bmatrix} M_0(t,1) \\ M_0(t,0) \end{bmatrix} = \begin{bmatrix} \hat{\alpha}_0\hat{\alpha}_1 p & \hat{\alpha}_0\hat{\alpha}_1(1-q) \\ \hat{\alpha}_0(1-p) & \hat{\alpha}_0 q \end{bmatrix} \begin{bmatrix} M_0(t-1,1) \\ M_0(t-1,0) \end{bmatrix},$$

or, defining

$$B \equiv \begin{bmatrix} \hat{\alpha}_1 p & \hat{\alpha}_1(1-q) \\ (1-p) & q \end{bmatrix},$$

we have

$$(3.13)\qquad \begin{bmatrix} M_0(t,1) \\ M_0(t,0) \end{bmatrix} = \hat{\alpha}_0 B \begin{bmatrix} M_0(t-1,1) \\ M_0(t-1,0) \end{bmatrix}.$$

Note from (3.12) that $M_0(0, s) = P_0[S_0 = s]$. Thus (3.13) has the solution

$$\begin{bmatrix} M_0(t,1) \\ M_0(t,0) \end{bmatrix} = \hat{\alpha}_0^t B^t \begin{bmatrix} \pi_0 \\ 1-\pi_0 \end{bmatrix}.$$

Solving for the roots of $|\mu I - B| = 0$, we see

$$\mu_1 + \mu_2 = q + p\hat{\alpha}_1,$$

$$\mu_1\mu_2 = \hat{\alpha}_1(-1 + p + q).$$

Following Chiang (1980, pp. 148–152), write

$$(3.14)\qquad B^t = T \begin{bmatrix} \mu_1^t & 0 \\ 0 & \mu_2^t \end{bmatrix} T^{-1}$$

where

$$T = \begin{bmatrix} (\mu_1 - q) & (\mu_2 - q) \\ (1-p) & (1-p) \end{bmatrix},$$

$$T^{-1} = \frac{1}{(\mu_1 - \mu_2)(1-p)} \begin{bmatrix} (1-p) & (q - \mu_2) \\ -(1-p) & (\mu_1 - q) \end{bmatrix}.$$

The expected value of the level of a series that follows a Markov trend in logs is then seen to be

$$(3.15)\quad E_0\hat{N}_t = \hat{n}_0[M_0(t,1) + M_0(t,0)]$$
$$= \hat{n}_0 \cdot [1 \quad 1]\hat{\alpha}_0^t B^t [\pi_0 \quad 1-\pi_0]'$$
$$= \frac{\hat{n}_0\hat{\alpha}_0^t\{(k_0-\mu_2)\mu_2^t - (k_0-\mu_1)\mu_1^t\}}{(\mu_1-\mu_2)}$$

where

$$k_0 \equiv [\mu_1\mu_2/\hat{\alpha}_1][\pi_0 + \hat{\alpha}_1(1-\pi_0)]$$
$$= [-1+p+q][\pi_0 + \hat{\alpha}_1(1-\pi_0)].$$

Normalizing $\mu_1 > \mu_2$, we see that, as in the case of a Markov trend in levels, the long-run growth rate is independent of information about the initial state:

$$\lim_{t\to\infty} \frac{E_0\hat{N}_{t+1}}{E_0\hat{N}_t} = \hat{\alpha}_0\mu_1$$

but a change in the current state exerts a permanent effect on the future level of the series,

$$(3.16)\quad \lim_{t\to\infty} \frac{E_0\{\hat{N}_t|\pi_0=1\}}{E_0\{\hat{N}_t|\pi_0=0\}} = \frac{\mu_1-(-1+p+q)}{\mu_1-\hat{\alpha}_1(-1+p+q)}.$$

From (3.15), the present value is

$$(3.17)\quad E_0\sum_{t=0}^{\infty}\beta^t\hat{N}_t = \frac{\hat{n}_0(1-k_0\beta\hat{\alpha}_0)}{1-\beta\hat{\alpha}_0(p\hat{\alpha}_1+q)+\beta^2\hat{\alpha}_0^2(-1+p+q)\hat{\alpha}_1}.$$

4. ESTIMATION, FILTERING, AND SMOOTHING

4.1. *Stochastic Specification*

Several options are available for combining the trend term n_t with another stochastic process. Here I discuss the approach that results in the computationally simplest maximum likelihood estimation.

Suppose we have observations on a time series $\{\tilde{y}_t\}$. Specify

$$(4.1)\quad \tilde{y}_t = n_t + \tilde{z}_t$$

where n_t is as given in (2.1) and (2.2) and $\tilde{z}_t$ follows a zero mean ARIMA$(r,1,0)$ process:

$$(4.2)\quad \tilde{z}_t - \tilde{z}_{t-1} = \phi_1(\tilde{z}_{t-1}-\tilde{z}_{t-2}) + \phi_2(\tilde{z}_{t-2}-\tilde{z}_{t-3}) + \cdots$$
$$+\phi_r(\tilde{z}_{t-r}-\tilde{z}_{t-r-1}) + \varepsilon_t.$$

I take $\{\varepsilon_t\}$ to be an i.i.d. $N(0, \sigma^2)$ sequence that is independent of $\{n_{t+j}\}$ for all j. Differencing (4.1) and rewriting (4.2) we obtain

$$(4.3) \qquad \begin{aligned} y_t &= \alpha_1 s_t + \alpha_0 + z_t, \\ z_t &= \phi_1 z_{t-1} + \phi_2 z_{t-2} + \cdots + \phi_r z_{t-r} + \varepsilon_t, \end{aligned}$$

where $y_t \equiv \tilde{y}_t - \tilde{y}_{t-1}$ and $z_t \equiv \tilde{z}_t - \tilde{z}_{t-1}$.

The econometrician is presumed to observe y_t but not z_t or s_t. I first discuss a filter whereby the econometrician can draw probabilistic inference about the unobserved state s_t given observations on y_t, and then show how evaluation of the sample likelihood is a natural byproduct of the filter. The analysis is closely related to the discussion by Cosslett and Lee (1985), who derived a recursion to evaluate the likelihood function for the case where (4.3) is a standard stationary regression equation with no lagged dependent variables.

4.2. *Filtering*

The *basic filter* accepts as input the joint conditional probability

$$P[S_{t-1} = s_{t-1}, S_{t-2} = s_{t-2}, \ldots, S_{t-r} = s_{t-r} | y_{t-1}, y_{t-2}, \ldots, y_{-r+1}]$$

and has as output

$$P[S_t = s_t, S_{t-1} = s_{t-1}, \ldots, S_{t-r+1} = s_{t-r+1} | y_t, y_{t-1}, \ldots, y_{-r+1}]$$

along with, as a byproduct, the conditional likelihood of y_t:

$$f(y_t | y_{t-1}, y_{t-2}, \ldots, y_{-r+1}).$$

Note well the notation: $[s_t, s_{t-1}, \ldots, s_{t-r+1}]$ refers to the r most recent values of s whereas $[y_t, y_{t-1}, \ldots, y_{-r+1}]$ denotes the complete history of y observed through date t. By "$P[S_t = s_t, S_{t-1} = s_{t-1}, \ldots, S_{t-r+1} = s_{t-r+1} | y_t, y_{t-1}, \ldots, y_{-r+1}]$" I refer to a vector consisting of 2^r elements. For example, suppose $r = 4$. The element indexed by (1, 0, 1, 1) denotes the probability that $S_{t-1} = 1$, $S_{t-2} = 0$, $S_{t-3} = 1$, and $S_{t-4} = 1$. These 16 probabilities sum to unity by construction, and represent an inference about the unobserved state $(s_{t-1}, s_{t-2}, s_{t-3}, s_{t-4})$ based on observations of y through date $t-1$. The algorithm is as follows.

STEP 1: Calculate

$$\begin{aligned} P[S_t &= s_t, S_{t-1} = s_{t-1}, \ldots, S_{t-r} = s_{t-r} | y_{t-1}, y_{t-2}, \ldots, y_{-r+1}] \\ &= P[S_t = s_t | S_{t-1} = s_{t-1}] \times P[S_{t-1} = s_{t-1}, S_{t-2} = s_{t-2}, \ldots, \\ &\qquad\qquad S_{t-r} = s_{t-r} | y_{t-1}, y_{t-2}, \ldots, y_{-r+1}] \end{aligned}$$

where $P[S_t = s_t | S_{t-1} = s_{t-1}]$ is given by (2.2). (Note $P[S_t = s_t | S_{t-1} = s_{t-1}] = P[S_t = s_t | S_{t-1} = s_{t-1}, S_{t-2} = s_{t-2}, \ldots, S_{t-r} = s_{t-r}, y_{t-1}, y_{t-2}, \ldots, y_{-r+1}]$ by the independence and first-order Markov assumptions.)

STEP 2: Calculate the joint conditional density-distribution of y_t and $(S_t, S_{t-1}, \ldots, S_{t-r})$:

$$f(y_t, S_t = s_t, S_{t-1} = s_{t-1}, \ldots, S_{t-r} = s_{t-r} | y_{t-1}, y_{t-2}, \ldots, y_{-r+1})$$
$$= f(y_t | S_t = s_t, S_{t-1} = s_{t-1}, \ldots, S_{t-r} = s_{t-r}, y_{t-1}, y_{t-2}, \ldots, y_{-r+1})$$
$$\times P[S_t = s_t, S_{t-1} = s_{t-1}, \ldots, S_{t-r} = s_{t-r} | y_{t-1}, y_{t-2}, \ldots, y_{-r+1}]$$

where we know

$$f(y_t | S_t = s_t, S_{t-1} = s_{t-1}, \ldots, S_{t-r} = s_{t-r}, y_{t-1}, y_{t-2}, \ldots, y_{-r+1})$$
$$= \frac{1}{\sqrt{2\pi}\,\sigma} \exp\left[-\frac{1}{2\sigma^2}((y_t - \alpha_1 s_t - \alpha_0) - \phi_1(y_{t-1} - \alpha_1 s_{t-1} - \alpha_0) - \cdots - \phi_r(y_{t-r} - \alpha_1 s_{t-r} - \alpha_0))^2 \right].$$

STEP 3: We then have

$$f(y_t | y_{t-1}, y_{t-2}, \ldots, y_{-r+1})$$
$$= \sum_{s_t=0}^{1} \sum_{s_{t-1}=0}^{1} \cdots \sum_{s_{t-r}=0}^{1} f(y_t, S_t = s_t, S_{t-1} = s_{t-1}, \ldots, S_{t-r} = s_{t-r} | y_{t-1}, y_{t-2}, \ldots, y_{-r+1}).$$

STEP 4: Thus

$$P[S_t = s_t, S_{t-1} = s_{t-1}, \ldots, S_{t-r} = s_{t-r} | y_t, y_{t-1}, \ldots, y_{-r+1}]$$
$$= \frac{f(y_t, S_t = s_t, S_{t-1} = s_{t-1}, \ldots, S_{t-r} = s_{t-r} | y_{t-1}, y_{t-2}, \ldots, y_{-r+1})}{f(y_t | y_{t-1}, y_{t-2}, \ldots, y_{-r+1})}.$$

STEP 5: The desired output is then obtained from

$$P[S_t = s_t, S_{t-1} = s_{t-1}, \ldots, S_{t-r+1} = s_{t-r+1} | y_t, y_{t-1}, \ldots, y_{-r+1}]$$
$$= \sum_{s_{t-r}=0}^{1} P[S_t = s_t, S_{t-1} = s_{t-1}, \ldots, S_{t-r} = s_{t-r} | y_t, y_{t-1}, \ldots, y_{-r+1}].$$

One could start up the algorithm with

$$P[S_0 = s_0, S_{-1} = s_{-1}, \ldots, S_{-r+1} = s_{-r+1} | y_0, y_{-1}, \ldots, y_{-r+1}]$$

though evaluating this expression proves to be somewhat involved computationally. I have instead in this paper adopted the simpler expedient of starting the filter with the unconditional probability $P[S_0 = s_0,\ S_{-1} = s_{-1}, \ldots, S_{-r+1} = s_{-r+1}]$, evaluated as follows. Set $P[S_{-r+1} = 1]$ equal to the limiting probability π of the Markov process from equation (2.7), and of course set $P[S_{-r+1} = 0] =$

$1-\pi$. Then for $\tau=-r+2,-r+3,\ldots,0$ calculate

$$\begin{aligned}P[S_\tau=s_\tau,\ S_{\tau-1}=s_{\tau-1},\ldots,S_{-r+1}=s_{-r+1}]\\ =P[S_\tau=s_\tau|S_{\tau-1}=s_{\tau-1}]\\ \times P[S_{\tau-1}=s_{\tau-1},\ S_{\tau-2}=s_{\tau-2},\ldots,S_{-r+1}=s_{-r+1}].\end{aligned}$$

The final product of this subiteration,

$$P[S_0=s_0,\ S_{-1}=s_{-1},\ldots,S_{-r+1}=s_{-r+1}],$$

is then used as input for the basic filter for $t=1$. The iteration on the basic filter is then repeated for $t=1,2,\ldots,T$.

For some applications, one might want to allow the possibility of a permanent change in regime (e.g., $q=1$). For such applications, we should not set $P[S_{-r+1}=1]$ from equation (2.7), but should instead treat it as a separate parameter (say π_{-r+1}) to be estimated along with the others.

It is easy to verify that the output of the filter is always a well-defined probability distribution with the terms nonnegative and summing to unity.

Neftci's (1982) algorithm for dating business cycle turning points can be obtained as a special case of the basic filter by setting $q=1$ and $r=0$.

One byproduct of the filter is evaluation of the conditional likelihood in Step 3. The sample conditional log likelihood is

$$\begin{aligned}\log f(y_T,y_{T-1},\ldots,y_1|y_0,y_{-1},\ldots,y_{-r+1})\\ =\sum_{t=1}^{T}\log f(y_t|y_{t-1},y_{t-2},\ldots,y_{-r+1})\end{aligned}$$

which can be maximized numerically with respect to the unknown parameters $(\alpha_1,\alpha_0,p,q,\sigma,\phi_1,\phi_2,\ldots,\phi_r)$, and optionally π_{-r+1} as described above. Obviously the model is unidentified in the sense that the decision of which state to call state 0 and which to call state 1 is arbitrary. I normalize by letting state 1 be the fast growth state and state 0 be the slow growth state, achieved by setting $\alpha_1+\alpha_0>\alpha_0$ or $\alpha_1>0$.

The logic of the filter is equally valid under much more general specifications. With n rather than 2 states, the input to the filter is a vector consisting of n^r elements, and the summations in Steps 3 and 5 are over $(0,n-1)$ rather than $(0,1)$. The autoregressive parameters (ϕ) can also be made a function of the regime by replacing ϕ_j in Step 2 with $\phi_j(S_t)$ or $\phi_j(S_{t-j})$. In my (1988) paper I applied the algorithm with the standard deviation $\sigma(S_t)$ also a function of the regime, and extended the estimation theory to a multivariate context where the econometrician wishes to impose the cross-equation restrictions implied by rational expectations. Higher-order dynamics for the regime shift are also conceptually straight-forward—e.g., replace $P[S_t=s_t|S_{t-1}=s_{t-1}]$ in Step 2 with $P[S_t=s_t|S_{t-1}=s_{t-1},\ S_{t-2}=s_{t-2}]$. That is, instead of multiplying each of the 16 numbers in the input to the filter by $p,q,1-p$, or $1-q$ (depending on the value of s_t and s_{t-1}) one multiplies by one of $p_{11},p_{12},\ldots$ depending on the value of s_t,s_{t-1}, and s_{t-2}.

Such extensions are in principle straight-forward. Any problems are chiefly numerical. Identification of the parameters characterizing the dynamics of S_t (p, q, and α_1) separately from those of the Gaussian component ($\phi_1, \phi_2, \ldots, \phi_r$) depends on nonlinearities in the data. There is a practical limit on how complicated we can permit the dynamics for both the regime shift and the Gaussian component to become and still have hope of obtaining useful results.

The relation between my approach and that of Sclove (1983) should now be stated more precisely. Let $y \equiv (y_1, \ldots, y_T)'$, $s \equiv (s_1, \ldots, s_T)'$, and $\theta = (\alpha_1, \alpha_0, p, q, \sigma, \phi_1, \phi_2, \ldots, \phi_r)'$. My filter evaluates $f(y|\theta, y_{-r+1}, \ldots, y_0)$ and maximizes with respect to θ. The MLE $\hat{\theta}$ is then used in a final pass through the filter to draw probabilistic inference about s. Sclove, by contrast, would calculate $f(y, s|\theta, y_{-r+1}, \ldots, y_0)$ and maximize with respect to both θ and s. Thus the output of my algorithm is a sequence of conditional probabilities, and the output of Sclove's maximization is an imputed historical sequence for s. Sclove's empirical application also opted for the other end of the trade-off between a rich parameterization of the dynamics for the Gaussian component and that for the Markov component. He assumed no autocorrelation for the Gaussian component, whereas I allow four lags; Sclove tested for up to nine different regimes, whereas I permit only two.

4.3. *Smoothing*

Another byproduct of the basic filter is inference about the state s_t based on currently available information,

$$P[S_t = s_t | y_t, y_{t-1}, \ldots, y_{-r+1}] = \sum_{s_{t-1}=0}^{1} \sum_{s_{t-2}=0}^{1} \cdots \sum_{s_{t-r+1}=0}^{1} P[S_t = s_t, S_{t-1} = s_{t-1}, \ldots, S_{t-r+1} = s_{t-r+1} | y_t, y_{t-1}, \ldots, y_{-r+1}].$$

Alternatively, one can obtain a more reliable inference about the lagged value of the state using currently available information. For example, using the output from Step 4 of the basic filter, one can calculate an *r-lag smoother*:

$$P[S_{t-r} = s_{t-r} | y_t, y_{t-1}, \ldots, y_{-r+1}] = \sum_{s_t=0}^{1} \sum_{s_{t-1}=0}^{1} \cdots \sum_{s_{t-r+1}=0}^{1} P[S_t = s_t, S_{t-1} = s_{t-1}, \ldots, S_{t-r} = s_{t-r} | y_t, y_{t-1}, \ldots, y_{-r+1}].$$

A full-sample smoother can be obtained from adapting a suggestion made by Cosslett and Lee (1985) in a slightly different context. Suppose that instead of using

$$P[S_{t-1} = s_{t-1}, S_{t-2} = s_{t-2}, \ldots, S_{t-r} = s_{t-r} | y_{t-1}, y_{t-2}, \ldots, y_{-r+1}]$$

as input into the basic filter, we used in its place

$$P[S_{t-1}=s_{t-1}, S_{t-2}=s_{t-2},\ldots, S_{t-r}=s_{t-r}|S_\tau=\hat{s}_\tau,$$
$$S_{\tau-1}=\hat{s}_{\tau-1},\ldots, S_{\tau-r+1}=\hat{s}_{\tau-r+1}, y_{t-1}, y_{t-2},\ldots, y_{-r+1}]$$

for some $\tau \leqslant t-1$ and for some choice of $(\hat{s}_\tau, \hat{s}_{\tau-1},\ldots, \hat{s}_{\tau-r+1})$ to be specified shortly. Running through the steps of the basic filter, it is easy to verify that the output of the filter would in this case be

$$P[S_t=s_t, S_{t-1}=s_{t-1},\ldots, S_{t-r+1}=s_{t-r+1}|S_\tau=\hat{s}_\tau,$$
$$S_{\tau-1}=\hat{s}_{\tau-1},\ldots, S_{\tau-r+1}=\hat{s}_{\tau-r+1}, y_t, y_{t-1},\ldots, y_{-r+1}]$$

with byproduct

$$f(y_t|S_\tau=\hat{s}_\tau, S_{\tau-1}=\hat{s}_{\tau-1},\ldots, S_{\tau-r+1}=\hat{s}_{\tau-r+1}, y_{t-1}, y_{t-2},\ldots, y_{-r+1}).$$

Bearing this in mind, the *full-sample smoother* can be obtained as follows.

STEP 1: Run through the basic filter for $t=1,\ldots,T$ and store the resulting sequences $P[S_\tau=s_\tau, S_{\tau-1}=s_{\tau-1},\ldots, S_{\tau-r+1}=s_{\tau-r+1}|y_\tau, y_{\tau-1},\ldots, y_{-r+1}]$ and $f(y_\tau|y_{\tau-1}, y_{\tau-2},\ldots, y_{-r+1})$ for $\tau=1,2,\ldots,T$.

STEP 2: For each τ and for each possible value of the vector $(\hat{s}_\tau, \hat{s}_{\tau-1},\ldots, \hat{s}_{\tau-r+1})$, repeat the following:

(a) Set

$$P[S_\tau=s_\tau, S_{\tau-1}=s_{\tau-1},\ldots, S_{\tau-r+1}=s_{\tau-r+1}|S_\tau=\hat{s}_\tau,$$
$$S_{\tau-1}=\hat{s}_{\tau-1},\ldots, S_{\tau-r+1}=\hat{s}_{\tau-r+1}, y_{t-1}, y_{t-2},\ldots, y_{-r+1}] \tag{4.4}$$

equal to unity if $s_\tau=\hat{s}_\tau$, $s_{\tau-1}=\hat{s}_{\tau-1},\ldots, s_{\tau-r+1}=\hat{s}_{\tau-r+1}$ and zero otherwise.

(b) Repeat the basic filter using (4.4) to start the iteration and iterate over $t=\tau+1,\tau+2,\ldots,T$, storing the output from Step 3 of the basic filter as $f(y_t|S_\tau=\hat{s}_\tau, S_{\tau-1}=\hat{s}_{\tau-1},\ldots, S_{\tau-r+1}=\hat{s}_{\tau-r+1}, y_{t-1}, y_{t-2},\ldots, y_{-r+1})$.

(c) The smoothed probabilities are given by

$$P[S_\tau=\hat{s}_\tau, S_{\tau-1}=\hat{s}_{\tau-1},\ldots, S_{\tau-r+1}=\hat{s}_{\tau-r+1}|y_T, y_{T-1},\ldots, y_{-r+1}]$$
$$= P[S_\tau=\hat{s}_\tau, S_{\tau-1}=\hat{s}_{\tau-1},\ldots, S_{\tau-r+1}=\hat{s}_{\tau-r+1}|y_\tau, y_{\tau-1},\ldots, y_{-r+1}]$$
$$\times\frac{f(y_{\tau+1}|S_\tau=\hat{s}_\tau, S_{\tau-1}=\hat{s}_{\tau-1},\ldots, S_{\tau-r+1}=\hat{s}_{\tau-r+1}, y_\tau, y_{\tau-1},\ldots, y_{-r+1})}{f(y_{\tau+1}|y_\tau, y_{\tau-1},\ldots, y_{-r+1})}$$
$$\times\frac{f(y_{\tau+2}|S_\tau=\hat{s}_\tau, S_{\tau-1}=\hat{s}_{\tau-1},\ldots, S_{\tau-r+1}=\hat{s}_{\tau-r+1}, y_{\tau+1}, y_\tau,\ldots, y_{-r+1})}{f(y_{\tau+2}|y_{\tau+1}, y_\tau,\ldots, y_{-r+1})}$$
$$\times\cdots\times\frac{f(y_T|S_\tau=\hat{s}_\tau, S_{\tau-1}=\hat{s}_{\tau-1},\ldots, S_{\tau-r+1}=\hat{s}_{\tau-r+1}, y_{T-1}, y_{T-2},\ldots, y_{-r+1})}{f(y_T|y_{T-1}, y_{T-2},\ldots, y_{-r+1})}.$$

5. MAXIMUM LIKELIHOOD ESTIMATES FOR U.S. GNP DATA

The above technique was applied to U.S. postwar data on real GNP. The variable used for y_t was 100 times the change in the log of real GNP for

TABLE I

MAXIMUM LIKELIHOOD ESTIMATES OF PARAMETERS AND ASYMPTOTIC STANDARD ERRORS BASED ON DATA FOR U.S. REAL GNP, $t = 1952:\text{II}$ TO $1984:\text{IV}$

Parameter	Estimate	Standard error
α_1	1.522	0.2636
α_0	−0.3577	0.2651
p	0.9049	0.03740
q	0.7550	0.09656
σ	0.7690	0.06676
ϕ_1	0.014	0.120
σ_2	−0.058	0.137
ϕ_3	−0.247	0.107
ϕ_4	−0.213	0.110

$t = 1951:\text{II}$ to $1984:\text{IV}$.[6] Numerical maximization of the conditional log likelihood function led to the maximum likelihood estimates reported in Table I. Also reported are asymptotic standard errors.[7]

One possible outcome that might have been expected a priori would associate the states $s_t = 0$ and 1 with slow and fast growth rates for the U.S. economy, corresponding to decade-long changes in trends. In fact, however, the sample likelihood is maximized by a negative growth rate of −0.4% per quarter during state 0 and a positive growth of $(\alpha_0 + \alpha_1) = +1.2\%$ during state 1. These values clearly correspond to the dynamics of business cycles as opposed to long-term variations in secular growth rates. Indeed, the first- and second-order serial correlation in logarithmic changes of real GNP seem to be better captured by shifts between states rather than by the leading autoregressive coefficients, as indicated by the fact that $\hat{\phi}_1$ and $\hat{\phi}_2$ come out remarkably close to zero. Negative coefficients at lags 3 and 4 suggest the possibility that the method used by the Bureau of Economic Analysis for deseasonalizing introduces spurious periodicity when applied to data generated by a nonlinear process such as this one. These coefficients further suggest that investigating a higher-order Markov process for the trend might also be a fruitful topic for future research.

Figure 1 reports the estimated probability that the economy is in the negative growth state ($P[S_t = 0]$) based on currently available information (panel A) and information available one year later (panel B). A full sample smoother (not shown) was also calculated. The probabilities from the full-sample smoother differed very little from those of the four-lag smoother in panel B. The average absolute difference between these two smoothed series was .016, with the maximum difference occurring in the second quarter of 1956; (the four-lag smoother

[6] The level of GNP is measured at an annual rate in 1982 dollars. Data are from *Business Conditions Digest*, February, 1986, p. 102, Series 50. The order of lags r was set arbitrarily to 4; the basic filter was thus started for $t = 1952:\text{II}$.

[7] Maximization was achieved by a Davidon-Fletcher-Powell routine. Convergence to the global maximum reported in Table I proved relatively robust with respect to a broad range of start-up values. Second derivatives of the log likelihood were calculated numerically, from which asymptotic standard errors were constructed. I would like to thank Kent Wall for use of his DFP algorithm and Steve Stern for use of his second-derivative program.

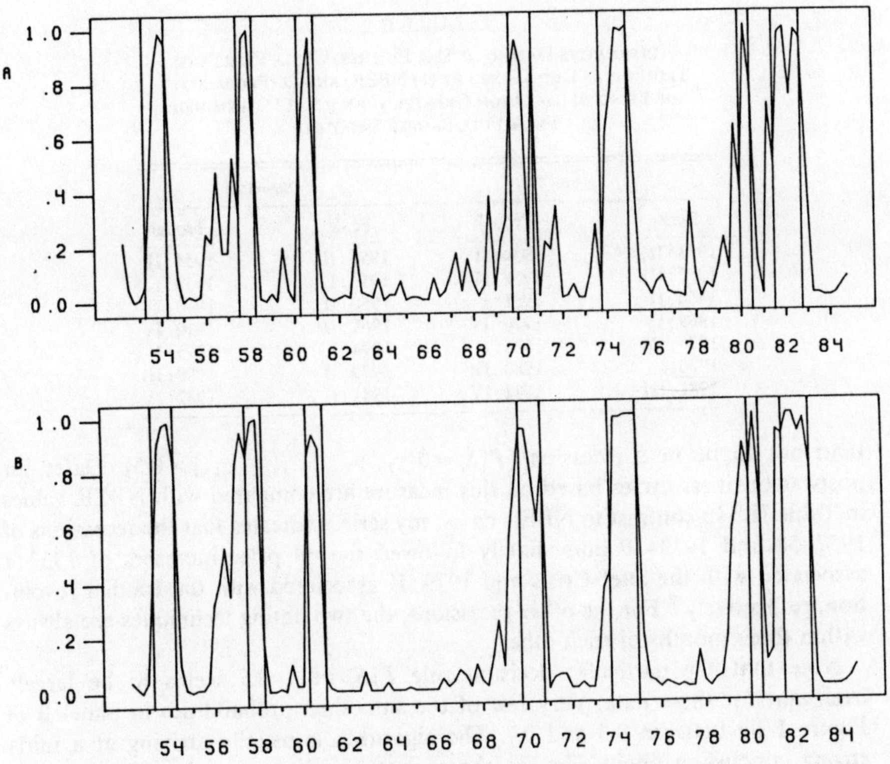

FIGURE 1.—Inferred probability that $S_t = 0$.

Panel (A) reports the inferred probability that the economy was in the falling GNP state at date t using information available at the time ($P[S_t = 0 | y_t, y_{t-1}, \ldots]$). Panel (B) reports the inferred probability that the economy was in the falling GNP state at date t using information available 4 quarters later ($P[S_t = 0 | y_{t+4}, y_{t+3}, \ldots]$).

puts the probability of contraction at .40 for this quarter, whereas the full-sample inference was .15). This suggests that reasonably precise estimates are available from the four-lag smoother associated with the basic filter itself, and it may be unnecessary to employ the full-sample smoother for many applications. Another reasonable alternative to the full-sample smoother is to augment the basic filter with a few additional lags on s.

6. ESTABLISHING THE DATES OF HISTORICAL BUSINESS CYCLES

The specific inferences about the historical incidence of growth states generated by the filter and smoother correspond extremely closely to conventional dating of business cycles, and indeed could be employed as an independent objective algorithm for generating such dating. A sensible metric might be based on whether the econometrician would conclude that the economy is more likely

TABLE II

ALTERNATIVE DATING OF U.S. BUSINESS CYCLE PEAKS AND TROUGHS AS DETERMINED BY (1) NBER, AND (2) PROBABILITY OF BEING IN RECESSION GREATER THAN 0.5 AS DETERMINED FROM FULL-SAMPLE SMOOTHER

NBER		Smoother	
Peak	Trough	Peak	Trough
1953 : III	1954 : II	1953 : III	1954 : II
1957 : III	1958 : II	1957 : I	1958 : I
1960 : II	1961 : I	1960 : II	1960 : IV
1969 : IV	1970 : IV	1969 : III	1970 : IV
1973 : IV	1975 : I	1974 : I	1975 : I
1980 : I	1980 : III	1979 : II	1980 : III
1981 : III	1982 : IV	1981 : II	1982 : IV

than not to be in a recession ($P[S_t = 0 | y_T, y_{T-1}, \ldots, y_{-r+1}] > 0.5$). Dates for postwar business cycles based on this measure are compared with NBER values in Table II.[8] In contrast to NBER dates, my series indicates that the recessions of 1957–58 and 1979–80 immediately followed the oil price increases of 1957 : I associated with the Suez Crisis and 1979 : II associated with the Iranian revolution, respectively.[9] For the other recessions, the two dating techniques are always within three months of each other.

Note that the particular decision rule $P[S_t = 0] > 0.5$ seems to be largely irrelevant for these data. Very few of the smoothed probabilities in panel B of Figure 1 lie between 0.3 and 0.7. The algorithm is usually arriving at a fairly strong conclusion about whether the economy is in a recession. The implicit histogram would also seem to suggest that the filter is not simply fitting parameters to an arbitrary nonlinear process, but rather reflects an underlying pattern in the data of dichotomous shifts between the expansion and contraction phase.

Another interesting implication of the Markov framework is that one can calculate from the maximum likelihood parameter estimates the expected duration of a typical recession and compare this predicted magnitude with the historical average. Conditional on being in state 0, the expected duration of a recession is

$$\sum_{k=1}^{\infty} kq^{k-1}(1-q) = (1-q)^{-1}$$

or 4.1 quarters. The historical average duration of a recession was 4.7 quarters during the postwar period according to the NBER figures. The expected duration of an expansion is likewise $(1-p)^{-1}$ or 10.5 quarters, compared with an average of 14.3 quarters in NBER dating.

[8] NBER business cycle dates are reported in *Business Conditions Digest* published by the Department of Commerce.

[9] My (1985) paper provided a detailed discussion of these events.

Series:

$y_t = 100 \cdot \ln(\mathrm{GNP82}_t/\mathrm{GNP82}_{t-1})$
$t = $ 1952:III–1984:IV

Sample Autocorrelogram:

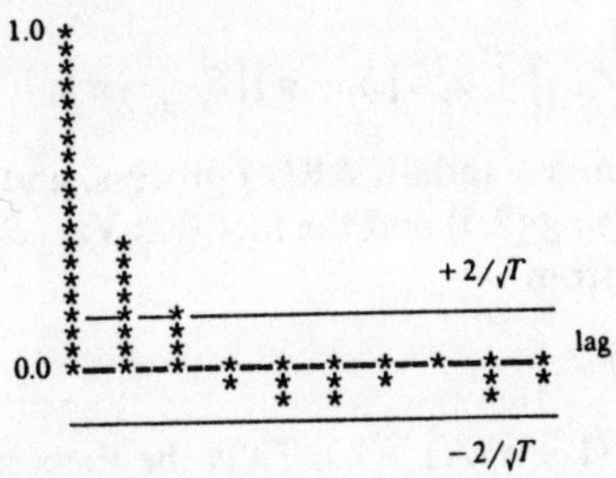

Series

$$y_t = -.3577 + 1.522 s_t + z_t$$
$$z_t = .014 z_{t-1} - 0.58 z_{t-2} - .247 z_{t-3} - .213 z_{t-4} + \varepsilon_t, \quad \varepsilon_t \sim N[0, (.769)^2]$$
$$P[S_t = 1 | S_{t-1} = 1] = .9049$$
$$P[S_t = 0 | S_{t-1} = 0] = .7550$$

Population Autocorrelogram:

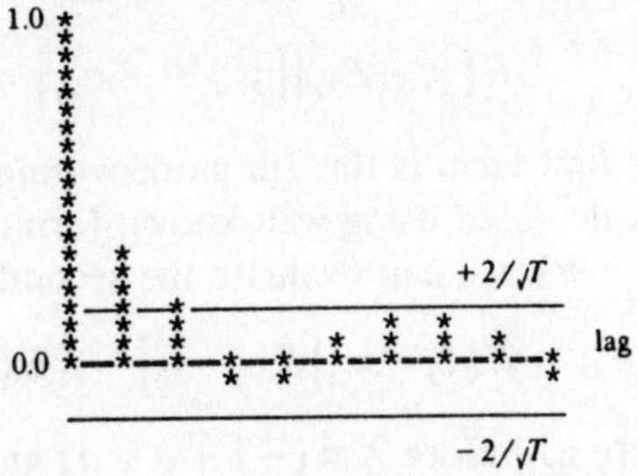

Sample Regression Coefficients for AR(4) (Standard Errors in Parentheses):

$$y_t = \underset{(.129)}{.555} + \underset{(.089)}{.312} y_{t-1} + \underset{(.093)}{.122} y_{t-2} - \underset{(.092)}{.116} y_{t-3} - \underset{(.089)}{.081} y_{t-4} + u_t, \quad \hat{\sigma}_u = 0.99$$

Sample Autocorrelogram of Residuals from AR(4) Regression:

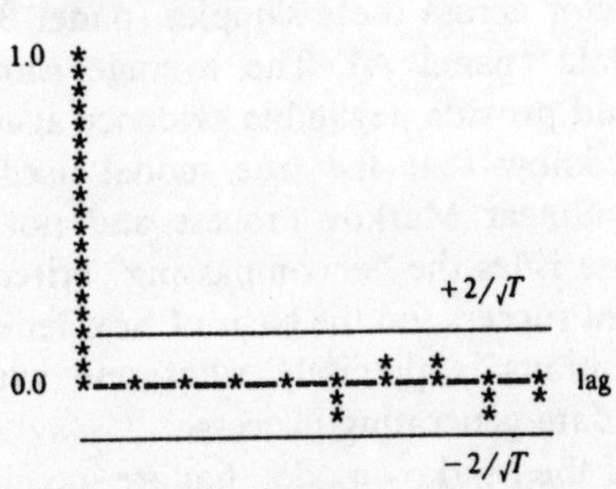

Expected Value of Sample Regression Coefficients for AR(4):

$$y_t = .589 + .293 y_{t-1} + .069 y_{t-2} - .104 y_{t-3} - .042 y_{t-4} + u_t, \quad \sigma_u = 0.98$$

Expected Value of Sample Autocorrelogram of Residuals from AR(4) Regression

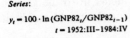

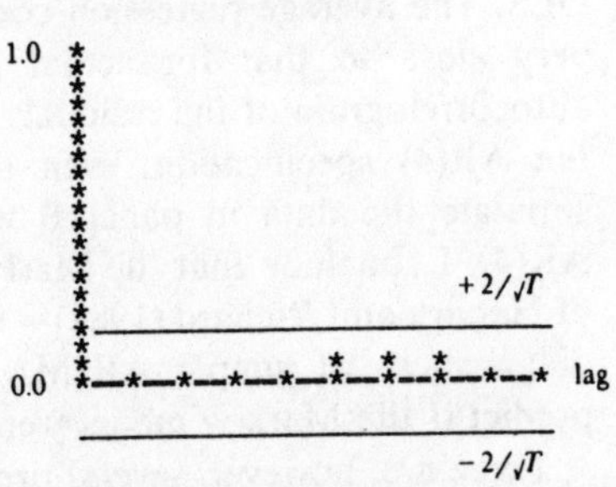

FIGURE 2.—Comparison of actual GNP data with predictions of Markov model of trend.

7. COMPARING LINEAR AND NONLINER MODELS OF GNP GROWTH

The Markov model offers a nonlinear alternative to linear representations such as the Box-Jenkins ARIMA specification (used by Beveridge and Nelson (1981), and Campbell and Mankiw (1987a, b)) or the unobserved components (UC) models of Harvey and Todd (1983), Watson (1986), and Clark (1987). One might well ask why, if the Markov model were the true data-generating process, do parsimoniously parameterized linear models seem to have fit the data so well?

Panel A of Figure 2 reports the sample autocorrelogram of actual postwar changes in the log of quarterly real GNP. Indeed this looks much like that predicted for low-order ARIMA processes.[10] An AR(4) model fit to the growth rate of real GNP exhibits only the most modest autocorrelation of residuals (Figure 2, panel A).

What would these same diagnostics be expected to reveal if the data were in fact generated by the Markov model? The Markov model posits that $y_t = \alpha_1 s_t + \alpha_0 + z_t$ with z_t a zero-mean Gaussian AR(r) process and $E(S_t) = \pi$. From the independence of S_t and z_t we know

$$E[y_t - Ey_t][y_{t-j} - Ey_{t-j}] = E[z_t z_{t-j}] + \alpha_1^2 E[S_t - \pi][S_{t-j} - \pi].$$

The first term is the jth autocovariance from a standard AR(r) process, and can be calculated using well-known formulas. Using (2.5) and the fact that $\text{Var}(S_0) = \pi(1-\pi)$, we can evaluate the second term from

$$E[S_t - \pi][S_{t-j} - \pi] = \lambda^j \pi(1-\pi)$$

where as before $\lambda \equiv (-1 + p + q)$ and $\pi \equiv (1-q)/(1-\lambda)$. Thus the theoretical autocorrelogram of data generated by a Markov model is known. Panel B of Figure 2 plots this function for the MLE parameter values of Table I. It would clearly be extremely difficult to distinguish the Markov model from a simple linear alternative on the basis of the observed autocorrelations in a sample the size of postwar quarterly data.

Figure 2 also reports some Monte Carlo results. For each of 1000 samples of size $T = 130$ generated by the Markov model, an AR(4) specification was fit by OLS. The average regression coefficient vector across these samples (panel B) is very close to that for actual postwar data (panel A). The average sample autocorrelogram of the residuals again would provide negligible evidence against the AR(4) specification, even though we know that the true model used to simulate the data in panel B was the nonlinear Markov process and not an AR(4). I conclude that the Markov model satisfies the "encompassing" criterion of Hendry and Richard (1982)—the apparent success (on the basis of Box-Jenkins diagnostics) of simple ARIMA representations is precisely what one would predict if the Markov model were the true data-generating process.

There are, however, several predictions of the Markov model that are inconsistent with an ARIMA or linear UC specification. The Markov model asserts that forecasts of the log of GNP that are restricted to linear functions of lagged values will be suboptimal; additional useful information is alleged to be contained in the nonlinear function $P[S_{t-1} = 1 | y_{t-1}, y_{t-2}, \ldots]$ which summarizes the inference drawn the previous period about the unobserved state variable S_{t-1}. The intuition for the sign and magnitude of the predicted effect is as follows. If the Markov model were true and we knew that the economy was in the expansion phase of the cycle last period ($S_{t-1} = 1$), we would forecast

$$E[(\alpha_0 + \alpha_1 s_t) | S_{t-1} = 1] = \alpha_0 + \alpha_1 p$$

[10] For example, Watson (1986) settled on an ARIMA(1, 1, 0) specification for the log of GNP, Campbell and Mankiw (1987b) preferred a (2, 1, 2), and Clark (1987) selected (0, 1, 2).

whereas when the economy was in recession last period,

$$E[(\alpha_0 + \alpha_1 S_t)|S_{t-1} = 0] = \alpha_0 + \alpha_1(1 - q).$$

The difference in the forecast growth rate of the economy knowing that the economy was in expansion rather than recession last period would thus be on the order of $\alpha_1(p - 1 + q)$, or about 1% faster GNP growth forecast when the economy was in expansion last period.[11] The Markov model therefore predicts that the lagged output of the basic filter,

$$X_{t-1} \equiv P[S_{t-1} = 1 | y_{t-1}, y_{t-2}, \ldots, y_{-r+1}]$$

should enter statistically significantly with a positive coefficient when added to the AR(4) representation for GNP growth. The ARIMA or UC specifications predict that it should have coefficient zero. When one performs this regression on actual postwar GNP data, one finds (standard errors in parentheses)

$$\begin{aligned} y_t = -\underset{(.294)}{.199} - \underset{(.1609)}{.0721}\, y_{t-1} - \underset{(.10088)}{.00639}\, y_{t-2} - \underset{(.0927)}{.1815}\, y_{t-3} \\ - \underset{(.0917)}{.1639}\, y_{t-4} + \underset{(.590)}{1.670}\, X_{t-1} + u_t. \end{aligned}$$

The t statistic associated with the null hypothesis that GNP growth rates were truly generated by an AR(4) model is 2.83, though X_{t-1} being a generated regressor, it is unclear what distribution theory is appropriate for interpreting this statistic.[12] The change in forecast is on the order of 1% of GNP.

Another prediction of the Markov model that is inconsistent with an ARIMA or UC specification concerns the heteroskedasticity of the residuals. The intuition is as follows. If the data were truly generated by the Markov model and we knew that the economy was in expansion last period ($S_{t-1} = 1$) along with knowing past values for ε_{t-j}, then the expected squared error in forecasting log GNP this period would be given by

$$E[\varepsilon_t^2] + E\{[(\alpha_1 S_t + \alpha_0) - (\alpha_1 p + \alpha_0)]^2 | S_{t-1} = 1\} = \sigma_\varepsilon^2 + \alpha_1^2 p(1 - p).$$

[11] This discussion (which rederives eq. (2.5) from first principles) is intended purely as an aid to the intuition. The formula in the text does not literally give the expected value of the coefficient in the regression that follows. One can of course arrive at the precise effect expected by adding s_{t-1} to the AR(4) regression of the Monte Carlo simulations described earlier. Its expected coefficient turns out to be 1.08.

[12] One might think it more natural to test the AR(4) specification against the Markov alternative as a conventional nested hypothesis. When $\alpha_1 = 0$, the growth rates in states 0 and 1 are the same. Thus, an AR(4) model for first-differences of the data obtains as a special case of the Markov specification, and one might think of using a likelihood ratio, Wald, or Lagrange multiplier test. Unfortunately, the usual regularity conditions for establishing asymptotic properties of these tests fail to apply here. Under the null hypothesis that $\alpha_1 = 0$, the parameters p and q are unidentified. When p, q, and α_1 are all treated as separate parameters, the information matrix is singular under the null hypothesis and the MLE's $\hat{p}$ and $\hat{q}$ cannot be regarded as consistent estimates of any population values. Furthermore, the derivative of the log likelihood with respect to α_1 is also zero at the constrained MLE. Davies (1977), Watson and Engle (1985), and Lee and Chesher (1986) have discussions of how one might try to construct asymptotic test statistics that are robust to these issues.

By contrast, if we knew that the economy was in recession last period,

$$E\left[\varepsilon_t^2\right] + E\left\{\left[(\alpha_1 S_t + \alpha_0) - (\alpha_1(1-q) + \alpha_0)\right]^2 | S_{t-1} = 0\right\}$$
$$= \sigma_\varepsilon^2 + \alpha_1^2 q(1-q).$$

Since $p > q > 1/2$, the model therefore predicts that an AR(4) forecast will have a smaller variance when the economy was in expansion last period than when the economy was in recession last period, the expected difference being on the order of[13]

$$\alpha_1^2\left[p(1-p) - q(1-q)\right] = -.229.$$

Thus, the Markov model predicts that in a regression of the square of the AR(4) residuals on a constant and the lagged filter output, the latter should enter statistically significantly and with a negative sign. The ARIMA or UC models predict homoskedastic errors and a coefficient of zero. In actual postwar GNP data one finds (standard errors in parentheses)

$$\underset{}{\hat{u}_t^2} = \underset{(.299)}{1.570} - \underset{(.369)}{.813}\, X_{t-1} + e_t, \qquad R^2 = .03654,$$

where $\hat{u}_t$ is the estimated residual from the AR(4) regression in panel B of Figure 2. The Breusch-Pagan (1979) test of the null hypothesis of homoskedastic errors is $1/\{2[(\hat{\sigma}_u^2)^2]\}$ times the explained sum of squares from this regression, which comes out to 5.17. Engle (1982, p. 1000) proposes calculating $TR^2 = 4.75$. Again abstracting from the generated regressor problem, both statistics should be $\chi^2(1)$ (whose 5% critical value is 3.84) under the null hypothesis that the data were generated by an AR(4) model with Gaussian homoskedastic errors. The data thus reveal evidence of the kind of conditional heteroskedasticity predicted by the Markov model and inconsistent with the ARIMA or UC specifications. Again the heteroskedasticity is economically large; (the squared residuals from an AR(4) are twice as large on average when the preceding period's inference about s_{t-1} pointed confidently to a recession).

8. ON THE CONSEQUENCES OF BUSINESS CYCLES FOR THE LONG RUN LEVEL OF OUTPUT

Much effort has recently been devoted to measuring the effect of an unanticipated increase in GNP on the optimal forecast of the level of GNP at an arbitrarily long time horizon. This question holds interest for two reasons. The first concerns the nature of the business cycle and its persistence; the second pertains to the response of consumers and firms to changing business conditions. I discuss the implications of my Markov parameterization for each of these issues in turn.

[13] Again, this discussion is meant primarily to highlight the intuition and not to derive the precise magnitude expected; the innovation of the AR(4) model is not simply $\varepsilon_t + (s_t - E_{t-1}S_t)$. From Monte Carlo simulations on data truly generated by the Markov model, the expected coefficient on s_{t-1} in the Breusch-Pagan regression that follows turns out to be $-.345$.

TABLE III

PREVIOUS ESTIMATES OF THE EFFECT OF AN UNANTICIPATED 1% INCREASE IN REAL GNP ON THE FUTURE LEVEL OF GNP AT AN ARBITRARILY LONG TIME HORIZON

BASIC WOLD REPRESENTATION: $(1-L)\tilde{y}_t = \mu + \psi(L)u_t$		$\psi(1)$
ARIMA$(p,1,q)$ *MODELS*: $\psi(L) = [1+\theta_1 L + \cdots + \theta_q L^q]/[1-\phi_1 L - \cdots - \phi_p L^p]$		
Watson (1986)	ARIMA(1,1,0)	1.68%
Clark (1987)	ARIMA(0,1,2)	1.62%
Campbell and Mankiw (1987b)	ARIMA(2,1,2)	1.49%
LINEAR UNOBSERVED COMPONENTS MODELS: $\psi(L)u_t = e_t^{\tau} + (1-L)\kappa(L)e_t^c$		
Watson (1986)		0.57%
Clark (1987)		0.64%
BIVARIATE MODEL: (univariate representation implied by bivariate process for GNP growth and level of unemployment)		
Evans (1987)	ARIMA(6,1,3)	0.55%
COCHRANE'S NONPARAMETRIC ESTIMATE:		
Campbell and Mankiw (1987a)		0.80% to 1.27%

8.1. *On the Nature and Persistence of the Business Cycle*

Nelson and Plosser (1982) and Campbell and Mankiw (1987a, b) were interested in the extent to which recessions represent temporary deviations from potential output with the shortfall largely made up during the subsequent recovery. Earlier approaches to this question were ultimately based on the standard linear representation for a nonstationary series $\tilde{y}_t$:

$$(1-L)\tilde{y}_t = \mu + \sum_{j=0}^{\infty} \psi_j u_{t-j} = \mu + \psi(L)u_t.$$

The permanent effect on the level of the series of a current innovation u_t is given by

$$\lim_{j\to\infty} \frac{\partial E_t \tilde{y}_{t+j}}{\partial u_t} = \sum_{j=0}^{\infty} \psi_j = \psi(1).$$

Previous researchers sought a finite-sample approximation to $\psi(L)$ based on Box-Jenkins methods, linear unobserved components models, bivariate models, and nonparametric tests. A sampling of estimates based on these techniques is provided in Table III.[14]

By contrast, the Markov model is fundamentally nonlinear and provides an alternative perspective on the basic question about business cycles posed by these researchers. We can write this model in the form

$$(1-L)\tilde{y}_t = (\alpha_0 + \alpha_1 s_t) + [\phi(L)]^{-1}\varepsilon_t.$$

Notice that the two fundamental sources of randomness, S_t and ε_t, are allowed to

[14]See also Cochrane (1987, 1988), Campbell and Deaton (1987), and Gagnon (1988). For comparison, the AR(4) model fit to GNP growth in panel 1 of Figure 2 implies $\psi(1) = 1.31$.

have very different implications for the future path followed by $\tilde{y}_t$. The earlier discussion argued that we could associate S_t with the business cycle directly, and ε_t with other factors contributing to changes in output. The permanent effect of the non-business-cycle component ε_t is given by

$$\lim_{j \to \infty} \frac{\partial E_t \tilde{y}_{t+j}}{\partial \varepsilon_t} = \frac{1}{\phi(1)} = \frac{1}{1 - .014 + .058 + .247 + .213} = 0.66.$$

On the other hand, if at date t the economy is in a recession ($S_t = 0$) rather than the growth state ($S_t = 1$), the consequences for the long-run future level of (100 times the log of) real GNP is given by equation (3.4):[15]

$$(5.1) \quad \lim_{j \to \infty} \left\{ E_t[\tilde{y}_{t+j} | S_t = 1] - E_t[\tilde{y}_{t+j} | S_t = 0] \right\}$$
$$= \frac{\alpha_1(-1 + p + q)}{(2 - p - q)}$$
$$= \frac{1.522(-1 + .9049 + .7550)}{(2 - .9049 - .7550)} = 2.953$$

or about a 3% drop in GNP.

We can gauge the importance of Jensen's inequality for such calculations by using equation (3.16), which, in contrast to (5.1), forecasts the level rather than the log of GNP. Notice that for the MLE's in Table I, the term $\hat{\alpha}_1$ in equation (3.16) is estimated to be $\exp(1.522/100) = 1.01534$. The eigenvalues are $\mu_1 = 1.01138$ and $\mu_2 = 0.66264$. Thus from (3.16),

$$\lim_{j \to \infty} \left\{ E_t[\exp(\tilde{y}_{t+j}/100) | S_t = 1, z_t] \div E_t[\exp(\tilde{y}_{t+j}/100) | S_t = 0, z_t] \right\}$$
$$= \frac{1.01138 - (-1 + .9049 + .7550)}{1.01138 - (1.01534)(-1 + .9049 + .7550)} = 1.0297$$

virtually the identical 3% change predicted in eq. (5.1).

8.2. *Implications for the Permanent Income Hypothesis*

A conceptually separate reason for interest in the magnitudes in Table III arises from a desire to understand the spending habits of consumers. Here Deaton (1986) and Campbell and Deaton (1987) raise the issue as to whether an unanticipated 1% increase in income rationally signals a greater than 1% increase in permanent income. The magnitudes in Table III are then used to evaluate theories of consumption behavior as distinct from theories of the business cycle per se. Watson (1986) showed that different finite-parameter approximations to a

[15] This calculation holds the current level of GNP constant, and calculates only the "signalling" consequences of the recession for future GNP. If instead one wanted a dynamic multiplier (the future *and present* consequences of a shift from $S_t = 1$ to $S_t = 0$ with the history of ε's and all past s_{t-j} constant), one should add α_1 (or 1.522%) to the values reported in the text.

given process can yield strikingly different answers to this question. In this spirit I examine $\psi(1)$ for the linear Wold representation for my Markov process,

$$(8.1) \qquad y_t = \alpha_0 + \alpha_1 S_t + [\phi(L)]^{-1}\varepsilon_t = \mu + \psi(L)e_t.$$

Note from (2.3), (2.13), and (8.1) that y_t has the spectrum

$$(8.2) \qquad f(\omega) = \frac{\sigma_\varepsilon^2}{(1-\phi_1 e^{i\omega} - \cdots - \phi_r e^{i\omega r})(1-\phi_1 e^{-i\omega} - \cdots - \phi_r e^{-i\omega r})} + \frac{\alpha_1^2[p(1-p)\pi + q(1-q)(1-\pi)]}{(1-\lambda e^{i\omega})(1-\lambda e^{-i\omega})} = \sigma_e^2 \psi(e^{i\omega})\psi(e^{-i\omega})$$

where our task is to calculate $\psi(1)$. From (8.2) we see

$$f(0) = \frac{\sigma_\varepsilon^2}{(1-\phi_1 - \cdots - \phi_r)^2} + \frac{\alpha_1^2[p(1-p)\pi + q(1-q)(1-\pi)]}{(1-\lambda)^2} = \sigma_e^2 \cdot [\psi(1)]^2.$$

Using the maximum likelihood estimates in Table I, we calculate

$$(8.3) \qquad \sigma_e^2 \cdot [\psi(1)]^2 = .261 + 2.277 = 2.538.$$

We further know (e.g., Anderson (1971, p. 422))

$$\sigma_e^2 = \exp\left[\frac{1}{2\pi}\int_{-\pi}^{\pi} \log f(\omega)\, d\omega\right]$$

which one calculates to be .9703 by numerical integration of (8.2). Thus

$$\psi(1) = \left[\frac{\sigma_e^2 \cdot [\psi(1)]^2}{\sigma_e^2}\right]^{1/2} = 1.62.$$

This estimate is completely dominated by the contribution of the business cycle variable (see the second term in the sum on the right-hand side of (8.3)).

It is also straightforward to calculate the effect a recession would have on permanent income if consumers knew with certainty that a recession had started, that is, calculate the effect of a recession on the cumulative discounted value of future output flows. From equation (3.17), the ratio of the discounted value of the trend term when $\pi_0 = 1$ to the value when $\pi_0 = 0$ is given by[16]

$$\frac{1-(-1+p+q)\beta \cdot \exp(\alpha_0/100)}{1-(-1+p+q)\beta \cdot \exp[(\alpha_0+\alpha_1)/100]}.$$

[16] Recall that in the case of a Markov trend in logs, the stochastic specification is multiplicative, not additive ($\hat{y}_t = \hat{n}_t \hat{z}_t$) and so use of this formula is only strictly valid for $E_t \hat{z}_{t+j}$ constant. It does seem to offer a useful benchmark, however, for summarizing a key feature of these empirical estimates. See also the preceding footnote.

Using $\beta = 0.99$ for the quarterly real discount factor, this expression comes out to 1.029 for the empirical estimates in Table I; that is, the certain knowledge that the economy has gone into a recession is associated with a 3% drop in permanent income.

9. CONCLUSIONS

This paper explored the possibility that growth rates of real GNP are subject to autocorrelated discrete shifts. Empirical estimation suggested that the business cycle is better characterized by a recurrent pattern of such shifts between a recessionary state and a growth state rather than by positive coefficients at low lags in an autoregressive model. Indeed, statistical estimates of the economy's growth state cohere remarkably well with NBER dating of postwar recessions, and might be used as an alternative objective method for assigning business cycle dates. A move from expansion into recession is associated with a 3% decrease in the present value of future real GNP and similarly portends a 3% drop in the long-run forecast level of GNP.

Department of Economics, Rouss Hall, University of Virginia, Charlottesville, VA 22901, U.S.A.

Manuscript received November, 1986; final revision received June, 1988.

REFERENCES

ANDERSON, T. W. (1971): *The Statistical Analysis of Time Series*. New York: John Wiley and Sons, Inc.

AOKI, MASANAO (1967): *Optimization of Stochastic Systems: Topics in Discrete-Time Systems*. New York: Academic Press.

BEVERIDGE, STEPHEN, AND CHARLES R. NELSON (1981): "A New Approach to Decomposition of Economic Time Series into Permanent and Transitory Components with Particular Attention to Measurement of the 'Business Cycle'," *Journal of Monetary Economics*, 7, 151–174.

BOX, G. E. P., AND GWILYM M. JENKINS (1976): *Time Series Analysis: Forecasting and Control*, Revised Edition. San Francisco: Holden-Day.

BREUSCH, T. S., AND A. R. PAGAN (1979): "A Simple Test for Heteroscedasticity and Random Coefficient Variation," *Econometrica*, 47, 1287–1294.

BROCK, W. A., AND CHERA L. SAYERS (1988): "Is the Business Cycle Characterized by Deterministic Chaos?" *Journal of Monetary Economics*, 22, 71–80.

CAMPBELL, JOHN Y., AND ANGUS DEATON (1987): "Is Consumption Too Smooth?" NBER Working Paper No. 2134.

CAMPBELL, JOHN Y., AND N. GREGORY MANKIW (1987a): "Permanent and Transitory Components in Macroeconomic Fluctuations," *American Economic Review Papers and Proceedings*, 77, 111–117.

——— (1987b): "Are Output Fluctuations Transitory?" *Quarterly Journal of Economics*, 102, 857–880.

CHIANG, CHIN LONG (1980): *An Introduction to Stochastic Processes and Their Applications*. New York: Krieger.

CLARK, PETER K. (1987): "The Cylical Component of U.S. Economic Activity," *Quarterly Journal of Economics*, 102, 797–814.

COCHRANE, JOHN H. (1987): "Spectral Density Estimates of Unit Roots," Working Paper, University of Chicago.

——— (1988): "How Big is the Random Walk in GNP?" *Journal of Political Economy*, 96, 893–920.

COSSLETT, STEPHEN R., AND LUNG-FEI LEE (1985): "Serial Correlation in Discrete Variable Models," *Journal of Econometrics*, 27, 79–97.

DAVIES, R. B. (1977): "Hypothesis Testing When a Nuisance Parameter is Present Only Under the Alternative," *Biometrika*, 64, 247–254.

DEATON, ANGUS S. (1987): "Life-Cycle Models of Consumption: Is the Evidence Consistent with the Theory?" in *Advances in Econometrics, Fifth World Congress*, Vol. II., ed. by T. F. Bewley. New York: Cambridge University Press, pp. 121–148.

DIEBOLD, FRANCIS X., AND GLENN D. RUDEBUSCH (1987): "Scoring the Leading Indicators," Federal Reserve Board, Special Studies Paper No. 206.

ENGLE, ROBERT F. (1982): "Autoregressive Conditional Heteroscedasticity with Estimates of the Variance of United Kingdom Inflation," *Econometrica*, 50, 987–1007.

ENGLE, ROBERT F., AND C. W. J. GRANGER (1987): "Co-Integration and Error Correction: Representation, Estimation, and Testing," *Econometrica*, 55, 251–276.

ENGLE, ROBERT F., DAVID LILIEN, AND RUSSELL P. ROBINS (1987): "Estimating Time Varying Risk Premia in the Term Structure: The ARCH-M Model," *Econometrica*, 55, 391–407.

EVANS, GEORGE W. (1987): "Output and Unemployment Dynamics in the United States: 1950–1985," Working Paper, Stanford University.

GAGNON, JOSEPH E. (1988): "Short-Run Models and Long-Run Forecasts: A Note of the Permanence of Output Fluctuations," *Quarterly Journal of Economics*, 103, 415–424.

GALLANT, A. RONALD, AND GEORGE TAUCHEN (1987): "Seminonparametric Estimation of Conditionally Constrained Heterogeneous Processes: Asset Pricing Applications," Mimeographed, North Carolina State University.

GOLDFELD, STEPHEN M., AND RICHARD E. QUANDT (1973): "A Markov Model for Switching Regressions," *Journal of Econometrics*, 1, 3–16.

GRANGER, C. W. J. (1983): "Forecasting White Noise," *Applied Time Series Analysis of Economic Data*, in *Proceedings of the Conference on Applied Time Series Analysis of Economic Data*, Oct. 13–15, 1981, Arlington, VA, ed. by Arnold Zellner. Washington, D.C.: U.S. Department of Commerce, Bureau of the Census, pp. 308–314.

HAMILTON, JAMES D. (1985): "Historical Causes of Postwar Oil Shocks and Recessions," *Energy Journal*, 6, 97–116.

——— (1988): "Rational-Expectations Econometric Analysis of Changes in Regime: An Investigation of the Term Structure of Interest Rates," *Journal of Economic Dynamics and Control*, 12, 385–423.

HARVEY, A. C. (1985): "Trends and Cycles in Macroeconomic Time Series," *Journal of Business and Economic Statistics*, 3, 216–227.

HARVEY, A. C., AND P. H. J. TODD (1983): "Forecasting Economic Time Series with Structural and Box-Jenkins Models: A Case Study," *Journal of Business and Economic Statistics*, 1, 299–307.

HENDRY, DAVID F., AND JEAN-FRANCOIS RICHARD (1982): "On the Formulation of Empirical Models in Dynamic Econometrics," *Journal of Econometrics*, 20, 3–33.

HINICH, MELVIN J., AND DOUGLAS M. PATTERSON (1985): "Evidence of Nonlinearity in Daily Stock Returns," *Journal of Business and Economic Statistics*, 3, 69–77.

KING, ROBERT, CHARLES PLOSSER, JAMES STOCK, AND MARK WATSON (1987): "Stochastic Trends and Economic Fluctuations," NBER Working Paper No. 2229.

LEE, LUNG-FEI, AND ANDREW CHESHER (1986): "Specification Testing when the Score Statistics Are Identically Zero," *Journal of Econometrics*, 31, 121–149.

LIPTSER, R. M., AND A. N. SHIRYAYEV (1977): *Statistics of Random Processes, Volume I: General Theory*. New York: Springer-Verlag.

NEFTCI, SALIH N. (1982): "Optimal Prediction of Cyclical Downturns," *Journal of Economic Dynamics and Control*, 4, 225–241.

——— (1984): "Are Economic Time Series Asymmetric over the Business Cycle?" *Journal of Political Economy*, 92, 307–328.

NELSON, CHARLES R., AND CHARLES I. PLOSSER (1982): "Trends and Random Walks in Macroeconomic Time Series: Some Evidence and Implications," *Journal of Monetary Economics*, 10, 139–162.

QUAH, DANNY (1986): "What Do We Learn from Unit Roots in Macro Economic Time Series?" Working Paper, MIT.

SCLOVE, STANLEY L. (1983): "Time-Series Segmentation: A Model and a Method," *Information Sciences*, 29, 7–25.

SICHEL, DANIEL E. (1987): "Business Cycle Asymmetry: A Deeper Look," Mimeographed, Princeton University.

STOCK, JAMES H. (1987): "Measuring Business Cycle Time," *Journal of Political Economy*, 95, 1240–1261.

TONG, HOWELL (1983): *Threshold Models in Non-linear Time Series Analysis*. New York: Springer-Verlag.

WATSON, MARK W. (1986): "Univariate Detrending Methods with Stochastic Trends," *Journal of Monetary Economics*, 18, 49–75.

WATSON, MARK W., AND ROBERT F. ENGLE (1985): "Testing for Regression Coefficient Stability with a Stationary AR(1) Alternative," *Review of Economics and Statistics*, 67, 341–346.

WECKER, WILLIAM E. (1979): "Predicting the Turning Points of a Time Series," *Journal of Business*, 52, 35–50.

[17]

DIAGNOSTIC CHECKING ARMA TIME SERIES MODELS USING SQUARED-RESIDUAL AUTOCORRELATIONS

BY A. I. MCLEOD

Department of Statistical and Actuarial Sciences, The University of Western Ontario

AND

W. K. LI

Department of Statistics, University of Hong Kong

Abstract. Squared-residual autocorrelations have been found useful in detecting non-linear types of statistical dependence in the residuals of fitted autoregressive-moving average (ARMA) models (Granger and Andersen, 1978; Miller, 1979). In this note it is shown that the normalized squared-residual autocorrelations are asymptotically unit multivariate normal. The results of a simulation experiment confirming the small-sample validity of the proposed tests is reported.

Keywords. ARMA time series; diagnostic checking; nonlinear time series; portmanteau test; testing for statistical independence.

1. INTRODUCTION AND SUMMARY

The ARMA (p, q) model for n observations $z_1, \ldots, z_n$ of a stationary mean μ time series can be written

$$\phi(B)(z_t - \mu) = \theta(B)a_t, \tag{1.1}$$

where

$$\phi(B) = 1 - \phi_1 B - \cdots - \phi_p B^p,$$

$$\theta(B) = 1 - \theta_1 B - \cdots - \theta_q B^q,$$

where μ is the series mean and B is the backshift operator on t. The polynomials $\phi(B)$ and $\theta(B)$ are assumed to have all roots outside the unit circle and to have no factors in common. The standard large-sample estimation theory (Whittle, 1961; Hannan, 1970) requires that the a_t's be independent and identically distributed with finite variance.

A very useful procedure for checking the adequacy of a fitted ARMA model is based on testing the estimated innovations or residuals, $\hat{a}_t$, for whiteness. Box and Pierce (1970) obtained the distribution of the residual autocorrelations function

$$\hat{r}_a(k) = \sum_{k+1}^{n} \hat{a}_t \hat{a}_{t-k} \Big/ \sum_{1}^{n} \hat{a}_t^2 \tag{1.2}$$

0143–9782/83/04 0269–05 \$02.50/0
JOURNAL OF TIME SERIES ANALYSIS Vol. 4, No. 4

and suggested the portmanteau statistic

$$Q_a = n \sum_{i=1}^{M} \hat{r}_a^2(i) \tag{1.3}$$

for testing the whiteness of the residuals. Under the assumption of model adequacy, Q_a is approximately $\chi^2(M-p-q)$ provided M and n are large enough (McLeod, 1978). Davies, Triggs and Newbold (1977) and Ljung and Box (1978) demonstrated that the modified statistic

$$Q_a^* = n(n+2) \sum_{i=1}^{M} \hat{r}_a^2(i)/(n-i) \tag{1.4}$$

provides a closer small-sample approximation to $\chi^2(M-p-q)$.

Granger and Andersen (1978) suggested that the autocorrelation function of the square of a time series could be useful in identifying non-linear bilinear time series. Granger and Andersen (1978, p. 86) found some series modelled in Box and Jenkins (1976) in which the squared residuals appear to be autocorrelated even though the residuals do not. In this situation, Granger and Andersen suggested that improved forecasts could be obtained by fitting a simple bilinear model to the residuals of the fitted ARMA model. Nonlinear time series modelling methods of Yakowitz (1979a, b) and Tong and Lim (1980) may also prove useful in this situation. Miller (1979) also reported, when modelling a mean daily riverflow series, that the residuals of a fitted ARMA did not appear to be autocorrelated although the squared residuals seemed significantly autocorrelated. When precipitation covariates were included in this model, Miller found that this difficulty was apparently eliminated. The present authors have also noticed numerous other hydrological and economic time series in which the squared residuals of the best fitting ARMA are significantly autocorrelated even though the usual residual autocorrelations do not suggest any model inadequacy.

The autocorrelation function of $\hat{a}_t^2$ is estimated by

$$\hat{r}_{aa}(k) = \sum_{t=k+1}^{n} (\hat{a}_t^2 - \hat{\sigma}^2)(\hat{a}_{t-k}^2 - \hat{\sigma}^2) \Big/ \sum_{t=1}^{n} (\hat{a}_t^2 - \hat{\sigma}^2)^2, \tag{1.5}$$

where

$$\hat{\sigma}^2 = \sum \hat{a}_t^2 / n.$$

In the next section, it is shown that for fixed M,

$$\sqrt{n}\, \hat{\mathbf{r}}_{aa} = (\hat{r}_{aa}(1), \ldots, \hat{r}_{aa}(M)) \tag{1.6}$$

is asymptotically normal as $n \to \infty$ with mean zero and unit covariance matrix. A significance test is provided by the portmanteau statistic

$$Q_{aa}^* = n(n+2) \sum_{i=1}^{M} \hat{r}_{aa}^2(i)/(n-i) \tag{1.7}$$

which is asymptotically $\chi^2(M)$ if the a_t are independent. In the final section, simulation experiments which suggest the small-sample applicability of these results are reported.

2. DISTRIBUTION OF SQUARED-RESIDUAL AUTOCORRELATIONS

Suppose that n observations, $z_1, \ldots, z_n$, of a time series are generated by an ARMA (p, q) model in which the innovations a_t are independent and identically distributed and for which $\langle a_t^8 \rangle$ exists, where $\langle \cdot \rangle$ denotes mathematical expectation. Let $\boldsymbol{\beta} = (\phi_1, \ldots, \phi_p, \theta_1, \ldots, \theta_q, \mu, \sigma^2)$ denote the true parameter values and let $\hat{\boldsymbol{\beta}}$ denote the least squares or Gaussian maximum likelihood estimates. Let $\dot{a}_t$, $t = 1, \ldots, n$ denote the residuals corresponding to arbitrary parameter values $(\dot{\phi}_1, \ldots, \dot{\phi}_p, \dot{\theta}_1, \ldots, \dot{\theta}_p, \dot{\mu})$ and let $\dot{\sigma}^2 = \sum \dot{a}_t^2 / n$.

The squared-residual autocorrelations for lag k can be written

$$\dot{r}_{aa}(k) = \dot{c}_{aa}(k) / \dot{c}_{aa}(0) \tag{2.1}$$

where

$$\dot{c}_{aa}(k) = \sum_{t=k+1}^{n} (\dot{a}_t^2 - \dot{\sigma}^2)(\dot{a}_{t-k}^2 - \dot{\sigma}^2)/n, \qquad k \geq 0. \tag{2.2}$$

Let $\hat{c}_{aa}(k)$ and $c_{aa}(k)$ be defined similarly.

The following lemma may be established by straightforward calculation (Li, 1981).

LEMMA

$$\partial \dot{c}_{aa}(k) / \partial \beta_i = \mathcal{O}_p(1/\sqrt{n}) \tag{2.3}$$

THEOREM. *For fixed M, $\sqrt{n}\, \hat{r}_{aa}$ is asymptotically $N(\mathbf{0}, \mathbf{1}_M)$ as $n \to \infty$, where $\mathbf{1}_M$ is the M by M identity matrix.*

PROOF. Expanding $\dot{c}_{aa}(k)$ in a Taylor series about $\dot{\boldsymbol{\beta}} = \hat{\boldsymbol{\beta}}$,

$$\hat{c}_{aa}(k) = c_{aa}(k) + \sum_i (\hat{\beta}_i - \beta_i)\, \partial \dot{c}_{aa}(k) / \partial \beta_i + \mathcal{O}_p(1/n). \tag{2.4}$$

Since $\partial \dot{c}_{aa}(k)/\partial \beta_i = \mathcal{O}_p(1/\sqrt{n})$ and $\hat{\beta}_i - \beta_i = \mathcal{O}_p(1/\sqrt{n})$, it follows that

$$\hat{c}_{aa}(k) = c_{aa}(k) + \mathcal{O}_p(1/n). \tag{2.5}$$

From Theorem 14 of Hannan (1970, p. 228) $\sqrt{n}(c_{aa}(1), \ldots, c_{aa}(M))/\gamma_{aa}(0)$ is asymptotically $N(\mathbf{0}, \mathbf{1}_M)$, where $\gamma_{aa}(0) = \langle (a_t^2 - \sigma^2)^2 \rangle$.

Expanding $\dot{r}_{aa}(k)$ about $\dot{c}_{aa}(0) = \gamma_{aa}(0)$ and $\dot{c}_{aa}(k) = \hat{c}_{aa}(k)$,

$$\hat{r}_{aa}(k) = \hat{c}_{aa}(k) / \gamma_{aa}(0) + \mathcal{O}_p(1/n). \tag{2.6}$$

The theorem now follows (using result 2c.4.12 of Rao 1973).

REMARK. The asymptotic variance of $\hat{r}_a(k)$ differs dramatically from that of $r_a(k)=\sum a_t a_{t-k}/\sum a_t^2$ due to the effect of estimating $\boldsymbol{\beta}$ (Box and Pierce, 1970; Dŭrbin, 1970; McLeod, 1978). However, it should be noted that this phenomenon does not occur with squared residuals.

3. SMALL-SAMPLE SIMULATION

The small-sample applicability of the results is examined for the AR (1) models:

$$z_t = \phi z_{t-1} + a_t, \tag{3.1}$$

where $t=1,\ldots,n$; $n=50$, 100, 200; $\phi=0$, $\pm.3$, $\pm.6$, $\pm.9$ and the a_t's are independent $N(0,1)$ random variables. The random number generator Super-duper (Marsaglia, 1976), was used in conjunction with the transformation of Box and Muller (1958) to generate the a_t's. Each of the 21 models was simulated 10 000 times using an exact simulation technique (McLeod and Hipel, 1978). The parameter ϕ was estimated by the sample lag-one autocorrelation. The empirical variances of $\hat{r}_{aa}(1)$ and Q^*_{aa} with $M=20$ are shown in table I. Note that the variance of Q^*_{aa} is too large while that of $\hat{r}_{aa}(1)$ is too small. The approximation is much better for $n=200$ than $n=50$.

TABLE 1

EMPIRICAL BEHAVIOUR OF $\hat{r}_{aa}(1)$ AND Q^*_{aa}

		Number of Rejections at Nominal 5% Level		Empirical Mean	Empirical Variance	
n	ϕ	$\hat{r}_{aa}(1)$	Q^*_{aa}	Q^*_{aa}	$\hat{r}_{aa}(1)$	Q^*_{aa}
50	−.9	258	447	17.91	0.0164	49.00
50	−.6	298	458	18.03	0.0167	50.75
50	−.3	293	474	17.90	0.0167	50.71
50	0	255	520	17.98	0.0162	54.09
50	.3	278	448	17.83	0.0164	50.10
50	.6	305	490	17.97	0.0166	52.86
50	.9	290	456	17.84	0.0166	51.69
100	−.9	365	521	18.70	0.0087	49.82
100	−.6	352	509	18.64	0.0091	49.16
100	−.3	387	535	18.74	0.0092	49.01
100	0	372	492	18.65	0.0088	47.90
100	.3	373	492	18.65	0.0090	47.62
100	.6	349	473	18.57	0.0088	48.19
100	.9	375	516	18.55	0.0091	48.17
200	−.9	412	536	19.19	0.0046	46.06
200	−.6	399	497	19.03	0.0046	46.17
200	−.3	401	551	19.23	0.0046	47.49
200	0	423	502	19.23	0.0048	45.01
200	.3	450	535	19.26	0.0048	46.49
200	.6	428	494	19.18	0.0048	45.63
200	.9	418	492	19.18	0.0048	45.74

The empirical levels of tests using $\hat{r}_{aa}(1)$ and Q^*_{aa} at the nominal 5% level was also examined. Table I shows the number of times $|\hat{r}_{aa}(1)| > 1.96/\sqrt{n}$ and $Q^*_{aa} > 31.41$ ($M = 20$). The 95% confidence interval for the number of rejections is 500 ± 43 (Conover, 1971, p. 111). The test using Q^*_{aa} is slightly less than the lower limit 4 times whereas the test using $\hat{r}_{aa}(1)$ is always conservative although the approximation clearly improves with larger *n*.

The above experiments were repeated using the exact innovations to calculate $r_{aa}(1)$ and Q^*_{aa} instead of the residuals. As expected, no significant difference in the pattern of behaviour already described in Table I was found.

REFERENCES

BILLINGSLEY, P. (1961) The Lindeberg–Levy Theorem for Martingales. *Proceedings of the American Mathematical Society*, 12, 788–792.

BOX, G. E. P. and M. E. MULLER (1958) A Note on the Generation of Random Normal Deviates. *Ann. Math. Stat.* 29, 610–611.

BOX, G. E. P., M. E. MULLER and G. M. JENKINS (1976) *Time Series Analysis Forecasting and Control*, 2nd ed. Holden Day: San Francisco.

CONOVER, W. J. (1971) *Practical Nonparametric Statistics.* Wiley: New York.

DAVIES, N., C. M. TRIGGS and P. NEWBOLD (1977) Significance of the Box–Pierce Portmanteau Statistics in Finite Samples. *Biometrika*, 64, 517–522.

DURBIN, J. (1970) Testing for Serial Correlation in Least Squares Regression When Some of the Regressors are Lagged Dependent Variables. *Econometrika*, 38, 410–421.

GRANGER, C. W. and A. P. ANDERSEN (1978) *An Introduction to Bilinear Time Series Models.* Vandenhoeck and Ruprecht: Gottingen.

HANNAN, E. J. (1971) *Multiple Time Series.* Wiley: New York.

LI, W. K. (1981) *Topics in Time Series Modelling.* Ph.D. Thesis, The University of Western Ontario.

LJUNG, G. M. and G. E. P. BOX (1978) On a Measure of Lack of Fit in Time Series Models. *Biometrika*, 65, 297–303.

MARSAGLIA, G. (1976) Random Number Generation. In *Encyclopedia of Computer Science*, edited by A. Ralston. Petrocelli and Charter: New York, pp. 1192–1197.

MCLEOD, A. I. and K. W. HIPEL (1978) Simulation Procedures for Box-Jenkins Models. *Water Resources Research*, 14, 969–975.

MCLEOD, A. I. and K. W. HIPEL (1978) On the Distribution of Residual Autocorrelations in Box–Jenkins Models. *J. R. Statist. Soc. B* 296–302.

MILLER, R. B. (1979) Book review on 'An Introduction to Bilinear Time Series Models', by C. W. Granger and A. P. Andersen. *J. Amer. Statist. Ass.* 74, 927.

RAO, C. R. (1973) *Linear Statistical Inference and Its Applications*, 2nd ed. Wiley: New York.

TONG, H. and K. S. LIM (1980) Threshold Autoregression, Limit Cycles and Cyclical Data. *J. R. Statist. Soc. B* 42, 245–292.

WHITTLE, P. (1961) Gaussian Estimation in Stationary Time Series. *Bull. Int. Statist. Inst.* 33, 105–129.

YAKOWITZ, S. (1979a) A Nonparametric Markov Model for Daily River Flow. *Water Resources Research*, 15, 1035–1043.

YAKOWITZ, S. (1979b) Nonparametric Estimation of Markov Transition Functions. *Ann. Statist.* 7, 671–679.

[18]

Biometrika (1986), 73, 2, *pp.* 461-6
Printed in Great Britain

Nonlinearity tests for time series

BY RUEY S. TSAY

Department of Statistics, Carnegie-Mellon University, Pittsburgh, Pennsylvania 15213, U.S.A.

SUMMARY

This paper considers two nonlinearity tests for stationary time series. The idea of Tukey's one degree of freedom for nonadditivity test is generalized to the time series setting. The case of concurrent nonlinearity is discussed in detail. Simulation results show that the proposed tests are more powerful than that of Keenan (1985).

Some key words: Concurrent nonlinearity; Nonlinear time series; Tukey's nonadditivity test; Volterra expansion.

1. INTRODUCTION

Recently there has been a growing interest in studying nonlinear time series. In particular, various tests for testing linearity have been proposed to illustrate the non-linear nature of certain well known processes (Subba Rao & Gabr, 1980; Hinich, 1982; Maravell, 1983; Hinich & Patterson, 1985) and to support the need for nonlinear time series models (Granger & Andersen, 1978). Recently Keenan (1985) adopted the idea of Tukey's (1949) one degree of freedom test for nonadditivity to derive a time-domain statistic, as an alternative of the frequency-domain statistics, e.g. bispectrum, for discriminating between nonlinear and linear models. Keenan's test is motivated by the similarity of Volterra expansions to polynomials, and is extremely simple both conceptually and computationally. However, as shown by Keenan's simulation in Table 1 of his paper, the power of his test could be very low.

In the present paper, we propose a modified test that retains the simplicity of Keenan's test yet is considerably more powerful. The new test statistic is given in § 2, and § 3 reviews numerical comparisons via simulation. Section 4 is devoted to the concurrent nonlinearity model for which Keenan's test fails, and § 5 briefly discusses the autoregressive-moving average models.

2. A TEST OF LINEARITY

A stationary time series Y_t can be written, in its very general form, as

$$Y_t = \mu + \sum_{i=-\infty}^{\infty} b_i e_{t-i} + \sum_{i,j=-\infty}^{\infty} b_{ij} e_{t-i} e_{t-j} + \sum_{i,j,k=-\infty}^{\infty} b_{ijk} e_{t-i} e_{t-j} e_{t-k} + \ldots,$$

where μ is the mean level of Y_t and $\{e_t, -\infty < t < \infty\}$ is a strictly stationary process of independent and identically distributed random variables. Obviously, Y_t is nonlinear if any of the higher order coefficients, $\{b_{ij}\}$, $\{b_{ijk}\}, \ldots$ is nonzero. For such a series, the proposed tests of this paper and that of Keenan (1985) are based on the following argument. Suppose, for the illustrative purpose, that b_{12} is nonzero. Then this nonlinearity will be distributionally reflected in the diagnostics of a fitted linear model if the residuals of the linear model are correlated with $Y_{t-1}Y_{t-2}$, a quadratic nonlinear term. In practice, since the orders of the higher order coefficients, if any, are unknown, Tukey's (1949) nonadditivity test simply uses the aggregated quantity $\hat{Y}_t^2$, the square of the fitted value of Y_t based on the entertained linear model, to obtain quadratic terms upon which the residuals can be correlated. This ingenious idea is extremely valuable when the sample size is small, because it only requires one degree of freedom. One disadvantage of using aggregated quantities, however, is that aggregation often loses potentially useful information. Thus, it seems preferable to employ disaggregated variables when the sample size is large or moderate, as is the case for most time series analyses.

The test proposed here is motivated by the above consideration and it consists of the following steps.

(i) Regress Y_t on $\{1, Y_{t-1}, \ldots, Y_{t-M}\}$ by least squares and obtain the residuals $\{\hat{e}_t\}$, for $t = M+1, \ldots, n$. The regression model will be denoted by

$$Y_t = W_t\Phi + e_t, \tag{2·1}$$

where $W_t = (1, Y_{t-1}, \ldots, Y_{t-M})$ and $\Phi = (\Phi_0, \Phi_1, \ldots, \Phi_M)^{\mathrm{T}}$ with M being a prespecified positive integer, n the sample size, and the superscript T denoting the matrix transpose.

(ii) Regress the vector Z_t on $\{1, Y_{t-1}, \ldots, Y_{t-M}\}$ and obtain the residual vector $\{\hat{X}_t\}$, for $t = M+1, \ldots, n$. Here the multivariate regression model is

$$Z_t = W_tH + X_t,$$

where Z_t is an $m = \frac{1}{2}M(M+1)$ dimensional vector defined by $Z_t^{\mathrm{T}} = \mathrm{vech}\,(U_t^{\mathrm{T}}U_t)$ with $U_t = (Y_{t-1}, \ldots, Y_{t-M})$ and vech denoting the half stacking vector. In other words, Z_t^{T} is obtained from the symmetric matrix $U_t^{\mathrm{T}}U_t$ by the usual column stacking operator but using only those elements on or below the main diagonal of each column.

(iii) Regress $\hat{e}_t$ on $\hat{X}_t$ and let $\hat{F}$ be the F ratio of the mean square of regression to the mean square of error. That is, fit

$$\hat{e}_t = \hat{X}_t\beta + \varepsilon_t \quad (t = M+1, \ldots, n) \tag{2·2}$$

and define

$$\hat{F} = \{(\Sigma\,\hat{X}_t\hat{e}_t)(\Sigma\,\hat{X}_t^{\mathrm{T}}\hat{X}_t)^{-1}(\Sigma\,\hat{X}_t^{\mathrm{T}}\hat{e}_t)/m\}/\{\Sigma\,\hat{\varepsilon}_t^2/(n-M-m-1)\}, \tag{2·3}$$

where the summations are over t from $M+1$ to n and $\hat{\varepsilon}_t$ is the least squares residual for (2·2).

Obviously, this procedure reduces to Keenan's if one aggregates Z_t, with weights determined by the least squares estimate of (2·1), to become a scalar variable. Notice that a by-product of this disaggregated approach is that from the regression (2·2) one can easily identify the significant nonlinear terms to be incorporated in the model. Thus, the proposed testing procedure can be used as a diagnostic tool for building linear or nonlinear time series models.

THEOREM 1. *Let Y_t be a stationary autoregressive process of order M satisfying the model*

$$(Y_t - \mu) = \sum_{i=1}^{M} \Phi_i(Y_{t-i} - \mu) + e_t,$$

where the e_t's are independent and identically distributed random variables with mean zero, variance σ_e^2, and finite fourth moment. Then, for large n, the statistic $\hat{F}$ defined in (2·3) *follows approximately a F distribution with degrees of freedom*

$$\tfrac{1}{2}M(M+1), \quad n-\tfrac{1}{2}M(M+3)-1.$$

Proof. Let $\Phi_0=(1-\Phi_1-\ldots-\Phi_M)\mu$ and $\Phi=(\Phi_0,\Phi_1,\ldots,\Phi_M)^T$. Then the least squares estimate $\hat{\Phi}$ of (2·1) converges to Φ almost surely under the conditions of the theorem (Lai & Wei, 1983). Using this result and Slutsky's Theorem (Bickel & Doksum, 1977, p. 461), and adopting an argument similar to that of Lemma 3.1 of Keenan (1985), it is clear that to prove the theorem it is sufficient to show that

$$n^{-\frac{1}{2}} \sum_{t=M+1}^{n} X_t^T e_t. \tag{2·4}$$

converges in distribution to a multivariate normal random variable, where X_t is given in (2·2). Since X_t depends only on $\{Y_{t-j}, j>0\}$ which is independent of e_t, $X_t^T e_t$ forms a stationary and ergodic martingale difference process. The asymptotic normality of (2·4) then follows from a multivariate version of a martingale central limit theorem (Billingsley, 1961). The associated covariance matrix is the limit of $n^{-1}\Sigma X_t^T X_t$. Finally, the large-sample F distribution of the testing statistic $\hat{F}$ of (2·3) follows from an argument similar to that of the usual analysis of variance. □

Note that the limit of $\{\frac{1}{2}M(M+1)\}\hat{F}$ is a chi-squared random variable with degrees of freedom $\frac{1}{2}M(M+1)$. This is a straightforward generalization of Corollary 3·1 of Keenan (1985). In practice, we prefer to use the approximate F distribution.

3. Comparison

In this section we use simulation to compare the F test of § 2 with Keenan's test. For simplicity, the six models of Keenan (1985) are used in this study. They are:

Model 1, $Y_t=e_t-0·4e_{t-1}+0·3e_{t-2}$;
Model 2, $Y_t=e_t-0·4e_{t-1}+0·3e_{t-2}+0·5e_te_{t-2}$;
Model 3, $Y_t=e_t-0·3e_{t-1}+0·2e_{t-2}+0·4e_{t-1}e_{t-2}-0·25e_{t-2}^2$;
Model 4, $Y_t=0·4Y_{t-1}-0·3Y_{t-2}+e_t$;
Model 5, $Y_t=0·4Y_{t-1}-0·3Y_{t-2}+0·5Y_{t-1}e_{t-1}+e_t$;
Model 6, $Y_t=0·4Y_{t-1}-0·3Y_{t-2}+0·5Y_{t-1}e_{t-1}+0·8e_{t-1}+e_t$.

The e_t's are independent $N(0, 1)$ random variates generated from the GGNML subroutine of the IMSL package. Table 1 gives a summary in terms of empirical significance levels

Table 1. *Empirical frequencies of rejection of the null hypothesis of linearity*; $n=70$, 204; $M=4$, *and* 350 *replications. Nominal significance level,* 0·05.

	$n=70$		$n=204$	
True model	Keenan	F test	Keenan	F test
(a) Linear				
Model 1	0·063	0·066	0·051	0·054
Model 4	0·060	0·066	0·051	0·046
(b) Nonlinear				
Model 3	0·366	0·509	0·843	0·971
Model 5	0·534	0·760	0·811	0·986
Model 6	0·549	0·707	0·857	0·934
Model 2	0·100	0·166	0·097	0·217

and powers. For each model, the results are based on 350 replications of two combinations of $n = 70$, $M = 4$ and $n = 204$, $M = 4$. It is clear that the proposed F test is more powerful than Keenan's test in identifying the nonlinear models while the empirical significance levels of the two tests are reasonable and remain comparable for the linear models.

4. CONCURRENT NONLINEARITY

A striking result of Table 1 is that both Keenan's test and the F test are not powerful in handling Model 2, which contains a concurrent nonlinear term $e_t e_{t-2}$. In this section, we consider the problem of concurrent nonlinearity in further detail.

Obviously, the failure of Keenan's test and the F test is, to a large extent, because the constructed variable Z_t of step (ii) of § 2, hence X_t of step (iii), does not contain concurrent nonlinear terms. We therefore consider in step (ii) the variable $\hat{A}_t = (Y_{t-1}\hat{e}_t, \ldots, Y_{t-M}\hat{e}_t)$ and define in step (iii) the statistics

$$\hat{R}_t = \hat{A}_t \hat{e}_t - U_t \sigma_e^2, \tag{4·1}$$

$$\hat{C} = \frac{(\Sigma \hat{R}_t)(\Sigma \hat{R}_t^{\mathrm{T}} \hat{R}_t)^{-1}(\Sigma \hat{R}_t^{\mathrm{T}})/M}{\Sigma \hat{e}_t^2/(n - M - 1)}, \tag{4·2}$$

where, again, $U_t = (Y_{t-1}, \ldots, Y_{t-M})$ and summations are over t from $M+1$ to n. The motivation for using $\hat{A}_t$ is obvious, and that for $\hat{R}_t$ will become clear in the following proof.

THEOREM 2. *Under the conditions of Theorem* 1, $\hat{C}$ *of* (4·2) *follows approximately a F distribution with degrees of freedom M and* $n - M - 1$, *provided that n is sufficiently large.*

Proof. Using the consistency property of the least squares estimates in the same way as in Theorem 1, we need only show the asymptotic normality of the statistic

$$n^{-\frac{1}{2}} \sum_{t=M+1}^{n} R_t^{\mathrm{T}} = n^{-\frac{1}{2}} \sum_{t=M+1}^{n} \{Y_{t-1}(e_t^2 - \sigma_e^2), \ldots, Y_{t-M}(e_t^2 - \sigma_e^2)\}^{\mathrm{T}},$$

where R_t is the theoretical counterpart of $\hat{R}_t$. Let $\mathcal{F}_{t-1} = \{Y_{t-1}, Y_{t-2}, \ldots\}$ be the σ-field generated by the available information at time $t-1$. Then, it is clear that (i) $E(R_t^{\mathrm{T}} | \mathcal{F}_{t-1}) = 0$ and (ii) each component of R_t forms a stationary martingale difference process with constant variance $(\kappa - 1)\sigma_e^4\{\mathrm{var}(Y_t) + \mu^2\}$, where κ is the fourth cumulant of e_t. The expected asymptotic normality follows, again, from Billingsley's (1961) martingale central limit theorem. Furthermore, since the process $\{Y_{t-j}e_t^2; j = 1, \ldots, M\}$ is stationary and ergodic, $n^{-1} \Sigma R_t^{\mathrm{T}} R_t$ converges in probability to the variance-covariance matrix of R_t. □

Note that the limiting distribution of $M\hat{C}$ is chi-squared with M degrees of freedom. The critical value of a chi-squared table, therefore, can be used when n is large. Here we use the F distribution to match with that of § 2. In practice, σ_e^2 of (4·1) is unknown. However, under the null hypothesis of linear model, it can be estimated by the residual mean square of error of the regression (2·1).

Table 2 compares Keenan's test, the F test of § 2 and the concurrent C test of Theorem 2. Here Model 1 is used to show the significance level and Model 2 to illustrate the power of each test in recognizing the concurrent nonlinear model. Again, 350 replications of each model were used for a given sample size. It is clear from the table that the concurrent C test increases the power markedly over the other two in identifying concurrent nonlinear models, especially when the sample size is moderate or large. None of the tests, however, is very powerful when the sample size is small.

Since Z_t is a function of U_t that is orthogonal to $\hat{e}_t$, $\hat{C}$ of (4·2) in fact can be defined in terms of the residual $\hat{\varepsilon}_t$ of (2·2). That is, one may replace $\hat{e}_t$ by $\hat{e}_t$. This substitution allows us to use the F test of (2·3) first and then switch to $\hat{C}$, if necessary, for concurrent nonlinearity. The numbers in parentheses in Table 2 give the corresponding results based on $\hat{\varepsilon}_t$. For Models 1 and 2, the effect of the F test of (2·3) on the performance of $\hat{C}$ is negligible.

Table 2. *Empirical frequencies of rejection the null hypothesis of linearity*; $n = 70, 140, 204$; $M = 4$, *and* 350 *replications. Nominal significance level,* 0·05

	$n=70$			$n=140$			$n=204$		
Model	K	F	C	K	F	C	K	F	C
				(a) Linear					
Model 1	0·037	0·069	0·074 (0·091)	0·049	0·054	0·054 (0·066)	0·066	0·066	0·046 (0·069)
				(b) Nonlinear					
Model 2	0·100	0·166	0·326 (0·320)	0·103	0·166	0·663 (0·751)	0·097	0·217	0·820 (0·911)

K, Keenan's test; F, F test; C, concurrent C test. Values in brackets use $\hat{\varepsilon}_t$.

5. Autoregressive-moving average models

In practice autoregressive-moving average models are often used in time series analysis with parameters estimated by the maximum likelihood method. In this case the proposed F test, or the concurrent C test, can be employed as a diagnostic tool for checking the linearity assumption of the process. We summarize the result as follows. Proof uses the same techniques as for Theorem 1, together with consistency properties of the maximum likelihood estimates.

Theorem 3. *Suppose that Y_t is a stationary and invertible* ARMA (p, q) *process, say,*

$$(Y_t - \mu) = \sum_{i=1}^{p} \Phi_i (Y_{t-i} - \mu) + e_t - \sum_{i=1}^{q} \Theta_i e_{t-i}, \qquad (5·1)$$

where $\{e_t\}$ is a sequence of independent and identically distributed $N(0, \sigma_e^2)$ random variables. Let $M = p + q$ and $Z_t = \text{vech}\{U_t^T U_t\}$, where $U_t = (Y_{t-1}, \ldots, Y_{t-p}, \hat{e}_{t-1}, \ldots, \hat{e}_{t-q})$ with $\hat{e}_{t-i}$'s being the residuals for model (5·1) *fitted by maximum likelihood. Then, for large n, $\hat{F}$ defined similarly to* (2·3) *follows approximately a F distribution with degrees of freedom $\frac{1}{2}M(M+1)$ and $n - \frac{1}{2}M(M+3) - 1$.*

Acknowledgements

The author wishes to thank the Editor for comments that improved the presentation of the paper, and the ALCOA Research Foundation for partial financial support.

References

Bickel, P. J. & Doksum, K. A. (1977). *Mathematical Statistics: Basic Ideas and Selected Topics.* San Francisco: Holden-Day.

BILLINGSLEY, P. (1961). The Lindeberg–Lévy theorem for martingales. *Proc. Am. Math. Soc.* **12**, 788–92.
GRANGER, C. W. J. & ANDERSEN, A. P. (1978). *Introduction to Bilinear Time Series Models.* Gottingen: Vandenhoeck and Ruprecht.
HINICH, M. J. (1982). Testing for Gaussianity and linearity of a stationary time series. *J. Time Series Anal.* **3**, 169–76.
HINICH, M. J. & PATTERSON, D. M. (1985). Evidence of nonlinearity in daily stock returns. *J. Bus. Econ. Statist.* **3**, 69–77.
KEENAN, D. M. (1985). A Tukey nonadditivity-type test for time series nonlinearity. *Biometrika* **72**, 39–44.
LAI, T. L. & WEI, C. Z. (1983). Asymptotic properties of general autoregressive models and strong consistency of least squares estimates of their parameters. *J. Mult. Anal.* **13**, 1–23.
MARAVELL, A. (1983). An application of nonlinear time series forecasting. *J. Bus. Econ. Statist.* **1**, 66–74.
SUBBA RAO, T. & GABR, M. M. (1980). A test for linearity of stationary time series. *J. Time Series Anal.* **1**, 145–58.
TUKEY, J. W. (1949). One degree of freedom for non-additivity. *Biometrics* **5**, 232–42.

[*Received May* 1985. *Revised October* 1985]

[19]

Non-Gaussian State–Space Modeling of Nonstationary Time Series

GENSHIRO KITAGAWA*

A non-Gaussian state–space approach to the modeling of nonstationary time series is shown. The model is expressed in state–space form, where the system noise and the observational noise are not necessarily Gaussian. Recursive formulas of prediction, filtering, and smoothing for the state estimation and identification of the non-Gaussian state–space model are given. Also given is a numerical method based on piecewise linear approximation to the density functions for realizing these formulas. Significant merits of non-Gaussian modeling and the wide range of applicability of the method are illustrated by some numerical examples.

A typical application of this non-Gaussian modeling is the smoothing of a time series that has mean value function with both abrupt and gradual changes. Simple Gaussian state–space modeling is not adequate for this situation. Here the model with small system noise variance cannot detect jump, whereas the one with large system noise variance yields unfavorable wiggle. To work out this problem within the ordinary linear Gaussian model framework, sophisticated treatment of outliers is required. But by the use of an appropriate non-Gaussian model for system noise, it is possible to reproduce both abrupt and gradual change of the mean without any special treatment.

Nonstandard observations such as the ones distributed as non-Gaussian distribution can be easily treated by the direct modeling of an observational scheme. Smoothing of a transformed series such as a log periodogram can be treated by this method. Outliers in the observations can be treated as well by using heavy-tailed distribution for observational noise density.

The algorithms herein can be easily extended to a wider class of models. As an example, the smoothing of nonhomogeneous binomial mean function is shown, where the observation is distributed according to a discrete random variable. Extension to a nonlinear system is also straightforward.

KEY WORDS: Filter; Smoothing; Smoothness prior; Likelihood; Akaike information criterion; Nonlinear system.

1. INTRODUCTION

A non-Gaussian smoothing methodology for time series analysis is introduced here. The method is based on non-Gaussian state–space modeling and is particularly relevant for time series that could not be analyzed satisfactorily by the conventional time series models.

This work was originally motivated by Akaike (1980), who treated smoothing problems with many parameters within the context of a Bayesian general linear model framework. The origin of the smoothing problem can be traced back to Whittaker (1923), who suggested that the solution balance a trade-off between infidelity to the data and infidelity to a difference equation constraint. Shiller (1973) approached the impulse response function estimation of econometric data by distributed lag modeling and introduced the term smoothness priors. In these approaches the selection of the trade-off parameter, although critical, was left to the discretion of the investigator. The novelty of the Akaike paper was the determination of the smoothness trade-off parameters by maximizing the likelihood of the Bayesian model. This was an objective solution to the smoothing problem that had otherwise been treated subjectively. Obviously, many dynamic models for a gradually changing system can be treated by this method. Typical applications of the method are seasonal adjustment of economic time series (Akaike 1980; Akaike and Ishiguro 1980), binary response curve estimation (Ishiguro and Sakamoto 1983), cohort analysis (Nakamura 1982), spectral estimation (Kitagawa and Gersch 1985a), and transfer function estimation (Gersch and Kitagawa 1984).

In Kitagawa (1981) it was shown that the problem of modeling time series with drifting mean value, originally treated in the Bayesian linear model, can be expressed in state–space model form and that the associated convenient filtering and smoothing methodology can be exploited. Elsewhere, various time series models in state–space form for the analysis of nonstationary time series have been presented. In Kitagawa (1981), Gersch and Kitagawa (1983), and Kitagawa and Gersch (1984) the analysis and prediction of nonstationary in mean time series by state–space modeling was treated. Kitagawa (1983) and Kitagawa and Gersch (1985b) dealt with time-varying autoregressive coefficient modeling and spectral estimation of nonstationary covariance time series. Kitagawa and Takanami (1985) treated a state–space model for the extraction of a micro earthquake signal from noisy data.

All of these models can be expressed as linear and Gaussian state–space models and hence the conventional filtering and smoothing methodology could have been successfully applied. But there are various problems for which linear Gaussian modeling is inadequate. In the problem of trend estimation, the trend sometimes has jumps in addition to smooth and gradual changes. In this case, a simple linear Gaussian model with small system noise variance cannot detect jumps. On the other hand, a model with a large system noise variance can produce inappropriate wiggles in the estimated trend. Outliers in the observation are another source of poor estimates. To treat such situations within the linear Gaussian model framework, it is necessary to develop a complicated model that takes into account both smooth changes as well as jumps in the parameters and the existence of outliers. But if we use heavy-tailed distribution for the system noise and observational noise, then we can handle these sources of

* Genshiro Kitagawa is Associate Professor, The Institute of Statistical Mathematics, Tokyo 106, Japan. This work was partially supported by a grant from the Japanese Ministry of Education, Science and Culture. The author wishes to thank the editors and referees for careful review and helpful suggestions; W. Gersch, D. F. Findley, and T. Yanagimoto for helpful comments; H. Akaike for encouragement; and T. Takanami for the use of his seismic data.

Journal of the American Statistical Association
December 1987, Vol. 82, No. 400, Theory and Methods

difficulty with simple models. The smoothing problems that are present in the estimation of power spectra, time-varying variance, and nonhomogeneous binomial (or Poisson) mean apparently require formulation with non-Gaussian noise. Furthermore, nonlinear models, such as a ship's nonlinear maneuverability model and a storage model for river flow, inevitably require non-Gaussian distribution treatments even when both the system noise and the observational noise are Gaussian. The development of methodologies for treating systems with non-Gaussian distributions thus is an important problem.

The primary objective of this article is to reveal the importance of non-Gaussian models in various problems of time series analysis. Simple examples only are shown here, related to my earlier work with others. These simple examples show the significant distinction between Gaussian modeling and non-Gaussian modeling. A secondary objective of this article is to present a methodology for non-Gaussian time series models. Specifically, shown here are a non-Gaussian version of filtering and smoothing algorithms in addition to numerical synthesis of the algorithms.

There have been a lot of attempts to filter non-Gaussian or nonlinear systems. The extended Kalman filter, the second-order filter, expression by Fourier series, Edgeworth expansion or Gram–Charlier expansion, and the Gaussian sum filter (Alspach and Sorensen 1972) are well-known approaches. All of these filters approximate the non-Gaussian distribution by one or several Gaussian distributions or by some parametric function and are known to be satisfactory in various nonlinear problems (Anderson and Moore 1979). Nevertheless, the possibility and necessity of improving nonlinear or non-Gaussian filtering methodology remain. Here the non-Gaussian system is treated in a very primitive way. The probability density function is approximated by a piecewise linear function, and the necessary operations on the density are realized by numerical computations. This kind of direct method was attempted in an early stage of the development of nonlinear filters (Bucy and Senne 1971; de Figueiredo and Jan 1971). But because of the recent development of fast computing facilities, it is now practical to use direct numerical methods. My method is free from Gaussian and linearity assumptions, and I can also derive a smoothing algorithm. To illustrate the utility of this method, I will show some simple examples. But they are just a fragment of a vast field of possible applications.

In Section 2, the non-Gaussian state–space model is shown, along with basic non-Gaussian filtering and smoothing algorithms. Some numerical aspects involved in the synthesis of the digital filter and smoother are considered in Section 3. The identification problem, the estimation of parameters of the non-Gaussian system, and the comparison of several candidate models are considered in Section 4. Section 5 is devoted to some applications where some non-Gaussian smoothing problems are considered as typical examples and contrasted with Gaussian models. Section 6 is devoted to some discussion. In particular, the possibility of extending the method to a higher-dimensional system and nonlinear systems is discussed.

2. NON-GAUSSIAN STATE–SPACE MODEL, FILTERING, AND SMOOTHING

Consider a system described by the state–space model

$$x_n = Fx_{n-1} + Gv_n, \qquad y_n = Hx_n + w_n, \qquad (2.1)$$

where F, G, and H are linear transformations $R^k \to R^k$, $R^l \to R^k$, and $R^k \to R$, respectively, and v_n and w_n are independent white noise sequences with probability density functions $q(v)$ and $r(w)$, respectively. They are not necessarily Gaussian. The initial state vector x_0 is distributed on R^k according to the density $p(x_0)$. The conditional density of x_n, given observations $(y_1, \ldots, y_m) = Y_m$, is denoted by $p(x_n \mid Y_m)$.

The recursive formulas for obtaining one-step-ahead prediction and filtering densities can be derived as follows: one-step-ahead prediction (time update),

$$\begin{aligned} p(x_n \mid Y_{n-1}) &= \int_{-\infty}^{\infty} p(x_n, x_{n-1} \mid Y_{n-1})\, dx_{n-1} \\ &= \int_{-\infty}^{\infty} p(x_n \mid x_{n-1}) p(x_{n-1} \mid Y_{n-1})\, dx_{n-1}; \end{aligned} \qquad (2.2)$$

filtering (observation update),

$$\begin{aligned} p(x_n \mid Y_n) &= p(x_n \mid y_n, Y_{n-1}) \\ &= p(x_n, y_n \mid Y_{n-1})/p(y_n \mid Y_{n-1}) \\ &= p(y_n \mid x_n) p(x_n \mid Y_{n-1})/p(y_n \mid Y_{n-1}), \end{aligned} \qquad (2.3)$$

where $p(x_n \mid x_{n-1})$ is the density of x_n given the previous state vector x_{n-1}, $p(y_n \mid x_n)$ is the density of y_n given x_n, and $p(y_n \mid Y_{n-1})$ is obtained by $\int p(y_n \mid x_n) p(x_n \mid Y_{n-1})\, dx_n$.

Similarly, consider the expression for the joint density of x_n and x_{n+1}, given the entire observation sequence Y_N,

$$\begin{aligned} & p(x_n, x_{n+1} \mid Y_N) \\ &= p(x_{n+1} \mid Y_N) p(x_n \mid x_{n+1}, Y_N) \\ &= p(x_{n+1} \mid Y_N) p(x_n \mid x_{n+1}, Y_n) \\ &= p(x_{n+1} \mid Y_N) p(x_n, x_{n+1} \mid Y_n)/p(x_{n+1} \mid Y_n) \\ &= p(x_{n+1} \mid Y_N) p(x_{n+1} \mid x_n) p(x_n \mid Y_n)/p(x_{n+1} \mid Y_n). \end{aligned} \qquad (2.4)$$

From (2.4) we obtain the following formula for smoothing:

$$\begin{aligned} p(x_n \mid Y_N) &= \int_{-\infty}^{\infty} p(x_n, x_{n+1} \mid Y_N)\, dx_{n+1} \\ &= p(x_n \mid Y_n) \int_{-\infty}^{\infty} p(x_{n+1} \mid Y_N) \\ &\quad \times p(x_{n+1} \mid x_n)/p(x_{n+1} \mid Y_n)\, dx_{n+1}. \end{aligned} \qquad (2.5)$$

In the linear Gaussian case, the conditional densities $p(x_n \mid Y_{n-1})$, $p(x_n \mid Y_n)$, and $p(x_n \mid Y_N)$ are characterized by the means and the covariance matrices, and (2.2), (2.3), and (2.5) thus are equivalent to the well-known Kalman filter and the fixed-interval smoothing algorithms (Anderson and Moore 1979; Kalman 1960). In the non-Gaussian or nonlinear case, however, it is necessary to evaluate the non-Gaussian densities explicitly at each step. For the synthesis of the aforementioned algorithms, it is necessary to numerically realize transformation of densities, convolution of densities, and the Bayes theorem (product of two densities and normalization).

3. NUMERICAL SYNTHESIS OF THE ALGORITHMS

In this section I show a numerical realization of the filtering and smoothing algorithms shown in the previous section. Only the formula for the one-dimensional system, $k = l = 1$, is shown. In principle, it is not difficult to generalize this formula to a multidimensional system. The main reasons for focusing on the simplest case is to avoid notational complexity. Even with this simplest case, it is possible to exhibit the significant merit of non-Gaussian modeling. The multidimensional case is discussed in Section 6.

In this approach, each density function is approximated by a piecewise linear (first-order spline) function. Each density is specified by the number of segments, location of nodes, and the value at each node. It is assumed that the density vanishes outside the two outermost nodes. Specifically, the following notation is used: For one-step-ahead prediction density, $p(x_n \mid Y_{n-1})$, the number of segments is kp, the nodes are xp_{n_i} $(i = 0, \ldots, kp)$, and the values at the nodes are p_{n_i} $(i = 0, \ldots, kp)$. For filtering density, $p(x_n \mid Y_n)$, the number of segments is kf, the nodes are xf_{n_i} $(i = 0, \ldots, kf)$, and the values at the nodes are f_{n_i} $(i = 0, \ldots, kf)$. For smoothing density, $p(x_n \mid Y_N)$, the number of segments is ks, the nodes are xs_{n_i} $(i = 0, \ldots, ks)$, and the values at the nodes are s_{n_i} $(i = 0, \ldots, ks)$. For system noise density, $q(x)$, the number of segments is kq, the nodes are xq_i $(i = 0, \ldots, kq)$, and the values at the nodes are q_i $(i = 0, \ldots, kq)$. For observational noise density, $r(x)$, the number of segments is kr, the nodes are xr_i $(i = 0, \ldots, kr)$, and the values at the nodes are r_i $(i = 0, \ldots, kr)$.

Some comment on the choice of nodes is in order here. The outermost nodes, x_0 and x_k, are usually determined subjectively so that the essential domain of the state density is covered by this region. Strictly speaking, every density is truncated. Although it is possible to cover the whole domain by a proper transformation of a variable, in my experience this truncation does not cause severe problems unless too small an interval $[x_0, x_k]$ is selected. In the simplest version, the node schemes are equispaced and the same spacing is used for all of the density functions, $p(x_n \mid Y_{n-1})$, $p(x_n \mid Y_n)$, and $p(x_n \mid Y_N)$. The nodes are defined by $x_0, x_0 + h, x_0 + 2h, \ldots, x_0 + kh = x_k$ with $h = (x_k - x_0)/k$. For these densities, a considerably large number of nodes is necessary. (For the examples given in Sec. 5, $k = 200 \sim 400$ are used.) How far out the extreme nodes should be positioned depends on the type of noises, with heavy-tailed distribution requiring a wider range. The interval between the nodes is set equal to the one for the state density. When the noise density has a very sharp peak, however, some care is required in numerical integration. Some remarks on this point and on the improvement of node schemes to increase accuracy and reduce the number of nodes needed are given in Section 6.

These values at the nodes naturally define the entire function under the piecewise linearity assumption on the function. These functions are denoted by $p_n(x)$, $f_n(x)$, $s_n(x)$, $q(x)$, and $r(x)$, respectively. Using this notation, the filtering and smoothing algorithms are realized as follows.

One-Step-Ahead Prediction. For each $x = xp_i$ $(i = 0, \ldots, kp)$, from (2.2) and $v_n = G^{-1}(x_n - Fx_{n-1})$, $p_n(x)$ is obtained by

$$\begin{aligned} p_n(x) &= \int_{-\infty}^{\infty} p(y \mid Y_{n-1}) p(x \mid y)\, dy \\ &= \int_{-\infty}^{\infty} f_{n-1}(y) q(G^{-1}(x - Fy))\, dy \\ &= \sum_{i=1}^{m} \int_{y_{i-1}}^{y_i} f_{n-1}(y) q(G^{-1}(x - Fy))\, dy, \end{aligned} \tag{3.1}$$

where $\{y_0, y_1, \ldots, y_m\}$ is the ordered set that is obtained from the union of two sets $\{xf_{n_0}, \ldots, xf_{n_k}\}$ and $\{G^{-1}(x - Fxq_{n_{kq}}), \ldots, G^{-1}(x - Fxq_{n_0})\}$. Since $f_n(y)$ and $q(G^{-1}(x - Fy))$ both are linear functions on the interval $[y_{j-1}, y_j]$, each integral is given by

$$\begin{aligned} &\int_{y_{j-1}}^{y_j} f_{n-1}(y) q(G^{-1}(x - Fy))\, dy \\ &= [f_{j-1}q_{j-1} + \{f_{j-1}(q_j - q_{j-1}) \\ &\quad + q_{j-1}(f_j - f_{j-1})\}/2 \\ &\quad + (f_j - f_{j-1})(q_j - q_{j-1})/3] \\ &\quad \times (y_j - y_{j-1}) \end{aligned} \tag{3.2}$$

or, approximately, by

$$(f_{j-1}q_{j-1} + f_j q_j)(y_j - y_{j-1})/2. \tag{3.3}$$

Here $f_j = f_{n-1}(y_j)$ and $q_j = q(G^{-1}(x - Fy_j))$.

Filtering. For each $x = xf_i$ $(i = 0, 1, \ldots, kf)$, $f_n(x)$ is obtained by

$$f_n(x) = p_n(x) r(y - Hx)/C. \tag{3.4}$$

Here y is the given observation at that stage and C is the normalizing constant given by

$$\begin{aligned} C &= \int_{-\infty}^{\infty} p_n(x) r(y - Hx)\, dx \\ &= \sum_{i=1}^{m} \int_{y_{i-1}}^{y_i} p_n(x) r(y - Hx)\, dx \end{aligned}$$

$$= \sum_{i=1}^{m} \{p_n(xf_i) r(y - Hxf_i) + p_n(xf_{i-1}) r(y - Hxf_{i-1})\} \times (xf_i - xf_{i-1})/2. \quad (3.5)$$

Smoothing. For each $x = xs_i$ $(i = 0, 1, \ldots, ks)$, $s_n(x)$ is obtained by

$$s_n(x) = f_n(x) \int_{-\infty}^{\infty} s_{n+1}(y) q(G^{-1}(x - Fy)) \div f_{n+1}(y)\, dy$$

$$= f_n(x) \sum_{i=1}^{ks} \int_{y_{i-1}}^{y_i} s_{n+1}(y) q(G^{-1}(x - Fy)) \div f_{n+1}(y)\, dy, \quad (3.6)$$

where $\{y_0, \ldots, y_l\}$ is the ordered set that is obtained from the union of $\{xs_{n+1,0}, \ldots, xs_{n+1,ks}\}$, $\{xf_{n+1,0}, \ldots, xf_{n+1,kf}\}$, and $\{G^{-1}(x - Fxq_0), \ldots, G^{-1}(x - Fxq_{kq})\}$. The integral in the summation is given by

$$[\log(1 + \Delta c c_1^{-1})\{a_1 b_1 \Delta c^{-1} - (a_1 \Delta b + b_1 \Delta a) c_1 \Delta c^{-2} + \Delta a \Delta b c_1^2 \Delta c^{-2}\} + (a_1 \Delta b + b_1 \Delta a)\Delta c^{-1} + \Delta a \Delta b(.5\Delta c^{-1} - c_1)](y_j - y_{j-1}) \quad (3.7)$$

or, approximately, by

$$(a_1 b_1 c_1^{-1} + a_2 b_2 c_2^{-1})(y_j - y_{j-1})/2. \quad (3.8)$$

Here

$$a_1 = s_{n+1}(y_{j-1}), \quad a_2 = s_{n+1}(y_j),$$

$$b_1 = q(G^{-1}(x - Fy_{j-1})), \quad b_2 = q(G^{-1}(x - Fy_j)),$$

$$c_1 = f_{n+1}(y_{j-1}), \quad c_2 = f_{n+1}(y_j),$$

$$\Delta a = a_2 - a_1, \quad \Delta b = b_2 - b_1,$$

and $\Delta c = c_2 - c_1$.

4. MODEL IDENTIFICATION

The non-Gaussian model presented in the previous section generally has some unknown parameters. The best choice of the parameters can be found by maximizing the log-likelihood that is defined by

$$l(\theta) = \log p(y_1, \ldots, y_N) = \sum_{n=1}^{N} \log p(y_n \mid y_1, \ldots, y_{n-1}) = \sum_{n=1}^{N} \log p(y_n \mid Y_{n-1}). \quad (4.1)$$

Here each $p(y_n \mid Y_{n-1})$ is the quantity that appeared in (2.3) and can be evaluated by (3.5).

Given several candidate models, each including a specification of the types of the density of system noise or observational noise, the model with the minimum value of the Akaike information criterion (AIC),

$$\text{AIC} = -2 \max l(\hat{\theta}) + 2(\text{number of free parameters}), \quad (4.2)$$

is considered as the best model. This criterion enables comparison of different models. It should be noted that even when the number of free parameters is the same in different models, the comparison of the values of maximum likelihood of different models is not well founded without Akaike's interpretation of likelihood that naturally derived the AIC (Akaike 1973).

5. NUMERICAL EXAMPLES AND DISCUSSIONS

5.1 Estimation of Shifting Mean Value

We consider the data artificially generated from the following model:

$$Y_n \sim N(\mu_n, 1)$$

$$\begin{aligned} \mu_n &= 0, & n &= 1, \ldots, 100, \\ &= -1, & n &= 101, \ldots, 250, \\ &= 1, & n &= 251, \ldots, 350, \\ &= 0, & n &= 351, \ldots, 500. \end{aligned} \quad (5.1)$$

The data are shown in Figure 1. The problem is to estimate the shifting mean value function, μ_n.

For this type of data, we use the model

$$\Delta^k t_n = v_n, \quad y_n = t_n + w_n. \quad (5.2)$$

Here Δ is the difference operator defined by $\Delta t_n = t_n - t_{n-1}$ and v_n and w_n are white noise sequences that are not necessarily distributed as Gaussian. For simplicity, we assume that the difference order, k, is 1. It is obvious that (5.2) is the special form of the state–space model (2.1)

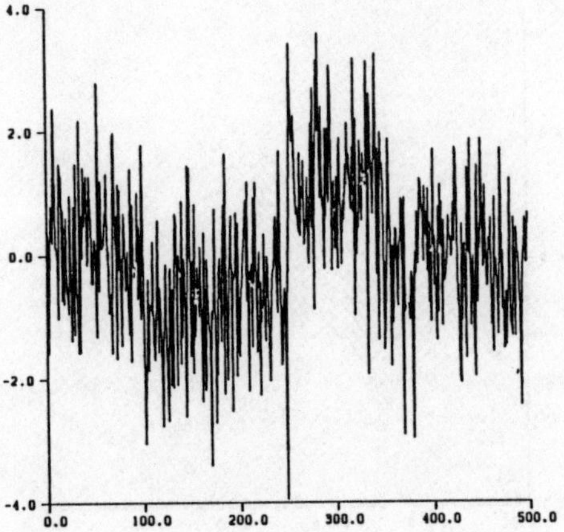

Figure 1. Artificially Generated Data With Shifting Mean Value.

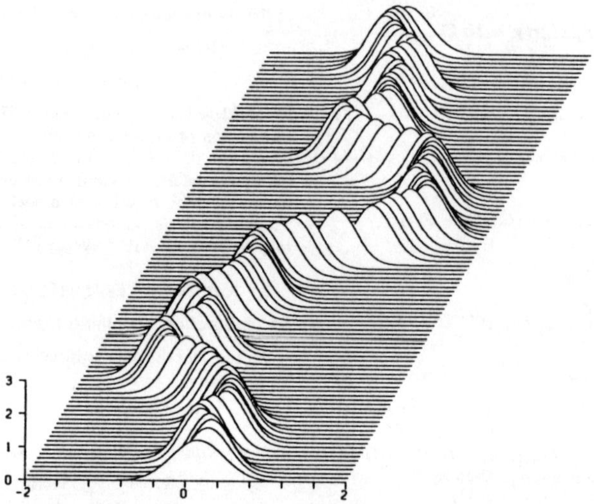

Figure 2. Estimated Densities $p(x_n \mid y_n)$ (n = 5, 10, . . . , 500) by the Gaussian Model, τ^2 = .0122, σ^2 = 1.043.

with $x_n \equiv t_n$, $F = G = H = 1$. We considered the following model class:

$$\text{Model}(b)\text{: } v_n \sim Q(b, \tau^2), \quad w_n \sim N(0, \sigma^2). \quad (5.3)$$

Here $N(0, \sigma^2)$ denotes the Gaussian distribution with mean 0 and variance σ^2 and $Q(b, \tau^2)$ denotes the distribution of the Pearson system, which has the density $q(x; b, \tau^2) = C(\tau^2 + x^2)^{-b}$ with $\frac{1}{2} < b \leqq \infty$ and $C = \tau^{2b-1}\Gamma(b)/\Gamma(\frac{1}{2})$. This family naturally links two distributions, Cauchy ($b = 1$) and Gaussian ($b = \infty$). Here we tried five models: $b = \frac{3}{5}, \frac{3}{4}$, 1, 2, and ∞. In numerical computations, the outermost nodes we used are $x_0 = -4$, $x_k = 4$, $k = 400$. The maximum likelihood estimates of τ^2 and σ^2 for the Gaussian model, Model (∞), were $\hat{\tau}^2 = .0122$, $\hat{\sigma}^2 = 1.043$, and the AIC of the model was 1,501.03. Figure 2 shows the marginal posterior density $p(x_n \mid Y_N)$ versus time n. As a natural result of the Gaussian assumption, the densities obtained have identical shape, except for both ends of the time interval where the densities become slightly broader. Figure 3 shows the mean (bold) and ±1, 2, 3 sigma intervals of the $p(x_n \mid Y_N)$. The estimated mean value function becomes a wiggly curve and does not reflect the sudden change of the mean value. In the Gaussian case, the ordinary Kalman filter can be applied, yielding the exact log-likelihood value, −748.773. The difference of two log-likelihoods, .156, reflects the effect of numerical integration, piecewise linear approximation, and truncation of densities.

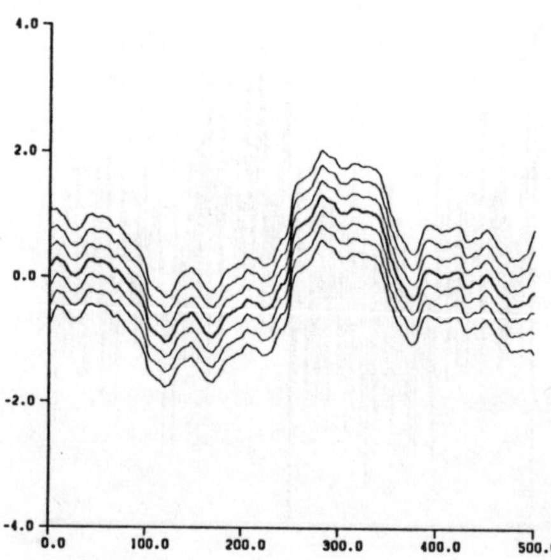

Figure 3. Estimated Mean and ±1, ±2, ±3 Sigma Intervals by the Gaussian Model.

The maximum likelihood estimates of τ^2 and σ^2, the log-likelihoods, and the AIC's of the non-Gaussian models are listed in Table 1. The AIC of Model (.75) is 1,487.89, which indicates that this non-Gaussian model is better than the Gaussian model. Figure 4 shows the marginal posterior density $p(x_n \mid Y_N)$ versus time n. We see that, unlike the Gaussian filter, the shape of the density varies with time.

Table 1. Summary of Fitted Models

b	$\hat{\tau}^2$	$\hat{\sigma}^2$	*Log-likelihood*	*AIC*
.6	1.3×10^{-8}	1.024	−741.988	1,487.98
.75	2.2×10^{-7}	1.022	−741.944	1,487.89
1.0	3.48×10^{-5}	1.022	−742.248	1,488.50
2.0	1.05×10^{-2}	1.018	−745.251	1,495.50
∞	1.22×10^{-2}	1.043	−748.517	1,501.03

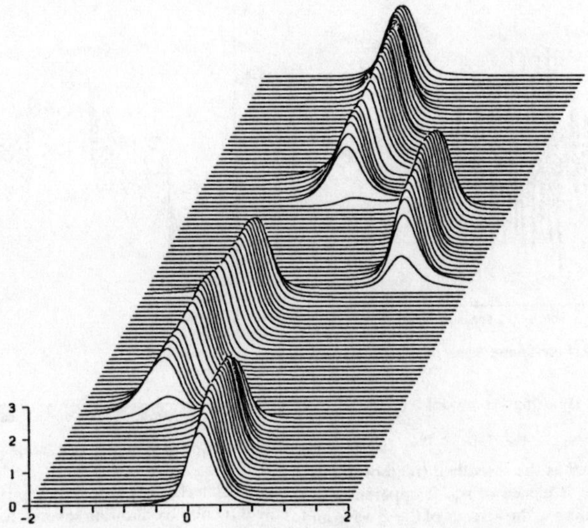

Figure 4. Estimated Densities $p(x_n \mid Y_n)$ (n = 5, 10, ..., 500) by the Non-Gaussian Model, b = .75, τ^2 = 2, 2 × 10^{-7}, σ^2 = 1.022.

In particular, when the shift of the mean value occurs, the density becomes heavy-tailed on one side, even bimodal, reflecting the transient mode. Figure 5 shows the median (bold curve) and .13, 2.27, 15.87, 84.13, 97.73, and 99.87 percent points of the density functions that correspond to −3, −2, −1, 1, 2, and 3 sigma points of Gaussian density, respectively. By comparing with Figure 3, it becomes clear that Model (.75) can yield smoother curves than Model (∞) and that it can also express the jump of the mean level automatically. It can also be seen that when a large deviation from the mean value occurs but the true mean value does not change, it affects the outermost .13 or 99.87 percent point only and does not affect the median at all. This reveals that the non-Gaussian model "explains" the large deviation by having a heavier tail on one side rather than shifting the distribution itself. These multimodal or skewed distribution and jump of the mean value are the typical phenomena we can see in non-Gaussian modeling.

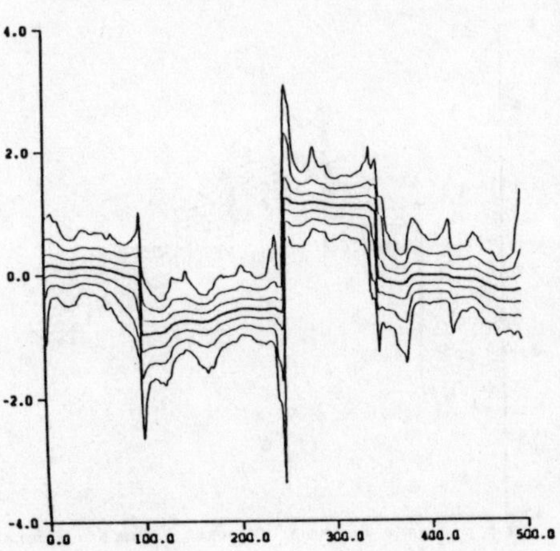

Figure 5. Estimated Median and ±1, ±2, ±3 Sigma Intervals by the Non-Gaussian Model.

It should be remarked that the posterior densities and percentile points given in this section are based on the marginal posterior densities, and their joint coverage is generally different from the joint posterior densities.

5.2 Estimation of Changing Variance

Figure 6 shows the whitening filter output of a micro earthquake observed at Hokkaido, Japan. The problem here is the estimation of the changing variance (envelope function) of the time series, $y_n, \ldots, y_{2N}$. In Kitagawa and Gersch (1985b), the following procedure was applied for estimation.

Assume that y_n ($n = 1, \ldots, 2N$) is the white noise sequence such that $y_n \sim N(0, \xi_n^2)$ and $\xi_{2m}^2 = \xi_{2m-1}^2$. By the transformation

$$s_m = (y_{2m-1}^2 + y_{2m}^2)/2, \qquad u_m = \ln s_m, \qquad (5.4)$$

$u_m - \ln \xi_m$ becomes the independent random variable that is distributed as the logarithm of an exponential distribution (χ^2 distribution with 2 df). Since the mean and the variance of the logarithm of the exponentially distributed random variable are given by ζ and $\pi^2/6$, respectively, where ζ = .57721 is the Euler constant, the observational noise density was approximated by a Gaussian distribution

1038 Journal of the American Statistical Association, December 1987

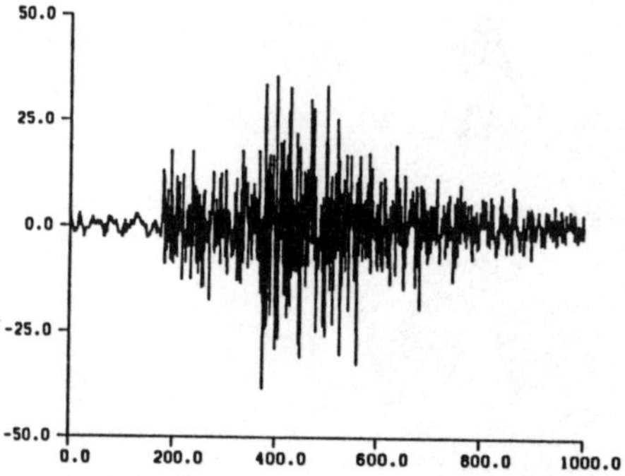

Figure 6. Filter Output of Earthquake Signal (Hokkaido, Japan).

with these moments. By using the model

$$\Delta^k t_m = v_m, \qquad u_m = t_m + w_m, \tag{5.5}$$

$\ln \xi_{2m}^2$ can be estimated as the smoothed trend of the u_m.

Figure 7 shows the sequence of u_m. It apparently has two jumps corresponding to the arrivals of the *P* wave and the *S* wave. Since the density of the observational noise is known in this case, the model has only one parameter, τ^2, the variance of the system noise. The maximum likelihood estimate of the parameter was $\tau^2 = .04318$, and the AIC = 1,861.64. The estimated mean value by this model is wiggly (Fig. 8). If we use a smaller value of τ^2, we can get a smoother curve, but that curve cannot follow

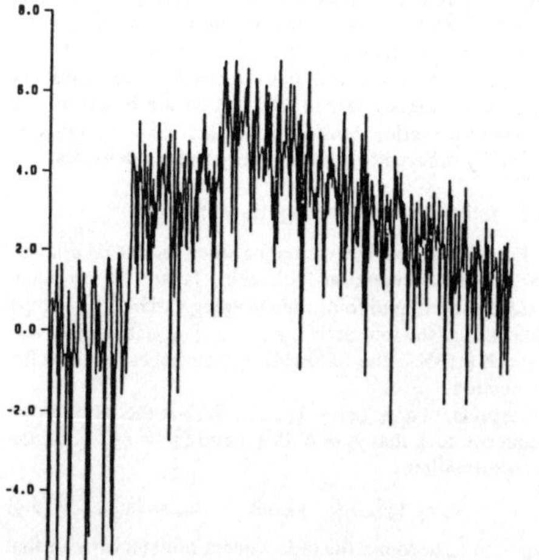

Figure 7. Transformed Series, u_n.

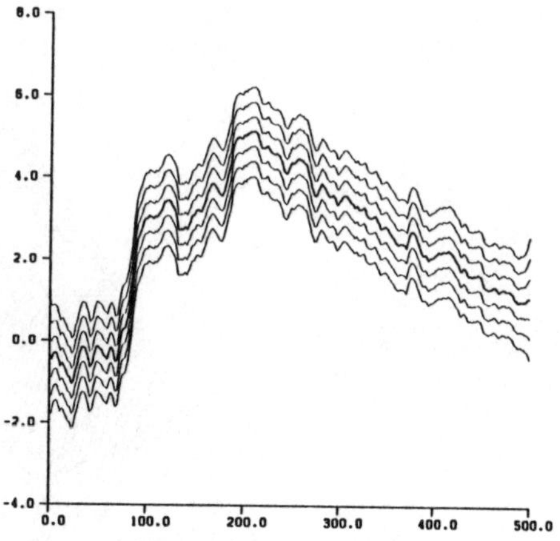

Figure 8. Changing Log-Variance Estimated by the Gaussian Model.

the sudden change of the variance. It is possible to alleviate the difficulty by allowing several outliers in system noise, but that requires the positioning of outliers and thus is applicable only when we know the position of the outliers beforehand or when an objective and effective outlier detection procedure is available (Akaike et al. 1985). Figure 9 exhibits the result by a non-Gaussian model,

$$q(x) = \tau\{\pi(\tau^2 + x^2)\}^{-1},$$

$$r(x) = .5 \exp\{x - .5e^x\}. \tag{5.6}$$

The maximum likelihood estimate of τ^2 was .000112. The value of the AIC (=1,718.15) indicates that in this case the non-Gaussian model is significantly better than the Gaussian model. The estimated curves are much smoother

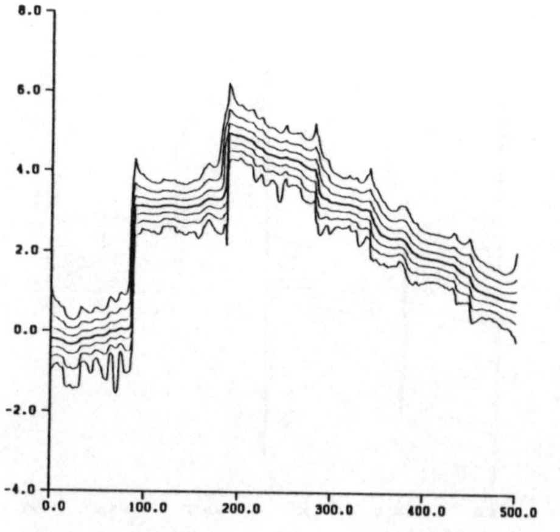

Figure 9. Changing Log-Variance Estimated by a Non-Gaussian Model.

Table 2. Number of Occurrences of Rainfall Over 1 mm in Tokyo, 1983–1984

	Day																														
Month	1	2	3	4	5	6	7	8	9	10	11	12	13	14	15	16	17	18	19	20	21	22	23	24	25	26	27	28	29	30	31
January	0	0	1	1	0	1	1	0	0	0	0	0	0	0	1	0	0	1	1	0	1	1	0	0	0	0	0	0	0	0	1
February	0	1	0	0	0	0	0	0	0	0	0	1	1	0	0	0	2	1	0	0	0	0	1	1	0	1	0	0	0		
March	0	1	1	0	0	0	0	0	0	2	0	0	1	1	0	2	1	0	1	1	1	0	1	2	0	0	1	1	1	1	1
April	2	0	0	1	1	0	1	2	0	1	1	1	0	0	1	2	1	0	2	1	0	1	0	0	0	0	0	1	0	0	
May	1	1	0	0	0	1	1	0	0	0	0	0	1	1	1	2	2	0	0	0	0	0	1	1	1	0	0	0	1	0	0
June	0	0	0	1	0	1	0	0	0	2	1	1	2	1	0	1	2	2	0	2	2	1	1	1	2	2	2	1	1	0	
July	0	0	1	0	1	1	1	2	1	0	1	1	0	0	2	1	1	1	1	2	2	0	1	0	0	0	0	1	1	0	0
August	0	0	0	0	0	0	0	0	0	0	0	0	1	1	1	1	1	1	0	1	2	1	0	0	0	0	0	0	0	1	0
September	1	0	0	0	1	0	1	1	1	2	0	0	0	1	2	2	0	1	1	2	2	1	0	1	1	1	1	1	1	0	
October	0	0	0	0	1	0	0	0	1	0	2	1	1	0	1	1	1	0	2	1	1	1	1	0	0	0	1	0	0	0	0
November	0	0	0	0	0	1	1	0	1	1	0	0	0	0	1	1	0	0	1	1	0	0	0	1	0	0	0	0	0	0	
December	0	0	0	0	0	0	0	0	0	0	1	0	0	0	0	1	1	1	0	0	0	0	1	0	0	0	0	0	0	1	1

NOTE: February 29 had only one observation.

than the ones in Figure 8. This figure clearly shows that the non-Gaussian models with heavy-tailed noise distributions have the ability to estimate both smooth change and jump of parameters simultaneously. That was not possible with a simple Gaussian model. The robustness of the non-Gaussian models to large deviations is more visible in this example. Because of the nature of the sampling distribution of u_m, it frequently has large deviations on the negative side. For the Gaussian model, they act as outliers. As a result, the estimated curves become wiggly. For the non-Gaussian model given in (5.6), however, they are no longer outliers and do not severely affect the estimates. In Figure 9 we see that only the lowermost .13 percent curve is affected by these large deviations.

5.3 Nonstationary Binary Process

In the formulation of our state-space model, for simplicity we assumed that the random variables have density functions. But actually we only need to compute the convolution and Bayes theorem shown in (2.2) and (2.3). Thus we can also handle discrete distributions. As an example, we will show a problem concerning estimating the time-varying mean of a nonstationary (nonhomogeneous) binary process. This problem was considered earlier by Ishiguro and Sakamoto (1983).

Table 2 shows the number of occurrences of rainfall over 1 mm in Tokyo for each day during the past 2 years (1983–1984). The problem is to estimate the probability, p_n, of occurrence of rainfall on a specific calendar day, which is believed to be gradually changing with time (or with the value of explanatory variables). The estimates obtained from only two samples per day are hopelessly irregular (Fig. 10).

The model for the smoothed probability of occurrence is in general given by

$$\Delta^k q_n = v_n, \qquad z_{l_n}(m_n \mid q_n) = \binom{l_n}{m_n} p_n^{m_n}(1 - p_n)^{l_n - m_n}. \tag{5.7}$$

Here $q_n = \log\{p_n/(1 - p_n)\}$, l_n is the number of observations at the nth time point, m_n the number of occurrences of an event at the nth time point, and $z_l(m_n \mid q_n)$ the probability mass function of the binomial distribution. In the original treatment, the transformation from p_n to q_n was applied to guarantee that $0 < p_n < 1$ (Ishiguro and Sakamoto 1983). In our method, this is not an essential requirement, since it is easy to restrict the state space.

It can be seen that, for this system with discrete observations, the analog of the filtering Equation (2.3) is given by

$$p(q_n \mid Y_n) = C^{-1} z_{l_n}(m_n \mid q_n) p(q_n \mid Y_{n-1}) \tag{5.8}$$

with $C = \int_{-\infty}^{\infty} z_{l_n}(m_n \mid q_n) p(q_n \mid Y_{n-1})\, dq_{n-1}$. The obtained result is shown in Figure 11. The estimated rainfall probability reveals the character of weather in Tokyo: dry winter, unsettled spring, clear sky in May, rainy season in late June to mid-July, stable hot summer in late July through August, generally fine but with an occasional typhoon in September and October. It should be noted that the estimated 50% curve resembles the one obtained from 4 years of data (1981–1984) and 10 years of data (1975–1984), although the ±sigma intervals differ, depending on

Figure 10. Number of Occurrences of Rainfall for Each Day of the Year in Tokyo, 1983–1984.

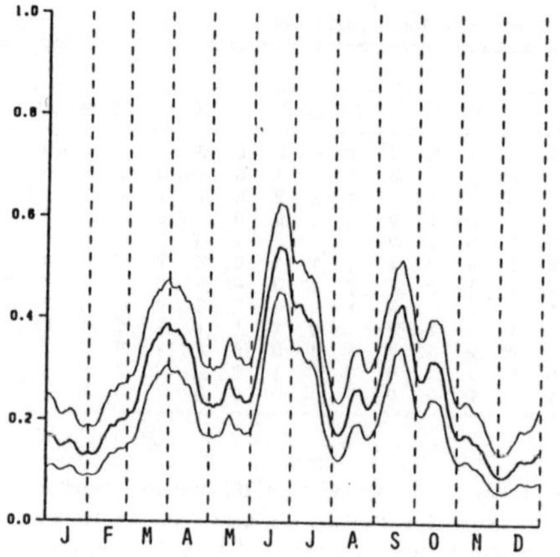

Figure 11. Estimated Binomial Mean Function of Rainfall in Tokyo.

the number of observations. Unlike the procedure used by Ishiguro and Sakamoto (1983), here we are free from the Gaussian assumption and the quadratic approximation to the likelihood function. It is clear that we could apply the same method to a nonstationary Poisson process.

6. CONCLUDING REMARKS

All results shown in this article are obtained by using a simple one-dimensional state vector. In principle, it is straightforward to extend the formula given in Section 3 to higher dimensions. Much computation is required, however, because the convolution of density functions and the curse of dimensionality is a serious problem. To mitigate this problem, various numerical techniques are needed. The use of a variable mesh has a significant effect on reducing the number of nodes. In this method, several intervals around the node attaining the maximum posterior density are further divided into fine mesh. With only 50%–100% addition to the original nodes, the improvement of the accuracy is significant, which eventually results in the reduction of the number of nodes. This mesh is especially useful for a noise density that has a very sharp peak. The results shown in Section 5 were obtained by this method. A moving mesh was also tried. Here the positions of the nodes are shifted so that the maximum a posteriori estimate of the state becomes the center of the mesh. This scheme is useful when the state is drifting. A higher-order spline approximation to the (logarithm of the) density functions is another possibility. According to my experience, in the one-dimensional case the number of nodes could be reduced by as much as a factor of 10 by the use of a third-order spline approximation. But to date, the extension of the third-order spline to higher dimensions has not been numerically stable. In retrospect, I feel that too much time was spent developing faster computing algorithms for multidimensional systems. It might be a better strategy to use a faster computer instead of making such effort to refine the algorithm.

In Section 3, exact and approximation formulas for the necessary integrations in prediction [(3.2), (3.3)] and smoothing [(3.7), (3.8)] were shown. In my experience, if we carefully select the nodes for the system noise $q(v)$, the approximated formula for prediction is sufficiently accurate. Furthermore, in smoothing, the exact formula is not very stable for the tails of the smoothing density, where a very small value of one-step-ahead prediction density occurs. The use of an integration formula, such as the Gaussian integration formula, for filtering and smoothing formulas instead of linear approximation to the densities is also possible. The improvement of the numerical method for necessary integration is left for further study.

Wahba (1980) showed an automatic procedure for the smoothing of the log periodogram. As a natural application of the model for smoothing the changing variance used in Section 5.2, we can also smooth the log periodogram by using a state–space model with $w_n \sim \log \chi^2$ and $v_n \sim$ Cauchy or Gaussian distribution or whatever. Wahba approximated the log χ^2 distribution by a Gaussian distribution with the same first and second moments as those of log χ^2. With our method we can directly apply the log χ^2 distribution.

It is also possible to extend our procedure to nonlinear systems. A typical nonlinear phenomenon can be seen, for example, in ecological data (e.g., the Canadian lynx data), sunspot data, or many varieties of air pollution data. These series each exhibit the approximate repetition of a pattern but the period is not clearly defined. Although such series are frequently modeled by autoregressive, autoregressive moving average, or autoregressive plus sinusoidals models (Campbell and Walker 1977), none of those models seems quite satisfactory for prediction with more than one lead time (Tong 1982). For a time series with quasi-periodic character, one might use a model like

$$\Delta^k t_n = v_n,$$

$$y_n = \sum_{j=0}^{m} a_j \sin(\omega n + t_n)$$

$$+ \sum_{j=1}^{m} b_j \cos(\omega n + t_n) + w_n.$$

Since this system has nonlinearity only in the observation model, the necessary modifications to the filtering formula are simple.

In conclusion, by the use of non-Gaussian models and non-Gaussian filters and smoothers, we can deal with time series with a variety of characteristics (nonstationarity, nonlinearity, outliers, continuous, or discrete) that have been difficult to analyze by the conventional linear Gaussian models. Although our non-Gaussian filter and smoother involves much more computation, it will be possible to mitigate this problem through the use of fast computing facilities and by the development of faster algorithms.

[*Received December 1985. Revised March 1987.*]

REFERENCES

Akaike, H. (1973), "Information Theory and an Extension of the Maximum Likelihood Principle," in *Second International Symposium on Information Theory*, eds. B. N. Petrov and F. Caski, Budapest: Akademiai Kiado, pp. 267–281.

——— (1980), "Likelihood and Bayes Procedure," in *Bayesian Statistics*, eds. J. M. Bernardo, M. H. De Groot, D. V. Lindley, and A. F. M. Smith, Valencia, Spain: University Press, pp. 143–166.

Akaike, H., and Ishiguro, M. (1980), "Trend Estimation With Missing Observations," *Annals of the Institute of Statistical Mathematics*, Ser. B, 32, 481–488.

Akaike, H., Ozaki, T., Ishiguro, M., Ogata, Y., Kitagawa, G., Hamada, Y.-H., Arahata, E., Katsura, K., and Tamura, Y. (1985), *Computer Science Monographs*, TIMSAC-84 Part 1, 22, Tokyo: Institute of Statistical Mathematics.

Alspach, D. L., and Sorenson, H. W. (1972), "Nonlinear Bayesian Estimation Using Gaussian Sum Approximations," *IEEE Transactions on Automatic Control*, 17, 439–448.

Anderson, B. D. O., and Moore, J. B. (1979), *Optimal Filtering*, Englewood Cliffs, NJ: Prentice-Hall.

Bucy, R. S., and Senne, K. D. (1971), "Digital Synthesis of Nonlinear Filters, *Automatica*, 7, 287–289.

Campbell, M. J., and Walker, A. M. (1977), "A Survey of Statistical Work on the McKenzie River Series of Annual Canadian Lynx Trappings for the Year 1821–1934, and a New Analysis," *Journal of the Royal Statistical Society*, Ser. A, 140, 411–431.

De Figueiredo, R. J. P., and Jan, Y. G. (1971), "Spline Filters," in *Proceedings of the 2nd Symposium on Nonlinear Estimation Theory and Its Applications*, San Diego, pp. 127–141.

Gersch, W., and Kitagawa, G. (1983), "The Prediction of Time Series With Trends and Seasonalities," *Journal of Business & Economic Statistics*, 1, 253–264.

——— (1984), "A Smoothness Prior Method for Transfer Function Estimation," in *23rd IEEE Conference on Decision and Control*, pp. 363–367.

Ishiguro, M., and Sakamoto, Y. (1983), "A Bayesian Approach to Binary Response Curve Estimation," *Annals of the Institute of Statistical Mathematics*, 35-B, 115–137.

Kalman, R. E. (1960), "A New Approach to Linear Filtering and Prediction Problems," *Transactions of ASME, Journal of Basic Engineerings*, 82D, 35–45.

Kitagawa, G. (1981), "A Nonstationary Time Series Model and Its Fitting by a Recursive Filter," *Journal of Time Series Analysis*, 2, 103–116.

——— (1983), "Changing Spectrum Estimation," *Journal of Sound and Vibration*, 89, 433–445.

Kitagawa, G., and Gersch, W. (1984), "A Smoothness Priors–State Space Modeling of Time Series With Trend and Seasonality," *Journal of the American Statistical Association*, 79, 378–389.

——— (1985a), "A Smoothness Priors Long AR Model Method for Spectrum Estimation," *IEEE Transactions on Automatic Control*, 30, 57–65.

——— (1985b), "A Smoothness Priors-Time Varying AR Coefficient Modeling of Nonstationary Covariance Time Series," *IEEE Transactions on Automatic Control*, 30, 48–56.

Kitagawa, G., and Takanami, T. (1985), "Extraction of Signal by a Time Series Model and Screening Out Micro Earthquakes," *Signal Processing*, 8, 303–314.

Nakamura, T. (1982), "A Bayesian Cohort Model for Standard Cohort Table Analysis," *Proceedings of the Institute of Statistical Mathematics*, 29, 77–99 (in Japanese).

Shiller, R. (1973), "A Distributed Lag Estimator Derived From Smoothness Priors," *Econometrica*, 41, 775–788.

Tong, H. (1982), "A Note on Using Threshold Autoregressive Models for Multi-Step-Ahead Prediction of Cyclical Data," *Journal of Time Series Analysis*, 3, 137–140.

Wahba, G. (1980), "Automatic Smoothing of the Log Periodogram," *Journal of the American Statistical Association*, 75, 122–132.

Whittaker, E. T. (1923), "On a New Method of Graduation," *Proceedings of the Edinburgh Mathematical Society*, 41, 81–89.

[20]

J.R. Statist. Soc. B (1986)
48, *No.* 1, *pp.* 79–88

A Non-Gaussian State Space Model and Application to Prediction of Records

By R. L. SMITH† and J. E. MILLER‡

Imperial College, London, UK

[Received April 1984. Revised December 1985]

SUMMARY

We develop a class of state space models for censored data. The basic model assumes an exponential distribution for the observations, conditionally on unobserved state variables. The model may be generalised by allowing transformations. We develop an application to the prediction of records. This is illustrated with some athletics data, though we also discuss briefly the possibility of more general applications connected with extreme values.

Keywords: ATHLETICS RECORDS; EXTREME VALUE DISTRIBUTIONS; STATE SPACE MODELS; PREDICTION

1. INTRODUCTION

State space models for time series have been extensively developed and applied in many directions, in particular to engineering and to econometric time series. Harvey's books (1981a, 1981b) are one good source of information about the Kalman filter and its use in modelling. Harrison and Stevens (1976) presented a Bayesian approach which has been the theme of much recent work. Meinhold and Singpurwalla (1983) gave an elegant Bayesian development of the Kalman filter, and there have also been numerous generalisations to non-linear or non-Gaussian models, e.g. J. Q. Smith (1979, 1981), West (1981), A. F. M. Smith and West (1983), West, Harrison and Migon (1985).

In this paper we develop a class of models, generalising work of J. Q. Smith (1979) and Bather (1965), for censored data in which the observations are assumed, possibly after transformation, to be exponentially distributed conditionally on some unobserved state variables. Although the models themselves are somewhat specialised, they do highlight what we believe to be some general issues in this kind of modelling. Our work is oriented towards a particular and somewhat novel application, the prediction of records.

The subject of records in random sequences has given rise to some beautiful mathematics. Glick (1978) gave a survey. A particularly striking result is the main theorem of Goldie and Rogers (1984), the proof of which has been much simplified by Vervaat (1985). Statistical work includes the use of record counts as a nonparametric test of trend (Foster and Stuart, 1954; Glick, 1978) and recent work of Dunsmore (1983) on the modelling and prediction of records. Most of this existing work, however, is concerned with records in i.i.d. sequences, which is very often not an appropriate assumption. Some recent work by Ballerini and Resnick (1985) and De Haan and Verkade (1985) is concerned with records in sequences including a trend component. De Haan (1984) describes the connection with extremal processes.

In this paper we consider the following problem. Suppose a variable is measured at discrete times, to give a series $Y_1, \ldots, Y_N$. We observe, however, not the whole sequence Y but only the records, i.e., the sequence of successive minima (or maxima). The problem is modelling or predicting the Y sequence based on observed records.

† *Present address*: Department of Mathematics, University of Surrey, Guildford, Surrey GU2 5XH.
‡ Now with IBM U.K. Ltd., Croydon, Surrey.

 0035–9246/86/48079 $2.00

To fix ideas, suppose we are talking about records for running. We may let Y_n denote the best performance (i.e. the minimum time taken to run a particular race) in year n; the records are successive minima of $\{Y_n\}$. Note that, in this formulation, if a record is broken more than once in a year, then only the best value for that year is counted.

Statistical modelling for such a series may be developed from the observation that, for any year in which the record is not broken, the best performance in that year is a censored value: we know only that it is bigger (or smaller) than the current record. Using this fact, if we have a model for Y then we may define the likelihood function for the unknown parameters based on the observed record values and record times. From there we may proceed by either maximum likelihood or Bayesian analysis.

R. L. Smith (1985) has exploited this idea to fit models in which the Y_n are independent (but not identically distributed) random variables. Our interest here is in extending this work to allow certain forms of dependence among the Y_n. More precisely, we develop a class of state space models for which many of the relevant calculations may be made without resort to approximations, and which therefore seem particularly appropriate to use in this context.

The potential applications of this kind of modelling are, we believe, much broader than the one considered in detail here. Many problems of extreme values are associated with some form of censoring. For example Glick (1978) mentions applications to materials strength testing, and there are applications in hydrology and oceanography in which only the most extreme (not necessarily record) observations are recorded. Existing literature on the prediction of extreme values is mostly concerned with probabilistic approximations, in particular the extensive work on "Slepian models" by Lindgren and co-workers (see Leadbetter, Lindgren and Rootzen, 1983). Our interest here is in the inferential aspect. More generally, our work extends the class of available models for non-Gaussian time series and may suggest further extensions in future work.

2. A CLASS OF STATE SPACE MODELS FOR CENSORED LIFE DATA

A general state space model may be described by two components:

(a) an unobserved parameter sequence $\{\theta_n, 1 \leqslant n \leqslant N\}$, evolving stochastically.

(b) conditionally on $\{\theta_n\}$, independent observations $\{X_n, 1 \leqslant n \leqslant N\}$, where X_n has conditional density $p(x_n | \theta_n)$ with respect to some dominating measure.

The main difficulty is to specify (a) and (b) in such a way that the resulting conditional distributions of θ_n and X_n remain computationally tractable. Bather (1965) analysed this problem, but it is not easy to find models satisfying Bather's conditions. West (1981) avoided the difficulty by using approximations to the conditional distributions. His models retain the normal assumptions on $\{\theta_n\}$, but allow the conditional distributions $p(x_n | \theta_n)$ to be non-normal. An application to the monitoring of kidney transplant patients is described by A. F. M. Smith and West (1983). A different approach was taken by J. Q. Smith (1979, 1981). He abandoned the traditional random walk model for $\{\theta_n\}$ in favour of a class of "steady forecasting models" based on conjugate priors and exact conditional distributions. A difficulty with these models is that, although forecasts for one step ahead are easily calculated, there is no simple formula for m-step forecasting, $m > 1$.

Our approach is based on a specific model which is a development of one first introduced by Bather. We shall use the notation $E(\theta)$, $G(\alpha, \beta)$, $B(\alpha, \beta)$ to denote, respectively, the exponential distribution with parameter θ and the gamma and beta distributions with parameters α, β. Our basic model is as follows:

1. θ_0 has prior distribution $G(\alpha_0, \beta_0)$.
2. For fixed n, $1 \leqslant n \leqslant N$, conditionally on θ_{n-1} and $X^{n-1} \equiv \{X_i, 1 \leqslant i \leqslant n-1\}$, we have

$$\theta_n = \theta_{n-1}\rho_n\xi_n \tag{2.1}$$

with $\xi_n \sim B(\gamma_n\alpha_{n-1}, (1-\gamma_n)\alpha_{n-1})$. Here ρ_n and γ_n are non-random quantities which may depend on X^{n-1} though not on θ_{n-1}.

3. Conditionally on θ_n, $X_n \sim E(\theta_n)$.

It is easy to develop recursive updating relations for this model. Suppose, as an inductive hypothesis, that the conditional distribution of θ_{n-1} given X^{n-1} is $G(\alpha_{n-1}, \beta_{n-1})$, where α_{n-1} and β_{n-1} are functions of X^{n-1}. For $n = 1$, X^{n-1} is empty and the hypothesis is true by assumption. Given the hypothesis for n, we have

$$(\rho_n \theta_{n-1} \mid X^{n-1}) \sim G(\alpha_{n-1}, \tau_n \beta_{n-1}), \quad (\tau_n = 1/\rho_n)$$

$$(\theta_n \mid X^{n-1}) \sim G(\gamma_n \alpha_{n-1}, \tau_n \beta_{n-1}),$$

and, after an application of Bayes' theorem,

$$(\theta_n \mid X^n) \sim G(\gamma_n \alpha_{n-1} + 1, \tau_n \beta_{n-1} + X_n).$$

Therefore the inductive hypothesis is verified, and the recursive updating relations are

$$\alpha_n = \gamma_n \alpha_{n-1} + 1, \quad \beta_n = \tau_n \beta_{n-1} + X_n. \tag{2.2}$$

So far we have not made any allowance for censoring. We now do this by assuming that X_n is either observed, in which case we write $\delta_n = 1$, or is the censoring point of a right-censored observation, in which case we write $\delta_n = 0$. The foregoing analysis remains valid except that the application of Bayes' theorem yields

$$(\theta_n \mid X_n) \sim G(\gamma_n \alpha_{n-1} + \delta_n, \tau_n \beta_{n-1} + X_n)$$

so that (2.2) becomes

$$\alpha_n = \gamma_n \alpha_{n-1} + \delta_n, \quad \beta_n = \tau_n \beta_{n-1} + X_n. \tag{2.3}$$

The conditional distribution of X_n given X^{n-1} may also be obtained. To take the uncensored case first, we have

$$(\theta_n \mid X^{n-1}) \sim G(\gamma_n \alpha_{n-1}, \tau_n \beta_{n-1}), \quad (X_n \mid \theta_n) \sim E(\theta_n)$$

so that, writing down the joint conditional density of $((\theta_n, X_n) \mid X^{n-1})$ and integrating out θ_n, we have

$$p(X_n \mid X^{n-1}) = \frac{\gamma_n \alpha_{n-1} (\tau_n \beta_{n-1})^{\gamma_n \alpha_{n-1}}}{(\tau_n \beta_{n-1} + X_n)^{\gamma_n \alpha_{n-1} + 1}}, \tag{2.4}$$

a Pareto distribution on $0 < X_n < \infty$. If X_n is a censored value, the preceding formula must be integrated from $x = X_n$ to ∞ to obtain

$$p(X_n \mid X^{n-1}) = \left(\frac{\tau_n \beta_{n-1}}{\tau_n \beta_{n-1} + X_n} \right)^{\gamma_n \alpha_{n-1}}. \tag{2.5}$$

These formulae have two main uses. First, they give directly the predictive distribution on which one-step forecasting is based. Secondly, they enable us to write down the joint density of the observations

$$p(X_1, \ldots, X_N) = \prod_{n=1}^{N} p(X_n \mid X^{n-1}) \tag{2.6}$$

which is the basis for any form of model verification. In the present paper we shall use this formula explicitly to estimate unknown hyperparameters in the γ_n's, ρ_n's and (shortly to be introduced) ϕ_n's.

As a final generalisation of the model, we assume that what is observed is not X_n but Y_n, where Y_n is related to X_n by a 1-1 transformation

$$X_n = T(Y_n \mid \phi_n)$$

depending on some additional parameter ϕ_n. Examples within this framework include the two-parameter Weibull distribution for Y_n with ϕ_n as the shape parameter ($T(y\,|\,\phi) = y^{\phi}$) and the Gumbel distribution with (see Section 3) ϕ_n as the scale parameter ($T(y\,|\,\phi) = e^{\pm y/\phi}$). If the joint density of $X_1, \ldots, X_N$ is given by (2.6), then the joint density of $Y_1, \ldots, Y_N$ is given by

$$p(T(Y_1\,|\,\phi_1), \ldots, T(Y_N\,|\,\phi_N)) \prod_{n=1}^{N} \left\{\frac{\partial T}{\partial Y_n}(Y_n\,|\,\phi_n)\right\}^{\delta_n}, \tag{2.7}$$

assuming differentiability of T.

In the following discussion, we shall assume that $\phi_n (1 \leqslant n \leqslant N)$ is a single unknown scalar parameter ϕ, and that $\rho_n \equiv \rho$ and $\gamma_n \equiv \gamma$ are also constants independent of n. The equations (2.4)–(2.7) then enable us to write down the joint density of $Y^N = (Y_1, \ldots, Y_N)$ as a function of ϕ, ρ, γ. This function may also be interpreted as a likelihood function $L(\phi, \rho, \gamma\,|\,Y^N)$. The hyperparameters ϕ, ρ, γ may be estimated in two ways: (i) by positing a prior density $\pi(\phi, \rho, \gamma)$ and computing the posterior density which is proportional to $\pi(\phi, \rho, \gamma)\,L(\phi, \rho, \gamma\,|\,Y^N)$; (*ii*) more simply, by maximising L with respect to ϕ, ρ, γ and thus obtaining "maximum likelihood" estimators ϕ, ρ, γ. A. F. M. Smith (1983) gives a Bayesian justification for the second approach by arguing that, in large samples, the estimators thus obtained will be close to the Bayes estimators obtained by the first approach.

We now turn to the prediction problem. In this we shall treat ϕ_n, ρ_n and γ_n as known, though a fully Bayesian approach would be to compute the predictive distributions conditionally on the unknown hyperparameters and then to integrate with respect to the posterior distributions of the hyperparameters.

We deal first with the case of no censoring. The exact distribution of $X_{N+m} (m > 1)$ conditional on X_N is given by the expression

$$p(X_{N+m}\,|\,X^N) = \int \cdots \int \prod_{n=N+1}^{N+m} p(X_n\,|\,X^{n-1})\,dX_{N+1} \ldots dX_{N+m-1} \tag{2.8}$$

using (2.4) together with (2.2) for the integrand. If ρ_n and γ_n do not depend on X_{n-1}, we may proceed as follows. By (2.1) and the independence of $X^N, \xi_{N+1}, \ldots, \xi_{N+m}$, we have

$$E\{\theta_{N+m}^{-t}\,|\,X^N\} = E\{\theta_N^{-t}\,|\,X^N\} \prod_{n=N+1}^{N+m} [\rho_n^{-t} E\{\xi_n^{-t}\}]$$

$$= \frac{\beta_N^t \Gamma(\alpha_N - t)}{\Gamma(\alpha_N)} \prod_{n=N+1}^{N+m} \left\{\rho_n^{-t} \frac{\Gamma(\alpha_{n-1})\Gamma(\gamma_n \alpha_{n-1} - t)}{\Gamma(\alpha_{n-1} - t)\Gamma(\gamma_n \alpha_{n-1})}\right\}$$

(assuming $t < \gamma_n \alpha_{n-1}$ for $N + 1 \leqslant n \leqslant N + m$) and

$$E\{X_{N+m}^t\,|\,\theta_{N+m}\} = \Gamma(t+1)\theta_{N+m}^{-t}$$

so that

$$E\{X_{N+m}^t\,|\,X^N\} = \Gamma(t+1) E\{\theta_{N+m}^{-t}\,|\,X^N\}.$$

In the "steady state" case $\rho_n \equiv \rho$, $\gamma_n \equiv \gamma (< 1)$, $\alpha_n \equiv \alpha = 1/(1-\gamma)$, this reduces to

$$E\{X_{N+m}^t\,|\,X^N\} = \Gamma(t+1)\beta_N^t \frac{\Gamma(\alpha - t)}{\Gamma(\alpha)} \rho^{-mt} \left\{\frac{\Gamma(\alpha)\Gamma(\gamma\alpha - t)}{\Gamma(\alpha - t)\Gamma(\gamma\alpha)}\right\}^m, \tag{2.9}$$

$-1 < t < \gamma\alpha$. Equation (2.9) gives the Mellin transform of the conditional distribution of X_{N+m} given X^N. Conditional moments may be read off directly so long as they are finite.

In the case where future observations may be censored, this analysis is not correct. There are two difficulties: (i) future values of α_n depend on future values of δ_n and are therefore no longer deterministic, (ii) the updating rule for β_n depends on the observed (possibly censored) value of X_n and not on the value which X_n would take if it were not censored. We have been unable to resolve these difficulties analytically, and have therefore resorted extensively to simulation as a means of generating predictive distributions.

We conclude this section with some general comments on state space models. Bather (1965) assumed that $\{\theta_n\}$ is a Markov chain with specified transition kernel. Thus, within Bather's framework it is possible to determine the joint distribution of $\theta_1, \ldots, \theta_n$ for any n. J. Q. Smith (1979, 1981) did not assume a Markovian structure but merely the existence of an updating rule

$$p(\theta_n \mid X^n) \rightarrow p(\theta_{n+1} \mid X^n) \tag{2.10}$$

for transforming the conditional distribution of θ_n given X^n into that of θ_{n+1} given X^n. Specifically, Smith considered the case where the r.h.s. of (2.10) is proportional to a power of the l.h.s. In Smith's models, the joint distribution of θ_n and θ_{n+1} is undefined. At first sight this seems to be a defect of this class of models.

We argue that this is not the case. The predictive distribution of X_{n+1} given X^n may be obtained from the formula

$$p(X_{n+1} \mid X^n) = \int p(\theta_{n+1} \mid X^n) p(X_{n+1} \mid \theta_{n+1}) d\theta_{n+1}.$$

Note that this formula requires that we specify $p(\theta_{n+1} \mid X^n)$, but not $p(\theta_{n+1} \mid \theta_n)$. But, using (2.6), we may then find $p(X_{N+m} \mid X^N)$ for all $m > 1$. This shows that it is possible to do m-step forecasting, for any m, without specifying more than the updating rule (2.10). This observation was the starting point of a study by Key and Godolphin (1981), though their primary concern was with a quite different aspect of the problem. Indeed, the predictive distributions of X_{n+1} given X^n, for $0 \leqslant n \leqslant N-1$, contain all the information that is verifiable from the data. Explicit relations for the joint distributions of the θ_n's, including Bather's transition kernels and our (2.1), are not identifiable from observations on $\{X_n\}$ alone.

Thus we have the apparent paradox that an equation such as (2.1), whose correctness cannot be verified from the data, may nevertheless give correct answers when used in prediction. What matters is that the predictive distributions, (2.4) and (2.5), are correct. Dawid (1984) gives a general discussion of this phenomenon which he calls "Jeffreys' Law".

We might also add that a Bayesian viewpoint is by no means essential to this whole approach. What we have done is to specify a family of conditional distributions based on (2.4), which may be fitted and tested using classical techniques. On the other hand, equation (2.4) would be difficult to interpret if it were not for the Bayesian derivation.

3. APPLICATION OF STATE SPACE MODELS TO RECORDS

In the records context, the series $Y_1, Y_2, \ldots$, are themselves minima (or maxima) from some larger set of random variables, so it seems natural to apply one of the extreme value distributions (Gumbel, 1958). Among these, the Type I or Gumbel distribution with c.d.f. $F(x) = \exp(-e^{-x})$ for maxima, $1 - \exp(-e^{x})$ for minima, is the most widely used and will be adopted here. The appropriateness of the Gumbel distribution for track records is examined by R. L. Smith (1985); there is some discrepancy, as might be expected, in the lower tail.

We therefore consider a model in which the series $Y_1, \ldots, Y_N$ are transformed to $X_1, \ldots, X_N$ via $X_n = T(Y_n \mid \phi)$ where

$$T(y \mid \phi) = \exp(\pm y/\phi),$$

the + sign being taken with minima and the − sign with maxima. In that case, if Y_n has a Gumbel distribution with scale parameter ϕ, then X_n is exponential. We take $\gamma_n \equiv \gamma$, $\rho_n \equiv \rho$ to define the model in terms of three hyperparameters ϕ, γ and ρ.

For a first analysis, we take $\gamma = 1$. In that case the model is just a Bayesian version of a Gumbel model with linear drift. The Bayesian framework is a natural one within which to develop predictive distributions.

First assume that ϕ and ρ are known, with $\rho > 1$, and take $X_n = \exp(+Y_n/\phi)$. By results in Section 2, $(\theta_N \mid X^N) \sim G(\alpha_N, \beta_N)$, where

$$\alpha_N = \alpha_0 + \sum_{n=1}^{N} \delta_n, \quad \beta_N = \rho^{-N}\beta_0 + \sum_{n=1}^{N} \rho^{n-N} X_n.$$

If Z_n denotes the record in year n, then for $y < Z_N$, $m \geqslant 1$,

$$P\{Z_{N+m} > y \mid \theta_N\} = P\{X_{N+r} > e^{y/\phi}, 1 \leqslant r \leqslant m \mid \theta_N\}$$
$$= \exp\left[-\sum_{r=1}^{m} \{\theta_N \rho^r \exp(y/\phi)\} \right].$$

But $E\{\exp(-t\theta_N) \mid X^N\} = (1 + \beta_N^{-1} t)^{-\alpha_N}$. Therefore

$$P\{Z_{n+m} > y \mid X^N, \phi, \rho\} = [1 + \beta_N^{-1} \exp(y/\phi)\rho(\rho^m - 1)/(\rho - 1)]^{-\alpha_N}. \tag{3.1}$$

Equation (3.1) gives the predictive distribution of Z_{N+m} for each $m \geqslant 1$. Predictive quantiles may be obtained by equating (3.1) to a constant (e.g. 0.5 for the median), and solving for y.

In the case that ϕ and ρ are unknown but have a posterior distribution, we replace (3.1) by

$$P\{Z_{N+m} > y \mid X^N\} = \int P\{Z_{N+m} > y \mid X^N, \phi, \rho\} p(\phi, \rho \mid X^N) d\phi d\rho. \tag{3.2}$$

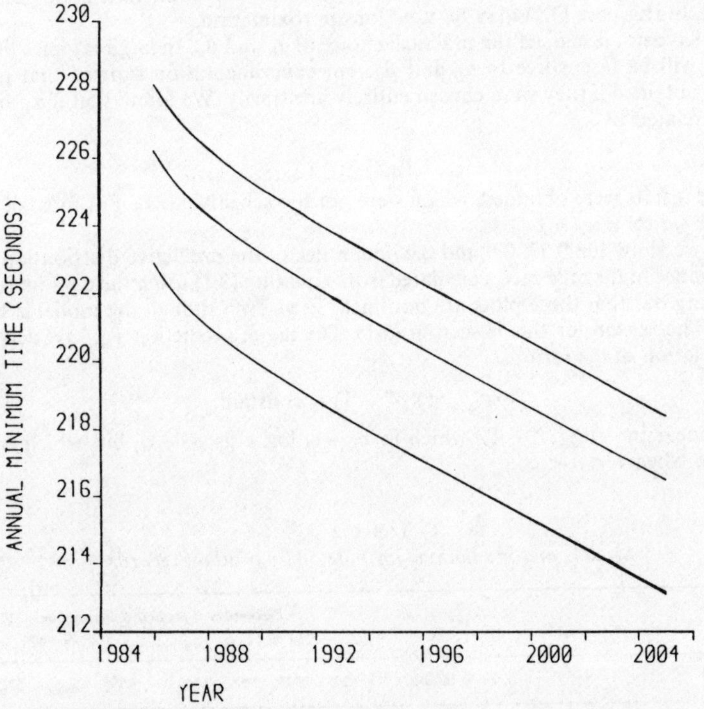

Fig. 1. 0.95, 0.5, 0.05 quantiles of predictive distribution for annual minima, mile race, 1986–2005 based on $\gamma = 1$ model.

TABLE 1
Men's world mile and marathon records

(a) Mile (time in seconds):

Year	*Record*	*Year*	*Record*	*Year*	*Record*
1931	249.2	1945	241.3	1966	231.3
1933	247.6	1954	237.9	1967	231.1
1934	246.7	1957	237.2	1975	229.4
1937	246.4	1958	234.5	1979	229.0
1942	244.6	1962	234.4	1980	228.8
1943	242.6	1964	234.1	1981	227.3
1944	241.6	1965	233.5	1985	226.3

(b) Marathon (time in minutes):

1909	162.52	1952	140.72	1965	132.00
1913	156.12	1953	138.58	1967	129.62
1920	152.60	1954	137.67	1969	128.57
1925	149.03	1958	135.28	1981	128.22
1935	146.70	1963	134.47	1984	128.08
1947	145.65	1964	132.20	1985	127.20

Quantiles of the predictive distribution may be obtained by solving for y in (3.2). In practice, we would usually expect (3.2) to be close to (3.1) with the "maximum likelihood" estimators $\hat{\phi}$, $\hat{\rho}$ submitted. In this case (3.1) may be used for approximation.

So far we have not discussed the practical choice of α_0 and β_0. In large samples theposterior distribution will be insensitive to α_0 and β_0, but experimentation showed that nonsensical results were obtained if they were chosen entirely arbitrarily. We found that if α_1 and β_1 were taken to be related by

$$\beta_1 = \alpha_1 X_1$$

then sensible results were obtained, which were not too sensitive to α_1. For most of the results which follow we took $\alpha_1 = 1$.

In Fig. 1, we show the 0.95, 0.5 and 0.05 quantiles of the predictive distribution of annual best performance in the mile race, calculated from equation (3.1) using the data in Table 1. It is worth pointing out that these plots are not linear in m, even though the model is based on a linear drift. The reason for this is seen in (3.1). The lag-m prediction y_m, say, depends on m through a relation of the form

$$\exp(y_m/\phi)(\rho^m - 1) = \text{constant}.$$

Thus y_m is linear in $-\log(\rho^m - 1)$, which is $\simeq -m \log \rho$ as $\rho \to \infty$, but which is a convex function of m when $1 < \rho < \infty$.

TABLE 2
Models and predictions for mile and marathon records

					Percentiles of predictive distribution					
					10 years			*20 years*		
	γ	ϕ	ρ	$\phi \ln(\gamma\rho)$	95%	50%	5%	95%	50%	5%
Mile	0.79	1.06	1.98	0.48	224.9	221.4	218.2	222.9	217.5	213.3
Marathon	0.84	1.98	1.64	0.64	124.1	118.9	113.1	120.2	113.4	106.6

For the remaining results we drop the constraint $\gamma = 1$ and fit the model both to the mile records and also the marathon records in Table 1, the results of which are summarised in Table 2. The hyperparameters ϕ, ρ and γ were estimated by maximum likelihood, as described in Section 2. In the case of γ, the constraint $0 < \gamma \leqslant 1$ was imposed. The reason for this is that the case $\gamma > 1$ corresponds to α_n growing exponentially fast. Since α_n is a measure of the amount of information we have about θ_n, this does not seem reasonable. Also shown in Table 2 is $\phi \log(\gamma\rho)$: this is the mean annual improvement.

The predictions of Table 2 were obtained by simulation of the fitted model. One thousand replications were taken to generate a range of simulated records at the ten- and twenty-year time lags, the 5th, 50th and 95th sample percentiles being shown. Various attempts were made to avoid simulation by using approximations based on (2.9) or (3.1), but none of our attempts was close to the simulated values. Therefore, based on our present knowledge we believe simulation is the only reasonable way of predicting records using these models. Plots of the simulated quantiles for the next twenty years in the mile race are given in Fig. 2. Note that here, in contrast to Fig. 1, we are predicting records and not annual minima.

The predictions look reasonable for the mile records, but less so for the marathon records. In the latter case the procedure predicts times of under two hours within the next twenty years, which few athletics experts would regard as a reasonable prediction. Closer examination of the data shows nearly perfect linearity up to 1969, but virtually no improvement since then. It is hard to imagine why there would be such a qualitative change.

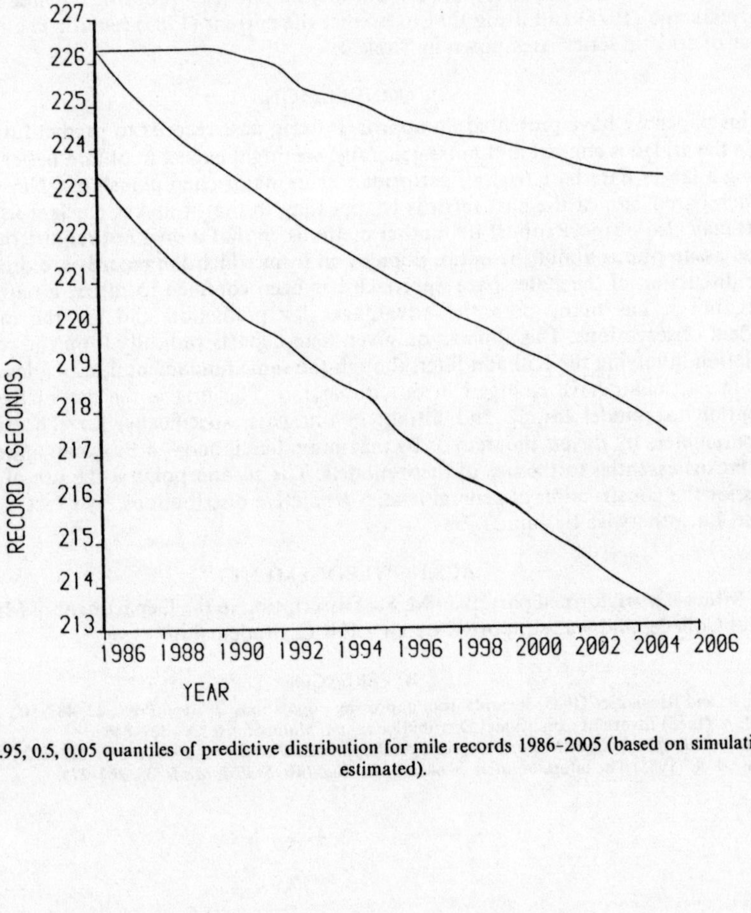

Fig. 2. 0.95, 0.5, 0.05 quantiles of predictive distribution for mile records 1986–2005 (based on simulation with γ estimated).

TABLE 3
Predictions of current records from ten years ago

Event	*Current record*	*Percentiles of prediction interval*		
		95%	50%	5%
Men's mile	226.3	229.4	225.4	221.4
Men's 400 m	43.80	43.7	43.3	42.4
Men's 1500 m	209.45	208.6	207.0	204.1
Men's long jump	8.90	8.90	8.90	9.15
Men's high jump	2.41	2.30	2.38	2.46
Men's shot put	22.62	21.93	23.42	24.45
Men's javelin	104.80	95.6	101.5	106.2
Men's marathon	127.20	126.4	120.4	114.0
Women's long jump	7.43	6.99	7.12	7.34
Women's high jump	2.07	2.01	2.07	2.14
Women's shot put	22.53	23.0	24.3	25.4
Women's javelin	75.40	71.4	73.5	77.2

Although the simulations give reasonable results overall, some of the individual replications behaved anomalously, with the values of X_n rising instead of falling. This seems to be inherent in the model, the result of an occasional very small value of ξ_n.

As a check on the actual performance of our method, we tried re-fitting the model to data up to ten years ago (1975) and using that to predict the current (1985) record. The results, for a number of athletic series, are shown in Table 3.

4. CONCLUSIONS

In this paper we have presented an approach using past records to predict future records. Both in the athletics context and more generally, we might expect to obtain better predictions by using a larger data base (e.g. all performances in major championships). Nevertheless, an approach based on just the past records is appealing in that it makes efficient use of limited data. It may also be more robust than other methods, in that it does not require that we make detailed assumptions about the entire population from which the records are drawn.

Our discussion of the state space approach has been confined to rather a narrow class of models, but it has many potential advantages for prediction and for the modelling of dependent observations. The application given here departs radically from the conventional formulation involving the Kalman filter, though the same fundamental principles apply. Two points in particular have emerged in our discussion. The first is the use of the predictive distribution for model testing and fitting; in our case, specifically, for the estimation of hyperparameters by Bayes' theorem or by maximum likelihood—a Bayesian approach being by no means essential to the use of these models. The second point is the use of state space models for the construction of general m-step predictive distributions, by exact calculation if possible, but otherwise by simulation.

ACKNOWLEDGEMENT

J. E. Miller's work formed part of an M. Sc. Dissertation in the Department of Mathematics, Imperial College, and was supported by an S.E.R.C. Studentship.

REFERENCES

Ballerini, R. and Resnick, S. (1985) Records from improving populations. *J. Appl. Prob.*, **22**, 487-502.
Bather, J. A. (1965) Invariant Conditional Distributions. *Ann. Math. Statist.*, **36**, 829-846.
Dawid, A. P. (1984) Statistical theory: The prequential approach. *J.R. Statist. Soc.* A, **147**, 278-292.
Dunsmore, I. R. (1983) The future occurrence of records. *Ann. Inst. Statist. Math.*, **35**, 267-277.

Foster, F. G. and Stuart, A. (1954) distribution-free tests in time series based on the breaking of records (with discussion). *J.R. Statist. Soc.* B, **16**, 1-22.
Glick, N. (1978) Breaking records and breaking boards. *Amer. Math. Monthly*, Jan. 1978, 2-26.
Goldie, C. M. and Rogers, L. C. G. (1984) The *k*-record processes are i.i.d. *Z. Wahr. verv. Geb.*, **67**, 197-211.
Gumbel, E. J. (1958) *Statistics of Extremes.* New York: Columbia U.P.
Haan, L. de (1984), Extremal processes and record values. In *Statistical Extremes and Applications*, (J. Tiago de Oliveira, ed.), Reidel, Dordrecht, 297-309.
Haan, L. de and Verkade, E. (1985) On extreme value theory in the presence of a trend. To appear.
Harrison, P. G. and Stevens, C. F. (1976), Bayesian forecasting (with discussion). *J.R. Statist. Soc.* B, **38**, 205-248.
Harvey, A. C. (1981) *The Econometric Analysis of Time Series.* Oxford: Philip Allen.
Harvey, A. C. (1981) *Time Series Models.* Oxford: Philip Allen.
Key, P. and Godolphin, E. J. (1981) On the Bayesian steady forecasting model. *J.R. Statist. Soc.* B **43**, 92-96.
Leadbetter, M. R., Lindgren, G. and Rootzen, H. (1983). *Extremes and Related Properties of Random Sequences and Processes.* New York: Springer.
Meinhold, R. J. and Singpurwalla, N. D. (1983) Understanding the Kalman filter. *Amer. Statistn*, **37**, 123-127.
Smith, A. F. M. (1983) Comment on a paper by DuMouchel and Harris. *J. Amer. Statist. Ass.*, **78**, 310.
Smith, A. F. M. and West, M. (1983) Monitoring renal transplants: an application of the multiprocess Kalman filter. *Biometrics*, **39**, 867-878.
Smith, J. Q. (1979) A generalization of the Bayesian steady forecasting model *J.R. Statist. Soc.* B, **41**, 375-387.
——(1981) The multiparameter steady model. *J.R. Statist. Soc* B, **43**, 256-260.
Smith, R. L. (1985) Forecasting records by maximum likelihood. In preparation.
Vervaat, W. (1985) Ignatov's Theorem: A new and short proof. To appear.
West, M. (1981) Robust sequential approximate Bayesian estimation. *J.R. Statist. Soc.* B, **43**, 157-166.
West, M., Harrison, P. G. and Migon, H. S. (1985) Dynamic generalized linear models and Bayesian forecasting. *J. Amer. Statist. Ass.*, **80**, 73-97.

Name Index